Evolution and "the Sex Problem"

*American Narratives during
the Eclipse of Darwinism*

Bert Bender

THE KENT STATE UNIVERSITY PRESS

KENT & LONDON

Frontis: *Creative Evolution.* In *The Song of the Lark* Cather dramatizes one of Thea Kronborg's "rapid evolutions" when she sees a majestic eagle soaring into the light. Celebrating this symbol of Bergson's creative evolution, Cather sings, "O eagle of eagles! Endeavour, achievement, desire, glorious striving of human art!"

© 2004 by The Kent State University Press, Kent, Ohio 44242

ALL RIGHTS RESERVED

Library of Congress Catalog Card Number 2004008855

ISBN 0-87338-809-7

Manufactured in the United States of America

08 07 06 05 04   5 4 3 2 1

Library of Congress Cataloging-in-Publication Data

Bender, Bert.

Evolution and "the sex problem" : American narratives during the eclipse of Darwinism / Bert Bender.

p.   cm.

Includes bibliographical references (p.   ) and index.

ISBN 0-87338-809-7 (alk. paper) ∞

1. American fiction—20th century—History and criticism. 2. Literature and science—United States—History—20th century. 3. Darwin, Charles, 1809–1882—Influence. 4. American fiction—English influences. 5. Evolution (Biology) in literature. 6. Mate selection in literature. 7. Narrration (Rhetoric) 8. Sex in literature. I. Title.

PS374.S33B46 2004

813'.5209—dc22   2004008855

British Library Cataloging-in-Publication data are available.

For Judith and Todd

and all those included in

my mother's last words,

"Family! Family! Family!"

Contents

Preface   ix

Acknowledgments   xv

Introduction: In a Dark Time   1
"Man's Place in Nature," Life Itself, and the Sex Problem 8   Aspects of the
Sex Problem 12   Modern Psychology and the Sex Problem 16

1 Frank Norris on the Evolution and Repression of the Sexual Instinct   30
Joseph Le Conte's Version of Darwinian Theory and His Emphasis on Sexual
Reproduction 32   Norris's Battle with the Theory of Sexual Selection 35
Norris and the Repression of the Sexual Emotions 47

2 "The Chaos of His Brain": Evolutionary Psychology in *The Red Badge of Courage*   52
Crane and William James 56   Evolutionary Progress, the "Throat-Grappling
Instinct," and the Emotions 57   Sexual Selection and the "Law of Battle" 62

3 Jack London and "the Sex Problem"   72
London's Early Explorations of Sexual Selection: *A Daughter of the Snows*, *The
Kempton-Wace Letters*, and *The Sea-Wolf* 73   *Martin Eden* and *The Valley of the
Moon*: Havelock Ellis, Freud, and the Ecological Vision 78   The "Bawling of
Sex" in *The Little Lady of the Big House* 91

4 Theodore Dreiser, Science, and "It"   116
The Problem and Solution: The Evolutionary Tangle and Evolutionary
Progress 119   Carrie's Choice and the "Distant Wings" of Beauty 121
"A Real Man—A Financier" 126

5 "The Varieties of Human Experience": Sexual Intimacy, Heredity, and Emotional Conflict in
Gertrude Stein's Early Work   135
Heredity and Female Choice in *The Making of Americans* (1903) 138
Q.E.D.: The Howling Wolves of Love 140   "The Nature of Woman" in
Fernhurst: The "Deepening Knowledge of Life and Love and Sex" 146
Three Lives: Anna's "Strange Coquetry of Anger and Fear" 148   "The Gentle
Lena": The Tyranny of Matchmakers and the Father-Instinct 153
Melanctha: "Too Complex with Desire" 155

6 Sex and Evolution in Willa Cather's *O Pioneers!* and *The Song of the Lark*   163
Creative Evolution and Sex 166   Marie and Alexandra: Beyond Sexual Selection in *O Pioneers!* 168   "Dreamers on the Frontier" 172   Sexual Desire in *The Song of the Lark* 176   Sex and Sublimation in *The Power of Sound* 179   Sexual Selection, Marriage, and Evolutionary Play 181

7 "Under the Shell of Life": Sherwood Anderson and "the Call of Sex"   189
The Darwinian Pattern in Anderson's Fiction 194   Sexual Difference: "The Maleness of the Male" 195   Sexual Difference: The Woman "Strong to Be Loved" 200   Reflections of Freud and Havelock Ellis in Anderson's Presentation of Sex 207   "The Hidden Wonder Story": The Unconscious and Anderson's Transcendental Naturalism Sexual Violence, Play of Mind, and Transcendence in *Winesburg, Ohio* 216

8 "His Mind Aglow": The Biological Undercurrent in Fitzgerald's *Gatsby* and other Works   224
"Love or Eugenics" 225   *The Riddle of the Universe*: Accident, Heredity, and Selection 226   Sexual Selection in *The Great Gatsby* 232

9 Harlem, 1928: The Biology of the Black Soul and the "Rising Tide of Rhythm"   244
W. E. B. DuBois's *Dark Princess*: The Talented Soul 250   Jessie Fauset's *Plum Bun*: A "Biology [that] Transcends Society!" 257   Nella Larsen's *Quicksand*: Darwin, James, Freud, and the Psychology of Mixed Race 264   Claude McKay's *Home to Harlem*: The "It's a Be-Be Itching Life" Blues 272   Rudolph Fisher's *The Walls of Jericho* and the "Rising Tide of Rhythm" 283

10 V. F. Calverton and the Principles of Red Love   298

11 "To Be Alive": John Steinbeck's *The Log from the Sea of Cortez* and *The Wayward Bus*   312
The Log from the Sea of Cortez: Ecology and Man's Place in Nature 315
Sweetheart's "Rear End" and the Marriage Problem in *The Wayward Bus* 320

12 "Night Song": Africa and Eden in Hemingway's Late Work   329
Courtship and Anthropology in Africa 333   Dark Eden 342

Afterword   358

Works Cited   362

Index   376

Preface

American novelists have long explored human nature in the light of Darwinian thought. Indeed, aside from religious beliefs, no other idea or cluster of ideas has ever provoked so strong and sustained a literary response as Darwin's theory of evolution. Yet our novelists' work with these ideas is scarcely known. Although it is widely accepted that Darwin initiated "the greatest of all scientific revolutions" (Mayr 501), even now, nearly eighty years after the Scopes trial, our culture resists evolutionary theory. We resist it in public education, where the word "evolution" is unacceptable in many biology classes, and the forty-third president of the United States can strengthen his political base by announcing that he does not believe in evolution. "Why?" John Steinbeck asked in 1941, "Why do we so dread to think of our species as a species?" (*The Log from the Sea of Cortez* 219).

The resistance to biological thought in academic, literary, and cultural studies is more complicated. It is entrenched in a long series of literary theories from the New Criticism of the mid-twentieth century to the latest trends in postmodern theory and in the simplistic belief that literary Darwinism yields only a brutish essentialism. Among the many reasons for examining our novelists' interest in evolutionary thought, one seems especially important. Their explorations of human nature are among our culture's earliest efforts to comprehend the Darwinian reality on which our emerging ecological awareness is founded. Only two of the writers discussed here were truly ecological thinkers (Jack London and John Steinbeck), but all of them took the first step toward ecological awareness by studying the human being in the evolutionary stream. Writing from their different social points of view, they constructed a great variety of American narratives and aligned them with particular varieties of evolutionary theory from their own times. Thus, their narratives are among our culture's first attempts to construct what E. O. Wilson calls a "true evolutionary epic" (*Consilience* 264–65) or what Loyal Rue calls "everybody's story," the basis of "a new wisdom tradition that couples an evolutionary cosmology to an ecocentric morality" (xiii).[1]

Evolution and "the Sex Problem" is a study in both literary history and that part of the history of science that concerns itself with the cultural assimilation of scientific thought. It completes a fifteen-year investigation of the American literary response to Darwin that should serve as a guide to America's major evolutionary narratives.

In a previous volume (*The Descent of Love*), the first book on Darwin and American literature and the first to explain how powerfully the theory of sexual selection appealed to the literary imagination, it was necessary to devote many pages to explaining what the theory of sexual selection is and why *The Descent of Man, and Selection in Relation to Sex* would have provoked such an immediate response among novelists such as William Dean Howells and Henry James. It emphasized the Darwinian influence in novels of courtship and marriage in the 1870s and 1880s, skipped over the "naturalists" because their interest in Darwin had been taken for granted (though never examined), and more briefly suggested how Darwin's theories of sexual selection, the evolution of race, and the expression of the emotions continued to interest novelists throughout the first quarter of the twentieth century. Because of that work and a number of other recent studies of Darwin and literature, and because the theory of sexual selection is now being much more widely discussed than ever before, it is no longer as important to argue that writers *were* interested in Darwinian materials or to explain why they would have been.[2] We are a bit freer to examine how our novelists have represented human nature within the community of common descent.

The present volume, therefore, begins in the 1890s and examines the ways in which fifteen writers over a period of about sixty years explored Darwin's "one general law leading to the advancement of all organic beings." The first requirement of Darwin's one law is to "multiply": "multiply, vary, let the strongest live and the weakest die" (*The Origin of Species* 208). That the human being exists within the community of common descent and must not only multiply but do so in accord with the workings of sexual selection led to the late nineteenth-century view that "sex [is] the central problem of life," as Havelock Ellis wrote in 1897. The literary careers discussed here help prove Ellis's prediction that "coming generations" would regard sex, "with the racial questions that rest on it . . . as the chief problem for solution" (*Studies in the Psychology of Sex* 1:xxx).

In demonstrating the thesis that a broad range of American writers explored sexual reality in the context of evolutionary thought, several themes are developed: (1) that the "naturalists" (Frank Norris, Stephen Crane, Jack London, and Theodore Dreiser) continued the realists' exploration of Darwinian courtship and the question that T. H. Huxley had posed in his title, *Man's Place in Nature* (1863); (2) that they and many successive writers were determined to sound the nature of *life*, particularly the two forces thought to drive it: love and hunger (or the reproductive and nutritive functions); (3) that several of the writers discussed in this book are best seen as having explored the sex problem and the meaning of life during the period known in the history of science as "the eclipse of Darwinism," basing their narratives on various anti-Darwinian assumptions that they found in theories by Joseph Le Conte, Peter Kropotkin, and Henri Bergson, for example; (4) that, responding to Darwin's analysis of sex and "the cerebral system," they were especially interested in the psychological aspects of the sex problem and often produced narratives of great introspection; (5) that writers early in the twentieth century explored Freud's theories of sex and the subconscious in the "historical perspective" provided by present-day historians—that "Freud's theory of mind is the embodiment of a scientific age imbued with the rising tide of Darwinism" (Sulloway 497); (6) that the most important specific aspects of the sex problem for these writers are the problems of male violence and jealousy, the female's power to select, the connection between sexual selection and the evolution of racial difference, the psychological problems of hysteria and repression, the problem of heredity, and the nature of bisexuality; (7) that a number of African American writers embraced Darwinian evolution as a powerfully liberating theory of life (as did a number of women in the 1880s and 1890s); (8) that Jack London's and John Steinbeck's explorations of evolution and the sex problem led to some of the most important writing on ecology in American literature; and (9) that John Steinbeck's and Ernest Hemingway's fictional explorations of life and sex during the 1940s and 1950s seem related to the renewed power of Darwinian thought at the time of the "Modern Synthesis" of natural selection and genetics as described by Julian Huxley in *Evolution: The Modern Synthesis* (1942).

Because this book is intended to reach a wide range of readers, including those interested in the role of science in cultural history, those interested in the literary history of this period, and those with special interests in particular writers, a word about methodology and the proportions of the chapters is in order. Some readers interested mostly in the way the main themes reflect on cultural or literary history, in general, will want to skim or even skip chapters on certain authors. However, readers with special interests in particular writers will probably require sufficiently detailed treatments of those authors in order to judge the truth of the general thesis. Readers with special interests in the naturalists, for example, or the Harlem Renaissance, or in certain writers such as Gertrude Stein or F. Scott Fitzgerald, will find that the relevant chapters here reveal how profoundly evolutionary thought (variously interpreted) figures in particular works and careers. Moreover, most readers might be unfamiliar with many of the novels discussed here, notable exceptions being *The Red Badge of Courage* and *The Great Gatsby*. Therefore, these novels are discussed through the use of plot summaries that are intended to familiarize readers with the novels. More important, these discussions interweave many quotations from the novels in order to demonstrate the novelists' use of significant terms and typical scenes as they construct their plots of evolutionary change. One aim of this study is to show how novelists who believe in evolutionary progress, for example, tend to dramatize progressive change by tracing their characters' success in dealing with certain evolutionary obstacles. Such obstacles—particular aspects of the sex problem—might be the male's jealousy or sexual violence, the female's need to select a superior male, or a character's struggle with the psychological pitfalls of repression or hysteria. In this way, the general problem for novelists wishing to plot evolutionary progress is to imagine a couple (often thought of as "new" men or women) who can lead the way into an improved future through the promise of their reproductive success. Novelists who are not particularly committed to evolutionary progress often set aside the problem of attaining reproductive success. Instead, such writers might dramatize a character's education (often his or her disillusionment in "love"). Others, such as Steinbeck and Hemingway, resisted our culture's efforts to repress or transcend Darwinian evolution and the sex problem. Rather, by embracing evolutionary biology and the human's place in the community of common descent, they found new ways to celebrate life itself.

Finally, regarding the proportion of these chapters, the chapter on Jack London is longer than most because his exploration of the sex problem, including its role in his ecological vision, is the most informed and comprehensive in American fiction. Similarly, the chapter on Sherwood Anderson is rather long because he is the central figure from the period when novelists were exploring the intermingling streams of Darwinian and Freudian thought. Because the chapter on the Harlem Renaissance discusses five novelists, it, too, is rather long. And the chapter on Dreiser is shorter than might be expected because a number of scholars have already examined different aspects of his interest in science.

Notes

1. Although, like Rue and Wilson, I am contending that the "true" ecological or evolutionary epic must be founded on Darwinian theory, it does not follow that all Darwinians would inevitably come to understand ecology in the way that we do today (or in the ways that Jack London and John Steinbeck did). It is doubtful that even Darwin or Ernst Haeckel, who coined and defined "ecology" as the study of the interrelations of organisms in the Darwinian struggle for existence, could have foreseen what ecology means for us. T. H. Huxley is an excellent example of how even a hardcore Darwinist could not foresee ecological problems as we know them today. As Mark Kurlansky writes, Huxley participated in three commissions on international fisheries from the 1860s to the 1880s, and in the last of these he claimed that "any tendency to over-fishing will meet with its natural check in the diminution of the supply, . . . this check will always come into operation long before any thing like permanent exhaustion has occurred" (122). The best case for acknowledging the Darwinian basis in the developing field of ecocriticism is to be found in Glen A. Love's *Practical Ecocriticism: Literature, Biology, and the Environment.*

2. Two important books in literary theory have appeared in recent years: Joseph Carroll's *Evolution and Literary Theory* and Robert Storey's *Mimesis and the Human Animal: On the*

Biogenetic Foundations of Literary Representation. Related to this work and included within it are the chapters contained in *Biopoetics: Evolutionary Explorations in the Arts*, edited by Brett Cooke and Frederick Turner. As Turner concludes in his chapter from this volume, for example ("An Ecopoetics of Beauty and Meaning"), "Essentially, I am calling for the abandonment of a good part of the present activities of the literary academy and the beginning of a new literature, a new poetics, and a new criticism based upon the evolving universe and our own leading part in it" (137). While I admire and certainly recommend this new work in literary theory, I do not want to suggest that workers in this field will necessarily appreciate my own quite different approach to literary studies. Whereas proponents of biopoetics are interested in exploring the unconscious presentation of Darwinian issues in the work of pre-Darwinian writers such as Jane Austen, my purpose is to show how post-Darwinian writers have *consciously* sought to keep pace with developments in science that have emerged not only in evolutionary biology itself but in anthropology, sociology, modern psychology, and ecology. Somewhat similar to the work I undertake here are two recent book-length studies of particular American authors and Darwin: Robert Faggen's *Robert Frost and the Challenge of Darwin* and Brian E. Railsback's *Parallel Expeditions: Charles Darwin and the Art of John Steinbeck*. Among the several recent articles on Darwin and literature are Brian Boyd's "Jane, Meet Charles: Literature, Evolution, and Human Nature" (in the field of biopoetics) and Friedemann Ehrenforth's "Music, Religion, and Darwinian Science in *The Damnation of Theron Ware*." While I would urge students of late nineteenth- and early twentieth-century literature to consult *The Descent of Man* in order to familiarize themselves with the theory of sexual selection, there are a number of excellent recent discussions of sexual selection, such as Helena Cronin, *The Ant and the Peacock: Altruism and Sexual Selection from Darwin to Today;* John Alcock, *Animal Behavior: An Evolutionary Approach;* David Buss, *The Evolution of Desire: Strategies of Human Mating;* Helen Fisher, *Anatomy of Love: The Natural History of Monogamy, Adultery, and Divorce;* Matt Ridley, *The Red Queen: Sex and the Evolution of Human Nature;* and Geoffrey Miller, *The Mating Mind: How Sexual Choice Shaped the Evolution of Human Nature.*

Acknowledgments

Four chapters of this book were previously published as articles: the chapter on Frank Norris, in *Nineteenth-Century Literature*; the chapter on Willa Cather, in *Prospects: An Annual Journal of American Cultural Studies*; the chapter on Gertrude Stein, in *Amerikastudien*; and the chapter on F. Scott Fitzgerald, in *Journal of American Studies*. The chapter on Jack London appeared in an abbreviated form in *Jack London: One Hundred Years a Writer*, edited by Sara S. Hodson and Jeanne Campbell Reesman. I am grateful to the editors and readers who were involved in seeing the foregoing work into print. I presented an abbreviated version of the chapter on Stephen Crane at an annual conference of the American Literature Association, an organization whose work in furthering American literary studies is invaluable.

I am grateful to a number of colleagues, friends, and former students who expressed their interest in this work, sometimes providing much needed encouragement and often providing helpful comments and suggestions. Thanks especially to Glen A. Love for his supportive interest in this project, particularly the parts that converge with his own work in ecology and literature; to Scott Donaldson for reading and suggesting revisions to my chapter on Fitzgerald; and to Bickford Sylvester for his shared interest in Hemingway and for introducing me to the Kent State University Press. Four other colleagues in Fitzgerald and Hemingway studies have provided helpful insights and encouragement in this work: James L. W. West III, Gerry Brenner, Joseph Flora, and Robert W. Lewis. William E. Hummel read and provided helpful suggestions on my introduction. Thanks also to Craig Gable, editor of the *Rudolph Fisher Newsletter*, for reading my chapter on Fisher and for suggesting a few revisions, and to Paul Sorrentino, editor of *Stephen Crane Studies*, for his words of encouragement. For their shared interest in African American literature, I am grateful to two colleagues at Arizona State University, Neal Lester and Keith Miller. And for their interest in this project from their different disciplinary points of view, I am grateful to the evolutionary biologist and my colleague at Arizona State University, John Alcock, and to the historian of science, Michael Ghiselin.

One of the most gratifying forms of encouragement I have received in this work came from a number of former students who picked up on my interest in Darwin and went on to do excellent related work on their own: Deirdre Pettipiece Ray,

Friedemann Ehrenforth, Maximilian Werner, Matthew Evertson, Kathleen Hicks, John McKinn, Arlon Benson, Leslie Wootten, Edgar Alosbaños, Tricia Farwell, and Gary Walker.

I very much appreciate the expert guidance and support I have received in this project from Joanna Hildebrand Craig, the assistant director and acquiring editor at the Kent State University Press, and Kathy Method, the managing editor. Thanks also to Matthew Enertson and Christine Francis for their help with the index. It was a great pleasure to have worked once again with my friend Tony Angell on this, our third project; his five striking drawings illustrate some of the main themes in this study, bringing a touch of clarity, economy, and distinction to my lengthy analyses. Finally, I cannot sufficiently express my thanks to Judith Darknall, my wife, for her companionship and for the patience, interest, and support she has shown over the several years that found me distracted by and absorbed in this work.

Introduction: In a Dark Time

> In a dark time, the eye begins to see,
> I meet my shadow in the deepening shade;
> I hear my echo in the echoing wood—
> A lord of nature weeping to a tree.
> —Theodore Roethke, "In a Dark Time"

Immediately after Charles Darwin presented his fully developed theory of sexual selection in *The Descent of Man, and Selection in Relation to Sex* (1871), novelists began to examine idealized love, courtship, and marriage in a new light. Exploring this view of life, William Dean Howells and Henry James laid the foundations of American literary realism with such works as *Their Wedding Journey* (1871) or *A Foregone Conclusion* (1874), and "The Madonna of the Future" (1873) or *Roderick Hudson* (1874). In these early exploratory years, they and other writers shared their culture's wariness and confusion about Darwin's complex theory, but many read him rather closely. After all, he had laid a most impressive foundation in the *Origin of Species*, and the courtship behaviors he later theorized in *The Descent of Man* were obvious if not comic. Indeed, when magazines such as the *Atlantic Monthly* and *Galaxy* were emphasizing their interest in science, novelists who aspired to be realists were obliged to demonstrate their authority in interpreting the Darwinian view of life. Inevitably, they engaged in the social debate over sexual difference and the supposed evolutionary hierarchies of sex, race, class, and culture.

In the 1870s and early 1880s, for example, writers tended to take shelter in the idea of "civilization," from which privileged point of view one could contemplate "barbarians," "savages," and, less frequently, the "lower" animals. At first it was amusing for some of these early writers to critique love and even motherhood in "the light of common day," to use Howells's phrase, especially in noting the slightly animalistic aspects of human courtship.[1] If one could not conclude that civilization would continue its ascent on the wave of evolutionary progress, as many believed, one could rest assured that it would at least endure—a little unpleasantly perhaps—as the struggle for existence demanded strength. Still, examining marriage as the institution on which civilization was founded, the realists focused their attention on certain inherent problems in what Darwin called "the sexual struggle" (*The Descent of Man* 2:398). The main elements in the theory of sexual selection that so interested the novelists were the male's passion, jealousy, and combativeness; the female's power to select the superior male; the biology of sexual attraction in ornamentation, music, and dance; and, in general, the highly controversial issue of sexual difference in both body and mind, as that was sadly distorted in the development of Victorian sexual science and racial science.[2] The greatest question, of course, was what the theory of common descent revealed about the human mind. In the following paragraph from Darwin's "General Summary," one feels the shock that transformed psychology and the modern psychological novel:

> He who admits the principle of sexual selection will be led to the remarkable conclusion that the cerebral system not only regulates most of the existing functions of the body, but has indirectly influenced the progressive development of various bodily structures and of certain mental qualities. Courage, pugnacity, perseverance, strength and size of body, weapons of all kinds, musical organs, both vocal and instrumental, bright colours, stripes and marks, and ornamental appendages, have all been indirectly gained by the one sex or the other, through the influence of love and jealousy, through the appreciation of the beautiful in sound, colour or form, and through the exertion of a choice; and these powers of the mind manifestly depend on the development of the cerebral system. (*The Descent of Man* 2:402)[3]

By the 1890s both Howells and James—but especially younger novelists such as Harold Frederic, Kate Chopin, Frank Norris, and Edith Wharton—were beginning to present much darker stories of sexual love. At the same time, the growing resistance to Darwin's theories of natural and sexual selection had emerged as the movement Peter J. Bowler describes in *The Eclipse of Darwinism: Anti-Darwinian Evolution Theories in the Decades around 1900* (1983). Indeed, in a subsequent book, *The Non-Darwinian Revolution*, Bowler calls for a "new historiography of evolutionism" in order to show that throughout the late nineteenth and early twentieth centuries "Darwinism itself was absorbed into nineteenth-century progressionism" and therefore "that Darwin's theory cannot be made the scapegoat" for the rise of materialism at that time (199). "Only after the emergence of the synthetic theory in the

1940s," Bowler concludes, "did anything like a Darwinian interpretation of human evolution begin to take shape" (150).[4]

The American fiction surveyed here reflects but does not exactly parallel this movement in the history of science. This is a literary history of writers' ways of presenting the human narrative in the evolutionary context. For histories of science during this period, one must consult works such as Ernst Mayr's *The Growth of Biological Thought* or Bowler's *The Eclipse of Darwinism*. As both these historians explain, theorists during the eclipse, in general, refuted the theories of natural and sexual selection in a number of ways, mainly through the revival of Lamarckism but also through orthogenesis (the belief in linear, nonadaptive evolution put forth by Theodore Eimer, for example) and mutationism (notably advanced by Hugo De Vries). It is instructive to review the varieties of Lamarckism that Bowler describes during this period. However, the main evolutionary theorists who excited the imaginations of most of the writers discussed here now scarcely figure in histories of science, particularly the (more or less) Lamarckians Joseph Le Conte and Henri Bergson, but also other evolutionists who attracted large general readerships during those years, such as Peter Kropotkin (*Mutual Aid*) and Ernst Haeckel (*The Riddle of the Universe*).

Also, these novelists' presentation of the evolutionary "reality" is further complicated in this important way: they were responding not only to Darwinian or the "anti-Darwinian evolution theories" of their time but also to the tradition of Darwinian courtship novels that had developed among the realists such as Howells and James. Among the clearest examples of later novelists beginning their careers by attempting to answer or rewrite the courtship narratives of their precursors are Sherwood Anderson (responding to Howells), Willa Cather (responding to Kate Chopin), and Hemingway (responding to Henry James). But by the 1890s young writers setting out to follow or displace the realists found that they had inherited a number of typical problems, themes, or scenes that had been developed in the realists' courtship novels. Broadly speaking, these included scenes that pictured the entangled world, including suggestions of the human being's animal origins; scenes or plots that projected views of primitive culture and (possibly) evolutionary progress; scenes or plots exploring many aspects of the problem of sexual difference; scenes tracking the woman's way of selecting the male and the attributes for which she selected him; scenes dramatizing elements of Darwinian psychology, such as instinctive or unconscious behavior and the expression or concealment of emotions; and many scenes of Darwinian courtship behavior, such as those featuring aggressive, eager, and possessive males and coy females; males participating in the "law of battle"; or scenes of music and dance that dramatized Darwin's theories on sexual attraction and biological beauty.[5] The most prominent of such Darwinian scenes carrying over into the fiction from the 1890s onward are scenes (or at least patterns of imagery) of nature entangled, scenes of males wielding their powerful hands, scenes of women engaged in the selection of mates, and scenes of music and dance. Such scenes or themes became the stuff from which courtship novels could be constructed, with the younger novelists' added variations on the themes, according to their own sensibilities or more recent readings in evolutionary thought.

Still, despite the extensive Darwinian heritage (in theory and fiction), most of the writers surveyed here through the 1930s were generally attuned to the eclipse of Darwinism (the exception being Jack London) and would be better termed "evolutionists" than "Darwinists"; it is for this reason that this book is titled *Evolution and "the Sex Problem"* rather than *Darwin and "the Sex Problem."* Moreover, even though Darwin's theory of sexual selection was generally ignored if not ridiculed by evolutionary biologists during the eclipse, toward the end of the nineteenth century evolutionary theorists, psychologists, and novelists were in general agreement on two points: First, that sex could be studied only within the context of evolutionary theory, as in works like *The Evolution of Sex* by Geddes and Thomson (1889) or *Sexual Dimorphism in the Animal Kingdom: A Theory of the Origin of Secondary Sexual Characters* by Joseph T. Cunningham (1900).[6] Second, they agreed that sex was the main problem to be explored. As Havelock Ellis remarked in his preface of 1897, "I regard sex as the central problem of life.... [It]—with the racial questions that rest on it— stands before the coming generations as the chief problem for solution. Sex lies at the root of life, and we can never learn to reverence life until we know how to understand sex" (*Studies in the Psychology of Sex* 1:xxx [hereafter, *Studies*]).

This general view of evolution and "the sex problem" is especially evident in Frank Norris's *Vandover and the Brute* (1894–95) and *McTeague* (1899); in Jack London's remarks that he considered himself a specialist "on sex" (Hamilton 83) and that he had long "studied the sex problem even it its 'most curious ways'" (*Letters of Jack London* 1042); in Sherwood Anderson's remark that he had joined with other writers of his time, such as Theodore Dreiser, in an effort "to tackle the problem of sex" (*Memoirs* 467); and in F. Scott Fitzgerald's emphasis on "the problem of sex" (*This Side of Paradise* 280). Moreover, these writers' different views on evolution and sex suggest how the fiction of this period reflects the eclipse of Darwinism. One well-known exponent of an anti-Darwinian theory in the 1890s was Joseph Le Conte, who revered Darwin but also projected a view of transcendent love beyond Darwinian sexual selection. As will be explained in chapter 1, Le Conte exerted a powerful influence on his student Frank Norris. While Jack London briefly flirted with Le Conte–like views on evolutionary love (*The Sea-Wolf*), he was one of American literature's most perceptive and devoted Darwinians, as will be shown in chapter 3. He was a voracious reader in this field, especially, and kept abreast of the rapidly emerging treatises on evolution and sex, from theories by August Weismann,

Ernst Haeckel, Mendel, and Peter Kropotkin to related work in psychology by Havelock Ellis, Otto Weininger, and Sigmund Freud.

Readers who remember London mainly for *The Call of the Wild* would be surprised to survey the range and volume of his personal library, now housed at the Huntington Library and partly reflected in David Mike Hamilton's volume, *"The Tools of My Trade": The Annotated Books in Jack London's Library*. London was certainly the chief American writer of these years to resist the eclipse of Darwinism. In *The Little Lady of the Big House* (1915), for example, he took the opportunity to deride Henri Bergson's new and at that time highly appealing *Creative Evolution* for its "glittering veils of . . . metaphysics" (244–45). Moreover, Sherwood Anderson's familiar identity as one of the first Freudians in American literature should be qualified not only to note that London had explored the Freudian landscape quite impressively in *The Little Lady of the Big House*, four years before Anderson published *Winesburg, Ohio* (1919), but also to emphasize that from Anderson's point of view (and those of other writers at that time) Freud's theory of sex and the subconscious seemed to be a natural development of Darwin's theory of sexual selection and the mind. In this way, Anderson's view (and London's, for example) is in general accord with Frank Sulloway's conclusion that, in its "proper historical perspective, Freud's theory of mind [should be seen as] the embodiment of a scientific age imbued with the rising tide of Darwinism" (497).[7] As will be shown in chapter 12, this tide was cresting in 1920 when Hemingway (not yet twenty years old) was advised by his friend Ted Brumback to take a course of self-study in psychology, for it would be "invaluable to you in your writing. . . . It's so damn interesting. . . . You learn how people think, what they do when certain things happen, and how you are like or unlike them. . . . You can learn how to assign motives for every action." Quoting these remarks, Michael Reynolds notes that Brumback advised Hemingway to read William James and Freud (*The Young Hemingway* 121), but he emphasizes that Hemingway was most excited in these years by what he gleaned from Sherwood Anderson's interest in sex and, most important, from his intense study of Havelock Ellis.

Other novelists early in the century expressed their particular interest in a number of other evolutionary theorists beyond Darwin, Le Conte, and Bergson (whose *Creative Evolution* was a profound inspiration to Willa Cather), suggesting that American literature has drawn much more deeply on scientific thought than is often assumed. Many of these theorists were highly influential, either in evolutionary biology itself or in fields like psychology or anthropology that had become oriented according to principles of either Lamarckian or Darwinian evolution. For example, William James is especially important in the work of London, Stephen Crane, Gertrude Stein, and Nella Larsen. August Weismann's devastating blow to Lamarckism influenced many writers, especially London. Similarly, Ernst Haeckel was of special interest to London, Dreiser, Anderson, F. Scott Fitzgerald, and Claude

McKay. Havelock Ellis influenced many writers, especially London, Anderson, and Hemingway. Freud influenced nearly every writer from London to Hemingway. Peter Kropotkin was consulted by London, Larsen, and V. F. Calverton. Herbert Spencer, Sir John Lubbock, Elmer Gates, and Jacques Loeb influenced Dreiser. Franz Boas was especially important to certain novelists associated with the Harlem Renaissance. Robert Briffault was powerfully influential to Calverton and John Steinbeck, and W. C. Allee was of special interest to Steinbeck.

In addition to these theorists, the novelists discussed here reflect their interest in many other works in popular psychology or science, such as Lothrop Stoddard's *The Rising Tide of Color against White World-Supremacy* (which exerted an unfortunate influence on Fitzgerald but which Rudolph Fisher mocked), Otto Weininger's *Sex and Character* (Jack London and Gertrude Stein), and George Bernard Shaw's speculations on the woman as husband hunter in *Man and Superman* (Jack London, McKay, and others). In sum, American literary history has ignored these novelists' interest in evolutionary biology and its related fields. Three, for example, were particularly interested in marine biology—Dreiser, Stein (both of whom were drawn to the Woods Hole Oceanographic Institution, she in what was part of her formal education in the sciences), and Steinbeck (whose well-known relationship with the marine biologist Edward Ricketts resulted in their collaboration on *The Log from the Sea of Cortez*). Among the writers studied here, the general interest in science is especially impressive in the careers of Gertrude Stein (whose studies with William James, publications in scientific journals, and rather lengthy but uncompleted work in medical school at Johns Hopkins are well known) and Rudolph Fisher, who earned a master's degree in biology from Brown University and a medical degree from Howard University, coauthored articles in scientific journals, and headed the department of roentgenology at International Hospital in Manhattan.

This leads to two other related themes in *Evolution and "the Sex Problem."* First, whether or not a particular novelist drew on one of the specifically anti-Darwinian theories, such as Le Conte's, Bergson's, or Kropotkin's, all the novels treated here *begin* with Darwin. That they should do so during the eclipse of Darwinism is not proof that they were oblivious to the important developments in evolutionary biology of their own time (that is, the anti-Darwinian theories of evolution). Even during the eclipse, much of Darwinism survived. As Ernst Mayr emphasizes, "Natural selection was not totally condemned" during the eighty years after the *Origin of Species*: "Many biologists admitted, 'Of course, natural selection occurs, but it cannot be the exclusive causal factor in evolution'" (525). Among the theorists consulted by novelists discussed in these pages, Le Conte, Haeckel, and Kropotkin could all be so classified. Also, although many theorists during the eclipse and most evolutionary biologists today identify Darwinian evolution as the theory of natural selection, and although "the theory of natural selection was the most revolutionary concept advanced by Darwin," it is misleading to think of *the* Darwinian "revolution" as including only the theory of natural selection (Mayr 507). In Ernst Mayr's view, "Darwin's thought ushered in several intellectual revolutions," and that "the first one is that by including man in the phyletic tree of common descent, Darwin took away from man his privileged position in nature assigned to him in the Bible and in the writings of virtually all philosophers" (508). This is certainly the sense reflected in Freud's famous remark about Darwin's great "biological blow to human narcissism" (*Standard Edition* 17:141), and the idea of our common descent is the essential underlying assumption in virtually every novel to be discussed in the following pages.

For such reasons, even the most anti-Darwinian novels acknowledge and then attempt to find solutions for key aspects of the sex problem as Darwin had defined them in the theory of sexual selection. These are the same problems, essentially, that realists such as Howells and James had dramatized in their courtship novels: the male's combativeness, sexual passion, jealousy, and possessiveness; the female's power to select the superior male; the power of biological beauty in courtship; and questions of sexual and racial difference. Often in novels from the 1890s through the 1920s authors present these aspects of the sex problem as part of "the entangled bank" of life that Darwin had described. In this way they identify either the problems to be *dis*entangled or transcended through evolutionary progress, or define those with which we must simply learn to live. Thus, for example, Norris describes a scene of courtship as a "confused tangle of waving arms . . . [and] tangled legs" (*The Octopus* 782); London describes an androgynous heroine as she rides a stallion bareback, remarking that her "flowing and tangled" hair "seemed tangled in the black mane" (*The Little Lady of the Big House* 104); Cather describes a jealous male (a "buck of the beer-gardens") who "got himself in such a tangle that . . . his love . . . [was] bitterer than his hate" (*O Pioneers!* 143); Fitzgerald in *The Great Gatsby* describes how Daisy's "evening dress [became] tangled among dying orchids on the floor beside her bed" (158) and how Nick "became entangled in [a] wild strident argument" between Tom Buchanan and his lover (40); and in *Dark Princess* DuBois gives us a black hero who wants "to get his hand into the tangles of this world" (42), mainly by learning to "see beneath the unlovely surface of this racial tangle" (59).

The second related theme developed here is that these novelists played a significant role in our culture's exploration of Darwinian evolution. In their own special field of the fictive imagination, exercising "the primal instinct of narrative, of continuous scenario invention," as E. O. Wilson defines it, they helped us to realize the implications of our common descent (Rue ix). They contemplated the human being in the evolutionary stream and gave us early versions of the human narrative that some now urge us to construct as "the epic of evolution" (Rue xii). In this work they tested and often resisted or distorted aspects of evolutionary thought as they knew it.

Moreover, in exercising the fictive imagination, they produced exploratory insights of the sort that such theorists as William James, Havelock Ellis, and Sigmund Freud sought at times to verify in their *own* readings of imaginative literature. That is, they shared "in the exploration of the living organism" that Ellis spoke of in the preface to his last volume of *Studies in the Psychology of Sex*. There, retrospectively justifying some of the work in his own distinguished career, he quoted "one of the greatest masters in the exploration of the living organism, William Harvey, [who] wrote a few weeks before his death: 'Nature is nowhere accustomed more openly to display her secret mysteries than when she shows traces of her workings apart from the beaten path.'"

Like Ellis, many of the novelists discussed here willingly risked offending the general public as they sounded the meaning of life and the reality of sexual love. Even though some, such as Willa Cather, W. E. B. DuBois, and Jessie Fauset, seem clearly to have distanced themselves from work like Ellis's, they expressed their general, implicit agreement with his feeling that "that which is true of Nature in general is true of the impulse of sex in particular, and [that] none of the explorations, however unfamiliar, recorded in this volume will be devoid of instruction" (*Studies* 2:2:v). Indeed, the value of these novels as exploratory work in modern psychology often inheres in their autobiographical dimensions, often in ways that suggest the case histories upon which Ellis and Freud based their conclusions. In work by Jack London, Sherwood Anderson, Theodore Dreiser, Nella Larsen, and Ernest Hemingway, especially, we are treated to several intensely self-analytical or confessional narratives. These courageous and often embarrassing self-explorations address humanity's timeless need for coherent narratives of our existence.

"Man's Place in Nature," Life Itself, and the Sex Problem

All of the writers discussed here addressed the post-Darwinian questions suggested in the titles of T. H. Huxley's *Man's Place in Nature* (1863) and Ernst Haeckel's *The Riddle of the Universe at the Close of the Nineteenth Century* (1900). However, it is important to note that the soundings of *life* undertaken by these writers are developments in a century-long response to evolutionary thought that first addressed problems defined by Lyell and Lamarck. In 1850, shortly before the *Origin of Species*, Alfred, Lord Tennyson, contemplated the fossil record and the fact that Nature was *not* "so careful of the type." Yet, even though he felt that "Nature red in tooth and claw . . . shrieked against his creed," he could affirm his faith in a Christian universe (*In Memoriam*, sec. 56). Similarly, in 1851 Melville's Captain Ahab raged at the violent creative power: "Look! See yon Albicore!" he exclaims, "Who put it into him to chase and fang that flying-fish? . . . Who's to doom, when the judge himself is dragged to the bar?" Melville's angry God destroys Ahab, and Ishmael goes on to celebrate "the ungraspable phantom of life," in part by classifying the whales according to his playful natural theology (as pre-Darwinian biology was known).[8]

Writing at or after the close of the nineteenth century, however, the writers discussed here were inclined to share Haeckel's sense that the theory of evolution as established by the "great scientist" Charles Darwin had provided "the key to 'the question of all questions,' to the great enigma of 'the place of man in nature'" (*Riddle of the Universe* 4–5). Indeed, a surprising number of these writers were drawn to Haeckel's influential book—London and Fitzgerald, for example, or Claude McKay, who recalled how he discovered "suddenly like a comet . . . the romance of science in Huxley's *Man's Place in Nature* and Haeckel's *The Riddle of the Universe*" (*A Long Way from Home* 12). Few of these writers subscribed to Haeckel's faith in what he called "our realistic monism" (*Riddle of the Universe* 382). But at some point in their careers, often early on, these writers expressed their desires for some higher evolutionary meaning in life. For Norris, "the Truth" is revealed in the anti-Darwinian principles of growth and altruistic love; for Dreiser, in "the flash of [beauty's] distant wings" in *Sister Carrie* (368); for Willa Cather, in a soaring golden eagle, her image of the Bergsonian creative spirit—the "achievement, desire, [and] glorious striving of human art" (*Song of the Lark* 277); for Sherwood Anderson, in his character Beaut McGregor's quest for an answer to "the riddle of the Universe" in "the instinctive passion that bursts in the orgasm of battle" or in the powerful sense of unity he feels in imagining masses of marching men (*Marching Men* 66, 149); or for W. E. B. DuBois in his vision of "the real and darker world . . . that was and is to be" when "the Darker Peoples" from around the world unite (*Dark Princess* 246).

For Hemingway in the mid-1950s, however, the desire for higher meaning in life leads only to gestures like this one after he had killed an African lion: lying beside the lion, he "talked to him very softly," asked it to "pardon" him, drew a fish (the Christian symbol) in the dust, and then "rubbed it out with the palm of [his] hand" (*True at First Light* 169). It seems that Steinbeck's and Hemingway's more hardened perceptions of life reflect something of the revival of Darwinism that began in the "new synthesis" of the 1940s. Expressing his great admiration for Darwin in *The Log from the Sea of Cortez*, Steinbeck describes how in the "life water . . . everything ate everything else with a furious exuberance" and how the animals "reproduce all over the place" (48), acting out their "two major preoccupations: first survival, and second, reproduction" (70). With that view of life, Steinbeck can see the promise of ecological awareness, a theme that Jack London had been the first to explore in the American fiction surveyed here (especially in *The Valley of the Moon* and *The Little Lady of the Big House*). But although Hemingway was also highly focused on life's two major preoccupations, he was far less interested in political or ecological issues than in expressing his determination to engage life on its own terms—to know, taste, and celebrate it.

One cannot appreciate Steinbeck's and Hemingway's mid-twentieth-century soundings of life without seeing them in relation to the way writers earlier in the century were repulsed by the elemental violence of life. Presenting his character Wolf Larsen, for example, Jack London describes his strength as being "alive in itself, the essence of life in that it is the potency of motion, the elemental stuff itself . . . that which . . . lingers in the shapeless lump of turtle-meat and recoils and quivers from the prod of a finger" (*The Sea-Wolf*, chap. 2). At the same time, Gertrude Stein was exploring sex in the context of the idea that "being living" is "the struggle for existence" (*Everybody's Autobiography* 243). And in a similar vein, as the Freudian era emerged, Sherwood Anderson wrote of "the call of sex" (*Marching Men* 81) and of a character who remarks, "I have seen under the shell of life and I am afraid" ("Seeds" 30). For Theodore Dreiser, the frightful life force is best termed "It": "Whatever It is, life-spark or ego, that sits at the centre and does the deciding . . . 'polymorphous perverse' (to use Freud's apt phrase) in infancy and later. . . . Dark central force that rules in our midst, that sings whether we will or no, plays, whether we will or no, decides, whether the circumstances seem propitious or no, reads, dreams, mourns. . . . It!" (*Theodore Dreiser: A Selection of Uncollected Prose* 221–23). And during the same years the young Fitzgerald was writing of sex as a "rather unpleasant overpowering force . . . part of the machinery underlying everything" (*This Side of Paradise* 238); it is the key element in his view of "life," which he described as "that sound out there, that ghastly reiterated female sound . . . active and snarling" and moving "like a fly swarm" (*The Beautiful and Damned* 260). From a different social point of view, Fitzgerald's friend Claude McKay celebrated the so-called primitive sexuality of blacks, making a blues melody, in effect, from the idea, "It's a be-be itching life . . . and we're all sons of it" (*Home to Harlem* 35).

For many writers the most troubling problem to arise in evolutionary and sexual theory early in the twentieth century was the oppressive emphasis on heredity. This had resulted from the late-nineteenth-century work by Weismann, Haeckel, and others but especially from the rediscovery of Mendel. Although Mendelian genetics was a welcome discovery for Jack London, who heartily embraced it as a rancher who practiced selective breeding, others, such as Anderson, Stein, and Fitzgerald, were deeply disturbed. In Anderson's *Poor White* (1920), for example, Hugh McVey struggles to "conquer his ancestry [and] change the fact that he was at bottom poor white trash" (254); and several of Stein's characters seem locked within their hereditary makeup, finding that "it is a dreary business this living down the tempers we are born with" (*Making of Americans* [1903] 147). For Fitzgerald, however, the problem of heredity took on an even more threatening aspect when he was studying at Princeton, where students were asked to give their family histories in order to further the university's studies in eugenics. In Fitzgerald's view, such eugenic histories defined absolute class distinctions and barriers to one's hopes to marry up. Thus, one of

Fitzgerald's characters confesses his sin of "not believing he was the son of [his] parents" ("Absolution" 187), and Jay Gatsby's tragedy derives largely from his effort to deny his parentage and spring "from his Platonic conception of himself" (*The Great Gatsby* 104). As he studied Gatsby, Fitzgerald was reflecting on Ernst Haeckel's analysis of the reproductive drive, "that powerful impulse" whose point "is not the 'embrace' . . . or the amourousness connected therewith; it is simply the introduction of the spermatozoa into the vagina" (*Riddle of the Universe* 139). At the moment of conception, Haeckel emphasized, the individual's hereditary fate is sealed. Thus, Daisy Buchanan of East Egg is not impressed with Gatsby's house in West Egg. For such reasons Fitzgerald was more than a little appalled in contemplating the way that Gatsby and Daisy Buchanan are "possessed by intense life" (102). Both their love and the hereditary laws that shaped and ultimately separated them are merely part of the "persistent organ sound" of the deep summer night on which Gatsby first appears in the novel, when "the full bellows of the earth blew the frogs full of life" (25).

If, as it seems, Fitzgerald is comparing his characters' love life with that of mating frogs, he touches on one of the most disturbing revelations about life and the sexual impulse that had come to light in modern psychology—and that figured as one of the chief aspects of the sex problem in the studies of Havelock Ellis and Jack London. In the first pages of his *Analysis of the Sexual Impulse*, Ellis refers to the 1865–66 work published by Friedrich Leopold Goltz, explaining how Goltz had confirmed earlier research on the sexual instinct in frogs. According to this research (also cited by William James in the early pages of *The Principles of Psychology*), "during coitus [the male] will undergo the most horrible mutilations, even decapitation, and resolutely continue the act of intercourse" for up to ten days, "sitting on the back of the female and firmly clasping her with his forelegs." Moreover, Goltz found that when male frogs were exposed simply to pieces of a female's flesh, they were attracted by "every part of the female"—and that the male was alive to this attraction not by means of "any special organ, but by the whole of his sensitive system" (*Studies* 1:2:4).

How might one respond to such astonishing revelations about the sexual instinct? Surely, the community of descent cannot include both frogs and man. This was Ellis's conclusion, in effect; for while he begins his "analysis of the sexual impulse" by noting that "the term 'sexual instinct' may be said to cover . . . the phenomena of reproduction which man shares with the lower animals," he goes on to explain that in "recent years there has been a tendency to avoid the use of the term 'instinct'" (1:2:1–2). Inevitably, Ellis was obliged to acknowledge that "the facts on which Darwin based his theory [of sexual selection] lie at the very roots of our subject, and we are bound to consider their psychological significance." But Ellis can disentangle himself from the most disturbing implications of our common descent by remarking that "Darwin . . . was not a psychologist" and that "he certainly injured his theory of sexual selection by stating it in too anthropomorphic language" (1:2:22, 24). However, reflecting his own interest in these most alarming explorations of the nature or sex, Jack London opens his last and darkest novel—*The Little Lady of the Big House* (1915)—with a scene in which the hero, Dick Forrest, is reading a book "entitled 'Commercial Breeding of Frogs'" (4). As will be explained here in chapter 3, London was attempting to connect this idea with Ellis's way of exploring the sexual impulse in the human touch, especially in reference to the question of female choice. And, writing only eleven years later in *The Sun Also Rises*, Ernest Hemingway began with the idea that Ellis had taken up immediately after his discussion of the frog's sexual impulse. Reporting a study of human males that had concluded that "the sex feeling exists unmodified by absence of the sexual organs," Ellis notes that "when castration is performed without removal of the penis, it is said that potency remains for at least ten years afterward" (1:2:10). Hemingway reflected on the meaning of love by creating a hero who had everything but the penis he had lost in World War I and by pairing him with the most promiscuous woman in American literature until that time.[9]

Aspects of the Sex Problem

Sex had become a problem first because it had emerged as the essential element of human nature in the context of evolutionary thought. Like all other species that reproduce sexually, the human must comply with Darwin's "one general law leading to the advancement of all organic beings,—namely, multiply, vary, let the strongest live and the weakest die" (*Origin of Species* 208). Yet simply to study or explore sex posed an important problem for all these writers, from Darwin on. The cultural resistance to the study of sexual selection is evident in the later editions of *The Descent of Man*, where Darwin felt obliged to add, "No excuse is needed for treating this subject [of sexual selection] in some detail; for, as the German philosopher Schopenhauer remarks, 'the final aim of all love intrigues, be they comic or tragic, is really of more importance than all other ends in human life. What it all turns upon is nothing less than the composition of the next generation. . . . It is not the weal or woe of any one individual, but that of the human race to come, which is here at stake.'"[10] Similar apologetic statements appear in Ellis's prefaces and his foreword to the 1936 edition of *Studies in the Psychology of Sex*, where he recounts his well-known difficulties with the censorship of his work, as well as in the prefaces to similar works such as August Forel's *The Sexual Question* (1908). Nearly every novelist discussed here met with at least some such resistance. Indeed, considering this aspect of the sex problem it is not surprising that Darwin's theory of sexual selection was followed by Freud's theory of sexual repression.

At first, the general problem for novelists was how to construct courtship plots that would produce "the human race to come," as Schopenhauer put it, but with an eye toward evolutionary progress. This required courtship plots in which authors imagined new men and women, arranged for them to be selected, and then sent these promising couples on into the evolutionary future. Notable examples of this narrative strategy are found here in Frank Norris's *The Pit*, London's *The Valley of the Moon*, Anderson's *Poor White*, and all the novels discussed here from the Harlem Renaissance, except Nella Larsen's *Quicksand*. Even if a novelist could not share the enthusiasm for new couples whose reproductive success would yield the future generations, he or she was often tempted to do the impossible, that is, to dramatize evolution in action within the development of a single character's life. Thus Dreiser describes Carrie practicing her "evolutions" (281), and Cather tells how the "rapid evolutions" in the life of her heroine, Thea Kronborg, dazed an observer (*Song of the Lark* 438). Gradually, however, novelists such as London, Dreiser, Fitzgerald, Nella Larsen, Steinbeck, and Hemingway lost their faith in evolutionary or social progress and sought mainly to dramatize how the "machinery under everything" operates in their characters' lives (to use Fitzgerald's phrase): if they could not conceive of progress, they could trace their characters' awakenings to their sexual natures, their encounters with the psychological pitfalls of repression and hysteria, or their growing disillusionment in modern love.

Especially in the novels that project pathways to evolutionary or at least social progress, but in several others as well, the most troublesome aspect of the sex problem is the one that Darwin takes up immediately in his chapter, "Principles of Sexual Selection." There, discussing secondary sexual characters (structural and instinctual differences between the sexes, aside from their reproductive organs), he singles out the male's "special organs of prehension so as to hold [the female] securely" (1:253). In the work of many novelists, from Howells and James to Dreiser and Rudolph Fisher, the human male's hands serve this purpose, as well as the purpose of engaging in Darwin's essential law of battle among males for the possession of the female. Taking this up as his first subject in the chapter "Secondary Sexual Characters of Mammals," Darwin notes that even "the most timid animals, not provided with any special weapons for fighting, engage in desperate conflicts during the season of love" (2:239).

Although there are relatively few outright battles among males competing for females in these novels (notable exceptions being those in Norris's *McTeague* and *The Octopus* or McKay's *Home to Harlem*), Stephen Crane seems to draw on this Darwinian element in his study of battle in *The Red Badge of Courage*. However, in all of these novels, the hero wields powerful hands. Indeed, the image of the male's hand grasping the female's is so characteristic in the fiction of this period that it seemed essential to include here Tony Angell's drawing to illustrate the decisive moment in *The Great Gatsby*, for example, when Nick Carraway sees that Tom Buchanan's powerful "hand had fallen upon and covered [Daisy's] own" (152). For novelists like Fitzgerald who envision no evolutionary progress, the powerful, jealous, possessive male simply prevails in the inherent sexual struggle that Darwin had described. In other novels the hero is obliged to wield strong hands, but they are civilized or somehow subdued, as in Norris's *The Pit,* in which the character Jadwin's powerful hands are gloved, or in Fisher's *The Walls of Jericho,* in which the hero Shine's hand is wounded. But from another, more self-consciously anti-Darwinian point of view, V. F. Calverton embraces views of the anthropologist Robert Briffault (and others such as Margaret Mead), denying that sexual jealousy among males actually exists in nature or in the primitive communistic community.

Related to such studies of the male's passion are those that explore the male's polygamous desire. Again, novelists hoping to project evolutionary progress find ways of restraining that tendency, as in Norris's hero, the financier Jadwin, who seems to have no sexual appetite at all aside from what he channels into the marketplace. One of the most interesting of such maneuvers is in Jack London's *The Valley of the Moon.* The heroine of this novel knows instinctively how to solve "the prenuptial problem of selecting a husband"; but London then draws on Havelock Ellis's analysis of the evolution of modesty in order to instruct his heroine in how to negotiate "the post-nuptial problem of retaining a husband's love" (117) through the seductive use of her delicate underclothing. At about the same time, however, Willa Cather restrains one adulterous male (as well as his married lover) by arranging for the jealous husband to murder them (*O Pioneers!*); or she creates a strong heroine, Thea Kronborg, who simply keeps her several suitors at a safe distance (*The Song of the Lark*). And a number of male novelists give us heroes who seem created mainly to demonstrate that the male's polygamous desire is a natural fact, as in Dreiser's financier Frank Cowperwood (*The Financier*), Anderson's John Webster (*Many Marriages*), Steinbeck's Juan Chicoy (*The Wayward Bus*), or Hemingway's persona (in his fictional memoir *True at First Light*), all of whom simply find opportunities to satisfy their polygamous desire.

As for the female's role in sexual selection, the main problem is in her selecting the most promising male. In *The Pit,* for example, Norris devotes his first chapters to dramatizing his heroine Laura's careful evaluations of her suitors. And like many of the novelists here, Norris invests her power to select with teleological significance—the altruistic love that *draws* humanity upward, as Joseph Le Conte (and others) believed.[11] Laura knows that Jadwin is the superior male, according to Norris's interpretation of what evolutionary progress will bring, and one of her suitors embodies the sexual villainy and weakness that Norris specifies in his name, Corthell. Similarly, though Jack London envisioned no teleological pattern in *The Valley of the Moon,* he dramatizes his heroine's process of selecting a mate from among her several suitors, one of whom she selects *against* partly because of his brutal hands and another because his hands are too soft. But in London's earlier autobiographical novel, *Martin Eden*, the hero's disillusionment over what it means to be selected contributes to his eventual suicide. Even as late as 1928, the problem of the female's power to select was a key element in the novels of the Harlem Renaissance. Nella Larsen, for example, was strongly affected by the idea that "no people can become civilized until the woman has the power of choice among males," as an influential white novelist had put it.[12] Reflecting his belief in the same idea in *Dark Princess*, DuBois arranges for his heroine to select the black hero partly because of his impressive performance in knocking down a white man who had made a pass at her. The question for all these novelists from Norris to DuBois was precisely as Darwin had articulated it in his reference to "the human race to come." And for the novelists of the Harlem Renaissance the sex problem was an inextricable part of "the problem of the color line" that DuBois claimed was "the problem of the Twentieth Century" ("The Forethought," *Souls of Black Folk* [1903]). Like DuBois himself, other Harlem novelists saw the promise in Darwin's analysis of racial difference as unfixed and largely dependent upon sexual selection.[13]

As novelists developed these lines of thought in the early decades of the twentieth century, the woman's power to select became more and more complicated with her increasingly aggressive sexuality, both in terms of her role as a competitor in the sexual struggle and in terms of her liberated sexual desire. At the same time there is a related development in novels by men in which the hero's sexual reluctance reflects his fear of both the assertive female and his own nature as a violent competitor. Such characters appear in several narratives by Sherwood Anderson, in Gertrude Stein's "Melanctha," and in Fitzgerald's portrait of Nick Carraway, for example. But, in regard to the woman's role in the sexual struggle, in *Sister Carrie*, for example, Dreiser studies Carrie's moves in sexual partnering as the essential element in her general struggle for existence and for social position. Others, such as London, explore the Shavian concept of the woman as the aggressive husband-hunter. And some, such as Fitzgerald, McKay, and Hemingway, dramatize scenes of what might be called the law of battle among females for possession of the male, Fitzgerald referring to this as "the first law of woman" ("Diamond Dick and the First Law of Woman"). Hemingway portrays Mary Hemingway's willingness to kill his "fiancée" (Debba) if that relationship gets out of hand (*True at First Light*), and McKay describes naked women engaged in a "hen fight" over a man (*Home to Harlem*).

In novels of the early twentieth century, fewer women than one might expect are sexually uninhibited. That is, only a few women characters seem to reflect Kate Chopin's groundbreaking explorations of her heroine's uninhibited sexual desire in *The Awakening* (1899) or Hemingway's portrait of the promiscuous Brett Ashley in *The Sun Also Rises* (1926). Among the most liberated women characters of these years are London's Paula Forrest (*The Little Lady of the Big House*) and Stein's Melanctha (*Three Lives*). More frequently, women characters during these years of emerging Freudianism seem sexually repressed. Indeed, Havelock Ellis devoted much of his energy to liberating the modern woman from such restraints, as in his "The Evolution of Modesty" and "The Sexual Impulse in Women" (major sections in the volumes of *Studies in the Psychology of Sex*). Similarly, fewer women than one might expect contemplate motherhood and childbearing with anything like the agonizing "revolt against the ways of Nature" that Edna Pontellier had expressed in *The Awakening* (chap. 37). The most notable example of a woman repelled by her reproductive function is Nella Larsen's character Helga Crane, whose childbearing leaves her with only scorn and hatred for her former "belief in the miracle and wonder of life": Helga concludes that "for Negroes at least [life was] only a great disappointment" (*Quicksand* 130). More typically, women characters of these years either minimize their desire for children of simply refuse to reproduce. For example, one of Fitzgerald's characters thinks that "the intolerable sentiment of child-bearing" is a menace to her beauty, concluding that "motherhood was also the privilege of the female baboon" (*The Beautiful and Damned* 392–93). And Willa Cather regards marriage and motherhood as pitfalls that her heroine can rather easily avoid in *The Song of the Lark*. While Cather's narrative strategy seems related to her exploration of her own lesbian interests, it also reflects her attraction to Bergson's *Creative Evolution* (explained here in chapter 6). Like others from these years during the eclipse of Darwinism, she was drawn to Bergson's theory of evolution because it virtually erased Darwin's theory of sexual selection. Embracing Bergson, one could transcend sexual violence; from another point of view, a number of early Freudians were drawn to Bergson because "the *élan vital* became a pleasant way to define the libido" (Hale, *Freud in America,* 243). However, the psychological aspects of the sex problem in early twentieth-century American fiction are so complex that it will help to discuss them separately, as though they were separable. In fact, as emphasized throughout this study, after Darwin's analysis of sex and the cerebral system it was virtually impossible to explore the sex problem without reference to the evolution of mind.

Modern Psychology and the Sex Problem

Writing that Darwin had dealt a great "*biological* blow" to mankind's "narcissistic illusion," Freud took credit for having shown "that the life of our sexual instincts cannot be wholly tamed."[14] But, as Michael Ghiselin remarks, even though "the insight that the brain is the slave of the gonads is attributed with good reason to Freud, for it was he who rammed an unpalatable truth down the throats of an indignant humanity, it helps to put matters in better perspective when we realize that the Freudian revolution was implicit in the Darwinian" (*The Economy of Nature and the Evolution of Sex* 219). This perspective is not yet sufficiently developed in American literary history. In fact, Howells and James were exploring the Darwinian landscape of sex and the unconscious during the 1870s, when the young Freud was also beginning to study *The Descent of Man*. Moreover, because the eclipse of Darwinism in American literary history extends into the Freudian era, it is necessary to enlarge Frederick J. Hoffman's landmark study, *Freudianism and the Literary Mind* (1945). Hoffman was apparently unaware that Darwin was one of the major "Precursors of Freud" (the title of his chapter 11) and therefore presented a misleading account of "the reception of Freudian theory" among American writers (vi). Referring to "the ordinarily slow process of transferring an interest from scientific journals to the popular consciousness [which] was made even slower by the preoccupation with questions of war and peace" surrounding World War I, Hoffman argues that "the real penetration of Freudianism" into the literary mind came only in the 1920s (56).

But Hoffman's formulation vastly underestimates the intellectual vitality of Jack London, whose *The Little Lady of the Big House* is the earliest and one of the most impressive Freudian novels in American literature. Indeed, Hoffman's sense of the slow process by which the literary imagination engages scientific thought repeats the miscalculation of earlier literary historians who concluded that Darwinian thought exerted no significant influence on American fiction until the 1890s. Moreover, Hoffman ignores the fact that, from the point of view of writers such as London, Dreiser, Anderson, and Fitzgerald, Havelock Ellis's *Studies in the Psychology of Sex* provided a resounding accompaniment to the "Freudian" theme in the early-twentieth-century exploration of sex. One cannot read the fiction of this period—or for that matter, Freud's own early work in comparison with his late work—without appreciating the extent to which Freudianism was and remains an even more unstable and contested term than Darwinism.

One dimension in London's exploration of the sexual unconscious in *The Little Lady of the Big House* concerned an idea that he later underscored in Edwin Bissell Holt's *The Freudian Wish and Its Place in Ethics* (1915). Holt (an assistant professor at Harvard who had been greatly influenced by William James) produced one of the most popular early books on psychoanalysis that was very well known among New York intellectuals (Hale, *Freud and the Americans*, 426). For London, one of Holt's most interesting ideas was the suggestion that the Freudian wish is an expression of the unconscious soul, which Holt compared to the almost mystical sensitivity that had impressed him in Darwin's description of the tips of roots in *The Power of Movement in Plants*. Related varieties of the unconscious soul appear in Willa Cather's transformation of the *élan vital* in the musical career of Thea Kronborg and in DuBois's argument that the souls of black folk find voice in the "sorrow song" rather than the primitive and libidinous blues.

More in the mainstream of the rising tide of Darwinism, as felt in the modern psychological novel, are two aspects of the sex problem that earlier writers had incorporated in novels of courtship and marriage—the drama of expressed or concealed emotions and the role of music and dance in courtship. A number of writers from these years were especially inventive in dramatizing their characters' conflicts with each other in their expression or concealment of emotions. Crane, London, and Stein, for example, continued to develop the materials that the earlier novelists had mined from Darwin's *The Expression of the Emotions in Man and Animals*. Stephen Crane's *The Red Badge of Courage* drew on both Darwin and William James to produce one of American literature's first and most impressive studies in what we have come to call evolutionary psychology. Moreover, London (*The Little Lady of the Big House*) and Stein (*Q.E.D.*) demonstrated how these Darwinian materials—already brilliantly exploited by Harold Frederic in *The Market-Place* (1899)—could be incorporated, compellingly, in exploratory fiction that had begun to move well beyond William James toward the Freudianism that we are told did not emerge until the 1920s.[15]

All the novelists discussed here include scenes of music or dance as they explore the psychology of sex. But novelists interpreted the musical phenomenon in distinctly different ways. For example, Cather keys on the idea of sublimation in music. As will be explained here in chapter 6, this idea (often attributed to Freud) can be traced to Edmund Gurney's *The Power of Sound* (1880), a work founded directly on Darwin's theory of music and a landmark in the history of aesthetics. Only a few years after Cather's heroine transcends her sexual nature through musical sublimation, however, Claude McKay draws on Darwin's theory of music in order to affirm the supposed black sexual primitivism that other Harlem novelists vehemently rejected. Whereas DuBois, for example, claimed that the African American's truest form of musical expression was the "soul song" ("sorrow song" or "slave song"), McKay celebrated the blues as a distinct element in the black's psychological good health as compared with that of the sexually repressed whites.

At about the same time that McKay was transforming Darwin's theory of the sexual origins of music into a rather raunchy blues melody, Havelock Ellis argued in one of his most popular books, *The Dance of Life* (1923), that life itself is a dance. Taking up this principle of sexual selection that courtship novelists had been dramatizing since the early 1870s, Ellis contributed to the literary discussion of primitivism during the Jazz Age. Like Cather, however, he tended to sublimate the sexual motive, suggesting that, in the dance of life "we are all engaged . . . in creating the spiritual world" (xi–xiii). Ellis speculates, with special attention to dance "among primitive peoples," that dance is "a kind of sexual selection . . . embodied in unconscious eugenics . . . aid[ing] the higher development of the race" (46–47). While writers such as McKay or Fitzgerald (who purchased *The Dance of Life*) would have rejected Ellis's optimistic views on eugenics and "the future race," they would have agreed with Ellis's suggestion that evolution and sex were at the center of modern art. The merging Darwinian and Freudian theme is evident in Ellis's assertion that "the external features of the male and his external activities . . . have been developed out of the impulse of repressed organic sexual desire striving to manifest itself ever more urgently in the struggle to overcome the coyness of the female" (110). And it is hard to imagine any artist of the 1920s who would not have not been intrigued by Ellis's more interesting thought that

> on the psychic side there has been a parallel impulse, if of later development, to carry on the same task in forms of art which have afterwards acquired an independent activity and a yet further growth dissociated from this primary biological function. We think of the natural ornaments which adorn male animals from far down in the scale even up to man, of the additions made thereto by tattooing and decoration and garments and jewels, of the parades and dances and songs of musical serenades found among lower animals as well as Man, together with the love-lyrics of savages, furnishing the beginnings of the most exquisite arts of civilisation. (110)

If the foregoing elements in modern psychological fiction were clearly derived from Darwinian concepts long tested in realist and naturalist fiction, others seemed distinctly new: the problems of hysteria, repression, autoerotism, androgyny, and the connection between love and pain. But in their proper perspective, these, too, can be seen as having arisen in the development and eclipse of Darwinism. As will be suggested in chapter 1, the resistance to Darwin's theory of sexual selection led authors such as Norris to imagine evolutionary steps by means of which the human being could transcend what they considered the animalistic evil of the sexual instinct. Norris did this in part by presenting sexual animalism as dirty (*Vandover and the Brute*) or decadent (as in his villainous character Corthell). Accordingly, Norris saw great promise in characters who could repress the animal instincts or in those whom he could present as "clean" if not essentially chaste.

Very early in the new century, however, the emerging idea that *repression* was the great threat to civilization included a new interest in the normality of the sexual impulse. After a late-nineteenth-century emphasis on the scientific study of sexual pathology, the new field of sexology began to qualify earlier work on perverse childhood sexuality. Then, largely through the influence of Albert Moll and Havelock Ellis, a "new and largely Darwinian conception of sex" made it possible for "sexuality in childhood" to be understood "as a biologically normal and prerequisite part of human maturation" (Sulloway 279, 309–10). Thus, in his widely disseminated and frequently reprinted *Love's Coming-of-Age* (1896), Edward Carpenter included chapters called "The Sex-Passion" and "The Intermediate Sex," for example, in order to correct "the notion of the uncleanness of Sex" (26).[16] And in the following year Havelock Ellis announced in the general preface that he was determined to present the actual facts of sex and "from the investigation of the facts . . . to ascertain what is normal and what is abnormal, from the point of view of physiology and of psychology. We want to know what is naturally lawful under the various chances that befall man, not as the born child of sin, but as a naturally social animal" (*Studies* 1:1:xxx). In the fiction of this period these developments are reflected in many ways. For example, in the way Jack London provides for his heroine's education in natural sexuality in *The Valley of the Moon*; in Sherwood Anderson's remark in *Dark Laughter*, "The dance of life! . . . Listen, do you hear the music?" (92) and in the way he presents the repressed wife as more animalistic than her polygamous husband John Webster in *Many Marriages* (190); and in McKay's aside to his reader that "you," too, would prowl the streets of Harlem "if you were a black kid [like his hero, Jake Brown] hunting for joy in New York" (*Home to Harlem* 30).

Beginning with Stein's "The Good Anna" (*Three Lives* [1909]) and London's *The Valley of the Moon* (1913), nearly every novel here surveyed includes portraits of characters suffering from sexual repression. In the manner of Ellis's many case studies and, especially, the famous case of Anna O., many of these fictional case studies could be "unraveled like a novel," as Nathan Hale describes Freud's very impressive method of presenting his study of Anna O. in his lectures at Clark University in 1909 (6). The full collection of such portraits in American fiction (extending in the novels covered here to Steinbeck's *The Wayward Bus*) echoes the "denunciation of civilized repressions" that Freud delivered in his final Clark lecture (Hale 11). As Freud warned in the Clark lectures that "we ought not to go so far as to fully neglect the animal part of our nature" (qtd. in Hale 12), Stein showed how her good Anna's "arduous and troubled life" reflected her "high ideals for canine chastity and discipline." Poor Anna sought furiously to restrain the sexual activities of "all the wicked-minded dogs" (*Three Lives* 12–13). In 1915 Cather's Mrs. Archie (*The Song of the Lark*) is so stingy that her husband "could never get thick cream for his strawberries" and sometimes has to go all the way to Denver because he is "hungry" (33). In 1928 DuBois gives us another such woman who drives her husband to distraction because, shortly after their marriage, she has "an electric log put in" their fireplace (*Dark Princess* 142). In 1930 one of V. F. Calverton's characters, a priest, is so threatened by an attractive parishioner's uninhibited sexuality (and her flirtation with the socialist ideals of free love that Calverton was advocating) that he is driven to murder her. And in 1947 Steinbeck gives us a woman who habitually washes her combs, brushes, and wedding ring in ammonia water while, in other ways, she "strangled" her husband's libido (*The Wayward Bus* 62, 288).

All these case studies of repression are obvious features of the Freudian landscape in American fiction but also, though less obviously, of the Darwinian landscape. The connection is evident in London's effort to imagine a new woman in *The Valley of the Moon*. Saxon Brown's evolutionary success depends not only on her power to select a husband and then retain his love but also on her ability to survive encounters with hysteria and repression—related aspects of the sex problem that London viewed as key symptoms of the social ill in industrial America. In the laundry where she works, Saxon sees a fellow worker fling "wild glances, like those of an entrapped animal" after hearing others talk of going "love dancin'," while "the forewoman strode the isles with a threatening eye for incipient breakdown and hysteria" (3–5). Similarly, Stein's portrait of the good Anna reflects her formal studies with William James, her brief studies in marine biology, her own publications on hysteria (cited by Havelock Ellis), her tribute to Darwin as "the great man of the period that [framed] my youth" (*Everybody's Autobiography* 242), and, in *Fernhurst*, the reasoning behind her critique of the "naive realism" (44) that limits her characters' "knowledge of life and love and sex" (4).

A darker aspect of the sex problem as explored by these novelists involves modern psychology's analysis of the sexual impulse and pain. And once again this analysis develops from Darwinian insights, as is evident in Havelock Ellis's opening remarks on "Love and Pain" (a major section of his second volume in *Studies in the Psychology of Sex*): "The chief key to the relationship between love and pain [is] to be found in animal courtship" (1:2:66). In the first place, Ellis notes, "the zoölogical root of the connection between love and pain" must be traced to the male's combative nature and the pleasure the female takes in it (60). On this point he cites not only Freud's remarks in *Three Contributions to the Theory of Sex* that the excitement boys experience in playful wrestling reveals "one of the roots of sadism" but also, more disturbingly, a study that concludes that "the pleasure of battle and murder is so predominantly an attribute of the male sex throughout the animal kingdom that there can be no question about the close connection between this side of the masculine character and male sexuality" (70). All this leads to the ideas on "the love-bite" and "lycanthropy" (werewolfism) that, as noted here in chapter 1, were reflected in Norris's interest in McTeague's nibbling of his wife's fingertips and in Vandover's lycanthropy (*McTeague* and *Vandover and the Brute*). Again, however—and in contradiction to Norris's way of presenting these phenomena—Ellis considers the love-bite "as the *normal* manifestation of the connection between love and pain" and stipulates that it crosses into "the frontier of the abnormal" only when one exhibits "a conscious desire . . . to draw blood, a real delight in this process, a love of blood" (120, emphasis mine).

In addition to Norris's early work with some of these materials, many other writers explored the connection between love and pain, as in Stein's emphasis on the good Anna's "varied pleasures and pains," particularly her tendency to scold: "truly she loved it best when she could scold" (37). Some writers seem to include references to the sadomasochistic theme mainly to demonstrate that they are up to date in their psychological research. With a reference to "Dr. Freud," for example, one of Anderson's characters contemplates his wife's "want[ing] him to beat her" and then asks himself, "am I becoming a Sadist?" (*Dark Laughter* 53). And both Carl Van Vechten (*Nigger Heaven*) and Claude McKay (*Home to Harlem*) arrange for their heroes to encounter similar women, Van Vechten's hero succumbing to such temptations while McKay's hero moves beyond them in disgust. Of all the writers here, however, only Hemingway touches the uttermost depths of the evolutionary past regarding the modern analysis of love and pain. As Ellis notes, "we have but to go sufficiently far back, or sufficiently far afield, in the various zoölogical series to find that manifestations which, from the human point of view, are in the extreme degree abnormally sadistic here become actually normal." Ellis is referring to "the beginning of animal life in the protozoa [when] sexual conjugation itself is sometimes found to present the similitude, if not the actuality, of the complete devouring of one organism by another" (*Studies* 1:2:127).[17] Hemingway does not gives us any scenes of cannibalism, but, as will be suggested here in chapter 12, the darkness of his Africa and his oceanic Eden always includes reminders of the inherent violence of the two hungers (the nutritive, in the need to kill and eat, and the reproductive). He gives us repeated images of his lovers eating foods like eggs and artichoke hearts, and he offers us only glimpses of our submerged evolutionary past, as in the image of David Bourne putting "his salty mouth against" Marita's and, in kissing her breasts, remarking that "they taste like the sea" (*The Garden of Eden* 241).

Finally, one of the most disturbing and yet liberating aspects of the sex problem for novelists of these years is the question of androgyny. This question as well originated in Darwin's analysis of the evolution of sexual difference and related research. As he wrote in *The Descent of Man*:

> It has long been known that in the vertebrate kingdom one sex bears rudiments of various accessory parts, appertaining to the reproductive system, which properly belong to the opposite sex; and it has now been ascertained that at a very early embryonic period both sexes possess true male and female glands. Hence some extremely remote progenitor of the whole vertebrate kingdom appears to have been hermaphrodite or androgynous. (1:207)

In fiction from the last decades of the nineteenth century this idea figured in the general critique of love and underscored the possibility of degeneracy in the male, as in Harold Frederic's analysis of Theron Ware's ineffectual manhood. Bringing in references to Darwin's theories about the evolution of hermaphroditism in plants, Frederic dramatized Theron's inability to do "the work of selection" (*Damnation of Theron Ware* 228, 323). Kate Chopin and Edith Wharton seem to have found in the theory of bisexual normality a natural way of blurring the lines of sexual difference and permitting their women to select males for their less virile and somewhat effeminate beauty, and Charlotte Perkins Gilman saw it as justifying her claim that our culture erred in its unnatural emphasis on absolute sexual difference.[18]

At the same time that Chopin, Frederic, and Gilman were drawing on Darwin's theory of bisexuality, the idea was beginning to enter modern psychology through the work of Richard von Krafft-Ebing, Wilhelm Fliess, Ellis, and Freud. Tracing this development, Frank Sulloway writes, for example, that "it was Wilhelm Fliess who first convinced Freud that all human beings are bisexual," leading Freud to conclude that "without taking bisexuality into account I think it would be scarcely possible to arrive at an understanding of the sexual manifestations that are actually to be observed in men and women" (183–84).[19] A brief passage from Ellis's revised edition of *Sexual Inversion* (first published in 1897) provides a convenient example of how early twentieth-century novelists were inclined to view the subject. Having traced the way the idea of bisexuality had been a subject of "medicophilosophic" speculation from ancient times through the writings of Schopenhauer, Ellis writes:

> Then the conception of latent bisexuality, independently of homosexuality, was developed from the purely scientific side (by Darwin and evolutionists generally). In the next stage this conception was adopted by the psychiatric and other scientific authorities on homosexuality (Krafft-Ebing and the majority of other students). Finally, embryologists, physiologists of sex and biologists generally, not only accept the conception of bisexuality, but admit that it probably helps to account for homosexuality. In this way the idea may be said to have passed into current thought. (*Studies* 1:4:314)

It is not so easy, however, to do justice to the variety of ways in which early-twentieth-century novelists explored this idea. In *The Little Lady of the Big House*, London, for example, is interested, as Chopin had been (though there is no evidence that he knew of her), in the way his heroine is attracted by the more feminine features of her lover's beauty, as compared with her husband's more traditional masculinity. Writing only a few years later, Anderson explored his heroes' fear of and withdrawal from their inherent violence as males, as in "The Man Who Became a Woman." In *Poor White* and *Dark Laughter* his heroines' development depends in part on what they learn from lesbian friends (but not in explicitly erotic relationships), and in his famous sympathetic portrait of a repressed homosexual in the Winesburg story "Hands," he apparently drew on the controversial theory among sexologists of possible male and female brain centers.

In *The Great Gatsby* Fitzgerald hints that Nick Carraway's being "half sick between grotesque reality and savage frightening dreams" (154) derives in part from his confused sexual identity. Fitzgerald's hint, I suggest, includes Nick's identity as a "sport," which seems a reflection of the idea, as Ellis put it, that "sexual inversion may . . . fairly be considered a 'sport,' or variation . . . which we see throughout living nature, in plants and animals" (*Studies* 1:4:317). More interestingly, perhaps, but also more difficult to interpret, are the narrative strategies of writers such as Claude McKay, Willa Cather, and Gertrude Stein, whose sexual orientations must have complicated their presentations of the courtship plot. Of the works discussed, only one by Stein addresses her lesbian interests openly, in the early autobiographical piece *Q.E.D.* (though she delayed its publication), and less openly in her studies of Anna and Melanctha in *Three Lives*.[20] It was of course much more difficult to write from this point of view in Stein's and Cather's lifetimes than in our own, but both these women were no less liberated by Darwinian insights into the ambiguities of sexual identity than were London and Anderson, as reflected, for example, in Stein's reference to a character's interest "in the varieties of human experience and her constant desire . . . to partake of all human relations" (*Fernhurst* 19).

Hemingway too was emboldened in his exploration of androgyny by what he found in Ellis and Darwin. Although discussions of androgyny or gender have dominated criticism on Hemingway ever since *The Garden of Eden* appeared in 1986, his interpreters rarely sense that his interest in this part of the sex problem is related to the history of evolutionary thought. Lacking this perspective, Hemingway's readers tend to ignore or misinterpret the darker depths of his work. As Hemingway's most distinguished biographer suggests, in reference to the "dark heart of Africa [that] beats deeply within his writing," the subject "he studied first, last, and always was that strange animal, his fellow man" (Reynolds, "Ernest Hemingway, 1899–1961," 47–48). Hemingway is an important contributor to our culture's long meditation on the meaning of our common descent, of man's place in nature, and of the nature of the human mind. And as our culture's exploratory work in evolution and the sex problem has focused on "the development of the cerebral system," as Darwin put it, it is worth considering the following passage from *The Expression of the Emotions in Man and Animals*, for here we can sense how Darwin also felt what Freud called the great biological blow to human narcissism. Describing how people express the feeling of helplessness by shrugging the shoulders, raising the open palms of the hands, elevating the eyebrows, and opening the mouth, Darwin writes:

> I may mention, in order to show how unconsciously the features are thus acted on, that though I had often intentionally shrugged my shoulders to observe how my arms were placed, I was not at all aware that my eyebrows were raised and mouth opened, until I looked at myself in a glass; and since then I have noticed the same movements in the faces of others. (264)

Evolutionary Psychology. In *The Expression of the Emotions in Man and Animals* Darwin tells how he had "looked at [himself] in a glass" in order to study the expression of helplessness or impotence. Seeing his raised eyebrows and open mouth, he realized "how unconsciously the features are thus acted upon" and later "noticed the same movements in the faces of others."

The American fiction surveyed here is best seen in this light, as a series of ever-deeper soundings of the self in life and love. In 1851 Ishmael could recall the story of Narcissus, consider his own reflected image in the water, and contemplate "the ungraspable phantom of life" ("Loomings," *Moby-Dick*). But after 1859 the quest for self-knowledge plunged into the dark past. It certainly has been a dark time for our culture since Darwin regarded the reflected image of his own animal helplessness. Dark as in William James's "zoological psychology" (*Principles of Psychology* 307) or "evolutionary psychology" (149), which he launched on the idea that "selection is the very keel on which our mental ship is built" (640). And darker yet in the soundings by Freud and by innumerable other psychologists and writers such as London, Anderson, Stein, Larsen, and Fitzgerald.

"Who are you, Martin Eden?" demands London's autobiographical character in repeated scenes in front of the looking glass (*Martin Eden* 145). "'What kind of a brain lay behind there,' was his insistent interrogation" (68). Similarly, writing on what he called "the universal narcissism of men" (139) a few years later (in the essay "A Difficulty in Psycho-Analysis" from 1917), Freud imagined speaking to his ego: "Turn your eyes inward, look into your own depths, learn first to know yourself" (143). In none of these self-explorations, however, is there a darker image of life than Hemingway gives us from his Africa or Garden of Eden. In these last works, especially *The Garden of Eden*, with its profuse imagery of characters contemplating their mirrored selves, Hemingway develops the modern analysis of narcissism beyond what Havelock Ellis had suggested in the last volume of *Studies in the Psychology of Sex* (which Hemingway, a longtime reader of Ellis, purchased when it appeared in 1936). There, tracing the history of thought on the subject of narcissism, Ellis arrives at Freud's most recent conclusion on the subject, that narcissism "becomes 'the libidinal complement to the egoism of the instinct of self-preservation, a measure of which may be attributed to every living creature'" (2:2:357–58). Whereas for Freud this conception of self-love and the instinct for self-preservation led to a theory of psychic disorders that would enable us to "avoid falling ill in future" ("A Difficulty in Psycho-Analysis" 142–43), Hemingway locates the *normal* self squarely within the community of descent—wherein there is no remedy for the instinct of self-preservation.

Still, if this was a dark time in modern thought, there is also a glimmer of illumination in the works by Steinbeck and Hemingway. Produced during the years when the new synthesis in evolutionary biology had begun to renew the sense of grandeur in the view of life Darwin celebrated in his conclusion to the *Origin of Species*, works such as *The Log from the Sea of Cortez*, *The Wayward Bus*, *True at First Light*, and *The Garden of Eden* seem also to have emerged from an eclipse of Darwinism in our literary exploration of human life and love. As though reclaiming man's place in nature, Steinbeck celebrates the "life water" in all its "furious exuberance" (48) and urges us to accept the ecological fact "that man is related to the whole thing" (218). And Hemingway was determined to realize and celebrate what it means to be *alive* by fully embracing the two forces that move the world, as Freud put it, "hunger and love" (Sulloway 254). In Hemingway's dark world everyone *must* kill and eat. Still, tracing this violent life to its ocean origins, he celebrates the idea that the sun "makes great deep prisms in the blue water" (*Old Man and the Sea* 44). Hemingway proclaims that, with courage, one can "make love and listen to the [African] night" and even join in the high dark laughter of the hyena's "night song" (*True at First Light* 309).

Notes

1. Edwin H. Cady quotes Howells's remark on how the American novel should keep "in the light of common day an action whose springs are in the darkest fastnesses of the human soul" (*The Light of Common Day* vii).

2. Cynthia Eagle Russett's *Sexual Science* is an indispensable work on this subject. Equally important in the later development of American literary realism is the question of racial difference, with its concern for miscegenation. On this general subject, John S. Haller's *Outcasts from Evolution* is an excellent guide to the racial science of the times.

3. For a recent study of sexual selection and the mind, see Geoffrey Miller's *The Mating Mind*. Explaining how the theory of sexual selection "was neglected for a century after Darwin and why it was revived only in the 1980s," Miller argues that, while present-day "evolutionary biologists and evolutionary psychologists . . . know about sexual selection," most have overlooked "its power, subtlety, and promise for explaining human mental traits" (15).

4. Bowler notes in *The Eclipse of Darwinism* that in the "classic survey of the modern synthesis," *Evolution: The Modern Synthesis* (1942), Julian Huxley "coined the term 'eclipse of Darwinism' to describe the situation at the turn of the century when many biologists had turned their backs on selection" (5).

5. Such problems, scenes, and themes are described in my *The Descent of Love*, 17–25. It is also important to consider another explanation of why such elements might recur in fiction or indeed why they often appear in earlier fiction that could not have been influenced by Darwinian theory. As Brian Boyd argues in "Jane, Meet Charles," in reference to Jane Austen, we should not be surprised to note that "Austen focuses overwhelmingly on female choice" (16). Commenting on the theory of mind advanced in contemporary evolutionary psychology, Boyd concludes that "even in the work of a writer who seems aloof from biology and remote from the humanly universal, much can be interpreted in terms of biologically evolved characteristics of human life, rather than as no more than the product of a particular cultural moment" (23). A keen observer of life, "Austen draws deep on our whole biological heritage. . . . She does not ignore biology; no major writer can" (23).

6. Bowler describes how Cunningham's "survey of secondary sexual characters," such as antlers or bright coloration among males, was "aimed at demonstrating their Lamarkian origin," in an effort to refute Darwin's theory of sexual selection. "His theory was based on use-inheritance and the continued effect of habit in stimulating those parts of the body most used in courtship and mating" (*The Eclipse of Darwinism* 90).

7. Referring to Sulloway's work on Freud, Bowler argues that while Freud might have thought of himself as building on Darwinian theory, "it was the developmental, not the

Darwinian, view of evolution that played the most vital role in the origin of this most disturbing facet of modern thought." Bowler believes that Ernst Haeckel's "recapitulationism, perhaps the most blatant late nineteenth-century expression of the analogy between growth and evolution" played a much greater role in the shaping of Freud's thought (*The Non-Darwinian Revolution* 192). As far as the literary response to Darwin is concerned, however, late nineteenth-century and early twentieth-century writers before Freud were clearly exploring Darwin's theory of the mind as he presented it in *The Expression of the Emotions*. See, for example, my discussions of Harold Frederic, Kate Chopin, and Edith Wharton in *The Descent of Love*.

8. Chapters 132 ("The Symphony") and 1 ("Loomings"). See my *Sea-Brothers* for an interpretation of *Moby-Dick* from this point of view.

9. For a discussion of *The Sun Also Rises* as a response to the theory of sexual selection and to Ellis's analysis of the sexual impulse, see chapter 13 in my *The Descent of Love*. Hemingway joked with Fitzgerald about his gratitude to Fitzgerald for having helped him place *The Sun Also Rises* with Scribner's: "I am asking Scribner's to insert as a subtitle in everything after the eighth printing

THE SUN ALSO RISES (LIKE YOUR COCK IF YOU HAVE ONE)
A greater Gatsby
Written with the friendship of F. Scott Fitzgerald (Prophet of THE JAZZ AGE)"

Baker, *Ernest Hemingway: Selected Letters, 1917–1961*, 231. Although Hemingway could joke about this, his serious purpose with the novel was to produce "a treatise on basic loneliness and the inadequacy of promiscuity" (767–68).

10. This is from the Modern Library edition of *The Descent of Man* (891), a volume that contains both the sixth edition of *The Origin of Species* and the fourth edition of *The Descent of Man*.

11. Discussing other evolutionary theories of the time, such as John Fiske's *The Ascent of Man* (1894), Richard Hofstadter remarks that in Henry Drummond's *Natural Law in the Spiritual World* (1883) "the first few chapters of evolution may be headed the Struggle for life, [but] the book as a whole is a love story" (*Social Darwinism* 97).

12. See Thadious M. Davis, *Nella Larsen*, 153. As explained later in this book, Larsen and a number of other Harlem novelists responded to the novel *Birthright* by the white southerner T. S. Stribling.

13. In *The Descent of Man* Darwin concludes the chapter "On the Races of Man" by remarking that it can "be shewn that the differences between the races of man, as in colour, hairyness, form of features, &c., are of the nature which it might have been expected would have been acted on by sexual selection" (1:250).

14. Freud explained that Copernicus dealt the first great blow, "the *cosmological* one," and Darwin the second, "the *biological* blow to human narcissism." But "the two discoveries—that the life of our sexual instincts cannot be wholly tamed, and that mental processes are in themselves unconscious and only reach the ego and come under its control through incomplete and untrustworthy perceptions—these two discoveries amount to a statement that *the ego is not master in its own house*. Together they represent the third blow to man's self-

love, what I may call the *psychological* one" ("A Difficulty in the Path of Psycho-Analysis" [1917], *The Standard Edition of the Complete Psychological Works of Sigmund Freud*, 17:143).

15. For a discussion of Frederic's work in conjunction with Darwin's theory of the emotions, especially in his novel *The Market-Place*, see chapter 10 in my *The Descent of Love*.

16. As Hale notes in *Freud and the Americans*, another side of the development that included Carpenter's famous book were those who resisted such "civilized" morality (which they associated too easily with Freud) by advocating sexual hygiene from a different point of view. Participating in "medical campaigns against venereal disease and . . . reticence," they advocated "purity" rather than license. Hale cites a negative review of Carpenter's book by one well-known representative of the more conservative point of view, referring to the review as "one of the clearest statements of American moralism" regarding the sex problem at that time (338–39).

17. On the subject of "reproduction by cannibalism" in modern psychology, see also "The Phylogeny of Sex" (Sulloway 290–96).

18. These issues are discussed in my *The Descent of Love*, where it is suggested that, while one of Wharton's women characters is attracted to a slightly effeminate lover, her husband wields his traditional male strength to control her choice (323–26); Kate Chopin's Edna Pontellier selects a lover whose beauty Chopin distinguishes from traditional masculinity (218–19); and Gilman's *Women and Economics* (1898) is founded on Darwin's theory of the evolution of sexual difference (202–3, 391–92).

19. Sulloway's full discussion of this subject is especially interesting (158–84).

20. Outside of the works discussed here, other authors dared to write more openly of homosexuality. A notable example is Richard Bruce Nugent's contribution to the Harlem Renaissance, "Smoke, Lilies, and Jade," first published in the short-lived literary magazine *Fire!!* (1926) and reprinted in David Levering Lewis, *The Portable Harlem Renaissance*, where Lewis describes the story as "the scandal of the Harlem Renaissance, an impressionistic celebration of androgyny, homosexuality, and drugs."

1 Frank Norris on the Evolution and Repression of the Sexual Instinct

Frank Norris's interest in evolution and the sexual instinct is so well known that there would seem to be little more to say on the subject. His grotesque if not darkly comic portraits of the human animal in *Vandover and the Brute* and *McTeague* are prominent features in the landscape of American Naturalism. When, for example, "the male virile desire in [McTeague] tardily awakened, aroused itself, strong and brutal" (*Novels and Essays* 281), "the foul stream of hereditary evil" (285) drove him to kiss his unconscious patient Trina "grossly, full on the mouth" (284). Making a similar point in his 1896 essay "Theory and Reality," Norris complained of the literary "idealists [who] . . . close their eyes to the fact that men *and women* are after all only human," adding that "even this word 'human' is misleading," as it obscures the fact that the human being "is, and for countless generations will be, three-quarters animal, living and dying, eating and sleeping, mating and reproducing even as the animals" (*Novels and Essays* 1104). And in "A Plea for Romantic Fiction" (1901) he called on novelists to plumb the "depths of the human heart, and the mystery of sex, and the problems of life, and the black, unsearched penetralia of the soul of man" (*Novels and Essays* 1168–69).

Norris's critics have certainly examined his interest in evolution and the sexual instinct, but with only rare brief reference to the theory of sexual selection.[1] A better approach to Norris's presentation of sexual love, however, would be to examine it as part of a prolonged development in American fiction that began in an immediate response to Darwin's *The Descent of Man, and Selection in Relation to Sex* in 1871, first in the courtship novels of W. D. Howells and Henry James. The problem is that most historians of American literature have misjudged the force of Darwinian theory in the 1870s and 1880s and have simply overlooked the theory of sexual selection. When Darwin is mentioned at all in literary discussions of sexuality, it is usually with the assumption that his work merely confirmed age-old observations in life and literature about the male's sexual eagerness and the female's coyness in courtship. Such assumptions obscure Darwin's profound contributions to literary realism. By locating the study of sex within the larger evolutionary reality that he had established in the *Origin of Species*, by demonstrating the surprising complexity of the sexual struggle, and by providing innumerable fascinating observations from animal behavior and evolutionary anthropology, Darwin offered novelists a wealth of absolutely new materials for presenting the reality of courtship and marriage, for critiquing idealized love or motherhood, and for engaging in the increasingly widespread social debate over racial and sexual difference.

Novelists during these years kept impressively abreast of developments in the new evolutionary studies of sex: in *A Foregone Conclusion* (1874), for example, Howells had begun to explore the unconscious expression and repression of the sexual instinct. This was the year after Freud began his career as a medical student at the University of Vienna, where he enrolled in a class, General Biology and Darwinism. Similarly, around the 1890s, as Norris was beginning his brief career, evolutionists were exploring the new sexual reality in works like "The Genesis of Sex" (1879) by Joseph Le Conte, Norris's revered professor at Berkeley; Freud was publishing *Studies in Hysteria* (with Josef Breuer in 1895), announcing that he had begun to understand the underlying significance of *Oedipus Rex* (1897), and preparing for the publication of *Three Essays on the Theory of Sexuality* (1905). In the new field of sexology (in which Darwin was universally acknowledged as the founding theorist) Havelock Ellis was publishing volumes like *Man and Woman* (1894), *Sexual Inversion* (1897), and *Sexual Selection in Man* (1905). During the same years Harold Frederic was referring to Darwinian experiments in the evolution of sexual difference as he studied Theron Ware's failure "in the work of selection" in *The Damnation of Theron Ware* (1896); Kate Chopin was exploring Edna Pontellier's sexual nature in *The Awakening* (1899), including Edna's repression and expression of sexual emotions and her power to select a lover outside her marriage; Jack London was beginning his career as a novelist (*A Daughter of the Snows* [1902]) by studying a woman who "believed in natural selection and in sexual selection" (86); and Edith Wharton was beginning to explore the implications of Darwinian sexuality in volumes like *The Descent of Man and Other Stories* (1904).[2]

Frank Norris was certainly caught up in this exciting new current of thought. But his readers give too little attention to developments in evolutionary theory during that time, tending to regard his Zolaesque portraits of Vandover or McTeague as self-evident studies of sexual beasts. However, far from simply reiterating a crude Darwinism of sexual animality, Norris was participating in a larger cultural movement to resist or transform Darwinian theory that is known to historians of science as the "eclipse of Darwinism." As Peter J. Bowler has shown, cultural responses to Darwin's offensive theories did not end with such immediate and impressive counterarguments as St. George Mivart's *On the Genesis of Species* (1871), but they continued especially in a number of anti-Darwinian evolution theories in the decades around 1900. Moreover, Bowler explains, these theories (to a large extent varieties of Lamarckism) were paradoxically "precipitated by movements *within* Darwinism" (*The Eclipse of Darwinism* 42)[3] Later in the twentieth century the eclipse of Darwinism yielded to a revival of Darwinism in American social thought, and as part of this movement over the last thirty years, the theory of sexual selection has become increasingly accepted as a fundamental principle in evolutionary biology and evolutionary psychology.[4] Because of the recent revival of Darwinian thought, literary historians are now in a better position to examine various novelists' interest in sexuality at around the turn of the century in order to see, for example, that for older novelists like Howells, as well as younger ones like Chopin, Frederic, Norris, and Wharton, the unavoidable problem was how to depict the human being's entanglement in the struggle of sexual selection. This chapter seeks to explain how Norris contended with and sought to transcend the troubling theory that was and continues to be the basis for further explorations of the sexual reality.

Joseph Le Conte's Version of Darwinian Theory and His Emphasis on Sexual Reproduction

In his efforts to reconcile the conflict between religion and evolutionary theory, Joseph Le Conte insisted that most of the objections to evolution are actually only objections "to some *special theory* of evolution—Darwinian, Spencerian, Lamarckian, or other" (*Evolution* 269). He was especially careful to distinguish his own views from those of the neo-Darwinists—the new "class of biologists . . . such as Wallace, Weismann, and Lankester, who out-Darwin Darwin himself in their exaltation of . . . natural selection" (92–93). For his own part, Norris seems much less aware than Le Conte of the contending varieties of evolutionary theory. But in expressing his certainty that his theory reflects "reality" or "the Truth," he shared Le Conte's faith that a true realism is available to the evolutionist who recognizes the underlying "one reality, spirit" (329).[5] Moreover, Norris shares Le Conte's faith that the Lamarckian factors of evolution assure slow "race-improvement" through the useful changes that are produced by education in each generation and are then "to some extent inherited and accumulated in the race" (98). As Norris addresses this issue in "The Responsibilities of the Novelist" (1902), the evolutionary lift of education will be provided by "the Pulpit, the Press, and the Novel" because each of these possesses the power to discern the "Truth" and improve the unenlightened (*Novels and Essays* 1209–10).

But while Le Conte was struggling to balance Darwinian selection with the Lamarckian possibilities that had grown more tenuous than ever, he could buoy his spirits more effectively by focusing attention on recent developments in embryology that led him to believe that the principle of growth is directed by the vital forces that are "resident in the egg itself" (*Evolution* 8). Indeed, he opens *Evolution* by asserting that the growth or development of the egg "is *the* type of all evolution" (3). This evolutionary principle is evident in Norris's repeated imagery of the seed farm and the sprouting wheat in *The Octopus*. But the social implications of Le Conte's emphasis on the egg and the growing tree of evolution are far more extensive in both his and Norris's work than one might imagine, involving not only Le Conte's and Norris's faith in the spiritual thrust of evolution but also their views on courtship, gender, race, class, and the meaning of love.

Le Conte began to assert his authority in the study of sex a decade before he published his influential *Evolution*. In "The Genesis of Sex" he addressed the question that he admitted was still veiled in obscurity and barely alluded to by evolutionists—the "genesis of sex in ontogeny" (in the embryo) and its recapitulation of "the genesis of sex in phylogeny" (168). After discussing the similarity between ordinary growth and the lowest forms of nonsexual reproduction, and then tracing the evolution of sexual difference in plants and animals as Darwin had done in *The Descent of Man* and other works, Le Conte begins to invest sexual difference and the sexual instinct with a spiritual force that transcends Darwin's theory of sexual selection:

> The sexual differences—i.e., the difference between male and female individuals of the same species—become greater and greater as we rise up in the scale. They are also greater, we believe, in the higher as compared with the lower races of man, and in the cultivated classes as compared with the uncultivated classes. From this sexual difference springs sexual attractiveness, and from this lowest root, it is not too much to say, springs much if not all our noblest altruistic nature. For, as our physiological functions are primarily divisible into two great groups, viz., the nutritive and the reproductive, the one including all that assemblage of functions which conserve the individual life, the other all that assemblage of functions which conserve the continuous life of the species, so all our psychical functions are also primarily divisible into two groups, the egoistic and the altruistic—the one concerned only about the well-being of self, the other about the well-being of the race. (176–77)

Norris clearly echoes this discussion of the nutritive and reproductive functions (the appetite for food and the sexual appetite) in his development of the character Annixter in *The Octopus*. Initially an "intolerant selfish man" with stomach problems, who constantly eats prunes, Annixter unites with Hilma Tree (the very principle of growth in Le Conte's frequent references to the "tree of evolution"), overcomes his stomach problems (apparently), and is soon transformed by the atmosphere of love into a generous, kind, and forgiving man. To use Le Conte's more extravagantly spiritual terms in *Evolution*, Annixter's "mighty transformation" (*The Octopus* 973) is caused by a force "*drawing* [him] upward" rather than by the force of purely organic evolution, which is "a *pushing* upward and onward from *below* and *behind*" because, "in a word, organic evolution is by the law of *force*, human evolution by the law of *love*" (*Evolution* 88). But before this can happen in Norris's imagination, Annixter and other characters in his novels must struggle with what Le Conte calls the three selective factors of organic evolution. In Le Conte's hierarchy of factors, these three arose later in evolutionary time than the Lamarckian factors ("pressure of the environment," and "use and disuse of parts") and precede the latest and highest factor, reason. All of these selective factors (natural selection, sexual selection, and physiological selection), Le Conte emphasizes, "are conditioned on reproduction" (81).

For students of Norris and of the American response to Darwinian thought, a brief consideration of these factors in Le Conte's view of evolution is worthwhile because they help explain several elements in Norris's plots as well as a significant strain of racist theory in America around the turn of the century. The factor of natural selection needs no explanation, except to note that Le Conte and Norris identify it with the nutritive appetite; and it is at work in many scenes in Norris's novels, from McTeague's eating and fishing, to the more panoramic scenes such as that of "the feeding of the People" in *The Octopus* (979).

The theory of sexual selection continued to be a formidable obstacle to evolutionists like Le Conte who wanted to project a universe of love, as well as to novelists of the 1890s like Howells, Harold Frederic, and Norris, who wished to capture the reality of civilized courtship and marriage while either questioning or attempting to preserve the idea of love. Sexual selection is an *obstacle* because, as Le Conte remarks in the first of his several discussions of it, it "acts in two ways, by the law of battle and the law of attractiveness. The strongest or the most attractive males alone, or mainly, leave offspring, which, of course, inherit their peculiarities" (*Evolution* 75). Noting that sexual selection does not operate "among many lower animals which are hermaphroditic," and that "the law of battle is most conspicuous among mammals" (75), Le Conte goes on to surmise that sexual selection is a relatively recent (i.e., higher) factor because it is "connected with a higher development of the psychical nature. This is especially true where splendor of color or beauty of song determines the selection" (85). In his construction of ascending factors, then, Le Conte imagines that "next, and last, and only with the appearance of *Man*, another entirely different and far higher factor was introduced, viz., *conscious, voluntary cooperation* in the work of his own evolution—a conscious, voluntary striving to *attain an ideal*" (86). This process of ascendance first through sexual selection (in which strength and beauty are essential elements) into a far higher state of psychic development is traceable in Laura Jadwin's experience in *The Pit*.

Le Conte's third selective factor, physiological selection ("the most important advance in the theory of evolution since Darwin"), had been presented only recently—in 1886 by George John Romanes, who maintained that Darwin did not account for the origin of species, but only for the origin of adaptive structures (75–76). According to Romanes, physiological selection originates new species when crossbreeding with the parent stock is blocked, thus sexually isolating the new species (78). For Le Conte, the special importance of physiological selection was that it seemed to reinforce his long-held views against the mixing of races. Le Conte was born and raised in Georgia, where before the Civil War he was "a legatee of a large plantation and four dozen slaves," and his southern heritage seems clearly reflected in his theory of race (Stephens xiii). In "The Genesis of Sex" he warned that "the mixing of primary races is bad, and [that] such mixed races, as weaker varieties in the struggle for life, must perish" (178). Then, finding support in Romanes, he reiterated this idea more fully in *Evolution* and then more fully yet in 1892 (when Norris studied under him at Berkeley) in "The Race Problem in the South." Emphasizing in *Evolution* Romanes's point that no organ is so subject to variation as the reproductive, Le Conte maintained that "sexual repugnance . . . exists between the primary races [as] the psychical sign" that they should not mix (244); as he explained in an earlier essay, "extreme types" like "the Teutonic and the negro" are "most certain to produce inferior result by mixture" ("The Effect of Mixture of Races on Human Progress" 94).[6] Readers familiar with Norris's fiction will recall many moments in which people of mixed race, especially (not to mention Jews or people of color in general), are depicted as weak and inferior, most notably perhaps in Norris's description of "the wretched, sickly child" born to Maria Macapa and the red-headed Polish Jew Zerkow in *McTeague*: "a strange, hybrid little being, come and gone within a fortnight's time, yet combining in its puny little body the blood of the Hebrew, the Pole, and the Spaniard" (431). Here Norris brutally enforces the religious stricture that Le Conte reiterates in *Evolution*—that "the way of evolution toward the highest . . . from lowest man to the ideal, the divine man . . . is a very *straight and narrow way*. . . . Once get off the track, and it is *impossible* to get on again" (90).[7]

Norris's Battle with the Theory of Sexual Selection

The importance of the sexual instinct in Le Conte's *Evolution* is reflected in all of Norris's novels. But between 1894, when he began working on *Vandover* and *McTeague*, and 1902, when he published *The Pit*, there is a clear development in his determination first to bring the sexual beast to life and then—projecting his vision of evolutionary progress—to subdue it or cleanse it of its grosser animal features. Finally, in *The Pit*, there is scarcely a remnant of the "foul stream of hereditary evil," the "panther leap of the animal," or "the fury of a young bull in the heat of high summer" that had awakened in McTeague (284–85)—only a virtually sexless love that could begin to realize Le Conte's theory of altruism in "The Genesis of Sex." But in all these novels Norris works self-consciously with the elements of sexual selection that Le Conte touched on (the law of battle and the roles of beauty and music in sexual attraction) and that Norris had seen appropriated as elements in the courtship plots of novelists like Howells, James, and Harold Frederic. The female's power to select the superior male is of far greater interest to the courtship novelists than it is to Le Conte. Presenting the principle of female choice in their various ways and from their different points of view, these novelists could construct a seemingly endless variety of heroines and plots, from James's story of Isabel Archer in *The Portrait of a Lady* (1881) to Frederic's portrait of Celia Madden in *The Damnation of Theron Ware* (1896).

When Norris worked with the evolutionary materials in *Vandover and the Brute* he began his peculiar but systematic transformation of the essential elements of sexual selection by reconstructing a Darwinian scene of "love-antics or dances" (*The Descent of Man* 2:343). Whereas in Darwin and in any number of novels that Norris knew, the male strives to be selected by exhibiting his prowess in dance. Norris creates an extended scene of dance in which Vandover is selected *against* by the woman he would impress (Turner Travis) but not because he is a poor dancer. Rather, his reputation for his affair with another woman (Ida Wade) figures as the reason for his failure, and another male (Geary) succeeds at the dance because he is simply more organized and industrious. He had filled his dance card in advance: "I've got every dance promised. . . . Ah, you bet, I don't get left on any dance. That's the way you want to rustle" (*Novels and Essays* 139). While "a swarm of men gathered about each of the more popular girls. . . . pushing [and] elbowing . . . like brokers in a stock exchange," Geary "walked about calmly, smiling contentedly" (139–40). In the "snarl and whine" of the orchestra (138), the dance heated until "the girls' faces [were] flushed and perspiring, their eyes half-closed, their bare, white throats warm, moist, and alternately swelling and contracting with their quick breathing"; "the heavy perfume of the flowers [and] the cadence of the music . . . reacted in some strange way upon their oversensitive feminine nerves," causing a "hypnotic effect" of "hysterical pleasure the more exquisite because mixed with pain" (141). But soon Vandover realizes that "some strange and dreadful change had taken place," that he was regarded with aversion and repulsion (146–47). Norris's note of mixed pleasure and pain is not an element in Darwin's theory of sexual selection, but it was theorized as such by other writers at the turn of the century, such as Havelock Ellis, whose remarks on the love-bite parallel Norris's dramatization of this behavior in *McTeague*. When McTeague would bite Trina's fingers "with his immense teeth, . . . this brutality made Trina all the more affectionate," arousing "in her a morbid . . .

love of submission . . . to the will of an irresistible, virile power" (479). As Ellis and others explained it, the connection between love and pain, courtship and blood, derives from the fact that "combat is of the very essence of animal and primitive human courtship" (*Studies* 1:2:121).[8]

In *McTeague* Norris presents one of his most extensive scenes dramatizing the elemental law of battle among males for possession of the female. While he had appropriated and then transformed the Darwinian scene of dance in *Vandover*, here his only departure from the Darwinian principle is in arranging for the males' battle after McTeague has already prevailed over his friend Marcus by coming "between him and Trina." Now Marcus fears, he "was coming between him and Selina," his new woman (422). On their picnic outing, then, after a shooting match had awakened a spirit of rivalry in the men, Marcus and McTeague take up other forms of competition, the "little feminine cries of wonder" urging them on (424). Having won in the shot put, McTeague "strut[s] back and forth in front of the women, his chest thrown out" until, "glorying in [their] admiring glances," he causes Marcus and the other males to suggest a wrestling tournament (424–25). This is an essential feature in Darwin's discussion of the law of battle, where he quotes an anthropologist's explanation that in ancient times it was "the custom . . . for the men to wrestle for any woman to whom they [were] attached, the strongest party always [carrying] off the prize," and in his further discussion of the law of battle among human males Darwin remarks on occasional cases of reversion among present-day males in which the canine teeth give further evidence that "as man gradually became erect, and continually used his hands and arms for fighting with sticks and stones . . . he would have used his jaws and teeth less and less" (*The Descent of Man* 2:324–25). In Norris's "terrible scene," "the brute . . . in McTeague . . . leap[s] instantly to life, monstrous," and he breaks Marcus's arm. Norris takes note of McTeague's "salient chin," his "gripped jaws," and the "sudden flash of bright-red blood," writing that when "the bestial fury lapsed," the females were duly impressed: Selina "giggle[d] hysterically" and "cried out with a peal of laughter: 'Oh, what a way for our picnic to end!'" (427–30).

The change in Norris's fiction after *McTeague* and *Vandover*, frequently noted, seems a logical development in his effort to subdue the human beast that by now he had brought more fully to life than any other American writer. Whether it was because he wanted to trace the full range of human evolution (as Le Conte had done), beginning with the animalistic Vandover and McTeague and ending with at least the prospects for an ideal, altruistic future in the new world, whether he had decided to follow Howells's lead (after beginning to read him seriously at Harvard in 1894) in projecting a more civilized if not altruistic future for American courtship, or whether, for more personal reasons such as his own love affair and marriage (reflected in *Blix* [1898]), he wanted to project a higher view of love—for whatever reasons, he began in his next novel to imagine a civilized hero who could eventually embody ideal love. But the necessary first step in this project was to free the hero from the threat of over-civilization or degeneration by reviving his own primitive instincts. Thus, by exposing his character Wilbur in *Moran of the Lady Letty* (1898) to the primitive reality, Norris enables his hero not only to destroy the beast that Norris projects in other beings such as "the Chinaman," but also, immediately thereafter, to arouse the Viking woman's (Moran's) love by subduing *her* in a "fight once and for all" (219). Especially in such moments, as Pizer has noted, Norris's masculine-feminine ethic is "an important weakness in . . . his work" (*Novels of Frank Norris* 178), as is his particular brand of turn-of-the-century racism. But the point here is that in projecting his hero's animalistic "joy of battle [and] horrid exhilaration of killing" in the high service of Anglo-Saxon supremacy (*Moran* 215), Norris is well on his way to freeing his characters from the gross animalism inherent in the theory of sexual selection—as is reflected in the difference between McTeague kissing Trina "grossly, full on the mouth" (284), and the chaste lovers' kissing each other on the mouth in *Blix* (331). Thus, following Le Conte's theory that evil is a necessary condition of evolution (*Evolution* 365), arising from the lower stages of existence (369), Norris created early characters whose "evil instincts" and "foul ordure" reside in their primitive sexuality" (*McTeague* 283–84).

Because the evolutionary stream can proceed only through the selective or reproductive factors that Le Conte theorized, Norris presents his hero and heroine in *Blix* as "two fine, clean animals" (237), especially—and repeatedly—Blix, whom Norris conceives as a kind of new Eve. "Her pink clean cheeks" are "redolent as new apples" (194), and Norris closes the book with their celebration of a New Year as they "step beyond the confines of the garden wherein they had lived so joyously and learned to love" (338). We are not to worry if an occasional "sudden male force [begins] to develop in Condy" (the young man), for "Blix . . . steadied him" (263); as her last name (Bessemer) indicates, she is the agent of the male's hardening and purification.

Similar ideas provide the foundation for *A Man's Woman* (1900), where both the man and woman are strong and vital. But the man (Bennett) demonstrates his superior physical strength and courage not only by his exploits as an arctic explorer but in a hideous scene of battle with a beast, the runaway horse who endangers the woman's (Lloyd's) life. She "saw the fearful thing done" as Bennett felled the horse with one "swift . . . terrible . . . blow" from (of all things, to make Norris's evolutionary point) his geologist's hammer (102–3). Lloyd is duly impressed with this male power and later exerts her own essential female power to help him regain his health, to avoid the threat of degeneration (she follows a friend's advice: "don't let him get soft; make him be a man and not a professor" [242]), and finally to resume his courageous work in the far north. Clearly a figment of Norris's sexual science, Lloyd must first overcome the female's evolutionary weakness, "the thinking faculties of her brain . . . a myriad of delicate interlacing wheels" that moved with too great "rapidity and intensity"; then, beginning "to feel instead of to think," she can give herself to the "nameless emotion" that Norris soon identifies as her instinct, her almost divine and virtually sexless love for Bennett, "as a mother feels for a son, a sister for her younger brother"(224, 244–45).[9]

Although many readers prefer Norris's more earthy realism in *Vandover* and *McTeague* to his sublimated rendering of sexual love in *Blix* and *A Man's Woman*, it is clear that the same evolutionary principles pertain in all these novels: the force of sexual selection drives both his primitive (or degenerate) as well as his more highly civilized characters. The crucial difference between these groups is that neither the primitive characters (McTeague, Trina, and those of "lower" or mixed race) nor the degenerate characters (e.g., Vandover) are capable of love. Like any number of late-nineteenth-century anthropologists who maintained that primitive people were incapable of love, Le Conte insisted that in the early stages of his progress, man, like other animals, was driven by "organic evolution" (particularly the nutritive instinct). Only at the higher levels of human evolution does "the law of *love*" arise (*Evolution* 86, 88). Thus McTeague and Trina do not so much love as "loaf" each other (323–24), a point Norris drives home in his Zolaesque scene of the wedding feast (380–85); and Trina has mainly a "hoasban" (388) rather than the kind of fatherly (but childless) husband Laura Jadwin will love in *The Pit*.

This is the point at which Norris begins his epic of the wheat: the transitional evolutionary time at which he imagines the law of *love* has emerged. In an evolutionary prologue in chapter 1 of *The Octopus*, Norris sends his writer Presley on a bicycle tour of the landscape, south into the old Ranch of the Dead (*El Rancho de Los Muertos*). There, in "the decayed and dying Mexican town" of Guadalajara, he meets an old Mexican who "sang an interminable love-song" and told of the "grand gentleman" named "De La Cuesta [who] held the grant of Los Muertos" in the old days: although he was a "devoted . . . respectful . . . [and] chivalrous" husband in a brilliant marriage that had been celebrated at the Mission, he did not love his wife (592–94).

In a strategic location on the northern edge of the old ranch, at the intersection of "the Lower Road and Derrick's main irrigating ditch," Pressley pauses to admire the "mammoth live-oak, the largest tree in all the country-side" (588); then, heading back north from Guadalajara, he moves on to visit his friend "Buck" Annixter, at the ranch where the novel's love will spring to life in the relationship between Annixter and Hilma (daughter of "Old Man Tree"). The Trees, of course, run the dairy that is located along the irrigation ditch midway between the mammoth live oak tree and the spring at the headwaters of Broderson Creek. The novel is fairly saturated with details of similar allegorical significance in Norris's evolutionary romance, according to which the love in Annixter's breast emerges synchronously with the sprouting of the wheat (at the end of chap. 2 in book 2). Even the love of

Annixter and Hilma Tree must pass through and withstand the struggle of sexual selection. First, however, it is important to note that in Norris's Le Contean vision of the evolutionary reality, "the seed had *already* been graded and selected" (618, emphasis mine). Norris writes that the wheat seed "was all of the white varieties of wheat and of a very high grade" (621), but this pertains equally to his human beings. He views the decayed Mexicans and other "primitive" peoples of color or mixed race as simply incapable of love, but an idealized, selfless, love will spring forth from Hilma Tree and Annixter, who is himself a seed or *"pip"* (712).

To put it more precisely, love can arise only between these Anglo-Saxons. It arises from "the lower dark places of [Annixter's] character" (868) but only under the influence of Hilma Tree's clean, "vigorous animal life"(642). As Hilma emphasizes, "I love *clean* things" (709). Always, in Norris's vision of transcendent evolutionary love, the greatest obstacle lies in "the lower dark places" of the male mind—whether it be De La Cuesta's, where the obstacle is insurmountable, or Annixter's. And this is precisely the problem that William Dean Howells had specified in his own confrontation with Darwin when he remarked of Bartley Hubbard that in "those fastnesses of [the male's] nature which psychology has not yet explored" there is "the sense of prey as to the girl whose love he has won" (*A Modern Instance* 40). As Darwin or Le Conte would express it more openly, the first principle of sexual selection is the male's necessary struggle in the law of battle for possession of the female. Although Norris protects Annixter from Howells's most serious charge against Bartley, that he is a promiscuous flirt, he does indicate at once that Annixter exhibits the Darwinian male's essential sexual jealousy. When Annixter looks into a mirror, thinking "What a mug!" and wondering whether "that fool female" will be around (641), he exhibits the male's insecure awareness that he must be selected, and after he sees Hilma being "astonishingly intimate" (642) with his ranch hand Delaney, he soon confronts and fires his competitor, remarking to himself, "that just about takes the saleratus out of *your* dough" (650).

Norris provides his most fully developed scene of the sexual struggle in chapter 6, the last chapter of book 1, which culminates in the "astonishing evening" of the barn dance (802). It all ends in a scene of "the uprising of The People. . . . the blind fury of . . . the brute, many-tongued, red-eyed, bellowing," and so forth (800); but it begins with a full-blown scene of Darwinian entanglement at the dance. And as Norris indicates through Vanamee's remark at the end of the chapter (and of book 1), this scene of "wild, clamouring pell-mell" with its "confused tangle of waving arms . . . [and] tangled legs" (782) suggests that there must have been "a dance in Brussels the night before Waterloo" (802). This is an appropriate follow-up to Vanamee's remarks on life earlier in the chapter, where he emphasizes that there is "something fundamental that we share with plants and animals" (749–50). True to Darwin's description of such scenes of love-antics or dances, in Norris's scene of "the most desperate love-making" (776), "the male instincts of possession . . . came twisting to the surface" (763).

But unlike Darwin, whose theory does not end in anything like transcendent love, Norris focuses on the "evil light" that flashes on Annixter's face as he at first struggles with the "hideous and abominable beast" (763). In this crucial period in his life, Annixter is finally selected by Hilma; then he realizes that "the wonderful thing [had] occurred" and that he was "never more alive to his surroundings" (782). But before he was selected, he found first that Hilma had been occupied with another partner, whose appeal was that of the most attractive peacock: "he wore the prettiest clothes!" she told the frustrated Annixter (779). Norris will not dress his eventually transcendent lover in this way, however, nor will he allow him the facility in dance that a sexier rival might display. Because Annixter knows that Hilma loves to dance, he reluctantly suggests that they dance, silently "wondering what kind of a spectacle he was about to make of himself" (780). Then, after his first clumsy attempts to dance, *chance* (an important element in every Darwinian narrative) provides him with the perfect opportunity for Norris's ideal male (783). A drunken primitive, the Irishman Delaney, rides into the barn on horseback, dressed in "bear-skin" or "hair trousers" with "his pistol holster low on the thigh" (781). Though Delaney tries to force Buck Annixter at gunpoint to "dance—dance all by hisself" (783), chance once again intrudes to prevent a fatal encounter and allow Buck to reign "enthroned in a circle of adulation" (especially by the women). "The Hero" in this idealized drama had not spilled blood (788). As always, Norris drives his evolutionary point home rather too bluntly by describing how this excitement recalled many stories of "the violent, wild life of the early days"; still his scene of present-day love-dances and antics dramatizes the essential "combative spirit amongst the men," who were "like young bucks excited by an encounter of stags . . . showing off before the does and fawns" (787).

Buck will live to marry and be even more fully transformed by love, its seed sprouting from his "lower dark places" as part of "the enigma of growth" (1084), and he dies heroically, trying to calm the mob with calls for the crisis to be settled peaceably (984). Had not the more primitive character Hooven fired the shot that set it all off, Annixter might have had a child with Hilma. But Norris seems reluctant to attempt description of the new child, who might embody the evolutionary promise. Realizing that there can only be "gradual evolution of the type through infinitely vast periods of time" ("Theory and Reality" 1104), Norris satisfies himself by arranging for something "better than romance": he will produce the dead woman "Angéle in the flesh" for the mystic Vanamee (*The Octopus* 1087), crush the villainous Berhman beneath a cascade of wheat, and send the wheat-loaded *Swanhilda* on its way to complete the great circle of manifest destiny (1094). No less remarkably, by exposing his writer Presley to the novel's expansive sweep of events and by bringing him finally to stand in the presence of Hilma Annixter, Norris completes a trans-formation that will save Presley from the greatest threat to his own existence. At the beginning of the novel Presley is certainly a candidate for classification as one of Max Nordau's degenerates. Possibly even of a "mixed origin," he has "the forehead of the intellectual," but "the impression conveyed by his mouth and chin was that of a delicate and highly sensitive nature, the lips thin and loosely shut together, the chin small and rather receding. One guessed that [his] refinement had been gained only by a certain loss of strength"; "morbidly sensitive" and "irresolute," he reveals, in short, that "his temperament was that of the poet" (583). But standing in the presence of Hilma's infinite capacity for love at the end of the novel, Presley shows that he has become a true man at last: "a longing to give the best that was in him to the memory of her, to be strong and noble because of her, to reshape his purpose-less, half-wasted life . . . leaped all at once within him, leaped and stood firm, harden-ing to a resolve stronger than any he had ever known" (1080). With a little help from Lamarck, perhaps this new manly novelist can provide the kind of evolution-ary thrust that Le Conte and Norris desire.[10]

Norris's final literary performance (*The Pit*) disappoints many of his critics be-cause it is so far removed from the epic landscape he had celebrated in *The Octopus*: "the great earth, the mother" in "its period of reproduction, its pains of labour, delivered of the fruit of its loins" (1084). But he should be credited for his attempt to sustain his transcendental evolutionary vision even in the pit or bowels of Ameri-can civilization. It is a mistake to conclude, as Pizer does, that the novel fails in part because its symbolism is disjointed or that the "violent and sensational symbols for the pit" (the whirlpool, military battleground, and combat of enraged animals) are in conflict with the subtler symbolism in the love story (*Novels of Frank Norris* 176). Rather, the novel is largely unified in its presentation of the natural violence that emerged in the evolutionary past, when the primitive organism—including the human embryo and the early "progenitors of man"—possessed a cloaca (*The De-scent of Man* 1:16, 207). In his effort to show "civilisation in the making, the thing that isn't meant to be seen, as though it were too elemental, too—primordial; like the first verses of Genesis" (*The Pit* 63), Norris could have done much worse than to compare the pit to "the mouth of some tremendous cloaca" (79). As the cloaca in certain birds, reptiles, fish, and mammals is the common cavity into which the in-testinal, urinary, and generative canals open, it makes fairly good biological sense for Norris to have used this term not only to define the pit but also to define the colossal task with which he presents his heroine, Laura. It will be for her alone to stand "forth like a challenger" and "battle with the Cloaca" (360). As the name Laura Dearborn suggests, she more than any other of Norris's female characters brings the promise of spiritual deliverance from the evolutionary evil that had destroyed Vandover and McTeague.

Laura's battle is twofold: first, in the courtship to which Norris devotes his first five chapters, she must exercise her power to select the superior male. Then, after the marriage at the end of chapter 5, she must first endure the loneliness caused by Jadwin's obsessive financial battles in the pit, and, in the greatest and most melodramatic test of her ideal strength, she must withstand the renewed efforts of a former suitor to win her from her husband. The second of her battles serves mainly to confirm the sanctity of her original choice. That is, by protecting her model marriage from the evolutionary evil identified in the other suitor's name, Sheldon Corthell, Norris can renew his faith in a key principle of sexual selection, the female's power to select. Through this power, embodied now in Laura as it had been in Hilma Tree, Norris fulfills Le Conte's proclamation that "human evolution [is drawn upward] by the law of *love*" (*Evolution* 88).

"Unquestionably beautiful," Laura has inherited "the blood of those who had wrestled with a new world," and she fully wields the power of her evolutionary superiority by attracting three suitors (*The Pit* 4, 65). Thus she enjoys a greater range of choices than any of Norris's other women, and Norris's initial question is, what kind of male will Laura select? What are the attributes of the male best fitted to join with this superior woman in leading humanity toward its higher evolutionary state? In dramatizing his own answers to these questions Norris affirms—but in key ways transforms—both Darwin's principle of female choice and his definition of the male's essential qualities in sexual selection.

In chapter 1 Laura meets the three males from whom she will choose: the "astonishingly good-looking" (15) young broker, Landry Court; the sensitive artist, Sheldon Corthell; and the nearly middle-aged financial "strong" man (11), Curtis Jadwin. In the context of chapter 1, set at a performance of Charles Gounod's opera *Faust*, it is clear that Norris works with the idea that Laura's initial conception of romantic love will complicate her choice, as she thinks to herself, "There was no such love as that to-day" (22). And there can be no question that Norris intends to present her with the problem of selecting the superior male. When the third of her suitors (Corthell) first appears and asks why she has not worn the flowers he had sent, she points to "a single American Beauty" on her gown and remarks that she *is* wearing one: "I tried to select the prettiest, and I think I succeeded—don't you? It was hard to choose" (17). Later, having for the moment set aside Landry Court (in part because he "conceived . . . love making" as involving "little domestic commotions" [50]), she wonders, "of the two existences, which did she prefer, that of the business man, or that of the artist?" (65). First, Norris explains, "it had been Sheldon Corthell. . . . Then Landry Court . . . and now—unexpectedly—behold, a new element had appeared—this other one, this man of the world, of affairs, mature, experienced" (77). Then, to heighten his drama of courtship and selection, Norris arranges at the end of chapter 4 for Laura to realize that she had been foolishly flirting with Landry, and Corthell and Jadwin, after which she sends letters of rejection to all three (142).

Soon, of course, she selects Jadwin, but for reasons that would have both impressed and amused Darwin. Norris repeatedly identifies Jadwin as the strongest and wealthiest of the three, and on this point Darwin would certainly agree that her eventual choice is a good one.[11] For other reasons, as well, Jadwin's Darwinian superiority is clear. Laura finds that the most attractive male is not the one who, like Corthell, promises a beautiful life, but the one who is conspicuous as a warrior in the heat of battle (65). Yet Darwin would have been amused to note the extent to which Norris plays upon and modifies what is still a little-known feature in the male's success or failure in the sexual struggle—the "secondary sexual character" he has evolved (his claws, if a lobster) by means of which first to capture and then grasp the female in copulation. As Darwin indicates at once in his initial discussion of sexual selection, the male's special organs of prehension have evolved because "he sometimes absolutely requires prehensile organs" to hold the female and to gain an advantage over other less well-endowed males (*The Descent of Man* 1:253–57). Throughout *The Pit* Norris includes innumerable references to Curtis Jadwin's large, powerful hands, as in Laura's impression on first meeting him: "He was a heavy-built man, would have made two of Corthell, and his hands were large and broad, the hands of a man of affairs, who knew how to grip, and above all, how to hang on. Those broad, strong hands, and keen, calm eyes would envelop a Purpose with tremendous strength" (33–34).[12] But in Norris's transformation of Darwin's point about the successful male's prehensile powers, Jadwin's powerful hands are a measure of his success as a financial warrior with great "holdings," rather than of the passion or sexual jealousy that Darwin had described in the male animal or that Norris had depicted in the more primitive McTeague. Reflecting her own primitive nature, Trina's "intuitive feminine fear of the male" had focused more and more on McTeague's "huge hands" (285–86), the "huge, red hands" (389) with which he will grip and break Marcus's arm and finally beat Trina to death. And because she is so primitive, Norris doubts whether she possesses the power to select that is wielded by the far more highly civilized Laura. Thinking perhaps of Le Conte's theory that the selective or reproductive factors of evolution arose only recently in evolutionary time, Norris asks, did Trina choose him for better or worse, or was she "allowed even a choice?" (326).

In the more highly evolved world of *The Pit*, Laura certainly has the power to select, and now Norris arranges for her to select a male whose powerful hands indicate that he is essentially free of the sexual passion that drove McTeague and Bartley Hubbard (in Howells's *A Modern Instance*). Although Norris is careful to note that Jadwin is a fan of Howells ("I *know* all those people," he remarks) and that he "never could rid himself of a surreptitious admiration for Bartley Hubbard," Norris clearly intends for his hero to be a far more highly evolved male than Bartley (*The Pit* 216). Whereas Bartley saw Marcia as prey, playfully grasped her wrists with such force that "his clasp left red circles," and, most telling, could not prevent himself from being a promiscuous flirt with a number of women before and after his marriage (*Modern Instance* 40, 14), Curtis Jadwin never looks at another woman nor fully participates in the essential scenes of sexual selection that Darwin had defined for the male, either scenes of love-antics and dances or of males engaged in sexual battle. Indeed, in his most passionate moment, it is only with *gloved* hands, that he "took [Laura] swiftly and strongly into his arms" and "kissed her *cheek* again and again" (179, emphasis mine).

In short, the mature man of about thirty-five whom Norris will have Laura select is somewhat beyond the age of the typical male's most tumultuous sexual urgency: on their first meeting "she had felt [Jadwin's] manhood more than her womanhood, her sex side" (35). By contrast, when Landry Court kisses her she feels "like a school-girl" (141), and, repeatedly, Corthell "stirred troublous, unknown deeps in her" that made it impossible for her to "forget her sex a single instant" (136). Jadwin certainly bears the stamp of Darwin's successful male, as underscored by Norris's frequent references to Jadwin's strong hands, his prowess as a warrior, his great wealth, and his effective mustache (the male's sexual ornament displayed not only by men and animals in *The Descent of Man* but by fictional characters thereafter such as Bartley Hubbard). He also displays similar signs of virility that were standard fare among novelists of that time, such as his prowess as a handler of unruly horses and his habit of smoking cigars. Still, Jadwin is so subdued in his reproductive nature that he exhibits absolutely no trace of the sexual jealousy that Darwin emphasizes as the essential element in the male's nature—most incredibly, even when Jadwin knows that Laura is spending a great deal of time with Corthell.

Norris protects all his males in *The Pit* from Darwin's law of battle by transferring the struggle from the sexual arena to the marketplace, where Jadwin prevails in a struggle that is still subliminally effective in influencing Laura. Similarly, in two memorable scenes involving the "great organ" in the Jadwin mansion (199), Norris takes up another of Darwin's principles of sexual selection, the power of music, but only to present it as evidence of degeneracy and evolutionary evil in Corthell's courtship behavior. In this way Norris transforms another typical scene in the novels of Darwinian courtship, as in Howells, James, Harold Frederic, and Kate Chopin, for example, sublimating these novelists' essential point that the power of music demonstrates the biological reality of human love in light of Darwin's theory of sexual selection and his theory of the emotions (*The Expression of the Emotions in Man and Animals*).[13] In the first of these scenes Jadwin shows a friend the great organ he had installed in Laura's favorite room of their mansion, demonstrating its power by inserting "one of those attachment things" and then sitting down to play it mechanically: "A vast preliminary roaring breath soughed through the pipes, with a vibratory rush of power. Then there came a canorous snarl of bass, and then, abruptly, with resistless charm, and with full-bodied satisfying amplitude of volume the opening movement of the overture of 'Carmen'" (201).[14] Norris writes that "the great-lunged harmony . . . fill[ed] the entire gallery," causing Jadwin's friend to shout, "That's bully, bully!" and Laura to appear, wearing a "single American Beauty rose" (201–2). Immediately following this scene Norris begins a lengthy discussion of the "great fact [that] had entered [Laura's] world" three years into her marriage—"her love for her husband" (203). And here, in one of his many oblique allusions to passages from the Bible, Norris writes that Laura's awakening came suddenly, when "she had seen a great light. Love had entered her world" (203), and she knew that "she belonged to [Jadwin] . . . forever, and the surrender was a glory" (205).

In contrast to this scene of Laura's chaste awakening, Norris later includes a lengthy melodramatic scene in which Corthell plays the "grand, noble organ" for her with his "long, slim hands," the music seeming "to flow, not from the instrument but, like some invisible ether, from his finger-tips themselves" (248–49). By this point in the novel Laura has suffered greatly in her loneliness because of Jadwin's preoccupation with his financial battles in the pit, and here Norris does his best to surpass Celia Madden's famous seductive musical performance in Harold Frederic's *The Damnation of Theron Ware*. Laura loves his performance and begs him to go on, and as Corthell plays the *Mephisto Walzer* of Liszt, commenting on its resemblance to Wagner, Norris insinuates his suggestion that this sort of music exemplifies the artistic degeneracy that Max Nordau had described. Laura is clearly affected by its "undercurrent of the sensual," the "feline, eager sentiment" that builds to "the very essence of passion . . . [and] voluptuousness" (249–50). And Norris's description of her emotional response to Corthell's performance, as distinct from Jadwin's, underscores his point that Corthell employs the power of music that originated when our "half-human ancestors" used it "during the season of courtship" in order to arouse "each other's ardent passions" (*The Descent of Man* 2:336–37). As Darwin noted in *The Expression of the Emotions in Man and Animals*, in people powerfully affected by music, the "eyes . . . become suffused with tears" and a "thrill or slight shiver . . . runs down the backbone and limbs" (217). Similarly, Norris notes that Laura responded to Corthell's performance with "intuitive quickness": "those prolonged chords of Liszt's, heavy and clogged and cloyed with passion, reached some hitherto untouched string within her heart, and with resistless power twanged it so that the vibration of it shook her entire being, and left her quivering and breathless, the tears in her eyes, her hands clasped till the knuckles whitened" (250).

That Norris was self-consciously drawing on Darwin's remarkable analysis of the power of music is not all that this analysis is meant to demonstrate, for any number of other novelists in the 1880s and 1890s did so as well. Rather, Norris confronts this feature of the male's behavior in sexual selection, as he had the law of battle, in order to subdue it. By dramatizing his point that Corthell can temporarily succeed in arousing Laura's "emotions and thoughts of a long-past age" (*The Descent of Man* 2:336)—to the point that she thinks that Corthell should select her pictures and music in the future (*The Pit* 251)—Norris demonstrates the high wisdom of his heroine's original selection of mates. Biologically, from Norris's point of view, Corthell's courtship behavior is tainted with "the foul stream of hereditary evil" that "flowed in [McTeague's] veins" (285). Thus he is unfit to accompany Laura into the vague evolutionary future that Norris reserves for his nearly ideal lovers. As the Jadwins proceed West from Chicago at the end of the novel, Norris suggests that they are part of the "resistless" Wheat, driven along the "ordered and predetermined courses from West to East" that will bear "Life and Prosperity to the crowded cities and centres of Europe" (419–20). As the emerging third Laura, who can ignore her "self," finally begins to see, the "change would be slow, slow—would be evolution, not revolution" (405).[15] But by now, at least, she and Jadwin are free of the cloaca and have survived what Le Conte called all "the selective factors [of evolution]—those of Darwin and Romanes—[that] are conditioned on reproduction" (*Evolution* 81).

Norris and the Repression of the Sexual Emotions

In admitting but then neutralizing specific features in Darwin's theory of sexual selection, particularly the male's sexual passion in the law of battle and in his appeal through beauty, dance, or music in courtship, Norris played a significant part in the larger movement in our culture that brought about the eclipse of Darwinism. Moreover, of Darwin's two main theories, Norris was far more troubled by the theory of sexual selection than by the theory of natural selection. He completely affirms the evolutionary value of strength, as embodied in Jadwin's strong hands, and charges his hero mainly with going temporarily crazy in the chaotic pit or, repeatedly word playing with Jadwin's name, of being jaded. And he readily admits that many must die or become extinct in order for evolution to proceed toward its transcendent end—especially the weak and those of certain "lower" or mixed races. But while he can forgive Jadwin his "jaded mind" (403) and even save him with the power of Laura's love, he absolutely condemns Corthell.

In projecting his vision of altruistic love, he was compelled to deny the frightening sexual reality that had emerged with *The Descent of Man*. In this regard, his response to the theory of sexual selection is far closer to Howells's *A Modern Instance* than to other novelists at the turn of the century, such as Harold Frederic, Kate Chopin, or Jack London. That is, as Howells had dispensed with his too emotional heroine and promiscuous hero (Marcia and Bartley Hubbard), giving the evolutionary future to the virtually sexless Athertons, Norris dispenses first with Vandover, then McTeague, and then even the promising Hilma Tree and the transformed Annixter in *The Octopus* before—in *The Pit*—entrusting the evolutionary future to the hands of a strong male with scarcely a trace of sexual desire and a heroine who selects against another male who "made her feel her sex" (34).

Although Norris strives to show that Laura and Curtis Jadwin are both involved in limited ways in the workings of sexual selection, he goes to extraordinary lengths to show that they are drawn "upward and onward from above ... by the law of *love*" that Le Conte had proclaimed (*Evolution* 88). This transcendent power is evident throughout the novel: in references to spiritualism that are linked to Jadwin's luck (128), in innumerable references to his "blessed sixth sense" (87), or chance, with his moves in the market (191), and in the timing of his fortunate arrival at crucial moments to block Corthell's efforts to seduce Laura (252, 410–11). The elements of chance and spiritualism are part of the same "infinite immeasurable power, onrushing in its eternal courses" that finally "shook the Pit in its grasp" (387). This, the ultimate male force in Norris's universe, "smashed" Jadwin (394), brought "Order—order, order" (393) to the "centre of the Nation ... between the oceans of the New World and the Old" (80), and finally allowed the chastened lovers to glimpse a "faint haze of light ... in the heavens" (420–21).

Norris's "faint haze of light" is a more restrained affirmation of the "infinite immeasurable power" in *The Pit* than is his outburst at the end of *The Octopus* about Anglo-Saxon progress, manifest destiny, and the Wheat's "Nirvanic calm" (934). There "Angéle was realised in the [sunlit] Wheat" (1087); but in the pit of civilization Norris can offer these lovers a glimpse of hazy light only by relying on the more strictly human power of repression that he found within Darwinism in *The Expression of the Emotions in Man and Animals* and that he reveres in Jadwin. Jadwin is seldom emotional, and Laura's first observation about him is that an expression of suspicion or distrust quickly crossed his face and faded as quickly—an instinct that told him "to keep out of strange young women's troubles" (11–12). Norris clearly associates Jadwin's control of his emotions with his strong grasp, especially when he drives the horses that threaten to "pull [his] hands clean off" (164). By contrast, Laura's effeminate drama teacher once tries to exert "a heroic effort to repress his emotion" before she finally has enough and silences him (117), and she herself once gives way to a violent "outbreak of long-repressed emotion" (45) and puts a group of meddling lady-deaconesses out of her house (44). Norris's point in all this is that Laura needs a strong man who will not make "her feel her sex" (35) or arouse all her "turbulent emotion" as Corthell does (251). In *Expression of the Emotions* Darwin explained, "Some actions ordinarily associated through habit with certain states of the mind may be partially repressed through the will" (28); moreover, he noted, "free expression by outward signs of an emotion intensifies it" and "repression ...

softens our emotions" (365). And of course for Darwin (and Norris as well), uncivilized or "savage" people express their emotions more openly than do civilized people, and women are more apt to express their emotions than men.[16] For Laura, perhaps, there is an ambiguous glimmer of hope in the conclusion that Darwin draws from some "curious cases" involving women. Having already observed that the "long-continued desire either to repress, or to increase, the action of the lacrymal glands is effectual," Darwin cites some remarkable cases regarding "women, of the power of the mind on the mammary glands; and still more remarkable ones in relation to the uterine functions" (*Expression of the Emotions* 339).

Norris's final response to the theory of sexual selection is most evident in his rendering of the sexual awakening. Whereas Kate Chopin's Edna Pontellier and Jack London's Martin Eden awaken to the disillusioning *significance* of beauty and sexual love as merely nature's decoys to make the species reproduce, McTeague, Trina, Hilma Tree, and Annixter suddenly and quite incredibly awaken (well into adulthood) to the fact that they even *have* sexual desire. Before Laura awakens she must first abandon her romantic misconception that love was "something that would shake [her] all to pieces" (*The Pit* 161); then, awakening after her marriage, she suddenly sees the "great light"(205)—that "Love had entered her world" (203). She takes "Jadwin her lover" to be infinitely inferior to "Jadwin her husband" (206), and Norris further transforms the husband into a "father" who has never conceived a child (308, 379, 416). In this way Norris's repression of the sexual instinct is a landmark in the eclipse of Darwinism. At the same time, it is a cultural landmark that would soon crumble as part of the development that gathered force after Sigmund Freud's visit to the United States in 1909. According to the distorted popular belief that arose within a decade, *repression* of the sexual instinct—not the instinct itself—was the darker source of our discontent.

Notes

1. In one of the earliest and still most insightful studies, Lars Åhnebrink noted briefly that "Norris's concept of sexual selection was probably colored by Darwinian thought," at least to the extent that in their exercise of female choice, Norris's women "selected the male who was the strongest and most attractive" (212). In 1953 Maxwell Geismar commented (without reference to the theory of sexual selection) on Norris's "popular Darwinism" in his simultaneous presentation of "the rut of love and the lust for blood" and on Norris's "debased Darwinism, in which sexuality was restricted to the inferior races as well as to the submerged 'brute' in man" (10–11, 64). But then, ignoring Norris's knowledge of the theory of sexual selection, Geismar claims that "the real psychological study in *Vandover and the Brute*," Norris's "most autobiographical novel," is of "an oedipal relationship through which a complete father fixation had concealed and repressed the incestuous drives for a 'dead' mother" (60, 62). More recently,

in one of the most important studies of Norris, Donald Pizer described the relationship between Norris's projection of the evolutionary reality and that of Joseph Le Conte (under whom Norris studied at Berkeley in 1892–93), making the essential point that both Le Conte and Norris were "absorbed [in] a particular contemporary system of belief," a more consoling, optimistic, and "malleable evolutionary theory" than Darwin's theory of natural selection—"Le Conte's evolutionary theism" (*The Novels of Frank Norris* ix, 4, 16). Accordingly, Pizer suggests that Norris was somewhat more directly under the spell of Le Conte than Zola, noting that in *The Octopus* (1901), especially, "Norris translated Christian love into propagation of the species" (131). Although Pizer does not explain Le Conte's central and extensive emphasis on the evolution of sex or the way in which both Le Conte and Norris draw on Darwin's theory of sexual selection, he does go on in a more recent piece to suggest that Norris's presentation of McTeague's mating with Trina "anticipates the contemporary field of inquiry known as evolutionary psychology" and "echoes" the evolutionary psychologists' theme that (quoting David Buss) we are "designed for individual survival and genetic reproduction" (Pizer, "The Biological Determinism of *McTeague* in Our Time," 30–31). Also studying Norris in relation to Le Conte in the chapter, "The Mystery of Instinct," William B. Dillingham concludes that "the heart of *The Octopus* is neither the railroad nor Darwin, but the creative and rejuvenating powers of instinct," including those instincts that cause women like Laura in *The Pit* (1903) to perpetuate what Dillingham calls Norris's "Philosophy of Masculinity" by being attracted to the physical and financial strength of men like Curtis Jadwin (65, 96). Finally, with rather more emphasis on Darwin and sexuality than that provided by either Pizer or Dillingham (but still with no reference to Darwin's theory of sexual selection), Joseph R. McElrath Jr. includes insightful sections on "Love: Predator and Prey," "Sexuality and the Victorian Male," and "Sexuality and the Victorian Female" in *Frank Norris Revisited*.

2. Discussions of Chopin's, Frederic's, and Wharton's work with the theory of sexual selection are indexed in my *The Descent of Love*.

3. For an illuminating discussion of the variety of theories of evolution around the turn of the century, see Bowler's outline of theories of evolution (7–10), his discussion of the several varieties of Lamarckism (chap. 4), and his discussion of "The American School" of evolutionary theorists, including Joseph Le Conte (chap. 6).

4. For the recent revival of Darwinism, see Carl N. Degler, *In Search of Human Nature: The Decline and Revival of Darwinism in American Social Thought*. The renewed interest in sexual selection in recent years among evolutionary biologists began in the late 1950s but did not gain much headway until the publication of Bernard Campbell, ed., *Sexual Selection and the Descent of Man, 1871–1971*.

5. In "Theory and Reality" Norris complained that a Mrs. J. R. Jarboe's novel *Robert Atterbury* proposed a theory that is only "a fine and admirable ideal" (that marriage, with no legal restraint on the birthrate, is "a crime against nature"); Norris insists that a novel "should tell a real story, of real people and places" (*Novels and Essays* 1103–4).

6. As Bowler remarks, a number of "American neo-Lamarckians" like Le Conte "were fervently committed to the biological justification of a hierarchy of human races" (19), and, as Bowler also notes, the best discussion of this tendency in Le Conte is contained in John S. Haller Jr.'s chapter on Le Conte in *Outcasts of Evolution: Scientific Attitudes of Racial Inferiority, 1859–1900*.

7. See also Le Conte's argument that degeneration is part of the "Law of Progress of the Whole" (13–15).

8. Here and in further references to this work, the volume numbers refer to the two volumes in the set and what the set terms "parts." This method differs from the set's confusing way of indicating the volumes and parts in its "cumulative index"). There is an odd parallel in Norris and Ellis. It is not clear what Norris might have known of Ellis when he worked on *Vandover* at Harvard, 1894–95, and when he revised it in 1899. One of the characters in *Vandover* is named Ellis, and in addition to Norris's remarks on hysterical pleasure and pain (which suggest Ellis's analysis of "Love and Pain"), Ellis's discussion of love and pain includes extensive remarks on "lycanthropy," Vandover's affliction (*Studies* 1:2:125–26). Ellis's "Part Two" of the *Studies* (*Analysis of the Sexual Impulse; Love and Pain;* and *The Sexual Impulse in Women*) was published in 1903. For a discussion of other late nineteenth-century sexologists' analyses of this phenomenon, see Frank Sulloway, *Freud, Biologist of the Mind,* chapter 8 ("Freud and the Sexologists"), where he discusses "protoplasmic hunger" and the relationship between reproduction and cannibalism among lower organisms (291), for example, and Freud's subsequent endorsement of "the 'cannibalistic' theory of sadism" (297).

9. For a moving and informative account of "sexual science," see Cynthia Eagle Russett, *Sexual Science: The Victorian Construction of Womanhood.*

10. For a discussion of Norris's self-conscious work with Nordau and the degeneration theme, see Pizer, *The Novels of Frank Norris,* 56–60, and for an example of Norris's work in this regard, see his "A Case for Lombroso" (1897) in Joseph R. McElrath Jr. and Douglas K. Burgess, eds., *The Apprenticeship Writings of Frank Norris,* 2:127–32.

11. Among women "in civilized nations . . . choice is largely influenced by the social position and wealth of the men" (*The Descent of Man* 2:356).

12. Discussions of the ways in which the male's prehensile power is dramatized in fiction by Howells, Henry James, Harold Frederic, Edith Wharton, and others are indexed in *The Descent of Love* under "prehensile power."

13. Discussions of such musical scenes in Howells, James, Frederic, and Chopin are indexed in *The Descent of Love* under "music."

14. Norris's emphasis on the "power" of this music suggests that he was familiar with Edward Gurney's development of the Darwinian theme in *The Power of Sound* (1880). See also the chapter here on Willa Cather.

15. For another even more explicit sense of the way Norris arranges for Laura to voice Le Conte's evolutionary theory and for both writers' sense of the crucial role of female choice, see her remarks in a conversation with Corthell: "The individual—I, Laura Jadwin—counts for nothing. It is the type to which I belong that's important, the mould, the form, the sort of composite photograph of hundreds of thousands of Laura Jadwins. . . . The type always grows better," and so forth (246). Compare this with Le Conte's remarks in *Evolution*: "The male represents the progressive, the female the conservative element. The one tends to divergent variation, the other to fixity of type by heredity" (262).

16. Darwin writes, for example, that "many savages do not repress the signs of fear so much as Europeans" (*Expression of the Emotions* 294); that, while "savages weep copiously from very slight causes," "Englishmen rarely cry" (153–54); that "of all expressions, blushing seems to be the most strictly human" (363); and that "women blush much more than men" (310).

2 "The Chaos of His Brain"

Evolutionary Psychology in The Red Badge of Courage

Many critical discussions of Stephen Crane refer generally and very briefly to his Darwinian views. Surprisingly few develop substantial analyses of the subject, and none focuses on the Darwinian issue that most interested Crane: the mind in evolution. Of course, he accepted the Darwinian scheme, in general, and emphasized environmental determinism in *Maggie, a Girl of the Streets* (Gibson 26–27), and of course he often reduced "the conduct of human beings to the level of animal behavior," projecting a rigorous, Darwinistic determinism in works like *Maggie* (Fitelson 186, 194). Reviewers of *The Red Badge of Courage* saw this at once; one, for example, complaining that it was "a study of the genus homo" by a member of the "animalistic school" who wanted to depict "the menagerie at feeding-time rather than human society."[1] Moreover, Crane, the disillusioned son of a Methodist pastor, was concerned with the cosmological questions that arose immediately after the *Origin of Species* in works like Huxley's *Man's Place in Nature* (1863) or, closer to his own day, in Alfred R. Wallace's *Man's Place in the Universe* (1903). In one well-known poem, for example, he registered his bitter rejection of social Darwinism (though he did not use this exact term) wherein those with opportunity and skill could claim "great heaps," while "only chance blossoms / Remained for the feeble." Why *shouldn't* "the beautiful strong" possess the wealth, proclaims the father in Crane's post-Darwinian garden ("The trees in the garden rained flowers," *Poems* 108).

In *The Red Badge of Courage*, however, Crane explored psychological questions arising from Darwin's prediction in the *Origin of Species* that "psychology will be based on a new foundation, that of the necessary acquirement of each mental power and capacity by gradation" (488). Darwin himself began to lay the new foundations in his later studies of the human mind, *The Descent of Man* and *The Expression of the Emotions in Man and Animals*. And in 1880, building on what he called Darwin's "triumphant originality," William James had begun to explore the "lower strata of the mind" and "the region of intelligence which man possesses in common with the brutes" ("Great Men" 443, 456). In 1890, the same year Stephen Crane published his first literary sketch, James published *The Principles of Psychology* and for all practical purposes began the study of human psychology in America (Degler 333).

Only three years later, at the tender age of twenty-two, Crane began *The Red Badge of Courage*. The question arises whether there is any relationship between this novel, long praised for its psychological realism, and the new psychology. That is, the question *should* arise. It has not yet been posed in Crane studies largely because American literary history has virtually ignored *The Descent of Man* and *The Expression of the Emotions*. Also, Crane's interpreters have tended to underestimate his intellect, suggesting that he was only an intuitive genius, or asserting, for example, that he read very few books (Gibson 25). Now, it is certainly true that we have no direct evidence that Crane ever read either Darwin or William James or much else for that matter. But there are similar myths of literary genius free from intellectual stimulation, for example, in studies of Henry James and F. Scott Fitzgerald.[2] A further reason why Crane scholars have paid so little attention to his own ideas is that studies of psychology in literature have long been dominated by Freudian analysis. Thus, for these and related reasons, studies of Crane's psychological realism in *The Red Badge* tend to emphasize his hero's "toils in the Oedipal family involvement" (Weiss 45) or the way his feelings of guilt indicate his literary inheritance from Hawthorne's Arthur Dimmesdale in *The Scarlet Letter* (McDermott 327).

It makes much more sense to approach Crane's psychological realism through the lens of late nineteenth-century psychology. In the first place, it is important to emphasize that Crane could rather easily have informed himself about the new psychology either by consulting Darwin's own texts or writings about him or by consulting James's formal studies of what he called "evolutionary psychology" (*Principles of Psychology* 149) or "zoological psychology" (307). It seems clear that Crane was familiar with James but that he was drawn even more to Darwin's *The Expression of the Emotions*. Also, Crane could have hardly missed the ways in which any number of psychological novelists of the 1880s and 1890s had begun to explore the Darwinian mind. Crane could not have known in composing *The Red Badge of Courage* that Darwin's American publisher (Appleton) would soon bring out his own novel, but as far as his general sense of Darwin's stature as a kind of modern Newton, he must have known that Benjamin O. Flower, the influential editor of the *Arena*, published a long essay on Darwin in 1893, assigning Darwin to "the loftiest niche in the temple of evolutionary thought" (352). Flower published many of the new writers, such as Hamlin Garland (who introduced Crane to Flower and who reviewed Crane's *Maggie* in the June 1993 issue of *Arena*), Frank Norris, and Crane himself ("An Ominous Baby" in May 1994 and "The Men in the Storm" in October 1994). Moreover, Crane's role in selecting the orchid design for the cover of his volume of poems, *Black Riders*, demonstrates his interest in the turn-of-the-century fascination with Darwin's theory of sexual selection as it pertains to flowers. As the artist, Crane's friend Frederic C. Gordon, wrote to Copeland and Day, "the orchid, with its strange habits, extraordinary forms and curious properties, seemed to me the most floral motive ['motif'] [sic], an idea in which Mr. Crane concurred before he left New York" (Wertheim and Sorentino 125). The widespread interest in this kind of flower imagery toward the end of the century derives from Darwin's (and before him his grandfather's) studies of the reproductive and other survival strategies of plants, as in Darwin's *The Various Contrivances by which Orchids Are Fertilised by Insects* (1862) and Grant Allen's popularization of such ideas in *The Story of the Plants* (1895). The new fascination with the evolutionary strategies of plants is reflected in images from *The Red Badge*, such as of shells exploding like "strange war-flowers bursting into fierce bloom" (40). In brief, then, even though Crane was only in his early twenties, he found himself rather near the center of his culture's efforts to comprehend the new and ever-changing Darwinian universe.

In our own time, of course, James's term "evolutionary psychology" refers to the controversial *new* school of scientific psychology exemplified in a variety of ways by the contributors to *The Adapted Mind: Evolutionary Psychology and the Generation of Culture* (1992), for example. However, the apparent newness of evolutionary psychology is due largely to the eclipse of Darwinism after about 1900 and, relatedly, to the rise of Freudianism. As Henry Plotkin notes in *Evolution in Mind: An Introduction to Evolutionary Psychology* (1997), while evolutionary theory was nearly irrelevant to psychological thought throughout most of the twentieth century, it was a powerful idea in late nineteenth-century psychology, especially in William James's contributions to the subject (24). Like Plotkin, contemporary evolutionary psychologists usually credit James for having undertaken the first systematic explorations of Darwin's theory of instincts and emotions. Among literary scholars, however, it is not so well known that a number of late-nineteenth-century novelists were also undertaking similar but certainly less systematic explorations of instincts and emotions. Among them, for example, were two writers whom Crane knew and admired, William Dean Howells and Harold Frederic. In an 1891 article for the *New York Tribune*, Crane reported on Hamlin Garland's lecture on Howells, including the point that Howells's *A Modern Instance* "is the greatest, most rigidly artistic novel ever written by an American, and ranks with the great novels of the world" (Wertheim and Sorentino 64–65). Later, having met and corresponded with both Garland and Howells, Crane referred to them as his "literary fathers" (*Correspondence* 62). Assuming that the aspiring Crane did indeed read Howells's great novel (famous as the first American novel to deal seriously with divorce), it is unlikely that he would have missed Howells's most penetrating insight about Bartley Hubbard, the first promiscuous hero in a well-known American novel. Howells wrote that in "those fastnesses of [a man like Bartley's] nature which psychology has not yet explored" (*Modern Instance* 40), the male regards his lover as prey; also, Crane might have noted Howells's suggestion (voiced by the character Olive Halleck) that Marcia Hubbard's "poor, feeble mind was such a chaos" (255). Similar suggestions appear in virtually all of Howells's courtship novels, as in many other novelists' efforts during the 1880s and 1890s to reflect the sexual reality in light of Darwin's theory of sexual selection. The novelists of these years certainly varied in the ways they presented their characters' unconscious compliance with the theory of sexual selection, just as contemporary evolutionary psychologists like Plotkin or Leda Cosmides and John Tooby approach their subject in different ways. But there can be little doubt that Crane's analysis in *The Red Badge* of "the chaos of [Henry Fleming's] brain" (95) resembles Harold Frederic's analysis of the "chaos of [Theron Ware's] mind" in *The Damnation of Theron Ware* (333). These two novelists, and others, were conducting early, independent explorations in what we know far more fully today as evolutionary psychology.[3]

The mental chaos in these characters' lives arises from their unconscious motivation and emotional tumultuousness in love and war. And it is clear that Crane and Frederic were quite aware that Darwin had treated these aspects of human behavior together in the workings of sexual selection and the expression of emotions—for example, in his explanations of how males comply with the law of battle for possession of the female, or of how "music affects every emotion" (*The Descent of Man* 2:323), as when our "half-human ancestors aroused each other's ardent passions, during their mutual courtship and rivalry" or when music "stirs up in us the sensation of triumph and the glorious ardour for war" (2:335–37). A central theme in both novels is that the heroes, Henry and Theron, pride themselves in their knowledge of how their minds work, yet demonstrate again and again their absolute failure at any kind of penetrating self-analysis. Once, realizing that in his aimless wanderings he had arrived outside Celia Madden's home, Theron muses on "the curious way in which people's minds all unconsciously follow about where impulses and intuitions lead" (*Damnation of Theron Ware* 183), and in thinking of Celia he wonders at "the wild and tropical tangle of moods, emotions, passions which had grown up in [her] strange temperament" (103), but in the end, he is absolutely humiliated because "his mind was full of tricksy devices for eluding [a] task of serious thought" (314). *The Red Badge of Courage* begins with Henry's efforts to solve mathematically the serious problem of whether he would run from a battle, and in this first effort at self-analysis he realizes that he cannot simply allow "the problem to kick its heels at the outer portals of his mind," for "as far as war was concerned he knew nothing of himself" (9–10).

Crane and William James

Of course there is an enormous difference between Crane's youthful, literary interests in this new psychology and James's systematic analysis. But it is worth emphasizing that for James and the novelists of those years, evolutionary psychology had only begun to explore an unknown world. Indeed, as William James emphasized in concluding his own formal study, "When . . . we talk of 'psychology as a natural science,' we must not assume that that means a sort of psychology that stands at last on solid ground." Then, pointing out that "at present psychology is in the condition of physics before Galileo," James cautions his readers that we must "understand how great is the darkness in which we grope, and never . . . forget that the natural-science assumptions with which we started are provisional and revisable things" (*Psychology* 467–68).[4] In his own gropings, James was far less interested in sexual passion than were novelists such as Frederic and Howells who reflected on the theory of sexual selection and sought to present what they took to be the reality of human nature, courtship, and marriage. Also, although James gave revolutionary emphasis to the instincts and emotions and in other ways qualified the "talk of man being the rational animal" (*Psychology* 351), he seems more confident than Crane (or Frederic) in the human's power of rational self-control, through attending to "reasonable ideas over others—*if they can once get a quiet hearing*" (451). To put it another way, although he was exploring the same mental territory as Freud toward the end of the century, James would have been far less inclined than either Crane and Frederic to appreciate Freud's purpose of proving "to the 'ego' of each one of us that he is not even master in his own house, but that he must remain content with the veriest scraps of information about what is going on unconsciously in his own mind" (*A General Introduction to Psychoanalysis* 296).

Even though there is no record that Crane did indeed read James's *Principles of Psychology* or *Psychology: The Briefer Course*, the chaos of Fleming's brain suggests Crane's implicit agreement with some of James's first principles, beginning with the idea that psychology is a natural science founded on Darwin's theory of evolution. Indeed, James's fundamental fact seems almost a recipe for the mental experience of characters like Henry Fleming or Theron Ware—that there is a stream of consciousness and that "the first and foremost concrete fact . . . [is] that *consciousness of some sort goes on. 'States of mind' succeed each other*" (*Psychology* 152). It follows from James's theory of "*the stream . . . of consciousness, or of subjective life*" (159) that the successive states of mind produce not only a multiplicity of selves but indeed a "rivalry and conflict of the different mes" and therefore a hierarchy of the "mes" (190). Readers familiar with *The Red Badge of Courage* might begin to recognize the theory of mind embodied in Henry Fleming. But if one reads further in James and notes his important chapters on the emotions and instincts, especially his remarks on fear, and if one recalls that Crane said that he intended *The Red Badge* to be "a psychological portrayal of fear,"[5] it seems increasingly likely that Crane actually did consult not only James but also the source on which James relies so heavily here, Darwin's *The Expression of the Emotions in Man and Animals*.

James's "striking theory of the emotions" was immediately singled out as "the most distinctive" of his "doctrines," as the *Atlantic Monthly* noted in its review (555–56). And early in his discussion of the emotions, James takes Darwin's lead from *The Expression of the Emotions*, emphasizing that "the emotions also have their bodily 'expression,' which may involve strong muscular activity (as in fear or anger, for example)" (*Psychology* 373). Then, describing fear, he quotes Darwin at length. Many details in the quote and especially its concluding sentence suggest almost the whole of *The Red Badge of Courage*: "In other cases there is a sudden and uncontrollable tendency to headlong flight; and so strong is this that the boldest soldiers may be seized with a sudden panic" (386).[6] Moreover, if Crane did read James's discussion of the emotions, he might have found a good reason for producing his own study of the emotions in fiction—that is, to do the work that James thought was outside the scope of his own scientific psychology. For the scientist, James thought, emotions "as inner mental conditions . . . are quite indescribable" (*Psychology* 373). He granted that when "emotions are described in novels, they interest us, for we are made to share them." But when it came to reading descriptions of the emotions in the classic works of psychology (374), James remarked that he would "as lief read verbal descriptions of the shapes of the rocks on a New Hampshire farm" (375). One wonders whether Crane did not echo this thought when he told his friend Corwin Linson of his response to reading some firsthand accounts by veterans of the Civil War: "I wonder that some of those fellows don't tell how they *felt* in those scraps. . . . [T]hey're as emotionless as rocks" (Wertheim and Sorrentino 89).

Evolutionary Progress, "the Throat-Grappling Instinct," and the Emotions

It is not being suggested here that Crane simply appropriated Darwin's or James's ideas on the emotions. By the 1890s these ideas did not belong to anyone in particular but had been largely assimilated, modified, twisted, or contested by our culture in many areas and in many ways. Crane's lexicon in *The Red Badge* and many incidents in the novel clearly demonstrate that he was attuned to the evolutionary controversy and adept in the language of evolutionary thought. The novel's many images of "tangled" humanity, for example, reflect Crane's interest, shared with many other novelists at that time, in Darwin's famous image of entangled life in *The Origin of Species*. For example, after Henry had run from his first battle, he joined a group of retreating soldiers who *had* engaged the enemy, and Crane writes, "the torn bodies expressed the awful machinery in which the men had been entangled" (*The Red Badge* 52).[7] Similar suggestions are unmistakable in Crane's remark on the "wild-eyed" expression on the men's faces: "it was the dominant animal failing to remember" how it came to this point (107) or in his image of the men musing upon their situation "with a hundred varieties of expression" (102). Such images and phrases clearly demonstrate that Crane was immersed in the Darwinian view of life. The question is, in his dramatization of this new view of life, what specific issues in evolutionary psychology or the expression of the emotions most concerned him and what can a clearer understanding of these issues contribute to the ongoing debate over Crane's final view of Henry? In remarking as Henry leaves the battlefield that "he was a man," does Crane suggest that Henry is now a different and better man as a result of his war experience?

Crane sets up his problem (and Henry's problem of proving to himself that he would not run from a battle) by raising the key question of evolutionary progress. Before Henry enlists, he fears that he will never have the opportunity to become a war hero in "a Greek-like struggle," for modern "men were better, or more timid. Secular and religious education had effaced the throat-grappling instinct" (5). Crane repeats this line (8) and reiterates the point in other ways: by noting how certain soldiers once evolved "powers of perception" (16), by noting how another "developed virtues" ("development" being a synonym for "evolution" in those years) in deciding to wash his shirt (1), and by describing how Henry's mind wavered when he imagined that his comrades were "all heroes," superior to him in their "development of the higher qualities" (14). At other moments, Henry suspected that they were all liars, "privately ... quaking" as much as he was himself, for his "emotions made him feel strange in the presence" of such swaggering heroes (14). Here Crane suggests that Henry is better served by his emotions than his intellect, and this is precisely the point in his innumerable references to Henry's mind or brain and in his many images of Henry or the other soldiers *trying* to think. Henry "strenuously tried to think" (22), his "brain [was] in a tumult of agony and despair" (46), "his mind flew in all directions" (49), "his disordered mind" distorted a forest scene (80), and his "ceaseless calculations" about his bravery "were all wondrously unsatisfactory" (13).

Then, working against the idea that evolutionary progress has lifted the human to such heights that he now scarcely bore what Darwin called "the indelible stamp of his lowly origin" (*The Descent of Man* 2:405), Crane underscores his extensive references to "the wild graspings of [Henry's] mind" (*The Red Badge* 125) with many images of the men as animals ("wild cats," "brazen game-cocks," "terrified buffaloes," and so forth) and, more important, with countless vivid descriptions of them *expressing* the full array of emotions that Darwin had analyzed in *The Expression of the Emotions in Man and Animals*. Indeed, if the subjective life is best understood as a stream of consciousness, as James put it, *The Red Badge* constitutes a veritable flood of expressed emotions: fear, anger, impotence, rage, astonishment, terror, horror, nervous laughter, pride, awe, desire, thrills of pleasure and joy, ecstasy, guilt, shame expressed through blushing, and so on. Crane certainly out-Darwins James in his presentation of the emotions, not only in dramatizing so many, but also in the attention he gives to particular themes in *The Expression of the Emotions* that James lets pass. In his treatment of these themes—(1) the expression of shame, (2) the concealment of emotions, and (3) the relationship between the sexual impulse and the passion for battle ("war-ardor," as Crane terms it)—Crane most distinguishes his own interests in evolutionary psychology from William James's.

Of these themes the one most obviously relevant to Crane's critique of courage is shame, an emotion about which Darwin has much to say but James very little. Crane introduces the theme at once in Mrs. Fleming's admonition to her son Henry that he do nothing in the war "that yeh would be 'shamed to let me know about" (195). Then, throughout the novel, he traces Henry's repeated encounters with shame. In one of Henry's last bouts with shame (over his having deserted the tattered soldier), "he blushed, and the light of his soul flickered with shame" (134). Here and elsewhere in such encounters Crane pursues two points: first, that Henry is anxious to conceal his emotions from his fellow soldiers, and second, that his instinctive self-concern prevents him from living up to the single ideal that only rarely survives in Crane's world—the deliberately compassionate or altruistic act. In *The Red Badge of Courage* only the tattered soldier exhibits true compassion, when he ignored his own (fatal) wounds to care for Henry. Henry blushes in remembering "the tattered soldier, he who gored by bullets and faint for blood, had fretted concerning an imagined wound in another . . . he who blind with weariness and pain had been deserted [by Henry] in the field" (134). A similar moment occurs in part 6 of "The Open Boat," when the correspondent plainly saw the imagined soldier who lay dying in Algiers and was "moved by a profound and perfectly impersonal comprehension." In such rare moments Crane allows that there is what he called a "mystic tie" that exists despite the cruelty and brutality of war.[8]

But Henry exhibits no such compassion in *The Red Badge of Courage*. When Henry does perform a few conventionally courageous acts in the heat of combat, Crane shows him as being merely swept along in what he calls the "wild battle-madness" (128). And it seems possible that his portrait of Henry is intended in part as a skeptical response to James's more optimistic remarks on "the strong-willed man," he

who hears the still small voice [of reason] unflinchingly, and who, when the death-bringing consideration comes, looks at its face, consents to its presence, clings to it, affirms it, and holds it fast, in spite of the host of exciting mental images which rise in revolt against it and would expel it from the mind. (*Psychology* 319)

By contrast, when Henry experiences his final encounters with shame, thinking of "his flight from the first engagement" and later of his abandoning the tattered soldier, "there were small *shoutings* in his brain about these matters" (134, emphasis mine). Responding to his shouting conscience, Henry seeks only to conceal his guilty blush and finally succeeds in "muster[ing] force to put the sin at a distance" from himself (135).

Not every reader will concede that Crane condemns Henry's moral failure and concludes the novel in ironic reference to Henry's thirst for "images of . . . eternal peace" (135). But it will help clarify the nature of Crane's psychological portrait to consider the emphasis he gives to Henry's efforts to read the emotions of his fellows and conceal his own. In dramatizing Henry's innate facility in the "language of the emotions," to use Darwin's term, Crane focuses his (and Henry's) attention on people's faces. As Darwin wrote, expressed emotions "reveal the thoughts and intentions of others more truly than do words, which may be falsified," and "of all parts of the body, the face is most considered and regarded, as is natural from its being the chief seat of expression" (*Expression of the Emotions* 364). For this reason, the face has "been subjected during many generations to much closer and more earnest self-attention than any other part of the body" (327). Also, Darwin wrote, "under a keen sense of shame there is a strong desire for concealment. We turn away the whole body, more especially the [blushing] face, which we endeavour in some manner to hide" (320). Again and again in the novel, as in this early instance, Henry struggled with his own fear and "studied the faces of his companions, ever on the watch to detect kindred emotions" (*The Red Badge* 16). In the scene above, his own emotions "made him feel strange in the presence of men" who approached battle "with nothing but eagerness and curiosity apparent in their faces," and he often thought these eager warriors were liars (14). Once, in an outburst of bravado, "he was secretly dumfounded at this sentiment when it came from his lips. For a moment his face lost its valor and he looked guiltily about him. But no one questioned his right to deal in such words, and presently he recovered his air of courage" (91). And in another scene, as the men disengaged from battle, they "began to show strange emotions. They hurried with nervous fear. Some who had been dark and unfaltering in the grimmest moments now could not conceal an anxiety that made them frantic" (116).

Beyond his emphasis on facial expressions and the concealment of shame, Crane also dramatizes other emotions and forms of expression that Darwin had described. Once, for example, when Henry "wrapped his heart in the cloak of his pride and kept the flag erect" (111), Crane seems to echo Darwin's remark that pride is the most plainly expressed of the emotions: "A proud man exhibits his sense of superiority over others by holding his head and body erect" (*Expression of the Emotions* 263). In this same passage Darwin remarks that "a peacock or a turkey-cock strutting about with puffed-up feathers, is sometimes said to be an emblem of pride." Similarly, Crane's soldiers "strut" (*The Red Badge* 8) and respond to bugles that call "like brazen game-cocks" (82), and in looking forward to the high pride he would enjoy in possessing the enemy's flag (81), Henry anticipates "an encounter of strange beaks and claws, as of eagles" (129). Also in this passage from *The Expression of the Emotions*, Darwin describes the expression of impotence, another emotion that interested Crane. For example, Darwin writes that when a man wishes to show that he cannot do something, or prevent something from being done, he often shrugs his shoulders and goes on to note that "Englishmen . . . shrug their shoulders far less frequently and energetically than Frenchmen or Italians do" (*Expression of the Emotions* 263–64). Similarly, in one of his own interesting passages of natural history, Crane describes how a Colonel MacChesnay responds when chastised by an angry general:

> The colonel was seen to straighten his form and put one hand forth in oratorical fashion. He wore an injured air; it was as if a deacon had been accused of stealing. The men were wiggling in an ecstasy of excitement.
>
> But of a sudden the colonel's manner changed from that of a deacon to that of a Frenchman. He shrugged his shoulders. (*The Red Badge* 118)

Witnessing this exchange, a "lieutenant . . . had listened with an air of impotent rage," but when he criticizes the general (after he had departed), the colonel rebukes *him*, and "the lieutenant made an obedient gesture" (118–19).

Of course such possible Darwinian echoes in Crane do not prove that he was more or less copying either Darwin or James. But the unquestionable similarities in these three writers' interest in the emotions indicate at least that Crane assumed Darwin's theory of the human mind's evolution by means of natural selection. Indeed, in his expressionistic study of the mind in evolution, Crane went about as far as he could go in the mid-1890s to depict the human reality that is still too offensive for serious consideration in many cultural strongholds. In accord with Darwin's theory regarding the "war of nature" (*The Origin of Species* 374), Crane suggested that the human being's essential motives were to kill and eat, as in a soldier's remark when the men lightened their loads: "Yeh can now eat, drink, sleep, an' shoot. . . . That's all yeh need" (21).[9] Pushing the idea even further, he noted, as Darwin does in *The Expression of the Emotions*, that when people unconsciously uncover the canine tooth in a snarl, sneer, or even a sardonic smile, they reveal their descent from "our semi-human progenitors [who] uncovered their canine teeth when prepared for battle" (251–52). In one battle, Henry "cried out savagely," crouching with "his teeth set in a cur-like snarl" (94), and in another, "they in blue showed their teeth" in "launch[ing] themselves as at the throats" of their enemies (129). Even prominent evolutionary theorists like Alfred R. Wallace would have balked at such suggestions in the expression of emotions that the human mind has evolved by "the necessary acquirement of each mental power and capacity by gradation" (*The Origin of Species* 488). But in Crane's more daring intention to dramatize how the mind is shaped not only by natural selection, but the other force in evolution, sexual selection, he knew that he could tread on *this* sacred ground only with the utmost caution.

Sexual Selection and the "Law of Battle"

Crane did not focus his thoughts on sexual selection to the extent that the courtship novelists of the 1880s and 1890s, such as Howells, Henry James, Harold Frederic, or Kate Chopin, did. But he made it clear that one of the forces to which Maggie fell victim was her instinctive attraction to a man like Pete, who "strutted upon the scene" like any Darwinian male fitted for survival in the "law of battle" and with all his sexual ornamentation. She noted his "bristling moustache of short, wire-like hairs," and the colorful attire (including "a red puff tie" and "patent-leather shoes") that "looked like murder-fitted-weapons": these details and "each curl of his lip" made it appear that he would be "invincible in fights," "a supreme warrior."[10] And in one of his last war stories, "The Clan of No-Name," Crane presents another view of the woman's sexual desire, her quickness to select a second lover after learning that her first choice had been killed in battle. When she asks the new but previously rejected lover, "How—how do I know you really—truly love me?" her "timorous glance made him the superior person in an instant"; then, "confident as a grenadier," he advanced, took "both her hands [and] kissed her" (*Poems* 251–52). In the world of men at war in *The Red Badge of Courage*, of course, there are no such intimate relations. But Crane was careful to indicate in several ways his awareness that natural and sexual selection are interwoven in the general war of life, especially in the male's physical and mental nature.

No one familiar with the elements of sexual selection can escape the fact of male violence according to the law of battle. In explaining sexual differences and discussing the male's secondary sexual "characters," Darwin acknowledges that in accounting for the evolution of certain structures of the male, for example, the large prehensile claws of certain oceanic crustaceans, it "is scarcely possible to distinguish between the effects of natural and sexual selection" (*The Descent of Man* 1:256–57). But he quickly adds:

> There are many other structures and instincts which must have been developed through sexual selection—such as the weapons of offence and the means of defence possessed by the males for fighting with and driving away their rivals—their courage and pugnacity—their ornaments of many kinds—their

organs for producing vocal or instrumental music—and their glands for emitting odours. (1:257–58)

Like many other writers of his time, Crane was struck by the essential union of power and beauty in Darwin's formulation. Kate Chopin's character Edna, for example, awakens to take in "the significance of life, that monster made up of beauty and brutality" (*The Awakening*, chap. 28). Similarly, Crane rails at the idea that the beautiful strong should prevail in life, yet in *The Red Badge* he notes that the homely face of the idealized, wounded, and tattered man "was suffused with a light of love for the army which was to him of all things beautiful and powerful" (53). This kind of love is generalized throughout the novel in such phrases as "war-ardor" or "war desire" (5), as when Henry searches his companion's faces for expressions of fear but is aware only of "some ardor of the air which was causing the veteran commands to move with glee, almost with song" (16). But if this ardor is diffused in nature, Crane locates it more specifically in the male's mind. Once, for example, when Henry is carried away by "swift pictures of himself" dying gloriously in battle, his "thoughts up-lifted him [and] he felt the quiver of war-desire" (64).

Thus, in a pattern of phrases and images more suggestive than "up-lifted" and "quiver" here, Crane indicates both his intent to define this as explicitly phallic power and his awareness that the only way to do so in the 1890s was symbolically. Like Howells, Henry James, Harold Frederic, and many of the others, he was adept at using the Victorian coded imagery of canes and hard-bitten cigars (as well as orchids). Although no observer of late-twentieth-century popular culture would mistake this kind of imagery in films such as *Dr. Strangelove* or *The Naked Gun*, there is a persistent odd tendency among Crane's interpreters to see him as an intellectual innocent. But in his efforts to deal with the male's sexual passion, as Darwin had defined it, his repeated image of "the red animal, war, the blood-swollen god" (*The Red Badge* 25, 69) is certainly part of a pattern that includes many references to the men's "impotency" (35), their wishes to "stand erect in battle" (26), and their "delicious" strutting when "swelled with . . . pride" (8).

Neither Darwin in *The Expression of the Emotions* nor certainly William James shares Crane's bold, fin de siècle literary interests in evoking phallic passion.[11] Darwin certainly has much to say about "the erection of hair" or feathers as animals express their anger or male combativeness, or about faces "gorged with blood" or flushed with blood. But Crane's wordplay is a purely literary device for making his impolite point about the male mind. In one revealing passage Crane writes, "When, in a dream, it occurred to the youth that his rifle was an impotent stick, he lost sense of everything but his hate, his desire to smash into pulp the glittering smile of victory which he could feel upon the faces of his enemies." Then, charging ahead (two sentences later), "the youth was not conscious that he was erect upon his feet," and here Crane refers to "the chaos of his brain," whose "one thought" at the time was to wonder if he had fallen down (95). Similarly, in another battle, "it had begun to seem to them that events were trying to prove that they were impotent," but in a moment, "the impetus of enthusiasm was theirs again. They gazed about them with looks of uplifted pride, feeling new trust in the grim, always-confident weapons in their hands. And they were men" (114–15).

In referring to the power of music as another aspect of these men's war ardor, however, Crane was on firmer theoretical ground. In both *The Descent of Man* and *The Expression of the Emotions* Darwin notes how music was employed by "the half-human progenitors of man, during the season of courtship, when animals of all kinds are excited by the strongest passions" (*The Descent of Man* 2:337) and also how music "likewise stirs up in us the sensation of triumph and the glorious ardour for war. These powerful and mingled feelings may well give rise to the sense of sublimity" (2:335). In one of several musical moments in this key in *The Red Badge*, Henry was "for a few moments . . . sublime" after thinking of himself as a glorious warrior and feeling "the quiver of war-desire." "In his ears, he heard the ring of victory. . . . The music of the trampling feet, the sharp voices, the clanking arms of the column near him made him soar on the red wings of war" (64). Again, emerging from another bout with his feelings of impotency, Henry is swept up in "a blare of heated rage, mingled with a certain expression of intentness on all faces. Many of the men were making low-toned noises with their mouths, and these subdued cheers, snarls, imprecations, prayers, made a wild, barbaric song that went as an undercurrent of sound, strange and chantlike with the resounding chords of the war-march" (35). And focusing on the expression of this kind of mingled sexual and combative passion in another such moment, Crane writes of Henry's terror in feeling that their fight was lost and that they would be overrun by "the blood-swollen god": "He had the impulse to make a rallying speech, to sing a battle-hymn, but he could only get his tongue to call into the air: 'Why—why—what—what's th' matter?'" (69). Many moments like this in Crane's war fiction register his ultimate sense of the meaninglessness of war and the grim comedy of man's place in nature. Here in *The Red Badge*, for example, he gives us the image "of a dead soldier" lying "upon his back staring at the sky" (24). He uses this image of a dead man's futile stare into the empty heavens even more powerfully in his story "The Upturned Face," and in the poem "War Is Kind" he drives home the point, "These men were born to drill and die" (*Poems* 81).

It would be a mistake to take Crane's bitter remarks about men "born to drill and die" as moral outrage directed only at belligerent males who should know better. In successive verses of "War Is Kind" he includes all the players in the reproductive struggle of life, admonishing a "maiden," "babe," and "mother" not to weep for a dead "lover," "father," or "son." And in the later war story, "The Clan of No-

Name," he emphasizes the maiden's role (Margharita's) in the tangled war of life, as Howells did in his own war story of 1905, "Editha." Both Margharita and Editha share Maggie's desire for a supreme warrior. In *The Red Badge of Courage*, of course, there are only fleeting references to the female's part. Still Crane gives it the emphasis it deserves by enveloping his story of warring life within opening and closing references to love. The hero who finally leaves the war with a "lover's thirst" went to war in the first place partly because of his subliminal sexual desire. "One night, as he lay in bed" before he enlisted, "the winds had carried to him the clangoring of the church-bell as some enthusiast jerked the rope frantically to tell the twisted news of a great battle. This voice of the people . . . made him shiver in a prolonged ecstasy of excitement" (6). His mother weeps when he tells her he has enlisted, but—like Maggie, Margharita, or Editha—she wants him to do nothing she would be ashamed of. "Jest think as if I was a-watchin' yeh," she says, and if "a time comes when yeh have to be kilt or do a mean thing, why, Henry, don't think of anything 'cept what's right, because there's many a woman has to bear up 'ginst sech things" (7).

Saying his goodbyes to schoolmates, he appreciated their wonder and admiration and "swelled with calm pride," and strutted (8). Like any gamecock, of course, he was aware that "a certain light-haired girl had made vivacious fun at his martial-spirit but there was another and darker girl whom he had gazed at steadfastly." She appeared to grow "demure and sad at sight of his blue and brass" and to express her interest by showing "a good deal of flurry and haste in her movement" (8). Crane ends this scene with a concise point that underlies the whole novel: "He often thought of it." There are other girls along the way—those included in the crowds that "fed and caressed" the enlistees: "he basked in the smiles of the girls" (8). Later, when a soldier tries to steal a horse from a farm, "a young girl rushed from the house," and seeing her stand there "with pink cheeks and shining eyes . . . like a dauntless statue," the soldiers "ceased to remember their own large war," "called attention to various defects" in the thief's "personal appearance," and "were wildly enthusiastic in support of the young girl" (17). Further along, having run in fear and then regained something of his self-respect, Henry imagined how his mother and the young lady whose admiring glance he carries in his memory would respond to his tales of "blazing scenes": he would destroy "their vague feminine formula for beloved ones doing brave deeds on the field of battle without risk of life" (88).

Thus, noting how Henry carries such images into his last two encounters, his most glorious moments, Crane reiterates his point that underlying Henry's war-ardor or war desire is the principle of sexual selection with its essential element, the law of battle. Even in describing what is certainly one of Henry's finest moments, Crane writes that "within him as he hurled himself forward, was born a love, a despairing fondness for his flag which was near him. It was a creation of beauty and invulnerability. It was a goddess, radiant, that bended its form with an imperious gesture to him. It was a woman, red and white, hating and loving, that called him with the voice of his hopes" (108).

As the novel builds toward its final dramatic encounter, then, chapter 20 ends with the soldiers celebrating in uplifted pride, with their "always-confident weapons in their hands. And they were men" (115). Chapter 21 ends with them knowing "that their faces were deeply flushing from thrills of pleasure" (121), and chapter 22 prepares for the final onslaught with imagery of the men standing "erect and tranquil" and of "the round, red discharges from the guns" (122). Continuing to underscore his psychological theme, Crane includes several references to the men's minds (122). A lieutenant "produced from a hidden receptacle of his mind new and portentous oaths"; Henry sometimes "prattled, words coming unconsciously from in him in grotesque exclamations," and Crane pictures the "savageness denoted in [the men's] expressions" as well as "the wild graspings of [Henry's] mind" (124–25). Preparing for the final assault, Henry expects to see the men "weary and stiffened" but sees instead their "unqualified expressions of assent." Then the men "sprang forward in eager leaps," with "new and unexpected force." Crane comments,

> A knowledge of its faded and jaded condition made the charge appear like a paroxysm, a display of the strength that comes before a final feebleness. The men scampered in insane fever of haste, racing as if to achieve a sudden success before an exhilarating fluid should leave them. (127)

Thus, they engage the enemy, and borne on "the swift wings of their desires," Crane writes that "there were subtle flashings of joy within [Henry], that thus should be his mind" (128). And the struggle ends when the men arrived "at the place of success" and "bellowed in an ecstasy" (130).

If Crane did not intentionally hint at an orgasmic end to this struggle, it is at least an orgy of "war-ardor" or, as he remarked of an earlier battle, a scene that "an ethereal wanderer" might take for "a scene . . . of some frightful debauch" (77). In either case, his intense analysis of Henry's chaotic brain throughout the novel suggests his belief that, first, these soldiers' expressions of their emotions verify Darwin's theory of common descent; second, that there are innumerable states of mind in the ongoing stream of consciousness; and third, that the sexual struggle, according to the principle of sexual selection, has helped produce a cerebral system that "not only regulates most of the existing functions of the body, but has indirectly influenced the progressive development of various bodily structures and of certain mental qualities," the first of which in Darwin's list is courage (*The Descent of Man* 2:398, 402).

It is important to remember that as an amateur evolutionary psychologist, Crane should be credited as understanding, with William James, "how great is the darkness in which we grope" (*Psychology* 468). But if we interpret the novel as Crane's exploration in this field, his final remarks about Henry are highly ironic—the idea that Henry "had *rid* himself of the red sickness of battle," that "the sultry night-mare was in the *past*," that "he had *been* an animal blistered and sweating in the heat and pain of war," and that now he can know "an existence of soft and eternal peace" (135, emphasis mine). Without Crane's irony, all this would serve to erase the "indelible stamp of [man's] lowly origin" (*The Descent of Man* 2:405), to halt the flowing stream of consciousness, and, in general, to mock the late-nineteenth-century scientific thought that questioned man's place in the universe. In view of the reflections on the theory of sexual selection that the novel contains, according to which "the season of love is that of battle" (*The Descent of Man* 2:48), the supreme irony is that Henry now "turned with a *lover's* thirst to images of tranquil skies" (135, emphasis mine). Nothing is more potentially violent than a male in love. Such images of the lover's thirst—like Maggie's pathetic need to see the supreme warrior Pete as "the beau ideal of a man"—are the stuff of romantic foolishness in virtually every work of American literary realism (*Maggie*, chap. 5). As Crane wrote in a draft to *The Red Badge*: "To seduce her victims, nature had to formulate a beautiful excuse."[12]

Moreover, Crane's conclusion about the "lover's thirst [for] images of tranquil skies" underscores the point he dramatizes repeatedly in the novel: that Henry's chaotic mind is marvelously equipped to deceive itself. His well-developed capacity for self-deception is comically evident when he "strenuously tried to think" about his flight from battle: "it occurred to him that he had never wished to come to the war. He had not enlisted of his own free will" but "had been dragged by the merciless government . . . to be slaughtered!" (22–23). And in a more analytical passage concerning how Henry was "unconsciously in advance" in one of the charges, Crane writes: "His mind took mechanical but firm impressions, so that afterward, everything was pictured and explained to him, save why he himself was there" (104–5). Deception, concealment, and mimicry are of course highly effective strategies for survival, as Henry seems to realize in the draft version: with the miraculous power to create dupes, Nature "could deck a hideous creature in enticing apparel" (Binder 49). In a sense, Crane's thoughts on the human capacity for self-deception (or Harold Frederic's remarks about the tricksy devices of Theron Ware's mind) seem to anticipate recent evolutionary psychologists' theories of the survival value of deceiving oneself, that, for example, "you can't leak your hidden intentions if you don't think they *are* your intentions" (Pinker 421).[13]

Although he is clearly interested in the chaotic mind's capacity for self-deception, Crane seems determined mainly to dramatize his characters' instincts and emotions and in this way to mock the idea of evolutionary progress. Crane's men are alive with the throat-grappling instinct, and even if young men like Henry can exhibit courage in the heat of battle, it is not because they are coolly determined to do so. Any animal is capable of courage or pugnacity, in Darwin's terms. For Crane, the human comedy is in denying our common descent, valorizing the human mind, and in overestimating one's significance in the universe. More important, Henry's tragedy (and the human tragedy) is his capacity to betray what Crane referred to as "the mystic tie" of selflessness (*Poems* 129), as when Henry abandons the wounded, tattered man. Because Henry finally saw his "vivid error" and yet mustered the "force to put the sin at a distance" (*The Red Badge* 135), it is hard to imagine that Crane shared Darwin's optimism about the evolution of the moral sense—that it might lead to "virtue . . . triumphant" (*The Descent of Man* 1:70–106).[14] Still, Crane might have found a glimmer of hope in Darwin's theory of the emotions: first and foremost in the fact that shame *is* in the repertoire of the emotions and that sometimes it is irrepressibly expressed in the blush. At the end of the novel, when "small shoutings in his brain" reminded Henry that he had run from battle, Crane writes that "for a moment he blushed, and the light of his soul flickered with shame" (134). Earlier, in the scene of abandonment that still haunts Henry, Crane referred to this as "the ghost of shame" (61). Thus, even in Henry, Crane can imagine a soul flickering to light when ignited by the moral sense. In this way Crane maintained, somewhat like the other American naturalists, that a soul of some kind could survive in the Darwinian reality.

The relationship between Crane's psychological realism in *The Red Badge* and the new evolutionary psychology will not be perceived by readers who adhere to the simplistic view that Darwinism consists only of the time-worn idea that nature is red in tooth and claw. Many will cling to the image of Stephen Crane as a youth who hated books and was willfully oblivious to the most compelling ideas of his time. It is also true, however, that Crane contributed to this myth, most notably when he wrote of *The Red Badge* that he did the fieldwork for his "psychological portrayal of fear" on the football field, where he "got [his] sense of the rage of conflict" (*Correspondence* 322). In this odd letter, in which he displays his pride that "George Wyndham, Under Secretary for War in the British Government" had compared him with Tolstoy and Zola as war novelists, he adds that his success in portraying the psychology of war might derive from the fact that "fighting is a hereditary instinct, and that [he] wrote intuitively." He drew on his heritage as a Crane, "a family of fighters in the old days," including the Revolution, where "every member did his duty," and he had "been very careful not to let any theories or pet ideas of my own creep into my work." "Preaching is fatal to art in literature," he continues, and in his own efforts "to give to readers a slice out of life," he keeps in mind Emerson's remark that "there should be a long logic beneath the story, but it should be kept carefully out of sight." Unless one is inclined to credit Crane for having formulated on his own the theory of mind that is projected in *The Red Badge of Courage*, there is reason to believe that one of the lessons he learned on the football field—or in the literary trenches or perhaps even in *The Expression of the Emotions in Man and Animals*—is that there are definite advantages in concealing one's play-book or one's blush.

Notes

1. This anonymous review from the *Nation* (July 2, 1896) is reprinted in Richard Lettis, et al., *Stephen Crane's* The Red Badge of Courage: *Text and Criticism*, 115–16.

2. Crane scholars know that there is no concrete record of Crane's having owned or read anything by William James or Charles Darwin. Neither the scholarly accounts of his brief studies at Lafayette College and Syracuse University nor the mass of biographical data gathered so helpfully in *The Crane Log*, for example, give us anything to go on here. In the absence of such factual material and because many readers still have a narrow view of influence, some will still prefer to imagine that Crane steadfastly closed his mind to "the greatest of all scientific revolutions," as Ernst Mayr refers to the development in science following *The Origin of Species* (501). For a counterargument to the myth that Henry James's aesthetic sensibility was untouched by mere ideas, see my case for his interest in Darwinian thought presented in *The Descent of Love*; here, chapter 8 later argues that Fitzgerald was much more interested in evolutionary thought than has been imagined.

3. Quotes from *The Red Badge* are from the University of Virginia edition. *The Damnation of Theron Ware* appeared in 1896, before Crane and Frederic began their brief friendship, and it is impossible that either influenced the other in the psychological analyses of Henry Fleming or Theron Ware. Readers who are primarily interested in literary studies but who also want to consult recent works on evolutionary psychology might begin with Plotkin and the highly regarded volume edited by Jerome H. Barkow, Leda Cosmides, and John Tooby, *The Adapted Mind*. But there are also two very interesting and readable recent volumes that have captured wide audiences: Matt Ridley's *The Red Queen: Sex and the Evolution of Human Nature* and Robert Wright's *The Moral Animal: Why We Are the Way We Are: The New Science of Evolutionary Psychology*. Stephen Pinker's longer *How the Mind Works* has also won a large, broad audience. Finally, as this chapter makes much of Crane's and William James's interest in the expression of emotions in relation to Darwin's exploration of the subject in 1872, readers might also want to consult Randolph M. Nesse's recent article, "Evolutionary Explanations of Emotions." Noting that "all biological phenomena require two separate kinds of explanation, proximate and evolutionary," and that there are still conflicting definitions of the emotions, Nesse proposes a "definition of emotions . . . based on [his] approach to understanding their evolutionary functions":

The emotions are specialized modes of operation shaped by natural selection to adjust the physiological, psychological, and behavioral parameters of the organism in ways that increase its capacity and tendency to respond adaptively to the threats and opportunities characteristic of specific kinds of situations. This formulation predicts that each emotion should correspond to a particular kind of adaptively significant situation that has occurred repeatedly in the course of evolution, and that the detailed characteristics of an emotional state can be analyzed as design features that increase the individual's ability to cope with the particular kinds of adaptive challenges that arise in this situation. (268)

4. This and further references to James in this chapter use *The Briefer Course* (cited as *Psychology*) rather than *The Principles of Psychology* on the theory that if Crane did consult James, he might have been more inclined to refer to this more recent and more accessible single volume. Scholarship on Stephen Crane has made too little of similarities between his view of life and William James's. Moreover, when scholars sometimes do note similarities between Crane's and William James's views, they tend to add at once that Crane would not have been up to reading James. In his introduction to the University of Virginia edition of *The Red Badge*, J. C. Levenson, for example, discusses the two together, even noting that Crane "was in 1893 in an avant-garde of the tough-minded"; but he adds immediately: "Not that Crane knew the work of [James or Chauncey Wright]; had he done so he might have handled his subject better" (lvii). A notable exception to this is Patrick K. Dooley, whose work on both figures leads him to a number of interesting conclusions, some involving James's ideas in *The Principles of Psychology*. See Dooley, *The Pluralistic Philosophy of Stephen Crane*, where references to James are indexed.

5. In an undated letter thought to have been written sometime in 1897 to John Northern Hilliard. *Correspondence of Stephen Crane*, 322.

6. James quotes Darwin's *Expression of the Emotions* (292), but students of Crane will be interested in Darwin's entire chapter 12, "Surprise—Astonishment—Fear—Horror").

7. This is the first use of "tangled" or "entangled" in the novel. Others occur on 63, 69, 80, 81, 83, and 92.

8. In the posthumously published poem: "Unwind my riddle. / Cruel as hawks the hours fly; / Wounded men seldom come home to die; / The hard waves see an arm flung high; / Scorn hits strong because of a lie; / Yet there exists a mystic tie. / Unwind my riddle" (*Poems* 129).

9. One of the many textual questions in *The Red Badge*, this passage is sometimes printed, "You can now eat and shoot, said the tall soldier to the youth. That's all you want to do" (*The Portable Stephen Crane* 209). That Crane was playing off Darwin's remark about "the war of nature" seems evident throughout the novel but especially in the "Discarded Chapter XII," as reprinted in the University of Virginia edition. There Henry once congratulates himself on the brilliance with which he had reasoned the way "Nature had provided the creations with various defenses and ways of escape that they might fight or flee, and she had limited dangers in powers of attack and pursuit that the things might resist or hide with a security proportionate to their strength and wisdom. It was cruel but it was war. Nature fought for her system; individuals fought for liberty to breathe. The animals had the privilege of using their legs and their brains. It was all the same old philosophy. He could not omit a small grunt of satisfaction as he saw with what brilliancy he had reasoned it out" (139–40).

10. These details of Pete's appearance from chapters 5 and 6 of *Maggie: A Girl of the Streets* are worth comparing with Darwin's description of the way pride is expressed. He notes, for example, that "the arrogant man . . . may show his contempt by slight movements, such as those before described, about the nostrils and lips. Hence the muscle which everts the lower lip has been called the *musculus superbus*" (*Expression of the Emotions* 263).

11. Crane is sometimes referred to as a "decadent, in a Beardsley vein" (Halliburton 270); this quality was certainly recognized by Copeland and Day, publishers of Crane's *The Black Riders* (1895), *The Yellow Book*, and Oscar Wilde's *Salome* (1894), with illustrations by Beardsley.

12. Binder, *The Red Badge of Courage*, 49; this passage is one of the points of contention in the long-standing debate over textual questions in the novel. For recent discussion of these issues, see articles by Michael Guemple and Robert M. Myers.

13. Referring here to Robert Trivers's work on the subject, Pinker writes that in "pursuing his theory of the emotions to its logical conclusion, [he] notes that in a world of walking lie detectors [another of our adaptive powers] the best strategy is to believe your own lies," and that "there is an obvious similarity to Freud's theory of the unconscious and the defense mechanisms of the ego (such as repression, projection, denial, and rationalization), though the explanation is completely different." On the subject of self-deception, see also Nesse's remarks on "the social emotions," for example: "Of particular interest is the possibility that the very 'irrationality' of these emotions may be essential to their adaptive functions. Love, anger, guilt, and anxiety can achieve their purposes only if they cannot easily be overriden by cognition" (284).

14. Darwin finds reason to believe that in future generations of mankind, "the social instincts" will grow stronger, to the point that "the struggle between higher and lower impulses will be less severe, and virtue will be triumphant" (*The Descent of Man* 1:104).

3 Jack London and "the Sex Problem"

Surely, I have studied the sex problem even in its "most curious ways."
—Jack London

As Jack London remarked toward the end of his career, he had "for many years specialized on sex."[1] But his work in this area is little known, in part because he is still widely mistaken as a writer with little intellectual heft who specialized in adventure stories of the far north. Many (but not all) London scholars acknowledge his interest in Darwin, but none has given due consideration to London's work with the theory of sexual selection. Indeed, scholarly work on Jack London shares the failure in American literary history in general to realize not only that there *was* a sex problem for writers of London's time but also why there *would* have been one. It is worth recalling that London (1876–1916) and Havelock Ellis (1859–1935) were contemporaries and that London began his brief writing career when Havelock Ellis's was at its height. They both explored the nature of sex in the context of Darwinian theory and in at least one case their magazine publications appeared side-by-side. London's very impressive library included several of Ellis's books, along with very many other works on evolution and sex.[2] In short, as a writer who "for many years specialized on sex," London undoubtedly agreed with Ellis's remark of 1897 that "sex [is] the central problem of life" (*Studies* 1:xxx). However, while London learned much from Ellis, he concerned himself with different aspects of the sex problem and, accordingly, conceived of possible solutions to the sex problem that were outside Ellis's range of interests.

From London's point of view, solutions to the sex problem involved not only the psychological and social issues that Ellis focused on in *Sex in Relation to Society* (1910) but also, to a much greater extent than for Ellis, the evolution of race; this was a question that was much more hotly debated in the United States than in England at that time. And, especially toward the end of his career, London took a much broader view of the sex problem than Ellis did, seeing it as the key to the world's ecological crisis. He worked on his own ranch to realize his hopes that selective breeding (Darwin's "artificial selection"), reinforced by the then new and very promising field of Mendelian genetics, could lead to more efficient farming and help alleviate the growing problem of worldwide hunger. And he addressed these issues in a series of agrarian novels. To put it another way, while Ellis revered Darwin and situated his study of sex within the context of evolution, London was much more interested in the larger biological questions—questions like those addressed by Huxley in *Man's Place in Nature* or by Ernst Haeckel in *The Riddle of the Universe at the Close of the Nineteenth Century*. And, much more than Ellis, London seems always to have kept in touch with the idea that there can be no evolution without reproduction: that the first principle of Darwin's "one general law leading to the advancement of all organic beings" is to *multiply:* "multiply, vary, let the strongest live and the weakest die" (*The Origin of Species* 208).

Darwin's theory of sexual selection is the essential element in each of London's novels of sexual love, from *A Daughter of the Snows* (1902), the heroine of which "believed in natural selection and in sexual selection" (86), to the last novel he lived to see in print, *The Little Lady of the Big House* (1916). But by the time he wrote this last novel, London knew much more about the sex problem than he did in 1902. For he kept abreast of the voluminous work in this new field, including especially the first volumes of Freud as they became available in translation. Thus, in his culminating work *The Little Lady of the Big House* (which he projected as being "all sex, from start to finish" [*Letters* 1135]), London produced an extensive analysis of sexual selection in the lives of his three lovers, explicitly addressing and routing the most attractive challenge to Darwin's theory of evolution at that time, Bergson's *Creative Evolution* (trans. 1911). He also presented his lovers within the larger biological reality, including the pressing issue of how to feed the world's exploding population. And, in one of the first American novels to take in Freudian theory, he explored the biological foundations of Freud's theory of sexuality. Indeed, taking all this into account, Jack London's studies in evolution and the sex problem are the most comprehensive and accomplished in all of American fiction.[3]

London's Early Explorations of Sexual Selection: *A Daughter of the Snows, The Kempton-Wace Letters,* and *The Sea-Wolf*

In *A Daughter of the Snows* London began to study the "elective affinity, sexual affinity, or whatever the intangible essence known as love is" (90). He produced a traditional plot based on the triangle: "Two men and a woman! The most potent trinity of factors in the creating of human pathos and tragedy!" (137). But, like his hero in this novel, Vance Corliss, London was in the early stages of "learning life [and] adding to his sum of human generalizations," and of learning how to reconstruct these ideas in fiction. Against a tiresome backdrop of remarks on the evolution of race (an unavoidable bugaboo in British and American evolutionary thought throughout London's career, especially during these years of imperial strife surrounding the Spanish-American War) London finally arranges for the heroine, Frona Welse, "a woman of fair Saxon type," to rely not only on the subconscious processes of selection but on her moral sense to accept Corliss. She will herself have to overcome a bout with hysteria, "a nervous condition" causing an emotional outburst when Corliss offends a young Indian woman. Corliss will come to understand Frona's race consciousness and see her "as the genius of the race" (147). The rival male fails because he lacked the appeal "that made the touch of [Corliss's] hand a pleasure to her" (88) and because he violated the code of selflessness that she had acquired in her "primitive life" (25) in Alaska, the "faith of food and blanket" (333). Clearly the twenty-five-year-old London strained to construct a meaningful tale in this first novel, but it is also clear that his "sum of human generalizations" about evolution and the sexual struggle at this early point in his career provided a solid foundation for his further explorations. He was well on his way to formulating a coherent view of the underlying question: man's place in nature. Moreover, he was already rather well attuned to the developing thought on the evolutionary issues involving sexual love that would emerge toward the end of his career in Freudian studies of hysteria, the subconscious, and sexual pleasure.

The following year London coauthored *The Kempton-Wace Letters* (1903) with Anna Strunsky. It is one of the clearest and most comprehensive studies of modern love in American fiction at the turn of the century, presented as a debate about love carried on through an exchange of letters. One of the correspondents is an exponent of romantic love, Dane Kempton (whose part Strunsky wrote), and the other is a scientific critic of "the romantic love malady," Herbert Wace (London's part). The debate arises when Wace writes of his anticipated marriage to a woman who "has health and strength and beauty and youth"; she "will certainly make a most charming wife and mother," one with whom Wace hopes to enjoy conjugal love (39) or conjugal affection (93). Making the case for "sex-comradeship" (138) as the solution to the problem of sexual love, Wace provides a succinct review of evolutionary theory, noting first that "there are two functions which all life must perform: Nutrition and Reproduction" (64) and that sex differentiation itself arose in the evolutionary struggle for life through a division of labor whereby the two sexes "shared the work of reproduction between them" (114–15). Wace then cites other details from *The Descent of Man* to illustrate, first, the violence of sexual selection inherent in the male's secondary sexual characters, such as the prehensile organs of insects or the tusks of the boar, and second, the adaptive function of male beauty in order to influence female choice, as in "the glowing incandescence of the stickle-back" or the colorful cock's strange antics in dance and his heartfelt song. Now having founded his position on Darwin's theory of sexual selection, Wace goes on to argue man's capacity to "take hold of life and mould and knead it into more beautiful and useful forms" through domestic selection (63–66). Wace knows the evolutionary value and use of this "erotic phenomenon" called "sexual madness," and he takes pride in managing his own love life with scientific detachment: "I . . . elect to choose my mate with my intellect" (68).

Kempton, on the other hand, defines modern love in different terms. He admires Wordsworth and Whitman, and he is especially taken by Schopenhauer's reference to the lover's "immortal part" (105), claiming that it justifies his feeling that "love is the God of my faith" (133). Kempton cannot deny "that sexual selection pertains," but he joins the debate in a way that gives the novel its keen edge in the evolutionary controversy at the turn of the century. Arguing that "the early facts of biology cannot include that which transcends them," that "Darwin at the conclusion of 'The Descent of Man'" was probably "overtaken by a feeling of incompleteness in the work" (75–76), and that true love is "a . . . spiritual . . . growth" (193), he indicates his inclination toward the Lamarckian views of Berkeley's famous professor, Loseph Le Conte (95). Wace, on the other hand, indicates that *his* biological education took an opposite direction at Berkeley, when he began to side with Weismann and the neo-Darwinians who claimed to have disproved the Lamarckian possibility (153).[4] He reveres the neo-Darwinian Ernst Haeckel as "that brave old hero of Jena" who defined love as the irresistible passion, "the same *powerful, unconscious,* attractive force which impels the living spermatozoon to force an entrance into the ovum in the fertilization of the egg."[5] In short, Wace claims that Kempton's view of sex is a futile attempt to "refine and sublimate" the "blind, unreasoning, and compelling" force of Nature's "eternal cry—PROGENY!" (207).

At the end of the novel Strunsky arranged for Wace's fiancée to reject him (she whom he had selected so coolly as a promising sexual comrade). And this underscores an aspect of the sex problem that London would continue to wrestle with throughout his career: the male's passion, jealousy, and violence. Wace is focused on the Darwinian principle of sexual difference whereby the male possesses the prehensile organs and superior strength, and he remembers that in "the love of [his own] whelpage," he too had reveled in being "indomitable in battle, invincible in love." Now, however, he is resolved to lay "the grip of my will over the passion" and will not sacrifice "honour and . . . right conduct" "for the sake of possession" (241–42). As a neo-Darwinian, London knew that this determination to cultivate a gentler maleness within oneself could not in itself yield future generations of gentler males. But Wace and future heroes such as Dick Forrest (*The Little Lady of the*

Big House) will take it as a matter of honor to restrain themselves in sexual love. Instead of using their prehensile power to possess mates, as in the primitive capture of wives, the agrarian heroes that London would later develop (Billy Brown in *The Valley of the Moon* and Forrest in *The Little Lady of the Big House*) will emulate Herbert Wace's determination to take hold of *life* through domestic selection—in agricultural ventures rather like London's own ranch.

Before London began to develop his agrarian vision, he explored other possible solutions to the sex problem in *The Sea-Wolf* (1904) and *Martin Eden* (1909). In these novels as well, he worked with the two principles of sexual selection, the male's violent passion, always the greatest obstacle in London's "fight . . . for higher civilization & culture" (*Letters* 1096)—and the female's power to select. But he approached these problems in different ways that reflect not only his own efforts to keep abreast of the developing thought in evolutionary biology but also, no doubt, the developments in his personal love life. In *The Sea-Wolf*, for example, with his spirits buoyed perhaps by his new relationship with Charmian, he attempted to dramatize evolution taking an upward turn through the agency of female choice. That is, willing a kind of belief in the power of sexual selection, or love, to lift evolutionary development to a higher level, as advocated by Joseph Le Conte, for example, London first subjected his over-civilized hero, Humphrey Van Weyden, to the reinvigorating forces of natural selection aboard Wolf Larsen's *Ghost*. Then having made Van Weyden a more-or-less-worthy competitor with the splendid Wolf, London introduces Maud Brewster as the determining factor in sexual selection. Of course she selects against the merely brutal but beautiful Wolf, and for Van Weyden, whose superiority inheres in his moral sense, the highest evolutionary development according to *The Descent of Man*. Thus, when Wolf dies of a blinding headache, London completes his plan of rendering the brutal male extinct. Then, sending the *Ghost* into the evolutionary future with the vigorous and highly developed lovers, Maud and Van Weyden, London ended his most optimistic—and ridiculous—narrative of sexual love.

Before leaving *The Sea-Wolf*, however, it is worth noting how Wolf Larsen's great physical beauty figures in London's plot. In several well-known scenes, Van Weyden remarks on Wolf's beauty, and on how "he caught [himself] looking at him in a fascinated way, for Wolf was beautiful in the masculine sense" (85). Again, when Wolf reads to him from Ecclesiastes, his "voice . . . reverberating deeply," Van Weyden was "charmed and held" (90). And again, commenting on Wolf's masculine perfection, Van Weyden describes how his "great muscles leaped and moved under the satiny skin" that, "thanks to his Scandinavian stock, was fair as the fairest woman's" (116). The first and most important idea in all this is that Wolf is the supreme male animal, possessing both strength and beauty, as Darwin had theorized. The charming voice is of course an essential part of this beauty. Still, in London's evolutionary romance, this supreme male will be selected against because of his deficient moral sense. London writes that Wolf was "a magnificent atavism" representing "the type that came into the world before the development of the moral nature" (81).

Because these issues in the theory of sexual selection are still relatively unknown among literary scholars, novels like *The Sea-Wolf* are often badly misunderstood. In a well-known recent study, for example (*Male Call: Becoming Jack London*), Jonathan Auerbach ignores not only London's interest in the theory of sexual selection but also *any* ideas he might have wanted to engage. Auerbach asserts that "the philosophical import" or "conceptual content" of dramatized conversations in London's novels is "far less interesting than . . . the heated passions motivating the exchange of ideas" (222). Accordingly, Auerbach concludes that *The Sea-Wolf* "charts London's turn from the death of the father to the finding of the oedipal mother/ mate, with the intense homoerotic interplay between Hump and Wolf . . . functioning as the uneasy, unstable passage of transition" (336). Moreover, making his point about London's homoerotic desire, Auerbach also seems unaware that the question of homosexuality and androgyny was a very important part of the sex problem as it was being explored at the turn of the century. Not only Havelock Ellis's *Sexual Inversion* or Edward Carpenter's *The Intermediate Sex* but also virtually every other work on the evolution of sex at that time began by acknowledging Darwin's theory of sexual selection (if only to circumscribe it within the animal realm),[6] including especially the idea that "it has now been ascertained that at a very early embryonic period both sexes possess true male and female glands. Hence some extremely remote progenitor of the whole vertebrate kingdom appears to have been hermaphrodite or androgynous" (*The Descent of Man* 1:207).

Every writer on evolution recognized this fact of human biology at the turn of the century, including the authors London read on sex, from Haeckel and Le Conte to Havelock Ellis, Otto Weininger, and Freud. Reviewing "The Theory of Sexual Inversion," Havelock Ellis, for example, wrote that "the conception of the latent bisexuality of all males and females cannot fail to be fairly obvious to intelligent observers of the human body," and he rested his theory on the work of "the great pioneers of the doctrine of evolution"—first Darwin then Weismann and Haeckel— "who ha[ve] in recent years clearly recognized the bearing on the interpretation of homosexuality of the fact that the ancestors of the vertebrates were hermaphrodites" (*Studies* 1:4:311–12). As Freud wrote in *Three Contributions to the Theory of Sex*, "a certain degree of anatomical hermaphroditism really belongs to the normal" and therefore that there is "an original predisposition to bisexuality" (*Basic Writings* 558). It is highly probable that when London, already familiar with Ellis, first read Freud he would have realized rather quickly what has been emphasized only recently in Freudian studies: that, as Frank Sulloway remarks, the new evolutionary vision pertaining to bisexuality that Freud acquired in his relationship with Wilhelm Fliess beginning in 1897 "reflects, in microcosm, the crypto-biological nature of

Freud's entire psychoanalytical legacy to the twentieth century" (237); moreover, Sulloway concludes, "By 1905, the bisexual theory of homosexuality had been advocated by most of the leading sexologists of Europe" (295).

Regarding Humphrey Van Weyden's fascination with Wolf's beautiful body, then, it is fair to conclude that in addition to the element of male beauty in sexual selection, London would have recognized a certain normalcy in Van Weyden's (and perhaps his own) feelings for the male body. London's interest in androgyny is part of a larger movement in early twentieth-century literature and psychology that was exploring the normalcy of androgynous desire. Indeed, like other writers of that day, such as Sherwood Anderson, London was interested in imagining boyish "new" women and gentler "new" men who might function within the range of normalcy to help human beings resolve one of the most important aspects of the sex problem—inflexible categories of sexual difference.

Martin Eden and *The Valley of the Moon:* Havelock Ellis, Freud, and the Ecological Vision

In *Martin Eden* London revisited "the love of my whelpage" that he had treated briefly as Wace in *The Kempton-Wace Letters*, when "life rioted in my veins" before "it was decreed that I should develop into an intellectual animal" (*Kempton-Wace* 209–10). But by now there were new issues in the emerging fields of sexology and psychology and he quickly incorporated them in his own work. To the extent that *Martin Eden* traces Martin's disillusionment regarding sexual love (in addition to his disillusionment with his phenomenal success as a writer and with socialism), London participates in the general development in American literature from this period that includes Kate Chopin's *The Awakening*, wherein young men or women despair after awakening to the implications of the Darwinian critique of love. Well on the way to his disillusioning education, Martin tells a clever, cultured professor of English from Berkeley, "you lack biology," the sense that everything is "subject to the law of evolution." The professor yields to this criticism and recalls that his former colleague, the "great . . . scientist and evolutionist, Joseph Le Conte," had once told him the same thing (291–94). At this high point in Martin's biological education we learn that, "thanks to the school of scientific philosophers he favored, he knew the biological significance of love; but by a refined process of the same scientific reasoning he reached the conclusion that the human organism achieved its highest purpose in love, that love must not be questioned, but must be accepted as the highest guerdon of life" (240–41). This refined reasoning, here associated with Le Conte, resembles the sublimated reasoning of Dane Kempton (according to Wace). But in *Martin Eden* London's view of this school of biological thought is suggested in the English professor's remark that Le Conte is dead (294). London had found a more recent and absorbing kind of "refined . . . scientific reasoning" to fill out his portrait of Martin in Havelock Ellis's *Sexual Selection in Man*, though London chose not to mention Ellis.[7]

In the early stages of Martin's development he comes to realize that Ruth, his idealized lover from a higher class, is not a goddess but mere clay, just as "subject to the laws of the universe" as he was (*Martin Eden* 139). Then, after learning about the biological significance of beauty and knowing that his youthful battles had been like those of "young bulls" (163), he realizes that "God! We are animals! Brute-beasts!" (179). In one of a number of introspective moments before the mirror, he sees not only that he has risen from the mud but also that, in his initial shock of self-recognition, he had experienced "a bit of hysteria and melodrama" (181–83). Subsequently, London writes of Martin's intimate moments with Ruth, noting that he soon divined that he had been following the right course in wooing her the old, primitive way: "the touch of his hand on hers was vastly more potent than any word he could utter. . . . [T]he touch of his hand, the fleeting contact, made its way directly to her instinct" (217). In such scenes of sexual intimacy, rather racy for that day, London writes that "life poured from the ends of [Martin's] fingers" with "the soothing balm of his strength"; Ruth frequently gazes at his muscular neck and is shocked to realize that she wishes to touch his neck so that "its strength and vigor would flow out to her" (219) or that she "desire[s] to place her hands on that sunburned neck" (42–43).

Presenting their sexual intimacy in this way, London apparently takes up Havelock Ellis's first point in *Sexual Selection in Man*, the "primitive nature of the sensory function of the skin" and "the main characteristics of the primitive sense of touch" (*Studies* 1:3:3, 6). As Ellis goes on to comment on the erotic appeal of hair to the touch, London notes how Ruth's "hair [would] brush [Martin's] cheek" and how she had "vagrant impulses" to "rumple his hair" (218). Ellis explains how the woman's need for strength is satisfied by the "fundamentally sexual sense of touch" and quotes both George Eliot and the famous American psychologist Stanley Hall (who brought Freud to America in 1909) to support his point. Echoing this passage in Ellis, perhaps, London writes that Ruth's doctor, Doctor Hall, won't permit her to take powders for her blinding headaches. Whereas Ellis quotes Hall's point that "the skin is 'not only the primeaval and most reliable source of our knowledge of the external world or the archaeological field of psychology' but a field in which work may shed light on some of the most fundamental problems of psychic action" (*Studies* 1:3:4); London writes that when Martin's "hands touched [Ruth's] head" with the "soothing balm of his strength," the pain went away. She fell asleep and then later told him, "You cured me completely" (*Martin Eden* 219). Indeed, at this point in his career, Martin seems intoxicated with the refined, scientific reasoning of writers like Le Conte or Ellis, because he concludes "that the human organism achieved its highest purpose in love . . . that must not be questioned." Finally, however, he will begin to "question love, sacred love" and wonder whether "love is so gross a thing that it must feed upon publication and public notice" (462). In this frame of mind, then, disillusioned to find that love is merely nature's reproductive thrust in sexual selection, he often sees women "appraising him, selecting him," and he laughs with the sickness that his friend Lizzie says is in his head, "Something's wrong with your think-machine" (455).

Like Edna Pontellier in *The Awakening*, Martin drowns himself, only with London's greater emphasis that this death remains violently within the Darwinian economy: when Martin jumps overboard, a bonita takes a piece out of his "white body." Here, remarking that "the sting of it reminded [Martin] why he was there," London addresses the question of man's place in nature by suggesting that life exists to feed on life (*Martin Eden* 480–81).[8] This was certainly a dramatic conclusion to London's story of Martin's disillusionment in love and in his success as a writer. But it would be a mistake to conclude that London himself was too disillusioned to go on or that he had given up his quest for a solution to the sex problem. On his way home from the *Snark* voyage in June of 1909 he began work on *Burning Daylight*, the first of his three ecological novels.[9] In December 1909 he was thinking of himself as "quite a farmer just now" (*Letters* 847), and he had begun to create Dede Mason, the first of his ecological heroines who, as he explained in reference to Saxon Brown (*The Valley of the Moon*), "gets the vision" and then "gets the man to see the vision as well"—Dede Mason's vision being the idea to cultivate eucalyptus trees (*Letters* 1014). As one critic has suggested, the women and the land in these novels "become almost indistinguishable embodiments of . . . fertility" (Watson 184), but London's sense of *fertility* can be grasped only within the full context of his evolutionary thought. In the first place, he links these heroines' visionary powers with the female's vital evolutionary role in sexual selection, as when Maud Brewster selects Van Weyden so that the two can continue their voyage into the evolutionary future aboard the *Ghost*. Second, London sees these heroines' fertility as only the promising part of what he called nature's "abysmal fecundity" (*Kempton-Wace* 67), the fundamental force without which neither life nor hope for further evolutionary development can exist. But he concerned himself more with the abysmal part of the sex problem, not only the inherent violence in the sexual struggle but also what he saw as the Malthusian crisis leading to the Great War.

Based on his work in these novels, London should be seen as one of American literature's first and most important ecological writers, for he anticipated the kind of ecological thought that emerged late in the twentieth century in the related fields of behavioral ecology, sociobiology, and evolutionary psychology. As John Alcock writes, evolutionary psychology is "a subdiscipline of sociobiology, which in turn . . . [is] part of an overarching behavioral ecology," and "evolutionary theory is at the heart of all three disciplines" (12). Although many present-day ecologists might object to this grouping of the three disciplines, or to E. O. Wilson's argument for "the biological basis of all social behavior" (*Sociobiology* 4), London would have embraced these ideas. A longtime admirer of Ernst Haeckel (who coined the term "ecology"), he would not only have affirmed Haeckel's definition of ecology as "the study of all those complex interrelations referred to by Darwin as the conditions for the struggle for survival" (Brewer 1), but he would have agreed with the exponents of evolutionary psychology that the human being is the most compelling subject in the field of behavioral ecology. As Ernst Mayr explained in 1982, "the part of sociobiology that is being attacked is that which deals with man," but London did not doubt for a moment that "man's social behavior [can] be compared with that of animals" (Mayr 598).[10] And, to maintain a focus on London as an ecologist, it is perfectly clear that he assumed E. O. Wilson's recent point that as we have "now begun to probe the foundations of human nature, revealing what people intrinsically most need, and why" we have entered "a new era of existentialism." Our first responsibility is to help "get *Homo sapiens* settled down and happy before we wreck the planet" (*Consilience* 297). There could be no better definition of London's purpose in his ecological novels. Moreover, *The Valley of the Moon* is one of the most impressive efforts in American literature to construct chapters in the kind of "true evolutionary epic" that Wilson envisions (265).[11]

Of course E. O. Wilson's theme "that humankind has created a planet-sized problem for itself" rests on a much deeper foundation of evolutionary thought than London could have known early in the twentieth century, involving the modern synthesis, in general, and Wilson's sense of the need for biodiversity (*Consilience* 277). But London focused his attention on that old part of the sex problem that Wilson revisits in warning of heedless population growth, emphasizing that "human beings [are] typical organisms in reproductive response" and will therefore expand to fill whatever might be added to the earth's carrying capacity through technological advances (289). London's firm grasp of these issues is most evident in his remarks on the outbreak of World War I, which tempered the optimism he felt when he had begun work on the ecological novels in 1909. Quoting him from these years before the war, Charmian remarked on his belief that a "solution to the great economic problems of the present age" was possible in "a return to the soil"; remarking on their own ranch, he said, "I see my farm in terms of the world, and the world in terms of my farm" (*Book of Jack London* 2:266). By December 1914, however, he wrote that no experience in his life had "affected [him] so profoundly" as the Great War: "It is a positive nightmare" (*Letters* 1389–90). Several months into the war, he explained why he believed that war "will always obtain on the planet":

(1) Man is an animal and lives upon the earth.
(2) Man must eat, and like any other animal, he is fecund.

(3) The habitable planet is only so large, and its size cannot be increased by man.

(4) Malthus' Law of Population still holds for man. Despite its wars and heavy emigration of the nineteenth-century, Europe increased population from 170,000,000 between the years 1800 and 1900.

(5) Man being an animal, a fecund animal, a fighting animal, he will be pressed against the means of subsistence, and when he is pressed too hard he will again and always draw the sword to crave out of other man's life a place for himself on the earth and in the sun. He had not at this date reduced his belly-need and his fecundity, and at present he is fighting more horribly and more colossally than he ever fought before. More superior devices for food-getting and shelter-getting [E. O. Wilson's "prosthetic dependence"] will merely enable him to live more crowded in the strictly limited habitable area of the planet. His fecundity will not diminish when he gets hungry because of pressure of population. (*Letters* 1508–9)[12]

Although London was not quite this pessimistic when he began work on his ecological novels in 1909, he had certainly focused his attention on the Malthusian theme. When he was well along in the composition of *Burning Daylight* (1909), he asked a correspondent, "Have you read *Expansion of Races*—by Dr. Woodruff, published by Rebman N.Y.? ... Malthus brought up to date. Most stimulating book I've read for a long while" (*Letters* 847). Working with this larger ecological problem in 1911, then, as he wrote *The Valley of the Moon* (1913), London created an evolutionary heroine, the fertile race mother he named Saxon Brown. Unfortunately, London's tiresome reiteration of this theme threatens to ruin the novel for many readers in our own time. There is too much of Saxon as "a flower of Anglo-Saxon stock" (104) or of her mental pictures of "the land-hungry Anglo-Saxon" (50). The best one can say about this part of the novel is that it comes with the territory of evolutionary thought during these years, from Frank Norris's *The Octopus*, to Freud's hopes "for the white nations upon whom the leadership of the human species has fallen" and F. Scott Fitzgerald's references to the rising tide of color in *The Great Gatsby* ("Thoughts for the Times on War and Death" 246).[13] In short, however dated and distasteful this view of racial evolution is today, it was an essential part of the evolutionary puzzle at that time and should not obscure three important points: first, that *The Valley of the Moon* is an ambitious ecological novel, dealing with "*all* those complex interrelations referred to by Darwin as the conditions of the struggle for existence" (Haeckel's phrase, emphasis mine) as London conceived them at that time; second, that London deserves a great deal of credit for ending his exploration of racial evolution in this novel with a critique of what he called "the Great White Way," and third, that *The Valley of the Moon* is yet another achievement in his premodernist exploration of the sex problem.

As a story of sexual love from the evolutionary point of view, *The Valley of the Moon* takes as its first principle the female's power to select. London constructs this foundation in book 1, where Saxon, by now having known the hero for some time, again asks herself the question: "*Is this the man?*" (42). By the end of book 1, the two are married. In book 2, the marriage is tested by the social strife in the urban environment and by Saxon's miscarriage. Toward the end of book 2 Saxon has the second part of her vision—that they should leave the overcrowded city and move to the land.[14] Threatened not only by the labor unrest, they narrowly escape being killed by typhoid from clams Saxon had dug in the marsh, an episode that serves as a final "mark against Oakland . . . the man-trap, that poisoned those it could not starve" (229). Book 3 traces their search for the fertile valley and their education in efficient, small-scale farming, and the novel closes with their setting up the farm and the announcement of Saxon's pregnancy.

Of course there are many autobiographical elements in this story (as in many of London's novels such as *Martin Eden* and *John Barleycorn*), notably London's own agricultural interests and the hopes he and Charmian had for the child she was nearly ready to deliver as he finished the novel. Sadly, the child lived for only two days. But while the novel reflects much of his own life, it was also an impassioned effort to dramatize what he said his philosophy and research had taught him, the fact that a return to the soil is the basis of economics (*Book of Jack London* 2:266). Moreover, as he recognized the elemental economics of his ecological vision, he was also quite aware of its larger social dimensions and in fact suggests that Billy's and Saxon's vision is essentially an effort to "perfect democracy" (*The Valley of the Moon* 333). As a character named Hastings (an obvious stand-in for London himself) remarks toward the end of the novel, "the way of the United States . . . is a veritable rape of the land" (349). Hastings is devoted to conserving and building up the soil, and London's hero in *The Little Lady of the Big House* concludes that, despite all his personal failures, "the land [on his farm] is better for my having been" (377).

In both these love stories, then, London's ecological vision proclaims the need for what the later, more famous ecologist, Aldo Leopold, described as a "land ethic," wherein the image of "man the conqueror" must give way to that of "man the biotic citizen" (*Sand County Almanac* 360).[15] As London explained in reference to his own farm, he believed that "the soil is our one indestructible asset" and devoted his energy to "rebuilding worn-out hillside lands that were . . . destroyed by our wasteful California pioneer farmers." And to realize this goal he had decided to farm without commercial fertilizer and to employ other agricultural techniques that "the Chinese have demonstrated for forty centuries" (*Letters* 1600–1601). But, unlike Leopold or other better known ecological writers, London presented his story of courtship leading to a stable and fertile marriage interwoven *as one narrative* with the story of his couple's quest for a viable economic relationship with the land. Doing so, while at the same time addressing the most troubling aspects of the sex problem as it was then understood, London assumed many of the Darwinian principles that gave rise to modern behavioral ecology, evolutionary psychology, and the kind of sociobiology that leads to E. O. Wilson's fear for the planet if Homo Sapiens does not settle down.

As London worked with the theory of sexual selection in bringing about the marriage of Saxon and Billy, he covered much of the familiar ground in stories of Darwinian courtship—the male's physical vigor and success in battle (Billy is a skilled boxer) and the graceful, attractive beauty of both lovers, as demonstrated in dance. Saxon is "a dream of a dancer" and Billy "danced beautifully": "the grace of those slow-moving, certain muscles of his accorded perfectly with the rhythm of the music," giving her "keen pleasure" and making her wonder for the first time, "*Is this the man?*" (13). But London was especially careful to deal with particular issues of the male's and female's sexuality that he considered obstacles to the ideal coupling he envisioned. First, he sought to refine what he always regarded as the chief obstacle to sexual love, the male's capacity for sexual violence, and as a solution to this part of the sex problem he drew once again on Havelock Ellis's analysis of sexual love. Second, he set out to deal with the more recent aspect of the sex problem that had appeared in studies of female hysteria arising from sexual repression. And here, too, guided in part by Ellis and through Ellis's discussion of hysteria by Freud, London found his own terms for defining his couple's love as innocently erotic and *natural.* "All that was needed was the proper soil," he counsels, "and their love would grow and blossom" (234). In this way London develops his analogy between the couple's healthy subconscious and the fertile land in their ecological vision.

London's solutions to both these aspects of the sex problem derive from the woman's vision, as essential accompaniments to her vision of their agrarian venture. Thus, in imagining an evolutionary solution to what London felt was the most disagreeable attribute in the male's sexual nature, he focuses repeatedly on Billy's hands and the way they appeal to Saxon. As she considers the other males from whom she might select a mate, their hands are crucial. Her most passionate suitor before Billy is Charley Long, by whom "she had been forced into almost slavery," particularly by his brutal beating of another male who had shown interest in her (37). But London relies on the essential evolutionary mechanism to remove this brutal male from the evolutionary stream—female choice: Long "was unlovely to [Saxon's] eye," mainly because of "the big blacksmith-hands and the thick strong fingers with the hair-pads on the backs to every first joint." Yet when she realizes that she hadn't been shocked to see "Billy fight . . . in the same primitive man-animal way," she senses (without analyzing it) that the difference resides in "the brutish-ness of [Long's] hands and mind" (45). Similarly, her eye for the male's hands figures crucially in her memory of others who had courted her: one "with the softest, cleanest hands" who was killed in a fight; two others (bookkeepers) with soft hands, who lost out for various reasons; and another whom she had thought she loved, a clerk who dressed attractively but who "was narrow-chested and skinny, and his hands were always cold and fishy." When this clerk asked to marry her, she refused, knowing it wasn't love because "somehow [she] couldn't see it" (72).

By contrast, when Billy and Saxon are introduced (he "with hat off and hand extended"), Saxon's first impression comes through the sense of touch, "as their hands clasped and she felt the teamster calluses on his palm" (12). Working in this way again with Ellis's theory of the primacy of touch and the woman's pleasure in it (from *Sexual Selection in Man*), as he had taken up this theme in *Martin Eden*, London overcomes the troublesome secondary sexual character with which Darwin had begun in his analysis of the male. With "her quick eyes," Saxon certainly found delight in other aspects of Billy's beauty, his eyes, nose, complexion, "large clean mouth . . . red lips" and "white, enviable teeth," but as is clear from the many, many references to Billy's and other males' hands throughout the novel, nearly everything depends on his hands: "As the touch of his hand had been good, so, to her, this subtler feel of all of him, body and mind, was good" (13). In short, London writes, she had found "a man she could love, hands and all" (76).

In view of all this it seems quite clear that London was closely following and developing Havelock Ellis's lead, pointing out that "Women are often very critical concerning a man's touch and his method of shaking hands. Stanley Hall . . . quotes a gifted lady as remarking: 'I used to say that, however much I liked a man, I could never marry him if I did not like the touch of his hand, and I feel so yet'" (1:3:192). Notably, however, in London's rendering of the male's nature there is a much stronger animal element than in the human male of Ellis's imagination. He brings this out in *The Valley of the Moon* by emphasizing Billy's way with horses, his having "always found with horses, dogs, and other folks, that what's natural is right" (78). Yet Billy is no mere sexual brute. Rather, he represents London's ideal solution to what he (unlike Ellis) always viewed as the most troublesome aspect of the sex prob-lem, the male's aggression and possessiveness. Because Saxon finds that Billy's are "the most beautiful hands in the world," "the old sex antagonism which [Saxon] had always experienced with men seemed to have vanished" (78).

If London's way of dealing with this part of the sex problem seems rather simple, it follows Darwin's principle that the male's sexual nature requires mainly that he be a passionate or "eager" and "efficient seeker" (*Descent of Man* 1:274); this under-scores London's faith in Saxon's instinctive wisdom as she deals with the female's "pre-nuptial problem of selecting a husband" (*The Valley of the Moon* 117). But in creating Saxon, London also shared Ellis's view that the female's sexual nature is more complex than the male's. As Ellis wrote in "The Evolution of Modesty" (the first of his volumes in the *Studies*), because the female must defend herself from the inevitable crush of many eager males, she evolved an underlying "complex emotional feminine organization to defend" (*Studies* 1:1:1). Thus, as London worked with this and related complexities in the female's sexual makeup, he sought solutions to two other problems: first, what he called the female's "post-nuptial problem of retaining a husband's love" (117), and second (but not in this order), the problem of female hysteria. These two problems will be more fully discussed later, but first it will help clarify London's approach to these issues to note that, in his general view of the sex problem, he shared Ellis's intention to examine what he took to be "the actual facts of sex" in order to "ascertain what is normal and what is abnormal," to "know what is naturally lawful" for the human being (*Studies* 1:xxx). Of course Ellis was censored for speaking so frankly about the nature of sex, but so was London. For example, he wanted to make the point, through Billy, that the social ill of prostitution would be alleviated if women were freer "to be lovin' their own husbands, an' havin' children they're not ashamed of, an' just bein' happy accordin' to their nature" (*The Valley of the Moon* 69). But when he offered an illustration of such natural, uninhibited sexual contact between husband and wife, he found that it was unacceptable to the editors of *Cosmopolitan*, who cut this scene from their serial edition: When Billy came home from work on the first night after their marriage, he came behind Saxon as she prepared dinner and "passed his arms under her arm-pits with down-drooping hands upon her breasts" (101).

Innocent as such scenes will seem today, it is worth noting that London designed them not only to offer a solution to prostitution but also to explore the question of female hysteria that had begun to dominate the study of sex by 1900. The subject of female hysteria is as old as literature, of course, but Ellis, Freud, and others had begun to interpret it in a new way. Ellis, for example, argued that hysteria could no longer be understood merely as "an unconscious expression of the sexual emotions." He referred to "Breuer and especially Freud, [who] have greatly aided the study of hysteria," citing Freud's point that "from whatever side and from whatever symptoms we start, we always unfailingly reach the region of the sexual life." But Ellis goes on to make the new psychoanalytical point by quoting Breuer's further assertion that hysterical individuals "suffer [from the sexual needs], and in large measure, indeed, they suffer precisely through the struggle with them, through the effort to thrust sexuality aside" (1:1:224). For London, then, the problem was how to conceive an evolutionary heroine who could avoid the modern neurosis of hysteria brought on by sexual repression. His ecological vision required a fertile heroine, and he demonstrates Saxon's psychological good health by dramatizing her success in surviving not just one but three bouts "with soul-sickening hysteria and madness" (59).

The novel opens with the first bout at the laundry where Saxon and her friend Mary work. The women are talking about going to a dance when one of the older workers falls to the floor, "drumming her heels [and] shrieking" (3–4). The episode passes, but "the forewoman strode the isles with a threatening eye for incipient breakdown and hysteria" (4). Thus, London adds to Freud's and Ellis's point that hysteria is related to the region of the sexual life by suggesting that it is exacerbated by the nerve-wracking pressures of the workplace. Saxon's second bout occurs in the home where she lives with her brother and sister-in-law Sarah. In this scene of tension in Sarah's *domestic* workplace, the problem arises when Saxon is preparing to go to the dance. Sarah claims that "It's a shame an' a disgrace the way some people can afford silk stockings" while she is left to toil day and night. Then, making the sexual point, she remarks that Saxon should have more natural shame than to be "a-runnin' with a prizefighter" (54–55). With "her breast rising and falling with staccato, mechanical movement," she slaps her husband and collapses "in the shrill, hoarse, monotonous madness of hysteria" (56–57). Saxon escapes this bout—exposure to "the shattering chaos of her sister-in-law's mind"—when Billy arrives and takes her away in a horse-drawn buggy, at once consoling her with the "nearness and comfort . . . of his body" and at the same time steadying "the nervous young animals" (59). The third bout takes place in the laundry again, as the envious women banter about Saxon's honeymoon.[16]

Although the subject of female hysteria was acceptable to *Cosmopolitan* (in trimming the novel for serial publication, it left in two of the three bouts), "the philosophy of love" London articulated through the character Mercedes Higgins certainly was not. Complaining to his editor that this material was cut in the serial publication "to the last line, semi-colon and comma," London claimed that he had treated this view of female sexuality as it "has never been exposited in fiction before" (*Letters* 1217). In the novel he clearly indicates that the Mercedes episode serves to educate Saxon on "the post-nuptial problem of retaining a husband's love" (117). But he certainly knew that the strange woman he had created in Mercedes would offend many readers.[17] Focusing on the nutritive and reproductive drives of life (the two kinds of hunger), Mercedes instructs Saxon in "the queer thing, this love of men" (108), explaining that a woman must keep the man's "appetite knife-edged and never satisfied" (115). And in a "softly throbbing voice" that "swelled . . . to love-cries barbarically imperious," Mercedes teaches Saxon that a woman's underclothes (her "dainties") are like "magical nets. No fisherman upon the sea ever tangled fish more successfully than we women with our flimsies" (115–16). Mercedes's love lessons delved into the sexual darkness so deeply that Saxon almost became hysterical. She "burned with a blush" and trembled with fear, nausea, and nervousness to the point that she nearly rejected the terrible but "magnificent" truths (117). However, because these lessons only "verified [Saxon's] own conclusions" in the "eminently rational philosophy of love" that she had already developed "instinctively, and consciously, too," she profits from the experience and learns how to keep Billy's sexual interest alive (117). As Ellis had explained, the evolution of modesty involved "the development of ornament and clothing" as enhancements to the female's powers of coquetry (1:1:82). Moreover, he adds that "It is the spontaneous and natural instinct of the lover to desire modesty in his mistress" (1:1:45). To place a more Darwinian point on this idea, as London does through Mercedes's instructions on how to entangle the male, Saxon demonstrates that the unruly male can be happily captured and held in the net of monogamy. Thus, even at the end of *The Valley of the Moon*, when Billy and Saxon have settled into their new life, London reminds his readers that Saxon still took time "for work on her pretties" (410).

Toward the end of book 2, before Saxon has her agrarian "vision," the couple is swept up in the social unrest that leads to a strike and Billy's imprisonment. Saxon feels "tangled in the conflict" (181) and sees only "the smudge of San Francisco, the smudge of Oakland, where men were . . . dying, . . . babies were dying, born and unborn, . . . and women were weeping with bruised breasts" (204), and she cannot "vision" a way out. Clearly, the sex problem and the social problem are inseparable in London's larger, ecological vision of life, and as the novel moves toward the fulfillment of his agrarian vision in book 3, he begins to offer his solutions to the kinds of problems he was considering in Woodruff's *Expansion of Races*: the explosion in the world's population as understood through Malthus and Darwin, the consequent world famine, and the paradox of birthrates growing in certain parts of the world while simultaneously diminishing in other parts of the world. But it is important to note that London's solutions were his own, and not in complete accord with Woodruff's or Ellis's or any other theorist's. While Woodruff, for example, seems hopeful that Darwin's vision of entangled life ("the mutual dependence of all living things," as Woodruff expresses it) will prove compatible with Kropotkin's theory of mutual aid, London was quite skeptical of what Woodruff calls "commensalism . . . based on mutual altruism" (231). London does include "Kropotkin's 'Fields, Factories and Workshops'" among the books Billy and Saxon consult as they set up their own operation. But according to his own ecological vision, the couple's essential lessons on how to farm come from foreigners, "natural-born farmers" like the Portuguese, Chinese, and Slavs, whom they see practicing "intensive cultivation" on small plots; from a woman named Mrs. Mortimer, who has discovered that the key to almost everything in the business of farming is in attracting a market, she by planting flowers with her vegetables so that passers-by will see them (268); and from Billy's and Saxon's relationship with Luther Burbank.

Multiply. Jack London ends *The Valley of the Moon* with an image of his ideal couple anticipating the birth of their child: "Together they gazed far up the side of the knoll where a doe and a spotted fawn looked down upon them." Their ecological quest ends only when they take the essential first step in Darwin's "one general law" of evolution—the need to multiply.

Aesthetically, *The Valley of the Moon* is not one of London's best literary performances, in part because of his ambition to project a holistic view of life (and because, as was often the case in his writing career, he wrote in haste). Still, it does project a coherent and impressively comprehensive solution to the problems of modern life as London understood them, including the explosion in the world's population, the threats of world war and famine, the conflict between the workers of the world and the forces of capitalism, the neuroses of civilized life, and the problems he imaged in Oakland's smudged skies and poisoned marshes. Writing of his plans for the novel's motif, "*back to the land*," he indicated that it would center on the sex problem: it would "begin as a love-story . . . [and] end as a love-story" (*Letters* 1007–8). The connection between the love story and the land is most clearly suggested in the character Hastings's words, "I love the soil" (350) and London's remark that with the proper soil Billy's and Saxon's love "would grow and blossom" (234). Fulfilling this prophecy, London closes this love story that is also an ecological narrative with an image of his ideal couple anticipating the birth of their child. Billy and the pregnant Saxon "gazed far up the side of [a] knoll where a doe and a spotted fawn looked down upon them from a tiny open space between the trees" (425). They have successfully mated, preserved their marriage, and returned to the land. But in London's view their ecological quest will conclude only when they have satisfied Darwin's first principle in the one general law of evolution—the need to multiply.

In his bold attempt to perfect democracy in *The Valley of the Moon*, London created a marriage that would endure largely by realizing the "sweet words" of "community property" (413).[18] This began in courtship when Saxon selected a man whose hands showed her that he was no rapist. London insisted that the male must retain his strength while loosening or softening the touch of his hand, and that both the male and female accept their natural sexuality, including even what Ellis termed "auto-erotism."[19] The new woman of this vision of life must therefore not only avoid the dangers of sexual repression and hysteria but also continue to work after the marriage to arouse and satisfy her husband's sexual appetite. Clearly, from London's point of view, the solution to the problems of American civilization lay in the fundamentals of sex and, in turn, in the unconscious. Finally, London's ecological vision, "back to the earth," is a call back to the instinctive body, and in this way his sense of evolutionary psychology offered a certain clarity to the emergent Freudianism of his time. Emphasizing the female's fertile instincts in sexual selection, he endowed Saxon with an inherent wisdom that protects her from the hysteria upon which modern psychology had focused its attention. Saxon is one of the first white characters in early twentieth-century fiction to maintain her psychic health through encounters with the "primitive." She wants "to be an Indian squaw" (71), and she is guided by the instruction in primitive love she receives from "the dark-skinned woman," Mercedes (108).[20] Thus by founding his radical ecological vision on Darwinian principles that were, for many other writers, in eclipse; by incorporating the latest insights into the darker reaches of the sex problem that he was finding in Havelock Ellis and Freud; by affirming the viability of the efficient farming as practiced by certain foreigners of color; and by recommending the principle of community property that came to American culture through Spanish law (a principle that still does not pertain in all parts of the United States); London told a story that he knew was bound to offend editors and readers "who [were] irrevocably pledged to the Great White Way" (*Letters* 1008).

The "Bawling of Sex" in *The Little Lady of the Big House*

By March 14, 1913, London had made extensive notes for what would be his master-piece on the sex problem. "It is all sex, from start to finish," he wrote to Roland Phillips, and it features a triangle of "cultured, modern" people who are "at the same time profoundly primitive." Believing "almost . . . that it is what I have been working toward all my writing life," he emphasized that it would have "all the guts of sex" and that "it will not be believed that I could write it—it is so utterly fresh" (*Letters* 1135). Then, "after mulling it over for a year," he had his title, *The Little Lady of the Big House*, and boasted to Phillips that his story of the triangle would be "in a setting that never before in the history of all the literature of all the world was ever put in print" (*Letters* 1322, 1328). Indeed, it was a fresh and almost unbelievable performance for London, and it is a pity that later writers of the twentieth century, like Sherwood Anderson, Hemingway, and Steinbeck, apparently never heard of it. In their own youth, each of these writers admired London's famous early work, especially *The Call of the Wild*, and when they were beginning their own careers the literary world was justly fascinated by James Joyce, T. S. Eliot, and D. H. Lawrence. On the eve of World War I, however, London produced a novel of impressive psy-chological intensity in which modern characters dance to the "noise of ragtime music and slangtime song" (*The Little Lady of the Big House* 118–19).

Moving beyond the work he had already begun in exploring the Darwinian un-conscious and Havelock Ellis's work on the sexual impulse, he became one of the first novelists to enter the murkier depths of the Freudian psyche. Throughout the novel but with increasing intensity in its final chapters, London found new ways to probe his characters' psyches as each unwittingly expressed or sought to conceal his or her conflicted motives and emotions. At the same time, almost anticipating Ernest Hemingway's art of the "iceberg" (leaving much unstated or beneath the surface of things), he found innovative ways to evoke the underlying structural re-alities of his story. As for the setting that he claimed was absolutely new in world literature, his point was that he would conduct this exploration of the sex problem on a ranch (very much like his own) that is a veritable laboratory for applied re-search on the nature of sex. As London wrote to a reader who had objected to the Darwinian themes in *Martin Eden*, "I breed too many horses, cows, pigs, sheep and goats, on my ranch here, to accept for a moment your baseless assertion that evolu-tion is wrong and is not" (*Letters* 1203), or as his hero (Dick Forrest) remarks in the novel, prefacing a discussion of the evolution of race and sex, "I am talking, not as a mere scholastic, but as a practical breeder with whom the application of Mendelian methods is an every-day commonplace" (257).

The psychological and biological elements are intertwined in London's analysis of sex as they were in a variety of other ways in the most recent treatises on sex that he had studied: in Havelock Ellis's *Studies in the Psychology of Sex*, Otto Weininger's *Sex and Character*, or August Forel's *The Sexual Question*, for example. And London's particularly Darwinian emphasis in presenting the biological and psychological elements is evident not only in the extensive references to artificial selection (in the selective breeding on the ranch) and to sexual selection (in the triangular drama) but also in his frequent reiteration of Darwin's theme of entanglement—as in Dick Forrest's remark that because "sex and soul are all interwoven and tangled together," it is impossible to "know yourself . . . your soul, your personality" when in elated moods of love. In such states, he argues, one thrills, vibrates, and dances "a mad orgy of the senses [without] knowing a step of the dance or the meaning of the orgy" (262–63).

But if few of London's readers recognize his Darwinian emphasis in the novel's many images of entanglement, even fewer seem prepared to recognize that his concept of the sex-entangled soul or personality reflects the sense of many early Freudians that the *unconscious* might well be all that we can identify as personality or soul. This idea is further suggested in the heroine's (Paula Forrest's) remark to the second man in the triangle (Evan Graham) about how she has learned to deal with her insomnia by applying knowledge gained from swimming in the ocean: "by not fighting the undertow . . . I . . . come quicker to unconsciousness from out the entangling currents. I invite my soul to live over again . . . the things that keep me from unconsciousness" (152–53). As London wrote these passages in 1914, deepening his own longtime explorations of sex and the unconscious after having taken in a good deal of the new psychology (as in Ellis, Richard von Krafft-Ebing, Albert Moll, August Forel, and Freud), he was anticipating a "Freudian" idea that he would underscore in a volume he could not have read until he purchased it the following year, Edwin B. Holt's *The Freudian Wish and Its Place in Ethics* (1915). As Holt speculated on "the *necessary implications* of [Freud's] discoveries, in the field of normal psychology," he asserted that "Freud's is actually the first psychology *with* a soul" (though certainly not anything that one might think of as a "ghost-soul"), for "if the unit of mind and character is a 'wish,'" and the wish is "something which the body as a piece of mechanism can *do*," then perhaps "the wishes *are* the soul" (48–49). London's and Holt's speculations on the unconscious soul will undoubtedly strike many contemporary theorists as naive or quaint, but they are representative of much of the early literary and cultural "groping" in these new "darknesses" that would continue in similar novels well into the 1930s, as in Conrad Aiken's *Great*

Circle (1933).[21] Moreover, in London's own gropings in 1914, he was intent on affirming the evolutionary reality of the subconscious in specifically Darwinian terms—as part of his explicit attack on "the glittering veils of Bergsonian metaphysics" in *Creative Evolution* (*The Little Lady of the Big House* 244–45).

One further passage that London underscored in Holt is worth noting as a prelude to the reading of *The Little Lady of the Big House* offered here because it resembles the most astonishing recent studies in the biology of sex that London brings into his novel at the outset. In his chapter on "The Physiology of Wishes," Holt comments extensively on Darwin's discussion of a root-tip's remarkable sensitivity, suggesting that this organic purposiveness is like a wish. He concludes his discussion with the following sentences that London marked:

> It is significant that Darwin concludes [*The Power of Movement in Plants*] with these words: "It is hardly an exaggeration to say that the tip of the radicle thus endowed, and having the power of directing the movements of the adjoining parts, acts like the brain of one of the lower animals; the brain being seated within the anterior end of the body; receiving impressions from the sense-organs, and directing the several movements." (62–63)

There is certainly no sexual element in this part of Holt's remarks on physiology, but it is the kind of thing that London had become interested in in the studies of the sexual touch that he had found in Havelock Ellis's *Sexual Selection in Man* and that he had incorporated in *The Valley of the Moon*: the idea that "the skin is . . . 'the primeval and most reliable source of our knowledge of the external world or the archaeological field of psychology'" (*Studies* 1:3:5). But it appears that in *The Little Lady of the Big House* London examined more closely the ground on which Ellis had based his *Analysis of the Sexual Impulse*, which he began by noting, "The term 'sexual instinct' may be said to cover the whole of the neuropsychic phenomena of reproduction which man shares with the lower animals" (1:2:1). Partly on the basis of a discussion of recent remarkable laboratory studies on the sexuality of frogs (the point London picks up in the opening pages of his novel), Ellis remarks that the sexual impulse

> is no longer a question of the formation of semen in the male, of the function of menstruation in the female. It has become largely a question of physiological chemistry. The chief parts in the drama of sex, alike in its psychic as on its physical sides, are thus supposed to be played by two mysterious protagonists, the hormones, or internal secretions, of the testes and of the ovary. Even the part played by the brain is now often regarded as chemical, the brain being considered to be a great chemical laboratory. (1:2:16)

Moreover, Ellis notes, "there is a tendency . . . to extend the sexual sphere" to include secretions from all sorts of glands—the thymus, the adrenals, and so forth—so that "it is possible that internal secretions from all these glands may combine to fill in the complete picture of sexuality as we know it in men and women" (1:2:16).

The research on frogs that contributed to Ellis's insights includes passages like the following:

> Spallanzani had shown how the male frog during coitus will undergo the most horrible mutilations, even decapitation, and yet resolutely continue the act of intercourse, which lasts from four to ten days, sitting on the back of the female and firmly clasping her with his forelegs. Goltz confirmed Spallanzani's observations and threw new light on the mechanism of the sexual instinct and the sexual act in the frog. By removing various parts of the female frog Goltz found that every part of the female was attractive to the male at pairing time, and that he was not imposed on when parts of a male were substituted. (1:2:4)[22]

Ellis's discussion of such experiments goes on at some length, largely in his effort to show that the sexual impulse is different from "the impulse to evacuate an excretion," although that seems to be the case with the frogs and to argue that among human beings "the impulse of contrectation" (in other words, the instinct to approach, touch, and kiss another person) plays a more important role in sexual love (1:2:21).

London introduces the subject of frogs on page 4 of his novel, noting that Dick Forrest "reached for a book entitled 'The Commercial Breeding of Frogs'" as he prepared to eat his breakfast. As he ate "he watched the hunting of [some] meat-eating yellow-jackets" preying on "a number of house-flies" that clung to the screen of his porch, then he marked his place in "Commercial Breeding of Frogs" and continued with other tasks in the management of his ranch. With this scene and many references in these opening pages to Forrest's successes in the breeding of livestock (for example, he smiles with pleasure in hearing the "throaty bawl" of a prize bull), London insinuates the Darwinian point that the nutritive and reproductive "instincts *and no others* [are] the primary basis of all animal behavior" (Sulloway 252). With such gestures in his opening pages London begins to suggest the massive subsurface structure of his novel, and by the time he returns to the subject of frogs in chapter 22, the novel's underlying biological and psychological principles have clearly shaped the plot. The triangular affair is rather fully developed, and Forrest has begun to sense that his wife and good friend are romantically engaged. This is the scene in which Forrest comments on how "sex and soul are . . . tangled together," a remark that develops from the houseguests' discussion of Mendel, the evolution of race and sex, the nature of woman, and the nature of the soul or personality. Suggesting London's interest in Freud's *The Interpretation of Dreams*, Forrest asks a guest, "what is your own personality when you sleep or dream? . . . When you are in love?" Then, pursuing his point that the soul or personality "is a vague and groping thing," he adds: "Possibly the bullfrog, inflating himself on the edge of a pond and uttering hoarse croaks through the darkness to a warty mate, possesses also, at that moment, a vague and groping personality" (*The Little Lady of the Big House* 262–63).[23]

The point of all these speculations is to shed light on the nature of sexual attraction as it leads to Paula's selection of the second male, Graham. Paula, whom one guest regards as "the soul of beauty" (340), has numerous musical encounters with Graham, and he once thinks that her odd behavior is so much "artist-dreaming . . . a listening to the echo of the just-played music in her soul" (206). In such moments and in the repeated scenes of music and dance, London develops the then well-known Darwinian principle that music and dance are crucial elements in courtship. Dick is certainly aware that Graham is a "beautiful dancer," but in detailing Paula's ardent awareness of "the closeness and tenderness of contact in the dancing" (347), London builds toward Dick's final sense that Paula's "very flesh has decided" that she prefers Graham as a lover (370). In this way London suggests that the sexual impulse in her flesh is somehow like that of the frogs Havelock Ellis remarks about or that, in the contact of their dance or their passionate kiss, "these minimal touch excitations represent the very oldest stratum of psychic life in the soul," as Ellis remarks in his analysis of the sexual touch (*Studies* 1:3:12).

As these materials suggest, London saw himself as a fellow explorer of the sexual terrain, working in his own field—fiction with a new psychological intensity—and in the Mendelian studies that he brought to bear in the selective breeding on his own ranch.[24] There is little question that he found many useful ideas in Ellis, for example, but neither is there any question that London's essential views on the sex problem differed significantly from Ellis's. London was far more willing to explore the human being's animal nature than was Ellis, who, while basing his whole study on Darwin's principles of evolution, insisted that "far from being animal-like, the human impulses of sex are among the least animal-like acquisitions of man" (2:3:130). And an even more important difference between London's and Ellis's views on sex is evident in London's emphasis on sexual reproduction, as in the way his characters Paula and Dick Forrest reflect Jack and Charmian London's disappointed hopes for children, and in his intention to illuminate his characters' sexual nature by setting the novel at the ranch, where the breeding of stock is the central concern. By contrast, Ellis certainly acknowledges that "the sexual impulse is very often associated with a strong desire for offspring," but he insists that "the reproductive instinct is not equivalent to the sexual impulse, though intimately associated with it, and though it explains it" (*Studies* 1:2:20).[25]

London interweaves the theme of reproduction throughout the novel from the moment in chapter 2 when a ranch employee watched as Forrest "diminished down the road" after lecturing him on how to raise his daughter. The employee thinks to himself, "but where's the kid of your own, Mr. Forrest?" (23). Similarly, toward the end of the novel, when Forrest realizes that Paula is drawn toward the other man, he wanders alone through her "secret patio." There he sees the fountain where "she kept her selected and more gorgeous blooms of [gold]fish." And noticing also the fountain's rollicking "life-sized babies wrought from pink marble," Forrest finishes a "cigarette and[,] retaining it dead in his hand," thinks "that was what she needed . . . children" (331–32). With "diminished" and "dead" in these scenes, London insinuates his evolutionary perspective—despite Forrest's expertise in selective breeding, he will enjoy no reproductive success himself. In the end, when the dying Paula tells Dick that she is sorry there were no babies, London describes how she "*nestled* her head" on a pillow and "drew her body up in *nestling* curves" (392, emphasis mine).

London's views on the evolutionary issues are clearly antagonistic to the then-recent and much more popular views put forth in *Creative Evolution*, where Bergson's few references to Darwin (and nothing at all on *The Descent of Man*) give the impression that there is no sexual struggle. The novel's several references to Bergson conclude with one character's assertion that Bergson is a "charlatan" whose popularity derives from his having touched up or "rosied" over the more disagreeable realities that Darwin had theorized (342–43). But aside from this important element in London's critique of sexual love (his adamant resistance to the eclipse of Darwinism during his time), three broad concerns that compelled his attention in this, his last and most extensive exploration of the sex problem, warrant special attention. The first two pertain to the key question of sexual difference that had led Darwin to formulate his theory of sexual selection: London's presentation of female sexuality in Paula Forrest and of male sexuality in Dick Forrest. The third is his analysis of his three characters' psychological conflict. In this he drew on both Darwin's *The Expression of the Emotions in Man and Animals* and the Freudian theory that he had managed to take in by 1914.

Paula: "We'll All Go Hunting."

The questions surrounding the evolution of sexual difference that Darwin addressed in formulating the theory of sexual selection were of far greater interest in public discourse during London's career than readers early in the twenty-first century tend to realize. Havelock Ellis had published *Man and Woman* in 1894, and the proliferation of further biological and psychological explorations of these issues is traceable in many of the texts London owned and marked, as well as in Ellis's continuing work on *Studies in the Psychology of Sex*. In fact, London's and Ellis's parallel interests in questions of sexual difference are evident in the August 1915 issue of *Cosmo-*

politan, where Ellis's article "Masculinism and Feminism" appears next to that month's installment of *The Little Lady of the Big House*. Although this juxtaposition of London and Ellis might seem fortuitous, it is certainly not incongruous, for both writers were self-consciously advocating forms of feminism. Referring to certain rhetorical feminists in his prefatory remarks, Ellis reminds his readers that "the champions of feminism have nearly as often been men as women" ("Masculinism and Feminism" 316). And as a growing number of feminist critics have noted in recent years, feminist values comprise a major portion of London's later work (Reesman 41).[26] It is not sufficiently recognized, however, that the fundamental feminist issue London embodied in his story of Paula Forrest is her freedom to exhibit and affirm her natural—that is, her animal—sexuality.

Paula's sexual freedom was certainly the most controversial aspect of the novel and was brought into focus for public view (and outrage) in one of Howard Chandler Christy's illustrations for the June installment of *Cosmopolitan*. The illustration is of Paula clad in a swimsuit and riding bareback the stallion Mountain Lad in a large cement water tank at the ranch, and it provoked a number of complaints from readers (*Letters* 1471, 1526).[27] But the illustration renders Paula's sexual animalism quite harmlessly, leaving out London's most shocking image of the modern woman's bold entry into the Darwinian arena of tangled sexuality:

> As she pressed her cheek against the great arching neck, her golden-brown hair, wet from being under, flowing and tangled, seemed tangled in the black mane of the stallion. But it was her face that smote Graham [the second man] most of all. It was a boy's face; it was a woman's face; it was serious and at the same time amused, expressing the pleasure it found woven with the peril. It was a white woman's face—and modern. (104)

Depicted in this way—her human nature tangled with the animal's, her female nature with the male's—Paula is a modern American woman at a historical point approximately midway between Edna Pontellier (in Kate Chopin's *The Awakening*) and Brett Ashley (in Hemingway's *The Sun Also Rises*). Edna, like "some beautiful, sleek, animal waking up in the sun," who selected two lovers outside her marriage, and Brett, the much more defiantly androgynous and sexually aggressive woman of the jazz age who selected any number of lovers.[28]

The essential similarity in these three modern women is their selection of sexual partners mainly for the male's beauty (in Edna's case, Robert; in Brett's, Romero). Paula, "the soul of beauty" (340), selects Evan Graham partly because he is a beautiful dancer and because of the physical features that London highlights in the juxtaposed portraits of the two men when Graham arrives on the scene (347). Graham is slightly taller than Dick, but it is his "grace of body and carriage," his "more . . . fulsome" and "redder" lips, and so forth, that catch Paula's eye. London hints that while both these attractive males have "mouths . . . [that] carried the impression of girlish sweetness," Graham (whose his first name, Evan, suggests Eve) is more intriguingly androgynous than Forrest, who "seemed a more efficient and formidable organism" and "dangerous" (99–100).

"Organism," in the context of the ranch's work in selective breeding and the house guests' several philosophical discussions of evolution and love, underscores London's study of Paula's power to select in relation to the Darwinian analysis of sexual difference. In repeated references to her "selected" goldfish (330), we know that she decided "to segregate [one gorgeous male] for the special breeding tank in the fountain of her own secret patio" (90); moreover, London writes that she is in charge of the horses on the ranch, notes that she can "breed them and mold them to [her] heart's desire" (148), and includes Dick's remark that *she* is the genius at selection (150). Whereas he can "muddle and mull over the Mendelian Law until [he is] dizzy," she "just knows it in some witch-like, intuitional way" (150). Forrest even remarks proudly, "She's as remorseless as any man when it comes to throwing out the undesirables and selecting for what she wants" (151).

By the end of chapter 13, acting on her instinctive sense, including her eye for erotic beauty, Paula selects Graham as her lover. At a swimming party in the water tank where Paula had ridden the stallion, Paula swims underwater, guests praise Graham as "a real fish man" for his own prowess as a swimmer, Paula and Graham discuss the "undertow" of "unconsciousness," and London closes the chapter with reference to a game of tag the guests have begun to play: Paula tagged Graham, cried "You're IT!" and plunged into the tank. But as this relationship develops from its initial playfulness toward the darker ending, when Paula kills herself, London again presents his view of the evolutionary reality in contrast to another popular interpretation of sexual love at that time—George Bernard Shaw's comic yet serious argument for Creative Evolution in *Man and Superman*, wherein Shaw replaced Darwin's image of the sexually aggressive male with the image of woman as the sexual hunter. When the houseguests consider questions of love, Madonna-worship, and woman, one guest asks, "Why is woman, in the game of love, always . . . the huntress?" Another responds, "That is just some of your Shaw nonsense" (265).

Still, in a later scene of introspection, as Paula looks at herself in a mirror, she cries out, "Oh, you huntress!" and admits "that Shaw . . . might be right" (310). But London pushes this idea further than Shaw does, causing Paula to realize that she is proud of her own sexual allure and her power in "living [and] thrilling" by having "two such men at heel" (310–11). More than what Shaw referred to as husband-hunting, London dramatizes Paula's sexual desire for two men at once and confronts the modernists' dilemma over the conflict between promiscuity (or free love or polyandry) and civilized marriage.[29] London emphasizes Paula's pleasure in

riding the stallion and in selecting the breeding stock, notes that Dick takes "pleasure in his wife's pleasure" in selecting stock (148), and that this enlightened, modern couple, Dick and Paula, "have one magic formula: *Damn the expense when fun is
selling*" (107). All this emphasis carries the Shavian point of the husband-hunting
woman toward the deeper waters that Freud explored in *Civilization and Its Discontents* (1930). Paula cannot make Graham appreciate "how tangled" the situation is
for her. And when Dick and Paula finally discuss it, she confesses her alarming self-
discovery: "Shaw and the rest must be right. Women are hunting animals. You are
both big game. I can't help it. . . . I want you. I want Evan" (367). Moreover, in confessing her desire for both men, Paula insists, "I am straight" (368); that is, London
suggests, although Paula is "excited [and] feverish" in her desire, she is not nervous,
abnormal, or neurotic (310).

In this way London brings Paula's natural sexual desire into the open, leaving
the males to admit their own occasional sexual interest in other women but confessing, as Dick does with "a slight twinkle in his eyes," that "while you [Paula] may
be polyandrously inclined, we stupid male men cannot reconcile ourselves to such
a situation" (368). But it would be a mistake to conclude that London wishes to
celebrate the kind of popular Freudianism that had already begun to emerge in the
erroneous view that Freud was advocating promiscuity. London was aware of Freud's
unhappiness over such "'Wild' Psychoanalysis" and included his own critique of it
in *The Little Lady of the Big House*.[30] Early in the novel Dick tells Paula that from the
commotion among the wild canaries on her patio he thinks "some free lover is trying to break up their monogamic heaven with modern love-theories" (84), and the
subject comes up more seriously in one of the houseguests' discussions when a guest
asks Forrest about the "boasted monogamic marriage institution of Western civilization" (271). Dick responds by explaining that, while he isn't exactly for free love,
he can "only answer with a hackneyed truism": "There can be no love that is not
free." He advocates a complicated free love that is not "merely [a] license of promiscuity" but a belief in both legal marriage and divorce, because "man, living in society, is a most complicated animal" (271–72).

Still, Dick's philosophical outlook is no solution to the triangular conflict displayed
in the novel. For that, London turns to Paula, who ends the conflict by shooting herself. This is no less problematic a conclusion than Kate Chopin's decision to have
Edna Pontellier drown herself in *The Awakening*. But it should be noted that London's
conclusion bestows on Paula the full humanity that another very prominent sexual
theorist had denied women. Indeed, London's presentation of Paula (as well as other
women in his last works) seems a pointed refutation of Otto Weininger's *Sex and
Character* (1906), which Jack and Charmian read and made marginal notes in together. Weininger maintained that woman is "soulless" (213), that "the Phallus . . . is
her supreme lord and welcome master" (299), and that her "unfaithfulness is an

exciting game, in which the thought of morality plays no part" (221). In contrast, London arranges for Paula to agonize over the hurt she causes Dick and to end their discussion about her polyandrous tendencies by remarking (ostensibly in reference to an excursion planned for the next day), "We'll all go hunting" (372). At the end, Dick had planned to kill *him*self, but he hears the shot and realizes, "*She beat me to it*" (382). Her greatest act of dignity, courage, and complicated humanity is to make it clear, as she dies dressed in her hunting outfit, not that she is repenting her polyandrous desire, but that she still loves *both* the men who have come to comfort her.

"Dick's Code"

As the pivotal figure in the novel's triangle, Paula reflects the emphasis on women of many early twentieth-century studies of the sex problem, as in such works known to London as Weininger's *Sex and Character*, E. Heinrich Kisch's *The Sexual Life of Woman*, Ellis's *Studies*, in general, and Freud's "The Case of Miss Lucy R" or "The Case of Miss Elisabeth v. R" in the volume, *Selected Papers on Hysteria*. But as a self-reflective explorer in what one authority in London's library termed the "Sex enlightenment [that] runs rampant at present" (Talmey 11), London was unrelenting in his study of the male, and his portrait of Dick Forrest develops his longstanding effort to restrain the male's essential secondary sexual character, according to Darwin's analysis—his prehensile power to possess the female. Forrest is much more aware of his sexual nature than was Billy Roberts in *The Valley of the Moon*, whose gentle hands appeal to Saxon but who still retains the identity of a successful competitor in his skill as a boxer, and Forrest has freed himself from the sexual violence or "Red Wrath" that caused London's character Darrell Standing to die for love in *The Star Rover* (1915). Convicted for murdering Professor Haskell in the laboratory at the University of California, Standing awaits his execution and explains that he died of love because Haskell "was a man. I was a man. And there was a woman beautiful" (290). London gives us glimpses of the rival lover's hand when, "unconsciously, Graham's hand went farther about [Paula's] shoulder" (307); he also pictures Paula "prisoning [Graham's] eager hand in hers" or thrusting "Evan's hand away" (321). But his theme in presenting Dick's prehensile power is that Dick has steadfastly committed himself to a "code" (319) whereby he won't compete with Graham (313). The "most horrible spiritual suffering [he] can imagine would be to kiss a woman who endured [his] kiss"; he cannot imagine "holding the woman one loves a moment longer than she loves to be held" (270). He is repulsed at the thought of laying "rough hands on love" (270), and, acting on his belief that "past love . . . gives no hold over the present" (319), he will "not lift a hand to hold" Paula (349). "My hands are tied," he tells her, "I can't put an arm to hold you" (370).

Dick (as a reflection of London himself) is a further development of Herbert Wace, who had also sought to rise above the sexual violence inherent in the male's prehensile organs (*Kempton-Wace* 171). But London's further study of the sex problem between 1903 and 1915 led him to be much more self-critically introspective in *The Little Lady of the Big House* than is generally recognized. The central irony of the novel is that, despite his highly efficient management of sexual energy on the ranch (through selective breeding of his stock or the control he has over his workers' lives), Dick cannot control the sexual entanglements in his own household. This theme runs throughout the novel, from the opening words, "He awoke in the dark," to his confession to Paula toward the end that, as a result of the affair and the discovery of his unexpected jealousy, he had come to laugh "all the books and all biology in the face" (363).

Although he had sensed the growing intimacy between Paula and Graham, Dick's shock of seeing Paula's "flash of quick passion" as she kissed Graham brought him "flat [to] the pavement" with a sense of "violent suffocation" (351); then he began to realize, "All I have learned of books and theory goes glimmering" (366). He is an efficiency expert in the selective breeding of prize livestock, priding himself in the ranch house that defied earthquakes (13) and where "every fence was hog-tight and bull-proof" (16). He celebrates "fecundity!" and tiresomely but ironically repeats his performance of the stallion's song, chanting "with mane tossing and foot-pawing" (228), "Hear me! I am Eros! I stamp upon the hills" (275). He even admits that experiments might work out "splendidly on paper, with decently wide margins for human nature," and still not avoid "the doubt and the danger [of] human nature" (287). Still, even as knowledgeable an expert in these matters as he is, Dick is struck down in witnessing his wife's sexual passion for another man and in feeling the sexual jealousy and possessiveness that he had denied. Whereas the novel opens with Dick having awakened in the dark to smile with pleasure in hearing "the distant, throaty bawl of [his prize bull] King Polo" (377), London ends the book by describing Dick's life in ruins as he lies awake, listening to the life on his ranch—"to all the whinnying and nickering and bawling of sex," to "the trumpeting of Mountain Lad and the silver whinny of the Fotherington Princess" (392).

Dick's "Book-Concealed" Stairway and Paula's "Secret Patio"

In his first novel on the sex problem, London had explored the subconscious processes of sexual selection (*Daughter of the Snows* 88). But between 1902 and late 1914, when he completed *The Little Lady of the Big House*, Sigmund Freud and others had deepened and complicated the exploration of the unconscious. London was of course intensely interested in these developments and was attempting to keep abreast of them as a contributing worker in his own field.[31] But while Freud's debt to Darwin was becoming somewhat less visible during these years (when he became a "crypto-biologist" even as his "psychoanalytic theories became *more* biological" [Sulloway 391]),[32] London's growing interest in psychoanalysis clearly reinforced the biological—that is, Darwinian—issues he had begun to address in 1902 . His characters are now more than ever exposed to the reproductive instincts that earlier characters had managed rather successfully in their civilized lives, through scientific self-knowledge or sublimation. However, London's latest characters are not troubled by the hysteria or neurosis that would result, as Freud was emphasizing during these years, from the repression of the sexual instincts. Even in *The Valley of the Moon*, where hysteria had victimized the more sexually repressed women, it proved to be a relatively minor obstacle in the freeing of Saxon Brown's natural sexuality. And in the much more modern and intensely psychological *The Little Lady of the Big House*, the threat of hysteria or neurosis seems beside the point. Working perhaps with Freud's observation that "in the normal vita sexualis no neurosis is possible" (*Selected Papers on Hysteria* 188), London writes in *The Little Lady of the Big House* that "the young people ragged and tangoed incessantly" (230) and that, in general, "the free and easy life of the Big House went on in its frictionless way" (210–11).

The problem for these modern characters is in acknowledging, acting upon, and coming to terms with the instinctive forces that reside in Paula's "secret patio" (330) and that Dick has hidden from himself by his scientific study of sex, as London suggests in references to Dick's "book-concealed" (177) stairway or the "concealed lighting" in his bedroom (2). Of course these subconscious forces prevail, causing Paula to confront and affirm her naturally aggressive sexual desire and Dick to reconsider the "bawling of sex" that rings out across his ranch at end of the novel. Clearly, London's ultimate psychological purpose here is to expose the underlying chaotic energy of the sexual life, but it is less clear that in doing so he develops two somewhat different Freudian points: that Dick Forrest's conscious, scientific study and application of Darwinian and Mendelian principles do not prepare him for what London calls the undertow of sexual disruption in his own life, and that each of the three players is engaged in reading the emotions expressed by the others while attempting to conceal his or her own.[33]

The Dick Forrest who at the beginning of the novel is "the center of a system which he himself had built and of which he was secretly very proud" (35), including a house that defied earthquakes (13), is none the less subject to the unconscious forces that leave him "with his love-world crashing around him" (375). Developing this (largely self-analytical) critique, London arranges for a guest to remark on how Dick is more "cocksure" in his evolutionary theory than Bergson (343), and he interweaves the language of Darwinian selection and the Freudian unconscious in a number of scenes. Once, for example, tracing Dick's thoughts after he had advised his sister-in-law on her own sex life, he catches Dick in a revealing moment: "turning off lights as he went, [he] penetrated the library, and while selecting half a dozen volumes on mechanics and physics, smiled as if pleased with himself" at the advice he had offered. "But, half way up the book-concealed spiral staircase that led to his work room," he suddenly stops in his tracks and "lean[s] his shoulder against the wall." A remark his sister-in-law had made produced "an echoing in his consciousness" that made him think of Paula's possible interest in Graham (177).

In an even more significantly Freudian scene of Dick's conscious mind attempting to conceal from itself a disturbing underlying thought, London describes Dick's visit late in the novel to Paula's secret patio. In the "fountain pools [where] she kept her selected and more gorgeous blooms of fish," Dick "glanced into the bathroom with its sunken Roman bath." London notes that Dick's response to this obvious suggestion of Paula's sunken sexual pleasure is that, "for the life of him he was unable to avoid seeing a tiny drip and making a mental note for the ranch plumber" (332). Further, when Dick notices the pink marble babies that "rollicked and frolicked" in the fountain, thinking, "that was what she needed . . . children," London suggests that, while Dick's sense of the fecund origins of sexual desire is true, it nevertheless shields him from the darker truth of Paula's desire. As London's earlier references to the breeding of frogs suggests that the sexual motive is indeed alive in Paula's flesh, here he extends that idea to include Freud's highly disturbing analysis of "the constitutional sexual predisposition of the child," which Freud regarded as being so "irregularly multifarious" that "it deserves to be called 'polymorphous perverse.'" Insights like this (from the text London owned, *Selected Papers on Hysteria*, [191] and from other passages he later marked in *Three Contributions to the Theory of Sex*) are reflected in London's description of the "live warm human babies" in Paula's fountain, one of whom "reached arms covetously toward the goldfish," while another "on his back laughed at the sky [and yet] another stood with dimpled legs apart stretching himself" (331).

But the point derived from Freud that proved most useful to London in this novel is the one with which he was probably already familiar, from Darwin's *The Expression of the Emotions in Man and Animals*, the text that Freud had also found so helpful in preparing his *Studies on Hysteria* in 1895.[34] In *Darwin's Influence on Freud*, Lucille B. Ritvo shows that "Freud [was] obviously well acquainted with [the] principles" (179) Darwin had set forth and explains that he "extended the study of the expressions of the emotions to include hysterical symptoms and verbal expressions" (191). Ritvo notes, for example, that certain "striking motor phenomena exhibited" by one of his patients "reminded Freud 'forcibly of one of the principles laid down by Darwin to explain the expression of the emotions—the principle of the overflow of excitation . . . which accounts, for instance, for dogs wagging their tails'" (184).

Like other novelists who developed an interest in *The Expression of the Emotions*, London realized how Darwin's observations could contribute to one's effort to dramatize psychological conflict.[35] Throughout *The Little Lady of the Big House*, but with increased intensity in the last half as the triangular drama develops, London focuses his energy on tracing (1) the characters' inadvertent expressions of their own emotions and their heightened interest in reading the emotions expressed by the other players, and (2) their consequent interest in concealing their own emotions from the others. As these characters express, read, and conceal their emotions, they reveal something of the behavior of Freud's patients (in a passage that London marked). But while Freud's patients attempted to conceal their obsessions once they had been made aware of their sexual origin, London insists that his characters are normal rather than hysterical or neurotic (*Selected Papers* 127). Thus, as they play out the drama of their conflicting sexual motives, they reveal London's more pressing interest in the foundations of Freud's theory of the emotions—Darwin's point that "expression" is a "branch of natural history" wherein the struggle for self-preservation is paramount (*The Expression of the Emotions* 12).

At an early point in the drama of expression between Paula and Graham, London positions Paula at the piano in a scene that obviously draws on the power of music in courtship that Darwin had explained. London writes:

> As [Graham] approached he caught the quick expression of pleasure in her eyes at the sight of him, which as quickly vanished. She made a slight movement as if to rise, which did not escape his notice any more than did her quiet mastery of the impulse that left her seated.
>
> She was immediately herself as he had always seen her. (211)

It is worth noting here that while London's reference to Paula's pleasure gives the scene a Freudian touch, it nevertheless remains within the realm of Darwin's analysis of the emotions expressed by lovers—that "with the lower animals we see the same principle of pleasure derived from contact in association with love" (*Expression* 213). As the triangular drama develops, London gives us such scenes as the following, which serves as a prelude to Dick's remark—in the houseguests' discussion of evolution and woman—that "sex and soul are all interwoven and tangled together" (263). In the early stages of this discussion London focuses on his three players:

> To look at Dick's face it would have been unguessed that he was aught but a carefree, happy arguer. Nor did Graham, nor did Paula, Dick's dozen years' wife, dream that his casual careless glances were missing no movement of a hand, no change of position on a chair, no shade of expression on their faces.

What's up? was Dick's secret interrogation. Paula's not herself. She's positively nervous, and all the discussion is responsible. And Graham's off color. His brain isn't working up to mark. He's thinking about something else, rather than about what he is saying. What is that something else?

And the devil of speech behind which Dick hid his secret thoughts impelled him to urge the talk wider and wilder. (260)

Throughout the last half of the novel London heightens his drama of the expression and concealment of emotions, mostly from Dick's point of view. Once, for example, he searches Paula's face and eyes for "the effect of the impact" of his own seemingly innocent remarks and finds "Graham's face . . . expressionless insofar as there was no apparent change of the expression of interest that had been there" (267). In later scenes London notes that "Dick knew her too long in all the expressions of her moods not to realize the significance of her singing" as she moves through the house" (285) and that he "had not failed to observe the flutter of alarm that shadowed her eyes so swiftly, and that so swiftly was gone" (290). In a final example of such scenes, one of London's most memorable, he dramatizes how Dick's self-confidence in concealing his own emotions is shaken in a moment of accidental introspection. Walking through Paula's studio he finds that "a portrait of himself confronted him." Paula had been painting it from a photograph, and London again suggests his interest in Darwin's discussion of emotions by bringing out one of the emotions that Darwin had noted in particular, Dick's "start" in noticing a difference between Paula's painting and the photograph:

With a start he looked more closely. Was that expression of the eyes, of the whole face, his? He glanced at the photograph. It was not there. He walked over to one of the mirrors, relaxed his face, and led his thoughts to Paula and Graham. Slowly the expression came into his eyes and face. Not content, he returned to the easel and verified it. Paula knew. Paula knew he knew. She had learned it from him, stolen it from him some time when it was unwittingly on his face, and carried it in her memory to the canvas. (333)

Indeed, it is fair to say that in this highly self-reflective novel, London had discovered a new, deeper subject matter that would have enriched his fiction had he lived further into the Freudian era to produce it—the sense, as Dick remarks to himself at this point, that "It would seem that all our faces are beginning to say new things" (334).

London did live to produce two memorable brief explorations of this new territory in 1916, "The Red One" and "The Kanaka Surf," and he "mapped out a new novel [*The Eternal Enemy*] that is on sex, and on sex with such a vengeance that I fear me The Cosmopolitan will have to prune some of the sex out of it" (*Letters* 1553).[36] But what possible solutions to the sex problem does London offer in *The Little Lady of the Big House*? This is the constant goal in the exploration of sex that he pursued throughout his career, as it was in his experimental farming. In this way, too, London resembles Dick Forrest, who remarks early in the novel that he would undertake postgraduate courses in the College of Agriculture because "[he] want[s] to do something. . . . something constructive" (73). To begin, London's most important general point in the novel is that in those years when Darwinism was being eclipsed by any number of anti-Darwinian evolutionary theories, only a Darwinian view of life—and emphatically not a Bergsonian one—will enable us to understand that there *is* a sex problem and that it is rooted in the entangled reality that Darwin had presented in his theories of natural selection and sexual selection. Darwin's analysis of the expression of the emotions, Freud's development and transformation of this insight in his psychoanalysis, and work in the new field of sexology, most notably in Havelock Ellis's *Studies in the Psychology of Sex*, all converged to underscore and deepen the Darwinian view that London had always championed, as in his tribute to Darwin's achievement at the conclusion of his *Origin of Species* (*Kempton-Wace* 177). London's orientation kept him aware of this development in the theory of sexuality: that "within the nascent sexology movement—itself largely inspired by Darwinism—virtually every important aspect of Freud's own theory of psychosexual development can be found" (Sulloway 276). Especially in his masterpiece on the sex problem, London saw more clearly than any other American novelist of his generation that, "in proper historical perspective, Freud's theory of mind is the embodiment of a scientific age imbued with the rising tide of Darwinism" (Sulloway 497).

London's first suggested solution to the sex problem is certainly to welcome continued scientific, psychoanalytical, and fictional exploration in the field, in the face of growing hostility among readers who were offended by Ellis, Freud, or D. H. Lawrence. Beyond this he suggests, rather tentatively, a number of more specific possibilities that can be singled out as threads in his larger tapestry of sex. First, to trace a line of thought that seems to run from Darwin through Freud's later writings (well beyond London's career), London maintains, as did Freud, that "the evolution of civilization [is] primarily at the expense of free sexual expression" (Sulloway 391). That is, London suggests that as the sexual impulse is undeniably chaotic and entangled by nature to the point of being "polymorphously perverse," the male, especially, "cannot lay rough hands on love" (270), and he calls on both his hero and heroine to practice self-restraint through a code like Dick's or even Paula's as she finally solved the triangle (320). Dick enforces this system of values in managing his personnel on the ranch—when he fired a man who was having an affair with another man's wife: "Smith had a perfect right to love the woman, and to be loved by her if it came to that," but "he had no right to hurt the group of individuals in which he lives" (319). A second suggested solution to the sex problem as manifested in the relationship between Paula and Dick is rather more in line with Havelock Ellis's views on the art of love or the kind of advice that the character Mercedes gives Saxon Roberts in *The Valley of the Moon*: she must solve "the post-nuptial problem of re-taining a husband's love" (117) by working with her "flimsies" to keep her husband's sexual "appetite knife-edged and never satisfied" (115–16). In *The Little Lady of the Big House*, however, London extends this obligation to the male, as well, showing repeat-edly that Dick is too preoccupied with his work to pay adequate attention to Paula. Once, for example, London writes that, "having tasted the pleasure of knowing [Paula] to be awake, Dick, as usual, forgot her in his own affairs" (82).

But more important, London interweaves the suggestion of a final, visionary solution that best characterizes his unique approach to the sex problem in its larger evolutionary context. Always interested in ethnology and the evolution of race, London had begun in recent years to develop a critique of American civilization (or what he called the Great White Way) by suggesting that it could renew itself by incorporating the wisdom of the "old Chinese," for example, or "other old and . . . dark-eyed foreign breed[s]," as in the methods of "intensive cultivation" that his hero and heroine learn in *The Valley of the Moon* (266). One aspect of this dark-skinned or primitive wisdom in *The Valley of the Moon* is the knowledge of sexual love that Saxon acquires from Mercedes. It is important to note that in London's imagination this sort of earth-wisdom constitutes an early expression of sexual primitivism that arose in the first years of Freudian fiction, wherein the overcivi-lized or neurotic whites are freed from their sexual inhibitions by exposure to the supposedly less inhibited lifestyles of primitive folk, such as the black people in Sherwood Anderson's *Dark Laughter*. London's own efforts to court the subcon-scious or the primitive mind were sparked during these years when, in 1911, the Yahi Indian Ishi, "the last wild man in North America," walked into the civilized world of Northern California.

As Charles L. Crow has recently noted, London "sensed an identity with Ishi" (47), but the sexual possibilities of this encounter in London's imagination are clear only in relation to the larger questions in the evolution of sex and civilization that London was exploring (53). London certainly did not see Ishi in the image of the promiscuous black people that Sherwood Anderson would help to popularize. Rather, in reading of Ishi's tribe in Stephen Powers's *Tribes of California*, London focused on the character of Red Cloud, whose "Acorn Song" he brings into *The Little Lady of the Big House* repeatedly (he used the song again in *The Acorn-Planter: A Cali-fornia Forest Play* [1916]). The song appears first toward the end of a section that traces the young Dick Forrest's education, representing the culminating wisdom that leads to his present agricultural project. London presents the song exactly as inscribed in *Tribes of California*:

The acorns come down from heaven!
I plant the short acorns in the valley!
I plant the long acorns in the valley!
I sprout, I, the black-oak acorn, sprout, I sprout! (78)

But as the novel develops, this song of the fecund world competes with another song that Dick now prefers to perform, the song of the stallion Mountain Lad, which begins, "Hear me! I am Eros! I stamp upon the hills!" London emphasizes that these two songs of fecundity define a deep conflict between Paula and Dick. When we see Dick first performing it for Paula, London notes that "for a flash of an instant . . . Paula knew resentment of her husband's admiration for the splendid beast," and she immediately asks that he sing "The Song of the Acorn" (85–86).

This kind of scene becomes quite tiresome in the novel, even though Dick's performances for the house guests are carried off with a saving degree of comic self-consciousness. But London's serious purpose is to suggest that Dick's "mutinous" performances of the stallion's song represent an aspect of his overbearing scientific mind that is related to the sexual violence of the Darwinian male. While Dick is repelled at the idea of forceful love, of "holding" Paula or causing her to "endure" his kiss, London suggests, again and again, that in his intensely scientific approach to agriculture and life, Dick unknowingly wields another secondary sexual character evolved for sexual combat that Darwin had described in male birds, the spurs. We first see Dick's spurs on the stairway that is hidden behind his "book-freighted" shelves: "he descended with care that his spurs might not catch" (11). Among many later examples of London's care with this pattern of imagery, we see Dick "stamping with jingling spurs through the Big House in quest of its Little Lady" (97). And the connection between the two songs and the idea of the male's spurs is evident in such moments as this one, late in the novel, when at one of the parties Paula requests, "Now, Red Cloud, the Song of the Acorn. . . . Put down your glass, and be good, and plant acorns," but Dick "stood up, shaking his head mutinously, as if tossing a mane, and stamping ponderously in simulation of Mountain Lad" (274–75).

With this pattern of imagery in the novel (echoing his earlier suggestion about Saxon's being like a "squaw" in *The Valley of the Moon*), London suggests that in the agricultural origins of North American civilization, as figured in the "Song of the Acorn," there existed a gentler kind of masculinity that could guide his modern Californians toward an enduring solution to the sex problem. The conflict between the "Song of the Acorn" and Mountain Lad's song of "Eros!" is resolved on Paula's deathbed when she asks Dick, whom she calls "Red Cloud," to sing "the song of Ai-kut, and of the Dew-Woman" (389). In the passages from *Tribes of California* that London marked, noting for example, "Ishi's tribe," and "Nishinam Adam & Eve" (in reference to lines about "Ai-kut . . . the first man"), London would have seen Powers's remark, "The California Indians anticipated Darwin by some centuries in the development theory, only substituting the coyote for the monkey" (339). London must have smiled at Powers's romantic claim for the Indians and his simplistic representation of Darwinian theory. But London was certainly reading of the California Indians with an awareness that ethnology, sexology, and psychoanalysis were intermingled in "the rising tide of Darwinism" (Sulloway 497).

More specifically, it seems, London was self-consciously projecting his own version of a feminist effort to solve the sex problem that was known to some Europeans at that time as the American Cult of Woman. As Ellis noted in his *Cosmopolitan* article "Masculinism and Feminism," one German writer was especially "appalled by what he sees in the United States. To him it is 'the American danger,' and he thinks it may be traced partly to the influence of the matriarchal system of the American Indians on the early European invaders" (317). But right up to the end of *The Little Lady of the Big House* London dramatized his own sense of how our culture might realize his feminist vision. It would require that we recognize both the male's and female's nature as hunters in the general bawling of sex. Also it requires a faith equal to London's own lifelong belief in Darwin's essential principle in the theory of sexual selection, the female's power to select and thereby exert a degree of control over the evolutionary future.

As in his memorable tribute to Darwin's conclusion to the *Origin of Species* (in *The Kempton-Wace Letters*), London's study of the sex problem shares Darwin's sense at the end of *The Descent of Man* that he knew "no fact in natural history more wonderful than that the female Argus pheasant should be able to appreciate the exquisite shading of the ball-and-socket ornaments and the elegant patterns of the wing-feathers of the male" (*The Descent of Man* 2:400–401). Even as World War I had begun to produce the sense of desolation that would emerge as *The Waste Land* or F. Scott Fitzgerald's sense that it had been "the last love battle" (*Tender Is the Night* 68),[37] London found reason to affirm Paula's sense of sexual beauty, even if it ended in her being attracted to the second male, Evan. London retained his faith in the idea that "the male Argus Pheasant [had] acquired his beauty gradually, through the females having preferred [the more beautiful males] during many generations," hoping, it seems, that even the human community might find a better way (*The Descent of Man* 2:401). One cannot mistake London's concluding image in *The Little Lady of the Big House* as more than a muted hope. It is far less promising than Saxon Brown's ecological "vision" in *The Valley of the Moon* or that novel's concluding image of the "doe and a spotted fawn" glimpsed through "a tiny open space between the trees." But Jack London closed his darkest and most highly complicated exploration of the sex problem with another of his many images of the female's power to "get the vision" when a trumpeting stallion elicits the novel's final note, "the silver whinny" of the mare.

Notes

1. In a letter to Edward Carpenter dated March 2, 1914, qtd. in Hamilton, 83. London was writing for a copy of Carpenter's *The Intermediate Sex*. The similar, earlier statement by London, in the epigraph to this chapter, is in a letter to Maurice Magnus dated October 23, 1911 (*Letters* 1042).

2. Ellis's "Masculinism and Feminism" and an installment of London's *The Little Lady of the Big House* appear side by side in *Cosmopolitan*, August 1915. For a sense of London's extensive reading in evolutionary biology, sex, and psychology, see Hamilton, *"The Tools of My Trade."*

3. This is not to deny that many of his books seem flawed, largely because he chose not to revise, or to suggest that his novels are as impressive in their artistry as certain other fictional presentations of sexual love, such as Henry James's *The Portrait of a Lady*, Kate Chopin's *The Awakening*, Edith Wharton's *The Reef*, or Scott Fitzgerald's *The Great Gatsby* (all of which explore the theory of sexual selection in different ways and from different points of view).

4. Wace's experience with Weissman reflects London's, of course, a glimpse of which is available in his letter to Cloudsley Johns in 1899:

> Have you read anything of Weissman's. He has struck a heavy blow to the accepted idea of acquired characters being inherited, and as yet his opponents have not proved conclusively one case in which such a character has been inherited. . . . Read him up, you will find him interesting. But it's heavy. If you have not studied evolution well, I would not advise you to tackle him. He takes a thorough grounding in the subject for granted. (*Letters* 106)

5. London's long-term interest in and sympathy with Haeckel is a subject not adequately explored in London scholarship. As David Mike Hamilton notes, London was interested in Haeckel for many years, to the point that he sent Haeckel a copy of *Before Adam* and received a postcard of thanks in return (16, 147, 188). In 1914 London wrote, "I have always inclined toward Haeckel's position. In fact, 'incline' is too weak a word. I am a hopeless materialist" (*Letters* 1339). The sense of London's reference to Haeckel in *The Kempton-Wace Letters* is echoed much later in Dick Forrest's remark that "man's consciousness is no greater a mystery than the reaction of the gasses that make a simple drop of water" (*The Little Lady of the Big House* 343).

6. Such is the approach in Le Conte's *Evolution*, for example, Havelock Ellis's *Sexual Selection in Man*, or another influential work from these years, *The Evolution of Sex* (1889), by Patrick Geddes and J. Arthur Thomson. In their opening chapter, "The Sexes and Sexual Selection," for example, Geddes and Thomson conclude that Darwin was "too glaringly anthropomorphic" (or to put it another way, too inclined to emphasize man's animal nature) and in their chapter "Psychological and Ethical Aspects" that "the hunger and reproductive attractions of the lowest organisms" give way to two "plane[s] of ascent" toward "altruism" whereby "sexual attraction ceases to be wholly selfish; hunger may be overcome by love;

love of mates is enhanced by love of offspring; love of offspring broadens out into love of kindred" (*The Evolution of Sex* 30, 296–97).

7. The following analysis differs from that of David Mike Hamilton, who surmised, based on evidence in *A Son of the Sun*, that London read Ellis sometime during 1911 (35). On December 28, 1910, London wrote to Charles F. Lowrie to defend himself against Katherine Dopp's claim that he had plagiarized her work, naming his "teachers as Darwin, Huxley, Spencer and all the school of evolutionists who . . . had promulgated their theories before she was dry behind the ears. Really, she vexes me, and reminds me of the abnormal females described by Havelock Ellis and other specialists" (*Letters* 962). The card catalog of London's books in the Huntington Library shows that he owned the six-volume set of *Studies in the Psychology of Sex* (Philadelphia: Davis, 1906–1910) as well as Ellis's *The New Spirit* (1890).

8. For an earlier example of London's meditation on life in these dark terms, see Van Weyden's thoughts on Wolf Larsen in chapter 2 of *The Sea-Wolf*: "My first impression . . . was . . . of his strength. . . . A strength savage, ferocious, alive in itself, the essence of life in that it is the potency of motion, the elemental stuff itself out of which the many forms of life have been molded; in short, that which writhes in the body of a snake when the head is cut off and the snake, as a snake, is dead, or which lingers in a shapeless lump of turtle meat and recoils and quivers from the prod of a finger."

9. Often referred to as his agrarian novels and sometimes as the Sonoma novels, the ecological novels are *Burning Daylight, The Valley of the Moon,* and *The Little Lady of the Big House.* Agrarian vision is Earle Labor's term in his "From 'All Gold Canyon' to *The Acorn-Planter*: Jack London's Agrarian Vision." This article is a major contribution to Jack London studies, but the discussion of London's ecological vision, below, develops Labor's insights by explaining how these novels address what London considered the underlying sex problem.

10. For a discussion of the controversy over sociobiology and evolutionary psychology since Mayr's remark in 1982, see Segerstråle's *Defenders of the Truth: The Battle for Science in the Sociobiology Debate and Beyond* (2000), and Alcock's *The Triumph of Sociobiology* (2001).

11. Referring to Homo Sapiens as "the mythopoeic species," with a "primal instinct of narrative, of continuous scenario invention," Wilson acknowledges the human need for religious epics, but he calls for an evolutionary epic to be composed "from the best empirical knowledge that science and history can provide of the real human story" (foreword to Rue, *Everybody's Story,* ix–x). Of course London's epic was limited by what he could know of science and history in 1911, but he is certainly aware throughout *The Valley of the Moon* that his narrative would require that his heroine give up her belief in the "law of God" that she had learned from her mother (204). Toward the end of the novel Saxon twice "parod[ies] an old hymn," singing, "De Lawd move in er mischievous way / His blunders to perform" (319, 330).

12. Despite these depressing remarks, there is no evidence that London had given up his ecological vision or his own practical efforts on his farm to help solve the world's problems. Because London and Freud both studied evolution and sex, it is worth comparing their thoughts on war. In "Thoughts for the Times on War and Death" (1915), Freud felt "swept . . . into the vortex of this war-time" and attempted to account for the "disillusionment of the war" (245). His disillusionment had arisen largely because "we had expected the great ruling powers among the white nations upon whom the leadership of the human species has fallen" to have continued to provide "technical advances in the direction of dominating nature," what with the "artistic and scientific acquisitions of the mind" (246–47). He goes on to argue

that, while we welcome illusions because they spare us emotional distress," "in reality, there is no such thing as 'eradicating' [the] evil tendencies [of human beings]. Psychological—more strictly speaking, psychoanalytic—investigation shows instead that the inmost essence of human nature consists of elemental instincts, which are common to all men and aim at the satisfaction of certain primal needs (252–53). But he ends his essay by remarking that "it is indeed a mystery" "why the national units should disdain, detest, abhor one another, and that even when they are at peace. . . . Possibly only future stages in development will be able to alter this regrettable state of affairs" (262). It seems fair to suggest that one of the reasons for the difference between London's and Freud's views on war in 1915 is that Freud's sense of the mystery of it all is related to his Lamarckian faith in the "acquisitions of the mind" and "development," whereas London had long since reached a different conclusion about the mechanisms of evolution and what we now think of as evolutionary psychology.

13. Fitzgerald introduces the problem in chapter 1 of *Gatsby* through the well-known remarks of Tom Buchanan on "The Rise of the Colored Empires."

14. The vision comes to Saxon as she and Billy watch a "moving picture show"—a "rural drama situated somewhere in the Middle West," toward the end of book 2. While from the reader's point of view in the late 1990s this might not seem a promising source of the saving vision, London had good reasons to imagine that the moving picture industry might eventually influence the country's development: about three months before he began writing the novel, he had begun negotiations "to sell the moving-picture-rights in *The Sea Wolf*" (*Letters* 1028).

15. Leopold's own sense of Darwin's fundamental role in founding ecological thought is too little appreciated. See, for example, his remark that by now, "a century . . . since Darwin gave us the first glimpse of the origin of species . . . we should have come to know that man, while captain of the adventuring ship, is hardly the sole object of its quest" (*Sand County Almanac* 116–17). Although the Darwinian foundation of Leopold's work is too little appreciated, there is a promising development in the field of literary study known as "ecocriticism," led mainly by Glen A. Love, who writes to encourage "serious interdisciplinary work between humanists and the sciences" (*Practical Ecocriticism* 47). The chapter "Ecocriticism and Science" is of particular interest.

16. Those who might want to track London's close reading in Ellis should compare this scene with a passage in Ellis's *Studies*. In his scene, London emphasizes the "vigilant" forewoman and describes the hysterical outburst in these terms: "The tense thread of human resolution [was] snapped" by "the wildest scream of terror [Saxon] had ever heard": a "strange black animal flapping great claw-like wings" had landed on Mary's shoulder, precipitating the women's riotous flight (92). This strange, melodramatic scene resembles Ellis's discussion of hysteria. London's reference to the "vigilant" forewoman seems to echo Ellis's remark in his second sentence on hysteria that "the subjects of hysteria really live in a state of pathological sleep, of vigilambulism," and the incident of the bat landing on Mary's shoulder resembles the example Ellis cites from Breuer, "in which a young girl of seventeen had her first hysterical attack after a cat sprang on her shoulders." If London did see this passage in Ellis, he would have been especially interested in the fact that Breuer's young woman had suffered her hysterical attack at exactly the scene at which she had escaped from the "hands" of an ardent male a few days earlier (1:1:221).

17. Even more recent critics such as Charles N. Watson Jr. object to Mercedes. In Watson's view, "although Saxon accepts much of what Mercedes teaches," Mercedes is a "Nietzschean"

figure (205), "a demon that must be exorcised before Saxon's (and London's) more optimistic spirit can reassert itself" (203). London fully affirms that Mercedes's instruction in the primitive "art" of love is a vital lesson without which Saxon's love life could not flower; Saxon needs it and draws on it to the last.

18. The question of community property comes up immediately after they are married, when Billy responds to Saxon's remark about their money as "your [Billy's] money": Billy "cried, 'It ain't mine. It's ourn.'" Saxon, with love in her voice, tells him, "that's one of the sweetest things you've said since we got married" (121). One of the authoritative works on the sex problem (one that London owned) is absolutely opposed to the idea of community property. Writing in *The Sexual Question*, August Forel remarks: "In my opinion, the first fundamental principles of civil marriage should be absolute legal equality of the two conjoints and complete separation of property. The momentary amorous intoxication of a woman should not allow a man to appropriate her property in whole or in part; only truly barbarous laws could permit such iniquity, and they should be banished from all the codes of civilized countries. Moreover, in countries where woman enjoys important rights, the community of property furnishes those who are unscrupulous with the means of completely despoiling their husbands" (370).

19. Making his case for the "natural" facts of sexuality in the first volume of *Studies in the Psychology of Sex*, Ellis follows his discussion of the evolution of modesty with lengthy parts on "sexual periodicity" and "auto-erotism," under which he treats hysteria. In his discussion of autoerotism, Ellis emphasizes that he is not limiting himself to "masturbation," rather, he remarks that when the "phenomena of auto-erotism" are considered in "a broad view" they are "the inevitable by-products of that mighty process on which the animal creation rests" (1:1:283). London seems to affirm this view of natural sexuality in moments like this, when, after noting that Billy thought of Saxon as "a thoroughbred, clean-cut and spirited," he concludes that with "the proper soil . . . their love would grow and blossom": then London has Saxon remark "I'm loving myself. . . . Because you love me . . . I love every bit of me, Billy, because . . . well, because you love every bit of me" (234).

20. London insinuates repeated references to Saxon as a squaw, as when another character tells Billy, "you got a squaw that is some squaw" (95). There is of course a parallel between Saxon's "dark-skinned" wisdom and the saving wisdom Billy and Saxon take in from the Portuguese, Slav, Chinese, and other dark-skinned farmers.

21. The remarks on gropings and darknesses and on Bergson are London's in *The Little Lady of the Big House* 263, 244–45. For a discussion of Aiken's *Great Circle* in this light, including a character's complaint, "What the hell's the difference between the soul and the subconscious and the unconscious and the will?" see Frederick J. Hoffman, *Freudianism and the Literary Mind*, 281–82. For a brief discussion of Holt and *The Freudian Wish* see Nathan G. Hale Jr.'s indispensable *Freud in America* (1:426–29).

22. As London had read William James rather closely, as well, he might have seen James's discussion of "the sexual act" in relation to both "Darwin's *Descent of Man*" and the research cited by Ellis. Referring to the research, James explains how frogs "show . . . a machine-like obedience to the present incitement of sense, and an almost total exclusion of the power of choice. Copulation occurs *per fas aut nefas*, occasionally between males, often with dead females, . . . and the male may be cut in two without letting go his hold" (*Principles of Psychology* 34–35).

23. Also in this passage on the "fog and mist . . [and] mystery" of personality, Dick notes that "there are seeming men with the personalities of women [and that] there are plural personalities," suggesting that London was interested both in William James's description of multiple personalities and the subject then much discussed in both evolutionary and Freudian theory of the human embryo's hermaphroditic nature.

24. This point is further suggested in an exchange between London and Upton Sinclair on the related subject of physical culture. London wrote to Sinclair on July 17, 1910, "Yes, I've been reading your 'Physical Culture' articles. But I have theories of my own. I'll expound 'em to you some day" (*Letters* 909). Sinclair later brought together articles like this in *The Book of Life* (1922), the two volumes (*Mind and Body* and *Love and Society*) of which suggest how these subjects, including a chapter, "Exploring the Subconscious," were essentially one for writers like London, Havelock Ellis, and Sinclair during these years. London expounded his own views on physical culture in the Carmel chapters of *The Valley of the Moon*.

25. One of Ellis's reasons for making this distinction is to free his subject from criticisms of "those who are unconsciously dominated by a superstitious repugnance of sex" and want to restrict sexual relationships to the reproductive purpose and thereby "veil the facts of the sexual life."

26. Imagining that her readers might respond, "What? Jack *London*, a *feminist*?" Reesman writes against the "typecasting [of London] as a writer of boy's books and machismo survival epics." See also Reesman's remarks that "although Clarice Stasz and Tavernier-Courbin, among others, have explored London's views on women as remarkably ahead of his time, the subject has generally been ignored" ("Irony and Feminism in *The Little Lady of the Big House*" 34).

27. See also London's letter to the editor of the *Atlantic Monthly*, complaining of a columnist's (Wilson Follett, though London did not know his name) remarks not about the serial illustrations but the novel's "erotomania," "in-growing concupiscence," and "perverted gusto" (*Letters* 1594; *Atlantic Monthly*, October 1916).

28. This passage is from chapter 23 in *The Awakening*. Discussions of Edna and Brett are indexed in my *The Descent of Love*.

29. For Shaw's retrospective view of his choice to leave the subject of "clandestine adultery" to others because it is "the dullest of all subjects" and of his choice to treat other aspects of sexuality such as "husband-hunting" as part of "the conception of Creative Evolution," see "My Own Part in the Matter" (*Back to Methuselah* xcviii). The difference between London's and Shaw's approach to these matters is suggested in Barbara Bellow Watson's remark that "in all [of Shaw's] plays, even though they are problem plays, sex is never a problem"; Watson offers this observation in distinguishing Shaw's from Freud's views on sexuality (*A Shavian Guide to Intelligent Women* 133).

30. London owned and made marginal notes in a copy of Freud's *Selected Papers on Hysteria and Other Psychoneuroses* (1912). In chapter 12 of this volume, "Concerning 'Wild' Psychoanalysis," Freud complains of the physician's "popular sense" of what the "sexual life" means—"namely, that under sexual demands nothing else is understood except the need for coitus or its analogy, the processes causing the orgasm or the ejaculation of the sexual product" (202).

31. Many of London's books on sex are listed in Hamilton's "*The Tools of My Trade*," but this excellent volume does not include many volumes on sex that London owned. For this, one needs to consult the card catalog to his library (at the Huntington Library), which in-

cludes works such as Albert Moll's *The Sexual Life of the Child* (1912) and, more important, several volumes by Havelock Ellis.

32. Sulloway explains in his chapter 12, "Freud as Crypto-Biologist: The Politics of Scientific Independence," this development in Freud's career. The idea that Freud's theories became *more* biological throughout his career seems reflected in Lucille B. Ritvo's study of Darwin and Freud, as well, where her appendix A, "Freud's References to Darwin," records an increasing number of references to Darwin after 1912.

33. As noted earlier, in her conversation with Graham in chapter 13, Paula talks of the "the entangling currents" of thought that she can escape by not "fighting" the "undertow" of her "unconsciousness" (152–53). A similar passage occurs in "The Kanaka Surf" (1916), when the man and woman are actually swimming in the ocean and the man advises her to "make yourself slack—slack in your mind." This story opens with the narrator's reference to Freud's point that, "where sex is involved," people "are prone sincerely to substitute one thing for another" and so forth (*The Complete Short Stories* 3:2417, 2396). In addition to London's reference to Freud in this story, several other references are indexed in *Letters*.

34. I know of no references by London to *The Expression of the Emotions*, but according to the card catalog of his library at the Huntington Library, he owned the eighteen-volume Appleton set of Darwin's works, and in David Mike Hamilton's appendix to *"The Tools of My Trade,"* London's library (as cataloged by Beatrice Barrangon Ragnor) contained nine books by Darwin in case 31 and five in case 32. A good deal of Freud's *Studies on Hysteria* is reflected in the existing, marked volume in London's library at the Huntington Library, *Selected Papers on Hysteria and Other Psychoneuroses*. Darwin's influential work was of interest to many psychologists during these years, for example, William James, whose index to *The Principles of Psychology* shows several references to *The Expression*; Hamilton includes London's notations in *The Varieties of Religious Experience* and *The Will to Believe*.

35. For discussions of Harold Frederic's and Edith Wharton's work with these Darwinian materials, see the chapters on Frederic's *The Market-Place* and Wharton's *The Reef* in my *The Descent of Love*.

36. This letter to Edgar G. Sisson, dated June 12, 1916, was written from Hawaii, where less than a month before London had finished "The Red One." As one critic has noted, "The Kanaka Surf," in which London refers to Freud, is in some ways a "miniature" of *The Little Lady of the Big House* (Lachtman 110). But in the rather voluminous commentary on "The Red One," it has not been remarked that that story's main character, a naturalist named Bassett, bears a resemblance to Dick Forrest—in the way that his scientific expertise regarding "the cosmic verity of sex" (*Portable Jack London* 326), as well as his certainty about "the psychological simplicities" (321) of the people he meets at Guadalcanal, fail to prepare him for his own encounter with "the grotesque, female hideousness" of an "unthinkably disgusting bushwoman" (325). London resolves this scientist's confrontation with the unconscious by beheading him.

37. As Dick Diver surveys a battlefield on the western front, he remarks, "Why this was a love battle—there was a century of middle-class love spent here. This was the last love battle."

4 Theodore Dreiser, Science, and "It"

For a full fifty years Theodore Dreiser was absorbed in evolutionary thought—from 1894, when he began reading John Tyndall, Thomas Huxley, and Herbert Spencer, until late in 1943, when he finished "My Creator," part of the uncompleted collection of scientific and philosophical musings called *Notes on Life*. His interest in science has been studied by a number of critics, most notably Ellen Moers, in *Two Dreisers* (1969), and Louis J. Zanine, in *Mechanism and Mysticism: The Influence of Science on the Thought and Work of Theodore Dreiser* (1993). In Moers's view, key points in the development of Dreiser's scientific thought include his experience in high school with Charles Kingsley's *Water Babies*, "Dreiser's first reading in post-Darwinian biology" (136); with Herbert Spencer's *First Principles* in 1894 (138); with Darwin's *Origin of Species* and *The Descent of Man* in 1896 (141); with Sir John Lubbock's *Ants, Bees and Wasps* (which Dreiser incorporated as "a kind of book review" in his story of 1899, "McEwen of the Shining Slave Makers") (143); with the physiological psychologist, Elmer Gates (whom Dreiser met early in 1900 and who, Moers believes, is reflected in Dreiser's portrait of the character Ames in *Sister Carrie*) (159–69); with Jacques Loeb's work in physiological psychology regarding chemical mechanism or tropism (dating from 1915) (240–55); and with his introduction, largely through a friendship with Abraham Brill that began in 1918, to Freudian theory (256–70). Emphasizing the roles of Gates, Loeb, and Freud, Moers develops her thesis that there were two Dreisers: the "heir to the whole nineteenth-century tradition" of "the normative novel" and "the austerely modern" novelist (vii). Zanine, on the other hand, draws on Moers's work but, emphasizing the mystical nature of Dreiser's thought, ends by more or less collapsing the two Dreisers into a single figure whose "interest in science was primarily a religious quest to find emotionally and spiritually satisfying answers to questions about human purpose and destiny" (2). Noting especially Dreiser's repeated tributes to Ernst Haeckel's *The*

Riddle of the Universe at the Close of the Nineteenth Century (1900), an extremely important element in his scientific thought that Moers and others have rather overlooked, Zanine reiterates Charles Child Walcutt's point that Dreiser represents the transcendental tendency (one of the two "streams") in American Naturalism. Pursuing this point, Zanine closes his study with a discussion of Dreiser's final sense of design in the universe (3), claiming that in his last years Dreiser completed his essentially religious quest by returning to "the realm of natural theology" (212), as in William Paley's *Natural Theology* (1802).[1] In "My Creator" Dreiser praised "the Creative Force itself" and the innumerable chemical and mechanical intricacies of "Design! Design! Design!" that he regarded as "miracles of my Creator—Nature" (*Notes on Life* 330–31).

Even these invaluable studies, however, do not tell the whole complicated story of Dreiser's passionate interest in science, for his wide-ranging speculations covered an extraordinary period in the history of science (especially biology) and social science that included, for example, the discovery of Mendelian genetics and the subsequent modern synthesis of Darwinian theory and genetics, as well as the emergence of Freudian psychology. The present chapter suggests the importance of an essential element in Dreiser's scientific thought that has eluded Moers, Zanine, and other major Dreiserians like Robert H. Elias, in *Theodore Dreiser: Apostle of Nature* (1949), or Donald Pizer, in *The Novels of Theodore Dreiser: A Critical Study* (1976). These critics have recognized Darwin's broad and unmistakable influence on Dreiser's thought but mainly in terms of the social Darwinism that Richard Hofstadter defined in his landmark study of 1945 (Pizer 9–10; Moers 138). Yet none has explored the role of Darwin's theory of sexual selection in Dreiser's presentation of the sexual reality nor the less important but related role of Darwin's theory of the emotions.[2] This limited sense of what Darwin meant to Dreiser clouds our understanding not only of his own presentation of human love and "the riddle of existence" (*The "Genius"* 251) but also his relationship with other realists, naturalists, and modernists in regard to these questions. It also obscures his role in our culture's continuing efforts to understand what Richard Dawkins refers to in the 1990s as "Darwinian selection and hence the baroque extravaganza that, on this planet, we call life" (xi).

Were he alive today, Dreiser would no doubt share Dawkins's awe at the "sinewy elegance" and "poetic beauty" of Darwinian theory—his sense that it "outclasses even the most haunting of the world's origin myths" (xi). He defiinitely shared Darwin's own sense of grandeur in view of evolution's "endless forms most beautiful and most wonderful" (*The Origin of Species* 489), and Haeckel's sense in *The Riddle of the Universe* that "the new sun of our realistic monism" had begun to reveal "the wonderful temple of nature in all its beauty" (382). And had Dreiser lived to take in the more recent developments in evolutionary biology, he would have certainly brought his sense of the "incomprehensible chemistry which we call *life,*" as he put it in *The Financier* (360), into line with the discovery of DNA and perhaps with something like Dawkins's theory of "the selfish gene." Moreover, he might have come to see that in the history of biology, Jacques Loeb's mechanistic theory of tropism has lost much of the meaning that he and even Ellen Moers attributed to it. Whereas Moers thought that "biological science today could not function without [Loeb's] concept" of tropism (250), Ernst Mayr concludes (*The Growth of Biological Thought*) that the study of "usually physico-chemical proximate causes" in biology (as in Loeb's studies of tropism) errs when it ignores "evolutionary causation": "The assumption of Julius von Sachs, Jacques Loeb, and other native mechanists that biology consists entirely of a study of proximate causations is demonstrably wrong" (73).[3]

Behind Dreiser's keen interest in science lay the far-reaching questions that continue to interest contemporary evolutionary biologists like Dawkins, no less then they had Darwin, Wallace, Haeckel, and Huxley in works like *Man's Place in Nature.* Dreiser would have adapted his views on science as new discoveries or theories emerged. But before examining the role of Darwinian theory in Dreiser's conception of sex and the riddle of existence, it is worth noting that Dreiser's approach to psychology and his response to Freudian theory both come more clearly into focus when one grasps the relationship between Darwinism and Freudianism that has been examined in recent years. Indeed, from Dreiser's perspective in 1919, Frank Sulloway's recent conclusion about Freud and the rising tide of Darwinism would have seemed obvious (497). In the unpublished manuscript "It," dating from 1918 to 1919, shortly after he had begun his relationship with Brill, Dreiser writes of Freud and the subconscious in terms that also reflect his interest in Gates's and Loeb's physiological psychology. Also, however, "It" clearly indicates Dreiser's sense of the underlying Darwinian reality. Acknowledging the possible influence of "psychic wounds in infancy or youth, repression or woes, which burst out later in retaliatory decision and works," Dreiser writes,

> Whatever It is, life-spark or ego, that sits at the centre and does the deciding (self-interestedly and selfishly always), there is no least evidence that we control It, Its wishes and instincts, but that It controls us. *It* is, or rather we are, for It is in us and we in It, "polymorphous perverse" (to use Freud's apt phrase) in infancy and later.

"It," he continues, "this internal spirit or chemic compound," makes "up Its mind," by "logic, reason, the workings of a free-willing and -thinking spirit, or only some internal and accidental chemical synthesis." And Dreiser is certain that "the biologic force shown in us" is "the same" in everyone because we respond, for instance, to the same stimuli (sex, hunger, ambition) and then in turn to all compulsions and inhibitions built up by this same biologos in the past via other forms of itself and in the same way. . . . Yes, down in the depths of the so-called unconscious, or the elements of which we are composed, rests or works the real representative of biologos. It is ever at work apparently, wishing, dreaming, ceaselessly planning. And of a sudden, growing weary of wishing or Its method of procedure finally thought out, It presents you, the general organization (the body), with Its idea. You are to do thus and so. . . . Dark, central force that rules in our midst, that sings whether we will or no, plays whether we will or no, decides, whether the circumstances seem propitious or no, reads, dreams, mourns. . . . It! (*Theodore Dreiser: A Selection of Uncollected Prose* 221–23)

Such moments in Dreiser underscore his sense, after reading Darwin in 1896, that Darwin's insights provided the basis of modern thought. Recalling his lifelong interest in science two years before his death, he wrote that, "Truly the endless variety of life—from amoeba to man; the three-toed, dog-sized horse to his present day, heavily hoofed descendant; the one time sea-going mammal of minute size that descended or ascended to be a whale: and so on *ad infinitum*—puzzled me to the point of reading Darwin, Haeckel, Spencer, Loeb, Lodge, Crookes, and who not else, Freud, Menninger, a long list" (*Notes on Life* 328). Yet in critical discussions of Dreiser's approach to psychology, writers like Moers have not recognized the logical continuity between Darwinian and Freudian ideas in Dreiser's thought. Thus, in her conclusion that Dreiser was in part a victim of Darwinian thought because "nothing in the work of the Victorian naturalists was dated more than their psychology" (144), Moers obscures the extent to which Darwin's theory of sexual selection was not only a fundamental element in Dreiser's thought throughout his career, but the way in which it continues to be a key element in the resurgent interest in evolutionary psychology today. As one of the major American novelists during the eclipse of Darwinism and the rise of Freudianism, Dreiser warrants closer scrutiny for having kept his finger on the pulse of Darwinian evolution and the sex problem.

The Problem and Solution: The Evolutionary Tangle and Evolutionary Progress

Few writers indulge so frequently and at such length in didactic or speculative digressions as Dreiser. But it should be noted in defense of his tiresome habit that, living at a time when theories abounded—from any number of variations on Darwinian themes to Christian Science and Freudianism—he was aware of the pitfalls in theorizing, even as he pressed on in his own efforts to solve the riddle of existence.

"Deep below deep lie the mysteries, and theories flourish like weeds in a garden," he wrote in the 1920 essay "Change" (*Hey Rub-A-Dub-Dub: A Book of the Mystery and Wonder and Terror of Life* 21 [hereafter *Rub-A-Dub*]). His hero in *The "Genius"* wonders at his lover's "philosophizing so! Basing a course of action on theorizing in connection with books and life" (556). In the same (largely autobiographical) novel, Dreiser notes his hero's efforts to understand life in flirtations with Christian Science, Alfred Russel Wallace's search for "a Divine Mind," Ernst Haeckel's concept of the "unconscious cell souls," and other theories of life (696–98). Then he comments: "the most dangerous thing to possess a man to the extent of dominating him is an idea" (700). The key to understanding Dreiser's thought (in everything he wrote: fiction, poetry, drama, essays, memoirs) is that, while he absolutely revered Darwin, he was himself much more akin to writers like Haeckel who launched their own probings for universal meaning from the foundation of Darwinian evolutionary theory.

Dreiser's well-known fascination with "life and mortal chemistry" (*Financier* 360) is best understood in the context Haeckel gives it in his first chapter, "The Nature of the Problem," in *The Riddle of the Universe*. Acknowledging the chemical basis of life, Haeckel subordinates it to the Law of Substance that "establishes the eternal persistence of matter and force . . . throughout the entire universe" and that "is nothing else than an eternal 'evolution of substance.'" But Haeckel emphasizes that "the immortal merit of establishing [this] doctrine on an empirical basis" belongs "to the great scientist Charles Darwin" (4). It is important here to note first, however, that despite Dreiser's reverence for Darwin, Haeckel, Spencer, and others like Loeb, his imagined solutions to the problem are his own, according to his own temperament, personal experiences, social biases, and readings, and second, that the solutions he projected in his courtship plots, essays, and "Notes on Life" emerged in various forms throughout his career. Still it is perfectly clear that for Dreiser the problem itself always arises from the challenge Darwin presented at the conclusion of *The Origin of Species*: "to contemplate [the] tangled bank" of life and "the war of nature" (373–74). "Oh, the tangle of human life!" Dreiser exclaims at the end of *Sister Carrie* (368), or as Frank Cowperwood in *The Financier* realizes (in another of Dreiser's innumerable reiterations of the idea throughout his life), "life . . . was an inexplicable tangle" (386), and, "Life was war" (575). Alternatively, he evokes the same troubled reality with his extensive use of ocean imagery, emphasizing Darwin's point that all species of life originated in the ocean and that the human being's early vertebrate ancestors were fish. He ends chapter 1 of *Sister Carrie* by depicting his heroine "rushing into a great sea of life and endeavour" (7), "a lone figure in a tossing, thoughtless sea" (8). Later, he ends chapter 1 of *The Financier* by answering young Frank's question, "How is life organized?" The lesson comes from a fish tank he observes daily, when a lobster catches and eats a squid. Dreiser closed the novel with the epilogue, "Concerning Mycteroperca Bonaci," in which he compared a fish (the Black Grouper) with the hero Cowperwood. As the grouper survives through its "almost unbelievable power of simulation" or deceptive coloration, Cowperwood survives through "subtlety, chicanery, trickery" (778).

As for his solutions to the problem, Dreiser took "consolation [in] knowing that evolution is ever in action," as he puts it in *Sister Carrie* (57). Like many others of his time (Frank Norris, for example, and Jack London in certain early works), he imagined that the problems that had arisen through natural selection would be ameliorated by evolutionary progress through sexual selection or love. But in Dreiser's view, the possibility of such progress is threatened by sexual repression. In "Neurotic America and the Sex Impulse" he insists that the sex impulse is about much more than the mere production of more children, rails against the sex-repression to be found in "all parts of America," and denies any distinction between love and lust, since "the one is but an intellectual sublimation of the other" (*Rub-A-Dub* 133–34). Then, still countering the forces of American sex-repression, Dreiser claims in "Marriage and Divorce" that "our so-called love (desire, passionate chemical response, physical and spiritual) becomes the most significant fact in the universe as we now understand it": only by freeing ourselves to express this love can we experience "complete chemical responsiveness to the universe" and thereby participate in "evolutionary progress" (*Rub-A-Dub* 223–24). Still, while he affirms the reality of evolutionary progress through love, thereby suggesting a solution for the human's entanglements in the war of nature, Dreiser never offers an individual character any lasting satisfaction in his or her own desire for what he calls the distant beauty. The following sections examine the ways in which Dreiser dramatizes "the mysteries of courtship" in the lives of Carrie and Cowperwood and his sense of both the mechanics and the mystic purpose of the sexual reality (*Sister Carrie* 38).

Carrie's Choice and the "Distant Wings" of Beauty

As Ellen Moers informs us, by November 1896 Dreiser "could paraphrase enough of Darwin on sexual selection to show that he had been through *The Descent of Man*" (141). Also, no doubt, by the time he began writing *Sister Carrie* in 1899 he had absorbed something of Howells's and other realists' ways of dramatizing the Darwinian courtship. In Carrie's successive experiences with the three characters Drouet, Hurstwood, and Ames, Dreiser traces a sequence of ascending types of males from which she might exercise the female's power to select: first the "rudimentary" Drouet (58), then the "stronger and higher" Hurstwood (82), and finally the detached Ames, who is beyond her reach but who "pointed out a farther step" (369). Ames had "unlocked the door to a new desire" (356), but refusing to allow

Carrie (or any character in his fiction) to rest fully satisfied in a relationship with anyone, Dreiser leaves her only with her longings for distant beauty (369). While only desire can propel the evolutionary progress that Dreiser envisions, none of his characters can be fully satisfied in the ever-changing evolutionary stream. Still, Carrie enjoys considerable progress in her own life. During her first hours in the "great sea of life" in Chicago, she met Drouet, and Dreiser shows him "luring" her with his card while she fails to realize that "she was drifting" (6). Soon, introducing her to "the mysteries of courtship," Dreiser dramatizes an essential primitive element of sexual selection when, "suddenly a hand pulled [Carrie's] arm and turned her about": Drouet had discovered her in a crowd and, using the male secondary sexual character that Darwin described in the ocean crustacean's claws, for capturing and holding the female, he begins the courtship in earnest (43). Dreiser emphasizes that at this stage of Carrie's life she has no choice; she is captured by the male, who "selected a table," extended some crumpled greenbacks "in his hand," and then put his "larger, warmer hand" over her own. Writing that Drouet too "was drawn by his [own] innate desire to act the old pursuing part," Dreiser remarks that "he could not help what he was going to do. He could not see clearly enough to wish to do differently," and he is capable of only rudimentary twinges of conscience (58).

In Hurstwood, Carrie "met a man who was more clever than Drouet in a hundred ways" (72). Thus, in his first effort to dramatize sexual selection at work toward its mystic end, Dreiser follows earlier realists like Howells and James in defining the superior mind as the ultimate criterion in the female's choice. Carrie now *has* a choice, and "almost unconsciously" she immediately begins to compare the two, noticing in particular a number of details in the elegance of Hurstwood's attire— suggesting Darwin's description of the peacock's ornamental beauty. The "mother-of-pearl bottons" and "shiny combination of silken threads," for example, clearly attract her attention, and Dreiser notes that "she was used to Drouet's appearance" (73). Hurstwood too is susceptible to what he sees in Carrie because of "the ancient attraction of the fresh" (79)—or, as Dreiser would term it in his later analyses of desire, the appeal of fresh varieties. But in *Sister Carrie*, Dreiser's first exploration of female choice, it is notable that in presenting the intellectual and vaguely disembodied Ames as the distant ideal, he acknowledges but muffles both Darwin's emphasis on the male's beauty and the male's involvement in "the law of battle" for possession of the female. Only in his last paragraphs does he refer to what Carrie had once perceived as Hurstwood's "original beauty and glory" and then only to make his point that she had now surpassed that stage in her evolution: "he could not have allured her" now (369).

As for the law of battle, it seems that Dreiser shares Howells's and other American realists' inclination to distance themselves from this most disagreeable of the male's roles in sexual selection—as Howells softens the fight between Bartley Hubbard and Henry Bird in *A Modern Instance*.[4] In Dreiser's version, as Carrie and the two men are engaged in conversation one night, "it was driven into Carrie's mind that here [in response to Hurstwood's entertaining talk] was the superior man. She instinctively felt that he was stronger and higher" and that Drouet was "defective." Poor Drouet "was not in the least aware that a battle had been fought" and that Carrie was "being wrested from him" (82–83). Still for all his superior qualities Hurstwood is never able to arouse what Dreiser calls "true" (211) or "great love" in Carrie (219). She apparently finds him acceptable, but once she meets the ideal male, Ames, she is immediately repulsed by Hurstwood—and with not even a hint of battle between the two males. Returning home after meeting Ames, she discovers that Hurstwood "was already in bed. His clothes were scattered loosely about," and she "retreated. . . . It was disagreeable to her" (238). The significance of this crucial moment in her life, as Dreiser emphasizes in closing the scene, is that it offers the promise of evolutionary progress: "Through a fog of longing and conflicting desires she was beginning to see. . . . She was . . . beginning to see" (238).

Writing that the "mental effect" of her meeting with Ames would never leave entirely, and that now "she had an ideal to contrast men by" (239), Dreiser at once undertakes to dispense with this inferior male (Hurstwood), as well. This is a familiar problem for the novelist wishing to project evolutionary progress through the vehicle of sexual selection and female choice, as Howells had finally killed off Bartley Hubbard in *A Modern Instance*, and Jack London would destroy Wolf Larsen with a terrible headache in *The Sea-Wolf*. Informing us that, suddenly, Hurstwood is over the hill, Dreiser explains that if a man is not "growing stronger, healthier, wiser," he begins "sagging to the grave side" (239).[5] Hurstwood took "the road downward," but the fatal blow to Hurstwood comes when Carrie experiences what Darwin would call antipathy for a particular male and refuses to sleep with him (244).[6] After the third night of her sleeping apart from him, once with the apology "I have a headache," Hurstwood felt the "grim blow" (261).

This power to act on her antipathy for a particular male and her rather successful career in the theater are all Dreiser will allow Carrie before the ambiguous ending, when he leaves her alone, rocking, dreaming, longing. Even before she hears the "the old call of the ideal . . . sounding" again in a subsequent meeting with Ames, she ignores the many offers from other men who are attracted by her notoriety (354). To allow her to be with Ames would be to deny the evolutionary principle that Dreiser preached himself and that he arranges for Ames to impart in his last words to Carrie: "'If I were you,' he said, 'I'd change'" (357). Ostensibly, he is referring to a change from comic to serious plays, but there is no mistaking the echo Dreiser sounded later in the opening sentence to his essay "Change": "If I were to preach any doctrine to the world it would be love of change, or at least lack of fear of it" (*Rub-A-Dub* 19). Nor is there any mistaking that he sees this as an absolute principle of evolution, for he calls on his readers to observe "the phenomena of geology and of biology," which show "how ready Nature is to quit one form of effort for another, once its uselessness has become apparent" (20). Dreiser's corollary is that desire, the lure of beauty, leads to change and, in the long run of evolution, change for the better: evolutionary progress. But of course this does not mean that, despite their desires, unfortunates like Drouet and Hurstwood will not be left behind. Even Carrie, who "practice[s] her evolutions" and makes her way beyond Drouet and Hurstwood to success in the theater world—even Carrie cannot achieve the ultimate evolutionary goal that Dreiser envisions (281). No one can, for as Dreiser suggests in his poem, "Protoplast," it is an elemental condition of life that one should seek "in mortal flesh, / A substance that is not flesh . . . / something that is eternal, / But will not rest / Or stay / In any form" (*Moods Philosophic and Emotional* 149–50).

It is important to keep in mind that while Dreiser's evolutionary optimism in *Sister Carrie* seems gray and disheartening as Carrie sits rocking and longing at her window, there *is* a window and Ames provides a sense of direction. But the abstract beauty of Ames's "very bright mind" so developed "in electrical knowledge" (237) and his marked lack of sexual passion (Carrie's "mind halted" at the "strong, clean vision" of Ames [293]) will disappear in *The "Genius"* and "The Trilogy of Desire." There, no less certain that even the unseemly elements in his characters' lives are contained in "some greater thing," an ultimately beneficent "Nature Herself," Dreiser will assert the value of simply promiscuous sexual desire or lust. His story of Carrie's awakening is oddly much more optimistic in addressing the question of man's place in nature and much more reserved in its portrayal of the female's sexual desire than was the story of Edna Pontellier that Kate Chopin published the year before. Both novels focus on the woman's sexual experience and her gradual awakening to the evolutionary reality. There are many more "awakenings" in Chopin's novel than in *Sister Carrie,* but the theme is unmistakable in Dreiser's novel when he writes, for example, that "awakening in her mind" was the sense of a "possible defect in herself," and then, "instinctively," a "desire to imitate" other women's better dress (76). Dreiser's key in this theme is in the title to chapter 37, "The Spirit Awakens: New Search for the Gate," and in his remark at the end that the oddly disembodied "Ames had pointed out a farther step" (369). By contrast, Chopin's key is in the idea that the Darwinian theorist in her novel (Dr. Mandelet) expresses when he sees Edna as a "beautiful, sleek animal waking up in the sun": realizing that she has taken a lover, he consoles her by speaking of Nature's "decoy to secure mothers for the race" (chaps. 23, 37).

While Chopin's meditation centers on the meaning of motherhood and the significance sexual desire, Dreiser's is unconcerned with these issues. Rather, when

Carrie practices "her evolutions" (281), once by posing before a mirror, Dreiser explains that *this* is the "outworking of desire to reproduce life" and that it is "the basis of all dramatic art" (117). Carrie does express her sexual antipathy for Hurstwood, as Edna does for her husband, but she never expresses anything like Edna's explicit erotic desire for Robert and Arobin. Moreover, these differences are brought into perspective in the authors' presentations of music's role in courtship and in their imagery of wings. Both Dreiser and Chopin develop Darwin's analysis of how music functions in courtship as among animals and our "half-human ancestors" who used it to arouse "each other's ardent passions" (*The Descent of Man* 2:337). It certainly functions this way in *The Awakening* and later in Dreiser's career, as in *The Financier*. In chapter 9 of *The Awakening* the music "sent a keen tremor down Mrs. Pontellier's spinal column"; and in Cowperwood's seduction of Aileen, Dreiser records that, when the two were dancing to "lovely music," "suddenly, as the music drew to its close," Cowperwood asked, "You like me?" Writing that Aileen "thrilled from head to toe at the question" and that "a piece of ice dropped down her back could not have startled her more"(*Financier* 238–39), Dreiser, like Chopin, echoes Darwin's observation that a "thrill or slight shiver . . . runs down the backbone and limbs of many persons when they are powerfully affected by music" (*Expression of the Emotions* 217). However, in his first effort to dramatize this sexual reality, in *Sister Carrie* Dreiser clearly aims to acknowledge the sexual power of music but then, emphatically, to sublimate it. The first words Dreiser gives us from Hurstwood on the night he meets Carrie at her home with Drouet are, "You ought to have a piano here" (72). Soon, Dreiser tells us, "Carrie was affected by music," and "certain wistful chords . . . awoke longings for those things which she did not have" (77). And when she and Ames listen to music together in their last meeting, Carrie is "touched by [a] feeling" that "reached her through the heart." Though *she* cannot say what it is about music or describe "the inexplicable longings which surged within her," Ames explains, "I know how you feel," and he counsels her not to worry "over the far-off things" (355).[7]

In the concluding scenes from these two meditations on sexual selection and the meaning of sexual desire, then, the authors' different views are clear. Before Edna drowns herself Chopin causes her to see "a bird with a broken wing . . . beating the air above, reeling, fluttering, circling disabled down, down to the water." But Dreiser addresses his reader with these words: "Ever hearkening to the sound of beauty, straining for the flash of its distant wings, [man] watches to follow, wearying his feet in traveling. So watched Carrie, so followed, rocking and singing" (368). Compared with Chopin's portrait of Edna, then, Dreiser's portrait of Carrie seems quite romantically distanced from his heroine's sexual nature. His subsequent analyses of the male's sexual nature are in a different key.

"A Real Man—A Financier"

> "The male shall seek the female."
> —*The Descent of Man*

Eleven years after he published *Sister Carrie* and immediately after finishing his frustrating lengthy work on *Jennie Gerhardt*, Dreiser began to focus on the male's sexual reality in the autobiographical *The "Genius"* and then in the "trilogy of desire" about Frank Cowperwood. Now, instead of emphasizing the element of female choice, his subject was the male's desire, the essential sexual passion as Darwin defined it in *The Descent of Man*. No doubt emboldened in part by the growing frank discussion of sex in the movement that included work by Albert Moll, Richard von Krafft-Ebing, Havelock Ellis, and Freud and perhaps as part of his own self-exploration and self-justification, he depicted the male's "leaning toward promiscuity" and questioned the viability of marriage and monogamy (*The Titan* 250). The vague but promising sense of the evolutionary impulse and its sense of direction he offered through the passionless male, Ames—as Carrie's longing for distant beauty—now emerged as the specific force inherent in the male's passionate and efficient search for mates. Darwin wrote that "the largest number of vigorous offspring will be reared from the pairing of the strongest and best-armed males, which have conquered other males, with the most vigorous and best nourished females, which are the first to breed in the spring"; and that in compliance with "the law . . . that the male small seek the female," males have necessarily become "efficient seekers" (*The Descent of Man* 1:271–74). Moreover, according to Darwin's compelling logic, "in order that [the males] should become efficient seekers, they would have to be endowed with strong passions. The acquirement of such passions would naturally follow from the more eager males leaving a larger number of offspring than the less eager" (1:274). For these reasons, Dreiser underscores his hero's procreative power in *The Financier* by remarking that "a real man—a financier . . . created" (85), just as he echoes Darwin's definition of the male as an "efficient seeker": Cowperwood's "mind . . . was tinged by a great seeking" (287).[8]

Readers familiar with the stories of Eugene Witla (in *The "Genius"*) and Frank Cowperwood might see nothing noteworthy in this observation about these characters' passionate seeking. Of course these characters have frequent sexual affairs and express their discomfort within the institution of marriage. Witla knew "the generally accepted interpretation of [monogamous] marriage, but it did not appeal to him" (*The "Genius"* 198). Similarly, Cowperwood refuses to believe that "a man was entitled to only one wife" (*Financier* 148) or, later in the trilogy, thinks himself "too passionate, too radiant, too individual and complex to belong to any one single individual alone" (*The Titan* 250). But even readers familiar with Dreiser's emphasis on the polygamous male will find it worthwhile to consider how this theme is often mis-interpreted by Dreiserians and how Dreiser's view of the polygamous male (particu-larly the financier) compares with other such views in American literary history.

Dreiserians tend to confuse matters when they fail to see that his "two principal kinds of human desire, the sexual and the aesthetic," are essentially *one* or when they imagine, for example, "that the Cowperwood trilogy breaks down awkwardly into the subject matters of finance and love," that Dreiser fails to explain "Cowper-wood's nature because . . . his . . . financial dealings . . . [lead] us to assume that his sexual activities and art collecting are not a quest for beauty but are rather further examples of his desire for possession and power" (Pizer, *Novels of Dreiser*, 24, 170). This approach to Dreiser mistakes what he meant by the "power of beauty" and the "terror of beauty" (*The "Genius"* 578). Beauty and power are unified in Dreiser's imagi-nation as essential traits of the single entity he called the "life force," "the creative force," or "God." The logic of Dreiser's formulation becomes clearer if we compare it with key ideas from the work of two theorists Dreiser held in highest esteem, Dar-win and Haeckel. First, as Darwin explained, power and beauty are essential ele-ments of sexual selection and therefore in the development of the human mind:

Courage, pugnacity, perseverance, strength and size of body, weapons of all kinds, musical organs, both vocal and instrumental, bright colours, stripes and marks, and ornamental appendages, have all been indirectly gained by the one sex or the other, through the influence of love and jealousy, through the appreciation of the beautiful in sound, colour or form, and through the exertion of a choice; and these powers of the mind manifestly depend on the development of the cerebral system. (*The Descent of Man* 2: 402)

Almost thirty years after Darwin's analysis of strength and beauty, during the years when Dreiser was projecting his vision of an evolutionary distant beauty in *Sister Carrie* and Norris was projecting his vision of transcendent, altruistic love in *The Octopus*, Haeckel moved beyond the connection between beauty and sexual choice to speculate on the relationship between a more generalized biological beauty and what he called "our monistic religion." Noting that "the remarkable expansion of our knowledge of nature, and the discovery of countless beautiful forms of life . . . have awakened quite a new aesthetic sense in our generation, and thus given a new tone to painting and sculpture," Haeckel asserts that

the nineteenth century has not only opened our eyes to the aesthetic enjoy-ment of the microscopic world; it has shown us the beauty of the greater objects in nature. . . . All this progress in the aesthetic enjoyment of nature—and, proportionately, in the scientific understanding of nature—implies an equal advance in higher mental development and, consequently, in the direction or our monistic religion. (*Riddle of the Universe* 341–42)

A comparison of these remarks by Darwin and Haeckel with Dreiser's thoughts on strength and beauty clarifies our sense of his relationship to scientific developments during these years of the eclipse of Darwinism. First, it is notable that Dreiser shared Haeckel's post-Darwinian interest in chemistry and microscopic life. Reader's familiar with Dreiser's remarks on microscopic life and sea life or his *Notes on Life* will sense the similarity, and it is clear that Dreiser's theme of the "incomprehensible chemistry which we call *life* and personality" (*Financier* 360) is related to the insights about biochemistry (and later, tropism) that he gained from his relationships with the physiological psychologists Elmer Gates and Jacques Loeb. But the important point here is that Dreiser's meditation on biological beauty, aesthetics, and mental development is firmly rooted in his Darwinian analysis of the male's strength and passion. Thus, in the passage from *The Financier* in which he remarks on the tinge of "great seeking" in Cowperwood's mind, Dreiser continues:

Wealth, in the beginning, had seemed the only goal, to which was shortly added the beauty of women. And now art, for art's sake—the first faint radiance of a rosy dawn—had begun to shine in upon him, and to the beauty of womanhood he was beginning to see how necessary it was to add the beauty of life—the beauty of material background—how, in fact, the only background for great beauty was great art. This girl, this Aileen Butler, her raw youth and radiance, was nevertheless creating in him a sense of the distinguished, and a need for it which had never existed in him before to the same degree. It is impossible to define these subtleties of reaction, temperament on temperament, for no one knows to what degree we are marked by the things which attract us. A love affair such as this had proved to be was quite as a drop of coloring added to a glass of clear water, or a foreign chemical agent introduced into a delicate chemical formula. (287)

As for the significance of Dreiser's emphasis on the financier's sexual passion in American literary history and in the history of our culture's response to Darwin's theory of sexual selection, it is important to remember that Dreiser did not invent the powerful financier as an American character. Indeed, Cowperwood is a descendant of the two earlier financiers portrayed by Harold Frederic and Frank Norris, whose work Dreiser knew and admired. Each of these financiers, Frederic's Stormont Thorpe in *The Market-Place* (1899) and Norris's Curtis Jadwin in *The Pit* (1903), wields great sexual power, and each knows instinctively how to prevail by mastering what Darwin called "the language of the emotions" (*Expression of the Emotions* 366). Frederic was

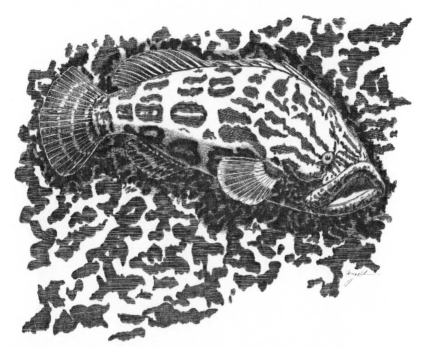

Marine Biology. One of many writers to draw on marine biology, Dreiser compared his hero in *The Financier* with a black grouper, Mycteroperca Bonaci, whose remarkable ability to adapt itself to conditions includes its power of simulation and power to deceive its prey by mimicking its environment.

more adept than either Norris or Dreiser at tracing his character's skill in reading his adversaries' emotions and concealing his own, but these successive psychological studies illustrate the way that, for American writers, Freudian psychology began to emerge from Darwinian theory.[9] Although Frederic conducts a very impressive study of Thorpe's mastery in the language of emotions, he does not develop a sense of his hero's unconscious repression or his conscious power to repress his sexual impulses.

By comparison, Norris emphasizes Jadwin's tight-fisted control or repression of his emotions, to the point that his sexual desire seems almost erased. Dreiser, however, was attuned to the popular Freudianism that was then emerging. Thus he is freer than the earlier writers to explore his hero's polygamous desire and even to affirm his hero's desire to satisfy himself with a great variety of women. Moreover, he explicitly affirms Cowperwood's strategic concealment of his sexual (and financial) affairs by comparing him with the Black Grouper, whose biological adaptation, its mottled markings and ability to change color, exemplify the "power to deceive" that is a part "of the constructive genius of nature" (*Financier* 778). The Black Grouper's facility in capturing "victim[s] of its beauty" is for Dreiser a compelling feature of "the creative power."[10]

Frederic's character Thorpe has no serious sexual rivals nor any pronounced interest in possessing other women, and his sexual appeal is mainly "the frank barbarism of power" (338) that can turn his wife's "brain to a sort of porridge" (162). In both Thorpe and Jadwin the male's powerful hands are repeatedly imaged as an essential feature of his sexual nature. Dreiser includes this feature in his portrait but for two interesting reasons gives it much less emphasis. In his first notable sexual conquest as a young man, with Mrs. Semple, Cowperwood impresses her with his "handsome body" and "his hands not large, but sinewy and strong" (*Financier* 98). True to Darwin's theory, "he caught her," "recaptured her," told her, "I'll take you down," and in this way made her realize "that she had never really lived before" (100–101). Other women in later episodes respond to "those strong hands" (*Titan* 120). But it is noteworthy that in Dreiser's effort to celebrate the unrestrained virile power, at a time when sexual repression was beginning to be perceived as a greater threat to personal and social health than sexual freedom, he uses the image of powerful-handed male brutality most emphatically to depict the enraged Puritan father, Edward Butler, who is determined to *restrain* his daughter's sexual life. Without suggesting that Butler is motivated by a Freudian desire for his own daughter, Dreiser underscores Butler's twisted fascination with sexual guilt, suggesting that this fixation is related to his work as a sewer contractor and that his brutal, prehensile power is a perversion of his own sexual nature. Butler closes his "big fist forcefully" (499), persists in "brutalizing" his daughter by hiring a spy and "hunting her down" (506), and puts out "a big, brown, horny hand" to restrain her (531). Dreiser's point about the brutal father is that "he did not know what love was" (533).

While both of Cowperwood's literary antecedents wield the male's prehensile power, neither exhibits anything that would pass in Dreiser's day as libidinous desire or a sexual appetite for other women. And another important distinction between these three portraits of the American financier arises from the authors' different views on evolutionary progress. Frederic is quite cynical about Thorpe's raw power and refuses to suggest that it will lead to evolutionary progress. Thorpe neither enjoys reproductive success nor shows any signs of developing a moral sense. However, Norris suggests that Jadwin's repressed sexual power makes him a fit companion for the ideal woman who had nearly succumbed to the sexual advances of another man. He then sends this chastened couple toward an evolutionary future whose glimmering promise arises as much from their victory over sex as from Jadwin's having left the financial pit. Unlike Frederic or Norris, then, Dreiser supports the male's polygamous seeking for more and more varieties of beautiful, young, strong women. He rewards Cowperwood's passionate seeking by giving him more and more women and by offering the ultimate evolutionary prize: offspring. Although Dreiser does not allow his hero to father many children with many different women, he does make it clear, unlike either Frederic or Norris, that in Cowperwood's first sexual conquest (of Mrs. Semple), "he wanted her physically and he felt a keen preliminary interest in the children they would have" (97). In this way Dreiser's trilogy of desire is a prolonged effort to affirm the vital but dark creative power that he saw in the male's "seeking." Comparing this force in nature with that embodied in the Black Grouper's "very remarkable ability to adapt itself to conditions," Dreiser suggests that evolutionary progress consists mainly in the organism's power to adapt. However, quite unlike Norris, Dreiser insists that this "constructive genius of nature . . . is not beatific" (*Financier* 778). In a later essay called "The American Financier" he even acknowledged what he called "the pathology of the genus financier," but he claimed that "it is a highly specialized machine for the accomplishment of some end which Nature has in view" (*Rub-A-Dub* 74).

Aside from his speculations on the question of evolutionary progress, though, Dreiser produced a narrative of the financier's life that develops through a number of Darwinian incidents in the drama of sexual selection. This is evident, for example, in the chapter, "Man and Superman," in *The Titan*, where his reference to Shaw's play and theme that women are the sexual hunters serves to refute that theme by dramatizing a Darwinian scene of the law of battle among males for possession of the female. Here, brazenly and with a peculiar kind of honor, Cowperwood overpowers the weakling Sohlberg in a contest for his wife, Rita, by challenging the husband to a duel and by displaying a "hand that . . . was hard and firm" (164). Similarly, there are many scenes of courtship by means of music and dance, others in which Cowperwood masters situations by concealing his emotions, and scenes of female choice. In the last chapters of *The Titan*, for example, the scenes of female choice are designed to prove that a young woman prefers Cowperwood for his mature power and financial genius rather than a charming young naval officer who is, paradoxically, "almost more of a battle-ship than he is a man" (*The Titan* 444). Thus the young woman does not select the handsome young lieutenant, for he is "in the tradition of American romance," as Dreiser puts it, that is, he lacks the appeal of Cowperwood who, despite his age, is "a real man" (460). Quite possibly as well, Dreiser's interest in dramatizing this reversal of the Darwinian expectation is related to his own well-known sexual vitality in his early forties. Knowing that such an outcome might provoke the reader's disbelief, he grants that it is part of "this queer, paradoxical, impossible world" (460), but as though to cover his bet, he arranges for yet another force in the Darwinian universe to assist the older man in his unlikely sexual conquest. There is an embarrassing incident that seems likely to "scare the Lieutenant away" from the young woman, and Cowperwood quickly sees the incident as "a fine windfall of chance" for himself (*The Titan* 455–56).[11]

Even over the next several years—between the time he published *The Titan* in 1914, met Abraham Brill in 1918, and then published "Neurotic America and the Sex Impulse" in 1920—Dreiser retained his sense that the sex question had originated in

Darwin's theory of sexual selection: that "Freud's theory of mind" had emerged "with the rising tide of Darwinism" (Sulloway 497). His theme in "Neurotic America" is that the whole American temperament is neurotic in its denial of "the biologic force" and the fact that "sex is the keynote to existence" (*Rub-A-Dub* 140). In another essay in the same volume he traces this issue to its source, as Darwin had asserted, to "the progenitor of the human race" who was capable of androgynous reproduction before the evolution of sexual difference (222). No matter whether the nation refused to be "enlightened" by such "eminent investigators as Krafft-Ebing, Ellis, [and] Freud," he argued, five years before the Scopes trial, "the sex impulse" would not be suppressed and would proceed pretty much as Darwin had explained it in *The Descent of Man*. Though Dreiser does not mention Darwin's name in this piece, his references to essential elements of sexual selection are unmistakable in his assertion that, sexually, human beings are "as avid and seeking as ever" (130), that love or lust "moves the seeker in every field of effort" (134), that this impulse acts by means of "every possible detail of ornamentation, comfort, and color" (135), and, underscoring his theme in the trilogy of desire, that, as "the bull seal still conquers his fifty or a hundred, and the weakling none"—neither is "man . . . temperamentally or chemically a monogamous animal" (137–38).

Notes

1. It makes much more sense to see the transcendental tendency in Norris and Dreiser, for example, in relation to developments within late-nineteenth-century evolutionary thought, itself, rather than in relation to the American Transcendentalists. Norris's famous teacher, Joseph Le Conte, for example, owed little if anything to Emerson but shared the desire of many other evolutionists to argue the compatibility of Darwinism with Christianity. In *The Eclipse of Darwinism: Anti-Darwinian Evolution Theories in the Decades around 1900*, Peter J. Bowler discusses Le Conte's role (and others, including Henri Bergson) who joined in a widespread resistance to the theory of natural selection.

2. Although Moers notes that by November 1896 Dreiser "could paraphrase enough of Darwin on sexual selection to show that he had been through *The Descent of Man*," she leaves the point undeveloped and never mentions *The Expression of the Emotions in Man and Animals* (141), and while in his first sentence Zanine notes that Dreiser "was born in 1871, the year that Darwin published *The Descent of Man*," he has nothing to say of either sexual selection or the expression of emotions (1).

3. The distinction between proximate and evolutionary causes is important in other areas of present day evolutionary biology, as in evolutionary psychology or Darwinian medicine. In *Why We Get Sick: The New Science of Darwinian Medicine*, for example, Randolph M. Nesse and George C. Williams write:

When proximate and evolutionary causes are carefully distinguished, many questions in biology make more sense. A proximate explanation describes a trait—its anatomy, physiology, and biochemistry, as well as its development from the genetic instructions provided by a bit of DNA in the fertilized egg to the adult individual. An evolutionary explanation is about why the DNA specifies the trait in the first place and why we have DNA that encodes for one kind of structure and not some other. . . . Proximate explanations answer "what?" and "how?" questions about structure and mechanism; evolutionary explanations answer "why?" questions about origins and functions. (6–7)

See also Henry Plotkin, *Evolution in Mind: An Introduction to Evolutionary Psychology*, 5–18, for example, and his discussion of causality wherein he uses the terms "proximate cause" and "historical cause" or "historical antecedence."

4. For a discussion of this scene from *A Modern Instance*, see my *The Descent of Love* (99–100).

5. Recounting the stages in life from infancy to old age, Haeckel summarizes his point that "Man's psychic life runs the same evolution—upward progress, full maturity, and downward degeneration—as every other vital activity in his organization" (147). For another example of how Dreiser views this kind of sudden decline in the context of love and courtship, consider his short poem, "The Courting": "Chemistry and mystery. / The Call of mood to mood, / of blood to blood. / Slang phrases and flares of poetry, / Silences that are simple and meaningless, / Silences that are crises. / An arm about a shoulder, a waist, a breast, / Taut nerves, / Tight breath, / Taut muscles. / And the beauty of youth discovered as passing. / And the beauty of life discovered as passing. / And the dread of the weariness of life without love. / And the dread of youth without love. / And kisses, kisses, kisses,—/ All the beauty of life discovered / At the edge of its decay" (*Moods Philosophic and Emotional* 271).

6. See Darwin's discussion of the female's preference for and antipathy toward particular males (*The Descent of Man* 2:113–24). For Kate Chopin's interest in this passage and idea, see my *The Descent of Love* 226–27.

7. For another of Dreiser's many remarks on music in this context, see his poem, "Music," in which he writes, "Of desire, yea, you [music] are the meaning" (*Moods Philosophic and Emotional* 317).

8. Dreiser frequently comments on the male's "seeking" in his nonfiction as well. In "A Counsel to Perfection," for example, he writes in biological terms of scientists' and philosophers' "seeking to wrest" from nature solutions to such problems as even "the secret of eternal life," and he advises all people to "accept as true the fabled statement made by 'God' in Genesis iii.14:19, and seek persistently and without too much reverence for some method of solving his own difficulties" (*Rub-A-Dub* 124). Similarly, in "Neurotic America and the Sex Impulse," he writes that love or lust "moves the seeker in every field of effort" and that, despite America's sexual anxiety, "the world apparently, or that part of it expressed by, in or through the sexes, is as avid and seeking as ever" (134, 130). Dreiser's poetry on love also reflects this sense, as in "Search Song" or "Protoplast"; in the latter, he writes: "My error consists, / If at all, / In seeking in mortal flesh / The likeness / Of what / Perhaps / Is Eternal" (*Moods Philosophic and Emotional* 371, 149).

9. For a discussion of Frederic's careful dramatization of Darwin's theory of the expression of the emotions, see *The Descent of Love* 274–85.

10. See also Dreiser's later essay on this theme, "Secrecy—Its Value"; this essay follows "Neurotic America and the Sex Impulse" in *Hey Rub-A-Dub-Dub*.

11. Here, like Howells in *A Chance Acquaintance* and *The World of Chance*, Dreiser suggests that the role of chance in Darwinian evolution (as in chance variation or shifts in environmental conditions) serves almost as a cosmic marriage broker. For a discussion of chance and of Howells's *Chance Acquaintance*, see my *The Descent of Love* 4, 18, 60.

5 "The Varieties of Human Experience"

*Sexual Intimacy, Heredity, and Emotional Conflict
in Gertrude Stein's Early Work*

> Her deepest interest was in the varieties of human experience and her con-
> stant desire was to partake of all human relations but by some quality of her
> nature she never succeeded in really touching any human creature she knew.
> —Gertrude Stein, *Fernhurst*

Gertrude Stein's well-known relationship with William James at Harvard and her subsequent formal studies in medicine at Johns Hopkins required that she be quite familiar with Darwinian thought. James, her mentor, fully acknowledged the Darwinian
foundations of his *Principles of Psychology*. In her later years Stein paid repeated tributes to Darwin's role in shaping her early work. On giving a copy of *The Descent of
Man* to Louis Bromfield (in 1937), she remarked on how near Darwin "had been when
[she] began knowing everything" (*Everybody's Autobiography* 242), and the following
year she wrote to another friend, "I still think Darwin the great man of the period
that [framed] my youth" (qtd. in Wineapple 61).[1] Her interest in evolution, in general, is widely noted, but this chapter offers a closer examination of her Darwinian
interests in order to illuminate her relationship to other writers of her time. In her
own short-lived career in psychology and in her subsequent occupation as a writer
Stein certainly knew that no study of psychology and sex could begin without a theory
of the evolution of human nature. Something of the relationship between William
James and Stein on this issue, for example, is suggested in his subtitle to *The Varieties
of Religious Experience* (*A Study in Human Nature*) and his prefatory remark that he
had originally thought of his projected lectures under the title "Man's Religious Appetites." Beginning with a discussion of religion and neurology, James was "inevitably . . . led" to conclude from "the merely biological point of view" that religion per-
forms an essential organic function, and because "creeds and faith-state" have such

an "extraordinary influence upon action and endurance" (49), felt "obliged . . . to class them amongst the most important biological functions of mankind" (399).

About two years after *The Varieties of Religious Experience* appeared, Stein was writing rather autobiographically of a character in *Fernhurst* whose "deepest interest was in the varieties of human experience" but with a "constant desire . . . to partake of *all* human relations (Fernhurst, Q.E.D., *and Other Early Writings* 19; emphasis mine).[2] Exploring her characters' sexuality in this and the other narratives she produced during the two years before she began *Three Lives*, Stein followed James's lead by entering the new depths of modern psychology that he knew were opening up but which he was not himself prepared to enter. Remarking in *The Varieties* that "the most important step forward . . . in psychology" during his career was the discovery of the "subliminal" consciousness, James extolled "the wonderful explorations by Binet, Janet, Breuer, Freud" and others "of the subliminal consciousness of patients with hysteria" (190–91). But much of the difference between his approach to the new psychology as compared with Freud's, Havelock Ellis's, or Stein's is suggested in his resistance to such "ideas that float in the air of one's time" as the "re-interpretation of religion as perverted sexuality" (18).

Although earlier in *The Principles of Psychology* he pioneered the field we now refer to as evolutionary psychology by building on Darwin's theories of instincts and emotions, he found it "a little unpleasant to discuss" the details of the sexual impulse (1055). He wrote that "of all propensities, the sexual impulses bear on their face the most obvious signs of being instinctive, in the sense of blind, automatic, and untaught," but he gave greater emphasis to "what might be called the *anti-sexual instinct*, the instinct of personal isolation, the actual repulsiveness to us of the idea of intimate contact with most of the persons we meet, especially those of our own sex" (1051–52). Regarding sexuality in this way and believing that "all human social elevation is [dependent] upon the prevalence of chastity," he saw chastity as one of the key measures of "the difference between civilization and barbarism" (35).

By the time Stein published *Three Lives* (1909), of course, Havelock Ellis had issued several volumes of his *Studies in the Psychology of Sex*, Freud's *Three Essays on the Theory of Sexuality* had appeared in English translation (1905), and Freud was making his historic visit to the United States. Psychology and sexuality were newly defined in modernist terms. This is not to suggest that Stein was in complete accord with either Ellis or Freud during these years or even much later in her life. Yet she certainly offered her own unique contributions in the modern effort to describe "the bottom nature" of "every kind . . . of men and women . . . and the way it was mixed up with the other natures in them," as she explained in reference to *The Making of Americans* (*Everybody's Autobiography* 266). Her publications on motor automatism in *The Psychological Review* in 1896 and 1898 were intended to develop James's speculations about the nature of the subconscious, as that had already been studied through the lens of "automatic writing," a recent discovery by the English psychologist and aesthetician of music Edmund Gurney (*Principles of Psychology* 200–210). In his enthusiasm for this new approach to the unconscious, James saw "the beginning of an inquiry which is destined to throw a new light into the very abysses of our nature" (208). Like others at this time, James was first interested in "'unconsciousness' in hysterics" (200), and Stein and her senior coauthor Leon Solomons carried the study further by urging, "We [have underestimated] the automatic powers of the *normal* subject" ("Normal Motor Automatism" 492, emphasis mine). They suggested that the automatic acts of ordinary people might indicate the presence of a second personality or the "so-called 'subliminal consciousness'" (493). That the normal mind might be divided in this way was part of the general development in evolutionary psychology that Darwin had foretold in *The Origin of Species* and that took shape in other ways during these years, as in Ellis's and Freud's conclusion that the normal human being's bisexual nature is evident in the embryo.

The following sections describe the main themes in Stein's response to the issues of Darwinian evolution early in her career within the limited period between 1903 and 1906. During that time, beginning about two years after she gave up her studies in medicine at Johns Hopkins, she produced "The Making of Americans Being the History of a Family's Progress" (her brief first version of *The Making of Americans*), then *Q.E.D., Fernhurst,* and *Three Lives.*[3] This approach will avoid dealing with her more difficult (and many think her most significant) works, but it traces what her interpreters recognize as "the first steps of Gertrude Stein's literary progress"(Katz i) and her initial "radical . . . exploration of sexual power, both heterosexual and lesbian" (Wagner-Martin 77).

It was a confusing period in her career. She was not only under the sway of both William and Henry James but was increasingly "steeped in naturalist novels" (Wagner-Martin 77). Also, she was initiating her radical exploration of sexuality during the years when the Freudian view of sexuality was beginning to emerge, along with the related new field of sexology. Further, as she was guided in this exploratory work by her own studies in psychology and medicine, she was also exploring her own intimate relations, especially regarding her affair with May Bookstaver (the subject of *Q.E.D.*). Moreover, she was beginning her career in fiction during the period when the eclipse of Darwinism was well underway. Stein based her early explorations of life, power, and sexual intimacy on the first principles that she derived from Darwin's theories of natural and sexual selection. As Darwin could reduce these to his point about the war of nature (*The Origin of Species* 374), Stein could reduce them to the general idea that "being living" is the "struggle for existence" (*Everybody's Autobiography* 243) or, later in her life, that "to live [World War II] is just what everybody has done since animal life began and not more or less complicated than that" (*Wars I Have Seen* 68).

Heredity and Female Choice in *The Making of Americans* (1903)

When Stein began "The Making of Americans Being the History of a Family's Progress," she set out to explore not only her own family's origins and progress but also the essential processes of human evolution. At this time, the terrain of evolutionary thought was dramatically changed from what it had been when William James had first explored similar questions in "Great Men, Great Thoughts, and the Environment" in 1880. Extolling "the triumphant originality of Darwin," James built on the theories of natural and sexual selection, acknowledged that in "the lower strata of the mind" the human being reveals his common descent "with the brutes" (443), and explained that evolutionary progress derives from selective pressures within particular environments, allowing for the survival of certain "accidental outbirths of spontaneous variation in . . . the excessively unstable human brain" (456). The environment, James maintained, "chiefly adopts or rejects, preserves or destroys, in short *selects* . . . the great man" (455). After the discovery of Mendelian genetics, James would have had to revise his version of how Americans are made, allowing the hereditary element a far greater role than had appeared to be the case in 1880. And this is an essential element in Stein's story of how "the new people [are] made out of the old."[4] Stein would always agree with James's point that environment plays a key role. "After all," she wrote, "anybody is as their land and air is" (*Wars I Have Seen* 258). But in 1903 she shared the anxiety that many Americans felt (and would feel for many years, as in the case of F. Scott Fitzgerald, for example) about what Ernst Haeckel referred to as "the chain of generations" (*Riddle of the Universe* 143).[5] This is the *evolutionary* reason behind Stein's remark about her character, Julia Dehning, and her often-quoted anecdote:

> [A] large part of our family history must be a record of [Julia's] struggle to live down her mother in her.
>
> There is an old story of a man who mercilessly and in his anger drags his father along the ground through his own orchard. "Stop," groans the broken old man at last "Stop! I did not drag my father beyond this tree."
>
> It is a dreary business this living down the tempers we are born with. (*The Making of Americans* 147)

As Stein realized, the only way to free oneself from the evolutionary chains was through further evolution or progress, and one's only hope to direct such progress was through the mechanism of sexual selection. Thus remarking that "the Dehnings had always had good instincts albeit these instincts sprang from peasant . . . sources," Stein immediately focuses her story on the time that "the daughters had grown ready to be wives" (138). The family's biological problem (it is also distinctly a problem of class in Stein's story) arises when the "bourgeois mind" feels "a little of the fervor for diversity" and responds with its search for an "attractive . . . strain of singularity"—that is, not just new blood but a new genetic strain that must have itself arisen according to its own evolutionary conditions, including chance or accidental variation.

At this point in Stein's account, there is a curious but understandable shift. Perhaps because she was herself beginning to realize that she was cut off from further evolutionary progress, in the sense that she would not transmit her "type" through sexual reproduction, Stein digresses from her narrative to identify with individuals in whom the new "strain of singularity" has arisen. Remarking that "it takes time to make queer people" (it seems unlikely that Stein uses the term in the present-day sense of *gay*) and that "custom, passion and a feel for mother earth are needed to breed vital singularity in any man and alas how poor we are in all these three"—she addresses her fellow "brother singulars." Identifying with such unusual types, she offers the consolation that "we are misplaced into a generation that knows not Joseph. We flee before the disapproval of our cousins, the courageous condescension of our friends" who sometimes "walk the streets with us" and seek "comfort [in] an older world accustomed to take all manner of strange forms" (152–53).

After this digression, Stein returns to her narrative of the Dehning daughters' marriages. And in pursuing this line of evolutionary thought she was quite aware that she was working within a rather long tradition of Darwinian courtship plots in American fiction. In relation to other novelists in this tradition, the one she had most in mind, it seems, was Henry James. She does not refer to him directly, as she does in other works from this period,[6] but the way she deals with the older daughter Julia's choice of suitors recalls James's treatment of that theme in *Washington Square*. James's approach to the principle of female choice in this and several other novels is essentially to deny it, following Darwin's and the evolutionary anthropologists' suggestion that the female lost much of her power to select when civilization originated with the capture of wives. In *Washington Square* James arranges for a nearly villainous father to prevent his daughter from foolishly marrying the beautiful young man she has selected, then he proves the paternal wisdom by verifying the father's suspicions that the suitor was only interested in the family fortune. Stein's approach is to bring a much kinder father and the daughter (Julia) into conflict on this issue, to show Julia's "struggle [successfully] . . . to bring her father to a slow consent," to reveal the suitor's (Hersland) true financial motives, and then to leave Julia trapped in what is bound to be a miserable marriage. No less critical than James was of the heroine's capacity to choose wisely, Stein writes that in the "ecstasy of loving and love, the intensity of feeling in the ardent young," it was not "with sober reason that [she] should judge of men" (159). Having proved herself to be too "strong in the passion of her eager young imagining" (159), Julia found finally that "she had to marry him and so she had to think it so [that "it was all as it had a little sounded good and best"] and she would think it so and did" (168).

Along the way, in describing Julia's courtship, Stein digresses again, this time in order to address young men, in general, who are involved in courtship. Her theme is that after the marriage further struggle is inevitable as the woman's family seeks to make the newcomer submit to their own traditions. "Young man if you are not of the strong of this earth beware," she advises, and addressing the "attractive and weak brother" she warns him "doubly" that in "the close life of the marriage" he will be doomed to unending "woe and loathsome sadness," for his wife will demand "power and support" (161–62). As she turns then to the remaining marriage, of Bertha Dehning, Stein reiterates another aspect of the ways in which strength and power determine, quite dismally, both the end of the courtship plot and the suffocating unhappiness of marriage. Her "astonishingly conventional" moral in Julia's case is that passionate women have mainly themselves to blame, for they "afflict their world with agitation, excitement and unrest," but she offers even less hope for "the other women [like Bertha], who know not passion" (169).[7] The passionate might know the discomfort of "the stomach overloaded," but Stein compares the passionless woman to "the empty stomach [that] can only weaken sadden and grow more helpless" (170). In either case the woman seems doomed to unhappy marriage. Without passion, then, Bertha concurs with her family's negative judgment and rejects her attractive and gentle lover because he has consumption. Now once again she is a "wealthy marriageable girl," but "the lover who came next had an easy, quick success." He is "the handsomest and biggest man in the most imposing bourgeois family in their set," a family named Lohms (no doubt suggesting *loam*), who "always filled rooms very full" and "blotted out all others with their solid solemn weight" (172). Stein treats this courtship so sketchily that it is impossible to tell whether Bertha actually used the female's power to select. She seems to suggest that, rather like James's Isabel Archer, Bertha chose foolishly and then fell into the trap of a deadly marriage.

Q.E.D.: The Howling Wolves of Love

In *Q.E.D.* Stein set aside the problem of female choice in heterosexual marriage, exploring instead her own sexual nature in the aftermath of her affair with May Bookstaver. It was for many reasons unpublishable at the time, and when it appeared in 1950 readers like Edmund Wilson concluded from it that the increasing vagueness and opaqueness in her work after about 1910 was due largely to the fact that the standards of the era had prevented her from writing openly about her lesbianism. Wilson credits Havelock Ellis's *Studies in the Psychology of Sex* for having helped "clear the air," and notes that while Stein's novel does not have much in common with Ellis's case histories, it does bring "us back to the brilliant young woman who . . . took psychology from William James" and "went through . . . five years of medical school at Johns Hopkins" (Hoffman, *Critical Essays*, 85–86).

She wrote the book at age twenty-nine, recreating the crucial period in her own life in terms that she explained a year or two later in reference to characters in *Fernhurst*:

> It happens often in the twenty-ninth year of a life that all the forces that have been engaged through the years of childhood, adolescence and youth in confused and ferocious combat range themselves in ordered ranks—one is uncertain of one's aims, meaning and power during these years of tumultuous growth when aspiration has no relation to fulfillment and one plunges here and there with energy and misdirection during the storm and stress of the making of a personality until at last we reach the twenty-ninth year the straight and narrow gate-way of maturity and life which was all uproar and confusion narrows down to form and purpose and we exchange a great dim possibility for a small hard reality. (*Fernhurst* 29)

Stein had sounded similar notes of "ferocious combat," "uproar and confusion," and the "storm and stress of the making of a personality" in her epigraph to *Q.E.D.*—the lines from *As You Like It* that begin, "Tell . . . what 'tis to love" and end: "'tis like the howling of Irish wolves against the moon."

The "small hard reality" in *Q.E.D.* (which means "that which was to be demonstrated," in mathematical terms, and here the main character's final recognition of "things as they are") is the result of the novel's conflict in the triangular affair between the couple Mabel and Helen and the third, autobiographical character, Adele. The hard reality is chillingly reflected in Stein's extensive use of war imagery, her interest in power, dominance, and submission, and her description of how Mabel wields her financial power to prevail in the struggle with Adele for possession of Helen. But if the novel's first principle is that love, as part of the struggle for existence, is essentially combat, its focus is on (1) the complex psychological struggle within Adele as she contends with her "moral sense," her desire for and yet "puritanic horror" of physical passion, and (2) the equally complicated struggle between Adele and Helen as they express or conceal their emotions. Thus the lovers demonstrate Stein's point that although "Adele had learned to love and Helen to trust . . . there was no real peace between them" (*Writings, 1903–1932*, 48).[8] Despite the truth of Edmund Wilson's observation about the prohibitive standards of 1903 regarding lesbian relationships, Stein writes that "to Adele's consciousness" there was "no obligation to conceal this relationship from her friends"; she is interested rather in "the undefined reason" that caused Adele and Helen to conceal their feelings from each other—"the convention of secrecy that governed their relations" (18–19).

Adele enters the novel in a state of evolutionary innocence, much like other fictional characters from this period who go on to encounter the complexities of their sexual natures such as Kate Chopin's Edna Pontellier in *The Awakening* or Jack London's Martin Eden. Exhibiting "the freedom of movement and the simple instinct for comfort that suggested a land of laziness and sunshine" (reflecting Stein's interest in the environmental influence of her experience in California and Baltimore), Adele "nestled close to the bare boards" of the ship's deck "as if accustomed to make the hard earth soft by loving it." With wriggling movements that serve "to adapt her large curves" to the hard deck, she murmurs "How good it is in the sun" (5). From her nest she engages in a discussion with Mabel and Helen, expressing her belief that the human's duty "consists in being reasonable and just," and objecting to her friends' opinion "that to be the mother of children is to be low."

Stein quickly reveals that Adele is not quite as naive as her initial portrait suggests. When Mabel tires of the discussion and gets up to leave, complaining that "the jar of that screw [ostensibly the ship's propeller] is unbearable," Adele says impatiently, "I always thank God I wasn't born a woman" (6). Then, confessing her discomfort with "the immensity of the ocean," and by extension, it seems, with the life that had originated there, she describes the intolerable confinement she feels on the ocean, which "offers no escape from the knowledge of the limits of your prison" (7). Like *screw* in this context, these remarks represent what Stein had come to understand of the very bottom nature of life as a result of her extensive studies in biology, particularly those at the Woods Hole Marine Biological Laboratory in 1897. With this essentially Darwinian insight, Adele has come to affirm Darwin's further point that evolution's highest product is the human being's moral sense, and, accordingly, to advocate the middle-class "ideal of affectionate family life [and] honorable business methods." One of her cardinal points is the need to "avoid excitements and cultivate serenity," and when Helen exclaims that this would mean cutting out passion, Stein brings her preliminary materials to bear on the novel's problem for solution (in the sense of Q.E.D.). Adele explains that she knows only two varieties of passion: what she called "affectionate comradeship" and a more intimate kind of "physical passion," which she regards with "an almost puritanic horror." Stein finishes setting up her problem by having Helen accuse Adele of leading a life "unlived . . . foolishly happy and content," thus eliciting Adele's response that she would welcome "an efficient teacher" (8).

Now the novel rather quickly traces the stages in Adele's experience as an affectionate relation gradually grows between her and Helen, leading to the point that Adele "suddenly awakened out of her long emotional apathy" (9) and soon realized further that "her moral sense had lost its importance" (11). Then, after Adele had "suddenly felt herself intensely kissed on the eyes and on the lips," she "stopped thinking" and concludes, "yes . . . I do begin to see," but Stein ends book 1 by suggesting that Adele's glimpse of this new life still leaves her in the dark (12–13). Enjoying the sun on her face while resting in Spain, Adele insists to herself that it is more than just sensuous delight. Further, she insists that Adele's brief flirtation with a motherly young Spanish girl represented perfect comradeship and that her glimpse with Helen resembles Dante's "divinely illuminated" vision of Beatrice.

The nub of Stein's question about Adele's psychological reality refers to her "puritanic horror" of intimate contact and back, in Stein's education, to what she had learned about the psychology of sex from William James. Leon Katz concludes that some years later, when Stein was writing of *The Making of Americans*, she "was in full flight from James and pragmatism" (Hoffman, *Critical Essays*, 149), but if she had not yet begun that flight when she was analyzing Adele in *Q.E.D.*, she was at least standing up to question James. In his chapter on instinct James wrote that, "of all propensities, the sexual impulses bear on their face the most obvious signs of being instinctive," in that they seem to be blind and automatic "because Nature urges that way," but he argues that "the facts are just the reverse." "The sexual instinct is particularly liable to be modified" by a number of factors, including what he calls "the *anti-sexual instinct*, the instinct of personal isolation, the actual repulsiveness to us of the idea of intimate contact with most of the persons we meet, especially those of our own sex" (*Principles of Psychology* 1053–54). Stein would have found many of James's conclusions about the sexual instinct questionable from her perspective,[9] but her main points of contention were that the sexual instinct was far more irresistible than he imagined. Indeed, she views it as no less powerful than the hunting instinct, about which James wrote that, "if evolution and the survival of the fittest be true at all, the destruction of prey and human rivals must have been among the most important of man's primitive functions" (1030).

This is not to suggest that Adele did not feel the Jamesian anti-sexual instinct, only that Stein's interest is in foregrounding and dramatizing the struggle between the sexual instinct and Adele's "instinct for intimacy without familiarity" (16). Adele's internal conflict is the important element in Stein's general view of love as combat, and it arises in Adele in response to a kiss from Helen "that seemed to scale the very walls of chastity," filling her with a sense of "battle and revulsion" and "fierce disgust" (39). Thus Adele is in the position of an early modernist, in that she is (in 1903) on the brink of articulating the Freudian view of such crises: she senses that her *inhibitions* (in her terms, "my puritan instincts") rather than the sexual contact itself pose a threat to her psychological well-being. As she explains to Helen, "somehow you have made me realise that my attitude in the matter was degrading and material, instead of moral and spiritual but in spite of you my puritan instincts say no and I get into a horrible mess" (40). (Stein's later story of Anna in *Three Lives* will examine a more disturbing pre-Freudian case of neurosis resulting from sexual repression.) Stein concludes that Adele's puritan instincts heighten the psychological conflict between these lovers—that is, their lovemaking becomes conflicted not because Adele experienced such revulsion again, but because "their pulses were differently timed." Adele had already fully satisfied her puritan longing for "clean simplicity" by visiting Boston, but when she realized that that way of life "was not earthy enough to be completely satisfying," she "returned to New York eager again for a world of greater complexity" in her intimacy with Helen (38). Now, recognizing the difference in their pulse-beats, her problem is the sort of thing that a late-twentieth-century reader might think could be remedied through marriage counseling: the problem of sexual incompatibility arising when a too-eager husband must learn to proceed more slowly in bed. Stein writes that Adele "could not go so fast and Helen's exhausted nerves could no longer wait. Adele found herself constantly forced on by Helen's pain. She went farther than she could in honesty and because she was unable to refuse anything to one who had given all" (40).

From Stein's point of view, of course, the thought of correcting this difficulty through counseling of some kind would have been absurd, particularly any suggestion that only the "husband" might be too fast. She understood the different rhythms of their pulses to have resulted mainly from the differences in their hereditary types, Helen, for example, being "the American version of the English handsome girl . . . a woman of passions but not emotions" (4). Stein treats this kind of sexual unhappiness as a result of hereditary difference more fully in her portrait of Melanctha in *Three Lives*, where Melanctha is too fast for her lover Jeff. Here her point is that the different pulses lead only to a further stage in the lovers' psychological struggle. The two had certainly struggled before the crisis brought on by the "kiss that seemed to scale the very walls of chastity." In an earlier crisis, when they talk of Helen's relations with Mabel, Stein relies on the laws of physics in calculating the nature of intimate combat: "When an irresistible force meets an immovable body what happens?" she asks and answers, "Nothing. The shadow of a long struggle inevitable as their different natures lay drearily upon them. . . . All that had gone before was only a preliminary. They had just gotten into position" (31). Even before *this* point Stein had presented the relationship in terms of racial strife, once, for example, when Adele had remarked on their "completely . . . different types," accusing Helen of being a "blooming Anglo Saxon" who would not hesitate "to stick a knife into a man"(22).

Long after these lovers had "gotten into position" and after the passionate kiss that provoked Adele's "fierce disgust," Stein sees the struggle as having escalated to a new level of psychological warfare: "All reactions had now to be concealed as it was evident that Helen could no longer support that struggle [of subduing her exhausted nerves]. Their old openness was no longer possible and Adele ceased to express herself freely" (40). And again, in dramatizing this stage in the war between them, Stein echoes William James's interest in the expression and repression of emotions but in ways that more fully acknowledge the underlying violence in James's source, Darwin's *The Expression of the Emotions in Man and Animals*. As Darwin concluded, his "theory of expression confirms to a certain limited extent the conclusion that man is derived from some lower animal form" (*The Expression of the Emotions* 365). Stein's apparent interest in revealing the underlying Darwinian struggle more vividly than James preferred to is undoubtedly related not only to their own differences in temperament but also to their difference in years. Writing at the age of forty-six, James acknowledged that "the relative sluggishness of my emotional life at present is" due in part to his years, "the invading torpor of hoary eld, or with the . . . routine of settled professional and domestic life" (1088).

Also, however, Stein shares the interest of many other novelists of these years (for example Harold Frederic, James, Edith Wharton, and Jack London) in dramatizing the expression or concealment of the emotions—the new "language of the emotions" that Darwin had defined.[10] In this late stage of the psychological warfare between Adele and Helen, then, Adele finds a way to conceal her feelings, and Helen claims that she need not conceal her emotions with Mabel, though she can certainly conceal her emotions in her conflict with Adele (49–50). Helen once instinctively attempts "to restimulate Adele . . . by all delicate charged signs as had for some time been definitely banished between them" (53). Adele thinks to herself that she might "have learned to read more clearly the small variations in [Helen's] looks and manner" (54), and Stein recreates a brief "drama of the eyes" in a silent exchange between the three women that captures the present state of the war between them. Mabel has now begun to play her winning hand of financial power in the struggle for Helen, and when Mabel sees Helen unconsciously express her appeal for comfort from Adele, Stein writes that "Helen was not conscious that there had been any betrayal and Adele did not enlighten her. She [Mabel] realised that such consciousness would still farther weaken her [Adele's] power of control" (55).

Ultimately, of course, Adele lacks the power to control the situation, and Stein ends her story of the triangular struggle among lesbians as a variation of Darwin's analysis of the law of battle among males for possession of the female. Stein casts both Mabel and Adele as masculine players. Mabel has the "manners of a gentleman" (15), and Adele, happy that she "wasn't born a woman" (6), once reflects on how she was once "soft-hearted and good natured," always preferring to let "the other man win." Now, however, in the battle for Helen, Adele finds herself "quite coldblooded and relentless" (34). Resoundingly in this novel Stein affirms Darwin's point that "the season of love is that of battle" (*The Descent of Man* 2:48), but she asserts that it applies as well in the world of lesbian love. Toward the end, when "Adele's domination was on the wane and Mabel was becoming the controlling power," Stein understands that Adele fails largely because her various powers, including her intellectual superiority, are no match for Mabel's financial strength (57). Taking all this in, Adele, who had entered the novel aware only of her "simple instinct for comfort" (5), discovers that "morally and mentally she was too complex" (32), that she was only a "grovelling human" (35), and even that she was now "eager . . . for a world of greater complexity" (38). Finally seeing "things as they are" and concluding that "it comes very near being a dead-lock," Adele bears a certain resemblance to other American characters from these years like Kate Chopin's Edna Pontellier and Jack London's Martin Eden whose first full taste of love had led toward their actual deaths (63).

"The Nature of Woman" in *Fernhurst:* The "Deepening Knowledge of Life and Love and Sex"

In *Fernhurst* Stein furthered her explorations in "the nature of woman" and "life and love and sex" through the narrative of another triangular affair. This one involved people she knew at Bryn Mawr—the philosopher Alfred Hodder, who left his wife for another professor, Mary Gwinn, and Gwinn's longtime companion, Martha Carey Thomas, the future president at the college. Stein's plot departs significantly from the actual affair, and two of her fictional characters, especially, seem vehicles for exploring her own reality: Miss Bruce (based on Gwinn) and the wife of Phillip Redfern (the counterpart of Hodder). Whether or not she wrote *Fernhurst* after *Q.E.D.*, the portrait of Miss Bruce seems to develop the kind of self-analysis that Stein undertook in her study of Adele. Whereas Adele had battled with her moralistic puritan instincts and responded in revulsion to the passionate assault on her chastity, Miss Bruce was also a kind of virgin, having "never succeeded in really touching any human creature." Still, she was not deterred by a puritan's instinct from pursuing "her desire . . . to experience the extreme forms of sensuous life and make even immoral experience her own" (19). Rather than fearing an assault on her chastity, she waited "for the hand that could tear down the walls that enclosed her and let her escape into a world of humans" (20).

With her deep "interest in the varieties of human experience" and " her constant desire to partake of all human relations" (19), Miss Bruce is evidently bisexual, but she resembles Mrs. Redfern in her capacity to feel and act on her sexual desire (Mrs. Redfern's desire being only heterosexual). In this way Stein suggests that these two represent an essential aspect of the female reality (in its "varieties") that Redfern, although "a student of the nature of woman," can never accept. As Miss Bruce cannot conceal her attraction to Redfern, the way "her body slowly fill[ed] with yearning and desire" (33), neither could Mrs. Redfern prevent herself from laying "her hand caressingly on [another boy's] head" on one "soft warm day [when] the ground was warm with young life and wet with spring rain" (26). She did this even in the presence of Redfern during their courtship, and it brought out the characteristic idealism that dogs him to the end. As a youth, he couldn't "conceal a start of surprise" when his future wife caressed the other boy, but his "ideals conquered his instincts" (that is, his instinct to knock off the other boy), and he persists in seeing her as a wonderful comrade in the new world (26–27). During his affair with Miss Bruce, when the two supposedly deepened their "knowledge of life and love and sex" (34), he remains blind to his own nature and "too ignorant of women's ways to see danger where danger really lay" (43). And after the affair "his instincts gave the lie to his ideals and his ideals to his instincts" (26). Stein writes, "He remained always a hopeless inextricable mess" (47–48).

Redfern's idealism regarding sexual "comradeship" in a "new world" (rather than what Stein took to be perilous intimacy in the Darwinian sexual struggle) reflects his naive belief in evolutionary progress, a theme that Stein reiterated throughout her life. In *Wars I Have Seen*, for example, she writes that "when evolution first began to be known . . . and everything was being understood . . . if everything was understood then there would be progress and if there was going to be progress there would not be any wars" (62). In *Fernhurst*, something like this view of life is the basis of Redfern's contribution to modern philosophy, the naive realism that Stein mocks through some of the college students' ironic comments. Once, after Redfern and Miss Bruce were obliviously "joined in rapt ecstasy in the center of a crowded streetcar," one student reports to others that "naive realism is most absorbing," and the general cry at student gatherings became, "Give us Redfern and the Bruce in the street-car doing naive realism!" (44). Moreover, Stein makes it quite clear at the outset of this "History of Philip Redfern, a Student of the Nature of Woman" (her subtitle), that her critique of naive realism is aimed at the general denial of Darwinian theory, a first principle of which is the evolution of sexual difference according to sexual selection. Indeed, Stein is almost strident on this point, complaining in her opening paragraphs of college women who conduct themselves "as if there were no sex and mankind made all alike and traditional differences were mere variations of dress and contour," and she wonders whether "the new woman [will] ever relearn the fundamental facts of sex," or whether "different things [will] never be recognized as different" (3–4).

Expressing such views on the facts of sex and the true nature of woman during these years, Stein found herself in conflict with other women—those, on one hand, who subscribed to the premise of Victorian sexual science that the stress of higher education posed a serious risk to young women's sanity and reproductive health. On the other hand, she was in conflict with those who rejected sexual science, often for very good reasons, but who also seemed to reject evolutionary theory as a whole.[11] Her general point, that sexual difference is an undeniable fact of evolutionary biology, is obviously complicated by her own sexual orientation, by her determination to further the emerging exploration of female sexual desire (as in work by Kate Chopin, Edith Wharton, Theodore Dreiser, or Jack London), and her familiarity with the currents in modern psychology that were giving rise to Freud's analysis of the libidinal instincts or Havelock Ellis's *Studies in the Psychology of Sex*. Also, in *Fernhurst*, there is a further suggestion that during these transitional years between her career as a medical student and her new one as a writer she was feeling an affinity more with Henry than with William James. She certainly never emulated either one without challenging his authority in her own field, and her approach to these towering figures seems evident in the similarities and differences between *Fernhurst* and James's *The Bostonians*.

The plots of both novels are based on sexual triangles in which a male vies with a feminist lesbian for another woman—Basil Ransom with Olive Chancellor for Verena Tarrant in James's novel. Both writers treat democratic idealism ironically, associating it with naive feminism, and resting their cases on fundamental facts of sex as determined by evolution. In *The Bostonians* James ridiculed the feminist Miss Birdseye (based on Elizabeth Peabody) and expressed his scientific views through his odd female character, Dr. Prance, and Stein criticizes the democratic education Redfern had received, wherein "inheritance was disregarded" in a program that advocated the "simple comradeship between the sexes" (23–24). Moreover, both writers view the triangle as a struggle for possession that is decided by strength. But while James gives the victory to his primitively virile though rational hero, indicating that Verena is by her female nature fated to submit to a powerful male, Stein makes a fool of the idealistic male (Redfern) and arranges for Miss Thornton, "with her instinct for the straight act to a desired end," to prevail over Redfern. By her strategy of informing Mrs. Redfern of her husband's affair and causing her to intervene, Thornton "regained all property rights in [the] shy learned creature" Miss Bruce. Thus, as distinct from what she had gathered from both her mentors in the Jameses, Stein presented a treatise on the nature of woman emphasizing that women, no less than Darwin's passionate males, are strongly motivated by sexual desire, not only the sexual instinct to mother or to submit to a powerful male, and that women are quite capable of defeating males in psychosexual warfare.

Three Lives: Anna's "Strange Coquetry of Anger and Fear"

In her early work on *Three Lives* in 1905 Stein furthered the kind of psychological self-explorations that she had completed in the earlier narratives, now including efforts to account for "The Making of an Author," with George Sand originally in mind (Wineapple 222). "The Good Anna," which she wrote first, is certainly the pioneer work that Donald Sutherland referred to as Stein's radical success in bringing "the language back to life" (40). This work undoubtedly reflects not only her interest in Flaubert's *Three Tales* (Wineapple 222) but also her interest in the Jamesian idea of the "specious present," as that was theorized by her acquaintance (also a student of William James) Alfred Hodder (Wineapple 190–91), and it reflects what she was learning from modern painters like Cézanne (Sutherland 32–35). But it is too little recognized that "The Good Anna" is also a landmark in Stein's efforts to move beyond William James's psychological interests to probe more directly the idea that was beginning to dominate modern psychology—that the sexual impulse was the key to analysis. Of course she had already touched on this subject in her paper (with Leon M. Solomons) on "Normal Motor Automatism." And James had begun to move in this direction, though only to a certain point. Whereas he had written of the *"antisexual instinct"* or "amativeness" as much less a force in the human psyche than "alimentation and defence" (*Principles* 294), he later published "a notice of one of the first articles by Freud and Breuer, on hysteria" in 1894 (Sutherland 2). In *The Varieties of Religious Experience* he mentioned "the wonderful explorations" by people like Breuer and Freud "of the subliminal consciousness of patients with hysteria" (191). "The Good Anna" explores the same psychological depths and takes the same approach to it that Josef Breuer (in 1880) and, later, Freud did in making Fräulein Anna O. "the founding patient of psychoanalysis" (Gay, *Freud Reader*, 61).

It has not been definitely ascertained that Stein knew of the case of Anna O. (though clearly she could have) or that this was actually the pattern for her own Anna. But even if Stein's biographers are correct in dating her initial enthusiasm or at least curiosity about Freud at around 1909 (Wineapple 316), there can be little doubt that Anna's "bottom nature" represents Stein's variation on a dominant theme in early twentieth-century psychology. Stein's analysis of Anna's strange life takes the approach not only of the naturalist writers whom Freud read and admired (for example, Ibsen, Zola, Strindberg) but also of Breuer's, Freud's, Ellis's, and many other psychologists' use of the case history. And she was certainly in step with these psychologists' sense that hysteria arises from sexual repression, as in the cases of Anna O. or Freud's Dora. This is the essential reason why Anna is "good"—that she is so opposed to the sexual "evil" that she battles in herself and in her pet dog Peter (*Three Lives* 12). Similarly, Anna battles the "badness" of her underling Sallie and the "bad [butcher] boy" (19–20); she is traumatized when "a mysterious, perhaps an evil man" (56) appears in the house of Mrs. Lehntman, "the only romance Anna ever knew" (54). Of course Anna is good also in the sense that she gives so much to others, especially the poor, but in Stein's view this kind of goodness is secondary, and is merely another aspect of Anna's many "strange," "queer," or "freakish" traits, all of which are symptomatic of her unconscious war against her instinctive self-interest

(29, 37). Anna finally dies because she is too tired "to eat more so that she would get stronger" (81), and her earlier efforts to help Mrs. Lehntman fix up her house "swallowed all Anna's savings" (55). Or, as Stein explains more ironically, "Miss Mathilda had to save her Anna from the many friends, who in the kindly fashion of the poor, used up her savings" (65).

Stein informs us in part 1 that it is largely because "the good Anna had high ideals for canine chastity and discipline" that she "led an arduous and troubled life." She persisted in her disciplinary efforts and, often by devising traps to catch the dogs by surprise, succeeded in making "all the wicked-minded dogs" slink away when she approached (12–13). And in part 2 Stein adds to the point about Anna's aversion to animal sexuality by noting repeatedly that "Anna had no strong natural feeling to love children" (25–26). As a kind of case history in the manner of Freud or Havelock Ellis, Stein's Anna exhibits a perverse kind of aversion to sexual passion that is quite unlike Adele's in *Q.E.D.* The note about Anna's lack of "strong natural feeling to love children" leads immediately to imagery of her "sharp resistance" and her "stiffened" body with "her lower teeth thrust a little forward"—and then to an extended scene of Anna traveling through a lush landscape "of new spring growth" in "the South." Stein attaches a theoretical commentary to this scene that provides the key to "The *Life* of the Good Anna," as part 2 is titled (emphasis mine):

> The languor and the stir, the warmth and weight and the strong feel of life from the deep centres of the earth, that comes always with the early, soaking spring, when it is not answered with an active fervent joy, gives always anger, irritation and unrest. (28)

Reiterating this idea, then, Stein elaborates her analysis of Anna's repression:

> To Anna . . . the steaming from the horses, the cries of men and animals and birds, and the new life all round about were simply maddening. . . .
>   At this time Anna, about twenty-seven years of age, was not yet all thin and worn. The sharp bony edges and corners of her head and face were still rounded out with flesh, but already the temper and the humor showed sharply in her clean blue eyes, and the thinning was beginning and begun about the lower jaw, that was so often strained with the upward pressure of resolve. (28–29)

Soon arrived at the end of this journey, Anna seems on the verge on an angry outburst at the aggravating little girl she has in her charge, but at the sight of her own employer, Miss Mary, she catches herself, and Stein describes her in this way: "her body and face [were] stiff with repression, her teeth closed hard and the white lights flashing sharply in the pale, clean blue eyes. Her bearing was full of the strange coquetry of anger and of fear, the stiffness, the bridling, the suggestive movement underneath the rigidness of forced control, all the queer ways the passions have to show themselves all one" (29). Among Anna's other queer ways or symptomatic behaviors, the most notable are that "truly she loved it best when she could scold" (37), that "her serving and her giving life went on, each with its varied pleasures and pains" (52), and that she maintains her strange relationship with her pets. She treats her dog Peter like either a son or a lover, "lov[ing] him well and spoil[ing] him as a good german mother always does her son" or loving him as "her good looking, coward, foolish young man," "the spoiled, good looking young man, of her middle age" (68). And the old dog "Baby" is her "baby" (75), who had been the "first gift from her friend the widow, Mrs. Lehntman" (73).

But Stein's most significant variation in exploring the theme of hysteria is reflected in her repeated reminder that "Mrs. Lehntman was the only romance Anna ever knew" and in her analysis of this relationship (52). Mrs. Lehntman is surely the embodiment of alluring female sexuality, "a good looking woman" with a "plump well rounded body, clear olive skin, bright dark eyes and crisp black hair," she was "magnetic" and "attractive" (30). As Brenda Wineapple notes, Mrs. Lehntman "encompasses sexuality in its broadest terms: in this case, premarital sex, abortion, lesbianism" (223).[12] For several reasons, then, not only because of the lesbian possibilities, Stein disrupts the relationship. For one thing, the relationship suggests Stein's general approach to the problem she addressed in the piece (recently attributed to her by Wineapple), "Degeneracy in American Women." There, noting the "lack of fecundity" and a diminution of "the ideal of maternity" in American women, she acknowledges normal or physiological sterility but is more critical of voluntary sterility, one kind of which is "the criminal abortion" (Wineapple 412–14). Moreover, when the Lehntman-Anna relationship begins to unravel, because Anna objects to Mrs. Lehntman's decision to adopt another baby (she already has two children of her own), Stein reiterates her point that Anna's lack of a "strong *natural* feeling to love children" is at the heart of the problem (emphasis mine). Mrs. Lehntman defends her decision by telling Anna, "If you had some [children], all your own, Anna, you'd see it don't do no harm" (44). This dispute over children, then, is "the grievous stroke" that finally destroyed Anna's "idealized affection" for Mrs. Lehntman, the "affair" that she thought "too sacred" to be told (46).

Introducing the scene in which this problem arises, Stein depicts the relationship in its highest state of excitement, from Anna's point of view, using the traditional imagery of Darwinian courtship. Anna appears at Mrs. Lehntman's home "one bright summer Sunday afternoon" rather like a Darwinian peacock: she is "much dressed up in her new, brick red, silk wait trimmed with broad black beaded braid, a dark cloth skirt and a new stiff, shiny, black straw hat, trimmed with colored ribbons and a bird. She had on new gloves and a feather boa about her neck"

(40). Noting that Anna's "spare, thin, awkward body" and "pale yellow face . . . made a queer discord with the brightness of her clothes," Stein suggests that the "queer discord" is in Anna's assuming *any* kind of seductive posture, because of her aversion to sexual intimacy. Yet as Stein traces the developing crisis in the relationship, she also clearly indicates that the bind from Anna's point of view is Mrs. Lehntman's inclination to enact the "ideal of maternity" within the bounds of a traditional heterosexual relationship. Referring to Anna's and Mrs. Lehntman's friendship, Stein writes that "in friendship, power always has its downward curve"; the struggle for power "goes by favour," allowing either party to "break away." "It is only in a close tie such as marriage," she theorizes, "that influence can mount and grow always stronger with the years and never meet with a decline. It can only happen so when there is no way to escape." In friendship, "there is always a danger of a break or of a stronger power coming in between" (54–55).

Now, "the stronger power" (and one cannot help wondering to what extent Stein means natural power) arises doubly, as "Anna's troubles came all of them at once," in the form of the evil man who appears in Mrs. Lehntman's life and in the decision of Anna's present employer (Dr. Shonjen) to marry. That this is an ominously natural power in Stein's view (the converging heterosexual relationships) is suggested in the odd scene that follows when Anna consults a medium on whether she should move from the Shonjen household into the home of Miss Mathilda. In answer to the lingering craze for spiritualism of the Madame Blatvasky type that aimed to transcend mechanistic evolution, Stein's medium "is always in her eating room [when] she has her trances." There (in the "eating room," we are repeatedly reminded), in the midst of "food that had fallen from the table" and "dirt that was scraped from off the shoes, and the dust that settles with the ages," the medium "choked several times and swallowed very hard" before blurting out her not so cryptic advice. "I see," she says, "I see—don't crowd on me . . . don't crowd on me . . . don't crowd on me," and so on (59–60). The meaning of this utterance in "The Good Anna" is that Anna must leave the traditional households for a new position with Miss Mathilda. While some might take this for what "the spirit" says, as Mrs. Lehntman insists, it is actually another memorable condensation of Gertrude Stein's long-held view of what it means to be "being living"—that is, to be involved in the Darwinian "struggle for existence" (*Everybody's Autobiography* 243). This aspect of the Darwinian war of nature, wherein the heterosexual couple retains its fierce grip on the only pathway to reproductive success, is, Stein suggests, just another part (along with actual warfare) of "what everybody has done since animal life began" (*Wars I Have Seen* 68).

As a case history in hysteria, then, "The Good Anna" is unique because it is entwined also with questions about what Stein considered degeneration in American women, and, in turn, the viability of lesbian friendships like that between Anna and Mrs. Lehntman. Always skeptical of love, Stein ended her story with that word, casting a pall over the lives of people like Anna, especially, whose psychic wounds and social circumstances make sexual intimacy only an icy void: "Miss Annie died easy, Miss Mathilda, and sent her love" (82). It is interesting to speculate on whether the story might have ended on a different note if "the standards of that era" had permitted her to portray lesbian relationships or if she had already formed her own kind of "marriage" with Alice B. Toklas. She might have suggested that such relationships can also yield a kind of enduring life if not love, or at least that, like conventional marriages, they could also "always grow stronger with the years" because there was "no way to escape" (54). But one is on firmer ground in remembering that in "Degeneration in American Women," as in each of her stories in *Three Lives*, Stein wrote down to women whom she considered lower by class or intellect. Charging that "the matrimonial and maternal ideal" was being abused, Stein held "the laboring classes" responsible, along with "the modern American woman" who "mistake[s] her education for cleverness and intelligence for effective capacity for the work of the world" (qtd. in Wineapple 413). But, adding that, "of course it is not meant that there are not a few women in every generation who are exceptions to this rule," Stein suggests not only her own sense of superiority but the possibility that the solution to a complicated case like Anna's is the superior individual's self-analytical insight into the nature of her sexuality. The kindest thing one can conclude about Stein's attitude toward Anna and other characters like the "earthy, uncouth, servile peasant creature old Katy" is that, were they *not* of such lowly origins, they might have learned from modern science and psychology that the sexual impulse is normal, but prone to grotesque if not neurotic distortion when it is too vigorously repressed (17). By relearning the "fundamental facts of sex," including the emerging awareness that there are many varieties of human experience, as she suggested in *Fernhurst*, one need not fear one's own inner life, and in this way one might find the strength not only to continue the struggle of "being living," but to prevail.

"The Gentle Lena": The Tyranny of Matchmakers and the Father-Instinct

Stein does not even faintly suggest that an enlightened view of the sexual instinct could have helped Lena endure "being living." One of the most dehumanized and helpless victims of life in the literature of this period, Lena is nearly incapable of knowing anything: "She did not really know that she did not like it" when men "would lay hold of her and roughly tease her" (246); "she did not think much about getting married" (254); "she did not really know what . . . was about to happen to her" (254); and "she did not seem to notice very much when [her babies] hurt her" (278). Indeed, it is a measure of how far our culture has come in its effort to acknowledge the

Darwinian "community of descent" that present-day ethologists and not only primatologists attribute more mental and emotional acuity to their subjects than Stein does to Lena. Both Frank Norris's McTeague and Trina and even Jack London's Buck in *The Call of the Wild* are far more complex than Lena, whom Stein classifies as an "earth-rough german" (244) with her characteristic "patient, old-world ignorance, and earth made pureness" (241). Lena exists mainly to make Stein's points that *some* girls can "really [have] no feeling about getting married," that the instinct to father is an ominous and more powerful force in life than the mother-instinct, and that the human family conspires to enforce the woman's reproductive service (252).

The plot of "The Gentle Lena" is controlled by the powerful woman, Mrs. Haydon, an American who returns from a visit to her German homeland with her niece Lena in tow. She is already married with three children of her own, but as her own daughters are still too young to marry, "the most important thing that Mrs. Haydon had to do" was "to get her niece, Lena married" (244). A primal force in nature, this "short, stout, hard built, german woman [who] always hit the ground very firmly and compactly as she walked"[13] is decidedly not a sensual earth-mother. (It seems to follow from Stein's view of the "patient" Germans as a type, including their reverence for authority, that no character in this story expresses any sensual or libidinous traits.) Rather, Mrs. Haydon embodies the female life force as was theorized by others at the turn of the century, like Otto Weininger, who wrote in *Sex and Character* (English translation, 1906) that woman is "altogether a match-maker" whose "only vital interest [is] that sexual unions shall take place." Indeed, he argued (in the famous book that impressed Stein so forcefully when she read it a few years after creating Lena), this is "the most common characteristic of the human female," to the extent that "the wish to become a mother-in-law is much more general than even the desire to become a mother, the intensity and extent of which is usually over-rated" (258–59).[14] Thus, as the essential tyrant in Lena's life, Mrs. Haydon arranges a marriage with an equally dull-witted and reluctant German, Herman Kreder.

Although Herman is not at all interested in women and runs away when his own dominating mother joins with Mrs. Haydon to force the marriage, he finally submits, partly because a third woman, his sister, pressures him as well. Concerned for his masculinity, she challenges him to be a "strong man" and sells him on the point that as a married man "you got somebody you can boss around when you want to" (265). After the marriage and the inevitable pregnancy, Lena lapses into depressed disarray, "letting herself go every way and crying all the time," and Stein shifts her focus to the developing power within the husband. His first important task (secondary in Stein's imagination to impregnating Lena) is in "getting really strong to struggle" in order to protect the developing fetus that is at risk from the terrible scoldings Mrs. Kreder inflicts on Lena. Because Herman "wanted strongly now to be a father" and to have a healthy son, he begins "to really make a strong struggle with his mother," succeeds in gaining his independence from his mother, and finds complete fulfillment as a father (275). He is not directly brutal toward Lena, but "he never really cared much about his wife. . . . The only things Herman ever really cared for were his babies" (278). He cares for them as an ideal mother, but Lena becomes more "dazed, and lifeless" than ever, shows no interest at all in her babies, and dies in giving birth to a fourth child (277). Far from missing her, Herman was "now always very happy . . . [and] very well content alone with his three children," a perfect example of Gertrude Stein's reiterated theme in later years that "there is too much fathering going on just now and there is no doubt about it fathers are depressing" (*Everybody's Autobiography* 133).[15]

Melanctha: "Too Complex with Desire"

In her fictional explorations of sexual intimacy between 1903 and 1906 Stein probed more and more deeply for the "bottom natures" of her characters, finally touching on the "real power in Melanctha's nature [that] came through her robust and un-pleasant and very unendurable black father," "a big black virile negro" (90). Stein's sense of an evolutionary hierarchy is reflected in a remark that she seems to attribute to one of the Haydon daughters in "The Gentle Lena": that to the American born German children, their "hard working, earth-rough german cousins were . . . ugly and dirty, and as far below them as were italian or negro workmen" (244–45). Through the character Jeff in "Melanctha," these depths extend to animals, when he thinks how they love "low in the streets together" (124). Although "Melanctha" is supposed to have won the appreciation of many African Americans when it appeared, it is impossible to read it today without being repulsed by its racist views. As Brenda Wineapple suggests, after having examined some of Stein's notes from her medical school days, Melanctha is "an amalgam of the sexuality and primitivism Stein asso-ciated with medical school, medical discourse, and May Bookstaver" (235), and many others have noted the similarity between Stein's analyses of sexual passion in *Q.E.D.* and "Melanctha." Stein's view of the "big black virile" male and of Melanctha's "nigger" friend Rose as representing "the simple, promiscuous morality of the black people" is certainly part of a tendency in evolutionary thought at the turn of the century, according to which people of color were regarded, even by some African Americans, themselves, as "outcasts from evolution" (86).[16] But Stein had also be-gun to explore the emerging view of sexual primitivism that would become increas-ingly seductive as popular Freudianism took hold: that both civilization and neuro-sis were products of sexual repression, and that the remedy for the white person's neurosis was evident in the black person's joyful and uninhibited sexual life.

These contradictory views on sex and race are the chief source of conflict in "Melanctha." They are evident first and most importantly in Melanctha's mixed racial heritage, her having "been half made with real white blood," though her real power came from her "big black virile" father, but they are also evident in the troubled mind of her lover, the mulatto Dr. Jeff Campbell, who explains to Melanctha that there are only two kinds of love: "one has a good quiet feeling in a family when one does his work, and is always living good and being regular, and then the other way of loving is just like having it like any animal that's low in the streets together" (124). Jeff is of course comfortable with only the former kind of love. But despite his preference for "hard scientific reading" (130) and his devotion to "taking care of the colored people" (124), he is also attracted to Melanctha's "strong kind of sweetness" (126). There is therefore a seductive appeal for Jeff or a character like Adele (or later for a writer like Sherwood Anderson in *Dark Laughter*) in the image of summers when "the colored people came out into the sunshine, full blown with the flowers," when "they shone in the streets and in the fields with their warm joy, and they glistened in their black heat, and they flung themselves free in their wide abandonment of shouting laughter" (208–9). Even Melanctha, because of her complex nature, is not altogether free to "do it" the way her pure black friend Rose "always liked to have Melanctha do it." Rose liked to see Melanctha come out into "the hot southern negro sunshine" with a black lover who chased her as she flew "like a bird," he trying to "catch" her and "put salt on [her] tail" and falling "full on the earth and roll[ing] in an agony of wide-mouthed shouting laughter." From Rose's point of view, this is the way: "to be engaged to him, and to have a good warm nigger time with colored men" (209).

As Stein begins to develop this essential conflict, however, it immediately branches in two directions—Melanctha's relationship with Rose, and, more emphatically, her relationship with Jeff—each with its own network of further complications. The story begins after the unhappy history of Jeff's and Melanctha's relationship (which Stein details throughout a long central part of the story), as Melanctha is about to lose her last place to "cling"—that is, in her relationship with Rose, who "had lately married." Stein first tells us how each of these women is "made," and then poses the general question that she addresses throughout the story. Melanctha's racial heritage is mixed, but Rose's is not. Rose "had been brought up by white folks," but "her white training had only made for habits, not for nature," Stein tells us, indicating her belief in hereditary determinism. "Rose had the simple, promiscuous morality of the black people," part of which, in one of Stein's most appalling racist points, is that Rose is so like a "simple beast" (86) that neither she nor her husband "thought about it very long" when their baby died (85). And now Stein poses her two-branched question, along with the suggestion of an answer that she will illustrate at length in the repetitive and confusing story to follow:

Why did the subtle, intelligent, half white girl Melanctha Herbert love and do for and demean herself in service to this coarse, decent, sullen, ordinary, black childish Rose, and why was this unmoral, promiscuous, shiftless Rose married, and that's not so common either, to a good man of the negroes, while Melanctha with her white blood and attraction and her desire for a right position had not yet been really married.

Sometimes the thought of how all her world was made, filled the complex, desiring Melanctha with despair. She wondered, often, how she could go on living when she was so blue. (86–87)

After repeating her question toward the end of the story, when Jeff's and Melanctha's relationship is in ruins (200), Stein answers it twice, writing that "the complex, desiring Melanctha" clung to Rose because of Rose's "solid, simple" nature (210) and because of "how all her [own] world was made" (212). Again and again Stein emphasizes that everything results from the way Melanctha is made, as when she told Jeff, "I certainly be glad to love anybody really worth, but I made so, I never seem to be able in this world to find him" (180).

Melanctha's complex nature is mirrored in her lover Jeff's complexity, but one of the most important ways in which Melanctha is "too complex with desire" is in exercising her female power to select. Whereas this had been a key principle in many earlier novels of Darwinian courtship—the woman's problem of selecting the most promising male—Stein suggests that no correct choice is possible (at least for Melanctha). Melanctha had "tried a great many men . . . before she was really suited," and she selects Jeff because "she found him good and strong and gentle and very intellectual" (109); he "was a strong, well built, good looking, cheery, intelligent and good mulatto" (125). These would all be promising qualities from the traditional Darwinian point of view, but they offer no solution to Melanctha's problem because of two further complications within herself that, in Stein's view, issue from her mixed race. First, Stein notes, Melanctha "always loved too hard and much too often," and this led to "denials and vague distrusts and complicated disillusions. . . . [She] would be sudden and impulsive and unbounded . . . and then she would suffer and be strong in her repression" (89). Second, in her complex desiring before her relationship with Jeff, Melanctha had had a relationship with Jane Harden. Both these complications surface early in her relationship with Jeff and then, because of his own unresolved inner conflict, eventually destroy the relationship.

Early signs of the essential trouble between them appear in a lengthy exchange when Jeff expresses his discomfort with Melanctha's kind of "real, strong, hot love," her way of getting "excited"; Jeff does not like to get excited (or be "like any animal that's low in the streets"), and he believes "in a quiet life for all the colored people" (122–24). They seem capable of dealing with this difference, but their first crisis arises when Jeff learns from Jane Harden "how Melanctha once had loved her" and "of all the bad ways Melanctha had used with her" (143). This discovery made Jeff begin "to feel very sick inside him" (144). After a brief breakup, caused by the revelation of Melanctha's bisexual desire, the two are together in a brief period of "warm sunshine," sometimes as if Jeff "was just waking from himself." "It was sometimes pure joy," but soon the more troublesome and eventually insoluble problem arises in Jeff's response to "the real, strong, hot love" (122) in which Melanctha had instructed him: something—"the disgust inside him" and his own sense of shame—"had made it all so ugly for him" (155–57). The key to this difference between them is again that, while Melanctha too had experienced brief episodes of repression, the "real power" within her (flowing from her black father) prevailed.

Jeff, having no dominant strain of blackness and having "really loved best science and experimenting," is more vulnerable to the kind of inner conflict that Stein had analyzed in the highly educated Adele and Redfern and in the much simpler Anna. Indeed, during a large central part of the story, Jeff dominates the narrative almost as the main (no doubt partly autobiographical) character. His encounter with the emotions of strong, hot love is far more intense than had been the case with Stein's earlier characters. But while his inner torment bears some resemblance to Anna's, he is better equipped through his racial makeup and education to survive the threat of hysteria when Stein places him in her typical setting for such crises. When "the warm moist young spring was stirring in him," Jeff "worked, and thought, and beat his breast," sometimes running "fast to lose himself in his rushing, and he bit his nails to pain and bleeding, and he tore his hair" (195). His brush with hysteria is short-lived, but Stein dwells at length on Jeff's struggle with the problem that, as Melanctha sees it, arises from his "awful [fear] about really feeling things way down in you" (123). Finally, however, Jeff is capable of resolving his inner conflict and to the extent not only that he survives his encounter with Melanctha and his own emotions but that he is stronger for having done so. Stein concludes her story of Jeff by writing that what he had learned from Melanctha "always more and more . . . helped him with his working for himself and for all the colored people" (207). It is important to note that, in reaching this rather fortunate state, Jeff had to deal with some of the same problems of modern love that had defeated other American characters at the turn of the century. Like Kate Chopin's Edna Pontellier and Jack London's Martin Eden, he confronted the question of ideal love, but successfully came to understand that he had "a real illusion in him," that he no longer loved "Melanctha any more now like a real religion, because now I know you are made just like all us others" (190–91). Sending him out of the novel, Stein remarks, "It was good that they now knew each other really": "Jeff had behaved right and he had learned to have a real love in him" (206).

We are left then with Melanctha and the puzzle of Stein's way of abandoning her. After the end of her relationship with Jeff, Melanctha was with other men, notably in a long relationship with a man named Jem Richards, but this ends for rather obscure reasons, mainly because "he did not like it when she wanted to . . . get really married" and because he "knew how to fight to win out better" (222–23). Left then to cling to Rose, Melanctha is again pushed away. Apparently acting to protect her own interest in her husband Sam and claiming that Melanctha does not "act the way it is decent and right" (232), Rose tells Melanctha that when Sam "comes home for his dinner he likes it when Rose is all alone there just to give him his dinner" (230). Stein then ends the story abruptly by reporting that Melanctha did not kill herself, as some had expected she would, but that she first had a bad fever and then a fatal case of consumption.

The clearest sign of Stein's final evaluation of Melanctha's life is in the crescendo of remarks about her relationship with Jem: first that her "joy made her foolish," then that her "love for Jem made her foolish," and then, repeatedly, that "surely her love had made her mad and foolish" (219–24). Especially in the context of Stein's (by this time) extensive effort to come to terms with the sexual instinct as Darwin had theorized it and in the context of other writers' similar efforts during these same years, one point seems clear: Stein was highly focused on the problem of heredity and traced Melanctha's despair to the "real power" that came to her through her father. She clearly identified her character's deepest bottom nature with the human's animal nature, for example through Jeff's remarks that Melanctha's way of loving is "like any animal that's low in the streets." Stein reinforces this suggestion about Melanctha's sexual nature through repeated references to her love of horses and in her description of Melanctha's interest in Jem as a young "buck" (216). Similarly, she writes that, "as a little girl [Melanctha] had had a good chance to live with horses," that she "always loved to be with horses," and so forth (91). And she returns to this point toward the end, when Melanctha takes up with the "buck" Jem, "who had to do with fine horses" (217).

Stein certainly does not hold Melanctha responsible for the way she is "made," as she suggests in her subtitle, "Each One As She May." But despite her unmistakable sympathy for Melanctha, her way of dealing with the human-animal reality is rather like what a number of other American writers had done in their responses to *The Descent of Man, and Selection in Relation to Sex*. As Howells had killed off—or, one might say, rendered extinct—Bartley Hubbard in *A Modern Instance* and as Frank Norris had disposed of Vandover and McTeague, Stein seems to push Melanctha into death and, in effect, the evolutionary past. By 1906 she had considered the costs of repressing the sexual instinct (as in Anna's battle with her dog's and her own inner impulses) but now she arranged for Dr. Jeff Campbell to confront and then successfully resolve that problem. Still, this left her with the problem in "the complex, desiring Melanctha" of her love for other women. All three of the women in this last story in *Three Lives*, Rose, Jane, and Melanctha, express their desire for other women. And Melanctha left Stein with the problem that she could never resolve: "being living" *is* a struggle.

There were undoubtedly many other troubling issues as she continued to find her own way of living with the evolutionary reality and especially "the fundamental facts of sex" as she put it in *Fernhurst*. Stein was inclined to put her faith in scientific solutions of some kind, rather in the way that Dr. Jeff Campbell had managed to survive. What she found so attractive in Otto Weininger's *Sex and Character* shortly after she finished *Three Lives* has been partly explained in studies by Katz, Wineapple, and others. But Weininger's way of fully acknowledging and then transcending Darwin's authority by means of his own spurious and finally mystical pronouncements would also have appealed to Stein, who initially revered but then took flight from her own mentor, William James. She had already anticipated Weininger's way of minimizing the mother instinct in favor of the matchmaking instinct. And given her long struggle with the problem of hereditary determinism, it is easy to see how she would have been drawn to Weininger's astonishing pronouncement that "it is possible for the progeny to be influenced by a man, although physical relations between him and the mother have not taken place," that, "just as Schopenhauer and Goethe were correct in their theory of colour, although they were in opposition to all the physicists of the past," so might he (Weininger) "be right against all the scientific men [i.e., Darwin, August Weismann, or Mendel] who deal with the problems of inheritance on a purely physical basis" (218). Weininger's thinking here is a particularly feeble example of the "anti-Darwinian evolution theories" that arose during those decades and brought about "the eclipse of Darwinism." One hopes that Stein eventually saw through Weininger's pseudoscientific and cruelly antifeminist approach to the evolutionary problems, as other writers did at the time— Jack London, for example. But we know also that at a later stage in her career she embraced yet another way of transcending Darwin and the post-Darwinian problems of heredity—in Henri Bergson's popular, more formidable, but short-lived *Creative Evolution*, in which Darwin's theory of sexual selection does not exist.[17]

Notes

1. Letter to Robert Haas. Similar remarks appear throughout *Wars I Have Seen* (1945). In these same years, Stein's brother Leo had reached a similar conclusion. Of course Gertrude and Leo had long since fallen out, and they disagreed on many things. But as Edmund Fuller notes in his edition of Leo's letters, papers, and journals, *Journey into the Self* (a title, by the way, that seems equally descriptive of Gertrude's career), Leo's notes for a "last book" included the preliminary remark that "this book has only one presupposition that need be mentioned: the doctrine of evolution." Fuller remarks that "the subject of [the projected

book] might well be said to have dominated his life. For this book was to have told the story of the long years of self-analysis" (299).

2. Subsequent references to *Fernhurst* are cited parenthetically by page number from this text.

3. Dating these early manuscripts before *Three Lives* is problematic. While I am following the standard dating based on Leon Katz's studies of the manuscripts, Brenda Wineapple's analysis of this question is convincing, as is her suggestion that *Fernhurst* might have been composed in 1903, instead of 1904–05, as Katz concluded (Wineapple 446–48).

4. *The Making of Americans* (1903), in Fernhurst, Q.E.D., *and Other Early Writings*, 137. Subsequent references to this work are given by page number from this volume.

5. Chapter 8 here will discuss Fitzgerald's interest in heredity and Haeckel's views on it.

6. In *Q.E.D.* the character Adele compares Helen to James's Kate Croy (54), and in *Fernhurst* several characters are engaged in analyzing "Swinburne, Oscar Wilde and Henry James" (12).

7. "Astonishingly conventional" is Leon Katz's phrase from the introduction to Fernhurst, Q.E.D., *and Other Early Writings*, xvi.

8. Further references to *Q.E.D.* are given parenthetically by page number from this text. Similarly, references to *Three Lives* will be given parenthetically in the text.

9. She could have had an interesting discussion with James on his points about the "antisexual instinct" in the form of women's coyness, for example, or his emphasis on the power of habits to modify instincts (a bit of Lamarckianism that would have been harder to argue after 1900), or his remarks on chastity and monogamy, or his belief that it is "a well-ascertained medical fact" that "the development of [the sexual appetite] in an abnormal way may check its development in a normal way" (*Principles of Psychology* 1052–55).

10. Darwin uses the phrase, "the language of the emotions," in order to explain how his evolutionary analysis shed new light on an old and well-known reality. Also, Stein agrees heartily with Darwin's assertion that the all-pervasive struggle for dominance is played out even within the individual psyche, wherein the "conscience" evolves as a result of "certain stronger or more enduring instincts" having prevailed over "others less strong and enduring" (*The Descent of Man* 1:73); moreover, she underscores his assertion that the language of the emotions further enacts the general struggle for life.

11. For a sensitive discussion of Stein's situation as these issues were contested, see Wineapple, especially 117–18, 180–81, and 409–10. Particularly relevant to this discussion is the early Stein manuscript that Wineapple discovered and printed for the first time, "Degeneration in American Women." Cynthia Eagle Russett's *Sexual Science: The Victorian Construction of Womanhood* is an indispensable guide to these issues and should be consulted by anyone who is trying to appreciate Stein's views on the nature of woman. For a discussion of two earlier American women novelists' efforts to deal with Darwinism and sexual science (Elizabeth Stuart Phelps and Sarah Orne Jewett) in a series of novels on women doctors, see the chapter "The Natural History of Doctresses" in my *The Descent of Love*.

12. Wineapple refers to Mrs. Lehntman's work with young women seeking abortions.

13. This kind of formidable, earth-shaking woman impressed Stein, who depicted Mrs. Dehning in this way as well: she was "fleshy but firmly compacted and hitting the ground as she walked with the same hard jerk with which she rebuked her husband's sins" (the first *The Making of the Americans* 140).

14. Stein's enthusiasm for Weininger is well documented and widely discussed but without reference to the way that it was a part of the early modernist study of sex or sexology that arose—in various forms—from Darwin's theory of sexual selection. The most important discussion of Weininger and Stein is by Leon Katz ("Weininger and *The Making of Americans*").

15. See also her discussion of her own father in this text (139–42) and her "Patriarchal Poetry" (collected in *Writings, 1903–1932*).

16. Although Richard Wright and Stein were said to have been on friendly terms, his story "Big Black Good Man" seems a perfect answer to her presentation of the "big black virile negro." For an admirable treatment of the evolutionary issues, see John S. Haller Jr., *Outcasts from Evolution: Scientific Attitudes of Racial Inferiority, 1859–1900*. These issues are discussed in reference to novels by Charles Waddell Chesnutt in my *The Descent of Love*.

17. A main document in tracing Stein's interest in Bergson is Mina Loy's "Gertrude Stein" in her *The Last Lunar Baedeker*; other brief discussions of Stein and Bergson are by Allegra Stewart in *Gertrude Stein and the Present* (especially on 14 and 84–85) and as indexed in Hoffman, *Critical Essays*.

6 Sex and Evolution in Willa Cather's *O Pioneers!* and *The Song of the Lark*

Studies of Willa Cather refer to Charles Darwin so rarely that one might conclude she hardly knew of him. But at least one recent interpreter has begun to discuss the Darwinian shadow in her work, describing the "Darwinist cartography" in the novel she published during the year of the Scopes trial, *The Professor's House* (1925), and noting the "striking parallels between Cather's mapping of America and that undertaken by her near contemporary, Thorstein Veblen" (Reynolds 130). Actually, Cather was quite familiar with the Darwinian landscape long before the years surrounding the Scopes trial. She did not study with a famous evolutionist during her university years, as did her contemporary, Frank Norris, but in a sense she was way ahead of Norris. In her high school years she explored the scientific world as a possible career, studying anatomy and circulation, dissecting animals in her own "makeshift laboratory," and referring to herself as "William Cather, M.D." (O'Brien, *Willa Cather*, 89, 107). As Sharon O'Brien writes, these early interests indicate something of Cather's discomfort with Victorian sex roles, her emerging lesbianism, and her attraction to medicine because "she associated the profession with the male role" (92). Yet to put it this way oddly diminishes Cather's intellectual acuity, and her sensitivity to the swirl of scientific and philosophical issues in early twentieth-century thought. In the novels she published in 1913 and 1915 these issues included, first, Darwin's theory of sexual selection at a time when it had given rise to and intermingled with Freud's theory of sexuality, second, the countercurrent of Bergson's *Creative Evolution*, and third, related aspects of evolutionary thought pertaining to the aesthetics of music and the theory of play.

At her high school graduation in 1890 Cather gave a speech that was indeed "a remarkable performance for a youngster of her time and place," as one of her biographers noted in publishing it for the first time in 1987 (Woodress 60). Beginning with a principle of evolutionary anthropology, she remarked that "all human history is a record of an emigration, an exodus from barbarism to civilization" and then went on to proclaim that "scientific investigation is the hope of our age" (60–62). She took her stand in the still-heated controversy between religion and science, arguing that "there is another book of God than that of scriptural revelation," and extolling the "record" of "the 19th century" (61) in tones that recall Edith Wharton's tribute "to the wonder-world of nineteenth century science."[1] Then, no doubt defending her own alarming interest in dissection, she argued that there can be no scientific progress—no "great anatomist or . . . brilliant naturalist" of the future—if students are prohibited from conducting experiments that "attempt to pierce the mystery of animal life" (62). Not long after voicing this defense of science, however, she entered the university, began to find her identity as a writer-journalist, and by 1894 was expressing a different attitude toward science. She objected to "encroaching realism and 'veritism' and all other literary unpleasantness" such as the "ape-like" characters in experimental novels by Zola; one of these, she quipped, might be taken as the author's "evolutionary grandsire" (*The World and the Parish* 137, 141). Resisting such representations of the Darwinian reality, Cather had begun to fight her own literary battle for fiction in which the "sensitive chord of the soul . . . vibrates" (*World and Parish* 140).

Still, in her very favorable response to novels by Frank Norris (*McTeague*) and Harold Frederic (*The Damnation of Theron Ware* and *The Market-Place*), she indicated that she admired certain writers' ways of dealing with Darwinian materials. She was particularly impressed with *Theron Ware*, which she thought was "as good as anything in American fiction," because it was the work of a "vigorous thinker" and was "full of [the kind of] brain stuff" that only "some [put] into science and a few, a very few, into literature" (*World and Parish* 711). One central bit of science that she would certainly have noted in *Theron Ware* touches on the evolution of sexual difference, in Dr. Ledsmar's Darwinian experiments on the evolution of sex pertaining to "hermaphroditism in plants" (228). Because of its reflection on human reality, the sexuality of plants was widely noted by turn-of-the-century novelists, and while Cather had objected to what she thought was Zola's heavy-handed treatment of flowers, she knew how to use similar biological materials to evoke her own, different sense of the natural order. Zola, she complained, "tells you about the color and shape and size, the calix and corolla, and the shape of the leaves. But he writes of them like a botanist, not a poet," with no appreciation of their "fragrance" or "color" (*World and Parish* 141). Whatever Zola might have done with the calyx, imagery of the calyx was of special interest to many women writers, like Kate Chopin, in their efforts to present the biological innocence of female sexuality.[2] But Cather's use of flower imagery in a crucial scene of growth and development in the life of Thea Kronborg (in *The Song of the Lark*) reveals a good deal of the strategy she had developed by 1915 in her own efforts to contend with the biology of sex.

Certainly one of the floweriest chapters in Cather (or indeed in American fiction), chapter 11 celebrates Thea's coming of age on her thirteenth birthday. Reminding us that Thea is now in her teens, Cather takes her heroine and her music teacher Wunsch into a garden that is in a heightened reproductive state: flowering "holly-hocks or the bleeding heart," "morning-glories," "sweet peas," "pansies," pink-flowering "tamarisks," and, most emphatically, bunches of "waxen yellow blossoms" of the linden trees. In this intensely fecund setting, the "sweetness [of the linden blossoms] embalmed all the air," attracting "bevies of wild bees [that] were buzzing" about them (*Song of the Lark* 74–75). Toward the end of the novel Cather will remind us that Thea's experience in the garden had shaped her identity (459). Wunsch had instructed her in "the speech of flowers," making her recite lines from Heine's "In the soft-shining summer morning" (to use the translation provided by Cather). Emphasizing the line, "The flowers they whispered and murmured," Cather underscores her theme that "The world is little, people are little, human life is little. There is only one big thing—desire" (75–77). Wunsch (desire) is moved by what Cather calls "the insidious power of the linden bloom!" and explains to Thea that everything begins with "*der Geist, die Phantasie*"—the inner "secret—what make the rose to red, the sky to blue, the man to love" (78).

By the end of the novel, Cather will have channeled Thea's emerging capacity for sexual desire into a process of passionate artistic growth that culminates in her career as a Wagnerian star. And she closes this memorable scene by confronting Darwin's theory of sexual difference, the obstacle that she knew she would have to overturn before presenting Thea's sexuality in this way. When Thea left Wunsch she "was shaken by a passionate excitement"; she had "not altogether [understood] what Wunsch was talking about," but she "knew, of course, that there was something about her that was different" (79). Then, wandering "for a long while about the sand ridges," she picked up some crystals and looked "into the yellow prickly-pear blossoms with their thousand stamens" (79). Gazing not at the (female) calyx but at the thousand male reproductive parts of the prickly pear blossom, Thea dramatizes Cather's point most clearly when she turned from the stamens to look "at the sand hills until she wished she *were* a sand hill" (79). Developing this theme throughout the novel, then, Cather continued the project (begun in *O Pioneers!*) of presenting a version of evolutionary thought wherein she could transcend the force of sexual selection that Darwin had theorized in order to explain the evolution of sexual difference.[3] Resisting Darwin on this point, Cather also contributed in her own way to the cultural dissemination of "anti-Darwinian evolution theories in the decades around 1900" (Bowler's subtitle to *The Eclipse of Darwinism*). In her efforts to pull this off— and in doing so not only to resist so much of what she found distasteful in naturalist and early modernist fiction, but perhaps to envision an evolutionary reality more accommodating to her lesbian orientation than the Darwinian view—she was greatly assisted by what she had found in Henri Bergson's *Creative Evolution*.

Creative Evolution and Sex

Writing on Cather in *Bergson and American Culture*, Tom Quirk concludes that she had developed an enthusiasm for *Creative Evolution* by September of 1912 (the year after *l'Evolution Créatrice* [1907] appeared in English translation) (124), and that in her next novel, *O Pioneers!* (1913), she produced "a biological epic" (138) or "vitalistic novel" (122) inspired by Bergson's *élan vital*. In his lengthy discussion of Bergsonian themes in *O Pioneers!* Quirk suggests that Cather paid tribute to Bergson by naming her heroine Alexandra Bergson, by emphasizing her "mysterious intuition" and "transcendent desire for a perfect and eternal love" (128), and, in general, by projecting "a mysterious, energetic life impetus [that] drives upward" (132), in opposition to the "downward" pull of a "patient and relentless necessity" (127). Moreover, Quirk notes that Cather's two forces correspond to "the two opposing forces" that Bergson elaborates "in *Creative Evolution*—the ascension of spirit and the descent of matter" (128). Similarly, Loretta Wasserman points out that Bergson was an important influence on Cather's thinking and that Cather expresses many of his ideas in her fiction.[4]

However, criticism on Cather and Bergson downplays her presentation of sex, largely it seems because Bergson has very little to say about sex in *Creative Evolution*. Also, it is still nearly unknown in American literary history that during Cather's career Darwin's theory of sexual selection was acknowledged and had been since 1871 as the fundamental theory of sexuality. Bergson confronted Darwin, arguing against the primacy of natural selection and chance variation and offering instead the *élan vital*.[5] However, proceeding as though *The Descent of Man, and Selection in Relation to Sex* did not exist, he all but erased the problem of sexual reproduction. Bergson's theory had many appeals that caused some to see him as "a prophet of the soul" and others to feel that he had released them from the "nightmare" of late nineteenth-century mechanistic thought;[6] after all, Bergson proclaimed that "man [has come] to occupy a privileged place" in nature, the difference between him and the animals being "no longer one of degree, but of kind," and, most wonderfully, he promised that in the *élan vital* there is a "tremendous push . . . behind each of us in an overwhelming charge able to beat down every resistance and clear the most formidable obstacles, perhaps even death" (*Creative Evolution* 182, 271). His theory of evolution took the sexual struggle out of human nature and helped resuscitate one's belief in an elevated kind of love. Similarly, but from another point of view, Nathan G. Hale

Jr. notes that when the Freudian view of sexuality began to trouble the modern imagination, "the *élan vital* became a pleasant way to define the libido for some psychoanalysts" (*Freud and the Americans* 243).

As Bergson's discussions of sexual reproduction are intended to evoke the *élan vital* and "the prolongation of the past into the present, or, in a word, *duration,*" they tend to dissolve the concepts of individuality and sexual difference in a mystic "*life . . . current passing from germ to germ through the medium of a developed organism*" (*Creative Evolution* 17, 27). In one discussion of the mother's ovum and the father's spermatozoon, he concludes

> that every individual organism, even that of a man, is merely a bud that has sprouted on the combined body of both its parents. Where then, does the vital principle of the individual begin or end? Gradually we shall be carried further and further back, up to the individual's remotest ancestors: we shall find him solidary with each of them, solidary with that little mass of protoplasmic jelly which is probably at the root of the genealogical tree of life. . . . In this sense each individual may be said to remain united with the totality of living beings by invisible bonds (43).

With this sense of the essential unity in life, then, Bergson can acknowledge "the numberless struggles that we behold in nature" but insist that "the original principle of life must not be held responsible" for this "discord, striking and terrible" (254–55). In this way he does not trouble himself with the nature of sexuality that Darwin had studied as the "reproductive struggle," wherein a violent order is inherent in sexual jealousy or the male's structural weaponry, for example. Nor does he concern himself with the anthropological issues that Darwin addressed so dramatically in *The Descent of Man*, such as the origin of marriage in the capture of brides. Bergson asserts at one point that "there is no striking utility in sexual generation" (59–60), and he insists that even though "the living" sometimes "turn upon themselves, borne up by the great blast of life," there is evolutionary "*progress*" and love:

> At times . . . in a fleeting vision, the invisible breath that bears [the living] is materialized before our eyes. We have this sudden illumination before certain forms of maternal love, so striking, and in most animals so touching, observable even in the solicitude of the plant for its seed. This love, in which some have seen the great mystery of life, may possibly deliver us life's secret. It shows us each generation leaning over the generation that shall follow. It allows us a glimpse of the fact that the living being is above all a thoroughfare, and that the essence of life is in the movement by which life is transmitted. (128)

Bergson's belief in such fleeting visions, sudden illuminations, or love as "the great mystery of life" was immediately rejected by Jack London, as it has been by virtually all evolutionary biologists for many years. But a number of writers such as Cather were spellbound.

Marie and Alexandra: Beyond Sexual Selection in *O Pioneers!*

Although *O Pioneers!* is "a vitalistic novel" (Quirk 122), it is far more concerned with sexuality than is *Creative Evolution*. Bergson's work of evolutionary philosophy is of course fundamentally different from Cather's novel, which was devoted to the development of character in a literary tradition based on the courtship plot. Working in this tradition, she was not overly constrained, as the variety of American courtship novels well known to her suggests—for example, Howells's *A Modern Instance*, James's *The Portrait of a Lady*, Jewett's *A Country Doctor*, Chopin's *The Awakening*, Frederic's *The Damnation of Theron Ware*, or Norris's *McTeague*.[7] While only two of these novels (Howells's and Frederic's) mention Darwin by name, all of them use Darwin's terminology in projecting their various interpretations of sexual love, and all deal with the central issues of sexual selection: sexual attraction, possession, the male's aggressive passion, combativeness, and jealousy, and the female's power to select. Even if Cather had never read *The Descent of Man, and Selection in Relation to Sex* (which, despite her early interest in evolutionary biology, may very well have been the case), she could not have read these novels without realizing that they all concerned themselves with the Darwinian elements of courtship. We can see her working with these elements in the early stages of her career, in her review of *The Awakening* and in two related stories that she published a few months later, stories that seem to be further responses to what she had disliked in Chopin. Reviewing *The Awakening*, she complained of Edna Pontellier's "over-idealization of love," describing it as a "disease" of people with "strong and fine intuitions." Cather criticized such "emotional people" because their possibly "rudimentary brains" respond inappropriately when "passions rise in the brain" by the brain's "badgering itself into frantic endeavors to love" (*World and Parish* 698).

In the courtship stories she wrote soon after this review, "The Dance at Chevalier's" and "Eric Hermannson's Soul," Cather produced Darwinian scenes of music and dance like those she might have noted in Howells, James, Norris, or Kate Chopin, and here her strategy is to let the overheated passions run wild before cutting them down. In the first story named above, the character Denis is a "remarkably attractive man," "an erotic poet undeveloped." One of "the pure animal products of nature" and "a dangerous force," he "was the lion of the French dances" and caused the heroine to blush "furiously."[8] Cather subdues this "dangerous force" by arranging for a jealous rival to murder him, thus leaving the heroine's "words of love, imperious as a whirlwind" to fall "upon deaf ears" (555). In the other story, the hero is a fair-haired rustic with "skin singularly pure and delicate," like an "amorous Prince" whose "fierce, burning blue" eyes were most "dangerous to women" (*Collected Short Fiction* 368). The heroine is swept off her feet by this beautiful male, who makes her fiancé (Jack Courtwell, of course) pale by comparison. Thus, giving in to "that desire to taste the unknown which allures and terrifies" (363), she is determined "to dance with him myself" (368). Clearly, she selects this lover, though Cather does not use the Darwinian term, as Chopin does in *The Awakening*. In one of many clear references to Chopin, when the heroine gives way to "the hoydenish blood of some lawless ancestor" and feels "the strength of the man . . . like an all-pervading fluid, stealing through her veins," Cather describes this as an "awakening" and asks, "But was it a curse, this awakening, this wealth before undiscovered, this music set free?" (375).[9] In this, perhaps Cather's most erotic but also comically distanced scene, the woman "laid her lips on his" and "held them there" while listening to "the deep respirations rattle in his throat" (378). But just as she submits to the "engulfing weakness" of the "riotous force under her heart" and feels "all the resistance go out of her body, until every nerve relaxed and yielded," Cather arranges for her to save herself from Edna Pontellier's fate in *The Awakening*. She suddenly draws back, "white with fear." It had been for her an unforgettable encounter with "Love's self" and "all that she was to know of love." Although Cather suggests that "God" might have helped the woman, she does not say that she had saved herself from "Satan," to use the young man's word (378). Rather, she had risen above "nature" or the warm "roots of life" (377).

As these stories from 1900 show, Cather acknowledged but sought to overpower the sexual reality as Darwin had explained it and as novelists like Chopin had interpreted it. But by 1912, when novelists had become even bolder in their treatment of sex and as the Freudian view of sex had begun to emerge, she began to conduct her war for sexual restraint on the higher ground of Bergson's evolutionary philosophy. Cather's war against sex has long been recognized by some of her interpreters but without reference to Darwin's theory of sexual selection or Bergson's refusal to consider it. Blanche H. Gelfant first articulated the point in her landmark 1971 article, "The Forgotten Reaping-Hook: Sex in *My Ántonia*." Analyzing the "fear of sex in Cather's world" (161), her heroes' "strong intuitive aversion to sex" (148), as exemplified in *My Ántonia*, Gelfant argues that "though the tenor of her writing is normality, normal sex stands barred from her fictional world" (147). Although Gelfant's analysis is widely accepted and reprinted in Cather studies, it is resisted or ignored by two prominent critics who approach her work from feminist or Bergsonian points of view. In her influential feminist biography, for example, Sharon O'Brien explains how Cather resisted "the culturally imposed contradictions between femininity and creativity" (*Willa Cather* 5) by demonstrating "that a female hero and a female author could write stories that both sprang from and transcended female experience" (434). Making this point, O'Brien acknowledges Gelfant's account of Cather's "discomfort with sexuality" (401n20) but considers it an example of how Cather is "mutilated by hostile critics" (396). However, Quirk explains that "by 1912, a strict evolutionism [i.e., "Darwinian evolutionism"] had loosened up enough to allow some creative principle to figure in one's biological destiny" (33), but he mentions neither Darwin's theory of sexual selection nor Gelfant's analysis of sex in Cather. The point here is that Gelfant's analysis of sexual aversion in Cather's work makes even better sense in the evolutionary context—that is, as part of Cather's (and Bergson's) efforts to transcend the Darwinian order.

Cather's approach to evolution and the sex problem in *O Pioneers!* is similar to Bergson's approach to Darwinian theory (without reference to sexual selection) in *Creative Evolution*. That is, as Bergson takes up Darwin's theory at once, arguing against natural selection and chance variation, Cather, working within a literary tradition in which Darwinian courtship was interpreted in various ways, dramatized key elements of Darwinian courtship, more or less as she had in the stories of 1900. Now, however, she could contain them within the context of her more elevated vitalistic novel, suggesting that in this transcendent view physical or animal sexuality will give way to the "tremendous push" of the *élan vital*, as Bergson had theorized: "The animal takes its stand on the plant, man bestrides animality, and the whole of humanity, in space and in time, is one immense army galloping beside and before and behind each of us" (*Creative Evolution* 271). In *O Pioneers!* Cather creates a "tremendous push" behind her mythic heroine, Alexandra Bergson, freeing her from the Darwinian sexual entanglement (from sexual *normality*, Gelfant would say) that destroys her counterpart, Marie Tovesky. In this first overly enthusiastic tribute to the *élan vital*, then, Cather begins with an epigraph (her poem, "Prairie Spring") that pays tribute to "Youth with its insupportable sweetness, / Its fierce necessity, / Its sharp desire." In the end she gives us Alexandra, a virginal mother figure with no children of her own nor prospects for having any, whose "heart" will be received one day into the "bosom" of the "fortunate country" (309). Cather promises in her closing words that a life cycle will then emerge when the land will "give [hearts like Alexandra's] out again in the yellow wheat, in the rustling corn, in the shining eyes of youth!" (309). In these new "shining eyes," apparently, there will be nothing of the "fierce necessity" or "sharp desire" in the original "Prairie Spring." Five years later, in her more famous earth mother, Ántonia, Cather would not absolutely deny the biological necessity of sexual reproduction (Ántonia reappears at the end with her impressive brood). Even then, however, Cather took great pains (partly through a pervasive pattern of castration imagery, as Gelfant notes) to repress or sublimate the sexual reality.

In part 1 of *O Pioneers!* "The Wild Land," Cather introduces Marie and Alexandra as children, but in an oddly sexual light. Her initial description of Alexandra signals her intent to resist the categories of sexual difference that Darwin had accounted for with the theory of sexual selection: Alexandra is a strong girl who seems to focus at once on the evolutionary future, seeming to know "exactly where she was going" and her deep blue eyes were fixed intently on the distance. Like a "young soldier," she wears a man's long ulster as though it really belonged to her, but she also wears a veil. When she unwinds the veil, an anonymous man is struck by her beauty and exclaims, holding the wet end of his cigar between his fingers, "My God, girl, what a head of hair!" When she "stabbed him with a glance of Amazonian fierceness," he dropped his cigar, and Cather notes that "his *hand* was still unsteady" (6, emphasis mine) when he took a glass from the bartender: "his feeble flirtatious instincts had been crushed" (8). The point is that in the presence of this strong girl, the man is unmanned in the sense that he lacks the secondary sexual character of prehensile power to possess the female, as Darwin had explained, and as novelists from Howells to Frederic, Norris, and Wharton had reiterated in depicting their various heroes' powerful hands. Cather closes this scene by remarking that "he suddenly wished himself more of a man" (8), looking forward to a later comment that Alexandra's "fate [is] to be always surrounded by little men" (181).

By contrast, as Alexandra is fated to overcome the laws of sexual selection and sexual difference, little Marie embodies and enacts them. Cather's first detail captures Marie's maternal instinct, as she makes a bonnet for a kitten. She is herself "like a brunette doll," dressed in a "red cashmere frock" with a "white fur tippet" that Alexander's brother (eventually Marie's adulterous lover) "fingered . . . admiringly" (11–12). With her "brown curly hair," "a coaxing little red mouth," and striking eyes the color of the "Colorado mineral called tiger-eye," she is also admired by her uncle's cronies, who encircle her in a ritualized drama of sexual selection: "They were all delighted with her, for they seldom saw so pretty and carefully nurtured a child. They told her that she must choose one of them for a sweetheart, and each began pressing his suit and offering her bribes; candy, and little pigs, and spotted calves. She looked archly into the big, brown, mustached faces, smelling of spirits and tobacco, then she ran her tiny forefinger delicately over [her uncle's] bristly chin and said, Here is my sweetheart" (12).

From these initial juxtaposed portraits of the two girls' sexual nature, everything in the novel develops. Cather reiterates her point in portraying the two together again in their maturity, in part 2, "Neighboring Fields." When Alexandra and her returned friend Carl visit Marie, now unhappily married, Alexandra remarks on seeing Marie, "Isn't she like a little brown rabbit?" (133), and as Carl watched the two, he thought that "they made a pretty picture in the strong sunlight" (135). As in the initial portrait, Cather captures Alexandra's sexual detachment, the girl-Amazon now a "woman . . . armored in calm" (135). And again the key element in Marie's portrait is her sexual animation, the child whose feminine allure was so heavily associated with animals (the kitten, the fur tippet, her tiger-eyes, and so forth) now a rabbit-woman whom Carl thinks of as "the alert brown one, her full lips parted, points of yellow light dancing in her eyes as she laughed and chattered" (135). Moreover, in this scene the three recall the times of the initial portrait, Marie confessing that she had thought Carl "very romantic" and Carl recalling the memorable toy that Marie's uncle had given her. This is Cather's image of the essential Marie. It was "some kind of a mechanical toy, a Turkish lady sitting on an ottoman and smoking a hookah," and "she turned her head backward and forward," Carl remembers. As Marie elaborates: "We wound our lady up every night, and when she began to move her head," everyone laughed. "It was a music-box, you know, and the Turkish lady played a tune while she smoked" (138–39). By the end of the novel, after Marie and her lover, Emil, are murdered by her jealous husband, Cather calls upon the calm Alexandra to make the moral point when she asks herself, "Was there, then, something wrong in being warm-hearted and impulsive like that? [She] hated to think so" (296). But the unstated Bergsonian point seems clear as well. Marie is one of the "supple" people who are "quick in adapting themselves to circumstances," Cather informs us, and especially in her association with the mechanical, flirtatious woman, she embodies the more primitive evolutionary process that must give way to the vitalistic force behind Alexandra (81). As Bergson remarked, "the Darwinian idea of adaptation by automatic elimination of the unadapted is a simple and clear idea. But . . . it has great difficulty in accounting for the progressive" (*Creative Evolution* 56). And reiterating this point in his subsequent discussion of "adaptation and progress," Bergson emphasizes that true "Evolution [that is, creative evolution such as the kind Cather projects] will thus prove to be something entirely different from a series of adaptations to circumstances, as mechanism claims" (101).

"Dreamers on the Frontier"

Many other details and incidents in *O Pioneers!* fill in Cather's larger myth of evolutionary progress beyond natural and sexual selection. In the sketchy account of Alexandra's ancestry, for example, Cather reinforces her own views by including other current ideas regarding the evolution of race, the superior Alexandra being of "clean" Nordic stock, as opposed to Marie's dark Bohemian background (132). As Alexandra remarks to her brothers in taking over the family responsibilities after her father's death, "we are better fixed" (than their Bohemian neighbors) "because father had more brains. Our people were better people than these in the old country" (68). Moreover, underlying Alexandra's ancestral background is a story of traditional Darwinian development but one in which Cather insinuates her own sex-transcending theme. As in Darwin's account of life originating in the sea, Alexandra's grandfather was a shipbuilder who, "when all was said . . . had come up from the sea himself, had built up a proud business . . . and proved himself a man" (24). His downfall was caused by a second marriage late in life, the result of an "infatuation," and his new "unprincipled wife" had "goaded him into every sort of extravagance" (23). Alexandra's father had also married "beneath" himself, although not quite as disastrously as his father, for Alexandra's mother was at least "a good housewife" (28). Thus it is that her father calls from his deathbed not for either his wife or sons but for Alexandra, to whose strong "hands" he "was content to leave the *tangle*" (25, emphasis mine). In using this resonantly Darwinian term here, Cather underscores her point that Alexandra will lead evolutionary progress to new levels beyond the Darwinian order, which in her family history had produced a sequence of unfortunate marriages. Arranging for Alexandra to take charge of the family's land, Cather writes that "for the first time, perhaps, since that land emerged from the waters of geologic ages, a human face was set toward it with love and yearning. . . . [T]he Genius of the Divide, the great, free spirit which breathes across it, must have bent lower than it ever bent to a human will before. The history of every country begins in the heart of a man or a woman" (65).

Conversely, from the moment we first see Marie as a child until she is murdered by her jealous husband, her life is determined by the workings of sexual selection: the primary obstacle, in Cather's view, to evolutionary progress. After the murder, Alexandra remarks that the jealous husband, Frank, had "got himself in such a tangle that for a long time his love [had] been bitterer that his hate" (305). In his youth he fully displayed the sexual ornamentation required of a Darwinian male: in a silk hat and a blue frock-coat, carrying a "little wisp" of a yellow cane, he was a veritable "buck of the beer-gardens" (143). He and Marie had been fatally attracted. Yet, paralleling her suggestion that only Alexandra is fated to transcend the sexual tangle, Cather arranges for three different characters to blame Marie for her own violent death. Marie blames herself for having selected Frank, explaining that she realized too late that "he ought to have [had] a different kind of wife"; now she "could pick out exactly the right sort of woman for Frank" (197). With a twisted moral sense, Alexandra does not blame Frank for the murder (294); rather, she blamed Marie, for it seemed wrong to be "warm-hearted and impulsive" (296). Finally, Alexandra's lifelong friend Carl (her husband-to-be after they reach the safety of middle age) remarks most sympathetically, "there are women who spread ruin around them through no fault of theirs, just by being too beautiful, too full of life and love" (304).

Like Alexandra's father, then, Cather leaves it to her heroine to lead us toward a transcendent evolutionary future such as the one Bergson had suggested in *Creative*

Evolution. Presumably the vitalistic "push" alone will deliver us, but Bergson argues that along the way we can console ourselves and perhaps even contribute to the inevitable progress by relying on the superior faculty of intuition, which he says "may enable us to grasp what it is that intelligence fails to give us, and indicate the means of supplementing it" (177). "It is to the very inwardness of life that *intuition* leads us," and by intuition, he means "instinct that has become disinterested, self-conscious, capable of reflecting upon its object and of enlarging it indefinitely" (176). This is the mystic faculty upon which Alexandra relies—instinct transcended as intuition, or instinct freed from the essential self-interested mechanisms of natural and sexual selection. At the end of the novel Cather locates it in Alexandra's "heart," and her friend Carl looks "wonderingly" at Alexandra as she experiences what one might call her evolutionary trance: "She was still gazing into the west, and in her face there was that exalted serenity that sometimes came to her at moments of deep feeling. The level rays of the sinking sun shone in her clear eyes" (308). In this reference to the western vision, Cather shares similar views by Americans like William Dean Howells that evolutionary progress proceeds toward the west, as Darwin had suggested in his reference to "the great stream of Anglo-Saxon emigration to the west" (*The Descent of Man* 1:179). However, Cather's preferred term for the faculty that leads in that direction is not instinct nor even intuition, but just a dream. As Cather remarks at the beginning of this final chapter in *O Pioneers!* "there are always dreamers on the frontier" (301). And when Carl arouses Alexandra from her visionary trance at the end, she refers vaguely to the developing dream that Cather had traced in Alexandra's career—a dream sequence that goes directly to Cather's central point that sexual selection is the chief impediment to further evolutionary progress.

In her first reference to the dream, Cather writes that Alexandra had had it repeatedly. When lying "luxuriously idle," she would have the "illusion of being lifted up bodily and carried lightly by someone very strong . . . a man, certainly . . . but like no man she knew. . . . She could feel him approach, bend over her and lift her, and then she could feel herself being carried swiftly across the fields" (206). Cather describes the dream here as "an illusion" not only because it dramatizes the romance of a maiden's rescue by a heroic prince, but because it dramatizes the idea of sexual possession, as in the theory of sexual selection, and because, in her first state, the dream-woman submits to the sort of sexual pleasure that destroys Marie. Thus Cather writes that "after such a reverie [Alexandra] would rise hastily, angry with herself, and go down to the bath-house that was partitioned off the kitchen shed. There she would . . . prosecute her bath with vigor, finishing it by pouring buckets of cold well-water over her gleaming white body which no man on the Divide could have carried very far" (206).[10]

Toward the end of the novel, after the murder and after Alexandra has reached middle age, Cather writes that Alexandra had again, more vividly than for many years, the old illusion of her girlhood, of being lifted and carried lightly by some one very strong. He was with her a long while this time, and carried her very far, and in his arms she felt free from pain. When he laid her down on the bed again, she opened her eyes, and, for the first time in her life, she saw him clearly. . . . His white cloak was thrown over his face, and his head was bent a little forward. His shoulders seemed as strong as the foundations of the world. His right arm, bared from the elbow, was dark and gleaming, like bronze, and she knew at once that it was the arm of the mightiest of all lovers. (282–83)

Transformed now into the figure of death, apparently this time the lover arouses no sense of anger or guilt in Alexandra. Rather, she "knew at last for whom it was she had waited, and where he would carry her," and she "told herself [that it] was very well" (283).

In her final reference to the dream, in her closing paragraphs, Cather traces its further development. Roused from her westering trance, Alexandra tells Carl that she is thinking of her recent dream but explains only, "I will tell you about it afterward, after we are married. It will never come true, now, in the way I thought it might" (308). Then, perhaps to give her heroine an earthly reward, or to offer a compromise for readers who would want a more conventionally happy ending, Cather allows Alexandra to lean "heavily on [Carl's] shoulder," murmuring, "I have been so very lonely, Carl" (309). This couple can "feel at peace with the world" and "be very happy"; they "haven't any fears" because "when friends marry, they are safe." That is, this aging couple "won't suffer like—those younger ones" (308).

In offering such a solution to the problem of sexual love, exemplified in Marie's tragic quest for "the remote, inaccessible evening star" (248), Cather was not the first American writer to leave us with a couple who seem sexually anesthetized. Howells, for example, had rid himself of the troublesome Bartley and Marcia Hubbard, giving us the distinctly passionless Athertons at the end of *A Modern Instance*. Nor was Cather the first to recommend marriage only in the safety of middle age. Elizabeth Stuart Phelps had suggested as much in *Dr. Zay*, during the same year (1882) that Howells gave us the Athertons, in telling of how her hero eventually learned to appreciate the "calm of an assured, long-married love [rather] than of a crude young passion" (256). But unlike these earlier contenders with the sex problem as Darwin had defined it, Cather was armed with the theory of *Creative Evolution*. Thus she imagined an earth-mother heroine who angrily sought to cleanse her body of its sexual taint, who "longed to be free from her own body" (282), who yet was sometimes "so close to the flat, fallow world about her [that] she felt, as it were, in her own body the joyous germination in the soil" (204), and—still more mystically—whose heart, having been received in the country's "bosom," will yield others like it "again in the yellow wheat, in the rustling corn, in the shining eyes of youth!" (309).

Sexual Desire in *The Song of the Lark*

Cather's story of "the evolution of an artistic self" (Introduction to *The Song of the Lark* xii) was "by her own standards . . . an overfurnished novel, stuffed with details, overwritten, overlong," as Sharon O'Brien remarks (vi). Still, I would argue, the novel is remarkably unified in its treatment of the sexual reality. By tracing a few of its central themes, I hope to show here how Cather harnessed her novel's sprawling energies in a direct assault on the sex problem that by 1915 was arising more disturbingly than ever, beyond Darwin's theory of sexual selection, in Freud's assertion that the "polymorphous-perverse disposition" is "a universal and primitive human tendency" (*Basic Writings* 592–93). There is no firm evidence that Cather had actually read Freud's *Three Contributions to the Theory of Sex* by the time she published *Song of the Lark* (1915), but in 1922, referring to D. H. Lawrence's *The Rainbow*, she complained of novelists who are too literal in presenting their characters' "mental reactions and . . . physical sensations," who indulge in studies of "bodily organs under sensory stimuli," and in 1923 she complained of modern novelists who go too far in "the process of chopping up [their characters] on the Freudian psycho-analytical plan."[11] In *The Song of the Lark* her references to Darwin are much more visible than possible ones to Freud. Still, the sexual undercurrent she tapped in the scene with Thea's music teacher Wunsch on Thea's thirteenth birthday brings to the surface a kind of desire with obvious Freudian possibilities, leaving Thea "shaken by a passionate excitement" and with the sense that she and Wunsch "had lifted a lid, pulled out a drawer, and looked at something" that they would always keep as "a secret" between them (*Song of the Lark* 79).

In seeking here to tap the sexual source of creative energy, Cather moved beyond what she seemed to recommend earlier in "Eric Hermannson's Soul" or *O Pioneers!* that sexual desire must be repressed. Now she seeks to transcend the sexual impulse by a complex form of sublimation. In *O Pioneers!* working with the assumption that the power of music is rooted in sexual desire, Cather had described how the young lover Emil was aroused by a musical performance, as in the tradition of Darwinian musical scenes that Cather knew, for example, in Chopin's *The Awakening* or Frederic's *The Damnation of Theron Ware*. In the "height of excitement," Emil was "too much alive" and rushed to meet his lover Marie (257). Then, arranging for the lovers' murder as they embrace, Cather enforced her sense—as distinct from Chopin's in *The Awakening* but rather like Tolstoy's in "The Kreutzer Sonata"—that the solution to sexual desire is in Alexandra's calm chastity. Similarly, writing in 1899, she had valorized Wagner's "warrior maidens, clothed in chastity and iron" (*World and Parish* 646). In *The Song of the Lark*, on the other hand, Cather defines the artist's intellectual and spiritual development as a process whereby young hearts must strive with passion toward an exalted ideal (479–80). Thus, in response to Thea's final triumphant Wagnerian performance, when "love impelled her" and her "inhibitions chanced to be fewer than usual," her former teacher Harsanyi becomes "nervous" and exclaims that Thea's "artist's secret" (475) is "passion" (477).

At the same time, suggesting her own vision of an evolutionary hierarchy and the evolutionary future, Cather writes that people on "different floors and levels [in the theater] . . . enjoyed [Thea's] triumph according to their natures" (478). In fact, because he "got greater pleasure" from the performance than anyone, her old friend, the "little Mexican" Spanish Johnny, was moved to such "*extasi*" that he had to be "repressed by his neighbors" (478–79). That is, he lacked Thea's more highly evolved power of sublimation through artistic expression. In *The Song of the Lark*, then, sublimation through art is both an intuitive and largely "disciplined endeavor" whereby the artist can *consciously* harness sexual passion or "the stream of life" that Spanish Johnny "embraced" with his smile (480), but that also "passed him" (479). When "the gates dropped" in Thea's triumphant performance, allowing the uninhibited Thea to touch the idea of sexual passion that was too often unavailable, she was able to "make it live" (478). In her moment of supreme artistry, she was conscious not only "that her body was absolutely the instrument of her idea" but also that this was the fruit of her having "kept [her body] so severely, kept it filled with such energy and fire. All that deep-rooted vitality flowered in her voice, in her face, in her very finger-tips" (478).

The process of sublimation that Cather envisions here in a complex amalgam of Bergson and Freud and, beneath these, of Darwin's theory of sexual selection, including a well-known theory of aesthetics in music that was founded on the theory of sexual selection. Indeed, the novel's sprawling proportions arise largely from Cather's ambitious effort to contain these then converging streams of evolutionary, psychological, and aesthetic thought in an overridingly Bergsonian story of artistic growth. She would show how the Darwinian and Freudian streams fed into the inspiring theory of art that she had found in *Creative Evolution*, where Bergson writes that the human eye can perceive only

the features of the living being, merely as assembled [but] not as mutually organized. The intention of life, the simple movement that runs through the lines, that binds them together and gives them significance, escapes it. This intention is just what the artist tries to regain, in placing himself back within the object by a kind of sympathy, in breaking down, by an effort of intuition, the barrier that space puts up between him and his model. It is true that this aesthetic intuition, like external perception, only attains the individual. But we can conceive an inquiry turned in the same direction as art, which would take life *in general* for its object, just as physical science, in following to the end the direction pointed out by external perception, prolongs the individual facts into general laws. (177)

Cather ends *The Song of the Lark* by figuring such "general laws" or "the intention of life" as "the stream of life that passed [Spanish Johnny] and the lighted towers that rose in the limpid blue of the evening sky" (479).

The kind of sublimation Cather envisions in *The Song of the Lark* is worth comparing with the way sublimation and Freudian sexuality were construed by a number of American psychoanalysts early in the century. Some of these, according to Nathan G. Hale Jr., "were in danger of stretching Freud's definition of sexuality in the direction of the Bergsonian Life Force. Following Jung, they tended to argue that a generalized energy preceded sexuality and was greater and more universal. Sexuality was not the source of sublimated energies; rather, evolution and progress were the sources of sublimation; sexuality was but one expression of primordial energy" (342–43). Cather's views resemble these except that for several reasons she gives greater emphasis to sexuality. In the first place she was working in a novelistic tradition that had long been exploring Darwinian sexuality and courtship, though certainly from different points of view. Second, in exploring the nature of Thea's musical artistry, she could draw on a theory of aesthetics in music that was founded on Darwinian selection—a theory of aesthetics that not only paralleled the novelists' work with music and courtship but also provided a link with the new Freudian interest in sublimation, as well. And, third, she could exploit a controversial suggestion in Freud's theory that the individual could consciously initiate the process of sublimation.

It is plausible to assume that Cather knew of Freud's theory in *Three Contributions to the Theory of Sex* in that, while sexual excitement can *result* from "the concentration of attention," it can also work "in a reverse direction . . . to influence the availability of voluntary attention." Thus he concludes that "the sublimation of sexuality, is accomplished," "*in health*," when "the attraction of the sexual motive-powers to other than sexual aims" passes through "the same paths through which sexual *disturbances* encroach upon the other functions of the body" (*Basic Writings* 603, emphasis mine). Working with this possibility, then, Cather could proceed as she had with Darwin's theory of sexual selection: she could draw on Freud in order to disarm Freud, transforming the libido into a more pleasant aspect of the *élan vital* in the manner of other Bergsonians. Thus, when she writes that Thea "was conscious [during her supreme performance] . . . that her body was absolutely the instrument of her idea" (*Song of the Lark* 478), she pushes the Freudian possibility to the point that many Freudians, like Ernest Jones, would have found absurd. As Hale explains, Jones wrote that "it was a commonplace . . . that sublimated sexual energies were applied to higher cultural ends. This was but an aspect of the conservation of energy. But the ordinary meaning, that of *consciously* seeking a sort of consolation in art or religion for disappointed love, was absurd. As Freud argued, one might initiate sublimation by conscious choice, but the process itself worked spontaneously and unconsciously" (342, emphasis mine).

Sex and Sublimation in *The Power of Sound*

While Darwin's influential theory of sexual selection is still nearly unknown among literary historians, historians of musical aesthetics are quite familiar with it. Discussing nineteenth-century emotional realism in his *History of Western Musical Aesthetics*, for example, Edward Lippman traces a development from Søren Kierkegaard's essay "The Musical Erotic" (1843) to Richard Wagner's voluminous writings on musical expression. Lippman notes that in *The Art-Work of the Future*, Wagner called for a revolutionary art that "is a faithful mirror of nature, a conscious pursuit of the only real necessity, *inner natural necessity*"; only when man's "life is shaped and ordered by true human nature and not by the willful law of state" will "genuine man . . . come into being" (246–47). Noting then how "the realistic conception of musical feeling assumed a more specifically biological character" in Herbert Spencer's "The Origin and Function of Music" (1857), Lippman goes on to describe Darwin's subsequent theory on the origins of music in sexual selection (in *The Descent of Man* and *The Expression of the Emotions in Man and Animals*) and how Edward Gurney "adopt[ed] Darwin's theory" in his influential *The Power of Sound* (1880). Here, Lippman concludes, Gurney opposed Spencer's views on music and produced a "treatise [that] remains one of the most impressive in the field of musical aesthetics."[12]

There is no indication by Cather's biographers or by Richard Giannone in *Music in Willa Cather's Fiction* that Cather ever read Gurney's *The Power of Sound*. The book was, however, well known during the years she was writing rather extensively on music and its title alone would have attracted her attention. Both Gurney and Cather assumed the vital connection between music, sexuality, and evolutionary theory, but Cather's views emerge in quite a different key. Gurney takes his thesis from Darwin's remark that "music has a wonderful power" to recall "those strong emotions which were felt during long-past ages, when . . . our early progenitors courted each other by the aid of vocal tones" (*Expression of the Emotions* 217). Cather would have been especially interested in Gurney's emphasis on sublimation and his disagreement, on the grounds of philosophy and evolutionary theory, with Wagner's theory of musical expression. Over twenty years before Freud developed his interest in sublimation, Gurney based his analysis of sublimation in music on the Darwinian principle that the "'powerful and mingled feelings' that music excites in us—emotions of tenderness, love, triumph, and ardour for war—'may well give rise to the sense of sublimity,' and that 'we can concentrate greater intensity of feeling in a single musical note than in pages of writing'" (119).[13] Proclaiming that "the *alpha* and *omega* of [music's] essential effect" is its "perpetual production in us of an emotional excitement of a very intense kind," Gurney emphasizes repeatedly that "we need scarcely doubt the power of Music to have become sublimated, as it were, out of the coarse definite passions and excitements" (120); that "the root and groundwork" of musical expression are to be found "in the fusion and sublimation of those strongest elementary passions and emotions which, according to Mr. Darwin's view, were associated with the primeval exercise of the musical faculty" (315); or that the "primitive passions" are the "germs for the marvellously sublimated emotions of developed Music" (316).

As Gurney developed this theory of music and sublimation, then, he was bound to take issue with Wagner, who subscribed to quite a different, decidedly pre-Darwinian, view of evolution and man's place in nature. At one point Gurney refutes the opinion of "the metaphysician Wagner" that "man's first utterances" expressed "the *noümenon* or true reality," arguing that it is "more probable" that "the wailings of an infant" express its "private feelings" (361).[14] And at another point he develops a lengthy discussion of what he asserts is Wagner's mistaken metaphysical interpretation of Elsa in *Lohengrin*—Wagner's belief that the interest "rests entirely upon a process in the heart of Elsa, which touches all the secrets of the soul" and "bursts like a cry of despair from the deep anguish of [her] heart" in questions of "Whence?" and "Why?" In Gurney's view, this kind of analysis presents "a mere metaphysical puzzle" that might be appropriate if "Elsa were a profound psychological study of a woman . . . driven by her nature . . . [to attempt] to read the riddle of her hourly life," but in fact "Wagner's Elsa has no secret self-questionings at all. She simply wishes, with female curiosity, to know an external fact which she has been told not to ask about" (381–83). In short, Gurney argues, Wagner's theory that music addresses the "utterly worn and barren" question "as to the meaning and object of existence" (383) obscures what we now know about the instinct for music and "its peculiar isolation" from "intellectual, moral, and external conditions" (399). The power of music "to awaken in thousands who are inaccessible to any other form of high emotion a mighty sense of beauty, order, and perfection" lies "in the fact that its utterances pass direct to the consciousness" (399).

If Cather were present in this one-sided debate between Wagner and Gurney, she would certainly have sided with Wagner, insisting that the erotic force does end in addressing his metaphysical riddle and suggesting that its solution lay in Bergson's *élan vital*. Writing on George Bernard Shaw's *The Perfect Wagnerite* over ten years before she came upon Bergson, Cather agreed that "Wagner always sought for some point of contact between his ideas and physical senses . . . [insisting] on the need for sensuous apprehension to give reality to abstract comprehension" (*World and Parish* 618). Years later, as suggested in her own story of how the Wagnerian Thea Kronborg manages her sexual energy, and in her enthusiastic preface to Gertrude Hall's *The Wagnerian Romances* (1925), Cather had come to see a kind of Bergsonian wisdom in Hall's concluding remarks on "the Bacchic dance, which stands . . . for the animal element in love" in *Tannhäuser* (386). Hall concedes that although "the love-music as a whole . . . carries it over the sacred music in beauty *of a sort*," Wagner counters it with "the power of the music of good," suggesting that "from a mysterious eternal bias of human nature man finally must prefer good. He has a soul" that will be drawn "on and upward" (386, emphasis mine).

Sexual Selection, Marriage, and Evolutionary Play

It is here conjectured that Cather found theoretical support in both Gurney and Freud for the sublimation of sexual desire that gives rise to Thea's Bergsonian artistic growth. But there is clear evidence that Cather contended with Darwin's theory of sexuality in several other theoretical ways, thereby reinforcing the process that she refers to once as Thea's "rapid evolutions" (*Song of the Lark* 438). Again, as in *O Pioneers!* working to free her heroine from submitting to the workings of sexual selection that lead naturally to marriage, she surrounded Thea with a number of interested but ineligible males: older or married males like Dr. Archie and Fred Ottenburg; the chaste and brotherly Ray Kennedy who dies in a train wreck; her friend Oliver Landry, who is as graceful and useless as the objects he collects; and other minor figures (445). Further, by including glimpses of several deadly marriages and of restrictive family ties, Cather underscores her point that Thea cannot or will not evolve through the normal means of sexual selection. Cather gives us the most significant of these marriages at the outset, indicating in a kind of cautionary tale that the barren marriage of Dr. and Mrs. Archie originated through sexual selection. A creation of those years when Darwinian and Freudian theory flowed as a single intermingled stream, Mrs. Archie suffers from sexual repression, as Cather indicates in noting that because of Mrs. Archie's stingy manner, Dr. Archie "could never get thick cream for his strawberries"; in fact, "she liked nothing better than to have Dr. Archie to go to Denver for a few days," where "he often went chiefly because he was hungry" (33). Underlying this Freudian trait in her makeup is a specifically biological analysis with a clear Darwinian twist. Cather describes Mrs.

Archie as one of those "little, mean natures [that] are among the darkest and most baffling of created things" beyond explanation, "the ordinary incentives of pain and pleasure do not account for their behavior" (34). Yet she explains with no uncertainty that as the former Belle White, Mrs. Archie had played her evolutionary hand quite effectively. Capitalizing on her beauty (underscored in "Belle") and her "millinery" interests, she had attracted a number of boys, and because "Archie was considered the most promising young man . . . Belle selected him." Indeed, "she made him fully aware that she had selected him," and Cather adds that "once she had married, fastened herself on some one, come to port,—it [her "prettiness"] vanished like the ornamental plumage which drops away from some birds after the mating season" (35).

The Archie marriage is no anomaly in Cather's view, for she characterizes the bleak marriage of Fred Ottenburg to Miss Beers in similar terms. Miss Beers was a "ripping beauty" who "darted about in magnificent furs and pumps and close-clinging gowns," "wriggled out of her moleskin coat," and "looked like a slim black weasel" (333–34). Cather goes no further than this to describe the courtship as a process of selection, but after the marriage fails she describes such courtships in Fred's life and his marriage as "entanglements." Although other girls found Fred attractive, he managed to keep out of entanglements, but for many years he remained "tied hand and foot" in the dead marriage, wondering "what . . . society get[s] out of such a state of things . . . except a tangle of irregularities" (397). Cather does not deny these Darwinian patterns in the nature of courtship and marriage; rather, she follows Bergson's principle that evolution by selection and adaptation is merely a "*mechanics of transformation*," his effort in *Creative Evolution* being "to show up to what point our theory goes along with pure mechanism, and when they part company" (32–33). For this reason she describes Belle White's "clicking laugh [that] sounded like a typewriting machine in action" (34), and after recording Miss Beers's remark that "one had to marry somebody, after all the machinery had been put in motion," she notes how the couple once sit "in a snug glass enclosure, with the steam sputtering in the pipes beside them" before being "jerked about in the cab for another hour" and finally leaving "by the latest fast train out" (335–36).

Although Cather does not analyze Thea's parents' marriage in such terms, she does emphasize Thea's and her mother's negative feelings about the family. Distancing herself from her family as a child, Thea did her siblings "the honor, she told herself bitterly, to believe that though they had no particular endowments, *they were of her kind*," and on one "stifling afternoon" she watched "the family go trooping up the sidewalk on the opposite side of the street" on their way to church (240). And if Thea feels apart from "the family band" (240), her mother looks back on *her* life to remark that "bringing up a family is not all it's cracked up to be. . . . The children you don't especially need, you always have with you, like the poor" (404).

Still, if the modern marriages of the Archies, the Ottenburgs, and the Kronborgs are mechanistic, sterile, or stifling, they are not as disastrous as the story of marriage that Thea's grandmother used to tell. Rather like the much longer and more vivid marriage story in *My Ántonia* that haunts Jim Burden (the story of the Russian bride and groom who were "sacrificed" to the wolves), this story from the old days in Norway seems to exist in Thea's memory as a warning about marriage and sexual passion heightened by music and dance. The summer after this couple's Christmas marriage, her husband caught her with another man, and at a gathering where everybody was dancing and singing by a bonfire near the edge of a cliff, "he danced his wife nearer and nearer the edge of the rock, and his wife began to scream so that the others stopped dancing and the music stopped; but Ole went right on singing, and he danced her over the edge of the cliff and they fell hundreds of feet and were all smashed to pieces" (279).

Arguing that Thea's artistic growth could not proceed if she married, Cather is especially inventive in employing two particular strategies to protect Thea from being smashed to pieces. In the novel's crucial part 4, "The Ancient People," Cather recalls the old story of the couple dancing off a cliff, explaining that "Panther Canyon was like a thousand others—one of those . . . fissures" that are "so abrupt that you might walk over the edge of any one of them on a dark night and never know what had happened to you" (297). Here Cather recalls the scene of Thea's sexual awakening on her thirteenth birthday, which is now retained in Thea's "mind and personality" as "memories of light on the sand hills, [and] of masses of prickly-pear blossoms," and Cather writes that here in Panther Canyon Thea will encounter things that will go "into her subconscious self and [take] root there" (301). A central part of this will involve her relationship with Fred Ottenburg. Before Thea learns that he is already married, this courtship builds to the most erotic experiences of her life, two passionate kisses. As a preliminary to this, Cather remarks repeatedly on nests in the canyon, noting how the ancient people had been "nest-building folk" (302), and how this had been Thea's "old idea: a nest in a high cliff" (298). At first Thea goes so far with her "intuitions about the women" that she could even "feel the weight of an Indian baby hanging to her back as she climbed" (302). But before Cather ends this pattern of allusions in Fred's realization, "you're not a nest-building bird" (317), she brings the two lovers to the very edge of the cliff in an odd scene that dramatizes her evolutionary point on just how Thea can avoid being smashed to pieces on the reality of Darwinian sexual difference.

In chapter 5 of "The Ancient People" Fred and Thea become "entirely absorbed in [a] game" whose evolutionary significance Cather suggests by enacting it at the base of the "crumbling ruin of [an] old watch-tower" on the edge of a cliff: the "tower . . . now threw its shadow forward" (309–10). Moreover, Cather suggests the game's sexual significance by depicting the "two figures nimbly moving in the light, both slender and agile . . . look[ing] like two boys" and by noting that "Thea's voice [was] high and excited," that "her face flushed with heat and excitement," that her face and throat were glowing, and that "she was breathing hard" (309–11). Eventually, when the game ends with Fred panting after a forceful kiss that made Thea only angry and hostile, Cather comments by way of an unseen observer named Biltmer. Though he was "embarrassed by the turn the game had taken," he concludes, "I guess that young lady can take care of herself" (312). In the game that brings this on, "Fred was teaching her to throw a heavy stone like a discus," and they threw the stones off the cliff. When Thea's turn came

> she snatched up a stone and stepped impatiently out on the ledge in front of him. He caught her by the elbows and pulled her back.
> "Not so close, you silly! You'll spin yourself off in a minute."
> "You went that close. There's your heel-mark," she retorted.
> "Well, I know how. That makes a difference." (310)

Cather's point in all this is that Thea learns in such play how to transcend Darwinian sexual difference and thus avoid being smashed to pieces. She quickly learns how to throw so effectively that Fred is moved to think that "there weren't many girls who could show a line like that from the toe to the thigh, from the shoulder to the tip of the outstretched hand." Indeed, he is so impressed that he remarks, "I'm going to make some single-sticks and teach you to fence. . . . You're light and quick and you've got lots of drive in you. I'd like to have you come at me with foils; you'd look so fierce" (311). This scene of unconventional courtship and eroticism is emphatically not one of sexual selection, as we see when "Thea selected another *stone*" rather than a male, and when she responds in anger to his forceful kiss (311, emphasis mine). She realized that she might have deserved what she got in the kiss, that is, by having unintentionally aroused him, but she is just learning how to "take care of herself." In sum, it is largely through what Thea *learns* in this story of her "rapid evolutions" that she can emerge in "The Ancient People" episode almost as a new species.

When, after their games, Fred heard her "call from the cliff," he looks up to see "her there between the sky and the gulf, with that great wash of air and the morning light about her," and he realizes that "Thea was one of those people who emerge, unexpectedly, larger than we are accustomed to see them." Giving him "the impression of muscular energy and audacity," she struck him as "a personality that carried across big spaces and expanded among big things" (320). Then as a coda to this chapter and to Fred's vision of Thea, Cather dramatizes Thea's evolutionary ascent beyond both "the ancient people" of Panther Canyon (the "nest-building folk") and her own present identity. Cather had begun the chapter by observing that "under the human world there was a geological world," and now, in a moment that suggest Bergson's belief in "vital impulsion" or the "new [that] is ever upspringing" (*Creative Evolution* 50, 164), "Thea sprang to her feet as if she had been thrown up from the rock by volcanic action." She had seen a magnificent eagle soaring above her into the light, and Cather pays tribute to the eagle as a symbol of Bergson's creative evolution: "O eagle of eagles! Endeavor, achievement, desire, glorious striving of human art!"

Cather was quite willing to admit her audacity in projecting this kind of rapid evolution, but she also knew that it was at least plausible in the realm of evolutionary theory at that time. It depends in the first place on what Bergson referred to as the "Neo-Lamarckism" that, alone among "the later forms of evolutionism . . . [is] capable of admitting an internal and psychological principle of development" (77), a principle on which he builds in *Creative Evolution* to assert that "consciousness appear[s] as the motive principle of evolution" (182). Moreover, this Lamarckian principle supported work in a new field of evolutionary theory that was pioneered by Karl Groos in *The Play of Animals* (1898) and *The Play of Man* (1899). And for the way that Groos's theory of play influenced early twentieth-century psychology, it is convenient to consider C. Lloyd Morgan's remarks in his chapter "Mental Factors in Evolution" in an anthology of essays by distinguished theorists, *Evolution in Modern Thought*. Claiming that "too much stress can scarcely be laid upon the dominance of emotion during the period of courtship and pairing in the more highly organized animals," Morgan explores the question, which he ends in affirming, "whether these psychological accompaniments of the pairing situation have influenced the course of evolution and whether [they] are themselves the outcome of evolution."[15] His investigation leads him to "the delicate and subtle relationship of instinct and educability—that is, of the hereditary and the acquired factors in the mental life, and he admits that "the full working-out" of this remains as "the task which lies before genetic and comparative psychology" (191). Still, like Cather, Morgan places great faith in the "psychological elements" that had been brought to light in Groos's studies of instinctive "play" (186–87). Referring to Groos's analyses of games involving "male sexual behaviour with all its biological and psychological implications," and to Groos's conclusion that "the utility of [such] play is incalculable . . . [in] the exercise it affords for some of the more important duties of life," Morgan claims "the essential biological value of play is that it is a means of training the educable nervetissue, of developing that part of the brain which is modified by experience and which thus acquires new characters . . . thus furthering the psychological activities which are included under the comprehensive term 'intelligent'" (188).[16]

Judging by Cather's emphasis on Thea's evolutionary play, it seems quite likely that Cather was trying in this way to dramatize a process of artistic growth for Thea in more concrete terms than she could have by relying on Bergson alone. Still, Thea's

educational games both depend on and reinforce Bergson's principle that consciousness (and not variation, selection, and adaptation) is "the motive principle of evolution" (182). "To the eyes of a philosophy that attempts to reabsorb intellect in
intuition," Bergson assures us, "many difficulties vanish or become light" (270). In
her enthusiastic agreement, Cather gave us a character who evolves beyond Darwinian sexual difference, and whose "head" is the subject of much admiration.
Wunsch the music teacher, for example, had exclaimed, "Ach! She have something
in there, behind the eyes" (72). And after this Cather repeatedly focuses on images
of Thea's illuminated head—as when, seeing her profile "in the lamplight," another
music teacher (Harsanyi) wondered, "where had he seen a head like it before?" (181).
Again, seeing Thea's head "in the light" at one of her performances, Dr. Archie
recalls how he "used to feel her head to try to locate" her amazing "difference." Each
time he looked at her he "felt . . . a fresh consciousness," and Thea's performance
moves Fred to imagine her as "emerging from one world into another" (370–72).

Throughout the novel, then, Thea acts on "the desire which formed in [her] in
early youth, undirected, and of its own accord" (401), dramatizing her own point—
contrary to Darwin's theory of sexual selection—that "who marries who is a small
matter, after all" (467). Writing that Thea eventually "entered into the inheritance
that she herself had laid up," Cather completes her extraordinary escape from biological heredity through sexual reproduction, from the sexual instinct (or libido),
and from Darwin's categories of sexual difference. In this sense Thea's "body" is
indeed "absolutely the instrument of her idea" (477–78).

Notes

1. Wharton, *A Backward Glance*, in *Edith Wharton: Novellas and Other Writings*, 856. For a
discussion of Wharton's interest in science and her special interest in Darwin's theory of
sexual selection, see my *The Descent of Love* (314–40).

2. For a discussion of this kind of flower imagery in Edith Wharton, Kate Chopin (as in
her character Calixta), and Zora Neale Hurston, see my *The Descent of Love* (228, 392–93n9).

3. Aside from the questions of the evolution of sex, itself, and of the separation of the
sexes, Darwin sought to explain the evolution of sexual difference in the "secondary sexual
characters" such as the male's larger size (in most species) and his "special organs of prehension so as to hold [the female] securely." Noting that such "modifications acquired through
sexual selection are often so strongly pronounced that the two sexes have frequently been
ranked as distinct species," he proceeded on the assumption that "such strongly-marked
differences must be in some manner highly important" (*The Descent of Man* 1:253, 2:399).

4. Loretta Wasserman, "The Music of Time," 227. Wasserman develops her point through
an analysis of *My Ántonia*.

5. Bergson takes up and then sets aside three "present forms of evolutionism," not only Darwinism or neo-Darwinism (the first he addresses) but also Gustav Heinrich Theodor Eimer's theory of orthogenesis or evolution, wherein "variations of different characters continue from generation to generation in definite directions," and neo-Lamarckism, "the only [recent form of evolutionism] capable of admitting an internal and psychological principle of development" (*Creative Evolution* 85, 86, 77). Discussions of these and other competing forms of "anti-Darwinian evolution theories" are indexed in Bowler, *The Eclipse of Darwinism*.

6. Quirk, quoting Woodbridge Riley and T. E. Hulme (55, 820).

7. For a discussion of the Darwinian elements in the first five of these, see my *The Descent of Love*.

8. In *Willa Cather's Collected Short Fiction, 1892–1912*, 547, 552–53. Unless otherwise noted, subsequent references to Cather's stories are cited from this volume, parenthetically by page number.

9. In chapter 13 of *The Awakening*, Edna Pontellier awakens from a nap in the island home of a woman who "had squatted and waddled there . . . gathering legends of the Baratrarians and the sea," and she remarks to her lover, Robert, that "the whole island seems changed. A new race of beings must have sprung up, leaving only you and me as past relics." And at a musical performance in chapter 9, Edna responds to the sexual power of music that Darwin had explained in *The Descent of Man* and *The Expression of the Emotions in Man and Animals*. For a discussion of this musical scene, see my *The Descent of Love*, 222–23.

10. This kind of ritual bathing is also significant in the life of Thea Kronborg in *The Song of the Lark*, except that Thea exhibits nothing of Alexandra's sense of sexual guilt. The pattern of Thea's bathing begins in part 4, "The Ancient People," when her baths in the stream at the Indian ruins in Panther Canyon "came to have a ceremonial gravity. The atmosphere of the canyon was ritualistic" (304); the pattern continues later in her career (427, 471). When John Steinbeck recreates this kind of bathing scene in the life of Eliza in his story "The Chrysanthemums," it indicates her neurosis of sexual repression, whereas Cather construes it as a scene of cleansing in preparation for the transcendent state.

11. *Willa Cather on Writing* 42; Bohlke, *Willa Cather in Person*, 58.

12. Lippman, *A History of Western Musical Aesthetics*, 270, 275–80, 283, 319. Similar discussions of Darwin and Gurney are indexed in Bojan Bujic, *Music in European Thought 1851–1912*, and Budd, *Music and the Emotions*. For a sense of how Darwin's theory of the origin of music retained its currency throughout Cather's life, see Diserens, *The Influence of Music on Behavior*, and Diserens and Fine, *A Psychology of Music*. In this later volume, for example, Darwin's theory is frequently discussed and qualified, as in a reference to Jules Combarieu's "work on the Evolution of Music" and Combarieu's belief that Darwin's theory does not include "all musical origins" and his belief "that the Sex impulse should be understood in a wider sense as something like the Libido of the psychoanalyst or the vital urge of Jung and Bergson" (35). My thanks to Friedemann Ehrenforth, who informed me of Darwin's influence in the theory of music. Part of Ehrenforth's own work on late nineteenth-century literature and the aesthetics of music is available in his "Music, Religion, and Darwinian Science in *The Damnation of Theron Ware*."

13. Gurney is quoting *The Descent of Man*.

14. Wagner's view on this question seems reflected in *The Song of the Lark* in Wunsch's

remarks to Thea (on her thirteenth birthday) about "the beginning of all things; *der Geist, die Phantasie*. It must be in the baby, when it makes its first cry" (78).

15. In Ernst Haeckel (with other editors), *Evolution in Modern Thought* 182, 185.

16. For a brief discussion of Groos and Freud and of Groos's influence on child psychology, see Sulloway 250–51.

This is not meant to imply that Cather had not gone directly to Groos, whose *The Play of Man* was published in translation in the United States by Appleton in 1901 and 1908. Morgan's essay did not appear until 1917 (two years after *The Song of the Lark*), but this discussion of this essay has been included here to show the idea of evolutionary play had considerable currency nearly two decades after Groos published *The Play of Man*. If she did go directly to Gross, she would have been interested in his way of dealing with Darwin, for he exemplifies the nimbleness with which an evolutionist could be both a Darwinist and an anti-Darwinist at around 1900. He notes the "steady and constantly increasing current against [Darwin's] teaching" and the way it has taken "a witty form, if one not dictated by good taste, in the saying that it is high time that biology recovered from its 'Englische Krankheit.'" He "regard[s] the cavalier treatment of the Darwinian doctrine as a mistake, and still prefer[s] to test special problems according to its light." He criticizes Weismann, "the leader of the neo-Darwinian school," yet also distances himself from "the Lamarckian principle" (369–72). But of particular interest to Cather would have been his analysis of music and courtship, in which he argues against Darwin's theory of music. Quoting Darwin on the theory about music's power to "excite in us . . . emotions of a long-past age," he writes, "Far be it from me to discard this hypothesis hastily," but he does go on to discard it (24). In his analysis of music and dance he cites W. H. Hudson's anti-Darwinian views and then quotes his own remark in his previous book, *The Play of Animals*: "Just as in the beast of prey instincts of ravenous pursuit are refined into the various arts of the chase, so [it is] from such crude efforts at wooing that courtship has finally developed in which sexual passion is psychologically sublimated into love" (266). And Cather would have approved of Groos's general emphasis on the developing intellect, as in this summary remark: "Play is the agency employed to develop crude powers and prepare them for life's uses, and from our biological standpoint we can say: From the moment when the intellectual development of a species becomes more useful in the 'struggle for life' than the most perfect instinct," natural selection will favor "individuals that play. Play depends . . . on the evolution of hereditary qualities to a degree far transcending this, to a state of adaptability and versatility surpassing the most perfect instinct" (375).

7 "Under the Shell of Life"

Sherwood Anderson and "the Call of Sex"

Sherwood Anderson is the most famous American writer of the 1920s to exhibit that decade's "insatiable curiosity about sex" (Hoffman, *The Twenties*, 22). He probed the lives of many characters in spiritual and psychic turmoil as they felt "the call of sex" (Anderson, *Marching Men*, 81). His friend Paul Rosenfeld referred to Anderson as a "phallic Chekhov," comparing him with Freud and Lawrence, Stieglitz and Picasso. All of them had been "forced by something in [that] age" to remind their audiences "that it is in the nucleus of sex that all the lights and the confusions have their centre, and that to the nucleus of sex they all return to further illuminate or further tangle" ("Sherwood Anderson" 79). If he was not *the* "American Freudian," his interest in sexual frustration or repression made him a "psychoanalyst by default," as Frederick J. Hoffman concluded in *Freudianism and the Literary Mind* (235).

Anderson certainly did play an important role in the early American response to Freudian theory, but that story is much more interesting and complicated than Hoffman or later literary historians have sensed. Hoffman's studies of that period do not take into account Darwin's theory of sexual selection, neither his chapter "Precursors of Freud," in *Freudianism and the Literary Mind,* nor his discussion of the Scopes trial in *The Twenties*. Yet, as Anderson's interest in "the call of sex" suggests, with its echo of London's *Call of the Wild*, he sought quite self-consciously to build on the literary explorations of sexual love that he criticized in the work of William Dean Howells and admired in the work of Jack London, Frank Norris, and especially Theodore Dreiser. In 1921 he explained to his new publisher that he "had come to novel writing through novel reading" (*Letters* 82). Years later, in his *Memoirs* of 1942, he recalled how he came to write and publish his first story ("The Rabbit-Pen" [1914]) as a critical response to Howells, who he thought was afraid of sex, that "tremendous force in life" (334). And elsewhere he wrote that Dreiser, Edgar Lee Masters, London, and Norris were "constantly in [his] mind" during those same years (*Story Teller's Story* 300).

As Anderson belonged to the generation of American naturalists (he and London were born in 1876, Crane and Dreiser in 1871, and Norris in 1870), it is not surprising that his views on sexual love were shaped by the underlying problems that arose in the post-Darwinian questionings about the meaning of life, as in Huxley's *Man's Place in Nature* or Haeckel's *The Riddle of the Universe*.[1] For example, the hero in Anderson's second novel, *Marching Men* (1917), thinks the answer to "the riddle of the Universe" might lie in finding a way to bring order to life by orchestrating the strength of men marching together in the cause of labor (61), feels "the call of sex" (81), and continues on a quest for "something . . . religious—a soul, a spirit" (281). Anderson wrote this clumsy and inconclusive flirtation with authoritarian power before he began to emerge as a "Freudian" novelist. But he seems to have understood, as did his friend and fellow pioneer in the Freudian novel Waldo Frank, that Freud belonged in the family of "nineteenth-century Titans," claiming that "in the perspective of cultural history, he will be seen as a contemporary of Darwin, Schopenhauer, Dostoevski, Marx" (Frank, *In the American Jungle*, 83–84).[2]

Failing to consider the significance of Frank's point about cultural history and the relationship between Darwin and Freud, even Anderson's recent (and excellent) biographer asks, "What did Anderson (or any of his friends, for that matter) know about homosexuality, or even sexuality? What other than that sexuality was a new and fascinating subject?" (Townsend 106). This, a comment on Anderson's treatment of homosexuality in the Winesburg story "Hands," reflects the broader failure of American literary history to recognize the extent to which Darwin's theory of sexual selection shaped American fiction after 1871. But it is also true that Anderson's reputation as a reluctant or inept reader has obscured our knowledge of his interest in theories of sexuality like Darwin's or Havelock Ellis's. He cultivated this reputation, remarking frequently on his background as a workingman, his informal education, and his distrust of intellectuals. For example, writing of "the great Sigmund Freud passion that swept through the American intellectual world during my time," Anderson recalls that many critics had concluded that he "had soaked [himself] in Freud" but maintains that "I had, at the time, never read Freud, had scarcely heard of him" (*Memoirs* 473). Thus, in his laudatory review of Anderson's *Many Marriages*, F. Scott Fitzgerald compared Anderson's achievement with James Joyce's, but remarking on Anderson's "transcendental naturalism," Fitzgerald still asserted that "Anderson feels too profoundly to have read widely or even well" ("Sherwood Anderson on the Marriage Question" 42–43).

A much more important assessment of Anderson's reading exists in Frederick J. Hoffman's doubt that psychoanalysis influenced *Winesburg, Ohio*: "there is no evidence [in anything by Anderson] which shows that he wrote with Freud's works, or a psychoanalytic dictionary, at his elbow" (*Freudianism* 254). Hoffman acknowledges that there is reason "to suspect that Anderson was quite well aware of the intellectualist version of Freud," that is, the version shallowly discussed by amateur analysts in Greenwich Village (238–39). And, citing Anderson's famous remark about not having read Freud, Hoffman remarks that if this is true, it would have been "indeed strange; for it was [Anderson's] habit to search out a man's works, once they had been referred to him" (*Freudianism* 236).[3] Nevertheless, Hoffman carefully develops his argument that Anderson was a "psychoanalyst" only "by default," making this point in order to support his excellent but—but from our present point of view— obvious case that "the literary Freudian was in no strict sense a psychoanalyst" (1).

Of course Anderson was no strict psychoanalyst, nor was he the kind of studious Darwinian that Jack London was. Indeed, there is no concrete record—as in the case of London's extensive library, where one can examine his marginal notes in many books—that Anderson ever owned or read books by Darwin, Freud, or Ellis. Regarding his possible reading of Darwin and Ellis, the record is even more obscure than in reference to Freud. There is an ironic remark (written in 1924) in *Sherwood Anderson's Notebook*: "I went along thinking of Darwin and the marvels of prohibition. 'We are a wonderful people, we Americans,' I thought" (104). And there is a reference to Ellis in his letter to Marietta D. Finley in 1926: having received three letters from different people in a single week "all about Ellis," Anderson wrote, "The man has something very definite and real for we moderns [*sic*]. For a time I thought him too much the preacher" (*Letters to Bab* 265).[4] Even when Anderson explains how he joined with others like Dreiser in an effort "to tackle the problem of sex," it would be foolish to conclude that his study of sex was as systematic as Dreiser's or London's (*Memoirs* 467). Still, Sherwood Anderson provides a notable example of one way in which the Darwinian and Freudian views of life and sexual love were interrelated for many Americans during the years of the Freudian craze and the Scopes trial.

Anderson's story "Seeds" reveals a good deal about how his sense of the Darwinian reality tempered his enthusiasm for the Freudian "cure." By the time he published the story in 1918 he had heard a good deal about Freud, beginning with his discussions in a circle of friends in Chicago in 1913, and "Seeds" is based on his meeting with the famous psychoanalyst Trigant Burrow in 1917.[5] The story begins with what would have been an unmistakable reference to Burrow (dropped from the story when it was collected in *The Triumph of the Egg* in 1921): "There was a Doctor from Johns Hopkins talked to me one day last summer concerning modern life and its universal insanity" (24). The narrator (obviously Anderson) goes on to tell how "for years [the doctor] had been trying to cure people of illness by the method called psychoanalysis," and of how this had become "the passion of his life." The doctor explains how he has "entered into lives . . . gone beneath the surface of the lives of . . . women especially" and that the only way he can begin to "get at things" is to love them (24–25). The doctor's certainty of his method provokes the narrator's anger and the two exchange insults, the narrator calling the other a fool because "the illness you pretend to cure is the universal illness" (25).

Then, after a break in the story, the narrator tells of an incident in Chicago that strengthens his belief in what he had told the analyst: one cannot "venture far along the road of lives . . . [and] expect love to be understood" (25). This incident was told him by another friend, LeRoy, who had "something very sweet in his nature" and who should be a writer because "he tells things with understanding" (26). It involved a woman he had known in a Chicago boarding house who "in a hundred ways . . . continually invited approaches that when made she repelled," violently; she would even stand "naked in the bathroom facing the hallway where the men passed up and down [and leaving] the door slightly ajar" (27). Giving something of her background, LeRoy explained, in terms that might have been expected from the psychoanalyst, that the woman had been raised with orphaned sisters in a situation where men never appeared. Inevitably, "she began to think and to dream of men . . . [and] wanted desperately to be loved by a man," but, as "she had thought too much and acted too little . . . 'what she wanted she could not achieve. The living force within her could not find expression. When it could not get expressed in one way it took another'" (29). The other men in the boarding house had whispered that "she may not know it but a lover is what she needs" (26). However, when the narrator remarked to LeRoy that *he* (LeRoy) "might have been her lover," because he had been kind to her and she wasn't afraid of him, LeRoy first became as shrill as the psychoanalyst had been and then said "quietly and softly, 'It isn't so simple.'" Of course "she needed a lover and at the same time a lover was not what she needed." Voicing Anderson's underlying criticism of the "Freudian cure," LeRoy explained, "The disease she had is, you see, universal. We all want to be loved and the world has no plan for creating our lovers." Then, telling the narrator that "I am myself like the woman," LeRoy explained, "I have seen under the shell of life and I am afraid" (30).

Something like LeRoy's fear of life resounds as a central theme in Anderson's explorations of the "sex call." A pattern of themes and incidents reveals that he was still haunted by many of the same problems that earlier novelists had addressed in their analyses of courtship and love in light of sexual selection—especially the male's violence and possessiveness. Because these elements of sexual selection remain "under the shell of life" and because evolution or "the world has no plan for creating" the kind of lovers we envision, many of Anderson's characters withdraw from sexual intimacy in fear or impotence. This is certainly not the *only* aspect of sexual disorder or unhappiness in Anderson's world. As he wrote to Burrow in 1919, "You and I know that the big story here is the story of repression, of the strange and almost universal insanity of society," and, as in *Poor White* and *Dark Laughter*, he frequently dwelt on the idea that American industry had drained off and twisted the creative force that he located in the sexual life (*Letters* 44). In another letter to Burrow in 1919 he spoke of a book he was planning that would loose his "fancies" in "indirection" in order to envision a way out "of the jangle and ugliness of industrial life"; he would call it *Industrial Vistas*, and it would apparently be a visionary work in the manner of Whitman's *Democratic Vistas* (*Letters* 50). In short, Anderson was quite in key with others in his circle of friends in imagining that early twentieth-century American life was hounded by a cluster of problems that threatened its psychosexual well being.

In *Our America* (1919), for example, Waldo Frank laid the foundation for his tribute to new writers like Edgar Lee Masters, Dreiser, and Anderson by explaining that "the industrial buccaneering that followed the Civil War, and . . . the damaging revelations of Charles Darwin" caused Americans to feel that "their whole structure of contentment [had] vanished. . . . Looking behind their fallen Idol, they found that Puritanism had hidden a festering mass of hideous repression. They found ugliness and sterility and disease playing beneath the white complexion of the moralists" (125). For his part. Anderson produced several narrative efforts to imagine ways of managing society's reproductive energy and of finding relief from the jangle and repression in America. Among these were his dreadful "dream of mankind galvanised by some great passion" in *Marching Men* (174), his Lawrencian celebration of sexual primitivism in *Dark Laughter*, and his exploration of the communist solution in *Beyond Desire*. But all his novels confront the restless sexual struggle under the shell of life and end ambiguously. His first hero's incredible quest (in *Windy McPherson's Son*) ends when he "stumbled up the steps and into the house" to rejoin his childless wife and their newly adopted children, and *Dark Laughter* ends with his hero and heroine moving on, for better or worse, into the "new life [that] had begun for them. Having experimented with life and love they had been caught" (299).

Such faltering and ambiguous endings demonstrate Anderson's reiterated theme that neither he nor any other novelist or theorist had yet solved "the problem of sex." Nevertheless, an analysis of Anderson's way of figuring sex will help to clarify our view of the 1920s in American fiction. The most important elements in Anderson's treatment of sex are, first, his sense of the underlying Darwinian reality; second, his presentation of sexual difference and his hope that new men and women might break through the troublesomely inflexible categories of sexual difference; third, his work with various Freudian themes; and fourth, his effort to transcend the sexual struggle and the libido by evoking Whitmanesque fancies of sexual mysticism. Finally, readings of two stories from *Winesburg, Ohio* will show how Anderson interwove these elements of the sex problem in what is generally regarded as his masterpiece.

Anderson sets his stories of people responding to the "sex call" against a general Darwinian background that is evident in his occasional references to "the struggle to exist" (*Marching Men* 310) and "the survival of the fittest" (*Poor White* 122) and in his frequent imagery of an entangled natural order that is reflected within his characters' minds. Early in *Poor White*, for example, he describes how on summer evenings young people in Bidwell put on "stiff white collars" and "white dresses" after "crawling over the fields between the rows of berries or pushing their way among the tangled masses of raspberry bushes. . . . Friendships begun between boys and girls in the fields ripened into love" (43–44). And early in *Many Marriages* John Webster thinks of "books [in which] one found a kind of refuge from the tangle of things in daily life" and of how men and women "were at times almost insanely anxious" to make love; might a time "come when men and women did that quite freely," he wonders, concluding that "it was difficult to try to think one's way through such a tangle of thoughts" (15–16). Clearly, such patterns of imagery also often reflect a sense of Freudian psychology, as in Freud's remarks on the "tangle of dream-thoughts" or "the net-like entanglement of our intellectual world" (*Basic Writings* 480). Similarly, Anderson's extensive use of sea imagery in *Many Marriages*, for example, reflects his sense of repression and the Freudian unconscious and at the same time his point about the origin of our species. Recalling his first sexual encounter with his repressed wife, John Webster tells how her eyes looked as though she had come "up to me, out of a deep buried place, out of the sea. . . . I have always thought of the place out of which she came as the sea" (115).[6]

Further exploring "the world-old problem of the sexes" (*Marching Men* 97), however, Anderson dramatizes important specific aspects of sexual selection, including the principle of female choice, the role of music and dance in courtship, and most importantly, the problems of sexual difference. In the Winesburg story "The Thinker" the character Seth thinks "it fine that he should be thus selected as the favorite of the richest and most attractive girl in town," and several years later in describing the relationship between Bruce Dudley and Aline Grey, Anderson writes, "well, she had selected him—not consciously. Things had happened" (*Dark Laughter* 252). As John Webster explains to his daughter, young men always dream of "some strange woman" who comes to them out of nowhere "bring[ing] with her new life. . . . There are many men standing about, all no doubt more deserving than yourself, but it is to you she comes, walking slowly, with her body alive" (*Many Marriages* 126). And among many references to music and dance in his stories and novels there is a notable scene in which a possessive father seeks to compete with his daughter's lover by thinking to himself, "I can sing her a more wonderful song." But when his daughter hears her lover's "booming voice float[ing] over the heads of the people" in an oratorical performance that echoes Darwin's analysis of emotions in response to music and oratory, the father sees his daughter "overcome with emotions," her body shaking "as with a chill" (*Marching Men* 301–2).[7] In reference to Anderson's interest in dance, there are many scenes like that of the wedding feast in *Poor White*, when the orchestra "began to play furiously," causing "a strange animal fervor [to sweep] over" one of the guests (297). Indeed, *dance* is one of Anderson's favorite words in his efforts to evoke the reproductive force in life. In *Dark Laughter*, especially, where he romanticizes "the dance of bodies" among the southern black people, he tiresomely reiterates his primitivist theme that these people's uninhibited sexual energy and psychic good health might show his neurotic whites the way (81). Obviously referring to Havelock Ellis's well-known treatment of this subject in *The Dance of Life* (1923), he writes, "The dance of life! . . . Dance the dance out to the end. Listen, do you hear the music?" (92).[8]

Anderson's exploration of the sex problem is largely a meditation on sexual difference. In general, his early novels, roughly through the time of *Many Marriages* (1923), deal with "the antagonism that so often exists between men and women" by imagining, as many novelists before him had done, how emerging "new" men and women could break through the existing strictures of sexual difference (*Poor White* 166). Later, as in *Dark Laughter*, when he had more fully entered the "Lawrencian orbit" (as Irving Howe describes it),[9] his work exhibits a discernible effort not so much to imagine new men or women, but to urge that his characters accept their sexual nature and free themselves of the sexual repression that wrecks Fred Grey's life in *Dark Laughter*. After Grey's wife had left him and their barren marriage for her new lover, the novel closes with an image of him trying to laugh: "He kept trying but failed" and could only sit "upright and rigid in bed" (309).

Sexual Difference: "The Maleness of the Male"

In his first published story, "The Rabbit-Pen" (in the July 1914 issue of *Harper's*), Anderson addressed the two sides of maleness that troubled him throughout his career: the male's nature as violent and possessive and a particular male's tendency to withdraw from that part of his nature in fear and impotence. About ten years later, in *Dark Laughter*, he referred to this question as "the maleness of the male" through his character Aline Grey's thoughts in observing her lover at work in her garden. She sometimes laughs secretly at both her lover and her repressed husband, but she is "infinitely relieved that [her lover] was not a Frenchman," presumably because he might have been a little too passionate (244). The main character in "The Rabbit-Pen" is an unmarried man, a successful novelist named Fordyce who walks through his friend's garden one day "imagining marriage" and is suddenly shocked to see a tragedy in his friend's rabbit pen. The father rabbit had killed one of the new litter, and the mother battled him furiously. Crying, "Help! There is murder being done!" he stands by "trembling and impotent" as the German housekeeper rushes from the house to seize the "huge and grotesque" male in her "strong grasp" and fling him aside. Well adapted to survive in the struggle for reproductive success, the father rabbit was trying to kill the young males, as the stableman explains. To use Anderson's phrase from "Seeds," Fordyce has been badly frightened by this glimpse under the shell of male life. Later we see Fordyce reading his own book and becoming "entangled in one of his own fancies . . . that never became realities": he "imagined himself the proud husband of . . . the housekeeper." But shortly after this the housekeeper tells him that she is leaving his friend's employ, and because Fordyce hesitated, she left before he could approach her as his possible wife. Again he "felt strangely impotent and incapable." As the story closes several months later, we learn that Fordyce has decided to "learn to speak the German language" in order to be able to understand what housekeepers and stablemen are talking about when they talk of "the doings of rabbits in pens" and "whisper secrets of life." And his friend tells him that after his housekeeper left, returning to Germany to marry Hans the stableman, his household had collapsed in disarray. His wife, Ruth, who "is all love and truth," simply cannot control his sons: they have decided to send the boys to a private school because "they are pretty hard to control."

Anderson worked with these two facets of the male problem throughout his career, the problems that writers from Howells to London had also addressed in their various ways: how to imagine males who are gentle but not impotent and incapable of succeeding in the reproductive struggle. In his own variations on this theme, Anderson tends to emphasize the male's need to overcome his fear of life and of his own maleness. Focusing again and again on the male's hands, Anderson, too, reveals his troubled awareness of the secondary sexual character that, in Darwin's analysis, enabled the male to grasp and hold the female. As the impotent Fordyce tells himself in "The Rabbit-Pen," "I should be taking things into my own hands," a lesson, by the way, in which the stableman *Hans* needs no instruction. (There will be much more to say about Anderson's interest in the male hand later in this discussion, with remarks on *Dark Laughter* and an analysis of the Winesburg story "An Awakening.") But another of Anderson's quintessential images of maleness is the stallion, and this, too, appears memorably in one of his first stories, "Vibrant Life" (1916).

In this very short story, a married "man of forty-five, vigorous and straight of body" sits up all night in a vigil over his dead brother. There with him is the woman who looks after his children and to whom he had introduced his brother some years ago. She and the dead brother (who "had been caught and shot in the home of a married woman") had been lovers. In the room the surviving brother sees a magazine picture of "a magnificent stallion" and tells the woman that he had once seen a "great animal" like that, full of "vibrant, magnificent life." Suddenly moving toward the woman and standing over her, he says, "We are like that." Then "with a low laugh he sprang at her," caught her, and after they had "struggled" and "stood breathless with hot startled faces," they hear the coffin crash to the floor and see the dead man's "staring eyes."

Readers familiar with Anderson's stories will recall many other references to stallions that are often played off references to geldings, as in the story of the young man's confusing and traumatic introduction to the sexual reality in "I Want to Know Why." He aches in thinking of the "raging torrent inside" the stallion Sunstreak and cannot understand why his friend Jerry would kiss an ugly woman like a prostitute who "looked a little like the gelding Middlestride, but not clean like him." Similarly, in the less well known but related story, "The Man Who Became a Woman" (in *Horses and Men* [1923]) Anderson examines the male reality through a young man's experience with stallions and geldings at a racetrack. But here Anderson more daringly explores the nature of bisexuality through his young man's confession that he sometimes had "a kind of contempt for all men, including myself" and that he once "turned into a girl." Having witnessed a terrifying scene of male violence, he had almost "vomited," but he found relief (one of the "sweetest feelings I've ever had in my whole life") in the stall with the gelding Pick-it-boy. He is struck with how "twisted-up human beings can become . . . because they are . . . not simple and clear in their minds, and inside themselves, as animals are, maybe."

In *Poor White* Anderson had included a brief scene of "a grey gelding" that had "hauled hundreds of young men and their sweethearts" but who is "thinking perhaps of his own youth and of the tyranny of man that had made him a gelding" (176). And part of Aline Grey's exploration of maleness in *Dark Laughter* includes her recollection of her life in Paris. "Something in French life [had] fascinated her. Little incidental things about life, the men's comfort-stalls in the open streets, the stallions hitched to dust-carts and trumpeting to mares, lovers kissing each other openly in the streets . . . a kind of matter-of-fact acceptance of life that the English and Americans seemed unable to come to" (167). And as for the rape that Anderson associates with the stallion in "Vibrant Life," it would seem that in contemplating this aspect of male violence over the years, Anderson was not just ambivalent but also engaged in a long effort to accept it as an undeniable part of the male's nature. There are certainly crude males in his stories, like John May in *Poor White*, whose assaults on women he seems to deplore. But Anderson's own struggle with this part of the sex problem is better represented by his character John Webster in *Many Marriages*, who forced himself on his wife on their wedding night. When they had first met, "there had been a rape of the unconscious self" when he accidentally walked naked into her room (165). And now in the turmoil of explaining his behavior to himself, his daughter, and his wife (whom he is about to abandon), he agonizes, "Why must one commit rape, rape of the conscious, rape of the unconscious?" (185).

In his stories and novels prior to *Many Marriages*, however, Anderson's main thrust was to imagine how the young male can claim his manhood and at the same time show signs of becoming a new man. Thus, his first hero's main problem as he matures is how to get "hold of *life*," not of just a particular woman, and thereby distinguish himself from his ineffectual father (*Windy McPherson's Son* 294, emphasis mine). Sam's father is only comically inept, not sexually impotent or repressed in the manner of Anderson's later characters, nor is he sexually dissolute. In the novel's repeated image, the father appears at a town ceremony, a tall military figure on horseback, whose duty is to sound a rousing call on his bugle. When he puts the bugle to his lips, however, there was "only a thin piercing shriek followed by a squawk" (24). But as Sam tries to get hold of life he must also avoid being distracted by the unhealthy, "aching hunger" that made most men dissipate their energy in unclean pursuits. Anderson's epic goal here is to theorize a way of "building . . . a bigger cleaner race of men" (294–95).

This is also the case in his second novel, *Marching Men*, in which Beaut McGregor's devotion to "some vast design" (85) transforms his "passion for reproduction" into the kind of "love [that] invaded his spirit" (124) when he imagined that he was "crying to [the marching men], touching them, caressing them" (149). Moreover, Beaut's efforts at this kind of transformation involve more than just Anderson's own fond recollections of his brief military experience in the Spanish-American War, as some have suggested. The militancy of his marching men is explicitly sexual, as Anderson suggests in noting that Beaut "didn't want to make love, he wanted relief. He would have much preferred a fight" (102). Again, when Beaut thinks that "the riddle of the Universe" is "how to achieve order out of our strange jumble of forms," he goes on to think of great generals in history and of the "instinctive passion that bursts in the orgasm of battle" (66). At many such moments, when "the old love of battle swept in on him," it is clear that part of Anderson's effort to understand the nature of maleness involves Darwin's law of battle among males competing for females (226). But in exploring a different way of contending with male belligerence in his first novel, Anderson arranges for his hero Sam McPherson to demonstrate his power as a man of affairs: part way through his career his future wife tells him, "You will have to be a new kind of father with something maternal in [you]" (178). Soon he begins "to understand how distorted, how strangely perverted, his whole attitude toward women and sex had been," and now realizes that sex "cleanses me! . . . Sex is a solution, not a menace" (180). The marriage fails, however, because his wife cannot have children. Still, his further, unbelievable quest for meaning in his life ends in his being a new kind of father-mother when he purchases three unwanted children from a prostitute and returns with them to resume his former life with his childless wife.

Anderson continued his efforts to imagine a new male in *Poor White*, where the issues are more complicated but in which the young man's hope to differentiate himself from his father remains a central concern. In this way Anderson addresses the problem of heredity, but he does not dwell on it as morbidly as Fitzgerald does in telling of Jay Gatsby's futile efforts to create his own hereditary identity. Still, Sam McPherson "would have invented a new ancestor" if he could (*Windy* 136), and Hugh McVey in *Poor White* cannot—even "by struggle and work"—"conquer his ancestry, nor change the fact that he was at bottom poor white trash" (254). In *Poor White* the hereditary problem for Hugh is that his obsession with his "animal-like" origins is a kind of hereditary guilt that renders him impotent. When he might have followed up on a sexual invitation from a schoolteacher, "his hands trembled," and "with a conscious effort he took *himself* in hand," saying "she's a good woman and you haven't the right" (235–37, emphasis mine). Moreover, in what should have been a moment of natural intimacy between Hugh and his eventual wife, Clara, he has "ugly thoughts" of "his father's shack," "the rancid smell of decaying fish and swarms of flies," and these memories bring "little lustful thoughts" that again make him ashamed of his poor white identity (274).

If Hugh is ever to develop into a successful man, then, he must overcome his sense of shame for his sexual nature and hereditary identity, but he never does. Even on his wedding night, after a guest at the party had declared, "On a wedding night someone's got to have the nerve to do a little love-making," he runs from the wedding bed (297). In Anderson's analysis, Hugh's problem is greatly exacerbated by his having made himself into an inventor of industrial machinery. "Thinking in iron" for so long (309), he now has the "disease of thinking" (361) that does not, however, afflict the working men, who "at night [go] boldly into the presence of the woman" (310). Presumably, the men's merely physical life protects them from the disease, and, as they are evidently lower in the evolutionary scale in Anderson's imagination, their sexual lives are comparable to those of birds. At one point Hugh realizes that the working people's marriages exhibit a natural settled reality that he had accidentally observed in the behavior of courting birds (314–15).

Interwoven throughout the novel, the imagery of courting birds appears most significantly when Hugh happened to see "a trivial thing. A male bird pursued a female among the bushes beside the road. The two feathered, living creatures, vividly colored, alive with life, pitched and swooped through the air. They were like moving balls of light . . . [and] there was in them a madness, a riot of life" (311). As Hugh finally begins to realize when he compares the workers' marriages with the birds,' such courtships and marriages require that "feathers" be "ruffled": "There has been pursuit and a pretense of trying to escape" (315). By imagining the birds as balls of light, Anderson mollifies the problem of rape, suggesting once again that the male's sexual aggression is both necessary and beautiful.

But Anderson also indicates that Hugh cannot relieve his "disease of thinking" by further thought, that is, by gaining such insights from natural history. By the end of the novel the best Anderson can offer us is the promise of a newborn child: the "man child" Hugh and Clara are expecting. Kicking strongly inside his mother, he represents "the struggle of the man of another generation striving to be born" (363). And the most positive influences in Hugh's pathway to manhood have been Clara's willingness to take the lead in their lovemaking, thereby overcoming his reticence, and her fierce and indomitable "mother spirit" when she sees him as "a perplexed boy hurt by life" (360). Then, at least she "who had been a thinker stopped thinking." Before this can lead to the promise of the new man-child and the closing image of the couple going "up the steps and in at the farmhouse door" (with its notable resemblance to the closing image in *Windy McPherson's Son*), Anderson has shown us this not-so-exemplary male in contrast to several even less attractive examples of manhood.

The most important of these is a character named Steve Hunter, an exploitative investor who lives by the catchphrase of economic social Darwinism, "the survival of the fittest" (122), and by contrast to the promised man-child, Anderson identifies Hunter as "the embryo industrial magnate" (110). But there are also Clara's father, whose "possessive passion . . . destroyed his ability to love" (139–40), and John May, who ruined Clara's "first attempt to run out to life" with his crude sexual assault on her (199, 147). At this stage in his career, then, Anderson's approach to the problem of imagining a new male was to begin with one like Hugh who was already alienated from his own identity as a male, to the point that he felt that some "wall . . . shut him off from humanity" (41). Then he could imagine a new woman who could help this troubled male find "the nerve to do a little love-making" and thereby reclaim his place in the community of life (297).

Sexual Difference: The Woman "Strong to Be Loved"

Anderson's novels emphasize the development of young men, but in the story of Clara Butterworth in *Poor White*, for example, he also devotes a good deal of thought to the young woman's development. The guiding principle in his meditation on the female and the sex problem is set forth in the Winesburg story "Tandy," its point being, "There is a woman coming," as the stranger in the story prophesies. Calling himself a lover who has "not found my thing to love," the stranger explains that the absence of this new woman—obviously of the evolutionary future—will make his "destruction inevitable," that is, his extinction, as of course no individual can reach into the evolutionary future without sexual reproduction. Speaking as Anderson's prophet of sexual evolution, the stranger claims, "Perhaps of all men I alone understand" that it is not "easy to be a woman [and] to be loved." Out of woman's "defeat [has been] born a new quality" for which he has invented the name "Tandy": "the quality of being strong to be loved." It will require both strength and courage and will mean being "something more than man or woman." Anderson had touched on this question repeatedly in *Marching Men*, in which a character comments on "the new kind of woman that is growing up" (92); the hero later thinks that Margaret Ormsby is "a new kind of womanhood, something sure, reliant, hedged about and prepared as a good soldier is prepared, to have the best of it in the struggle for existence" (189).

As it turns out in this novel, Margaret "does not stand the test" because her strength and beauty pale in a confrontation with a workingwoman and because she is dominated by her wealthy father (244). Later, in *Many Marriages*, John Webster's lover, Natalie Swartz, seems to fill the bill, the darkness in her name suggesting that she, like the brown women in the novel and the black people in *Dark Laughter*, is free of the sexual repression that has wrecked Mary Webster's life. Hoping to protect his daughter from his wife's fate, Webster explains the sexual longing that had drawn him to his wife long ago and that accounts for his decision to leave his wife for Natalie: a young man dreams of this new woman "clad in shining garments" who is "suddenly to come up to him out of nowhere and bring with her new life" (126). This fantasy of the male's being selected by a superior new woman takes an unexpected turn in *Beyond Desire*. As the hero Red Oliver thinks of "a woman, beautifully gowned, walking toward you," Molly Seabright "walks across the sunlit field toward" him. Embodying the agrarian values that underlie Anderson's critique of industrial America, she is "a farm woman, a work woman" clad "in an old worn calico dress" (245–46).

Anderson's long quest for the new woman, as for the new man, is shaped by particular evolutionary problems that had to be overcome before the old "antagonism . . . between men and women" could be eased (*Poor White* 166). Chief among these are first the woman's fear of men based on her early experience as a victim of sexual assault and her consequent lapse into submissiveness—the main kind of defeat from which her new quality will be born, to use the terms from "Tandy." Also, as the selector, she must learn how to play fair with men as the selector, so as not to "lead [characters like Beaut McGregor] into being a reproductive tool for her" (*Marching Men* 128). And she must recognize, as does the character Louise in *Beyond Desire*, that as the selector she has "something savage and ugly in [her] too" that causes her to fall "for you men in your uniforms" (337). Also, as with Anderson's males, his women need to overcome sexual repression, free themselves from the role of submissiveness, and be willing to take the leading role in sexual intimacy. However, Anderson's greatest source of optimism that the sexual antagonism might someday end is the fierce maternal instinct that figures in nearly all his work as the power in the "woman who [might] save" the troubled hero from himself, as in *Beyond Desire*, for example (305).

Four women who figure significantly in Anderson's novels are assaulted in their youth by overeager males, Clara Butterworth in *Poor White*, Mary Webster in *Many Marriages*, Molly Seabright in *Beyond Desire*, and Kit Brandon in *Kit Brandon*. Of these, only Mary is psychologically devastated by the assault, her husband's rape of her on their wedding night. He had concluded that "there came a time when fear must be put aside. One was a male and at the proper time went toward the female and took her. There was a kind of cruelty in nature and at the proper time that cruelty became a part of one's manhood." When Webster acted on this feeling and approached his wife, "he was on his knees like an animal" (183). The problem is that she had "said [what] almost everyone said"—that "after all man was not an animal. Man was a conscious thing trying to struggle upward out of animalism. . . . If one just let oneself go one became no better than a beast" (186). After the wedding night the marriage was permanently damaged by Mary's ensuing sense of shame. Though Anderson presents this sexual conflict from both points of view, he is clearly more sympathetic with John Webster's animalism and natural cruelty than with his wife's response to it, suggesting that, even in her repressive agony, she "was so much more like an animal than himself" (190). And there is no question that in comparison with Anderson's other victims of sexual assault, Clara Butterworth and Molly Seabright, Mary serves as his example of the woman who cannot be born anew out of her defeats.

In Clara's case, the aggressor is a cruder male than John Webster, yet his animalism is as innocent and natural as his name, John May, suggests. He and the other men on the farm eat "greedily like hungry animals," but in their sexual encounter both John and Clara are "young animals" (*Poor White* 146). In fact, Anderson holds Clara largely responsible for the sexual violence that ensues, she having flirted with May, having playfully thrown a corncob at him, and then having run laughingly into the shed where he assaulted her. Anderson writes that May "was a little amazed by her boldness but did not stop to ask himself questions. She had openly invited him to pursue her" (147). But this assault is certainly more willfully brutal than Webster's: after catching her, as "she lay trembling and weak in his arms . . . he took hold of the collar of her dress and tore it open. Her brown neck and one of her hard, round breasts were exposed" (147). However, striving to construe this as an ultimately positive experience in Clara's development, Anderson describes Clara's Tandy-like strength and courage: she does not submit to him, as her own mother "had submitted" and whose "life had been a story of submission" (293). Rather, Clara's "eyes grew big with fright [and] strength came back into her body" (147).

When, having fought back and broken free, she ran upstairs to her room, Anderson writes that "a farm dog followed her up the stairs and stood at her door wagging his tail," and his concluding point in regard to the whole incident is that "*for the moment* everything that lived and breathed seemed to her gross and ugly" (148, emphasis mine). Over the course of the novel other experiences will shape her development, particularly her companionship with a lesbian friend, but Clara becomes a kind of Tandy, marrying the hero Hugh McVey and ending the novel as the prospective mother of the new man-child.

When he gave us the character Molly Seabright twelve years later in *Beyond Desire*, Anderson was both more and less optimistic in projecting the evolutionary future. Molly remains single at the end of the novel, having had only a brief and nonsexual encounter with the hero. But before he is killed in a communist riot for a cause to which he is only vaguely committed, he repeatedly sees Molly in a "circle of light" as she milks a cow: her hands are "gripping teats—milk coming . . . the strong sweet smell of the milk, of animal life in the barn" (311). And as in the story of Clara, Molly's allure as the woman who came toward Red results largely from her having refused to submit to a would-be rapist in her youth. A young mountain man had attacked her, this time without her having teased him on as Clara had, but when he tried to throw her to the ground and before she escaped his grasp she had an even more frightening experience with the aroused male: she saw "his face pressed down close to her own for a moment, the queer determined terrible look in his eyes" (280). Still, with the natural power of self-renewal suggested in her name, Seabright, Molly overcame that ordeal. In a later episode Anderson pays a second tribute to Joyce's Molly Bloom (as he had remarked on "her night of animalism" in *Dark Laughter* [120]), writing that when Molly's "time to bloom had come," she consented to a sexual encounter with a married man she liked and who was her "own kind" (296). She became pregnant and secretly aborted the child, but she came back from this defeat, as well, to stand in the center of Anderson's circle of light as his most promising image of "woman's form" (312).

A second problem to be overcome in the evolution of Anderson's new woman was the way in which she exercises the key power of female choice in sexual selection. And in dealing with this issue he is no more consistent than he is in presenting the male's sexual eagerness as both brutal and, at the same time (apparently in an effort to rouse his timid heroes to effective manhood), harmless as the male bird's pursuit of the female. That is, while Beaut McGregor resists the idea of becoming a woman's reproductive tool, Red Oliver hopes to find "a strong woman [who] will suddenly see in me something, . . . hidden manhood I can't yet see or feel myself" (*Beyond Desire* 306). Tracing Clara Butterworth's development in relation to her power to select, Anderson note's first that she had begun "to take revenge upon men for their betrayal of her," as when John May had assaulted her. She began an experiment with a young school teacher and tempted him into kissing her in order to "find out, without risk to herself, the things she wanted to know about life"; this led to an expected confrontation between her and the school teacher and John May, who had observed them jealously. When May approached them Clara provoked the rival males into acting out the law of battle so that she might observe them. She picked up a rock, handed it to the schoolteacher, and said, "Hit him . . . don't be afraid. He's only a coward. Hit him on the head with the stone" (153–54). Her experiment is a disappointment, however, as the young schoolteacher runs away, and she returns to her home angry and alone, leaving the frustrated May to mutter, "She was making a bluff" (155). As Anderson put it several years later in *Beyond Desire*, remarking on the violence in sexual selection, whereby the female selects the dominant male, the woman's erotic attraction to the male's military uniform reveals something of her own savage and brutal nature, as well (337). In the earlier novel, however, wanting to present Clara's development beyond simple brutality, Anderson writes that when Clara talked with her friend Kate Chanceller (a lesbian) about her role in provoking the males' violence, "for the first time she got a sense of justice toward men" and realized that she hadn't been "square" with the schoolteacher. Thus, when she meets the hero, Hugh, she first plans "to use him for her own ends" (167) but soon "all thought of [that] had gone" (262), and eventually this helped them to consummate their troubled but finally promising marriage.

Later, in *Dark Laughter*, after Aline had been tempted unsuccessfully into a lesbian relationship with a woman named Esther, Esther counseled her, in quite a different spirit from Kate Chanceller's advice to Clara, that "you get what you reach out your hand and take. Women always do the taking—if they have the courage" (202). Thus Aline married Fred Grey, only to realize later "how many men [there are] in the world" and that her marriage for "money and position" had left her unhappy (135). Only after she had selected Bruce, because she "intended playing with him, exerting her power over him" (252), does she begin to realize how "infinitely glad" she was to have him (283). She had taken a younger, stronger, more handsome man as a lover and then recognized that she really loved her husband, Fred. Still, because she found "how very gentle and strong [Bruce] was" as a lover and how he brought "peace to the body, to the spirit too" (260), because he had impregnated her after her years of childlessness with her husband, because she realized that "things changed in nature" (261), and because the novel celebrates the vital "river life" on the "Mother Mississippi," where the motto is "Keep afloat! Keep afloat!" (100, 258)—for these reasons Anderson encourages Aline to join with the lover she has selected in the "grotesque dance of life" (90). Together, they "will be compelled to face new problems," but it will be "a new kind of life" (299).

In his first potential new woman, Sue Rainey, in *Windy McPherson's Son*, Anderson imagined a companion with whom his timid male could join in "service to mankind through children" but without giving in to "the hungry pursuit of pleasure" (177). Eventually they join in that cause after their own babies had died in birth by adopting children. In this tentative exploration of a possible marriage in the service to mankind but free from the sexual motive to reproduce, Anderson gives us a glimpse of Sue's ideal male, a beautiful man who "was past sixty but looked like a boy of twenty-five, not in his body, but in an air of youth that hung over him. . . . He was clean. He had lived clean, body and mind" (175–76). Cleansed of the sexual taint, this male exemplifies the wisdom Sam gains in his further quest, that "vice was openly crude and masculine . . . unclean and unhealthy" (296–97). Sam's ideal, then, is that "marriage is a port . . . a point of departure" for "the real voyage of life" (183). And Anderson certainly underscores his tentativeness about this new kind of life by closing the novel with the image of Sam as he "stumbled up the steps into the house." But before he could move this new couple beyond a mere sexual basis for cohering he realized that he could not bring them together in the first place without sexual union. And at this point Sue Rainey's emphatically androgynous nature plays a key role in bringing the reluctant hero to full life as a male. On first meeting her, Sam "had been pricked by a mild curiosity concerning her. . . . He knew that she was athletic, travelled much, rode, shot, and sailed a boat; and he had heard [that she was] a woman of brains" (164). Sporting these traditional masculine qualities, Sue is already like Tandy in that she is "something more than man or woman," and she is so "strong to be loved" that she takes the lead in their first lovemaking ("Tandy"). In order to help Sam (son of the ineffectual Windy McPherson) claim his natural masculinity, "she got her rifle and gave [him] his first lesson in marksmanship, his awkwardness making the lesson half a jest." Then, under the stars and in a "clean cold wind" they "lay down together for their first long tender embrace" (185).

By the time Anderson traced Clara Butterworth's sexual development four years later in *Poor White*, his analysis had become more complicated, including Clara's having to withstand the assault by John May and then, during her first years in college, her relationship with another male who "had nothing to urge upon her except the needs of his body" (163). At this point Clara meets Kate Chanceller, a woman who will teach her a great deal about life and love; she "wore skirts and had the body of a woman, [but] was in her nature a man" (165). Kate's function in the novel is to introduce the idea that Kate explains to Clara—that although "men hate such women" as herself, "they should watch and study us." For one thing, "being part women," she says, "we know how to approach women" gently and delicately; whereas men are too often "blundering and crude" (167). Although "something like lovemaking had happened between" Kate and Clara, their relationship is not burdened with the sexual antagonism that often exists between Anderson's men and women (298); thus, "in Kate's presence [Clara] became bolder than she had ever been with any one," telling her of her unhappy experiences with men (166). Moreover, in this closeness Clara hears Kate's advice about being fair in her dealings with men, and she learns valuable lessons on how to dress in style; as a result, when the hero Hugh sees them together, he thought that Clara's "dress was the most stylish thing he had ever seen" (253). In these several ways, then, Anderson exploits Clara's relationship with Kate in order to help Clara become "more than man or woman" (as he said of Tandy) and thus have the strength as a new woman to lead the hero toward psychosexual liberation from his sense of guilt as an animalistic poor white male. Along the way she realizes that "already [she'd] taken things too much into [her] own hands" (275), but determined to "put through this marriage," she persists in leading the way until she helps him find the required "nerve to do a little love-making" (297).

Since this is a major obstacle in Anderson's imagination, however, he gives us drawn-out descriptions of the couple's painful failures to consummate the marriage. On the wedding night, tired of waiting for him to make a move, she first speaks to him "sharply" and leads him to the bedroom; then she speaks to him "in a low, husky voice," and she finally breaks out in anger when he simply sits looking "into the darkness outside" (303–4). The following "evening was the hardest of their lives" and ends when Clara retreats to her room, where she kneels "just inside the door, waiting, hoping for, and fearing the coming of the man" (307–8). Finally, over a week later, even after seeing the male bird pursuing the female, when Hugh tried to do "the necessary thing in life" he once again "surrendered . . . the manhood in himself" (316–17). But as Clara's father realizes, in sympathy with the "defeated, frightened man," the only solution to this problem is for the woman to "put out her hand [and] reassure him" (310–11). Thus, his hovering "about . . . like a mother bird" over a fledgling "prematurely pushed out of the nest" (311), the father helps to bring about the desired end: when Clara finally "said softly and firmly" and obviously in the tones of a mother, "Come here, Hugh" (317). Obediently, he went toward her "like a boy caught doing a forbidden act," and "from him there was no protest and no attempt to escape the love-making that followed" (317). Anderson describes how Clara takes the lead by using the hand that had become identified as a key secondary sexual character of the male. "Her hand crept up and lay in his hand. It seemed unbelievably large. It was not soft, but hard and firm," and when she let "the hand [go] out of his and touched, caressed . . . his wet hair, his cheeks," Anderson writes that something stirred to life in Hugh. He remembers the "flight of the male bird . . . in pursuit," and then "the new thing he had found . . . inside himself . . . flew like a bird out of darkness and into the light" (318–19). Even now, however, Anderson suggests that this new life will not "run on forever" (319), so severe is Hugh's "disease of thinking" (361), and only by enlisting the aid of Clara's mother instinct, "fierce, indomitable, [and] strong," when she sees Hugh as a "perplexed boy hurt by life," can Anderson close the novel with his promise of the new man-child to be born (360).

Reflections of Freud and Havelock Ellis in Anderson's Presentation of Sex

Anderson was not alone among writers of the twenties to doubt that the Freudian cure could provide any meaningful relief for "the universal illness," the need to be loved ("Seeds"). Three whose work he knew and admired, Fitzgerald, Hemingway, and D. H. Lawrence, were also skeptics, Lawrence, for example, writing that, "while the Freudian theory of the unconscious and the incest motive is valuable as a *description* of our psychological condition," "the moment you apply it to *life* . . . the theory becomes mechanistic."[10] Nevertheless, Anderson realized that the Freudian theory of sex and the unconscious, along with other works like Havelock Ellis's *Sexual Selection in Man*, were further developments in the exploration of the sexual instinct, the emotions, and the unconscious that Darwin had begun in the *The Origin of Species; The Descent of Man, and Selection in Relation to Sex;* and *The Expression of the Emotions in Man and Animals*. Anderson had not necessarily studied these works. There is little indication, for example, that he was nearly as interested in *The Expression of the Emotions* as were other writers like Kate Chopin or Harold Frederic.[11] But, especially if one had followed the realists' and naturalists' studies of courtship and marriage, as Anderson had, the continuity between the Darwinian and Freudian theories of sexuality would have been evident, for example, in Freud's analysis of the psychology of the dream processes and in the first sentences to *Three Contributions to the Theory of Sex*. In the analysis of dreams, Freud expected to build on our "knowledge of the archaic inheritance of man" and to help "reconstruct the oldest and darkest phases of the beginnings of mankind" (*Basic Writings* 497). And he began his *Three Contributions to the Theory of Sex* by noting that "the fact of sexual need in man and animal is expressed in biology by the assumption of a 'sexual instinct.' This instinct is made analogous to the instinct of taking nourishment, and to hunger. The sexual expression corresponding to hunger not being found colloquially, science uses the expression, 'libido'" (*Basic Writings* 553).

Thus, it is not always easy to separate the Darwinian from the Freudian elements in Anderson's presentation of sexuality. His interest in the female's power to select, for example, seems to reflect how this traditionally Darwinian element in realist and naturalist novels was of much greater interest to him as a novelist than Freud's analysis of "object finding" or "object selection" in the individual's sexual development (*Three Contributions to the Theory of Sex*). Even here, however, there is reason to believe that Anderson drew on Freud's discussion of "The Sexual Object of the Invert" in his famous Winesburg story "Hands" at the same time that he sought to situate the story in a traditionally Darwinian setting. The story opens with an image of Wing Biddlebaum as his nervous hands seemed to be "arranging a mass of tangled locks" on his bald head. From the townspeople's point of view, Wing Biddlebaum's "shadowy personality [seemed] submerged in a sea of doubts," and his nervous fingers sometimes seemed to "wriggle, like a fish." As in the novel *Many Marriages*, this kind of sea imagery suggest both the character's original animal nature and a Darwinian-Freudian conception of the unconscious. Moreover, Anderson's sympathetic (though at the time very controversial) portrayal of Wing Biddlebaum suggests his awareness of Darwin's and then Freud's point that "a certain degree of anatomical hermaphroditism really belongs to the normal" and that it is a "long known anatomical fact . . . that there is an original predisposition to bisexuality" (Freud, *Three Contributions*, 558). And when Anderson explains that Wing "was one of those men in whom the force that creates life is diffused, not centralized," there is a discernible suggestion that he was aware of the controversy among sexologists about whether there were "male and female brain centers."[12] As a whole, then, in its emphasis on Wing's inability to "conceal his hands" or control "the nervous expressive fingers," the story seems clearly intended to explore the kind of Freudian reality, concerning inversion and repression, to which Anderson was exposed in his discussions of Freudianism with his Chicago friends. As he recalls in his *Memoirs*, "It was a time when it was well for a man to be somewhat guarded in the remarks he made, what he did with his hands." In one such discussion, he recalls, "when there were several of us gathered together in a room . . . in an unfortunate moment, I brought up the subject of homosexuality" (339).

At many other moments in his career there is similar evidence that Anderson was rather more than the "psychoanalyst by default" that Frederick J. Hoffman took him to be. Although Hoffman asked himself what kinds of suggestions exist in Anderson's work to indicate that he had thought about Freud, and although he admits that Anderson was "not unaware . . . of the subject matter of psychoanalysis, and [that] occasionally the language intrudes in his novels," he refers to very few such moments and has nothing at all to say about the story "Hands," for example.[13] The most famous of Anderson's references to Freud is in *Dark Laughter*, when, apparently through the mind of his character Bruce Dudley, he remarks on Dudley's life as a man in his thirties who is "enamored of a woman, his physical being all aroused." It "is a common enough sight," but in answer to the question, "Does it matter?" Anderson writes, "Men who have passed the age of thirty and who have intelligence understand such things. A German scientist can explain perfectly. If there is anything you do not understand in human life consult the works of Dr. Freud" (230). This ambiguous remark has been interpreted in various ways, Hoffman, for example, suggesting that Anderson seems to be saying to the reader, if you have found my characters hard to understand, "Dr. Freud has studied these matters calmly and scientifically, and he will aid you. But if you do go to him, you will have failed to understand much of what I wish to say to you" (*Freudianism* 255).

This seems a reasonable suggestion, except that Hoffman sees no irony in Anderson's note that Dr. Freud could explain anything about life, nor does he offer us any help in trying to understand what Anderson *does* wish to say about these characters. Anderson's ambivalence about Freud is clear enough. He certainly does suggest that Fred Grey (the ineffectual husband whom Aline leaves when she selects Bruce as a lover) is sexually repressed, and in the paragraph following his reference to Freud, Anderson traces Fred's problem to his having become hysterical during the war and, therefore, having killed a man: "he had been made hysterical because he had seen men in the raw" (230). And in analyzing Bruce's first, failed marriage to Bernice, he notes that "they hadn't any children because Bernice never wanted them"; she had her career as a writer and thought that he was "flighty" and not "very ambitious" (36). The point of his analysis of Bruce is that he had "never taken hold of life with his hands"—that is, that he had failed to accept the male's aggressive role in nature, according to Darwin's analysis (60). Anderson explains, "There was a disease of life due to men getting away from their own hands, their bodies too," but this is certainly not the case with Bruce's friend, the working man named Sponge (98). As his name suggests, Sponge is related to the large-clawed oceanic crustaceans that Darwin cites as his example of prehensile power having evolved as the male's means of capturing and holding the female. Anderson tells us that "with [Sponge] everything is down in his hands. He gets everything out of him through his hands. Take his woman away and he would get another with his hands"; he is not "the kind that makes a mess of his life" (125).

In his characteristic way, then, Anderson takes this essentially Darwinian point forward into a kind of Freudian analysis. Thinking about his sterile relationship with Bernice, Bruce wonders, "Did he have any special desire to torture Bernice and if he did, why? Now she wanted to have it out with him, to bite, strike, kick, like a furious little female animal," and recalling that sometimes he had the notion that "Bernice wanted him to beat her" (50), he wonders, "Am I becoming a Sadist?" (53).[14] Clearly Anderson is attempting here to emphasize the Darwinian element in Freud's analysis of sadism and masochism, wherein he asserts that "the pleasure in pain and cruelty" is present "in the normal individual. The sexuality of most men shows an admixture of aggression, of a desire to subdue, the biological significance of which lies in the necessity for overcoming the resistance of the sexual object by actions other than mere *courting*" (*Basic Writings* 569).[15] But, to return to Frederick J. Hoffman's unanswered question about what Anderson might want to say to us regarding all this—that is, beyond what Dr. Freud might be able to explain about life—even if Fred Grey could overcome his sexual repression and even after Bruce Dudley learns how to be more fully alive in his "maleness," the problem remains that what Anderson has seen under the "shell of life" is still enough to make him afraid and continue to ask the "fearful question! What does it mean? What is love?" ("Seeds," *Dark Laughter*, 286). Knowing that "the world has no plan for creating" the kind of gentle lovers one dreams of, the kind who would love one "long and

quietly and patiently," Anderson can only suggest that Bruce and Aline have succeeded in the struggle of sexual selection. She is pregnant by the new, stronger lover
she has selected in Bruce, and he, having learned to take hold of life with his hands,
has taken the woman from the weaker male. When Bruce and Aline passed "through
the gate [and] out of the garden" into their "new kind of life" (one of Anderson's
several suggestions that his characters have entered a modernity like that in *The
Great Gatsby* or *The Sun Also Rises*, in which both God and Love are dead), Anderson writes that "they had been caught" and "could not draw back" ("Seeds," *Dark
Laughter*, 300, 299).

There are many other suggestions in Anderson's fiction that he had explored
the sex problem in light of Freud and Havelock Ellis, suggestions that he included
in part, no doubt, merely to indicate to his readers and fellow writers that he had
been around. For example, he causes his introspective character Bruce to consider
the key problem in Freudian analysis in worrying that he "might wake up some
night, crying for mother, wanting her soft arms about me, my head on her soft
breasts. Mother-complex—something of that sort" (92). And two sentences later
in the same passage, remarking on "The dance of life!" Anderson displays his awareness that Freud and Ellis were colleagues who often referred to each other's work in
the same general analysis of the sexual instinct. Also, in *Many Marriages*, Anderson
explores a darker aspect of the sexual instinct that had interested others from William James to Jack London—the studies of the sexual instinct in frogs (and by extension, mammals) that Ellis discusses in *Analysis of the Sexual Impulse*. Reviewing
the well-known laboratory research on frogs, Ellis was interested in how the sexual
impulse was dispersed throughout the "whole of [the] sensitive system" (rather
like Freud's later theory of the "polymorphous-perverse disposition"), so that "by
removing various parts of the female frog Goltz found that every part of the female
was attractive to the male at pairing time" (*Studies* 1:2:4). As the character John
Webster thinks about his failed marriage with his repressed wife, Anderson writes
that "the truth was that he had got the notion into his head that there was in her a
kind of spiritual power divorced altogether from the flesh. Outside the house, along
the river banks, frogs were calling their throaty calls and once in the night some
strange weird call came out of the air" (*Many Marriages* 188). Soon, in an extended
passage that includes his typical sea imagery to represent the unconscious, as well
as a clear indication that Anderson had also considered Freud's theory of Eros and
the death wish from *Beyond the Pleasure Principle*,[16] Webster declares, "Now I accept the flesh first, all flesh" (189). Toward the end of this meditation, then, Anderson indicates once again that he is interested mainly in the underlying biological
insights that had provoked many writers to puzzle over man's place in nature or
the riddle of the universe. As Webster remarks to himself, "In one evening I have
managed to plunge pretty deeply down into the sea of life" (201).

"The Hidden Wonder Story": The Unconscious and Anderson's Transcendental Naturalism

In addition to the many indications that Anderson was intent on exploring the realm of the sexual unconscious in the wake of Darwin, the naturalists, Freud, and Ellis, there is a more pervasive and important psychological element in his work—his interest in what he called indirection or the fancy, which loosely resembles Freud's various "modes of indirect representation" in dreams (*Basic Writings* 370), or the "dream-phantasy" (528), or "the free indulgence of the psyche in the play of its faculties" (527), or the patient's "free association" in analysis (370). There is only a loose resemblance here; unlike Freud, Anderson was prepared to trust the unconscious as a source of possibly transcendent truth or wisdom, like that which drew him so powerfully to Walt Whitman and Whitman's celebration of his "fancy." While Freud held that "the unconscious is the true psychic reality" (542), one that, when acknowledged, "permits of successful therapeutic intervention in the curable forms of the psychoneuroses" (547–48), Anderson was inclined to place his faith in the unconscious as the expression of an essentially beneficent if often frightening and painful natural order that had become distorted by modern industrial life and repression.

To put it another way, Freud explained how the present perfection of the "psychic apparatus" owes its long process of evolution, or development, to the great physical needs or "exigencies of life" that first resulted in expression of the emotions (508–9). He also explained how, under the pressure of external reality and repression, the "treacherous expression" or "outlawed dream-thoughts" issued a psychic impulse that allowed for wish-fulfillment in the dream or hallucination (473). But Anderson held that the living force within his characters that "could not find expression" was not only a libidinous wish in search of fulfillment but also the cry of an isolated modern spirit in search of "light" ("Seeds"). As the character LeRoy explains in "Seeds," the distraught woman "was like a young tree choked by a climbing vine. The thing that had wrapped her about [her obsession with sex] had shut out the light." And as Anderson suggests here, the need to be loved is the primary or "universal illness," whereas the need for a lover is "after all, a quite secondary thing." Indeed, it seems, the modern analysis of the libido that sometimes made even Freud want to "get away from [his] rummaging in human filth" (*Basic Writings* 441) also left Anderson's character LeRoy in "Seeds" feeling "weary" and wanting "more than anything else in the world to be made clean" (31). And while Freud might well have analyzed Anderson's tendency to indulge his fancy in the manner suggested in "The Relation of the Poet to Day-Dreaming," Anderson was confident that his self-conscious plan to loose his fancy would make good sense to his friend the psychoanalyst Trigant Burrow.

In October 1919 Anderson wrote to Burrow of "a notion that can't fail to interest you," his plan "to write a book to be called *Industrial Vistas*":

It is to be the autobiography of a man's secondary self, of the queer, unnamed fancies that float through his brain, the things that appear to have no connection with actualities.

In me, and, I fancy, in most men, odd, detached fancies are born, blossom, sometimes like flowers, sometimes like evil-smelling weeds, then appear to pass.

My notion is that no man knows himself or can arrive at truth concerning himself except by what seems like indirection. I have a desire to take hold of indirection as a tool and use it in an attempt to arrive at truth.

Industrial Vistas, you see, because it is written out of the jangle and ugliness of industrial life.

By my plan and by indirection, you see, I hope to make an odd, insane-seeming man emerge into actuality. (*Letters* 50)

As I noted earlier, *Industrial Vistas* (which Anderson never produced) suggests Walt Whitman's *Democratic Vistas* and the kind of Whitman-inspired book that Anderson's friend Waldo Frank published this same year, *Our America*.[17] Anderson explained to Burrow his belief that "an analysis of America . . can best be achieved by the autobiography of the fanciful life of an individual" (*Letters* 50).

While readers have often noted the confused "groping" for emotional truths in Anderson's stories, it was mainly this approach that caused his friends and fellow Freudians Trigant Burrow and Waldo Frank to think of him as "an original psychologist in his own right" (Burrow, *A Search for Man's Sanity*, 559) or as a genius whose power "to incarnate . . . the inchoate emotions of his people" marked him as "a mature voice singing a culture at its close" (Frank, "*Winesburg, Ohio* After Twenty Years," 119–20). But Anderson's plan to use "indirection" is also key to his unique effort to transcend the Darwinian reality that he had begun to confront at the outset of his career in "The Rabbit-Pen." That is, in his accustomed transcendental naturalism (to use F. Scott Fitzgerald's phrase) Anderson does not project a view of altruistic, cosmic love as did Frank Norris, with help from Joseph Le Conte, nor does it project a Bergsonian version of the libido subsumed in the *élan vital*.[18] Rather, he sought to revive Whitman's sexual mysticism not only as a measure of what America had lost to the industrial sickness and sexual repression but also as the basis of his faith that the individual's physical and spiritual isolation can be eased, that—aside from mere sexual release—"the thing needed" in order to make "the mature life of men and women in the modern world possible" *does* exist ("Sophistication," *Winesburg, Ohio*).

Whitman's appeal for writers like Waldo Frank and Anderson lay largely in his celebration of sex and the body. For this reason Whitman had been the only member of his own generation to absorb the Darwinian blow with the equanimity he expressed in his remark of 1888 that "'Leaves of Grass' is avowedly the song of Sex and Amativeness, and even Animality" and his belief that a new attitude would emerge "towards the thought and fact of sexuality, as an element in character, personality, the emotions, and a theme in literature" (*Prose Works, 1892,* 2:727–28). In the following decades, then, Whitman's openness to sex exemplified the kind of good health that Frank, Anderson, and others like Edward Carpenter and Havelock Ellis understood in light of the new views on sexual repression.[19]

The Whitmanesque theme emerges in Anderson's first novel when his young hero Sam McPherson

> read Walt Whitman and had a season of admiring his own body and its straight white legs, and the head that was poised so jauntily on the body. Sometimes he would awaken on summer nights and be so filled with strange longing that he would creep out of bed and, pushing open the window, sit upon the floor, his bare legs sticking out beyond his white nightgown, and, thus sitting, yearn eagerly toward some fine impulse, some call, some sense of bigness and of leadership that was absent from the necessities of the life he led. He looked at the stars and listened to the night noises, so filled with longing that the tears sprang to his eyes. (*Windy McPherson's Son* 29)

Later, in Anderson's more mature work, the key Whitman text that seems reflected almost everywhere—from his stories of the grotesque lives in *Winesburg, Ohio* to his first fully "Freudian" (and, as many critics have noted, Lawrencian) novel, *Many Marriages*—is Whitman's visionary poem "The Sleepers." For example, when John Webster, the hero of *Many Marriages,* leaves his lifeless marriage for a relationship with another woman, he is not merely indulging in jazz-age promiscuity. As Anderson tells us in his *Memoirs,* "it wasn't exactly free love we wanted" (341), and in the same, essentially Whitmanesque, spirit Frank mocked people who were in those years flocking "to Greenwich Village where they bedded in Freudian freedom" (Frank, *Memoirs,* 144). Anderson called his book *Many Marriages,* "meaning to convey the feeling of contacts among people, of the flesh and not of the flesh—something deeply of the spirit that nevertheless has the flesh in it" (Anderson, *Memoirs,* 152). Thus, imagining that he might have many lovers and "many marriages," John Webster feels "certain that the possibility of human relationship had not even been tapped yet. Something had stood in the way of a sufficiently broad acceptance of life" (72). And in several instances in which he enacts a characteristic Andersonian scene, Webster walks alone through the village or city streets at night, imagining the lives of people in houses along the way. Once, for example, he went "in fancy" into his neighbor's house, went softly from room to room through the house. There was the old man asleeping beside his wife and in another room the son who had drawn up his legs so that he lay in a little ball. He was a pale slender young man. "Perhaps he has indigestion," whispered John Webster's fancy. In another room the two daughters lay in two beds set closely together. One could just pass between them. They had been whispering to each other before they slept, perhaps of the lover they hoped would come some time in the future. He stood so close to them that he could have touched their cheeks with his out-stretched fingers (71–72).

He thinks of the many houses and the "people [who] were sleeping in their beds. How many bodies lying and sleeping close together, babes . . . young boys . . . young women. . . . As they slept they dreamed. Of what did they dream? He had a great desire that what had happened to himself and Natalie [his lover] should happen to all of them" (77–78).

The following excerpts from Whitman's "Sleepers" provide a sense of the transcendent vision that buoys Anderson's naturalism and elevates his longing for intimacy beyond mere libidinous desire. The poem begins, "I wander all night in my vision,"

Stepping with light feet, swiftly and noiselessly stepping and stopping,
Bending with open eyes over the shut eyes of sleepers,
Wandering and confused, lost to myself, ill-assorted, contradictory,
Pausing, gazing, bending, and stopping.

How solemn they look there, stretch'd and still,
How quiet they breathe, the little children in their cradles.

The wretched features of ennuyés, the white features of corpses, the livid faces of drunkards, the sick-gray faces of onanists,
The gash'd bodies on battle-fields, the insane in their strong-door'd rooms, the sacred idiots. . . .
. . . .
The married couple sleep calmly in their bed, he with his palm on the hip of his wife,
    she with her palm on the hip of the husband,
The sisters sleep lovingly side by side in their bed,
The men sleep loving side by side in theirs,
And the mother sleeps with her little child carefully wrapt.

. . . .

The female that loves unrequited sleeps,

And the male that loves unrequited sleeps,

The head of the money-maker that plotted all day sleeps. . . .

. . . .

I go from bedside to bedside, I sleep close with the other sleepers each in
turn,

I dream in my dreams all the dreams of the other dreamers,

And I become the other dreamers.

Whitman's visionary intimacy with such persons (especially "the insane in their strong-door'd rooms [and] the sacred idiots") is a model for Anderson's approach to his grotesques in Winesburg.[20] Entering the lives of his characters, he, like Whitman, can "dream the dreams of the other dreamers." Of course Whitman wrote these lines long before Darwin had conceived of the theory of sexual selection or Freud his theory of repression, yet there is nothing in Anderson quite so boldly uninhibited as other of Whitman's lines here, such as "Darkness, you are gentler than my lover, his flesh was sweaty and panting, / I feel the hot moisture yet that he left me." Still, Anderson's fondness for the "Sleepers" theme in Whitman suggests how he had found his own way of transcending the naturalist or Darwinian reality by escaping from the walled-in self into psychic or spiritual intimacy with others; yet by indulging his Whitmanesque fancy, Anderson could explore a version of the unconscious life that also seemed to be in the new "Freudian" key.

In making this comparison, it would be mistaken to suggest that Anderson could sustain Whitman's vibrant faith in the spiritual reality wherein the beautiful sleepers "flow hand in hand over the whole earth from east to west as they lie unclothed," or in the idea that Whitman's "invigoration of the night," his mystic love, can make "the insane . . . sane" or "the poor distress'd head . . . free." Anderson's characters never realize such states of being healed (any more than do Whitman's ailing sleepers) nor are any cured through Freudian analysis. Moreover, Anderson can never rest in a vision of evolutionary progress wherein satisfactory new women and new men can free themselves from the constraints of natural selection and sexual selection. Sometimes, as in the Winesburg story "An Awakening," a character's fancy brings him glimpses of natural realities that ultimately defeat him. At best, characters like George Willard can sense the regenerative promise of the budding maple trees in Winesburg, noting that "the seeds are winged," and yet he realizes that "when the wind blows they whirl crazily about, filling the air and making a carpet underfoot" ("Departure"). Or, Anderson can relieve, if not transcend, the grotesque reality of modern life by showing that, in truth, a pathetic character like Wing Biddlebaum in "Hands," for example, is not the beast that Winesburg citizens believe him to be. Rather, Wing is only an "odd, insane-seeming man," to use Anderson's phrase from his letter to Trigant Burrow. Moreover, Wing's advice to the young George Willard expresses Anderson's Whitmanesque faith in the idea that George "must try to forget all [he has] learned" and overcome his tendency to be afraid of dreams. And in Wing's "wholly inspired" dream, "men lived again in a kind of pastoral golden age" in which a Whitmanesque bard presided: "Across a green open country came clean-limbed young men . . . to gather about the feet of the old man who sat beneath a tree in a tiny garden and who talked to them." As Anderson explains, he offers this story in hopes that he might "arouse the poet who will tell the hidden wonder story of the influence for which [Wing's] hands were but the fluttering pennants of promise."

Sexual Violence, Play of Mind, and Transcendence in *Winesburg, Ohio*

In two representative stories from *Winesburg, Ohio*, "An Awakening" and "Sophistication," one can examine the way Anderson worked with a number of issues involving the sex problem during the early years of his career, when he produced his masterpiece. "An Awakening" centers on the kind of experience that typifies so many post-Darwinian novels of courtship and marriage when a young person begins to realize his nature as an animal in the community of common descent, as well as something of the larger question involving man's place in nature. Many characters in novels from the 1870s through the first decades of the twentieth century "awaken" in such ways, some of the most famous examples being Kate Chopin's Edna Pontellier in *The Awakening* and Jack London's Martin Eden. Edna is like "a sleek animal waking up in the sun," and when Anderson's George Willard lingers in an alleyway, "smelling the strong smell of animals," he lets "his mind play with the strange new thoughts that [come] to him. The very rankness of the smell of manure in the clear sweet air awoke something heady in his brain." This awakening occurs when George is just beginning to realize his manhood and when he finds himself in a triangular relationship with Belle Carpenter. Anderson bases the story on the two general principles of sexual selection, the males' competition for possession of the female and the female's power to select. Unfortunately for George, Belle has already selected her man: she "occasionally walked out in the evening with George," but "secretly she loved another man." The other man is Ed Handby, whose last name identifies him as the superior male—with Darwinian prehensile power. Thus, Anderson focuses repeatedly on Handby's powerful hands and fists, including once when Handby "gripped [Belle's] shoulders with his strong hands." The trouble for George arises when Belle finds that Handby is not attentive enough. Then she begins to use George, letting "him kiss her to relieve a longing that was very insistent in her nature" and hoping also to arouse Handby's jealousy.

Apparently beginning to realize that he must take a more aggressive stance, George attempts to whip up his self-confidence by declaring to a number of "boys" gathered in the pool room to talk of women "that women should look out for themselves, that the fellow who went out with a girl was not responsible for what happened." In this scene George is eager for attention from the other would-be men, one of whom holds a cigar in his mouth and spits impressively on the floor. When George leaves the poolroom, he finds himself alone on the dark streets and so begins to talk aloud to himself. Then "in a spirit of play he reeled along the street imitating a drunken man and then imagined himself a soldier" with shining boots and a sword, and it is in this scene that his "aroused fancy" leads him, in the proximity of the animals and their strong smell, to feel that "something heady in his brain" "awoke." Now feeling "unutterably big and remade," he mutters to himself, "Death . . . night, the sea, fear, loveliness," and soon thinks that "if there were only a woman here I would take hold of her hand and we would run until we were both tired out."

Describing George's "aroused fancy" and the way he let "his mind play with the strange new thoughts that came to him," Anderson also notes that George had "the curious feeling of one revisiting a place that had been a part of some former existence." Here, it seems, Anderson is working with the idea in Freudian and early evolutionary psychology that instinctive play has an important psychological function, especially in the development of successful courtship behavior. In *The Interpretation of Dreams* and *Three Contributions to the Theory of Sex*, Freud frequently cites Karl Groos's work on play in support of his own theories. Commenting on "the free indulgence of the psyche in the play of its faculties," he also cites approvingly Havelock Ellis's remark that "the dream is '*an archaic world of vast emotions and imperfect thoughts*'" and "Sully's statement, that 'our dreams bring back again our earlier and successively developed personalities, our old ways of regarding things, with impulses and modes of reaction which ruled us long ago'" (*Basic Writings* 527–28). Each of these writers was interested in the same phenomenon but presented it in accord with his theory. Anderson does the same in this story, showing how George's play of mind clearly points the way to successful behavior in the male's sexual struggle—he must do battle and take hold of the female. But Anderson is also interested in how George, the aspiring writer, contributes to his own failure and further isolation by *indulging* his dreams or fancies. For example, when George leaves Winesburg in the final story, "Departure," his "mind was carried away by his growing passion for dreams"; "he closed his eyes" to Winesburg and began to use it as "but a background on which to paint the dreams of his manhood."

Thus, after his awakening in "An Awakening," George is soon "half drunk with the sense of masculine power." He tells Belle, "you've got to take me for a man"; then, "taking hold of her shoulder [he] turned her about and stood looking at her, his eyes shining with pride." At this point Belle looks over George's shoulder for Handby, whose jealousy she had hoped to arouse, and Anderson writes that George's "mind ran off into words" as he held "the woman tightly," whispering words into the still night like "lust and night and women." Worse, George "put his hands up in gratitude for the new power in himself and was waiting for the woman to speak." At this moment Handby appears. "Gripping George by the shoulder and pulling him to his feet, he held him with one hand" and then "sent the younger man sprawling away into the bushes." Anderson underscores this decisive defeat in the sexual struggle by writing that three times Handby caught George "by the shoulder [and] hurled him back into the bushes." After "Handby took Belle Carpenter by the arm and marched her away," the story ends with a reference to George, his "heart . . . sick within him," hating himself and "the fate that had brought about his humiliation. When his mind went back to the hour alone in the alleyway" when something within him had awakened, he was puzzled; he stopped in the darkness to listen for "the voice outside himself that had so short a time before put new courage into his heart."

In "Sophistication," when George is slightly older and "fast growing into manhood," "the voices outside of himself whisper a message concerning the limitations of life." Now he experiences "the sadness of sophistication" in realizing how countless generations of men before his time "have come out of nothingness into the world, lived their lives and again disappeared into nothingness." Courting Helen White in the summer of his eighteenth year he had tried to impress her with his manliness, boasting that "I'm going to be a big man, the biggest that ever lived here in Winesburg," but "the boy's voice failed" to carry his point. Now, in the story's present, Helen too is older and wiser, having been away to college for a year, and now she is "hunger[ing] to reach into the grace and beauty of womanhood." Another suitor is impressive, and she enjoys being seen with him, but he is "pedantic," condescending, and interested mainly in her money. She and George are in each other's thoughts, and as he goes to pay her a visit Anderson exposes him to images of the human-animal reality that had contributed to George's awakening in the earlier story. "People surged up and down [Main Street] like cattle confined in a pen," "young men with shining red faces walked awkwardly about with girls on their arms," and "fiddlers tuned their instruments" in a dance hall. Now these scenes oppress him with "the sense of crowding, moving life," and he falters in his intention to visit Helen, thinking that it makes no difference to him if she wants to be with the other suitor. Then, passing a livery barn, he "stopped in the shadows" listening to men talk of how the owner's "stallion, Tony Tip, had won at the Fair" that day. Pressing the phallic point further, Anderson describes how the owner of the stallion "pranc[ed] up and down" and boasted, tapping the ground with a whip and exclaiming, "Hell, quit your talking. . . . I wasn't afraid." George is somehow angered by the bragging man and continues on his way to Helen's house, where he arrives just after Helen has fled from the company of the pompous suitor into her garden. She is tired of "meaningless people saying words," and calls into the darkness, "Where are you, George?"

When George arrives, he is "still saying words" of self-encouragement but not to the effect that Anderson wrote of in "An Awakening," when George's "mind ran off into words." Now George immediately takes "hold of her hand," and Anderson leads the two into one of the most strangely beautiful but emphatically non-libidinous scenes of sexual intimacy he ever produced. It is the kind of experience he describes in the opening paragraphs of the story, the experience that comes to the young man in his "new sadness of sophistication." Already hearing the call of "death . . . with all his heart he wants to come close to some other human, touch someone with his hands, be touched by the hand of another." He wants a gentle companion and "most of all, understanding." Like the woman in the later story "Seeds," George and Helen need to love and be loved by a gentle person who is not exactly a lover because, Anderson makes clear in this story as well, they have in effect "seen under the shell of life and [are] afraid." In this story Helen and George feel this way at the fair ground, where the stallion Tony Tip had won the race that day and where "young girls [had] laughed and men with beards [had] talked of the affairs of their lives. The place has been filled to overflowing with life. It has itched and squirmed with life and now it is night and the life has all gone away. The silence is almost terrifying." In one's new "sadness of sophistication" and reflection, "one shudders at the thought of the mean-inglessness of life while at the same instant . . . one loves life so intensely that tears come into the eyes."

Bringing the two together in this way, then, Anderson insists that this experience transcends mere libidinous eroticism. And, although George "had reverence for Helen," and wanted "to love and to be loved by her" without being "confused by her womanhood," Anderson seems intent on denying the possible Freudian interpretation that his two young people only succeed for this brief time in sublimating their sexual desire. When George does take "hold of her hand," it is not in sexual possession. She "crept close" and when "a wind began to blow . . . he shivered. . . . In that high place in the darkness the two oddly sensitive human atoms held each other tightly and waited. In the mind of each was the same thought. 'I have come to this lonely place and here is this other,' was the substance of the thing felt."

Again, Anderson emphasizes that the thing that holds them together is not the frenzy of courtship that had so fascinated realists and naturalists in their critiques of sexual love after *The Descent of Man*—now by situating his couple far from the dancehall. There, "further down Main Street, the fiddlers, their instruments tuned, sweated and worked to keep the feet of youth flying over a dance floor." Anderson will not deny that the sexual impulse accounts for part of their intimacy, for he writes that "they kissed but that impulse did not last." Again, when George "put his hands on the girl's shoulders . . . she embraced him eagerly and then again they drew quickly back from that impulse." Mainly they feel mutual respect but also embarrassment when the sexual impulse arises; then, they begin to play. And here Anderson strikes an odd but characteristic note in his effort to accept the Darwinian analysis of the sexual struggle and the subsequent thought on man's place in nature, or as George feels "keenly," "his own insignificance in the scheme of existence." He transforms the Darwinian world into an Eden of the animal kingdom. In their embarrassed play, George and Helen "dropped into the animalism of youth. . . . In some way chastened and purified by the mood they had been in they became, not man and woman, not boy and girl, but excited *little* animals. . . . In the darkness they played like two splendid young things in a young world" (emphasis mine). This cannot make any evolutionary sense, of course, but is best understood as Anderson's determination to affirm the violence but also the essential innocence of the Darwinian reality—and at the same time to will his belief in Whitman's transcendental vision of the body.[21] Thus, he ends the story by explaining that "for some reason they could not have explained they had both got from their silent evening together the thing needed. Man or boy, woman or girl, they had for a moment taken hold of the thing that makes the mature life of men and women in the modern world possible." In such rare moments, Sherwood Anderson's lonely characters find refuge from the meaninglessness of life and the frightful violence beneath its shell, the universal illness for which mere sexual release is no cure.

Notes

1. Notable discussions of Anderson in relation to the naturalists are V. L. Parrington's brief notes in "Sherwood Anderson: A Psychological Naturalist" in *Main Currents in American Thought*, and Charles Child Walcutt's chapter on Anderson, "Sherwood Anderson: Impressionism and the Buried Life" in his *American Literary Naturalism: A Divided Stream*. Neither Parrington nor Walcutt discusses Darwin's theory of sexual selection, but in making his point about Anderson's naturalism, Walcutt refers to "his questionings, and his quiet, suppressed conclusions as to what orders our cosmos and what is man's place in it" (224).

2. Although Frederick Hoffman cites Freud's remark that his early work had developed in part from his interest in "the theories of Darwin" (*Freudianism* 3), he has very little to say about Darwin (and nothing about sexual selection). He certainly does not see Darwin as belonging to the group of nineteenth-century titans that Frank names.

3. It is clear from Anderson's letters and memoirs that he did read rather widely and that he drew heavily on what he could find in books. That he was a capable navigator in the world of books is evident, for example, in his story of his debate with Bertrand Russell in 1931 over the question of whether children should be raised by the state or by their parents. Commenting rather good-naturedly on the way he "did Russell dirt" in the debate, Anderson tells how he prepared for the debate by going "through his books. I remembered the old

saying, 'Oh that my enemy would write a book,' and Russell had written many books." Although it is hard to imagine that Anderson actually bested Russell in the debate, his further anecdote here suggests his superiority to Russell in other ways. After the debate, in response to Russell's expressed desire "to see the life of Harlem," the group went to dine in Harlem, and Anderson raised eyebrows by dancing with two of the black women in their party. He recalls how "Russell was shocked. He came and spoke to me about it. 'It isn't done, old chap.' He shook his head over my extraordinary behavior" (*Memoirs* 532–34).

4. Anderson's friend, the famous psychoanalyst Trigant Burrow, published similar remarks about prohibition and Darwinism the following year, as the Scopes trial was under way. Writing of the "personal equation" as an unconscious mechanism like sublimation and repression, Burrow was interested in such mechanisms that operate "*socially*"; prohibition was "too preposterous for words," he thought and compared it with the "socially unconscious fiasco . . . being enacted at the moment in the courts of Tennessee. Some people called Fundamentalists, failing to sense the personal element by which they are unconsciously prompted, are insisting upon the introduction of statutory measures whereby all of their Simian connections shall be repudiated by formal process of law," and so forth ("Psychological Improvisations and the Personal Equation" 182–83).

5. For Anderson's account of these meetings, "at the time Freud had just been discovered and all the young intellectuals were busy analyzing each other and everyone they met," see his *Memoirs* 339–46. For Burrow's account of the meeting see Hoffman, *Freudianism*, 238–39, and Burrow, *A Search for Man's Sanity*, 442–43, 558–62.

6. One of the innumerable possible sources of Anderson's interest in sea imagery to insinuate the Darwinian point about the origins of human nature is *The Education of Henry Adams*, which he began reading and commenting on shortly after it was published in 1918, and in which no reader could miss Adams's meditation on his relationship to the ganoid fish.

7. Darwin's remarks on music as a sexual appeal and of the emotional response to music and oratory are in *The Descent of Man*, 2:335–37, and *The Expression of the Emotions*, 217. Again, while there is no specific evidence that Anderson read these Darwinian texts, he could have seen these ideas dramatized in any number of courtship novels by Howells, Norris, or Dreiser, for example, and whether or not he talked with his friend the psychoanalyst Trigant Burrow about this aspect of Darwinian psychology, from Burrow's point of view *The Expression of the Emotions* was an important work (see his reference to it in 1925 in his selected letters, *A Search for Man's Sanity*, 94).

8. In *The Dance of Life* Ellis notes, for example, how the early Christians abhorred dance because of the "immodest and dissolute movements by which the cupidity of the flesh is aroused," and he continues: "But in nature and among primitive peoples it has its value precisely on this account. It is a process of courtship and, even more than that, it is a novitiate for love, and a novitiate which was found to be an admirable training for love. Among some peoples, indeed as the Omahas, the same word meant both to dance and to love. By his beauty, energy, his skill, the male must win the female, so impressing the image of himself on her imagination that finally her desire is aroused to overcome her reticence" (46).

9. In his chapter "In the Lawrencian Orbit" in *Sherwood Anderson*, Howe argues convincingly that "toward Freud Anderson could feel little warmth," but "he found in D. H. Lawrence . . . a vision of a more passionate life, a morality by which to affirm the body" (181).

10. From Lawrence's review of Trigant Burrow's *The Social Basis of Consciousness*, "A New Theory of Neuroses," 314. For a discussion of Hemingway's similar belief that "the psychoanalysts" had misinterpreted sexual passion and how he had intended *The Sun Also Rises* as "a treatise on basic loneliness and the inadequacy of promiscuity," see the chapter on him in my *The Descent of Love*, especially 343.

11. For discussions of these writers' interest in Darwin's theory of the emotions, see my *The Descent of Love*. It is possible at least that in Anderson's discussions of psychology with his friend Trigant Burrow, Burrow might have spoken of Darwin's book. As Burrow explained to William L. Phillips in 1949, correcting what he had said earlier to Frederick J. Hoffman regarding his (Burrow's) influence on Anderson, "Anderson was not uninfluenced by my talks with him on psychoanalysis." Burrow recalls in this letter how on one day in the summer of 1916, in particular, he and Anderson "sat there beside the brook and talked the livelong day, and our talk was entirely along psychoanalytical lines" (*A Search for Man's Sanity* 559). In his letter to Dr. L. Pierce Clark in 1925 Burrow wrote, "I wish you would remind your son again for me of Darwin's *Expressions of the Emotions in Man and Animals*" (94).

12. The quote about brain centers is from Freud (*Basic Writings* 559), where Freud expresses his disagreement with Krafft-Ebing on this point. As Anderson gives credence to this theory, it seems likely that he might have known or at least heard of Havelock Ellis's discussion of the subject in *Sexual Inversion*. Ellis describes the "view now widely accepted by investigators of sexual inversion": that "there has been a struggle in the centers, homosexuality resulting when the center antagonistic to that represented by the sexual gland conquers, and psychosexual hermaphroditism resulting when both centers are too weak to obtain victory" (*Studies* 1:4:312).

13. Hoffman's two examples to show that Anderson was "not unaware . . . of the subject mater of psychoanalysis" are Anderson's occasional references to a character's "unconscious self" and passages involving characters' dreams that "may imply . . . a study of Freud's dream-interpretation" (239).

14. Anderson explores this and other aspects of modern sexuality in chapters 19 and 20, which are set in Paris and involve scenes at the Quat'z Arts Ball. An American newspaper woman named Rose Frank tells Aline about the ball, "a kind of swoon, an orgy," in which people might say, "If you want to fight, all the better. I'll slug you. That's a way of making love. Didn't you know?" (185).

15. As for the male hand, a subject about which Freud has much less to say than Darwin, it is worth noting his analysis of the boy's "preference for the hand" in masturbation: it "already indicates what an important part of the male sexual activity will be accomplished in the future by the mastery impulse" (590). Another likely source of Anderson's thoughts on sexual cruelty is Havelock Ellis's section on "Love and Pain" in *Studies in the Psychology of Sex*, where he discusses, among other things, the love bite (1:2:84).

16. Anderson remarks, "There was a race toward the goal of death between the mind and body and almost always the mind arrived first. . . . Every one carried about, all the time, within himself life and death . . . two Gods sitting on two thrones," and so forth (192).

17. Frank was also inspired by Whitman because Whitman "found multitudes within his self, within all selves . . . [and because] he designated America as the home of this mystic revelation. . . . The unique in Whitman, and the irresistible appeal for me, was that he *naturalized* his sense of the cosmic Whole into the body and shape of America" (*Memoirs of Waldo Frank*

10–11). As he explains further in his *Memoirs*, "'The multitudes in Whitman,' I had called the penultimate chapter of [*Our America*]. . . . For the book's theme song, I quoted Whitman:

> None has begun to think how divine he himself is, and how certain the future is.
> I say that the real and permanent grandeur of These States must be their religion." (99)

In his tribute to Anderson, "*Winesburg, Ohio* after Twenty Years," Frank argues that Anderson's "suggested symbols" or, "if you will *indirections*," were lyric efforts to seek "Eternal truths" that could be found or expressed in no other way (118).

18. For a different description of Anderson's transcendental naturalism, see Charles Child Walcutt's chapter on Anderson in *American Literary Naturalism: A Divided Stream*, where he writes of Anderson as an "impressionist" of "the buried life." Also, in addition to Anderson's efforts to use indirection as his pathway to transcendent vision, he occasionally explored the stream of transcendental naturalism by evoking a midwestern variety of the fecund life force that Frank Norris had envisioned in his cycle of the wheat. In "his strange quest—to seek Truth, to seek God," Sam McPherson once hears from an old man that "'God is a spirit and lives in the growing corn'" (*Windy McPherson's Son* 246). He continued this line in later stories, as in "Out of Nowhere into Nothing" (1921) and "The Corn Planting" (1934), but the "lovely daughter of the cornlands" he gives us in "Out of Nowhere" can find no "son of the cornlands" to love her passionately (*Triumph of the Egg* 241, 267). While she "contained light" and "was a creator of light," she exists in the typical Andersonian state of loneliness that can find no relief either in anything like Norris's vision of the wheat's "ordered and predetermined courses from West to East" or in his story of the Jadwins' "love" surviving the threat of sexual hell (represented by the seductress Corthell) through their repression of the sexual impulse (*The Pit* 368).

19. As Frederick J. Hoffman notes in *The Twenties*, "Carpenter's *Love's Coming of Age* (1896) proved one of the most influential books of the scores that argued for a revision of sex morality" (230). Carpenter, also anticipating a kind of evolutionary progress in the sexual realm, writes that "however things may change with the further evolution of man, there is no doubt that first of all the sex-relation must be divested of the sentiment of uncleanness which surrounds it, and rehabilitated again with a sense almost of religious consecration; and this means, as I have said, a free people, proud in the mastery and the divinity of their own lives, and in the beauty and openness of their own bodies" (*Love's Coming of Age* 27).

20. A more frequently cited model for Anderson's Winesburg stories is Edgar Lee Masters's *Spoon River Anthology*. Masters's own interest in Whitman is evident in these poems as well as in his critical biography of Whitman.

21. Nor is there any evolutionary sense in his assertions elsewhere that *sexual repression* produces simian animalism among human beings. In the Winesburg story "Respectability" the character Wash Williams has become like "a huge, grotesque kind of monkey, a creature with ugly, sagging hairless skin below his eyes and a bright purple underbody" as a result of his fearful rejection of his wife's sexual appetite. And in *Many Marriages* Anderson describes John Webster's sexually repressed wife as "so much more like an animal then [Webster] himself" (190). At the same time, of course, he typically celebrates the stallion's sexual power and in *Poor White* presents the male and female birds as balls of light when they are caught up in innocent sexual pursuit.

8 "His Mind Aglow"

The Biological Undercurrent in Fitzgerald's Gatsby and Other Works

> They talked until three, from biology to organized religion, and when Amory
> crept shivering into bed it was with his mind aglow.
> —Fitzgerald, *This Side of Paradise*

Readers familiar with F. Scott Fitzgerald's early work might recall that in the years just before the Scopes trial he wrote of Victorians who "shuddered when they found what Mr. Darwin was about" (*This Side of Paradise* 151) or that he joined in the fashionable comic attacks on people who could not accept their "most animal existence," describing one such character as "a hairless ape with two dozen tricks" (*The Beautiful and Damned* 415–16). But few would guess the extent to which his interest in evolutionary biology shaped his work. He was particularly concerned with three interrelated biological problems: first, the question of eugenics as a possible solution to civilization's many ills; second, the linked principles of accident and heredity (as he understood these through the lens of Ernst Haeckel's biogenetic law); and third, the revolutionary theory of sexual selection that Darwin had presented in *The Descent of Man*. His concern with these issues underlies such well-known features in the Fitzgerald landscape as his insecurity in the social hierarchy (his sense of its "terrifying fluidity"), his emphasis on the element of time, his interest in "the musk of money," his interest in Spengler and the naturalists, and his negative portraiture of male violence.[1] The principles of eugenics, accidental heredity, and sexual selection flow together as the prevailing undercurrent in most of Fitzgerald's work before and after *The Great Gatsby*, producing more anxiety than love from the tangled courtships of characters he deemed both beautiful and damned.

By his second year at Princeton (1914), before he began to read the naturalists, Fitzgerald had taken in enough of the evolutionary view of life to see its relevance to the most fascinating subject for any youth of eighteen—sex. In "Love or Eugenics" he playfully wondered whether young men are most attracted by women of vigorous stock, with "plenty of muscle, / And Avoirdupois to spare," or by modern flappers who know the value of "good cosmetics" (*F. Scott Fitzgerald in His Own Time* 18). But Fitzgerald grew a good deal more serious about the biology of sex before he left Princeton in 1917. In the scene from *This Side of Paradise* in which Amory and his friend Burne Holiday talked about biology until Amory's mind was "aglow," the two came naturally to the question that gave eugenics its pressing relevance, the idea that "the light-haired man *is* a higher type," as Burne puts it (128). When Burne (patterned on Fitzgerald's friend Henry Slater) "voluntarily attended graduate lectures in philosophy and biology" (131), he might have heard Princeton's famous professor of biology Edwin G. Conklin lecture on phylogeny (with attention to Darwin and sexual selection) and ontogeny (with emphasis on Conklin's particular interest in eugenics). Conklin published a detailed outline for the course in general biology (*Laboratory Directions in General Biology*) and ended the section on ontogeny with this note: "All members of the class are invited, but not required, to fill out a Family Record blank, giving details of their own heredity for the use of the Committee on Eugenics" (78).[2]

Even if Fitzgerald or Burne-Slater never read this invitation, it is clear from *This Side of Paradise* that the subject was quite palpably in the air at Princeton, no doubt heightening what Fitzgerald's biographers have described as his insecurity in the social hierarchy. Indeed, Fitzgerald was so attuned to the subject of eugenics and heredity that he included a further brief, playful scene in his next novel: a young man accused of being an "intellectual faker" responds with the challenge, "What's the fundamental principle of biology?" When his accuser guesses, "natural selection?" the young man corrects him: "Ontogony recapitulates phyllogony [*sic*]" (*The Beautiful and Damned* 153–54).

The profound social consequences of this fundamental principle are reflected in much of Fitzgerald's work. Articulated by Ernst Haeckel, the idea was that a species' evolutionary development (phylogeny) is recapitulated in the individual's embryological development (ontogeny), revealing in the human embryo's gill slits, for example, our ancestral relationship with fish. But as Stephen Jay Gould notes, "Recapitulation served as a general theory of biological determinism" with a terrible appeal to many Americans who felt the pressure of immigration from Ireland and, especially, southern Europe. The American paleontologist E. D. Cope "preached [it as the] doctrine of Nordic supremacy": the "inferior" groups (including "races, sexes, and classes") were believed to be arrested in development at the level of the white male's child. Just as the white embryo's development recapitulated the human descent from lower forms, so did the white child's development recapitulate the development of the lower or "childlike" races (who were supposedly arrested at that stage) until, triumphantly, the white males, at least, would go on to exhibit their superiority as a race (*The Mismeasure of Man* 115).

One begins to see how the study of heredity might have appealed to Princetonians of those years, some of whom, like Fitzgerald, were so disturbed at seeing "the negroid streak creep[ing] northward to defile the nordic race" that they were overly receptive to popular and less scientific writers like Lothrop Stoddard.[3] Stoddard (referred to as "Goddard" by Tom Buchanan in *Gatsby*) welcomed the time when "biological knowledge will have so increased" that eugenicist programs might "yield the most wonderful results" (309); in the meantime, he advised, "migrations of lower human types like those which have worked such havoc in the United States must be rigorously curtailed. Such migrations upset standards, sterilize better stocks, increase low types, and compromise national futures" (308). As Fitzgerald wrote to Edmund Wilson from Europe in the summer of 1921, "Raise the bars of immigration and permit only Scandinavians, Teutons, Anglo Saxons + Celts to enter" (*Letters* 47).

The Riddle of the Universe: Accident, Heredity, and Selection

Since Fitzgerald referred to Haeckel's biogenetic law and as a reviewer complained of another writer's "undigested Haeckel," it will be worth considering what he seems to have gathered from his own copy of Haeckel's *The Riddle of the Universe at the Close of the Nineteenth Century* (1900).[4] Although Fitzgerald's critics have never discussed it, *The Riddle of the Universe* is much more reliable in suggesting the outlines of Fitzgerald's thought than is the text most frequently cited in this regard, Oswald Spengler's *The Decline of the West* (even though it did not appear in English until 1926). In a way, the books are similar in providing different but sweeping senses of destiny: Spengler's in his advocacy of "Goethe's form-fulfillment" as destiny (rather than Darwin's causality) and Haeckel's in his closing with Goethe's lines: "By eternal laws / Of iron ruled, / Must all fulfil / The cycle of / Their destiny" (231).[5]

But, in general, Haeckel's book does much more to bring together the two subjects about which Amory and Burne talked until their minds glowed in *This Side of Paradise*—biology and organized religion. *The Riddle of the Universe* deals with many of the key biological terms that figure in Fitzgerald's work before, in, and after *Gatsby*—like *accident, egg, descended, specimen, instinct, struggle, adaptation, selection, extinction,* and the name of Darwin, himself, whom Haeckel praises as "*the Copernicus of the organic world.*"[6] Haeckel's particular attraction for Fitzgerald, however, lay in his solution to the riddle of man's place in nature by explaining the related principles of accident, heredity, and selection (62).

Of these three, Haeckel emphasizes the role of heredity, advancing it in a larger context that dispenses with the superstition or primitive religions of revelation. Yet he explains "the embryology of the soul" and calls for a "new monistic religion," scientific and realistic, that will be revealed in "the wonderful temple of nature" (382 and chaps. 8, 19). Fitzgerald certainly seems attuned to Haeckel's criticism of primitive Christianity (which he would have especially appreciated after reading Harold Frederic's examination of it in *The Damnation of Theron Ware*, one of his favorite books), and in *Gatsby*, especially, he emphasizes the role of accident in ways that suggest that he was quite familiar with Haeckel's (and ultimately Darwin's) discussion of it. Haeckel, going well beyond Darwin's point about chance or accidental variation, insists that "all individual forms of existence . . . are but special transitory forms—*accidents* or *modes*—of substance" (216): "nowhere . . . in the evolution of animals and plants do we find any trace of design, but merely the inevitable outcome of the struggle for existence, the blind controller, instead of the provident God, that effects the changes of organic forms by a mutual action of the laws of heredity and adaptation" (268–69).

In *The Great Gatsby* Fitzgerald gives us, in place of a provident God, the gazing "eyes of Doctor T. J. Eckleburg" that were set there by "some wild wag of an oculist" who "then sank down himself into eternal blindness" (27–28). These are the eyes that peer out over the bleak figure of George Wilson when he is told that his wife Myrtle was killed in an accident and that provoke him to insist repeatedly, "God sees everything" (166–67). Fitzgerald's emphasis on accident becomes overwhelming in the closing pages of the novel, including Nick's remark that Gatsby "knew that he was in Daisy's house by a colossal accident" (156) and most resoundingly in his last image of the dead hero afloat in his pool: "A small gust of wind that scarcely corrugated the surface was enough to disturb [the water's] accidental course with its accidental burden" (170).

As a story of modern love, *Gatsby* is squarely within the tradition of American fiction that began to appropriate Darwin's theory of sexual selection immediately after *The Descent of Man*, beginning with W. D. Howells's *A Chance Acquaintance* (1873).[7] This is not to suggest that Fitzgerald had Howells particularly in mind, but he depicted Gatsby and Daisy in this way as they leave together after the confrontation between Gatsby and Tom Buchanan: "They were gone, without a word, snapped out, made accidental, isolated like ghosts even from our pity" (142). Rather than Howells, the American writers most on Fitzgerald's mind during these years were Frederic, Dreiser, Frank and Charles Norris, and Wharton—to name only a few who were quite self-consciously engaged in critiquing "love" from their various biological points of view. But, again, it would seem that the most immediate theoretical support for

Fitzgerald's own critique of love was *The Riddle of the Universe*, where Haeckel refers to Darwin's theory of sexual selection. Here, writing of the "eros" or "powerful impulse that . . . leads to . . . nuptial union," Haeckel emphasizes: "the essential point in this physiological process is not the 'embrace,' as was formerly supposed, or the amorousness connected therewith; it is simply the introduction of the spermatozoa into the vagina" (138–39).

Such remarks provide the kind of biological insight into modern love that caused many characters in American fiction at around the turn of the century to question love and motherhood, as Edna Pontellier did in *The Awakening*. Witnessing "the scene of torture" as her friend gave birth, Edna thought of her own experience in "awakening to find a little new life to which she had given being, added to the great unnumbered multitude of souls that come and go," and she feels "a flaming, outspoken revolt against the ways of Nature" (chap. 37). In *This Side of Paradise* similar insights provoke Amory's agonizing questions, "How'll I fit in? . . . What am I for? To propagate the race?" (215). And they lead his friend Eleanor to complain of the "rotten, rotten old world" where she remains "tied to the sinking ship of future matrimony" (237).[8] Then, voicing Fitzgerald's sense that the struggle of sexual selection is far more disturbing than what the Freudian craze had suggested in its apparent invitation to promiscuity, she remarks: "I'm hipped on Freud and all that, but it's rotten that every bit or *real* love in the world is ninety-nine per cent passion and one little soupçon of jealousy." Amory (already depressed about his purpose in life as a male) agrees that this "rather unpleasant overpowering force [is] part of the machinery under everything" (238).

Before going on to analyze what drives the machinery of love in *The Great Gatsby* (that is, the process of sexual selection, as Fitzgerald construed it), there is a final important point—the essential point—to make about Fitzgerald's interest in *The Riddle of the Universe*. Everything is determined by the accident of heredity—"the soul-blending at the moment of conception [when] only the latent forces of the two parent souls are transmitted by the coalescence of the erotic cell-nuclei" (142). Intent on showing his theory's "far-reaching consequences" regarding "our great question" of man's place in nature, Haeckel notes that "the human ovum, like that of all other animals, is a single cell, and this tiny globular egg cell (about the 120th of an inch in diameter) has just the same characteristic appearance as that of all other viviparous organisms" (62). Thus Haeckel concludes not only that the "law of biogeny" demonstrates our heritage back through the ape and all the higher vertebrates to "our primitive fish-ancestors" (65) but also that it "destroy[s] the myth of the immortality of the soul" (138). For Fitzgerald, though, Haeckel's conclusion that "each personality owes its bodily and spiritual qualities to both parents" raises questions not only about man's place in nature but also in the social hierarchy (138).

Haeckel's further conclusion about the accident of heredity demonstrates—as "in the reigning dynasties and in old families of the nobility"—that all individuals are held "in the chain of generations" (143).

For these reasons more than anything else, the imagery of eggs figures memorably in Fitzgerald's work, not only in the absolute barrier that exists between East Egg and West Egg in *Gatsby* but also in such earlier works as the unsuccessful play he produced in 1923, *The Vegetable*. There, one of the characters, Doris, explains that she plans to marry a man named Fish, and Fitzgerald heavily underscores both "Fish" and "egg." "Fish? F-i-s-h?" another character (Jerry) asks. When Doris explains that "these Fishes are very nice," he warns that she might have to live "right over his father's place of business." Doris is attracted not only by Mr. Fish's wonderful build but also by his habit of calling her "adorable egg." Confused again, the character Jerry asks, "What does he mean by that?" and Doris explains, "Oh 'egg' is just a name people use nowadays." After Jerry asks again, "Egg?" Doris wonders, "Does your father still read the Bible?" (25–28).[9] This apparently trivial exchange has its place in the play's larger plot, which tracks the vegetable-hero's failed accidental ascent to the presidency of the United States and his ultimate career as a postman. As the hero finally explains about postmen, "They not only pick 'em out—they select 'em" (134).

Even though Fitzgerald's work with the egg idea could not save *The Vegetable*, he did not give up on it. Before he wrote the play he had commented to Edmund Wilson that he thought Sherwood Anderson's *The Triumph of the Egg* was "a wonderful title" (*Letters* 49), and he made something much more serious of it in *Gatsby* than his readers have sensed. Aside from the East and West Egg material, he includes two other odd but meaningful scenes. In the first, sitting in the New York apartment where Tom Buchanan meets with Myrtle Wilson, Nick notes that "the only picture was an over-enlarged photograph, apparently a hen sitting on a blurred rock. Looked at from a distance however the hen resolved itself into a bonnet and the countenance of a stout old lady beamed down into the room" (33). Moments later Nick realized that it was a "dim enlargement" of Myrtle's mother that "hovered like an ectoplasm on the wall" (34). "Ectoplasm" is a succinct comment on Myrtle Wilson's place in the social and evolutionary hierarchies, its two meanings (according to the *Random House Dictionary*) being (1) "the outer portion of the cytoplasm of a cell," and (2) "the supposed emanation from the body of a medium." According to Haeckel, "the skin layer, or ectoderm, is the primitive psychic organ in the metazoa . . . the tissue-soul in its simplest form" (160).

The other "egg" scene in *The Great Gatsby* serves to gloss the well-known passage in which Tom Buchanan violently exclaims that "'The Rise of the Coloured Empires' by this man Goddard" shows how "civilization's going to pieces" (17).

Fitzgerald seems to discredit Tom's belief that "it's all scientific stuff; it's been proved" (17), but through Nick's observation as he and Gatsby enter the city, Fitzgerald suggests his own anxiety about the *Rising Tide of Color*. Crossing over the Queensboro Bridge, Nick sees "a dead man" pass "in a hearse" accompanied by friends with "the tragic eyes and short upper lips of south-eastern Europe," then "a limousine passed us, driven by a white chauffeur, in which sat three modish Negroes, two bucks and a girl. I laughed aloud as the *yolks* of their eyeballs rolled toward us in haughty rivalry" (73, emphasis mine). Nick's own anxiety is clear here when he stops laughing and thinks to himself, "Anything can happen now that we've slid over this bridge"; "Even Gatsby could happen, without any particular wonder," he concludes. But this is before Nick meets Gatsby's father, Mr. Gatz, or learns that Gatsby's "parents were shiftless and unsuccessful farm people [and that] his imagination had never really accepted them as his parents as all" (104).

Gatsby's effort to create himself—to spring "from his Platonic conception of himself"—can only fail in the biological universe that Haeckel described (104). And if Gatsby is a true "son of God" who "must be about His Father's Business, the service of a vast, vulgar and meretricious beauty," it is in the sense that he is destined to pursue Daisy's beauty according to the laws of sexual selection (104).[10] This force of beauty drives many of Fitzgerald's young men, as Dexter Green is "unconsciously dictated to by his winter dreams" of Judy Jones ("Winter Dreams," *Stories* 150). Even at age eleven, Judy was "beautifully ugly as little girls are apt to be" who "are destined . . . [to] bring no end of misery to a great number of men" (147); "she was arrestingly beautiful . . . [and the] color and the mobility of her mouth gave a continual impression of flux, of intense life, of passionate vitality" (152). Fitzgerald writes that the thing that made Dexter so susceptible to Judy's beauty was "deep in him" (161). Only when he was much older did Dexter realize that "long ago, there was something in me, but now that thing is gone. Now that thing is gone, that thing is gone" (168).

By 1922 Fitzgerald had freed himself somewhat from his earlier hero's conclusion in *This Side of Paradise* that "the problem of evil" was "the problem of sex" and that "inseparably linked with evil was beauty" (280). In *The Beautiful and Damned* beauty is simply part of the "machinery under everything"—an engine of sexual selection, and Fitzgerald identifies life itself as "that sound out there, that ghastly reiterated female sound" (150); "active and snarling," it moves "like a fly swarm" (260). In *The Great Gatsby* Fitzgerald anoints both Daisy and Gatsby with the power of beauty, but in both their cases, as in the "intense vitality" of Myrtle Wilson (which contains *no* "gleam of beauty" [35]), the underlying force is simply "life" (30). This is Fitzgerald's ultimate subject in *The Great Gatsby*: "the full bellows of the earth [that was blowing] the frogs full of life" at the moment on that evening in late spring when "the silhouette of a moving cat" drew Nick's eye to Gatsby for the first time (25). Later, when Nick leaves Daisy and Gatsby alone during her first visit to his house, he sees that they are "possessed by intense life" (102).

Fitzgerald dramatizes the process of sexual selection in the stories of Tom and Daisy Buchanan, Daisy and Gatsby, Myrtle and George Wilson, and Nick Carraway and Jordan Baker. The tangled web of conflicted life in which all the players exist has distinctive features and serious implications. First, everyone is subject to the anxieties that arise in the general, unending struggle for life. In Fitzgerald's presentation of the evolutionary reality everything is subject to change: accidents happen at any moment, men and women must struggle to win and then keep their mates, the tide of "lower" racial groups is on the rise, and civilizations themselves rise and fall. Moreover, in the individual's development through life, according to Haeckel, his or her psychic activity is subject to the same pattern of progress and decline. In Haeckel's five stages of man's psychic activity, the newborn develops self-consciousness, the boy or girl awakens to the sexual instinct, the youth or maiden up to the time of sexual intercourse passes through the "idealist" period, the mature man and woman engage in the founding of families, and then what he calls "involution" sets in as the old man or woman experience degeneration. As Haeckel dismally concludes, "Man's psychic life runs the same evolution—upward progress, full maturity, and downward degeneration—as every other vital activity in his organization" (146–47). Rather in this key, Nick Carraway on his thirtieth birthday looks forward to only "the promise of a decade of loneliness, a thinning list of single men to know, a thinning brief-case of enthusiasm, thinning hair." Having just witnessed the disastrous confrontation between Gatsby, Tom, and Daisy, who loves them both, he remarks, "So we drove on toward death through the cooling twilight" (143).

Second, in this universe of accident and change, every individual and every individual's "house" or line is fixed at the moment of conception—as in "the Carraway house," for example, "in a city where dwellings are still called through decades by a family's name" (184). And third, although people like Myrtle and Gatsby are not only free but also compelled to enter the struggle of sexual selection (their only means of elevating themselves in the social and evolutionary hierarchies), they nor any other characters in Fitzgerald's fiction can break the bonds of what Haeckel calls "the chain of generations" (143). As Fitzgerald put it in "The Unspeakable Egg" (1924), the comic story he wrote while *Gatsby* was in press, although a young woman might have her choice of "attractive eggs" and unattractive ones, the "unspeakable egg" itself determines that even in "Umerica, a free country," there are really no "chauffeurs and such that marry millionaires' daughters" (*The Price Was High* 132–34).

Sexual Selection in *The Great Gatsby*

While Fitzgerald's understanding of heredity and ontogeny seems to have originated in his informal exposure to such ideas at Princeton and his reading in *The Riddle of the Universe*, his familiarity with the theory of sexual selection probably came as much from the novelists he admired as from biologists like Conklin or Haeckel. Both of these biologists briefly discuss the secondary sexual characters (like "the beard of man, the antlers of the stag, the beautiful plumage of the bird of paradise") that, Haeckel remarks, "are the outcome of sexual selection" as Darwin had explained (*Riddle of the Universe* 139). For lengthier discussions of the theory of sexual selection, including courtship behavior, Fitzgerald might have turned to any number of sources, from *The Descent of Man* to Havelock Ellis's *Sexual Selection in Man* (a volume collected as part of his *Studies in the Psychology of Sex*) or Upton Sinclair's *The Book of Life* (1921). It is important to realize that, had he turned to these three, he would have seen distinctly different versions of the sexual reality. Ellis, for example, built on Darwin's theory but then strove to elevate the psychology of sex into the art of love and ultimately a transcendent religion in which the human's animal nature is scarcely perceptible, and Sinclair strove to emphasize the human's supremacy over nature by his greater power to combine in groups—as in "primitive communist society" (*Book of Life* 2:9–10). No less than the theory of natural selection, the theory of sexual selection was (and continues to be) susceptible to various interpretations, as different writers construed evolutionary theory in ways that reflected their particular points of view regarding gender, class, race, or political ideology, as well as their particular spiritual or psychological anxieties.

Whatever his sources, it is clear that Fitzgerald focused on the key principles of sexual selection that previous American novelists from Howells to Edith Wharton had depended on in constructing their own plots of courtship and marriage. Seeing the process in general, as he put it in *This Side of Paradise*, as the "rather unpleasant overpowering force that's part of the machinery under everything" (238), he emphasized the female's power to select the superior male and the male's struggle to be selected. Both the male and female in Fitzgerald's fiction wield the power to attract, often through music or dance—the female through her physical beauty and the beauty of her voice and the male through his strength or ornamental display. And like so many American novelists who had also worked with the Darwinian materials, Fitzgerald embraced Darwin's observation that civilized human beings select for wealth or social position. Also, as in Darwin and the many realist and naturalist novelists who took up his theory, the successful male is compelled to exhibit superior strength and to contest his strength with competing males in what Darwin called "the law of battle" for possession of the female. Finally, as part of a more recent development in literary interpretations of Darwin's theory, Fitzgerald was interested in (and considerably frightened by) the modern woman's aggressive sexuality—her occasional desire for more than one man and her recognition that she must engage in sometimes deadly competition with other females to win her man.

Working essentially with these points in *The Great Gatsby*, then, Fitzgerald constructed a plot with a fully natural ending: Gatsby fails in his romantic quest and remains a "poor son-of-a-bitch" because he denies his genetic identity and ignores the laws of sexual selection (183). Moreover, while Tom Buchanan retains physical possession of Daisy, his hand covering hers in "an unmistakable air of natural intimacy" (152), he continues in his "alert, aggressive way, . . . his head moving sharply here and there, adapting itself to his restless eyes" (186). And Nick, having exhibited much anxiety and ambivalence in his own sexual relations, having witnessed the violent, chaotic drama involving Gatsby, the Buchanans, and the Wilsons, and having realized that the most profound "difference between men . . . [is] the difference between the sick and the well" (131), Nick withdraws alone into the middle-west of his youth, "half sick between grotesque reality and savage frightening dreams" (154).

Fitzgerald takes his first step toward this natural ending with his epigraph. Here, carrying forward his interest in the sexual "machinery under everything" (from *This Side of Paradise*), he focuses immediately on the essential workings of sexual selection—the male's struggle in dance or ornamental display to be selected and the female's power to select:

> Then wear the gold hat, if that will move her;
> If you can bounce high, bounce for her too,
> Till she cry "Lover, gold-hatted, high-bouncing lover,
> I must have you!"

But before Nick enters into the story of Gatsby's effort to win Daisy, he begins by referring to his own clan's descent and telling of his own participation in a "counter-raid" in the "Teutonic migration known as the Great War" (6–7) ("the last love battle," as Fitzgerald later termed it).[11] Resulting in his feeling at "the ragged edge of the universe" (7), Nick's war experience has made him a wounded veteran in the larger sexual struggle about which Tom Buchanan is so anxious—that "the white race will be—will be utterly submerged" (17) in the rising tide of color, and ultimately that he stands to lose his wife to a "crazy fish" like Gatsby (110). If you "sit back and let Mr. Nobody from Nowhere make love to your wife," Tom complains, you might as well "throw everything overboard and have intermarriage between black and white" (137).

In his first chapter, then, Fitzgerald identifies his other main characters and sets them adrift in the fluid, evolutionary universe wherein "we [all] beat on, boats against the current, borne back ceaselessly into the past," as Nick remarks in the famous last line (189). Tom Buchanan, Daisy, and Gatsby all drift in and out of the novel as the dead Gatsby finally does in his swimming pool, where Fitzgerald surrounds him with other "poor ghosts" who "drifted fortuitously about" in this "new world" (169). Telling how by chance he had rented his house near the "pair of enormous eggs" in that "strangest [of] communities in North America" (9), a community to which Tom and Daisy had also drifted (and where Daisy will joke about accidentally arranging Nick's marriage to Jordan Baker), Nick begins to picture a tumultuous reality of high winds and rampant growth (23).

The "great bursts of leaves growing . . . just as things grow in fast movies" (8) are driven by the same cosmic force that blows the "frogs full of life" (25) and causes the Buchanans' "lawn [to start] at the beach and [run] toward the front door for a quarter of a mile, jumping over sun-dials and brick walks in burning gardens—finally when it reached the house drifting up the side in bright vines as though from the momentum of its run" (11). Developing this theme, Fitzgerald writes that the "fresh grass . . . seemed to grow a little way into the [Buchanan] house," suggesting that, like all life, it emerged from the sea and is related to the life force within the Buchanan line (12).[12] Later in the novel Nick describes how "the Buchanans' house floated suddenly" into view (149). This household's vital force throbs in "the enormous power of [Tom's] body" with its "great pack of muscle shifting" beneath his coat (11), and it has produced the child about whom Nick remarks, "I suppose she talks, and—eats, and everything" (21). Moreover, it is reflected in the "paternal contempt" of Tom's gruff voice, which seemed to say, "I'm stronger and more of a man than you are" (11). Within pages we learn of the first incident in which this dominant male, a "hulking physical specimen" (16), uses his "cruel body" to injure each of the three women in his life (11). He is responsible not only for Daisy's "black and blue" knuckle in this scene but also for another woman's broken arm (82), and he will go on to break Myrtle Wilson's nose (41). Ultimately, Fitzgerald's point is that Tom's brutal sexual power is alive in his house and that it is determinant in his struggles with both George Wilson over Myrtle and with Gatsby over Daisy. By contrast, no such force resides in Gatsby's fake "ancestral home" (162). Indeed, the futility of Gatsby's romantic denial of his biological identity and the violence of sexual selection is reflected in his well-trimmed lawn (which soon grew to be as long as Nick's after Gatsby's death) and the "thin beard of raw ivy" (188) that covers his "tower" (9).

Despite Tom's brutal strength, however, neither he nor any other individual in Fitzgerald's evolutionary world can rest secure. Frequently drawing attention to Tom's powerful hands (serving the Darwinian male's need to capture and hold the female), Fitzgerald notes that Tom "broke [Myrtle's] nose with his open hand" (41), that "he put out his broad, flat hand with well-concealed dislike" when introduced to Gatsby (122), and finally that "his hand [fell] upon and covered" Daisy's, signaling the end of his struggle with Gatsby (152). By contrast at this conclusive mo-

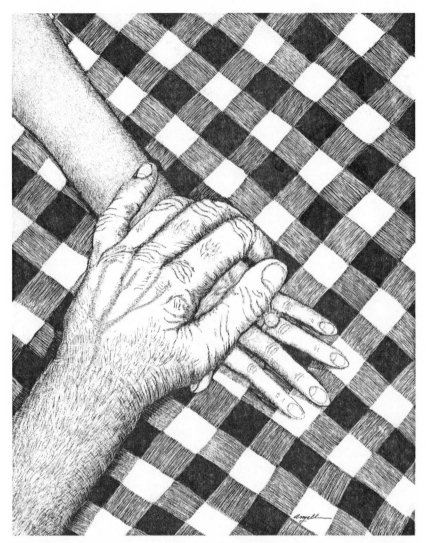

Prehensile Power. At the end of *The Great Gatsby* Fitzgerald dramatizes the end of the struggle between Gatsby and Tom Buchanan for Daisy. One of many writers who worked with Darwin's theme of the male's adaptive prehensile power to possess the female, Fitzgerald frequently describes Tom's powerful hands, here showing how his "hand had fallen upon and covered" Daisy's.

ment, Nick leaves Gatsby "with his hands in his coat pockets . . . watching over nothing" (153)—a fate that Fitzgerald had projected in the initial meeting between Gatsby and Daisy. In the first of three images of the would-be lover with his hands in his pockets in this brief scene, Nick describes Gatsby "pale as death, with his hands plunged like weights in his coat pockets" (91). Still, Fitzgerald emphasizes that in this world where "there are only the pursued, the pursuing, the busy and the tired" (85), Tom must be ever vigilant. As Nick observes in chapter 1, even with two women, "something was making [Tom] nibble at the edge of stale ideas as if his sturdy physical egotism no longer nourished his peremptory heart" (25), and when we see him last he continues in his restless, "alert, aggressive way, his hands out a little from his body as if to fight off interference" (186).

Also one of the "pursuing," Gatsby expresses his restlessness as well: "he was never quite still; there was always a tapping foot somewhere or the impatient opening and closing of a hand" (68). When told that "you can't repeat the past," he looks around "wildly, as if the past were lurking here in the shadow of his house, just out of reach of his hand" (116–17), and since Gatsby's past moment with Daisy is out of reach largely because of the inherent deficiency of his house, Fitzgerald presents Gatsby in a precarious state of balance: "he was balancing himself on the dashboard of his car with that resourcefulness of movement that is so peculiarly American" (68).

For similar reasons, in chapter 1 Fitzgerald depicts another of his main characters, the equally unattached and restless Jordan Baker, as "the balancing girl"; she had a way of holding her "chin . . . as if she were balancing something on it which was quite likely to fall" (13). Supplementing the precariousness of her social situation as a single woman who is both pursuer and pursued is her notably androgynous nature. A "small-breasted girl with an erect carriage" who looks "like a young cadet" (15) and whom Fitzgerald identifies as the other athlete in his group, she displays "a flutter of slender muscles in her arms" within the same sentence that captures the bright "lamp-light [on Tom's] boots" (22). As others have noted, Jordan's androgyny appeals to Nick, who "enjoyed looking at her" and seems part of Fitzgerald's effort to reveal Nick's own sexual ambivalence (15).

As Nick explains in chapter 1, he went east to learn the bond business (which Fitzgerald suggests includes the bonds of intimate relations). One of his reasons was to escape the rumors that he was engaged, and during his time in the east he breaks off with two other women. Nick has a history of being "privy to the secret griefs of wild, unknown men" (5–6) whose "intimate revelation[s]" sometimes "quiver[ed] on the horizon . . . marred by obvious suppressions" (34), and he will go on to tell of one of his most intimate moments in the east: when he reached out to touch Mr. McKee, the "pale feminine man" from the flat below Tom's and Myrtle's. Minutes later, Nick and McKee "groaned down in the elevator" together on the way to McKee's flat (41–42). And immediately after the strange brief scene in which Nick stands beside McKee's bed (where "between the sheets, clad in his underwear," McKee shows Nick some of his photographs), Nick finds himself "half asleep in the cold lower level of the Pennsylvania Station" (42). Aside from the possible reflections of Fitzgerald's and Nick's vague homoerotic desire that others have sensed in this scene, it would seem that Fitzgerald's emphasis on "down," "below," and "lower," represent another dimension in his view of the social and evolutionary hierarchy.[13]

Further suggested by Tom's remark when meeting Nick unexpectedly at lunch, "How'd you happen to come up this far to eat?" Fitzgerald's references to *up* and *down* in regard to Nick's biological activities suggest his susceptibility to degeneracy (78). This possible meaning is clearer in the uncorrected galleys, where Nick tells of having written the names of Gatsby's guests (names like Bull, Fishguard, Hammerhead, and Beluga) on an "old time-table [that was] degenerating at its folds."[14] That is, as a reference to Nick's sexual identity, the idea that he "groaned down in the elevator" suggests more than his possible moral degeneration, as someone like Max Nordau would emphasize. Rather, Jordan's androgyny and Nick's sexual ambivalence reflect on one of the darker aspects in the evolution of sex that Darwin brought to light in *The Descent of Man*: that "it has now been ascertained that at a very early embryonic period both sexes possess true male and female glands. Hence some extremely remote progenitor of the whole vertebrate kingdom appears to have been hermaphrodite or androgynous" (1:207). Fitzgerald was certainly aware of this idea from his having read of Dr. Ledsmar's Darwinian experiment about hermaphroditism in plants (*The Damnation of Theron Ware*) and probably from having read Haeckel's discussion of such rudimentary structures as "the nipple and milk-gland of the male" (265). Moreover, it seems that Fitzgerald hints at this aspect of Nick's sexual identity in Gatsby's repeated way of addressing Nick as "old sport." As Havelock Ellis concluded, "Whatever its ultimate explanation, sexual inversion may thus fairly be considered a 'sport,' or variation, one of those organic aberrations which we see throughout living nature, in plants and in animals" (*Studies* 1:4:317). At any rate, an important result of Fitzgerald's presentation of these possibilities in *The Great Gatsby* is that they contribute to Nick's being repelled by the chaotic nature of sex. "Half sick between grotesque reality and savage frightening dreams," he withdraws from both the brutal male force that nevertheless fascinates him in Tom Buchanan and from "the secret griefs of wild, unknown men," though they fascinate him as well (he frequently feigned sleep when the "intimate revelation was quivering on the horizon" [5–6]). He let one short affair with a girl "blow quietly away" when he was confronted with a violent male: "her brother began throwing mean looks in my direction" (61). Similarly, although he had come east to learn the bond business, when he found himself confined with the unlovely couples Tom and Myrtle and the McKees, Nick "wanted to get out and walk eastward toward the park." But "each time [he] tried to go [he] became entangled in some wild strident argument which pulled [him] back" (40). Still a resoundingly Darwinian term in the early 1920s, "entangled" in this scene leads immediately to Nick's thoughts on his own "share of human secrecy" and his feeling of being "simultaneously enchanted and repelled by the inexhaustible variety of life" (40). Then, in response to Tom's violent outburst (when he breaks Myrtle's nose), Nick leaves with the "feminine" McKee. As the scene in McKee's apartment ends, Fitzgerald suggests in the titles of the first two pictures in McKee's portfolio that Nick's under-lying story has to do mostly with "Beauty and the Beast" and "Loneliness" (42).

If Tom's brutal male power represents the beast in Fitzgerald's imagination, Daisy's voice is the deadly instrument of beauty. At the end of *This Side of Paradise* Amory had begun "to identify evil with . . . strong phallic worship" and concluded that "inseparably linked with evil was beauty," as in "Eleanor's voice, in an old song at night . . . half rhythm, half darkness" (280). There is certainly something of Eleanor's struggle with her female nature that lingers in Daisy: as Eleanor cried, "*why* am I a girl? . . . tied to the sinking ship of future matrimony" (*Paradise* 237), Daisy wept when she learned that her baby was a girl, thinking "the best thing a girl can be in this world [is] a beautiful little fool" (*Gatsby* 21). But even as she is aware of her biological entrapment (as Hemingway would later refer to it in *A Farewell to Arms* [139, 320]) she cannot refrain from voicing what is perhaps the most alluring appeal in American literature. Playing on Darwin's analysis of the sexual appeal of music and the voice, many writers had invested the female voice with such power, as in W. D. Howells's Lydia Blood and James's Verena Tarrant.[15] But whatever Fitzgerald's sources for this idea (Darwin, Haeckel, or any of the many "Darwin-ian" novelists), no writer dramatizes it more fully. He introduces the musical theme as part of the scene of natural history wherein the grass grows up from the beach into the Buchanan house and a sea breeze "rippled over the wine-colored rug, mak-ing a shadow on it as wind does on the sea" (12). Then Daisy began asking Nick

> questions in her low, thrilling voice. It was the kind of voice that the ear fol-lows up and down as if each speech is an arrangement of notes that will never be played again. Her face was sad and lovely with bright things in it, bright eyes and a bright passionate mouth—but there was an excitement in her voice that men who had cared for her found difficult to forget: a singing compul-sion, a whispered "Listen," a promise that she had done gay, exciting things just a while since and that there were gay, exciting things hovering in the next hour. (13–14)

In his innumerable references to Daisy's voice, Fitzgerald identifies it as the prin-ciple instrument with which she casts her spell over Gatsby, compelling his belief in the kind of love that cannot exist in Fitzgerald's view of life. As Nick notes even in this first scene, "the instant her voice broke off, ceasing to compel my attention, my belief, I felt the basic insincerity of what she had said" (22). But the "deathless song" of Daisy's voice held Gatsby "with its fluctuating, feverish warmth because it couldn't be over-dreamed" (101). And when Gatsby tells Nick that "her voice is full of money," Nick immediately realizes that "the inexhaustible charm that rose and fell in it [was] the cymbals' song of . . . the king's daughter, the golden girl" (127).[16]

As Daisy consciously or unconsciously wields her irresistible power, she becomes further entangled in the web of sexual struggle. When Gatsby left for the war after their brief romance, she had suddenly begun to date other men, only to find that, with her "evening dress tangled among dying orchids on the floor beside her bed . . . she wanted her life shaped . . . by some force," which soon proved to be the "force . . . of Tom Buchanan" (158–59), and even when she has not only Tom but possibly Gatsby, she looks back at Gatsby's house as she leaves the party, wondering, "what would happen now in the dim incalculable hours? Perhaps some unbelievable guest would arrive, a person infinitely rare and to be marvelled at, some authentically radiant young girl who with one fresh glance at Gatsby, one moment of magical encounter, would blot out those five years of unwavering devotion" (115). She is instinctively aware of "the first law of woman"—that she is a competitor in the sexual arena, as Fitzgerald had treated this subject in 1924 in "Diamond Dick and the First Law of Woman." Diana ("Diamond Dick") Dickey's "nickname survived"— "she had selected it herself"—and she lived up to it by threatening a sexual competitor with a revolver (*The Price* 69). "I think you've got my man" (82), she explains; "I wasn't made for anything like love" (79). No less a hunter than this Diana or perhaps even Hemingway's Margot Macomber, Daisy is implicated in Myrtle Wilson's accidental death, as Fitzgerald suggests in Nick's concern that if "Tom found out that Daisy had been driving . . . he might think he saw a connection in it—he might think anything" (152).[17]

Gatsby himself can never conceive of such a grim possibility, for he is determined to deny his origins and wants to believe "that the rock of the world was founded securely on a fairy's wing" (105). Nor can he accept the other part of his reality, as suggested in Fitzgerald's epigraph—that he was destined to perform the lover's dance in the biological struggle to be selected. He is always acted on by the natural laws he cannot accept, as when the "universe of ineffable gaudiness spun itself out in his brain" one night as "the clock ticked" and his "tangled clothes [lay] upon the floor"; then "an instinct toward his future glory" led him on his way, first to St. Olaf College and finally to his second opportunity to be selected by Daisy (105). Even then, "as if he were on a wire" (91), he seems unaware that his most effective moment comes, as Fitzgerald's epigraph and Darwin's theory suggest, when he proudly displays his ornamental attractions—the "many-colored disarray . . . [of] shirts with stripes and scrolls and plaids in coral and apple green and lavender and faint orange with monograms of Indian blue" (97–98). Not too subtly invoking the Darwinian idea when he has Gatsby explain that "a man in England . . . sends over a selection of things at the beginning of each season," Fitzgerald illustrates how effective is the power of beauty in sexual selection: "'They're such beautiful shirts,' [Daisy] sobbed, her voice muffled in the thick folds. . . . 'I've never seen such—such beautiful shirts before'" (97–98).

Certainly the most splendid peacock in American literature, Gatsby repeatedly wears his famous pink suit, has his man Klipspringer perform "The Love Nest" on the piano, and, in general, "deck[s] out [his illusion] with every bright feather that drifted his way" (100–101). Nothing could be gaudier to attract the female's eye for ornamental beauty unless it is perhaps the taxicab that appeals to Myrtle Wilson: "she let four taxi cabs drive away before she selected a new one, lavender-colored with grey upholstery [in which the party] slid out from the mass of the station into the glowing sunshine" (31). The image of phallic power and beauty is evident here, as it is in "Gatsby's gorgeous car . . . [of] rich cream color, bright with nickel, swollen here and there in its monstrous length with triumphant hatboxes," and so forth (68). But as Fitzgerald suggests in the line from "Ain't We Got Fun?" ("nothing's surer / The rich get richer" [101]), despite Gatsby's gorgeous ornamentation and phallic appeal, he is no match for Buchanan when they finally confront each other "with competitive firmness" (138).

Gatsby manages moderately well in the dance, with his "graceful, conservative fox-trot" (112), and Tom reveals himself to be no more impressive at this natural feat, in which, as Fitzgerald knew in *This Side of Paradise*, people are "selected by the cut-in system at dances, which favors the survival of the fittest" (58). More restrained in this dance with Daisy than at the first raucous event that Nick attended, Gatsby conceals his instinctive sense that music and dance can be effectively combined in what Darwin called "love-antics and dances" (*The Descent of Man* 2:68). There he had requested that the orchestra play the "Jazz History of the World," and it achieved its desired effect: "girls were putting their heads on men's shoulders . . . and swooning backward . . . into men's arms" (55). The trouble is, such primitive performances tend also to arouse the combative instincts that are inherent in the struggle for reproductive success. In a passage that Fitzgerald cut from the galleys, the "Jazz History of the World" is something like H. G. Wells's evolutionary *Outline of History*, providing "a weird sense that it was a preposterous cycle after all"—one "discord" after another (36).[18] In the novel, the scene ends with one fight leading to several others, and the frenzy of "dissension" and "flank attacks" subsides only when two "wives [are] lifted kicking into the night" (56–57).[19]

Of course this is the way the struggle will end in *The Great Gatsby*, with the stronger male prevailing not so much for his beauty or love, as Gatsby might have hoped, but for the superior physical and financial strength that inheres in his "house." Other American novelists had reached similar conclusions but in different ways: some of Howells's heroes in the 1870s, for example, who prevail over rival males because women select them for their *moral* as well as financial strength, or James's Basil Ransom, who prevails over weaker males (as well as a female competitor) because of his physical and *mental* power, or Harold Frederic's Joel Stormont Thorp because of his combined "nerve-force" and physical and financial strength, as well as the woman's attraction to his "frank barbarism of power," or Edith Wharton's Cobham Stilling in her story "The Choice" because of his sheer physical strength without financial wealth (Mrs. Stilling possesses the wealth).[20]

Unlike any of these, Fitzgerald's plot is quite in accord with "the fundamental principle of biology" that he alluded to in *The Beautiful and Damned*, Haeckel's "ontogenic fact" that in the "tiny globular egg cell" one is already bound within the "chain of generations." Representing a different strata from Daisy's, Gatsby "had no real right to touch her hand" (156), and when she saw his "huge incoherent failure of a house" (188), it simply fell "in like a card house at the disapproval in her eyes" (120). For such reasons Fitzgerald suggests in his closing paragraphs that there never has been a "new world," only the "old unknown world." The "fresh, green breast of the new world . . . pandered in whispers" to the first sailors, compelling their unwanted "aesthetic contemplation," and beauty is still part of the "machinery under everything" that drives us toward an "orgiastic future" (189). "The essential point," as Haeckel remarked, "is not the 'embrace' . . . or the amorousness connected therewith; it is simply the introduction of the spermatozoa into the vagina" (139). Thus the imagined "pap of life" at which Gatsby would "gulp down the incomparable milk of wonder" (117) is destroyed by the "accident" and by the grotesque reality of Myrtle's "left breast . . . swinging loose like a flap" (145).

Notes

1. Discussions of these elements in Fitzgerald's life and work can be found in Jeffrey Meyers, *Scott Fitzgerald: A Biography*, 1–3; James W. Tuttleton, "Seeing Slightly Red: Fitzgerald's 'May Day,'" 196; Matthew J. Bruccoli, preface to *The Great Gatsby*, xiv–xv; Scott Donaldson, *Fool for Love: F. Scott Fitzgerald*, 99–115 (quote on 101); John S. Whitely, "'A Touch of Disaster': Fitzgerald, Spengler and the Decline of the West," throughout his article; and Judith Fetterly, "Who Killed Dick Diver? The Sexual Politics of *Tender is the Night*," 124–26.

2. In his well-known book, Conklin builds toward his long last chapters on eugenics, arguing, for example, that "the promotion of human evolution [through eugenics] must be undertaken by society as its greatest work," and that "individual freedom must be subordinated to racial welfare" (*Heredity and Environment in the Development of Men* 348–49).

3. Letter from Fitzgerald to Edmund Wilson, dated July 1921, in *F. Scott Fitzgerald: A Life in Letters*, 46–47.

4. The "Fitzgerald Book Lists" in the F. Scott Fitzgerald Papers at Princeton University indicate that Fitzgerald owned and had signed a copy of *The Riddle of the Universe*, but that volume is not now contained in the university's Department of Rare Books and Special Collections. These book lists include no volumes by Darwin. In his enthusiastic review of Dos Passos's *Three Soldiers*, Fitzgerald cited Owen Johnston's *The Wasted Generation* as an example of a current war story that paled by comparison, in part because "it abounded with . . . undigested Haeckel" (*In His Own Time* 123).

5. Spengler definitely rejected modern evolutionary thought, criticizing the shallowness of Darwinism and referring to the "soulless and soul-killing generation of . . . Haeckel" (132); *The Riddle of the Universe*, 383.

6. Some of these words and other key terms in the Darwinian lexicon (like *tangle*) are traceable in Andrew Crosland, *A Concordance to F. Scott Fitzgerald's The Great Gatsby; Riddle of the Universe*, 252. As Haeckel notes here, he had first referred to Darwin in this way in 1868—long before Freud's more famous remark that after Copernicus's first great blow to human narcissism (by showing that the earth is not at the center of the universe), Darwin dealt the second or "*biological* blow" by proving the human's animal nature (Freud, *Standard Edition*, 17:141).

7. For a discussion of the Darwinian elements in *A Chance Acquaintance* and other novels of courtship and marriage by Howells, see my *The Descent of Love*.

8. Another example of Fitzgerald's biological critique of sexual love and motherhood is contained in these remarks about the character Gloria in *The Beautiful and Damned*:

> She knew that in her breast she had never wanted children. The reality, the earthiness, the intolerable sentiment of child-bearing, the menace to her beauty—had appalled her. She wanted to exist only as a conscious flower, prolonging and preserving itself. Her sentimentality could cling fiercely to her own illusions, but her ironic soul whispered that motherhood was also the privilege of the female baboon. So her dreams were of ghostly children only. (392–93)

9. It is worth recalling that when Tom Buchanan learns that Gatsby knows his wife, he complains that "these days . . . [women] meet all kinds of crazy fish" (110).

10. As many critics have remarked, Fitzgerald's earlier story "Absolution" (1924) represents a preliminary effort to deal with the problem of his and his characters' origins. As I would put it, Rudolph in that story exemplifies the kind of anxiety about his fixed evolutionary state that Gatsby and other characters in Fitzgerald experience. Rudolph confessed his sin "of not believing I was the son of my parents" and so imagined himself as Blatchford Sarnemington, a character who then "established dominance over him" (187, 189). As Haeckel might remark of such figures as Rudolph and especially Gatsby, the "boundless presumption of conceited man has misled him into making himself 'the image of God,' claiming an 'eternal life' for his ephemeral personality, and imagining that he possesses unlimited 'freedom of will'" (15).

11. In *Tender Is the Night*, as Dick Diver surveys a battlefield on the western front, he remarks: "Why this was a love battle—there was a century of middle-class love spent here. This was the last love battle" (68).

12. Elsewhere, in many places, Fitzgerald is far more explicit in suggesting the human link to fish and the sea. In "The Swimmers" (1929), for example, the character Henry Marston enjoys swimming and feeling like a "porpoise," and he thinks that Americans could better deal with their restlessness if they had developed "fins and wings"; he comments ironically on the American idea that we could "leave out history and the past," "inheritance or tradition" (*Bits of Paradise* 201). Similarly, in *Tender Is the Night*, Fitzgerald remarks that "Nicole had been designed for change, for flight with money as fins and wings" (311).

13. For other controversial but insightful studies of androgyny and homosexual possibilities in *The Great Gatsby* that have only recently emerged (especially in the scene with Nick and McKee), but not from the evolutionary point of view, see Fraser, "Another Reading of *The Great Gatsby*"; Thornton, "Sexual Roles in *The Great Gatsby*"; Wasiolek, "The Sexual Drama of Nick and Gatsby"; and Kerr, "Feeling 'Half Feminine': Modernism and the Politics of Emotion in *The Great Gatsby*."

14. Bruccoli, *The Great Gatsby: The Revised and Rewritten Galleys*, 47.

15. Discussions of Howells's, James's, and other novelists' uses of Darwin's observations about the sexual appeal of music and the voice are indexed in my *The Descent of Love*. Whether Fitzgerald caught it or not, Darwin referred to Haeckel's "interesting discussion of this subject, agreeing that "women . . . possess sweeter voices than men," but concluding "that they first acquired [these] musical powers in order to attract the opposite sex" (*The Descent of Man* 2:337).

16. Among the innumerable parallels in Fitzgerald's story of a naive male's destruction in an encounter with the sexual reality, compared with Harold Frederic's in *The Damnation of Theron Ware*, are Celia Madden's several musical performances and Theron's fascination with "Miss Madden's riches"; the "glamour" of wealth "shown upon her," the "veritable gleam of gold" (261). Both Fitzgerald and Frederic work with Darwin's point that human beings select for wealth and social position.

17. That Fitzgerald saw a good deal of Diana Dickey ("Diamond Dick") in Daisy is clear from his having taken two paragraphs of his description of Diana in the story to use in reference to Daisy in *The Great Gatsby* (Fitzgerald, *Trimalchio*, 180); in Fitzgerald's story "The Dance" (1926) another sexual struggle between women ends in murder because "all the girls are good friends . . . except when two of them are try'n to get hold of the same man" (*Bits of Paradise* 154).

18. Something of Fitzgerald's early attraction to the evolutionary view of life is evident in the interest he showed in Wells's *Outline of History, Being a Plain History of Life and Humankind*, which, he remarked in 1920, was "Most absorbing!" (*Correspondence of F. Scott Fitzgerald* 73).

19. For similar remarks by Fitzgerald on the role of music and dance in sexual selection, see "The Dance," which is set in a small town where life's affairs and scandals "live on all tangled up with the natural ebb and flow of outward life" (*Bits of Paradise* 140).

20. Discussions of these examples are indexed in my *The Descent of Love*.

9 Harlem, 1928

The Biology of the Black Soul and the
"Rising Tide of Rhythm"

The Harlem Renaissance played an important part in American culture's exploration of evolutionary thought. A highly complicated and conflicted movement of
the 1920s and early 1930s, the Renaissance was rooted in the late nineteenth-century careers of writers like W. E. B. DuBois, Charles W. Chesnutt, and Paul Laurence
Dunbar (whose 1902 novel, *The Sport of the Gods*, was set partly in Harlem). As
Arnold Ramperad concludes, the Renaissance flowered as a "youthful cultural movement that was an integral part of the Jazz Age and subject to many of the stresses
that simultaneously produced the Lost Generation" (199); other historians have
described important generational and cultural differences within the movement.[1]
But underlying these stresses and differences was a common assumption that narratives of race must either build on or contend with Darwin's theory of racial difference. Unfortunately, however, literary discussions of the Renaissance rarely mention Darwin, for many novelists embraced his theory of race as a powerfully
liberating force. Reiterating the power of fluid evolutionary change, Darwin dis-
puted not only the dogma that absolute race distinctions were part of biblical design but also the theory that they were set by environmental conditions in the evolutionary past. He wrote that the "so-called races of men" are not "constant," that
not all of "the characteristic differences between the races of man" can be accounted
for by "the direct action of the conditions of life" (such as environment); and that
such racial differences as color "are of the nature which it might have been expected
would have been acted on by sexual selection" (*The Descent of Man* 1:214, 248–50).

Thus, like many other writers of the 1920s, novelists of the Harlem Renaissance
worked with Darwin's theory of sexual selection, either celebrating or questioning
the new sexual freedom of the Jazz Age but with keener interest in its role in the
evolution of race. These novelists realized that the modernist discussion of race
and sex was founded in evolutionary thought, as in Havelock Ellis's remark that

"the question of sex—with the racial questions that rest on it—stands before the coming generations as the chief problem for solution" (*Studies* 1:lixxx). And agreeing with DuBois's more famous remark that "the problem of the Twentieth Century is the problem of the color line" ("The Forethought," *Souls of Black Folk*), they knew that this included not only the depressing history of black and white relations in America, but the problems of "passing" and of discrimination within the African American community according to gradations in skin color, as in the "blue vein society." Chesnutt was the first African American novelist to explore these issues in light of Darwinian thought in *The House behind the Cedars* (1900).[2]

In 1922 Darwinian theory was the keystone in the novel that had such an enormous impact on the Harlem Renaissance, T. S. Stribling's *Birthright* (Lewis, *Harlem Renaissance Reader*, 333, 762). In this novel (published three years before the Scopes trial), Stribling (a white southerner) criticizes a white southern gentleman's library for excluding any scientific works after the 1880s, "when Charles Darwin's great fructifying theory . . . began to seep into the South." This man's library contained only a single "notice of evolution . . . a book called 'Darwinism Dethroned'" (182). By the end of the novel Stribling's black hero, Peter Siner, a young M.D. from Harvard, has apparently drawn on the great fructifying theory, affirming his racial heritage. He is amazed and overjoyed to realize that "he had come out [of Harvard] just as he went in, a negro" (309) and along the way Stribling writes that "what Christ did for theology, Darwin did for biology,—he democratized it" (219).[3] But at the same time Stribling was interpreting racial science in this optimistic way, Lothrop Stoddard was arousing widespread hysteria within the white community over the problems of race and sex in his widely known book, *The Rising Tide of Color against White World-Supremacy* (1920). Finally, an additional and very important element in the fictional exploration of race and sex during these years was the great interest in sexual primitivism. This issue had emerged as an apparent corollary to popular Freudianism. Thus, in many almost obligatory scenes of music and dance in the Harlem novels, some writers, like DuBois and Fauset, devoted a good deal of energy to presenting the concept of black sexual primitivism as a figment of the neurotic white psyche. And other writers, especially McKay, celebrated the uninhibited black psyche as expressed in dance and the blues as the key to group survival.

The Renaissance produced twenty-six novels by African Americans (as Lewis figures, *Reader* xl), far too many to survey in a chapter of these proportions. But the five novels that appeared in 1928 (DuBois's *Dark Princess*, Jessie Fauset's *Plum Bun*, Nella Larsen's *Quicksand*, Claude McKay's *Home to Harlem*, and Rudolph Fisher's *The Walls of Jericho*) provide a snapshot of the varieties of evolutionary narratives that were produced by representatives of both the "genteel" and the "demotic" groups within the Renaissance (in Lewis's terms) and by both men and women at the height of the Harlem Renaissance.[4] Moreover, the novels of 1928 appeared after a turning point in the Renaissance that began in 1925 when Alain Locke published his land-mark anthology, "Dedicated to the Younger Generation," *The New Negro*. The following year saw Langston Hughes's "The Negro Artist and the Racial Mountain," Carl Van Vechten's highly influential and controversial novel *Nigger Heaven*, Wallace Thurman's short-lived literary magazine *Fire!!* and the symposium DuBois published in the *Crisis* (from March through November), "The Negro in Art: How Shall He Be Portrayed." The evolutionary theme that runs through this literature is especially evident in Locke's introductory essay, "The New Negro," the *Crisis* symposium, "The Negro in Art," and Van Vechten's *Nigger Heaven*.

Writing about "the vogue of the New Negro," Nathan Huggins notes that it resembled "a public relations promotion" aimed at the general public and "the Negro himself," and he objects to "the metaphor itself" (the New Negro) because it implies "some inadequacy in the past" (65). However, it would help clarify the relationship of the Harlem Renaissance to American literature in general to remember that the interest in the new man or woman was by the 1920s an old theme in American writing as it had begun to probe the question of human nature in light of evolutionary thought. Based on the belief in evolutionary progress, writers from William Dean Howells and Elizabeth Stuart Phelps to Frank Norris, Jack London, and Sherwood Anderson had sought to imagine new men and women who could lead the way to a more highly evolved civilization, especially regarding marital discord attributable to the promiscuous and brutal male. Others, of course, like Henry James, Harold Frederic, Stephen Crane, and Edith Wharton, scoffed at the idea of evolutionary progress or, as Fitzgerald puts it at the end of *The Great Gatsby*, the myth that there ever was a "new world." A similar disagreement over the meaning of *progress* or *new* or over how and to what extent the race might *uplift* itself runs throughout the Harlem Renaissance, as evidenced in the novels under discussion. And, while it is true, as Huggins notes, that the interest in the New Negro expressed "an urgent need for self-assertion and militancy" (65), one should remember that this sense of urgency among black Americans corresponded to the anxiety among white Americans over the evolutionary questions that underlay *The Rising Tide of Color against White World-Supremacy*.

In response to the Stoddard hysteria, Alain Locke wrote that the growing phenomenon of race consciousness among "the dark-peoples" "is a different thing from the much asserted rising tide of color" (*New Negro* 14). That is, blacks' "new internationalism" was largely a defensive maneuver in response to the Stoddard hysteria and was "not of our making"; moreover, Locke insisted, the movement need not be "damaging to the best interests of civilization," and it would be up to "the dominant races" to decide whether the movement would bring "Armadas of conflict or argosies of cultural exchange and enlightenment" (14). Finally, Locke's conception of the New Negro emphasized cultural exchange and the idea that the movement was "primarily an effort to recapture contact with the scattered peoples of African derivation." Such views underscore his alignment with Franz Boas's effort in early twentieth-century anthropology to counter what many took to be the biological determinism of Darwinian theory (15). Working in behalf of African Americans, he argued that "the traits of African culture as observed in the aboriginal home of the Negro," emphasized blacks' inherent personal initiative, talent for organization, imaginative power, and technical skill and thrift (qtd. in Degler, *In Search of Human Nature*, 77).[5] Indeed, this was an essential theme in Locke's groundbreaking anthology of "the first fruits of the Negro Renaissance" in *The New Negro*, which includes a section, "The Negro Digs Up His Past" (xvii). Locke's own contribution to that chapter, "The Legacy of the Ancestral Arts," reproduces examples of African art that demonstrate its influence on contemporary European artists like Matisse and Picasso.

From DuBois's different evolutionary point of view, it was always better to promote the higher achievements of the elite or the "talented tenth" of the black population. Voicing his opposition, especially, to Booker T. Washington's program for black education, DuBois felt that racial progress (for any race) would proceed only if the exceptional tenth were given their opportunity, as this would "make way for natural selection and the survival of the fittest" ("The Talented Tenth," *DuBois: Writings*, 843). Also to this end, he favored fiction that was avowedly propagandistic, emphasizing achievements of the more highly educated blacks. Although he had contributed his own chapter to *The New Negro* ("The Negro Mind Reaches Out," about his interest in Pan-Africanism, a subject he would treat fictionally in *The Dark Princess*), he complained that Locke's emphasis on Beauty would "turn the Negro renaissance into decadence" (qtd. in Rampersad 194). And he immediately took up this banner in his *Crisis* symposium, "The Negro in Art."

DuBois resisted the growing interest in uninhibited sexuality in literature, especially in works by white writers depicting blacks, as in Gertrude Stein's "Melanctha" and the more explicitly primitivistic and Freudian *Dark Laughter* by Sherwood Anderson. And he invited "artists of the world" to respond to such leading questions as, "Is not the continual portrayal of the sordid, foolish and criminal among Negroes convincing the world that this and this alone is really and essentially Negroid . . . ?" Disappointingly, scarcely anyone gave him the kind of response he wanted; in the main, there was only his assistant, Jessie Fauset, who wrote in the June 1926 *Crisis* that there was "emphatically . . . a grave danger" in response to "The Negro in Art" symposium question about "young colored writers" being "tempted to follow the popular trend in portraying Negro character in the underworld" (70–71). Even the aging Charles Waddell Chesnutt (to whom DuBois gave the last word in the symposium) did not feel the danger. Perhaps the most upsetting irony from DuBois's point of view was that his first respondent, Carl Van Vechten, ignored his leading questions, writing that it would be "completely inimical to art" to discourage novelists from depicting "the lower strata of the race" ("The Negro in Art," March 1926, 219).

Worse, before the symposium had ended, Van Vechten's *Nigger Heaven* appeared, provoking DuBois's review, "The most crushing . . . in the history of the *Crisis*" (Rampersad 196). DuBois began his review by calling "Carl Van Vechten's 'Nigger Heaven' . . . a blow in the face." He was outraged not only because "the author counts among his friends numbers of Negroes of all classes," but because "love is degraded" in the novel, "his women's bodies have no souls," and "life to him is just one damned orgy after another, with hate, hurt, gin and sadism" (Review 81–82).

But if DuBois and many others were driven into "apoplexy" by *Nigger Heaven*, others welcomed the novel. As Lewis notes, *Nigger Heaven* deepened the dichotomy within "literate Afro-America" (*Reader* xxx); the other side of the argument is best exemplified by Wallace Thurman's defense of the novel, where he wrote somewhat playfully that Van Vechten should be honored with "a statue on the corner of 135th Street and Seventh Avenue" ("Fire Burns" 47). Thurman's only complaint about the novel was that Van Vecthen "wavered between sentimentality and sophistication"— the sentimentality being in his portrayal of the heroine Mary Love. But it is important to note that the problem Van Vechten embodied in the well-named character Mary Love[6] was the key problem that evolutionary novelists from Howells to Sherwood Anderson and Claude McKay knew they were obliged to address in order to imagine the new men and women of the evolutionary future. That is, the problem in plotting the evolutionary future was to imagine a couple who were both strong enough to survive the environmental conditions of their present lives and then, at the end of the novel, to send them on their way toward achieving reproductive success in some brave new world.

The plot of *Nigger Heaven* expresses Van Vechten's caution to the New Negro: the promising relationship between Mary Love and the aspiring writer Byron Kasson fails (1) because she is not quite "capable . . . of amorous emotion," and (2) because he proves to be morally and artistically weak (54). As Van Vechten explains, "Mary confessed to herself . . . that she did not let herself go. She had an instinctive horror of promiscuity" (54), and Van Vechten suggests that Byron's failure as a weak male in the struggle for existence is his inability to select his material (202). After a white editor (apparently modeled on H. L. Mencken) humiliated him by criticizing his ability to "select a subject" (224), Byron "realized his impotence" (228), was later reduced to "impotent rage" (265) when cast aside by the lascivious Lasca Sartoris, and finally fired ineffectual pistol shots into "the ugly black mass" of a sexual competitor who had already been dispatched by the black underworld figure known as "the Bolito King" (284). The relationship between Mary and Byron had begun promisingly enough when Mary, who "was selective," saw Byron in a bathing suit (23, 54). His relatively light skin color was "her preferred tint," she was impressed with "the symmetrical proportions of his body" (24), and she would "unaccountably . . .

tremble" on hearing his voice (34). With these typically Darwinian elements of sexual attraction, then, this relationship seems well on its way until Van Vecthen begins to develop his Freudian analysis of Mary—his effort to isolate the "indefinable something in her makeup [that] interfered with the progress of a more intimate relationship" (88). And now the novel begins to develop the themes that DuBois thought were "degraded"—what Van Vechten refers to as the "dim, biological way" in which some of Mary's friends responded to jazz and "the beat of the African rhythm." Thinking her friends "savages at heart!" Mary had "forfeited her . . . primitive birthright," her claim to the vital force that was so appealing even to "a Picasso or a Stravinsky." Of course such music also "aroused her emotionally—but she was conscious of feeling it"; the "warm, sexual emotion . . . [was] hers only through a mental understanding" rather than being simply "instinctive" (88–90).

DuBois was most revolted by the "simply nasty" lovemaking between Byron and Lasca (252–53), when they revel in the sadistic pleasures of sexual passion that Havelock Ellis and Freud had found to be within the range of normality. But in Van Vechten's view, this kind of Freudian lovemaking was far less problematic in the evolutionary plot than Mary's having lost the instinct to kill her sexual rival, Lasca. That is, Van Vechten imagines that Mary *could* have controlled the evolutionary plot by killing her sexual rival—thereby both claiming the male as her own possession and at the same time rescuing him as a somewhat typical male who is apparently helpless to restrain his own sexual appetite. Mary knows that her friends enjoy something that is "more than a marriage," the "primitive consecration" that makes them willing to "fight—kill if need be—to retain the other's love," but this only makes her "feel her own lack more keenly than ever. How had she, during the centuries, lost this vital instinct?" (91–92). Again, when she later realizes that she "ought to kill" Lasca, she can only moan, "I want to, but I can't. What's wrong with me?" (167). Thus, having depicted an ineffectual hero, whom Mary should not have selected in the first place, and a heroine who had repressed her sexual instinct, Van Vechten was bound to offend many of his many readers.

Nigger Heaven helped stimulate the production of other varieties of the evolutionary plot, including the five novels of the Harlem Renaissance that appeared in 1928. As these novelists addressed "the problem of the color line," then, they constructed possible solutions within the evolutionary framework. Whether imagining mere survival or outright evolutionary progress through the mating of their new men and women, their solutions explored, first, the female's power to select the superior male, second, the problems of sexual selection in relation to the concern over "absorption" or "color prejudice within the race" (Lewis, *Vogue,* 237), and third, the possibility that the black subconscious would show the way, either as a primitive vital force that might be expressed in the blues or as a soul that endured in the soul song or spiritual.

W. E. B. DuBois's *Dark Princess:* The Talented Soul

W. E. B. DuBois's most insightful critic, Arnold Rampersad, concludes his discussion of *Dark Princess: A Romance* by insisting that the novel is "in the final analysis . . . a utopian exercise" reflecting "DuBois's vision of the ideal political, moral, and social world" (217). This point is amplified by showing how DuBois's vision of the darker world is in the tradition of American utopian novels that were constructed of evolutionary thought—from W. D. Howells's *A Traveler from Altruria* (1894) to Frank Norris's *The Octopus* or Jack London's *The Valley of the Moon.* Like the first two of these, *Dark Princess* is a love story, comparable especially to Norris's romance of altruistic love (*The Octopus*) in its interest in the real and darker world of the "seed" and growth and to London's novel in that both build on developments in evolutionary thought that extend into the Freudian era.

In his autobiographical *Dusk of Dawn* (1940) DuBois recalled his early interest while at Harvard in "evolution, geology, and the new psychology," how he was struck by "the biological analogy," and how his own study of psychology under William James had predated the Freudian era but had helped prepare him for it (590, 770). Of course at Harvard he also faced "scientific race dogma: first of all, evolution and the 'Survival of the Fittest.'" But, especially after further study helped him see how "race became a matter of culture and cultural history," he found that he could accept evolution and the survival of the fittest when the scientific calculations were plausible. He could not abide the "impossible" thousand years that certain evolutionists had concluded was sufficient to account for supposed differences between "advanced and backward races," or the confidence many racial scientists had in brain weight (625–26). By the time he wrote *Dark Princess,* all this was behind him, including his own impressive work in the scientific study of African Americans in the Atlanta University Studies, designed to counter the kind of racial science espoused by Joseph Le Conte and, in turn, Frank Norris. In short, David Levering Lewis errs in asserting that DuBois "embrac[ed] a patently nineteenth-century theory of race" (*When Harlem Was in Vogue* 7), for DuBois was acutely attuned to early twentieth-century theories of race. Indeed, he helped to construct them.

Still, there is no question that DuBois intended *Dark Princess* as racial propaganda. As he remarked in his 1926 essay "Criteria of Negro Art" (when he must have been at work on *Dark Princess*), "Whatever art I have for writing has been used always for propaganda for gaining the right of black folk to love and enjoy" (*Writings* 1000). "I do not care a damn for any art that is not used for propaganda," he exclaims. He offended some of his fellow writers in the Harlem Renaissance by arguing that "all Art is propaganda and ever must be, despite the wailing of the purists."[7] But surely this theory of art applies to some extent to virtually every evolutionary plot during this time, including those by some of his critics within the

Renaissance. Each of these novels had a political orientation and projected an interpretation of the evolutionary reality.

With its unquestionably wooden fictional apparatus, *Dark Princess* is devoted to establishing a political-evolutionary principle that can emerge only after darker peoples of the world rise up in resistance to the oppressive white European world order. Clearly an extension of DuBois's evolutionary logic in "The Talented Tenth," the idea is now enlarged to include his growing interest in Pan-Africanism and the Bolshevik Revolution, and it serves to revive his hero's (Matthew Towns) shaken faith in democracy. Towns had been "drifting logically and inevitably toward oligarchy." But through his heroine, the dark princess Kautilya, DuBois counters Towns's belief that "we can make life good [only] by compulsion" (283). Kautilya's response is that

> oligarchy as you conceive it is not the antithesis of democracy—it is democracy, if only the selection of the oligarchs is just and true. Birth is the method of blind fools. Wealth is the gambler's method. Only Talent served from the great Reservoir of All Men of All Races, of All Classes, of All Ages, of Both Sexes—this is real Aristocracy, real Democracy—the only path to that great and final Freedom which you so well call Divine Anarchy. (285)

Of course this is a romance, as DuBois clearly emphasizes in his title. It projects his vision that natural selection should proceed according to truth and justice to preserve the "talented" variations that emerge throughout the human community. He knew that other writers, such as Frank Norris, had also argued the legitimacy of romance in constructing evolutionary plots. And within the Harlem Renaissance DuBois is only a little more extravagant in presenting his evolutionary love story than are Fauset, McKay, or Fisher.

The plot of *The Dark Princess* develops in four parts: part 1, "The Exile," in which the black hero Matthew Towns leaves the United States after being rejected from medical school in New York because "white women patients [are not] going to have a nigger doctor delivering their babies" (4). In Germany he meets the heroine, Kautilya, a princess from India who is there to participate in the "Great Council of the Darker Peoples" from around the world, except for African Americans. Having heard in Moscow of an African American movement to resist white rule, she takes an interest in Matthew, and the two return separately to the United States. In part 2, "The Pullman Porter," Matthew is briefly involved with a black nationalist named Miguel Perigua (apparently a reflection of Marcus Garvey), becomes disillusioned with this approach to the race question, and then enters the black proletarian world as a railroad porter. There, a trivial incident with a white woman results in an encounter with the Ku Klux Klan, and Towns's friend and fellow porter is lynched.

Matthew then becomes involved in a plot of retribution to blow up a train, but he is saved when the princess appears and persuades him to give it up. He ends up in prison and the princess continues to explore black America, agreeing to deliver Matthew's message about his imprisonment to his aged mother in Virginia. In part 3, "The Chicago Politician," Matthew is pardoned after a light "colored" woman, Sara Andrews, secretary to a black politician in Chicago named Sammy Scott, convinces Scott to intervene in Matthew's behalf. Now, guided by Sara's political expertise, Matthew quickly rises in the world of Chicago politics, being elected to the Illinois state legislature and, almost, the U.S. Congress.

His alliance with Sara leads to their passionless marriage, but on the eve of his election to Congress, Kautilya appears again. By now she has entered the world of American labor and has assumed a high role in union leadership. She appears just in time to save Matthew once again from the corruption of political life, and DuBois celebrates their passionate reunion. In part 4, "The Maharajah of Bwodpur," Matthew and Kautilya are together in love, during which time we learn of Kautilya's background and her life's work in the cause for the darker world. But Matthew must return to Sara and satisfy his moral obligation in that passionless marriage. When this proves futile and the marriage ends in a divorce, Matthew and Kautilya are finally reunited—they having continued to correspond and she having concluded from her relationship with Matthew's mother in Virginia that the old woman is "Kali, the Black One; wife of Siva, Mother of the World!" (220). When Matthew finally goes to Kautilya and his mother in Virginia, Kautilya surprises him with their newborn son. Under the direction of the old mother, who declares "we'se gwine to make dis little man an hones' chile," the two are married. "The ancient woman" sings "the old slave song of world revolution," "I am seekin' for a City," while a robed contingency from India joins in celebrating this "Incarnate Son of the Buddha!"—"Messenger and Messiah to all the Darker Worlds!" (309–11).

Truly, as Arnold Rampersad remarks, "this queer combination of outright propaganda and Arabian tale, of social realism and quaint romance, is a challenge to the casual reader" (204). Rampersad is certainly the most helpful guide to DuBois's fiction in relation to his career as a whole. But I would suggest that there is an important answer to the question he poses about Kautilya's "doctine of deified love"—her remark to Matthew that "'Love is God, Love is God and Work is His Prophet'; thus the Lord Buddha Spoke.'" Noting that "neither Kautilya nor DuBois specifically explains the extent of this doctrine," Rampersad asks, "Does it mean primarily the love between persons? Is DuBois preaching a Christlike submission to political adversity?" His tentative answer is that "DuBois is echoing Plato as well as Buddha" in suggesting that hate is self-destructive "and love is a necessity of growth and harmony" (214–15). But DuBois was working not primarily with Plato but rather with evolutionary theory and its emphasis on sexual selection, especially within the tradition of American fiction that envisioned sexual love as the only pathway to evolutionary progress. As Rampersad notes, at least one of DuBois's earliest critics saw at once that DuBois was working with evolutionary thought. In 1911 William Stanley Braithwaite drew a comparison between Norris and DuBois and suggested that DuBois was projecting his belief "in some form of evolutionary optimism" (Rampersad 117, 181). But to develop these important points more meaningfully, it helps to recall that the mystic force that transforms Norris's hero Annixter is his love for Hilma Tree (*The Octopus*) and that Norris identifies this love with the spiritual force that causes "the great earth, the mother" in "its period of reproduction" to deliver "the fruit of its loins" (*Novels and Essays* 1084). And this same teleological force drives the wheat-laden *Swanhilda* to India in fulfillment of the manifest destiny of Anglo-Saxon supremacy (1094).

Just as Norris had sought (with the help of Joseph Le Conte's *Evolution*) to transcend the entanglement of Darwinian selection, DuBois gives us a hero in Matthew who wants "to get his hand into the tangles of this world" (42). Having met and seen the promise in the Dark Princess, he realizes that he had come to count "on this woman—on her subtlety and vision" to "see beneath the unlovely surface of this racial tangle" (59). But even toward the end of his quest he has it only partly right, writing to Kautilya, "I seem to see" that our purpose is "to straighten out the tangle and put the feet of our people . . . on the Path," the "first step" of which is "to reunite thought and physical work. . . . Work is God" (266). Then, after reading her response, that "Love is God, Love is God and Work is His Prophet," he remains in a state of confusion, unable to think: "He could not reason. He just sat and saw and felt in a tangled jumble of thoughts and words, feelings and desires, dreams and fears" (306). Then he makes his way to the home of his mother, "the Black one; wife of Siva, Mother of the World!" as Kautilya had proclaimed (221). And there, seeing their son, Matthew "went down upon his knees before [Kautilya] and kissed the sandals of her feet and sobbed" (307).

DuBois's vision of the Princess and the "Messiah to all the Darker Worlds" is an effective answer to Norris's vision of Anglo-Saxon supremacy (though *Dark Princess* is not without its own discriminatory taint, most notably in the Princess's confession that if their baby had "been a girl child, I must have left both babe and you. Bwodpur needs not a princess, but a King" [308]). But it is important to recognize how these two works of racial propaganda differ. DuBois locates the highest power not in the light of the rising sun (as Norris does) but in the "ancient woman" of "the Darker World." He transforms Norris's passion for the "seed farm" in *The Octopus* by arranging for Kaultilya, pregnant with their child, to proclaim from the old home in Virginia that the "seed that is hidden dark, inert, dead, will one day be alive, and here, here! . . . [T]he earth is rich and full and Love sits wild and glorious on the world" (282). Then, after writing to Matthew that Asian and African culture had "gone to seed" but proclaiming that "its re-birth is imminent" (285), she writes again from Virginia that "I want to see seed sink in the dead earth" (290). Also, however, DuBois clearly deploys his evolutionary propaganda beyond the racial issues that Norris had emphasized at the turn of the century (notably, Norris's theme of degeneration through racial mixture) in order to contend with other matters in the battlefield of the 1920s. Most importantly, perhaps, responding to the hysteria over the rising tide of color, DuBois ends his romance by emphasizing the fertility of the real and darker world with the birth of a new child to a dark couple from both sides of the globe (246). Moreover, in response to the idea voiced by Van Vechten's impotent hero in *Nigger Heaven*—that the white man's desire for "our women will eventually solve the race problem. We'll all be absorbed in the white race!" (183)—DuBois tells how Kautilya was "the last of a long royal line" threatened with "absorption by England" (243), and he describes his ideally "beautiful couple . . . in the brownness of their skins, in their joy and absorption in each other" (264).

But if DuBois's evolutionary romance projects a different future from those he knew in Norris and Van Vechten, it begins in the same way. He brings his couple together by means of an essentially Darwinian episode in the drama of race and sexual selection, when Matthew is feeling "a dreadful homesickness" for "black America" and at that moment feels the "first ecstasy" in seeing Kautilya: "First and above all came that sense of color" (7–8). As Darwin theorized, noting that there is no "universal standard of beauty with respect to the human body," it seems likely that "each race would possess its own innate ideal standard of beauty," for "men of each race prefer what they are accustomed to behold" (*Descent of Man* 2:353–54). Also, like any successful Darwinian male (and again as distinct from Van Vechten's ineffectual Byron), Matthew immediately displays his success in the law of battle for possession of the female when a boastful white American makes a pass at Kautilya: the white man's "hand had hardly touched her elbow when Matthew's fist caught him right between the smile and the ear. The American sat down on the sidewalk very suddenly" (10). Working with this idea, DuBois also brings in the traditional Darwinian imagery of the male's grasping hand but now identifying it as the imperial grasp. He had noted earlier in this scene that in the white man's first approach to Kautilya he could only place "his hand on the back of the empty chair" next to her (9) and later in the novel Kautilya tells of an unsuccessful, disabled English suitor who was "'always insistently arranging my cushions with his lone hand'" (237). And, following the initial episode of Matthew's heroics, DuBois underscores the Darwinian point about beautiful and combative males. In a scene in which Matthew and Kautilya are discussing how "brown women seem strangely attractive to white men . . . and this is the open season for them," Kautilya recalls the way "you knocked him into the gutter quite beautifully. . . . I had a curious sense of some great inner meaning to your act" (17).

As a contestant in the literary conflict *within* the Harlem Renaissance, though, DuBois knew that his most difficult problem would be how to emphasize Matthew's virility and Kautilya's fertility, her passion for the "seed," and at the same time protect his couple from the taint of primitive promiscuity. He was intent on maintaining that "ancient African chastity" had been lost only to "two centuries of systematic defilement of Negro women" and that twentieth-century America would be richer if "her vulgar music [were replaced] with the soul of the Sorrow Songs" (*Souls of Black Folk* 368, 370). In *Dark Princess* DuBois arranges for the couple's discussion of their ideal relationship—Matthew's pledge to "keep strong in body and clear in mind and clean in soul," and his supposition that their commitment to each other "is based on the physical urge of sex between us . . . the magnificent fact of our love . . . whatever its basis. . . . It rises from the ecstasy of our bodies to the communion of saints" (259–60). But writing this in 1928, DuBois knew that he had to do more than this to engage the discussion of the sex problem. Though he can avoid the Harlem scene as much as possible by setting his novel mostly in Europe, Chicago, and Virginia, he was obliged to at least acknowledge Harlem's famed night life in order to deny its vital reality. Thus, in a brief chapter of the Pullman section, Matthew and an excited minister visit a Harlem cabaret for a midnight lunch, entering to find it "close, hot, and crowded," with over "half the patrons . . . white." Although "the colored patrons seemed more at home and natural . . . some looked bored," and DuBois presents the sexual element as more essentially white than "primitive."

The dancing girl is "pale cream" and she first collects "all the cash in sight on the white side." DuBois describes her "sinuous, writing movement," her "astonishing blend of beauty, rhythm, and ugliness," and notes that "she sang her vulgar 'blues' with a harsh shrill voice that hardly seemed hers at all." Making her move for Matthew, whom she calls "Big Boy," the dancer seductively "slipped her hand in his," signaling that she and not Matthew is the sexual predator. Still, after he leaves with the minister (who serves to make DuBois's moral point, thus freeing the author from the charge of prudishness), Matthew returns for a liaison with the seductress. When he visits her once again, he danced with her and "drank the stuff that burned and rankled," but returning with her to her flat he "slipped his clothes off," clasped "his arms around her curving form [and] fell into dreamless sleep" (64–70). Thus this brief flirtation with the "nasty" nightlife of Harlem ends the next morning when the dancer expresses her "forgotten shame" and tells Matthew, "Good-by, Big Boy . . . you ain't built for the sporting game" (64); he then leaves her with a kiss on her forehead, and she remains for a long time "with that kiss upon her brow" (70).

In a more interesting and detailed maneuver as he works to acknowledge his hero's sexual need while also channeling it toward the dark princess, DuBois analyzes the sexual nature of Sara Andrews, the political strategist whom Matthew marries and divorces. Introducing her, DuBois makes the significant points that she is scarcely recognizable as "colored," that "she was not beautiful," and that "she gave an impression of cleanliness, order, cold, clean hardness, and unusual efficiency" (109). Predictably, then, we learn that she is sexually cold and "physically 'pure' almost to prudery," a point DuBois reiterates with a Freudian gesture to those who might have thought him too prudish to indulge in the new psychology (112). Not long after the grand wedding, Sara "had an electric log put in," despite Matthew's desire for "a fireplace with real logs." DuBois writes, "Matthew hated that log with perfect hatred" (142), and he shows the couple again in their library, noting that Matthew did not have the slightest interest in its well-bound books and describing Sara as she "closed the door and turned on the electric log" (155). Then in an important scene that brings together both the Freudian and Darwinian elements in DuBois's romance, he tells how Matthew remembered "shamefaced" his encounter with the Harlem dancer. Then, thinking of his loveless marriage, he "strove to evolve something in its place" and raises the subject of their having a baby, but Sara snaps "in uncomprehending astonishment," "Certainly not!" Still, DuBois takes this opportunity to distinguish his analysis of sex and race from those of the typical Freudians: though he has referred to her prudery, he insists that "Sara did not repress passion—she had no passion to repress" (153).

In this deft maneuver, DuBois lays claim to the blacks' purported "primitive" or subconscious vitality and suggests that the nearly white Sara is doomed to evolutionary sterility. Whereas Matthew had tried to "evolve" something in their marriage by suggesting that they have a baby, she evolved something else in her political efforts to advance Matthew's career by trying to win over "the high-placed white folk"; like one of her black guests at her fancy dinner party, she managed to attract "quite a select white clientele" (200). In his repeated use of the words "select" or "selection" in reference to Sara's career, then (for instance, 139 and 142), and in ways that exclude the passion of *sexual* selection, DuBois prepares for the point he makes most clearly through Matthew's remark: "Sara loves no one but herself. She can never love. To her this world-tangle of the races is a lustful scramble for place and power and show" (260). By contrast, when Kautilya comes to Chicago "to save [Matthew's] soul from hell" (209)—that is, from his ascent into the political hierarchy— the two withdraw under an onslaught of racial slurs about their "primitive passion" (218). Arriving then at his "attic nest," they "nestle" passionately, experiencing in "the ecstasy of [their] bodies" (220) a "resurrection of the spirit" and conceiving their baby in all animal innocence (260).

DuBois's final point about their sexual love is that the sexual instinct or libido itself does not govern the unconscious or determine the plot of this romance. In his view, rather, the unconscious is the deepest part of "the real and darker world . . . that was and is to be" (246). He reiterates this point (while also echoing the section in Locke's *The New Negro*, "The Negro Digs Up His Past") through Matthew's stint of work on the Chicago subway: "I am digging a Hole in the Earth . . . to make a path" (246) for the transport "of human souls" (264). Indeed, the driving vision of the book springs precisely from such unconscious depths when, in his first midnight meeting with the delegates from the darker world, Matthew is asked to defend his assertion that "the tint of a skin [does not] matter in the question of who leads" in world affairs. Making DuBois's long-held evolutionary point that "self-interest and the inclusion . . . of all really superior men of all colors" is the key, Matthew is forced to answer the question, what if this talent lies "buried among millions of men down in the great sodden masses of all men and even in Black Africa?" He answers, "It would come forth. . . . it would come forth." At this crucial moment, Matthew closes his eyes and hears "again the Great Song" he had heard in his youth, when his father led "the moaning singers in the Great Song of Emancipation." Suddenly, he "found himself singing . . . 'Go down, Moses!'" The song silences the skeptical delegates. Then, breaking the silence, Matthew repeats his point that "America is teaching the world one thing and only one thing of real value . . . that ability and capacity for culture is not the hereditary monopoly of a few . . . [but] for the majority of mankind if they only have a decent chance in life" (25–26). Now he "lapsed into blank silence, wondering how he had come to express the astonishing philosophy which had leapt unpremeditated from his lips" (27). When he recalls this moment with Kautilya much later in the book, Matthew denies that he said it: "It was said. I opened my mouth and it was filled." Thus the vision had come "to [Kautilya] like a great flash of new light" from "the son of slaves" (248). For DuBois, the souls of black folk find their essential voice in the spiritual or slave song. The darker world will survive by recognizing this unconscious force and not—as other Harlem novelists contended—the vulgar and libidinous blues (66).

Jessie Fauset's *Plum Bun:* A "Biology [that] Transcends Society!"

Jessie Redmon Fauset's important role in the Harlem Renaissance is unquestioned, especially her work as literary editor of the *Crisis* between 1919 and 1926. But critics like Huggins and Lewis have undervalued her fiction, emphasizing how Fauset used "the clichés of genteel realism to construct stories of the 'respectable' Negro middle class" (Huggins 146) or how, in treating the "passing" theme in *Plum Bun,* she parceled out the "lovers according to the shade of their skins," thus creating "the ultimate mulatto novel, belonging more to the school of Thomas Nelson Page than to that of Charles Waddell Chesnutt" (Lewis, *Vogue,* 235). Other critics more or less agree with these assessments but have also emphasized Fauset's interest in women's issues, "her keen awareness of the racism *and sexism*" that so often "lay beneath the surface in the cultural and literary politics of the 1920s and 1930s" (Davis, Introduction to

The Chinaberry Tree, xxx). Deborah McDowell, for example, explains how Fauset combined "passing and marriage as dual plots in a novel of female development" in order to explore her "prevailing theme: the unequal power relationships in American society" (xvi). Fauset's readers will be struck with the way her novels generally involve themselves not only with the complexities of color discrimination (within the black community and between black and white) but of sexual and class politics, as well, resulting in the confusion in her characters' lives that she underscored in the title of her first novel, *There Is Confusion.* Indeed Fauset sorted out these complex and perplexing issues by relying on certain principles of biological thought. Aligning herself with others from different points of view who addressed the social problems of that time, she developed her own argument for higher-class black women's power to distinguish themselves in the social struggle. Her general principle was that "biology transcends society!" (*The Chinaberry Tree* 121).[8] But as we shall see, she envisioned a particular form of evolutionary thought that transcended biology itself.

Plum Bun traces the life of Angela Murray from her childhood in Philadelphia in a family with a light-skinned mother who passes as white and a dark father and sister, through Angela's own passing in New York while studying to be a painter and pursuing an affair with a white man, to her successful development as an artist and her prospective marriage to another light-skinned artist who had also made his way up in the art world by passing as white. The novel's five-part structure ("Home," "Market," "Plum Bun," "Home Again," and "Market Is Done") develops the idea Fauset introduces in the nursery rhyme she uses as her epigraph: "To Market, to Market / To buy a Plum Bun; / Home again, Home again, / Market is done." In the concluding part, Angela enjoys artistic success, exhibits her racial integrity and moral stature (by acknowledging her own racial background while resisting the racial discrimination against a fellow artist), and succeeds in the quest for a suitable partner in marriage. In this way Fauset advances the idea in her title "Market Is Done": that life's most substantial rewards are not found in the marriage market of a capitalist and patriarchal culture. She identifies false, capitalistic values with Angela's wealthy white suitor, Roger Fielding. By contrast, Fauset's own values reside in the black home and community. And in projecting the kind of love that will hold black families together, she envisions a transcendental power of sexual selection—sexual selection with overtones of both Christian love and evolution through mutual aid. Even as she insinuates such values, however, Fauset arranges for only a certain class of blacks to attain greater heights in the social hierarchy, exhibiting the same theoretical self-contradictions as DuBois in elevating the talented tenth while also celebrating the socialist possibilities of the conclusive marriage (on May Day) in *Dark Princess.*

Introducing her heroine, Angela, Fauset immediately identifies the essential biological problem she will deal with in the novel. Angela had observed at a very early age that "the good things of life are unevenly distributed," that "certain fortuitous endowments, great physical beauty, unusual strength, a certain unswerving singleness of mind" are "bestowed quite blindly and disproportionately by the forces which control life" (12). From her mother, with whom she often passed for white at expensive shops and hotels, the mother responding to an "unquenchable instinct for life which thrived within her" (16), Angela learned that "the possibilities for joy and freedom" were perhaps "inherent in mere whiteness" (14). Now, having laid this groundwork, Fauset explores the psychology of passing, the material advantages as well as the psychic costs of concealing one's identity, in this way making her own contributions to modern psychology (along with those of other African Americans, especially Nella Larsen) by illuminating a field that Freud had not explored. Her approach, somewhat like Chesnutt's in *The House Behind the Cedars*, is first to free the passing individual from his or her possible feelings of guilt by suggesting that passing is an innocent, natural strategy for survival among those with the "fortuitous endowments" (or chance variation) of light skin color (12, 14). As Angela realizes toward the end of the novel, passing served her own selfish interests, but selfishness "'is one of the prerequisites for survival.' In 'passing' from one race to the other she had done no harm to anyone. Indeed she had been forced to take this action" (308).

Moreover, Fauset writes that Angela's dark father did not object to his own wife's passing, even when she cuts him in public. After one such incident, he tells her not to be ashamed for having pretended not to see him: "My dear girl," he consoles her. "I told you long ago that where no principle was involved, your passing means nothing to me" (19). Here the mother refers to her passing as "my old game of playacting," and Fauset reiterates this point throughout the novel by having the sisters act out a game of passing that they had played in their youth.[9] Ultimately, Fauset's guiding principle on this subject is her reiterated reference to the "mother's dictum" that "Life is more important than colour" (266). This is an earlier form of the principle Fauset's Dr. Denliegh would voice two years later in *The Chinaberry Tree* ("Biology transcends society!"), and Fauset gives it a certain sanctity early in *Plum Bun*. Already having remarked that the mother's "maternal instincts were sound," she creates a scene in which the mother is listening to the father's "virile, hearty voice" as he sings "The Dying Christian." In this setting the mother again counsels Angela about color and "the problem of living, just life itself you know" (55). The mother is utterly devoted to her husband and he to her. Despite their superficial differences in skin color, when they go to church or gather in their home to sing hymns the family is "as close and united as it is possible for a family to be" (25).

Before the novel can bring Angela "home again" (in part 4), she, like her eventual mate, will "become entangled with white people" and "conscious of living in an atmosphere of falseness, of tangled implications" (291, 271). The setting for these developments (in part 2, "Market," and part 3, "Plum Bun") is New York, where

Angela goes to study art, while passing. But in this novel the famous Harlem nightlife is even less visible than in DuBois's *Dark Princess*, where the hero briefly indulges in but then separates himself from that part of black life. In the first of the novel's three brief scenes in Harlem, Angela explores Harlem "on an exquisite afternoon," noting that "unquestionably there was something very fascinating, even terrible, about this stream of life—it seemed to her to run thicker, more turgidly than that safe, sublimated existence in which her new [white] friends had their being. . . . [T]his was fuller, richer . . . but . . . she was glad . . . that she had cast her lot with the dwellers outside its dark and serried tents" (96, 98). The second scene in Harlem is at night but not in a cabaret. Angela went there with her reluctant white lover to hear a talk by a man named Van Meier, an obvious stand in for DuBois. Again Angela "sensed that fullness, richness, even thickness of life," feeling that "The stream of living ran almost molten." She noticed especially a group of "the most advanced coloured Americans, beautifully dressed, beautifully trained" and, in contrast, "one section [where] loomed the dark, eager faces of West Indians," whose "features [were] so markedly different" from those of the other Americans that they had "a wild, slightly feral aspect" (216–17).[10]

In the third brief scene in Harlem, Angela accompanies her sister to a beauty shop in order to observe "these people whose blood she shared but whose disabilities by a lucky fluke she had been able to avoid." Angela is impressed with these people's power to endure, their "iron and blood," and she notices the "actresses" who "flitt[ed] in like radiant birds of paradise with their rich brown skins, their exotic eyes and the gaily coloured clothing which an unconscious style had evolved just for them" (326–28). According to the logic of Fauset's plot, however, the only suggestion of sexual vitality among these women is touched with the innocence of "paradise," as, in the second Harlem scene, the DuBois figure is described as "a god." While he speaks with a compelling beautiful voice (an essential feature in the theory of sexual selection), it is "cultured," and Fauset's point in the scene is that the speaker arouses the sexual interest of one of the white women. Recalling how she had tried unsuccessfully to "grasp" him (reversing the normal pattern of possession in sexual selection), the white woman wonders "what he would be like alone" (218–20). In this way, then, Fauset adheres emphatically to the advice she had offered in the symposium on "The Negro in Art" in the *Crisis*. In response to the question, "What are Negroes to do when they are continually painted at their worst and judged by the public as they are painted?" she wrote, "They must protest strongly and get their protestations before the public" (June 1926, 71–72). Thus, contradicting Van Vechten's or Sherwood Anderson's presentation of black promiscuity, throughout *Plum Bun* Fauset limits the libido strictly to the white psyche.

She insists that the black psyche is driven not so much by the reproductive instinct as by the general instinct to survive and be free, as when Angela's "subcon-

scious mind . . . codified: First, that the great rewards of life—riches, glamour, pleasure—are for white-skinned people only" (17). Moreover, it is only because Angela's
instinct for pleasure is associated with her whiteness that she becomes sexually involved with her white lover, Roger. Even in her childhood she had "missed the essential fact that her [darker] father and sister did not care for the type of pleasure"
that attracted her and her mother—that is, the pleasure of "riches, glamour" (18).
Of all the "black" women in the novel, only Angela participates in the processes of
sexual selection, and Fauset is clear in indicating that Angela's interest in the white
world and her erotic life with Roger are aspects of her selectiveness. Fauset shows
her one day as she is passing, with her mother, "slowly selecting another cake" (58),
and she notes that in New York Angela's "chosen thoroughfare" was on Fourteenth
Street near Union Square. Angela was "not sorry that she had chosen" Fourteenth
Street over Harlem (90), and Fauset brings Angela's selectiveness to its main point
when Angela first arrives in New York and considers how she might best acquire
the "power" that fascinates her (97). In this last scene (chapter 1 of "Market"), Angela realizes that if she were a man her opportunities for power would be greater.
But she simply wants a woman's power that she knows will come only with "money
and influence; indeed since she was so young," she reasons, "she would need even
protection; perhaps it would be better to marry . . . a white man" (88).

The idea of marrying a white man comes to her "out of the void," apparently as
part of her instinct for survival or the subconscious code about "the great rewards
of life" (17), and it leads to Fauset's feminist point (in Angela's calculations) "that
men had a better time of it than women, coloured men than coloured women, white
men than white women" (88). Fauset reiterates this point elsewhere in the novel, as
in a scene with Angela's white friend Paulette, who seems to make Fauset's feminist
point more forcefully (and with clearer lesbian overtones) than she would be comfortable with had it come from Angela: Paulette thinks that men are "nearly all animals. I'd rather have a good woman friend any day" (103). Still, Paulette's determination not to let "her feminity stand in the way of what she wants" serves to justify
Angela's efforts to pass into a position of greater power (105). Also, Fauset's feminist point is clear in her discussion of Roger's (Angela's white lover's) sexual appetite, when Paulette comments on his "impudence [in] expecting a woman to repress
or evoke her emotions just as he wants them! Hasn't a woman as much right to feel
as a man and to feel first?" (198). Ironically, this feminist point about the liberated
female libido comes from a white woman and not Angela, for, while Fauset identifies
Angela's effort to pass into the world of white power as part of the force of sexual
selection, she resists tainting it with the kind of promiscuous sexuality that throbs
only in the white veins of Roger or the woman who makes the pass at Van Meier.

Fauset underscores this point in her analysis of Angela, who "was naturally cold;
unlike Paulette, she was a woman who would experience the grand passion only

once, and perhaps twice in her life and she would always have to be kindled from without" (199). Indeed, this point is crucial to the meaning Fauset intended in the novel's subtitle, *A Novel without a Moral*, as she explains, "In the last analysis [Angela's] purity was a matter not of morals" but "of fastidiousness"—fastidiousness in the sense that, when "viewed in the light of the great battle she was waging for pleasure, protection and power," further sexual relations with Roger were simply "inexpedient" (199–200). Nevertheless, writing at the height of the Renaissance and the popular interest in Freudianism and primitive sexuality, it was important for Fauset to examine Angela's sexual nature more fully, acknowledging that she was a woman whose desire *could* be "kindled from without." Fauset's point, however, is mainly that Angela had never loved Roger. Once Angela had told him that she loves her *car*, and Fauset suggests that Angela's momentary passion with Roger helped her eventually to overcome her "fear of herself" (200). While she had been carried away "on a great, surging tide" of sexual emotions (especially in one scene on a "terrible" stormy night) to the point that she had been "appalled by her thoughts and longings" (203), she comes to realize that it had been "nothing but emotion" (200). As a result of her sexual experience, then, she avoids the kind of hysteria (the great bugaboo for any woman in the Freudian era) that Fauset exemplifies in the novel with her repeated references to one of Angela's childhood friends, Hetty Daniels. Demonstrating her familiarity with the typical Freudian theme, Fauset writes that Hetty's "great fetish was sex morality" and that this brought forth her symptomatic fits—when "her unslaked yearnings gleamed suddenly out of her eyes . . . wild and avid" (66). By contrast, as a result of her own experience with the sexual emotions, Angela demonstrates her psychological well-being by thinking that "now she herself was cognizant of phases of life for which Hetty longed but so condemned" (205).

Clearly, the pathway to power and evolutionary progress that Angela had considered in her decision to marry a white man will not do, in large part because her sexual experience with Roger made her recognize "his complete absorption of her, so completely, so exhaustively did his life seem to envelop hers" (203). Freeing herself from Roger, Angela casts about, thinking of her fellow art student and, at one time, potential lover, Anthony Cross. Anthony too is passing, but he and Angela had experienced an intimate moment earlier one spring day at Van Cortlandt Park. Fauset refers back to the scene repeatedly, for as the name of her well-chosen setting suggests, it represents ideal courtship. On this important day, "so new with the recurring newness of Spring," Anthony touched her hand and said, "I'm so content to be with you Angel. I may call you Angel, mayn't I? . . . I could get down on my knees and thank God for it" (140). The scene is replete with such religious possibilities, not the least of which is Anthony Cross's repeated reference to Angela (here and for the remainder of the novel) as Angel. Invariably, Fauset's critics call attention to the fact that when Angela passes, she goes by the name Angéle Mory, but the significance of the third name (Angel) given to her by Anthony escapes notice. It is an essential part of Fauset's design in presenting black sexual intimacy as absolutely different from the libidinousness of whites, a note that she first strikes in the novel in depicting Angela's mother "straining forward a little . . . to catch every note of her husband's virile, hearty voice" (55). At this moment he is singing "The Dying Christian" and one of the earlier hymns is "Am I a Soldier of the Cross" (21). When Anthony Cross and Angela meet again after the affair with Roger, Anthony expresses once more the chaste passion he had felt for her at Van Cortlandt Park, this time kissing her "slowly, with rapture, with adoration," and in the end—after prolonged problems resulting first from revealing his racial background and then from his previous but loveless engagement to Angela's sister Victoria—he and Angela are reunited on Christmas Day (281–82).

Still, this heavily Christianized relationship will not serve to advance Fauset's evolutionary plot, any more than DuBois's references to spirituals and the black soul alone could in *Dark Princess*. Rather, in developing the relationship between Anthony and Angela, Fauset projects a form of evolutionary progress (alternative to a more strictly Darwinian plot that might proceed through the traditional workings of natural and sexual selection) that preserves racial solidarity, denies the claim of black promiscuity, and solves the problem of patriarchal marriage: evolution according to the theory of mutual aid. Although there are no references in Fauset's work to Peter Kropotkin's *Mutual Aid*, there are multiple reasons to assume that she was aware of his famous theory of evolution. For example, her interest in developments in Russia is evident in *Plum Bun* in Paulette's repeated references to Russia and her trip there, in the character Jack Hudson's work as a correspondent in Moscow, and in a "conspicuously beautiful [Russian] poet" who attended a party where "such subjects as Russia, Consumers' Leagues" and so forth "figured most largely" (114). At this party the Russian poet can't "keep his eyes away from" a black woman named Miss Burden, who seems to think those gathered at this social event in Greenwich Village are completely out of touch with "the things that really matter, birth and death and hard, hard work!" Also, it seems likely that Fauset would have heard her colleague DuBois tell of meeting Kropotkin at the Universal Races Congress in London in 1911. But whether she got the idea of a marriage built on the principle of mutual aid from Kropotikin or from others who wrote on marriage during the early years of the century, in works that were very often highly optimistic about the new concept of marriage in Russia, there is no question that this marriage based on mutual dependency is cast in evolutionary terms.[11]

Angela gets the idea of such a marriage from her friend Rachel's dreams of a marriage in which both partners would "be absolutely dependent on each other," but Angela cannot imagine such a relationship, she with her own "work-room" in her life with Roger (214–15). Angela realizes that because of Roger's wealth and possessiveness, there would be no "mutual need" in their relationship (223), and she later tells Anthony, "I came to you because I needed you . . . and I thought you needed me" (284). When she realizes that Roger's life of leisure (he lives on his father's wealth) prevents him from being "a man, a real one . . . not afraid to go on his own," she sends him away with the words, "I want to work" (321–22). Also Fauset suggests that Roger's whiteness, his great wealth and sexual aggression, and Angela's initial attraction to the power he offers her are all part of the "Nordic . . . savage lust of power" (291). Thus, after hearing more from Rachel about lovers' "mutual fears and hopes," Angela finds that her thoughts are "constantly winging to Anthony" (247): "Together they would climb to happier, sunnier heights" (272). She would "struggle with him," and "she knew that the summit of her bliss would be reached in the days while she and Anthony were still poor and struggling" (272).

In this final solution to the problem presented by life—how to devise "a method of living" (252)—Fauset overcomes "the apparently unbridgeable difference between the sexes" (229) in a way that paralleled other theories of marriage during her time: by subjugating the male's sexual aggression to the principles that sexual relations must be "mutually pleasurable" (including the problem of birth control) and that civilization requires "divorce by mutual consent" (Ellis, *Studies,* 2:3:550, 462). But she also reverses the popular theory of black promiscuity, suggesting that only the white male (with the Nordic lust for power) is given to the libidinous "excitement of the chase" (191–92). Angela eventually comes to see black people as "powerfully, almost overwhelmingly endowed with the essence of life . . . [who would] survive because they did not know how to die" (309). Nor does Fauset blame light-skinned blacks for passing in order to survive, for this is only one of the tangled implications of color, one of the "traps" set for them by "Life" and the "accident of heredity." On one occasion, when Angela and Anthony are together, they discuss Angela's allegorical drawing, "Life" in these terms, but it is only a work in progress, and she does not know whether she will develop it (280). In the end, however, Angela and Anthony return to their roots, and Angela has sent Roger away so that she can work. Then Fauset arranges for another character to express his admiration for Angela's completed masterpiece—the drawing of "Life"—and to wonder "how [she] came to evolve it" (323–24).

Nella Larsen's *Quicksand:* Darwin, James, Freud, and the Psychology of Mixed Race

Although she published only two short novels, *Quicksand* (1928) and *Passing* (1929), Nella Larsen is justly considered one of the most brilliant writers of the Harlem Renaissance. Lewis, for example, believes that *Quicksand* is certainly "one of the three best novels of the Renaissance" (*Vogue* 231). She is among the most probing psychological novelists of her time and unsurpassed in her particular field—studying the woman of mixed race in the Freudian era. *Quicksand* is an intense and prolonged analysis (assumed to be largely autobiographical) of Helga Crane, a "black" woman with no close family ties who is neither black nor white but who is pulled in both directions at times and yet sometimes fears or hates both these "selves." Her fragmented sense of identity along racial lines profoundly exacerbates the disorientation already felt by the "normal" human subject who, according to William James's new "zoological psychology," must live with many contending selves.[12] Moreover, Helga is unavoidably drawn into the evolutionary struggle of sexual selection, and her supposed "primitive" nature draws her into a more disastrous encounter with the subconscious than she might have felt if she were only black or white.

That Larsen explores the field of mixed racial identity in the light of Darwinian, Jamesian, and Freudian theory will be evident only to readers who are attuned to these currents of thought and who are prepared to acknowledge that the psychological novel of the 1920s was often deeper and broader than the stream of consciousness. Larsen's biographer reveals she was prepared to navigate these waters, even though she never pursued a university degree. She was "by all accounts . . . extremely well read," so much so that one of the leading intellectuals involved in the Harlem Renaissance remarked on Larsen's "most extraordinarily wide acquaintance with past and current literature" (Davis, *Nella Larsen*, 163).[13] One revealing example of her interest in modern literature is her reference to the Danish scientist and novelist Jens Peter Jacobsen when she wrote to defend Walter White's novel *Flight* (1926).[14] If it was partly because of her own ties to Denmark that she had developed an interest in Jacobsen, it was also no doubt due to his reputation as "perhaps the most creative Darwinist in the Europe of his day" (Raphael xii). Jacobsen translated both the *Origin of Species* and *The Descent of Man*, and his novels were widely viewed as representations of "Darwinist biological ideas" (Jensen 149). Larsen was herself married to a distinguished scientist, the physicist Elmer Imes, and she had a close relationship with the brilliant doctor-scientist-novelist Rudolph Fisher. Moreover, her interest in other psychological novelists of her time, like Van Vechten, Gertrude Stein, and James Joyce, indicates that she was highly sensitive to the literary appropriation of the scientific thought of that era.[15] Regarding T. S. Stribling's novel *Birthright*, for example, Larsen's biographer writes that Larsen was "more affected than [fellow authors of the Harlem Renaissance, like Fauset or Walter White] by Stribling's statement, 'No people can become civilized until the woman has the power of choice among males. . . . The History of the white race shows the gradual increase of the woman's power of choice'" (Davis, *Nella Larsen*, 153).

Of course this Darwinian principle of the female's power to select had long been a staple in American fiction, and Larsen was acutely aware of the related psychological issues involving race and sex that Gertrude Stein had drawn on in the case studies she had presented in *Three Lives*, especially in "Melanctha." In the letter Larsen sent to Stein with the copy of *Quicksand*, Larsen wrote that she had read "Melanctha" "many times"; she thought it a "truly great story" and wondered how Stein could "so accurately have caught the spirit of this race of mine" (Gallup, *Flowers of Friendship*, 216). Through their mutual friend, Carl Van Vechten, she probably learned of Stein's having studied with William James, as she must have known of DuBois's Jamesian education. But whether or not she knew of these connections, she produced a psychological novel superior to those of DuBois, Van Vechten, or Stein in developing the Jamesian principle: "Selection is the very keel on which the mental ship is built" (*Principles of Psychology* 640).[16] James made this point in a discussion of "Forgetting" that prefigures Freud's more famous analysis of that phenomenon, but his reference to "selection" is a reminder to readers early in the twenty-first century that modern psychology in both James and Freud was founded on Darwinian theory. In the case of Helga Crane these materials come together in a life that does not exactly sink because of a faulty "keel" (though this accurately describes Henry James's study of Isabel Archer in *Portrait of a Lady*).[17] Rather, to use Larsen's metaphor, Helga sinks into psychological quicksands because she can never achieve the mental "security [and] Balance" that she repeatedly perceives in her purely white Danish relatives, and largely because of her disastrous experience in the struggle of sexual selection (79, 86).

The plot of *Quicksand* is fairly simple, but a summary at some length here will show how its main Darwinian, Jamesian, and Freudian threads are interwoven with Larsen's psychological insights as an African American woman—particularly her sense of how Helga feels racial "ties that were of the spirit" but that were "entangled with [more than the] mere outline of features or color of skin." They were "Deeper. Much deeper than either of these" (95). The novel opens when Helga Crane is so exasperated in her work as a teacher at Naxos (Larsen's fictional Tuskegee Institute, suggesting its Anglo-Saxon inclination) that she is preparing to resign. She cannot bear its machinelike approach to education; "life had died out of it" (4), as is evident in the way her fellow teacher had turned her "nice live crinkly hair" into "a dead straight, greasy, ugly mass" (14). Leaving Naxos will mean breaking up her engagement to James Vayle, who "fitted into his niche" there in quite a "naturalized" way, but she in undeterred (7). In her departing interview with the principal Robert Anderson, however, she experiences "something very like hysteria," finding herself moved by his "deep voice of peculiarly pleasing resonance" and "feeling a mystifying yearning which sang and throbbed in her" to do "service, not now for her people, but for this man" (19–20). Thus, in the opening chapters, Larsen identifies the essential analytical problems she will examine in Helga's life: first the feeling she has as "a despised mulatto . . . [of] something intuitive, some unanalyzed driving spirit of loyalty to the inherent racial need for gorgeousness," second, her puzzlement about "just what had happened to her" that was "so powerful, so compelling" in her interview with Anderson (questions that are answered largely by the theory of sexual selection, as in Helga's response to Anderson's voice), and third, the question (to be answered in terms of Freudian analysis) of why she had burst "into a rage so fierce, so illogical, so disastrous" that she now found herself "despondent, sunk in shameful contrition" (18, 22). Struggling with these related issues throughout the novel, then, Helga exhibits again and again the chief symptoms in Larsen's analysis: her constant flight from intimate situations with first one and then another of her racial communities, as she tries to find her own true niche, and her desperate blindness to the nature of her own sexual desire, as when "she didn't, *she told herself,* after all, like this Dr. Anderson" (22, emphasis mine). The question, as William James might have put it but with no thought of Larsen's excruciating circumstances of mixed race, is: which of Helga's various selves is she?

Leaving Naxos she tells Anderson, "I don't belong here" and embarks on the quest that Larsen specifies in her epigraph from Langston Hughes: "My old man died in a fine big house. / My ma died in a shack. / I wonder where I'm gonna die, / Being neither white nor black?" (21). Whereas Hughes's poem focuses on the "tragic mulatto," Helga's greater tragedy is that, with her fragmented sense of identity, she will never have anything like a stable self and will therefore never find security in either a house or a shack. Moreover, as Larsen analyzes Helga in this Jamesian manner, in reference to the problem of "personal identity"[18] (a problem that was irrelevant in Freudian analysis) and also in reference to the explicitly Freudian problem of sexual repression, she presents Helga's quintessential homelessness: she can rest secure in neither the white nor black community, nor in the black soul, nor in the divided psyche of the Freudian era.

Going first to Chicago, Helga is pushed away from her single surviving American relative, her Danish uncle Peter, because his wife is offended by Helga's blackness. She soon finds work as a prominent "race" woman's secretary, and this leads her to New York. Within a year there she feels that she has come home, for "Harlem, teeming black Harlem had . . . lulled her" into what she thinks is "peace and contentment" (43). Larsen's psychological point is that Helga "did not analyze this contentment"; thus, with the coming spring, she finds that "within her, in a deep recess, crouched discontent." She is "shocked to discover that, for some unknown reason," she is afraid of herself. Soon she begins to withdraw from Harlem, recoiling "in aversion from the sight of the grinning faces" on the hot swarming streets (46–48). Then, in an accidental encounter with Anderson, now a resident of New York, she feels "a sudden thrill," "a peculiar, not wholly disagreeable quiver ran down her spine"; she feels faint and "the blood rushed to her face" (49). Further in this scene—at a Harlem "health meeting"—she feels "a strange ill-defined emotion, a vague yearning" but also the same kind of quick "anger and defiant desire to hurt," "to wound," that had flared up in her in her first meeting with Anderson (50–51).

Now tiring of the way meetings like this always developed into discussions of the race problem, discrimination, and uplift, Helga once again fled (52). As "her frayed nerves grew keener," she finds Harlem increasingly a "hateful place where one lived in intimacy with people one would not have chosen had one been given a choice" (53). Now insinuating the question of the female's power to select, Larsen gives Helga both an opportunity to flee Harlem (as a result of a five thousand dollar gift from her Danish uncle, to ease his conscience while ending their relationship) and, at the same time, yet another encounter with Anderson. This time Helga and Anderson meet in the "vast subterranean room" of a Harlem cabaret. And here Larsen creates the kind of scene that was so objectionable to DuBois and Fauset. The people danced, "violently twisting their bodies" to the "thumping of unseen tomtoms" and "wild" music. Feeling that "the essence of life seemed bodily motion," Helga, too, is carried away, but when the music stops she withdraws in shame; she realizes that she had enjoyed it all, yet with "a conscious effort" "she [tells] herself" that she isn't "a jungle creature." Still, when she sees Anderson dancing with a beautiful woman who "swayed with an eager pulsing motion" to the "wild music from the heart of the jungle," Helga feels "a more primitive emotion" within herself (58–62). Once again she flies from the cabaret, next to be seen on the ocean liner that will carry her to Denmark and into the arms of her white relatives and a white suitor.

On the way to Denmark, relieved to be free of the people for whom she now felt "a great aversion," Helga exults in "belonging to herself alone and not to a race" (63–64).[19] But in one of her many characteristic moments, she recalls how she had fled from her original encounter with Anderson and how she had taken flight again from the cabaret. This gives rise to "a dim disturbing notion" that is so humiliating that she quickly dismisses it: she can't be "in love with the man," because "when one is in love, one strives to please," and she had repeatedly felt the urge to wound him (64). However, not realizing, as her analyst (Larsen) certainly does, "that cruelty and the sexual instinct are most intimately connected" (Freud, *Basic Writings*, 570), she cannot escape a "shadowy, incoherent" sense that "in a remote corner of her consciousness lurked" the image of Anderson and the sound of his "musical voice" (*Quicksand* 64). And as soon as the liner enters Danish waters she begins to pace nervously back and forth in her "rushing emotions," "nauseated," and "prey to sinister fears and memories" of being rejected by her white relatives in Chicago. Immediately, though, she begins to celebrate this new life in Copenhagen, feeling that "this was her proper setting" (64–67).

Again, as always in her life, her fleeting sense of security passes all too quickly when her relatives begin to capitalize on her exotic beauty, attempting to elevate their own social standing by marrying her to a prominent artist. Dressing her in bright colors and gaudy jewelry, they make her feel like "some new and strange species." Yet, while she feels "greatly exposed," she also enjoys "the compliments in the men's eyes" as they respond to her "exotic, almost savage" attraction (70). She soon realizes that "her exact status in her new environment" is that of "a peacock," and Larsen underscores her Darwinian point by noting how Helga is overwhelmed with new clothes that had been selected by her artist suitor: garments "which mingled indigo, orange, green, vermillion . . . blood-red, sulphur-yellow, sea-green," some with ornamental "great scarlet and lemon flowers," including "a leopard-skin coat." If Larsen was aware of F. Scott Fitzgerald's similar scene between Daisy and Gatsby, she turns it in a different direction by writing that, as distinct from Daisy's tearful response to the beautiful shirts, Helga feels "incited . . . incited . . . incited . . . incited" by all these "silks, feathers and furs" and by the "nauseous Eastern perfume" (74–75). Psychologically much more complex than Daisy, Helga nevertheless finds that this slightly nauseating beauty suited her, and she thinks that the trouble with American "Negroes" is that they denied their love of beauty in order "to be like their white overlords." When she recalls how stupid she had once been in thinking that she "could marry and perhaps have children" who would be only "more dark bodies for mobs to lynch," she puts that humiliating thought from her mind, for she now believes that "her mental difficulties and questionings had become simplified" (74–75).

Within a year, however, Helga yields to the "subconscious knowledge" that something is wrong. "What was the matter with her?" she wonders, "was there, without her knowing it, some peculiar lack in her?" (81). Soon her growing discomfort comes to a head when she is forced to confront "something in her which she had hidden away": at a circus she attended with her suitor, she sees a vaudeville act featuring two prancing "American Negroes . . . cavorting on the stage." She is "filled with a fierce hatred for the cavorting Negroes" but cannot help returning alone "again and again" to see them (82–83). And this leads immediately to the disintegration of her affair with the artist, whose proposal she now rejects after sensing that her origin has aroused "some impulse of racial antagonism" in him (84). Also, she had felt that he had made an inappropriate sexual advance, and even though he still takes her to select new garments, she selects against *him* for the best of Darwinian reasons—his lack of beauty—but with an African American twist. Helga becomes aware of her "curious feeling of repugnance" for him, rather like the white evolutionist Joseph Le Conte had construed as nature's warning against miscegenation, "*race-aversion*" ("The Effect of Mixture or Races" 101).

Larsen writes that Helga "was too amazed to discover suddenly how intensely she disliked" everything about him—the shape of his head, his hair, his voice, and even the line of his nose, which was broader than her own. Thus she delivers the ultimate evolutionary blow according to the theory of sexual selection, telling him, "I don't want you"; but Larsen also identifies Helga's repugnance for this man as part of the American experience. "I'm not for sale . . . to any white man," Helga tells him and will not "be owned. Even by you" (86–87). Then, moved also by hearing a performance of Dvořák's *New World Symphony* with its "wailing undertones" of the familiar spiritual, Helga realizes that "in the back of her troubled mind" there had always been a sense of "the irresistible ties of race," and she embraces this renewed "knowledge of almost sacred importance" (92–93). Thus, because Helga can never "be satisfied in one place," she embarks almost at once for the United States. Yet when the ship's "bells rang," "the gangplank was hoisted," and "the dark strip of water widened," "tears rose in Helga Crane's eyes, fear in her heart" (93).[20]

Of course her arrival in America will bring Helga into even more disastrous contact with the "ties . . . of the spirit," ties that entangled her much more deeply with the "dark hordes" than the merely visible features of race (95). In the first place, Helga's purpose in returning had been to attend the wedding of her best friend Anne to Robert Anderson. Much more insightful about her own sexual nature than is Helga, Anne realizes that beneath "the decorous surface of her new husband's mind" was a "lawless place where she herself never hoped or desired to enter" and where there was "a vagrant primitive groping toward something shocking" (94–95). Realizing also that Anderson could not so easily restrain this impulse in the presence of Helga, who had now grown more aware of her power as a result of her experience in Denmark, Anne is on guard. She knows that, in response to her own cool nature, Anderson could rather easily restrain the impulse which even he as one of the genteel talented tenth found "shameful" (95).

Inevitably, at a social gathering of genteel blacks and "Negrotarians" (as Zora Neale Hurston dubbed white supporters of the New Negro movement), Helga meets first her old suitor James Vayle, who reiterates his intention to marry her some day. To her remarks that it is sinful to bring black children into the world, more "creatures doomed to endure" the racial suffering, he replies that that is exactly the problem: "The race is sterile at the top," and if it is to get anywhere people like themselves must have the children (103). Quickly, she cuts Vayle short and escapes that encounter. But then, "it" happened: when she and Anderson bumped into each other in a hallway "he stooped and kissed her, a long kiss, holding her close. She fought against him with all her might. Then, strangely, all power seemed to ebb away, and a long hidden, half-understood desire welled up in her with the suddenness of a dream" (104). After describing how Helga was "consciously confused" and seized with "sudden anger," Larsen ends the scene by writing that Helga "went slowly down to the others." That is, she had at last entered the human (clearly the Freudian) world of "colorful dreams" and "emotional upheaval" that she had repressed from her first moment of "hysteria" in meeting Anderson. And she will never succeed in freeing herself from "the mental quagmire [or quicksand] into which that kiss had thrown her" (105–6).

Now the novel plummets to an abrupt and shocking conclusion that many readers have found problematic. Rather, it is an inventively bitter and ironic ending to the meditation on race and sex that Larsen presents in her psychoanalysis of Helga Crane. When Anderson and Helga meet again, "desire . . . burned in her flesh with uncontrollable violence," but she is devastated to learn that he, no less repressed than she, wants only to apologize. She "savagely slapped" him, and when we see her the next day, "her staggered brain [is] still wavering." Then failing to understand how she could have made such a fool of herself, she "jumped up and began hastily to dress herself." And here again Larsen underscores her psychological point by noting that Helga "couldn't go on with the analysis" (107–10).

Realizing that "her self-knowledge had increased her anguish," and "trying desperately to take some interest in the selection of her apparel," Helga goes out alone into the stormy night and soon falls helpless "into the swollen gutter" (110). But hearing a distant song that she had "heard years ago—hundreds of years it seemed" (111), she stumbles into a black church where Larsen creates a scene of primitive religion, like those she might have known in W. D. Howells's race novel *An Imperative Duty*, Harold Frederic's *The Damnation of Theron Ware*, or, more recently, Sinclair Lewis's *Elmer Gantry*, in which sex and religion are united in "almost Bacchic vehemence" (113). The "weird orgy" leaves her, "like one insane" or "unconscious," sunk further into Larsen's quicksand, "back [in] the mysterious grandeur and holiness of far-off simpler centuries" (113–14). Now she meets the repulsive, "rattish yellow" "Reverend Mr. Pleasant Green" and falls immediately into a sexual relationship with him.[21] She is attracted by his mind, which seemed secure in its concern with the soul but was actually at home in the material world and consumed with sexual longing for her. Suddenly fearing that she had "missed the supreme secret of life," Helga "deliberately stopped thinking," returned his advances, and provoked a "wild look" in his "bloodshot eyes" (115–16). Thus, "in the confusion of seductive repentance," she quickly marries Green and returns with him to the "tiny Alabama town where he was pastor to a scattered and primitive flock" (118). There Helga feels so much at home that at night, "emotional, palpitating, amorous, all that was living in her sprang like rank weeds . . . with a vitality so strong that it devoured all shoots of reason" (122).

But the inevitable reversal comes soon enough, after the birth of her twin sons, when we see her sick with "disgust at the disorder around her" in her "forlorn garden" (124). Green often tells her that his lovemaking is "a natural thing, an act of God," and others in the flock remind her that "et's natu'al fo' a 'oman to hab chilluns." But in writing of how the fourth baby appeared, a "little dab of amber humanity which Helga had contributed to a despised race," Larsen expresses an even more bitter sense of the meaninglessness of life and the female's reproductive role in evolution than Kate Chopin had in *The Awakening* (125, 127). (There, assisting a friend in childbirth, Edna Pontellier had felt "a flaming, outspoken revolt against the ways of Nature," recalling how she had herself awakened from the chloroform "to find a little new life to which she had given being, added to the great unnumbered multitude of souls that come and go" [chap. 37].) But in *Quicksand*, Helga scoffs at her former "belief in the miracle and wonder of life. Only scorn, resentment, and hate remained—and ridicule. Life wasn't a miracle, a wonder. It was, for Negroes at least, only a great disappointment" (130). Still, Larsen's anger is aimed not only at "the white man's God" (130) but at the disgusting Pleasant Green, for whom Helga's sexual "aversion" is so great that "between them the vastness of the universe had come" (129). And Larsen's anger seems aimed at men like DuBois as well, whose enthusiasm for the spiritual or slave song and the souls of black folk is implicated in Helga's descent into the bog of primitive religion and sexuality. Only insightful analysis, she suggests again and again—analysis that draws on Darwin, William James, Freud, *and* African American experience—could help Helga retain her sense of balance. As William James had remarked, "selection is the very keel on which our mental ship is built." Even now, when Helga "had to concede" that it was "all of her own doing, this marriage," she cannot endure the pressure of introspection. Instead, she dreams, in a clearly ironic reference to DuBois's soul songs or spirituals, that she would "escape from [this] oppression [and] degradation"—"by and by," "by and by." Thus she let "time run on. Away." The novel closes when Helga prepares to have her fifth child and is now mired permanently in the quicksand of her primitive life.

Claude McKay's *Home to Harlem:* The "It's a Be-Be Itching Life" Blues

The meaning of life and the black person's share in it is an underlying question in all the Harlem novels here examined, but Claude McKay was more determined than the other novelists to embrace the crucial sexual element in the evolution of race and to celebrate the primitive sexuality that was so offensive to what he called "the intellectual gang" in Harlem (*A Long Way from Home* 114). DuBois found *Home to Harlem* so nauseating that he wanted to bathe after reading it (qtd. in Giles 69); Charles S. Johnson complained that McKay "out-niggered Mr. Van Vechten" in the novel (qtd. in Watson 82), and, more recently, Nathan Huggins has written that the novel became a best seller (the first by an African American writer) "precisely because it pandered to commercial tastes by conforming to the sensationalism demanded by the white vogue in black primitivism" (126).[22] But such remarks obscure McKay's own intellectual acuity.

McKay's view of life began to take shape at a rather early age when, as a young man exploring his older brother's library in Jamaica, he discovered "suddenly like a comet . . . the romance of science in Huxley's *Man's Place in Nature* and Haeckel's *The Riddle of the Universe*" (*A Long Way from Home* 12). Growing up in Jamaica, he had "played at sex . . . in a healthy harmless way" and at the age of "seventeen or eighteen . . . became aware of the ripe urge of potency and also the strange manifestations and complications of sex"; at the same time, reading "a variety of books in [his] brother's library," he "became intellectually cognizant of sex problems" (245). With this kind of orientation, then, he began to develop what he later called the "clearly consistent emotional-realist thread" that runs throughout his career (250). Of course he realized that he had puzzled many of his sophisticated white readers who "couldn't understand the instinctive and animal and purely physical pride of a black person resolute in being himself and yet living a simple civilized life like themselves" (245). As he wrote of his character Ray in *Banjo* (1929), "a black man, even though educated, was in closer biological kinship to the swell of primitive earth life" (323).[23] And while readers today will certainly question the validity of his scientific views on black primitiveness, it is important to note that he was passionately committed to the idea that there is no conflict between literature and science. Arguing this point at length (in 1932) in a letter to his friend Max Eastman, whose *The Literary Mind: Its Place in an Age of Science* had made the case against science and for "literary truth," McKay insisted that "a real artist cannot but feel that his work is facilitated by the discoveries of science, even though Science should lay its operating hand upon his body and soul and lay bare the why and wherefore of his creative energy" (Cooper, *Passion of Claude McKay*, 152).

Home to Harlem traces the life of Jake, a "tall, brawny, and black" man, from the time he returns to Harlem after a disappointing period overseas (3). He had enlisted in World War I but deserted when he and his fellow black soldiers were not allowed into combat, and he then lived for a time in England. The novel opens with him aboard the freighter on which he is working his way back to the States, and McKay introduces a note of racial-sexual conflict that resounds throughout the chapter. The freighter has a "dirty Arab crew," and there is a hierarchy of race and class aboard; Jake regrets having gone to fight "in a white folks' war" in the first place; and he had become fed up with life in the East End of London, where so many other blacks had moved after the Armistice that "the price of sex went up" and racial and sexual conflict grew between black and white men: "Jake saw a big battle staged between the colored and white men of London's East End" (7). This situation recalls an earlier incident in McKay's life, when he wrote a letter to the editor of Britain's *Daily Herald* in 1920. Complaining about the article it had published by E. D. Morel, "Black Scourge in Europe: Sexual Horror Let Loose by France on Rhine," McKay asked "Why all this obscene, maniacal outburst about the sex vitality of Black men?"[24] Writing in 1928, McKay plots his hero's life as he moves beyond this background of racial and sexual strife. Jake had sickened of the race conflict in London and had begun to think of his English woman as "only a creature of another race." Thus, longing for the "chocolate-brown and walnut-brown girls [who] were calling him" with their "brown flesh draped in soft colorful clothes," their "brown lips [that] pouted for sweet kissing," and "brown breasts throbbing with love," he goes back home to Harlem (8).

In Harlem he immediately finds and sleeps with a beautiful woman named Felice, but he is just as quickly separated from her by accident. After further adventures in Harlem (largely sexual), Jake leaves Harlem for a short stint of work as a porter on the railroad. There he meets the bookish character Ray, who articulates many of the book's ideas. (Also in this section McKay advances the proletarian values that had already taken him on his famous pilgrimage to Russia, where he addressed The Third Communist International.) Jake then returns to Harlem, in the meantime freeing himself from a number of threatening encounters with a possible life as a "sweet man" and from encounters with alcohol and drugs. Now Jake meets up again with Felice, and McKay signals that he has solved the evolutionary problem of his plot: Jake's "mind was a circle containing the girl and himself only, making a thousand plans of the joys they would create together" (311). Having brought his promising couple together, then, McKay ends the novel by seeing them safely out of Harlem. If he does not exactly agree with his character who proclaims that Harlem is a "nigger hell" rather than "nigger heaven" (98–99), he does suggest that life in Harlem had become "too close and thick" for his ideal couple to thrive there (287).

In McKay's assessment, the underlying problem of life reverts to the kinds of questions he had confronted in his early reading of Huxley and Haeckel, involving *Man's Place in Nature* and the problem of heredity as an essential part of *The Riddle of the Universe*. Such questions are articulated in the novel by Ray, whose education and experience with racial and political turmoil in Haiti had "landed him into the quivering heart of a naked world whose reality was hitherto unimaginable" (224), who feels caught up "into a big whirl where all of life seemed hopelessly tangled and colored without point or purpose" (244), and whose last words in the novel are, "Why are we living?" (274). He found that his former spiritual masters—first Hugo, Zola, Stowe, and Dickens, and then Shaw, Ibsen, Anatole France, and Wells— "had not crossed with him into the new" (225–26). They had simply died, marching with "all their wonderful, trenchant, critical, satirical, mind-sharpening, pity-evoking, constructive ideas of ultimate social righteousness, into the vast international cemetery of this century" (226–27).

Ray had been moved by the modern writers James Joyce, Sherwood Anderson, D. H. Lawrence, and Henri Barbusse to question the very nature of art and literature if it "did not wrestle and sprawl with appetite and dark desire all over the pages." But he concludes that the only standing "giants in the new" are the great Russians of the late era, Gogol, Dostoievski, Tolstoy, Chekhov, and Turgeniev, who had survived "the grand carnage" because "the soil of life saved their roots from the fire. They were so saturated, so deep-down rooted in it." And this meditation leads him to McKay's question: "Could he create out of the fertile reality around him?" (228). Unfortunately, for a number of reasons—mainly his "impotence" and his inability to love either his deserving friend Agatha or black people in general—Ray cannot provide the creative energy to carry McKay's plot into the future.

McKay's problem, then, is to define the attributes that enable Jake to survive in the sprawling world of "appetite and dark desire," and the most important of these is that, like the great Russian writers, he is rooted in "the soil of life." That is, in the context of the Harlem debate over "The Negro in Art," McKay is determined first unabashedly to affirm his hero's primitive vitality but at the same time to view it in the larger context of life in general. This is the essential element in his alignment with the writers "in the new" with whom he identified (Joyce, Anderson, Lawrence, and Hemingway), the element he developed as the "consistent emotional-realist thread" throughout his career and that F. Scott Fitzgerald admired in *Home to Harlem*.[25] Thus, while Jake meets his eventual mate in the first brief scene in a Harlem cabaret, in his second, more extended scene of the cabaret life, McKay shows that the problem of sexual violence is the same the world over. Referring to fights they have witnessed between two women of different color (a "shiny coffee-colored" woman and a "putty-skinned mulattress") and their contending partners ("a potato-yellow man and a dull-black"), Jake tells his friend Zeddy: "The same in France, the same in England, the same in Harlem. White against white and black against white and yellow against black and brown. We's all just crazy-dog mad. Ain't no peace on earth with the womens and there ain't no life nowhere without em." Zeddy replies, "You said it, boh. It's a be-be itching life . . . and we're all sons of it" (33–35). Indeed, even these old buddies will confront each other in sexual conflict in the novel's last cabaret scene, in the chapter "Spring in Harlem," where McKay describes the dancers "shivering amorously, itching for their partners to come" (296).

McKay makes this point again and again in the novel, once, for example, with an eye toward the other Harlem novelists like DuBois or Fauset: "Honey, I lived in Washington and I knowed inside and naked out the stuck-up bush-whackers of the race," says a character named Miss Curdy. "They all talks and act as if loving was a sin, but I tell you straight, I wouldn't trust any of them after dark with a preacher." Agreeing with this view of reality, her friend Susy adds, "Nobody kaint hand *me* no fairy tales about niggers. Wese all much of a muchness when you git down to the real stuff" (164). And at the end of the novel, with an eye toward the "refined souls" of both races, McKay underscores his theme about "Simple, raw emotions and real":

that they might well "frighten and repel refined souls, because they are too intensely real, just as a simple savage stands dismayed before nice emotions that he instantly perceives are false" (338).

Now, having laid the foundation of Jake's plot by rooting it in the universal reality of raw life, McKay devotes his energy to showing, first, how his black hero must negotiate the same problems of sexual selection that had troubled the white heroes in many other novels, those for example by Jack London, Sherwood Anderson, or Ernest Hemingway (mainly the Darwinian problems of female choice and male sexual violence, and the Freudian problems of sexual repression and sexual perversion); and second, how a black hero's particular problems include both his inevitable immersion in racial-sexual conflict within a black community and, at the same time, his commitment to what McKay thought of as "group survival."

When Jake arrives in Harlem, "his blood . . . hot" and sniffing "the street like a hound" (10), he immediately takes his place "among the lowly of Harlem's Black Belt," (20), and McKay insists that "you would [too] if you were a black kid hunting for joy in New York" (30). The instant he enters a cabaret, "a little brown girl [Felice, his eventual mate] aimed the arrow of her eye at him as he entered," for "there was something in his attitude, in his hungry wolf's eyes, that went warmly to her" (11). Jake has been selected, but for vague reasons (the "something") that McKay wants also to define as love at first sight. McKay writes that "her shaft hit home," and when Jake goes to another woman, Rose, after being separated from Felice, he finds that "she had no spirit at all—that strange elusive something that he felt in himself" and that he had sensed in Felice, with whom "he had felt a reaching out and marriage of spirits" (41–42). Although McKay will certainly idealize this relationship (when the two are finally alone together in the "circle" of Jake's mind), he underscores his point that it arises according to the evolutionary force of sexual selection. Jake has the essential quality of the successful male: "there was something so naturally beautiful about his presence that everybody liked and desired him" (103); another woman responds to his magnetic touch, and another, "a traveled woman of the world," responds to him by exclaiming to a friend, "*Quel beau garçon! J'aimerais beaucoup faire l'amour avec lui*" (324–25). Moreover, in his effort to strengthen Jake's hand as an evolutionary player, McKay notes that he is not just like a "thoroughbred" (237) but a new variation, "one of those unique types of humanity" about whom "you would hardly wonder who were his father and mother and what they were like" (234).

Summing up his analysis of how Jake is selected by Felice, McKay writes that Felice "had met the male that she preferred and gone with him. . . . It was a very simple and natural thing. . . . However, she was aware that in her world women scratched and bit into each other's flesh and men razored and gunned at each other over such things" (306). That is, McKay reminds us throughout the novel, sexual selection includes not only the Darwinian problem of male combativeness in "the law of battle" for the possession of the female, but, less violently, female combativeness for the male. In one of his several efforts to rewrite Van Vechten's way of ending the sexual drama (when Byron fires impotently into the already dead body of his sexual competitor in *Nigger Heaven*), McKay has Jake prevail over his competitor (Zeddy) by pulling but choosing not to fire his revolver.

However, making his point about female combativeness, a theme that had developed in early twentieth-century literature beyond Darwin's emphasis on the male law of battle (as in Fitzgerald's "Diamond Dick and the First Law of Woman" and "The Dance"), McKay refers rather specifically to the then famous theory of George Bernard Shaw about women as husband-hunters. Jake has seen enough of men and women to know that, while men are certainly "ugly and brutal," a "woman could always go farther than a man in coarseness, depravity, and sheer cupidity. . . . *They were the real controlling force of life*" (69–70). Among the novel's many references to combative women, the most memorable is a long scene of two women engaged in a ferocious battle of sexual jealousy, "stark naked" because "it turn you' hands and laigs loose for action" (308–10). McKay comments that this scene is "perhaps a survival of African tribalism" (308) and that "a hen fight was more fun than a cock-fight" because "the hens pluck feathers, but they never wring necks like the cocks" (310). In *Home to Harlem* Felice is aware of this reality and is willing to defend her claim on Jake, but it is an indication of her evolutionary excellence—in McKay's terms, her "mystery" or "spirit" (70, 41)—that she never reverts to battle. Still, as a Darwinian female with the power to select and also the Shavian power to be "the real controlling force of life," she has the authority to tell Jake at the end of the novel, "You know I had the keys"—that is, the keys not only to her apartment, but, presumably, the evolutionary problem as McKay construes it (340).

Also, however, as a literary hero of the 1920s, Jake is obliged to avoid the Freudian pitfalls on the way to sexual success: the problem of sexual perversion that had defeated Van Vechten's Byron Kasson in his sadistic relationship with Lasca Sartoris or the kind of parasitic fetishism exhibited by the pimp Jerco in *Home to Harlem*.[26] McKay shows in a number of ways that Jake can successfully negotiate such issues, notably in his brief affair with the character Rose, who wants to make him her "slave" and who tells him that she loves him all the more when she succeeds in getting him to hit her (41); although this once brings "a nasty smile" to his face, Jake leaves her in disgust, for he "don't like hitting no womens" (117–18). Thus, McKay explains how Jake's good nature solves not only the problem of Darwinian sexual violence but the problem of Freudian perversion. He explains that the "miserable cock-fights"

> had always sickened, saddened, unmanned [Jake]. The wild, shrieking mad woman that is sex seemed jeering at him. Why should love create terror? Love should be joy lifting man out of the humdrum ways of life. He had always

managed to delight in love and yet steer clear of the hate and violence that govern it in his world. His love nature was generous and warm without any vestige of the diabolical or sadistic. (328)

Moreover, Jake's warm "love nature" frees him from both the problem of sexual repression and the modern malaise of spiritual desolation, as in T. S. Eliot's sense of Prufrockian impotence or "The Hollow Men." Jake stands in contrast to a tyrannous chef on the railroad, who "was a great black bundle of consciously suppressed desires" (16), and, more importantly, to Ray, who agonizes over the fact that he is "black and impotent" (154). On one tortuous night, Ray realizes that love might help him get to sleep but knows also that "he could not pick up love . . . on the street as Jake" could easily do (152). Then, desperately seeking relief by sniffing some cocaine (in the chapter "Snowstorm in Pittsburgh"), he lapses into deep sleep and an obvious Freudian dream: he turned into "a blue bird in flight and a blue lizard in love. . . . Taboos and terrors and penalties were transformed into new pagan delights, orgies . . . fetishes and phalli and all the most-high gods" (158). Still, in a later scene Ray provides an articulate analysis of his own psychological condition, one that links McKay's thoughts on this "be-be itching life" with the particular problems of the blacks. In a discussion of pimps and their way of life, which Jake thinks of as "stinking life" and another thinks of as "rotting human flesh," Ray cautions them about their "nice theories" and how "the things you call fine human traits don't belong to any special class or nation or race of people." His advice is to "keep your fine feelings" without trying "to make a virtue of them": "They'll become all hollow inside, false and dry as civilization itself" (242–43).[27]

A modern discontent, Ray cannot bring this good psychological advice to bear in his own life. But he helps make McKay's point that for African Americans especially the problems of race and sex are as inseparable as Charles Darwin and Havelock Ellis proclaimed them to be: for Ray (and presumably other repressed black people) the symptoms are that he can love neither Agatha, his more-than-worthy girlfriend, nor black people in general. Before finding psychological relief in his cocaine dream, Ray is repelled by the thought of his fellow workers on the railroad who snored "with masticating noises of their fat lips, like animals eating. . . . These men claimed kinship with him. They were black men like him. Man and nature had put them in the same race. He ought to love them and feel them (if they felt anything). He ought to if he had a shred of social morality in him," but he could not answer the question why he "should have and love a race" (152–53). Beneath this, in the novel's logic, is his inability to love *life*. Unlike Jake, who was sometimes "disgusted with life, but . . . never frightened of it" (105) and who, Ray realizes, loved life too much to destroy himself with alcohol or by taking up the life of a "sweet man" (222), Ray finds that "the more I learn the less I understand and love life" (274).

Thus McKay's earthy, working-class hero Jake embodies his message for black America and especially "the intellectual gang" of Harlem: not only that the individual's psychological well-being depends on his or her ability to remember that Sheba "was black but beautiful" (136), as Ray seems to know, but that in terms of group survival, "the Negro intelligentsia cannot hope to get very far if the Negro masses are despised and neglected."[28] In this sense *Home to Harlem* is "the real proletarian novel" that McKay considered it to be but in a way (calculated to offend the Talented Tenth) that fully celebrated "the unwashed of the Black Belt" in all their sexual primitivism and their essential voice in the blues.[29] McKay begins to make this case with his biological principle about group survival, that "it is a plain fact that the entire world of human- ity is more or less segregated in groups," family, tribal, national, racial, groups ac- cording to language and class—and "groups within groups" (*A Long Way from Home* 350). Of course, he insists, "no sane group desires public segregation and discrimina- tion," but it is a fact of life that will not be dissolved by "miscegenation and final assimilation by the white group" in time enough to provide "a solution for the great dark body of Negroids living in the present" (350–51). And in *Home to Harlem* McKay arranges for his more vital, uneducated hero Jake to instruct Ray in this fact of life: that group and racial difference is rooted in sex. Telling Ray about his preference for the Harlem brothels over the European ones he had frequented, Jake deplores the way the European brothels were "all straight raw business. . . . I prefer the niggers' way every time. They does it better." And when Ray indicates that he cannot appreciate the "difference of race" (dirty sex is dirty sex to him), Jake instructs him, "Youse crazy chappie. . . . There's all kinds a difference in that theah life" (201–2).

Forwarding this view in the context of the Harlem disagreement over race, class, and sexual primitivism ("The Negro in Art: How Shall He Be Portrayed"), McKay inevitably—and quite self-consciously—projects his own form of racism. One can begin to appreciate his effort in this regard by noting the way he draws the line be- tween black and white, as in his pointed references to Van Vechten's *Nigger Heaven*. The most effective of these references is a scene between the reunited Jake and Felice. Describing them together in "the nigger heaven of a theater" on Broadway, McKay writes: "They enjoyed the exhibition. There is no better angle from which one can look down on a motion picture than that of a nigger heaven" (315). More angrily, in *A Long Way from Home* he objects to Gertrude Stein's remark about Africa and evo- lution, that Africa "has a very ancient but very narrow culture and there it remains. Consequently nothing can happen" (349). McKay remarks that "the high priestess of artless-artful Art" is one of "the eternal faddists who exist like vampires" feeding on "Negro art" (*A Long Way from Home* 348–49), and, earlier in the memoir, remark- ing on his "aversion to cults and disciples" like those around Stein in Paris, he de- nied the value of Stein's "Melanctha" and said that "Esther [*sic*] Waters is more im- portant to me" (248).

In the disagreement among novelists of the Harlem Renaissance over which kind of music most truthfully represents the black voice, no novel does more with the blues than *Home to Harlem*. In the single short scene in a Harlem cabaret in *Dark Princess*, for example, DuBois suggests that the singer's "harsh, shrill voice" and the dancing "preach against themselves" (66–67). However, in more than a dozen musical scenes, *Home to Harlem* celebrates the blues. As Ray realizes once, the "melancholy-comic notes of a 'Blues'" are "the key to himself and to his race" (266). However, despite all Ray learns from Jake, with his "sure instinct for the right rhythm," Ray remains repressed and withdrawn (311).[30] Still, McKay's complicated theme with the blues in *Home to Harlem* demands closer scrutiny. It begins with McKay's characteristic single note of *life* and life as Darwin had defined it in reference to the origin of music in *The Descent of Man*. Echoing Darwin, McKay writes that when his "Black lovers of life [are] caught up in their own free native rhythm" they are "threaded to a remote scarce-remembered past, celebrating the midnight hours in themselves" (197). Moreover, McKay always insists, as Darwin does, that "musical cadences and rhythm" arouse "the emotions and thoughts of a long-past age" when they originated in "courtship and rivalry" and also that "the season of love is that of battle."[31] Thus, for McKay, the blues rhythm—as distinct from "musical-hall syncopation and jazz"—is necessarily "simple-clear and quivering. Like a primitive dance of war or love . . . the marshaling of spears or the sacred frenzy of phallic celebrations" (196–97).

After the very brief initial cabaret scene in which Jake and Felice meet, McKay plunges into the reality of courtship and rivalry as Jake, "hunting for joy" but separated from Felice, goes from one cabaret to another (30). At the first cabaret a singer croons the refrain, "I'm crazy, plumb crazy / About a man, mah man." McKay writes that "Dandies and pansies, chocolate, chestnut, coffee, ebony, cream, yellow, everybody was teased up to the high point of excitement. . . . 'Crazy, plumb crazy about a man, mah man.' . . . The saxophone was moaning it," the dancers "were acting it," and "Jake was going crazy." Then "a crash cut through the music," and the first of the novel's several "hen-fights" and "cock-fights" breaks out—"a raging putty-skinned mulattress" knocking the "shiny coffee-colored" singer to the floor, stamping and spitting on her and yelling, "That'll teach you to leave mah man be every time." At the side, "a potato-yellow man and a dull-black were locked," causing the proprietor to work "his elbow like a hatchet between them." As the men square off, McKay emphasizes the warlike violence by having them repeat the phrase "I acks you." Then one hurls the racial slur that goes to the source of McKay's analysis of the racial-sexual conflict he identifies in this chapter as our "be-be itching life." One of the combatants calls the putty-skinned woman a "white man's wench" (33).

McKay will not let us off this hook. For him it is the essential fact of natural history that DuBois pointed to but downplayed in proclaiming that "the problem of the Twentieth Century is the problem of the color line" or that Havelock Ellis similarly avoided in his study of "the question of sex—with the racial questions that rest on it." McKay insists that his audience face this fact, underscoring it in the penultimate chapter, "Spring in Harlem." Leading up to the moment when Jake and Felice are reunited in this cabaret scene, McKay describes how, at the first notes of the music, "showing all their teeth," the dancers "started shivering amorously, itching for their partners to come" (296). Whether or not he had Darwin's specific image in mind—of "the thrill or slight shiver which runs down the backbone and limbs of many persons when they are powerfully affected by music" (*Expression of the Emotions* 217)—there can be no doubt that he intends to strike a Darwinian primitive chord with the blues song, the keynote of his novel. He strikes this chord at length early in "Spring in Harlem" and then briefly reiterates it in the closing scene. The song of intraracial conflict is played by "black fellows" in the Sheba (a cabaret named for the queen who "reminded them that she was black but beautiful"):

Brown gal crying on the corner,
    Yaller gal done stole her candy,
Buy him spats and feed him cream,
    Keep him strutting fine and dandy.

Tell me, pa-pa Ise you' ma-ma,
    Yaller gal can't make you fall,
For Ise got some loving pa-pa
    Yaller gal ain't got atall

"Tell me, pa-pa, Ise you' ma-ma." The black players grinned and swayed and let the music go with all their might. The yellow in the music must have stood out in their imagination like a challenge, conveying a sense of that primitive, ancient, eternal, inexplicable antagonism in the color taboo of sex and society. The dark dancers picked up the refrain and jazzed and shouted with delirious joy. "Tell me, pa-pa, Ise you' ma-ma." (296–97)

As the scene draws to a close, we hear the lines from the singer (a "brown girl") that tell how her "chocolate" turns down the "yaller," "'Cause he knows there ain't no loving / Sweeter than his loving brown.'" Now seeing his "brown" Felice for the first time since they were separated early in the novel, Jake (whose last name is Brown) drops "the quadroon girl" he is dancing with and rushes to Felice, soon to stand together with her in the "circle" of his mind.

What can be said of McKay's discriminatory theme? First, that despite his complaints about DuBois's "racial propaganda," his own propaganda of the blues is only more artfully disguised. Also and more important, he sounds his blues note for the same high cause of DuBois's spirituals. Both writers ministered to a black spirit, but McKay places his faith in the darker reality of Darwinian thought. He fully embraces Ray's sense that "life seemed hopelessly tangled and colored without point or purpose" (244) and his own point (in reference to Suzy and Miss Curdy) that "the black woman had had her entanglements in yellow . . . [and] the mulattress hers of black" (61). But he argues on the one hand that the "yellow complex" resulted when "civilization . . . brought exotic types" into the race and on the other hand that characters like the "putty-skinned" Miss Curdy "did not realize that she could not help desiring black" (57, 61). He remarks of the "spade" woman, Suzy, that her "yellow complex" is "a hive of discontents" (57–58), and he writes that the black chef on the railroad is "a great black bundle of consciously suppressed desires" and loses his position because he plays around with yellow women (160). All of these problems result from white civilization, as the chef himself says, "This heah white man's train service ain't no nigger picnic" (124).

But the theme of this composition is Jake's proletarian and racial-sexual remark when the chef is brought down: "I hope all we niggers will pull together like civilization folks" (187). McKay's dominant chord is that, while love and rivalry are entwined in the heart of the natural world, they are also the primal source of racial harmony in the blues. For McKay, the blues cleanses, elevates, strengthens, and unites the black community. "Oh, 'blues, blues, blues,'" he intones in saving his character Zeddy (Zeddy with his "gorilla feet") from a lethal battle with another man. Just as the fight seems inevitable, a blues melody breaks out, and Zeddy joins in, "humming in harmony, barbaric harmony, joy-drunk, chasing out the shadow of the moment before" (54). Again, hearing the music, "Love is like a cocktail cherry," at another cabaret, "the women, carried away by the sheer rhythm of delight, had risen above their commercial instincts" to be simply "gorgeous animals" (108). And again, at "Aunt Hattie's," where Jake had gone "to feed," McKay brings in the song, "But we know who feel the pain, / Oh, ring the bell again," commenting that "the song was curious, like so many Negro songs of its kind, for the strange strengthening of its wistful melody by a happy rhythm that was suitable for dancing" (292). And yet again, toward the end of the novel, just before Jake and Zeddy are brought into sexual battle over Felice, McKay brings in a blues song that serves as a play within the play about buddies in sexual conflict. "Ise got the blues all ovah," but "I won't do a crazy deed 'cause of a two-faced pal," intones the black singer with a "triumphant note of strength that reigned over the sad motif" (321–22).

Triumphing even more completely over the discord according to skin color within the black community, McKay presents the final performance of his theme song, "Tell me, pa-pa, Ise you ma-ma." He writes that "it was a scene of blazing color. Soft, barbaric, burning, savage, clashing, planless colors—all rioting together in wonderful harmony." Describing this varicolored "assembly of Negroes," he asserts his deep biological principle, "Negroes are like trees. They wear all colors naturally" (320). Thus, even when this blues song of brown and yellow strikes the note of "eternal, inexplicable antagonism in the color taboo of sex and society," McKay insists that "the handful of yellow dancers . . . were even more abandoned to the spirit of the song" (297). Later, the black buddies Jake and Zeddy act out the words of the earlier song (the play within the play) and avoid their climactic battle, Zeddy telling Jake, "You was always a good man-to-man buddy" (333–34). And at last we see the cabaret crowd "all drawn together in one united mass, wriggling around to the same primitive, voluptuous rhythm" of "Tell me, pa-pa, Ise you' ma-ma" (337).

"Ise you' ma-ma," "Ise you' ma-ma," McKay's brown woman sings to the end. Like the brown heroine Felice who has selected the dark brown hero Jake Brown, she is confident that with the female's power to select in this "be-be itching life," she has the keys to the problem of the color line (340).

Rudolph Fisher's *The Walls of Jericho* and the "Rising Tide of Rhythm"

Of all the novelists discussed here, Rudolph Fisher was by far the most distinguished student of evolutionary biology. He earned a master of arts in biology degree from Brown University in 1920 and his medical degree from Howard University in 1924. While at Howard he taught embryology. After medical school he won a National Research Council Fellowship to study bacteriology at the College of Physicians and Surgeons at Columbia University, work that led to two coauthored articles in *Proceedings of the Society of Experimental Biology and Medicine* and *Journal of Infectious Diseases*. Later he conducted research in his special field, X-ray technology, served as head of the department of roentgenology at International Hospital in Manhattan, and conducted his own medical practice.[32] Along the way he helped pay his college tuition as a pianist, touring with his friend Paul Robeson, and published prizewinning short stories, three in the *Atlantic Monthly*. *The Walls of Jericho* was his first novel; a second, *The Conjure-Man Dies* appeared in 1932, two years before his untimely death from a stomach disorder that might have been related to prolonged exposure to X-rays.

Fisher's work deserves much more attention than it has received. Some scholars agree with David Levering Lewis that *The Walls of Jericho* is "one of the most thematically successful and enduring works of the Harlem Renaissance—to say nothing of the most enjoyable" (*Vogue* 229). But, partly because the recent renewed interest in the Harlem Renaissance has for good reason promoted the work of women like Fauset, Larsen, and Hurston, who had for too long been overshadowed by men such as McKay, Jean Toomer, or Langston Hughes, Fisher remains in relative obscurity.

Another reason for the relative obscurity of *The Walls of Jericho* is that Fisher's irony and his brilliance as a satirist mask the impressive blend of scientific and spiritual thought from which he constructed his plot. Something of his view of life and the race question is suggested by his background as both the son of a Baptist minister and a scientist and in the self-reflective character he created in *The Conjure-Man Dies* and the story "John Archer's Nose." The physician John Archer is interested in "the mixture of Christian faith and primitive mysticism" and supposes that "every religion is a confusion of superstitions" ("John Archer's Nose" 193). Fisher's characteristic effort, then, is to follow the advice of his memorable grandmother figure Miss Cynthie (in "Miss Cynthie"): "Be a preacher or a doctor. . . . If the Lord don't see fit for you to doctor the soul, then doctor the body," but the body and mind as shaped by evolution (*City of Refuge* 69).[33]

Indeed, the trajectory of Fisher's career is evident in the commencement speech he gave at Brown University in 1919, "The Emancipation of Science." There he argued that a "oneness of purpose . . . brings science and religion into harmony" and that science is devoted to "making . . . life worth living." Science "devoutly rever[es] its supreme ruler, which is law; persistently uphold[s] the principles of its savior, which is evolution; and constantly [finds comfort in its] holy spirit, which is truth" (*City of Refuge* xiv). That evolution might be a "savior" is of course a familiar though hardly uncontested theme in the American fiction I survey here, from Frank Norris's mystic evolution in *The Octopus* to DuBois's faith in the black soul in *Dark Princess*. But Fisher's unique take on this theme is evident in much of his work, as in his reference to "Tessie Smith's 'Lord Have Mercy Blues'" in the story "Blades of Steel"— it was "a curious mingling of the secular and the religious" (*City of Refuge* 141). Similarly, a curious mixture of science and religion is at the heart of *The Walls of Jericho* in the sermon that provides its title. Presenting his sermon on the biblical story, the preacher tells his audience—including Fisher's hero and heroine, Joshua (Shine) Jones and Linda Young, "I don't care the least little bit whether this thing ever happened or not," but whether it is a parable, a legend, or a myth, it has tremendous "spiritual value" (183–84).

The sermon is instrumental in Fisher's effort to bring his ideal couple together and to send them on their way into the future; that is, it is key to his way of diagnosing and solving what he thinks is the main problem that must be overcome before his own couple (like DuBois's, Fauset's, or McKay's) can continue in the quest for evolutionary salvation. But if the courtship plot provides the novel's structural foundation and Fisher's ultimate solution to the race question (the survival of the black couple "Shine" Jones and Linda Young, through their improved economic status and their prospective progeny), in his full cast of characters and subplots he treats related aspects of the sexual-racial problem with the fine, evenhanded satiric touch that disarms much of the racial tension within the novel. He suggests how some of these issues—for example the color conflict between the "yellow" working man Jinx and his black fellow worker Bubber—might be ameliorated, and he implies that other problems, notably the extreme racial hatred of the light-skinned black man Merrit and the racial fear of the white woman Miss Cramp, will be solved only when the characters who exemplify them live out their sterile lives. In the main, Fisher suggests that racial antagonism is an inevitable part of American life but that it is not as horrific as many thought it to be.

He opens the novel with a satiric reference to Harlem as "the dark kingdom's backwoods. A city jungle this . . . peopled largely by untamed creatures that live and die for the moment only. Accordingly, here strides melodrama, naked and un-ashamed" (4). In Patmore's Pool Parlor "the discussion concerned a possible race riot in Harlem" that would surely develop in response to a "Darkey's" decision to move into a white neighborhood (5–6). This will be Fisher's melodrama: the ram-pant racial hysteria of the time that was widely disseminated in Lothrop Stoddard's *The Rising Tide of Color against White World-Supremacy* (1920). The famous book (which DuBois must have been outraged to find cited his own work in order to make its racist case and which figured prominently in *The Great Gatsby*) warned of "a hideous catastrophe," the "gigantic race-war" (308) that would surely engulf the world if whites failed to heed "the peril of migration" by the colored races (236). Because "recent discoveries in biology" had shown that "heredity is far more im-portant than environment or education" (254), Stoddard warned, it was essential to realize that "crossings with the negro are uniformly fatal" and that all other races "are alike vanquished by the invincible prepotency of the more primitive, general-ized, and lower negro blood" (301).

Thus Fisher's fun with this melodrama in *The Walls of Jericho* begins when the upper-class black man named Merrit has decided to carry his assault to the white inner sanctum by moving into a house on "Court Avenue." Not that Merrit (light enough to pass for white) is at all interested in courting a white woman. He tells his alarmed friends, "I hate fays" (whites), "Always will. Chief joy in life is making them uncomfortable" (37), and even though Merrit had no specific sexual motive, Fisher is clear enough in remarking, "Court Avenue is a straight, thin spinster of a street which even in July is cold" (44). As Merrit tells his friends (one of whom believes that "progress is by evolution, not revolution"), "the extension of territory by vio-lence and bloodshed strikes me as natural enough" (36). Fisher's own view seems best represented in this exchange by the preacher Tod Bruce, who remarks, "It's the old story . . . war—conquest of territory" (41), suggesting that "the fays have a side too" and offering the idea that "nowadays . . . we grow by—well—a sort of passive conquest" (43).

As it works out in the novel, when Merrit does move into Court Avenue (much to the consternation of his new neighbor, the white spinster Miss Cramp, whose obsession with helping to uplift the blacks is a main target of Fisher's satire), his house is burned to the ground. But the surprise is that this was not the work of angry whites but instead of the black bootlegger and owner of the poolroom, Patmore, in revenge for an earlier financial wound he had received from Merrit. And in a similar reversal of the expected racial melodrama, although the white spinster still thinks that black men are deceitful in their efforts to "get into [white women's] homes—God knows for what purpose" (286), Fisher plays with Stoddard's image of the rising tide of color by describing dancers of all color variations being caught up in "a current of leisurely, compelling rhythm, a rising tide of rhythm" (82). In this scene at the General Improvement Association's Annual Costume Ball (for the cause of uplifting the race), the rhythmic music "floated couple after couple off the bank into midstream," and the only racial mixing in the dance occurs repeatedly when the white man Tony Nayle sweeps the black woman Nora Byle onto the floor—arousing the jealous anger of her appropriately named husband, the Hon. Buckram Byle (82). In his witty essay of the previous year, "The Caucasian Storms Harlem" (in *American Mercury*), Fisher produced a similar ironic reversal of white fear over the "peril of migration."

Although Fisher had created memorable cabaret scenes of primitive music and dance in his short stories, notably in "Common Meter," *The Walls of Jericho* contains only the dance scene at the costume ball. In this important scene—only loosely related to his central courtship plot—Fisher takes the opportunity to suggest a "philosophy of skin color" that furthers his efforts to allay Nordic fears of a migrating dark horde. At the same time, his philosophy defines problems of class and color conflict within the African American community that he believes will continue in the future but for which he will offer his own ameliorative advice. He begins by noting that no occasion brings together "a greater inherent variety" of types than does this annual ball: varieties mainly of class, "personal station," or "social standing" that range "from the rattiest rat to the dicktiest dicky" but also varieties of "personal appearance" that range in color from black to white (70).[34] Surrounding the dance floor on which all these varieties intermingle is a low terrace containing a "tangle" of tables where the "ordinary respectable people or rats" sit; in a balcony above sit "dickties and fays" who had "mounted the stairs" (70–72). His summative description is as follows:

> So swept the scene from black to white through all the shadows and shades. Ordinary Negroes and rats below, dickties and fays above, the floor beneath the feet of the one constituting the roof over the heads of the other. Somehow, undeniably, a predominance of darker skins below, and, just as undeniably, of fairer skins above. Between them, stairways to climb. One might have read in that distribution a complete philosophy of skin-color, and from it

deduced the past, present, and future of this people. . . . Out on the dance floor, everyone, dickty and rat, rubbed joyous elbows, laughing, mingling, forgetting differences. But whenever the music stopped everyone immediately sought his own level.

One great common fellowship in one great common cause. (74)

So much for Fisher's faith in the "Nigerrati's" high hopes.

Two of the novel's most important subplots are interwoven in this scene—the conflict of color difference between the two "rats," the yellow man Jinx and the black man Bubber, who work with the hero Shine as piano movers; and the economic difference between the dickty Merrit (a wealthy lawyer) and the ordinary working man Shine. Fisher's prescription for the second of these comes at the end of the novel when Merrit sets Shine up in his own business as a piano mover. This provides "what we Negroes need, a business class, an economic backbone" to fill in the social structure that now has only "extremes—bootblacks on one end and doctors on the other" (282–83). But before this can happen Fisher will have chastened Merrit for his extreme racial hatred and—at the same time—aroused Shine's sympathy for Merrit, when he sees Merrit in the ruins of his razed home, weeping over a lost picture of his black mother. So light-skinned that he can pass, Merrit reveres his black mother, whom he regarded as "a symbol of sexual martyrdom" victimized by the anonymous white father he hates (38).

Similarly, Fisher suggests that the enmity between Bubber and Jinx, whose yellow color seems to account for his own "querulous" nature and "murderous scowl" (6), is rooted in sexual conflict: speculating on the "nature of [their old] quarrel" (12), he asks rhetorically, had it begun "over a woman, hey?" (208). As a result, they now often exchange racial insults, Jinx, for example, claiming that Bubber's ancestors go "all the way back to the apes" (12). But, suggesting that their "extravagant enmity" is merely an "inverted" expression of their deeper mutual affection or "profound attachment"—a suppression necessitated by their distorted view of what it means to be a man, Fisher finally arranges for them to be sent into a cellar to have it out for good (11). When they emerge from this apparent descent into their subconscious past, Jinx falls to the floor because "his legs and feet [got] all tangled like those of a fly trying to escape sticky paper," and Bubber falls over his body, murmuring, "ain' nuthin' to fight about boogy. Ain't you my boy?" (210–11). In yet another of his delightful comic reversals of our expectations, Fisher reveals that these closely related buddies hadn't actually fought at all in the cellar, though they both appear near death. They are merely drunk from having found and consumed a bottle of whiskey.

Also in the long dance scene at the costume ball, Fisher brings together the hero and heroine (Shine and Linda) to act out the early stage of their courtship. And as he begins to develop this central plot, he provides further remarks on the evolution of race (in addition to the "complete philosophy of skin color" that he reads into the multileveled seating arrangement). For example, there are conversations between the various types gathered in the boxes upstairs on a number of issues pertaining to the race. These range from discussions of "The Negro's Contribution to Art and The Lost Sciences of Ethiopia" (35) to the debate over how Harlem should grow (by evolution, revolution, or passive conquest), to the social worker J. Pennington Potter's bombastic argument that "only admixture produced harmony between races" and that "social admixture . . . was the solution to all the problems of race" (98). But the most entertaining of these conversations is between Merrit and the professional uplifter Miss Cramp, who assumes he is white and is later shocked beyond belief to learn that she had been talking so intimately with a black—and worse, that he was actually moving into Court Avenue as her next-door neighbor. In their priceless, extended exchange, Miss Cramp goes on about how "primitive . . . primeval . . . [and] unspoiled by civilization" the blacks are, and Merrit agrees (his "eyes twinkled"), calling them "beautiful savages" and comparing their abandonment to what one might see at a Yale-Harvard football game (108).

Most interesting, though, is their discussion of the light-skinned blacks, about whom Miss Cramp expresses her naive theory of evolution. Their light skins must have developed over a few hundred years, which "isn't such a long time if you believe in evolution. I consider evolution very important, don't you?" In one of Fisher's finest satiric strokes, Merrit replies, "Profoundly so." Of course this black man's whiteness is a result of sexual selection and miscegenation. And when Miss Cramp theorizes that the change of color results from "chiefly the climate," Fisher writes that Merrit blinked and "then nodded gravely, 'Climate undoubtedly. Climate. Changed conditions of heat and moisture and so on'" (113).[35] Miss Cramp does not catch Merrit's sly suggestion about the "'heat and moisture'" of sexual contact between the races, and she marvels at the thought of environmental changes producing "a Negro with skin as fair as [Merrit's] own!" Merrit smiles (114). Earlier, looking forward to her fatal encounter with Merrit, Fisher describes Miss Cramp's background, recalling her "urge" for service and her near nervous breakdown from so much service to a variety of causes, and he remarks that although other dark-skinned people "had never approached her person, they had penetrated her intellect a little. But Negroes she had always accepted with horses, mules, and motors, and though they had brushed her shoulder, they had never actually entered her head" (62). Toward the end of the costume ball, however, she hears that Merrit is actually black, and "the statement transfixed Miss Cramp like a lance" (138).

Against this elaborate background of evolutionary material, Fisher brings his couple together in the traditional way, touching on the male's superior qualities, his powerful hands, and the female's act of selecting him. When Shine enters the novel "everybody looked" to see this "supremely tranquil young Titan," and we later learn of his appeal to women (12–13). "There had been girls aplenty: Sarah Mosely, Babe Merrimac, Lottie Buttsby, Becky Katz, Maggie Mulligan, and others" (80), a full assortment of ethnic types, with "the voluptuous Lottie Buttsby" serving to suggest that Shine's sexual appetite had found easy satisfaction (86). Fisher adds that "an acknowledged master of men is usually attractive to women" and that "there was no end of stories about what he could do with his hands" (80). In this passage Fisher touches briefly on the main problem in Shine's makeup that must be overcome before he and Linda end the novel together: Shine's "general philosophy of conduct, of being impenetrably hard, of repudiating sentiment and relaxing toward no one and nothing, shielded his spirit if not his body from the women he so far had known" (81). Too given to the kind of combative masculinity that also marks Jinx and Bubber, Shine has never loved. Through the health-giving sermon and Linda's good influence, however, Fisher gradually rehabilitates the promising male, whose strength and combative passion alone are enough to make Linda select him at the costume ball. Just as the bootlegger Patmore begins to dance with the reluctant Linda and just as the orchestra strikes up the tune, "Take You' Fingers Off It," Shine arrives on the scene to save the woman in distress, causing her "to fling herself impulsively toward him, uttering an inaudible but obvious plea" (131–32).

Thus, in this satirically melodramatic scene, Fisher makes the point that he reiterates throughout the novel, that the unsuppressed impulse is the key to this developing relationship. But it is important to note that "impulse" is Fisher's way of construing what, in the terms of the evolutionary and Freudian theory that underlay the Harlem novels, might be primitive instinct or the subconscious. The essential element in Fisher's analysis of the problems of race and sex, it is echoed sympathetically by the observers from the boxes above when they see Shine and Linda moving off together: they all "sighed prodigiously" and cried "Marvelous!" Moreover, Fisher suggests that because the sexual conflict is resolved without a scene of battle between the black men, the group's anxiety over the ominous rising tide of color is eased. For now in the "rising tide of rhythm" (the underlying racial impulse that shapes the whole of this long scene), all the "couples casually resumed dancing, and the stream, as if undisturbed, resumed its course" (82, 132).

After a series of misunderstandings and emotional miscues by both these lovers, and as both Linda's and the sermon's positive influences gradually affect Shine, Fisher brings them together for good. The scene takes place in a hospital where Shine had gone because of a slight injury sustained in an accident while moving pianos. It might have been fatal, had not Linda, in one of her saving impulsive acts, screamed out to warn him. Fisher writes of this incident that "miraculous as a vision," Linda stood before Shine (229). But if Linda's impulse is miraculous (an essential element in Fisher's evolutionary psychoanalysis), the hospital is at the same time a kind of church, where the injured Shine, sits on "a white metal pew" and notices the "mysteriously varicolored bottles and jars" of medicine. There he soon learns that Linda has also been rushed to the hospital and is being cared for in "Ward VII" (232–35). Now, repeatedly striking the note that this is "Ward VII," Fisher suggests that medical science is involved in the kind of evolutionary salvation that he had honored in his commencement address. And returning to the evolutionary point that so many other novelists had addressed in the courtship novels of his time, regarding the male's prime "secondary sexual character" (in Darwin's analysis), his power to grasp and hold the female, Fisher ends the courtship drama. Shine sits in Ward VII with Linda: "He reached out, not fully aware of his gesture and placed his great hand over hers on the bed. She placed her other hand on top of his," signaling that their relationship will not be crushed by the male's dominating power. Now, with imagery that draws on both the power of science and metaphysics, Fisher writes that this "was the closing of a switch, the making of a circuit through which leaped new, strange, shattering impulses" that were far more powerful than anything Shine had ever experienced with Lottie Buttsby. "For one brief, eternal moment that mere contact of hands as completely obliterated the surroundings as if their whole bodies had been fused in passionate, tender embrace" (260–61).

Even after this moment of evolutionary mysticism (with suggestions of "winged angels" and the "fragrance of roses"), Shine will have a final encounter with the characteristic hardness that Fisher isolates as the cause of his hero's inner conflict. In that critical moment, Shine's battle with his sexual rival Patmore, the novel's sermon and its evolutionary theory reinforce each other to resolve Shine's inner conflict and to project once again (as in the hospital scene) Fisher's vision of science and religion working in harmony. Shine's problematic hardness first arose as a possible obstacle between himself and Linda when she told him how Patmore had called Shine "a dirty rat." Then she "saw the change come over his face; saw the brows contract, the eyes gleam, the jaws tighten, the lips set . . . the bronze skin lose its life and turn dirty copper" (96). As Linda tells him later, "you think muscle's everything." Thus, with his sexual combativeness and the legendary power of his hands, Shine is a version of the troublesome evolutionary male (passionate and combative) that stalks the pages of American fiction from Howells's Bartley Hubbard to London's Wolf Larsen, and on to Fisher's character, Frimbo, in *The Conjure-Man Dies*.[36]

When Linda convinces Shine to accompany her to church, however, he hears a sermon from Tod Bruce that Fisher hopes will save such "ordinary people or rats" as Jinx, Bubber, and Shine. As Bruce explains, the goal of his lesson from the story of Joshua's battle "is the knowledge of man's own self," knowledge that is blocked by the "wall of self-deception." Illustrating his point, Bruce explains that "a man may . . . boast that he is evil and merciless and hard when all this is but a crust, shielding and hiding a spirit that is kindly, compassionate, and gentle." Thus, as every man has his own inner wall of Jericho, Bruce urges his listeners "therefore to besiege yourselves; to take honest counsel with the little fraction of God, of Truth, that dwells in us all." But it is important to note here that Bruce's "God" and "Truth" have more to do with Fisher's commencement remarks on science and its "holy spirit . . . truth" than with orthodox religion. As Bruce preaches, a man "may pledge himself to a religion when he is by nature a pagan, thus robbing himself and his generation of all that might come out of honest self-expression" (184–87). It is equally important to recognize that Fisher's faith in the imprisoned spirit resembles DuBois's in the black soul and McKay's in the spiritual love he created between Jake and Felice. In his own way, Fisher, too, strives to affirm a version of evolutionary and Freudian theory that can liberate the ordinary black community. He argues quite self-consciously that the black psyche is both innately healthy and compassionate in its primitive or "pagan" state; however, while Fisher's argument resembles the "Freudian" affirmation of the liberated sexual impulse that was so often admired in the "primitive" black, it includes his emphasis on compassion and once again illustrates his vision of science and religion working in harmony.

Clearly, though, Fisher's inner wall of self-deception is a variation of Freudian repression. This is the case with Jinx and Bubber, whose actual affection for each other Fisher compares with that of "Damon and Pythias." The problem between them is that under their present "order of life" there is a "required . . . suppression" that distorts their "normal manhood" and causes "hostility" to rise "into their consciousness." Their "concealed . . . profound attachment" and "extravagant enmity" are "a distortion of behavior so completely imposed upon them by their traditions and society that even they themselves did not know they were masquerading" (10–11). Finally arranging for them to emerge from their confrontation in the "cellar" with a clearer and saving sense of who they are, Fisher provides a chorus of suggestions that their conflict had been a psychological and spiritual betrayal (one onlooker cries "Judas Priest" and others, "for Chris sake" and "Jesus"). Similarly, in reference to his central plot (the courtship), Fisher writes that Shine once "had an impulse to catch [Linda] up and kiss her right there on the street corner oblivious to broad daylight and possible observation. Had he done so, spontaneously, on the crest of that emotional wave, the result would have been different," bringing the lovers together well in advance of the scene in Ward VII. "But the old habit of hardness . . . promptly clamped down on his exuberance and distorted his natural impulse into a presumably safer substitute" (197).

Linda too has her own troubles with this kind of repression, once when "something pinioned her arms that wanted to reach out to" Shine, causing her to think "how silly and impetuous she was, and . . . ashamed" (229–30). At another moment, seeing the wound on his forehead, she "reached impulsively toward it [but] checked the motion. 'No—'tisn't supposed to be touched, is it?'" (253). But the chief problem from Fisher's point of view is the potentially disruptive male—Shine, who, after Linda spurned him once, took out his frustration on his moving van, "Bess," who "became a willing mistress" (216). Fisher notes that Shine's "knowledge of women contained no therapy," so he became "more violent" and "worked harder" (215). But after this the two are united in Ward VII, and Shine learns that his old rival Patmore had assaulted Linda (the cause of her treatment in the hospital). And now Fisher leads Shine to his final test, his confrontation (enacting Darwin's "law of battle") with Patmore. "All the hatred [Shine] had ever felt for anybody . . . gathered in one single wave, advanced in one tidal onrush," his hatred "of all fays" and "of dickties in general," causing him to become "a madman with no notion of what he was doing, no sustained consciousness" (270–71). In the ensuing battle at Patmore's pool hall we see Shine again as "a gigantic madman," a monster of racial and sexual hatred, and Fisher describes the Darwinian combatants in a "senseless twist and tangle" (273). Significantly, Patmore shoots Shine in the left hand, but Shine prevails and finally stands poised with "his right arm [ready] to strike the exposed throat."

At this precise moment someone accidentally breaks "the great bar mirror" so that "the crash and jangle of the falling glass wall . . . snatched Shine out of madness. The sound transfixed him as if all the walls of the place had tumbled." Shine then "blinked" and for the first time saw that his opponent was "on his knees, gasping and helpless" (275–76). In this instant Shine (Joshua Jones) breaks through his inner wall of Jericho or self-deception, and Fisher stages the scene in an aura of evolutionary, psychological, and religious thought. Shine himself cannot be aware that he has acted out Fisher's solution to the evolutionary problem of restraining the violent male, or that he has resolved a rather "Freudian" inner conflict that resulted from his repressive hardness and made him "crazy 'bout" Linda (259). But Fisher does manage to subdue this titanic male, partly by disabling half his prehensile power, by helping him to learn through Linda's insight that "you're not hard or mean or tough . . . [but] just sacred," and by staging a fortuitous vision of the sermon's truth (256). Bruce had concluded the sermon by prophesying that when the "towering illusion tumble[s]" you will "straightway enter triumphant into the promised land" (187). Always maintaining that evolution is the savior of science, Fisher wills his belief in a compassionate rather than a violent or libidinous subconscious—and closes his novel with an image of the promising couple ascending into the evolutionary future.

They drive together in Shine's van on a road that "led up and over a crest beyond which spread sunrise like a promise . . . straight into the kindling sky." Shine is a lovely name for this glittering hero, the transfigured bootblack. Fisher describes the van carrying Shine and Linda as it recedes from our view: "Against that far background of light . . . [it] hung black and still a moment—then drop[ped] abruptly out of vision, into another land" (293).

Notes

1. The political, social, racial, sexual, and ideological complications and "stresses" within the movement are discussed in different ways and from different points of view by Nathan Irvin Huggins in *Harlem Renaissance* and David Levering Lewis in *When Harlem Was in Vogue*. See also Steven Watson, *The Harlem Renaissance*, and Eloise E. Johnson, *Rediscovering the Harlem Renaissance*. In his excellent introduction to his *The Portable Harlem Renaissance Reader* David Levering Lewis identifies three phases of the Harlem Renaissance: first, "The Bohemian Renaissance," 1917-23; second, "The Talented Tenth Renaissance" (or the "genteel" Renaissance), 1924-26, led by DuBois, Jessie Fauset, and Walter White; and third, "The Negro Renaissance" (or "the demotic Renaissance"), 1926-35, represented by Alain Locke, Langston Hughes, Nella Larsen, Claude McKay, and many others (xxx, xliii-v).

2. These evolutionary issues are discussed in the chapter "Race and Sexual Selection in Charles W. Chesnutt's *The House behind the Cedars*" in my *The Descent of Love*.

3. Stribling was not the only writer to think of Darwin as a great liberator. For example, in 1898 *The Outlook* had published a poem titled "Lincoln and Darwin" in which the poet (Frederick LeRoy Sargent) referred to the two as "emancipators both"; crediting Darwin with having taught us of "the *progress* which our fathers sought," he celebrates both men (who share the same birthday) as "hope's prophets."

4. Of course this focus on 1928 leaves out some of the most interesting and well-known fiction of the period, for example Walter White's *The Fire in the Flint*, Jean Toomer's *Cane*, James Weldon Johnson's *The Autobiography of an Ex-Colored Man*, Wallace Thurman's *The Blacker the Berry*, Langston Hughes's *Not without Laughter*, other novels by these five writers, and very impressive short fiction by Richard Bruce Nugent and Zora Neale Hurston. Also, unfortunately, my survey does not do justice to the rich presentation of "gay and lesbian affections" that is better represented in other works from the movement (Lewis, *Vogue*, xxii).

5. Zora Neale Hurston's work with Boas and her interest in African American folklore is well known, but Degler's discussion of Boas's interest in African Americans and his relationship with DuBois should be consulted by readers interested in the evolutionary issues underlying the Harlem Renaissance (see especially section 2, "The Sovereignty of Culture," 75–80).

6. Lewis surmises that Mary Love "can only have been confected from Jessie Fauset" (*When Harlem Was in Vogue* 185).

7. See, for example, Claude McKay's letter to DuBois (June 18, 1928): "I sympathize with and even pity you for not understanding my motive [in writing *Home to Harlem*, which DuBois had criticized], because you have been forced from a normal career to enter a special field of racial propaganda and, honorable though that field may be, it has precluded you from contact with real life, for propaganda is fundamentally but a one-sided idea of life. Therefore I should not be surprised when you mistake the art of life for nonsense and try to pass off propaganda as life in art!" (Cooper, *The Passion of Claude McKay*, 150).

8. In this scene, the heroine, Laurentine, confesses to the man she will eventually marry, Dr. Denleigh, not only that she is illegitimate, but that her father is a white man. Denleigh responds: "What bosh to talk to a physician! Biology transcends society! . . . I mean to say that the facts of life, birth and death are more important than the rules of living, marriage, law, the sanction of the church or of man."

9. Fauset refers to the game in which the darker Virginia approaches Angela as "Mrs. Henrietta Jones" (35, 47, 83, 159, 359); in the most serious instance, when Angela refuses to acknowledge her dark sister in order to protect her situation with her own white lover, Virginia is seriously hurt, but Fauset seems to forgive Angela, and Angela herself, when she (Angela) realizes that "that was the one really cruel and unjust action of her whole life" (308).

10. Fauset's image of the "feral" West Indians suggests what it was about her work that offended Claude McKay. Born in Jamaica, McKay wrote that "Miss Fauset is prim and dainty as a primrose, and her novels are quite as fastidious and precious" (*A Long Way from Home* 112).

11. The scant biographical work on Fauset sheds little light on her reading, but her work with the idea of marriage in *Plum Bun* seems quite in tune with the way it was discussed, especially in reference to Russia, during those years. In 1929, for example (the year after her novel appeared), Bertrand Russell remarks early in his *Marriage and Morals*, "There is no country in the world and there has been no age in the world's history where sexual ethics and sexual institutions have been determined by rational considerations, with the exception of Soviet Russia" (5). Closer to home, in his *The Bankruptcy of Marriage* (1928) V. F. Calverton called for greater "mutual independence in morals as well as in economics" in marriage, and argued that the "new morality which we find expressed in the independent position of woman, and the new marriage and divorce laws written into the legal code of Soviet Russia" constitute "the first strides in the direction of a new ethic" (37, 267). Calverton was famous for his interest in African American writing (he published an excellent anthology in 1929 that included work by Fauset). For a range of views on modern marriage see also *Sex in Civilization* (1929), edited by Calverton and S. D. Schmalhausen, with an introduction by Havelock Ellis. First published in 1902, Kropotkin's *Mutual Aid* has little to say about modern marriage, but his theory was obviously applicable to later analyses of the institution of marriage. He emphasized that "it is not love and not even sympathy upon which Society is based in mankind. It is the conscience—be it only at the stage of an instinct—of human solidarity. It is the unconscious recognition of the force that is borrowed by each man from the practice of mutual aid" (xiii–xiv).

12. James uses the term "zoological psychology" in his long, important chapter 10, "The Consciousness of Self," in *The Principles of Psychology* (307); within this chapter, the section "Rivalry and Conflict of the Different Selves" seems especially relevant to Larsen's psychological explorations.

13. "Extraordinarily wide" quotes Charles S. Johnson, who earned a Ph.D. in sociology from the University of Chicago, chaired the Department of Sociology at Fisk University, edited *Opportunity*, and wrote *The Negro in American Civilization: A Study of Negro Life and Race Relations in the Light of Social Research* (1930). Davis's biography is indispensable in shedding light on Larsen's still somewhat mysterious early life and education; see especially her preface, "The Search for Nella Larsen." The details of Larsen's life that are provided below are from Davis.

14. Recounted by Davis, *Nella Larsen*, 200–207.

15. References to Larsen's interest in these and other writers are indexed in Davis, *Nella Larsen*.

16. In discussing Larsen's interest in modern psychology, her biographer refers briefly to Larsen's "understanding of William James's explanations of the human thought process,"

but perhaps because she justifiably emphasizes the psychological materials in Larsen's second novel, *Passing*, Davis leaves the Jamesian possibilities in *Quicksand* untouched (310–11).

17. At the end of *The Portrait of a Lady* James describes Isabel's psychic turmoil after Goodwood's kiss as though she were going under after a shipwreck; for a discussion of the Darwinian possibilities in this novel, see the chapter, "Psychological Darwinism in *The Portrait of a Lady*" in my *The Descent of Love*.

18. *Quicksand* contains many suggestions of Larsen's interest in Jamesian psychology, far more than can be noted here. But anyone who consults James in relation to *Quicksand* will sense the similarity in their principles of psychology, especially in reference to James's chapter 10, "The Consciousness of Self," which contains a section on "The Sense of Personal Identity." For example, such remarks as the following (from James's discussion of the constituents of the self and the material self) seem reflected in Larsen's novel: writing of the body as "the innermost part of *the material self*," James remarks, "Our immediate family is a part of ourselves. Our father and mother. . . . When they die, a part of our very selves is gone. If they do anything wrong, it is our shame. If they are insulted, our anger flashes forth as readily as if we stood in their place. Our home comes next. . . . We all have a blind impulse to watch over our body, to deck it with clothing of an ornamental sort, to cherish parents, wife and babes, and to find for ourselves a home of our own which we may live in and 'improve,'" and so forth (280). Again, in reference to Larsen's observation about Helga's desire not so much for money as for "the things which money could give, leisure, attention, beautiful surroundings. Things. Things. Things" (67), it is worth comparing James's principle: "*The words* ME, *then, and* SELF, *so far as they arouse feeling and connote emotional worth, are* OBJECTIVE *designations, meaning* ALL THE THINGS *which have the power to produce in a stream of consciousness excitement of a certain peculiar sort.*" He goes on: "Our *interest in things* means the attention and emotion which the thought of them will excite, and the actions which their presence will evoke. Thus every species is particularly interested in its own prey or food, its own enemies, its own sexual mates, and its own young" (304). Finally, and more profoundly in view of Larsen's ultimate theme, especially in the novel's closing scenes of primitive religion, it is worth noting James's remarks on the self and the impulse to pray: "The humblest outcast on this earth can feel himself to be real and valid by means of this higher recognition [that is, in praying to one's god]. And, on the other hand, for most of us, a world with no such inner refuge when the outer social self failed and dropped from us would be the abyss of horror" (301).

19. "Aversion" is one of the many terms in Larsen's analysis that reflect her involvement in the debate over race and intermarriage around and after the turn of the century, as in Joseph Le Conte's insistence "that race-aversion" is nature's built-in mechanism for preventing racial crossing ("Effect of Mixture of Races" 94).

20. As an indication of the way Larsen was attuned to the literary currents of her time, it is worth noting how this scene reflects her admiration of James Joyce. At the end of "Eveline" (*Dubliners*), Eveline is at the pier ready to board a ship with her suitor, bound for Buenos Ayres. But when she hears the ship's "mournful whistle," "a bell clanged upon her heart" and she is overcome by fear: "all the seas of the world tumbled about her heart. . . . He would drown her."

21. Larsen plays on the significance of "green" and "pleasant" throughout the novel, suggesting that Helga had always misunderstood the natural world. In chapter one, for example,

she focuses our attention on Helga's "startling green and gold negligee" (9); on her way to her first meeting with Anderson, Helga walks through "the flat green," drawn to the shady side of it and seemingly unaware that the "radiant life" she feels among the trees includes the kind of sexual response she will soon have to Anderson (16), and later, when HehAa k;s returned to Harlem for her visit with Anne and Anderson, she is "pleasantly unaware" of the triangular conflict—or her own feelings for Anderson or of Anne's insight into the "lawless place" in her husband's psyche and the sexual feelings between him and Helga.

22. Although there is some truth in the remark that McKay "out-niggered" Van Vechten in the presentation of sex, that observation misses much of McKay's ironic response to Van Vechten—as in the difference between Van Vechten's opening description of "the Scarlet Creeper" and McKay's description of French men. The Scarlet Creeper "wore a tight-fitting suit of shepherd's plaid which thoroughly revealed his lithe, sinewy figure to all who gazed upon him, and all gazed" (3); but in writing of how men dress in the Harlem cabarets, McKay makes his hero Jake laugh to recall the way he had seen the French dress: "The French must consider the average bantam male killing handsome, and so they make clothes to emphasize all the angular elevated rounded and pendulated parts of the anatomy." (289).

23. Tracing the further development of his character Ray in *Banjo*, McKay pursues his essential biological theme about "black skin itching, black flesh warm with the wine of life, the music of life, the love and deep meaning of life" (50).

24. The letter, rejected by the *Herald*, was published in the *Worker's Dreadnought* on April 24, 1920, and is reprinted in Cooper, *Passion of Claude McKay*, 54–57.

25. Fitzgerald told McKay that *Home to Harlem* "was one of the two most worthy novels of the spring," and remarked upon "the emotion of the purely Harlem scenes" (qtd. in Cooper, *Claude McKay*, 246).

26. In the episode in *Nigger Heaven* Byron and Lasca refer to whips and knives in their lovemaking and draw blood with their fingernails (252–53). In the scene from *Home to Harlem* Ray describes how he had seen "Jerco kneeling down by the open wardrobe [of his woman Rosalind] and kissing the toe of one of her brown shoes. He started as he saw me and looked queer kneeling there" (257–58). But, while he wants to separate Jake from such forms of sexual expression, McKay insists that they are natural. Ray accepts Jerco's life as a pimp as one of "the many forms of parasitism," telling Jake that "all men have the disease of pimps in their hearts" and that he has himself been "forced down to the level of pimps and found some of them more than human"; and he tells the story of Jerco in a chapter called "He Also Loved" (241, 243, 244).

27. In "The Hollow Men" (1925) Eliot had written, "We are the hollow men. . . . Our dry voices, when / We whisper together / Are quiet and meaningless / As wind in dry grass." In a letter to Max Eastman in 1932 McKay criticized such "ultra modernists in poetry and prose" as T. S. Eliot, whom he thought was "pedantic and commonplace" (Cooper, *The Passion of Claude McKay*, 151).

28. For McKay's views on "Group Survival," see his essay of 1937, "For Group Survival" (in Cooper, *Passion of Claude McKay*, 234–39); *Long Way from Home* 351.

29. Letter of April 30, 1928, from McKay to James Weldon Johnson, qtd. in Lewis, *When Harlem Was in Vogue*, 227; *Home to Harlem*, 29.

30. In *Banjo*, however, the character Banjo will be instrumental in Ray's further liberation from himself. McKay writes of Banjo that "every chord in him responded to the loose, bistro-love-life" (11).

31. Darwin, *The Descent of Man,* 2:28, 2:336–37.

32. My source for this information is John McCluskey Jr.'s introduction to the volume he edited, *The City of Refuge: The Collected Stories of Rudolph Fisher,* which contains a bibliography of Fisher's work.

33. Fisher suggests that this wise old grandmother is a survivor in the struggle for existence: she "had accurately selected her own treasures out of the row of luggage [at the train station on her arrival in New York] and guarded them vigilantly" (68).

34. Like Van Vechten's *Nigger Heaven, The Walls of Jericho* contains what Fisher calls "An Introduction to Contemporary Harlemese *Unexpurgated and Abridged.*" Fisher defines "dicty" in its use as an adjective as "swell" and as a noun as a "high-toned person"; a "rat" is the "antithesis of dicty."

35. Fisher draws attention to this naive theory of climate again and again (123, 286).

36. Believing that "Psychology is really a branch of biology," Fisher's Dr. Archer discovers the conjure-man's dark secret—not only his belief in the primitive "rite of the gonad," but his practice of collecting male sex glands in order to treat himself with the "testicular extract" (176, 269, 291). Frimbo's resultant "hyper-sexuality" is his downfall: he dies when the jealous husband of his mistress shoots him. Fisher's plot disposes of this troublesome male, but he indicates his belief that the combative male continues to threaten social development in Harlem. At moments throughout the novel, and at its conclusion, he quotes "a gay young man . . . burst[ing] into song":

> "I'll be glad when you're dead, you rascal you—
> I'll be glad when you're dead, you rascal you—
> Since you won't stop messin' 'round,
> I'm go'n' turn you' damper down—
> Oh, you dog—I'll be glad when you're gone!"

10 V. F. Calverton and the Principles of Red Love

Now scarcely remembered in American literary history, V. F. Calverton (1900–1940) was one of the most influential figures of "the literary Left during the 1920s and 1930s," an "independent Marxist" who founded the *Modern Quarterly* (at age twenty-three) and edited it until his death (Wilcox 2).[1] He devoted his brief and intensely productive career to furthering his belief that "man can achieve a co-operative commonwealth in our industrial society" and that it would "include everyone . . . without restriction or discrimination as to race, color, or creed." He wrote this in the epilogue to the book he completed just before his death, *Where Angels Dared to Tread* (1941), a history of socialist and communist utopian colonies in the United States. By 1925, shortly after founding the *Modern Quarterly*, he had published a first book that immediately established his credentials as a formidable literary theorist, *The Newer Spirit: A Sociological Criticism of Literature*. Among his most important and enduring literary works (in addition to his work at the *Modern Quarterly*, where he published several writers from the Harlem Renaissance) are *An Anthology of American Negro Literature* (1929) and *The Liberation of American Literature* (1932). He also edited an impressive anthology of writings in anthropology, *The Making of Man: An Outline of Anthropology* (1931), and coedited two volumes with Samuel D. Schmalhausen that are still important landmarks in American cultural history, *Sex in Civilization* (1929) and *Woman's Coming of Age, A Symposium* (1931). In relation to these, Calverton's two volumes of fiction have little to offer present-day readers. But his collection of stories, *Three Strange Lovers* (1930), and his novel, *The Man Inside* (1936), provide important examples of how one could deal with the sex problem in the fiction of the 1930s through the lens of socialist evolutionary and anthropological theory.

Knowing that it was "dangerous . . . to touch upon the sex question in a serious manner—in America" in the 1920s, Calverton wrote admiringly of what he called "red love," the USSR's "attempt to meet the problem of sex as well as the problem of society with realistic candour" ("Red Love in Soviet Russia" 183). Having freed itself from crippling religious taboos, Calverton explained, "Soviet Russia [was] in the advance of the rest of the world in its attitude toward sex, marriage, and divorce" (188). Its enlightened social policies began by accepting "the ecstasy of sex-contact" and "the joy of erotic communion," including woman's full claim to "free association of the sexes on the basis of mutual attraction" (190), and these principles were being instituted in progressive social policies toward birth control and divorce (185).[2] Not long after writing this in the late 1920s, however, Calverton became disillusioned with the social reality in Russia. He denounced Stalinism and argued that "the significant truth of Marxism must be tested in the scientific world of fact and not in the closed chambers of authoritarianism" (qtd. in Wilcox 151). But his sense of the "scientific" facts remained relatively unchanged.[3]

We can begin to understand how he understood these "facts" by noting that his career emerged during the Freudian era and that he embraced a version of popular Freudianism. He began *The Bankruptcy of Marriage* (1928) with the chapter "The Jazz Age," in which he welcomed the idea that "repressions have been released" (12) even if it resulted in the contemporary "mad dance of youth, intoxicated with the swell of its new freedom" (11), for "we have known the costs of repression" (330) and "the general chaos of our era" bespeaks "the decline of an old morality and an old marriage order" (305). With Trotsky he believed that "the psycho-analytic theory of Freud . . . can be reconciled with materialism" ("Red Love" 183), but he also believed that "the psychoanalytic technique is individualistic, while the basic problem is social" (*Sex in Civilization* 282). In this regard he agreed with certain other Freudians of the time, for example Trigant Burrow, that "the neurotic mind . . . is fundamentally a reflection of maladjustment on the part of the group rather than on the part of the individual" (*The Passing of the Gods* 21). Citing the Electra complex as an example of the limitations of Freudian theory, he argued that it "may have deep meaning in certain patriarchal societies where the family is a close-knit unit, but it can have no meaning whatsoever in matriarchal societies where the position of the father is without real influence and power" (*The Passing of the Gods* 6).

Calverton's introductory essay in *The Making of Man* sets forth the evolutionary and anthropological principles that underlay his radical views on sex in civilization. He begins this piece by noting that "the growth of the science of anthropology is closely bound up with the development of the doctrine of evolution" (1), and he suggests his general agreement with Darwin's theory of evolution by asserting that "man is not as radically different from the animals as we have been all too prone to conclude. *Human tendencies not only go back far beyond the family; they extend to the simian horde*" (22). But he criticizes "the Darwinian theory of natural selection" for having "made survival synonymous with advance" and thereby proffering "the best justification of the *status quo* of nineteenth century Europe" (3–4). In this way he prepares to argue with Frederick Engels in *The Origin of the Family* (1884, trans. 1902) and, more important, with Robert Briffault in *The Mothers* (1927) that before the rise of the patriarchal family (and civilization's distorted emphasis on "wealth, and again wealth, and for the third time wealth . . . of the puny individual" [*Origin of the Family* 215], there was "the group marriage . . . in which whole groups of men and whole groups of women mutually belong to one another, leaving only small scope for jealousy" (42). Neither Engel nor Kropotkin, however, was the most authoritative theorist in the radical approach to sex and civilization as the Freudian era emerged. Calverton was entirely sympathetic with Kropotkin's beliefs that "unbridled individualism is a modern growth" and that social cooperation and mutual aid were to be promoted (*Mutual Aid* 88, xiii). But he knew that talk of the instinct of "human solidarity" was of limited value at a time when the sex problem was being analyzed in terms of Darwin's theory of sexual selection and Freud's study of the libido. Kropotkin had avoided discussing sexual selection and remarked that "it would be impossible to enter here into a discussion of the origin of the marriage restrictions" (88). For theoretical support on these crucial issues Calverton turned to Briffault, to whom he dedicated *The Making of Man*, calling him "one of the most amazing and original minds of our generation."[4]

Picking up Briffault's massive study today, it is easy to see how Calverton and others of his generation would have been overwhelmed; the three volumes of *The Mothers: A Study of the Origins of Sentiments and Institutions* contain approximately 2,500 pages, including a bibliography of nearly 200 pages and an index of 120 pages.[5] But it is not necessary to read all of this ponderous work in order to trace through the themes that Calverton found so compelling. Briffault begins with the theory that the "the human mind has a twofold origin": first, "from the evolution of organic life" (through "natural heredity"), and second, from a "development . . . under social conditions" that is not transmitted through "natural heredity" but mainly through language in "the social environment as a *traditional* inheritance" (1:1–3, emphasis mine). From this basis, then, he develops his main theme, that the "social characters of the human mind" derive from "the functions of the female" (her maternal instincts) and not the male, that this important development in social evolution predated "patriarchal societies," and that "no trace of patriarchal organisation is to be found in the animal world" (1:v). Thus, while relying heavily on Darwin's theory of common descent, he limits the role of "natural" or genetic heredity as that that was being emphasized by eugenicists like E. Grant Conklin (*Heredity and Environment in the Development of Man*) or Karl Pearson. Then, with support from Franz Boas and others, he argues that in primitive culture "a traditional heredity is superadded to natural heredity and its congenital instincts" (1:70). Denying the idea of hereditary genius, he asserts that even Darwin's "great achievement" reveals a greater "filiation" with "innumerable . . . spiritual ancestors" like Malthus, Lyell, and Lamarck than with Darwin's own "natural ascendants" (1:58).

This kind of foundation in evolutionary thought (as in Briffault's later book, *Rational Evolution (The Making of Humanity)* [1930]) was essential for progressive theories of social change. But Briffault's treatise on the mothers of the primitive human group (in group marriage and sexual communism) also rested on two essential elements of the sex problem—sexual jealousy and promiscuity—that were of special interest not only to anthropologists like Margaret Mead, but to many novelists of the 1920s and 1930s as well. Discussing polygamy and monogamy among animals (1:168), Briffault notes that in *The Descent of Man* Darwin argued "against primitive human promiscuity" partly on the basis of his "loose . . . wording and reasoning" (1:168) in reference to "monogamous habits among monkeys" (*The Mothers* 1:173). Refuting this view, Briffault cites a number of later studies (rather like the late-twentieth-century studies of bonobo chimpanzees) to claim that monkeys and, implicitly, "primitive" human beings are indeed promiscuous. Briffault was particularly unhappy with Darwin's theory that the dominant male in the human horde enforced his inherent sexual jealousy, thus preventing promiscuous intercourse (*The Descent of Man* 2:362). Both Briffault and Margaret Mead explicitly deny this aspect of the male's psychological nature. Referring to the "so-called sexual 'jealousy'" among such animals as male salmon or birds, Briffault argues that males do not battle, as Darwin thought, "for the possession of particular females, but for access to females in general" (*The Mothers* 1:181–82). The sexual impulse is best understood as hunger, he explains, and then goes on to discuss its cannibalistic nature as suggested in "the love-bite." Writing that "'love,' or sexual attraction, is originally and preëminently 'sadic,'" Briffault claims that it is more truthfully associated with "cruelty . . . and the spectacle of pain" than with "tender feelings." Thus he concludes that when "spent," the male will simply ignore the female, and her capacity for tenderness has nothing to do with her own sexual hunger but with her maternal functions. Even in cases of "murders through 'jealousy,'" he argues, the jealousy is probably only "a pretext for the outburst of the primary violence and homicidal tendency of 'love'" as sexual hunger (1:118–21).

In Briffault's view, then, the human female's sexual appetite is much greater than Darwin had generally allowed for, her "sexual instinct differ[ing] from that of the male chiefly through its periodicity" (3:253). Moreover, building on Darwin's theory that the human female lost her power of sexual selection when marriage originated in the capture of wives, he suggests that among primitive human beings, the female (like the peahen) still selects for beauty: primitive men exhibit a far greater "love adornment" than women (2:176–77). Yet at the same time he argues that "sexual selection and the discrimination of the qualities that govern it play scarcely any part in either the sexual relations of uncultured peoples or in their marriage associations," for this enables him to deny the nature of both male and female sexual jealousy and to link the development of sexual jealousy with the economic forces that gave rise to patriarchal monogamy (1:247).

As Calverton surveyed the sex problem, then, there was no more extensive or authoritative treatment of its evolutionary and anthropological aspects than Briffault's *The Mothers*. Nor was it difficult for him to find corroboration for this general approach to the nature of sex in the late 1920s, as with the contributors he included in *The Making of Man* such as Lewis Henry Morgan, Havelock Ellis, Freud, Edward Carpenter, Franz Boas, and Margaret Mead. In the piece by Margaret Mead, for example, we see that "romantic love as it occurs in our civilization, inextricably bound up with ideas of monogamy, exclusiveness, jealousy and undeviating fidelity[,] does not occur in Samoa" (599). Thus in his repeated remarks on the evils of monogamy as a patriarchal invention, Calverton emphasized that "the very nature of sex desire" will not tolerate "such enforced restriction," for "the craving for variation . . . has always been conspicuous in the sexual history of man" (*Bankruptcy of Marriage* 329). He believed that "we can intelligently consider the sexual character of the human species, female as well as male, only when we begin with the obvious fact that it is by nature promiscuous and becomes otherwise only as a result of social regulations" ("Are Women Monogamous?" in *Woman's Coming of Age* 479). And, realizing that some of the most compelling modern explorations of sex were being undertaken in fiction, by writers like James Joyce, Sherwood Anderson, and a number of writers from the Harlem Renaissance, Calverton attempted the same—first in *Three Strange Lovers* and then in *The Man Inside*.

"Mad with Beauty and Love"

In each of his three stories in *Three Strange Lovers* Calverton explored an aspect of what he took to be the madness of romantic love. In the first story, "The Strange Lover," he overturned the naive belief that sexual love between individuals can endure the stress of proximity and familiarity. In the second story, "The Return," he dramatized the male's sexual jealousy as a romantic perversion. And in "Thy Will Be Done," he presented the religious fear of female promiscuity in terms of repression and sublimation. As Leonard Wilcox justly concludes, this volume as a whole is Calverton's "most successful work of fiction" (91). And of these stories, "The Strange Lover" is Calverton's most impressive effort to present his own theory of red love within the context of other more prominent theories of sex during the 1920s. In the manner of Poe's deranged narrators in tales like "The Tell-Tale Heart," the unnamed narrator of "The Strange Lover" tells his story from a prison; "Poe is asleep with his shadow," he remarks in one of his "nonsensical ravings" (50). The self-confessed murderer of his fourth and last lover, he addresses her (Tess) through-out the story without remorse; indeed, he worships her, for by killing her he had preserved "a sacred, unfading beauty" (115). He concludes a brief prologue to the story by asking why people "take death so seriously and so tragically, when it led to a deathless beauty?" (20).

Building his story on this kind of conflict between love and death, Calverton develops the idea that Freud presented the same year in *Civilization and Its Discontents*. "The struggle between Eros and Death . . . is what all life essentially consists of" (69), according to Freud, "the instinct for destruction . . . provid[ing] the ego with the satisfaction of its vital needs and with control over nature" (68). Whether Calverton takes this idea from Freud is unclear and irrelevant, but there is no question that he does intend in this story to develop his own theme on the psychology of sex by playing it off the other contending psychological theories in the 1920s of Freud, Jung, Adler, and Havelock Ellis. The narrator is analyzed by a number of psychiatrists in the prison, but they knew that he "too had studied psychiatry" and that he "could pierce their pretensions without the least difficulty" (23). There is no question that the narrator is "mad," of course, but Calverton will demonstrate that the narrator's love-madness is based on a profound psychological reality that the psychiatrists are afraid to acknowledge. The psychiatrists demand to know "what kind of love is that?" that would cause the narrator to murder his lover, but the narrator meets them with the charge that they "are only using words to conceal subtlety and drive away [their] doubt" (28–29). His motive in the murder was to preserve the fleeting beauty in his love for Tess, because in a series of previous rela-tionships he had come to realize that "proximity kills passion. Passion dies with easiness of access. Passion cannot survive constant familiarity, and the inquisito-rial intimacies of a possessive life. . . . And love without passion . . . is not love at all" (81). Thus, as Freud might have explained, the narrator's "instinct of destruction . . . provide[s his] ego with the satisfaction of its vital needs and with control over na-ture" (*Civilization and Its Discontents* 68).

But the board of psychiatrists examining the narrator are not open to this view of psychology. Instead, in their interviews with the narrator, the psychiatrists note that he has a "fixation," giving the narrator an opportunity to instruct them on "all of the psychiatric aspects of a fixation" (62). And, with more specific reference to the various schools of psychiatry at the time, Calverton gives us their various diag-noses, as the narrator discovers them in the notations on their charts:

> The gland specialist was confident that my disorder was glandular and rec-ommended gonadic examination and treatment; the Fruedian was convinced that my ailment was a psychosis derived from the repressive influence of my mother, which manifested itself in the form of an Œdipus-complex; another

[apparently the Jungian] traced my difficulty to a frustration complex, of endopsychic character and intrauterine origin; another [apparently the Adlerian] felt that all that I had done was to have found an obvious way of compensating for my inferiority as a writer. (74)[6]

Of these various diagnoses, of course the oedipal theory enjoyed the greatest currency during these years, and for this reason Calverton deals with it at some length in order to set it aside as a superficial explanation of the narrator's plight. The narrator explains that as a boy he wasn't afraid of his dreams: "I remember loving my mother so much that the idea of killing my father consumed my dream-world for over a year." He recalls his mother's embarrassment and terror when he told her the details of his dream; but he "saw nothing wrong in it. A dream was a dream, and then too, my father had mistreated my mother, and I hated him for that.... I believe I could have killed him" (32). And he tells us later that after World War I he "had gotten over [his] childish affection for [his] mother, gotten over the restraints and repressions of [his] early environment" (48). And on another psychological theme, though with much less emphasis, the narrator tells of his interest in Schopenhauer on the problems of old age and how he had once given "a lecture on this topic . . . before a psychology class." They "were stunned by [his] logic" in explaining (with a nod to Dreiser, one of Calverton's favorite novelists) "that the katabolic processes after fifty had already begun to exceed the anabolic, that changes in tissue already ran to decay," and so forth (33). In order to avoid this kind of decay, he explains, he would willingly kill *himself* at sixty, just as he "had done what [he] did to Tess" (34).

The narrator's first lover, Nina, had appealed to him instantly and powerfully because of her dark "strangeness": "Dark-faced, with eyes a vivid, immutable ebony, and hair a soft, silken black, oriental in abundance, she fell upon my vision like something I had seen in a dream. We loved like pagans at first," he recalls. It was "the wonderful cleansing force of love . . . the whirl of ecstasy" (52–53). But when he saw her again, after the war, "the world [had] changed—or was it I that changed?" and on this point, as well, Calverton acknowledges but sets aside another modernist theory about the "death of love"—that the crucial blow was World War I. Although she had the same hair and eyes after the war, "something had passed out of her"; her "voice," especially, "seemed suddenly to have grown old"; she had lost "that intimate beauty which enchanted [him]"; "[his] kisses were anemic, and [his] fingers no longer tingled as [he] caressed her" (57–59). In short, without realizing that he has experienced what Calverton would describe as the normal sexual impulse with its biological demand for variation, the narrator concludes that he had "seen love turn into a living corpse": "beauty, intensity, eagerness, ecstasy, the spontaneity of emotion" had died (61). Only once, when he tries to explain himself to

Tess (whom he has already murdered), does he seem to grasp the biological significance of his motives. "Beauty lives in moments and not in eternities," he tells her, "and yet we, Tess, you and I, seek its survival" (46–47).

The narrator is clearly mad, but according to Calverton's diagnosis only because his natural urge for sexual variety is in conflict with both romantic love's demand for constancy and with the patriarchal enforcement of monogamous marriage. Whereas the story's psychiatrists "conceal" this sexual reality from themselves by means of their own favorite theories, the narrator seeks "the satisfaction of [his] vital needs." Moreover (echoing Freud's idea in *Civilization and Its Discontents*), the narrator seeks "control over nature" in humanity's time-honored way: religion. As Calverton explained in *The Passing of the Gods*, in religion "the ego" can find what it craves, "an assurance of 'everlasting life' as an escape from" the ravages of time (295); similarly, the narrator kills Tess in order to keep her "everlastingly beautiful," a constant object of his "adoration" and "worship" (107–10).

Calverton's second story, "Thy Will Be Done," is devoted entirely to bringing out the conflict between religion and the sexual impulse. The main character, the priest Father Angelo, is a study in sexual repression and sublimation in the tradition of such analyses in American fiction from William Dean Howells's Don Ippolito in *A Foregone Conclusion* (1874) to Harold Frederic's Theron Ware, or Sherwood Anderson's grotesque religious figures in *Winesburg, Ohio*.[7] Angelo wants to "become a reincarnation of Tertullian" in order to sound the early Christian warning that woman is "The Devil's Gateway!" (213).[8] He too is driven to murder a woman, Miriam, whom he has come to know through her lengthy confessions regarding her sexual appetite. During her confession in the climactic scene, both had become so sexually aroused that she bit his ear ("consuming him" in an expression of the primitive cannibalism that Briffault and countless others had theorized), and he thrust "his hand . . . deep into her body": then "Tertullian returned," and Angelo shoots Miriam. He had feared that the revolver would "explode or discharge," and in "his passion and fury" it had assumed "an unnatural hardness" (239–41). Poor Angelo had tried his best to save her soul from sex and socialism (her husband, Joe, and her lover, Jack, are unenlightened Marxists, and Angelo had warned her that "socialism is a sin" [177]), but she had driven him to this in a sequence of confessions about her sexual aversion to her husband and her rampantly consummated sexual desire for Jack. An embodiment of Ellis's idea in *The Dance of Life*, that humanity is profoundly involved in "the erotic dance of the animal world" (48), she confesses that sexual intercourse with Jack makes her a "new person, and I live in a world of wonder. Everything becomes bright and dancy, and my heart beats to a strange music within me" (195). Worse, she confesses that she soon developed a sexual aversion for Jack, too: the thrill was gone; his presence sickened her; she "was finished with him" (197). Yet when Angelo realizes that she had confessed "hundreds of such sins" and that "her persistent passion" was for "new" and "strange" men" (198), he finds in their subsequent sessions that his own "words [were] penetrating into her very flesh" (201).

Part of the way through "Thy Will Be Done" father Angelo senses that in "the concealed recesses of his soul" he had become jealous of Miriam's "hundreds of men," and Calverton associates this part of his madness with the fact that Angelo regards socialism as a sin and with his ties to ancient Rome, where the patriarchal family got its foothold in Western civilization (210). And in his final story, "The Return," Calverton sets aside the problem of religious repression and focuses entirely on a strange lover who is mad with sexual jealousy. At his death Calverton left a detailed outline for what he thought would be the first scientific book on jealousy, wherein he would argue that it was neither instinctive nor essentially connected with sex.[9] This was an essential principle in his theory of red love. And in this story once again Calverton admits Freudian possibilities in his study of his unnamed main character. He suffers after the death of his mother and has frequent bouts of hysteria, but his hysteria is much less an expression of Freudian sexual repression than of his anxiety over losing his lover to her own husband or to any of her many other lovers. Illustrating his theory that the normal male has no inherent sexual jealousy and that jealousy is only a social ill that followed the origin of the patriarchal family and economic individualism, Calverton writes that this character "wanted [his lover] madly" and knew "that he must have her all to himself" (150). He would "make her bend to his will . . . succumb to his strength" and whip her "into submission by his own mastery" (151–52). In the end the woman's wealthy husband claims possession of her and the hero is left to fantasize her return, when he might hear her foot touch again "the little Roman step leading into his room"—the threshold, according to the anthropologists, over which the early patriarchal groom carried his bride in ritual proclamation that she belonged to him alone (155).

The Man Inside

Set in the African jungle in the mid 1930s, *The Man Inside* follows the career of a scientific social reformer named Joli Cœur, who conducts hypnotic experiments on animals and the Xulu people in search of techniques for changing "the man inside"— that is, the human nature that he theorizes had been shaped over the ages by particular environmental conditions. The best one can say of Calverton's fantastic quest is that it was a serious effort (certainly not the only one in the 1930s) to contend with the problems of Western civilization that had arisen along with the careers of Hitler and Mussolini during the few years since he had published *Three Strange Lovers*. With the rise of Hitler and the intellectual barbarism that followed, the narrator of *The Man Inside* had become increasingly disillusioned with the future of Western civilization and so traveled to Africa in search of Joli Cœur and a "key to life" that no science, anthropology or any other, had yet provided for effecting human progress. The adventure he recounts supplies what was required, a theory of evolution, human nature, and the sexual impulse like that which justified Calverton's belief (expressed here through the character Joli Cœur) that "what they are doing in Soviet Russia is a close approximation" to what should be "done all over the world" (181).

Joli Cœur's theory of evolution acknowledges that "men are far more like animals than most of us are willing to admit" (93) but denies that nature is necessarily "red in tooth and claw" (96). Moreover, holding that environment is more important than heredity, that human nature is malleable, and that present human nature was created by environmental conditions over great spans of time, he realizes that what social reformers really need is a "technique that can effect change within [that is, human nature or "the man inside"] with electrical rapidity" (96). Based on his belief that the most important environmental force is the "psychological environment," he concludes that the key to rapid social change is through "suggestion" (208). "We must discard the false hypothesis ["of most radical arguments"] that the mind is a thinking mechanism," for in truth "the mind is a suggestible and not a logical organ" (112).

Thus, in his experiments on controlling the minds of animals and the Xulu people, Joli Cœur employs the methods of the Hitlers and Mussolinis, but for constructing a new social order along the lines envisioned by the "other social and revolutionary thinkers" whose works fill his library, for example, Marx, Lenin, Lester Ward, Thorstein Veblen, and Kropotkin (113–14). Clearly, Calverton understands that his program for mind control through suggestion is susceptible to abuse by dictators like Hitler or Stalin, and if Joli Coeur's African exploits suggest Joseph Conrad's Kurtz, the irony is not "unintended," as Leonard Wilcox concludes (205). Writing in an entirely different milieu of evolutionary theory and historical events from that which gave rise to "The Heart of Darkness" in 1902, Calverton had enlisted in "the battle of the world [that] is not a battle over ideas, but a battle over suggestion" (*Man Inside* 112). Naive, overheated, and appalling as it will certainly strike readers of today, his program was founded on his belief that neither the animal nor the human heart is *by nature* dark. Joli Cœur "proves" this point with experiments showing that when animals are well fed the "predatory propensities" (110) disappear and, similarly, that when the Xulu "children and adults were well-fed, they tended without exception to be amicable and generous by nature" (108). Then, by hypnotic suggestion, he can cause even the fiercest animals to become "docile, amicable, and cooperative, thereby demonstrating Kropotkin's theory that mutual aid is a more fundamental force in evolution than natural selection: his caged animals "tugged co-operatively at the pillars" of their cage until the pillars collapsed (129–30).

But if the predatory instincts involve the hunger of the stomach (as Calverton addresses that issue in the chapter, "The Stomach Speaks"), they also involve sexual hunger, and this is apparently Calverton's reason for setting the novel in Africa. As the narrator remarks at first (in the chapter, "Why I Fled to the Jungle"), "in the jungle . . . a man's real nature comes out" and he loses the inhibitions of civilized life (1–2). Consequently, he tells us, he likes the Xulus because they "have none of the hypocrisy and dishonesty" that civilization brings and because they exhibit "more actual love for one another" than do civilized people (10). Clearly, then, the Xulus' function in the novel is to verify the idea about primitive sexuality that was contested among the writers of the Harlem Renaissance and that Briffault propounded in *The Mothers*. Joli Cœur is especially interested in this aspect of their human nature, for he knows that "love . . . has played a larger part [than any other emotion] in the history of Western civilization" (227). Thus we see that "without exception" these uninhibited Xulus "had been having normal sex relations with one another ever since puberty, some pairing off into monogamous couples, others carrying on brief unions which exhausted themselves in quick spasmodic passions, and still others living as promiscuously as the animals in the jungle" (226).

As there are no "strange" or neurotic lovers among the Xulu (as in *Three Strange Lovers*), Joli Cœur finds perfect conditions for proving through his suggestive powers that romantic love in the Western tradition is an aspect of the madness that began with "the illusion of individuality" and solidified in our culture's patriarchal monogamy (182). He suggests to two young Xulus that they are in love, and when they go into the village, the villagers see their obsession with each other as "crazy" (235). From this Calverton concludes that Western love originated as a "cultural compulsion," like Joli Cœur's power of suggestion, and that it can be ameliorated by social policies such as those in Russia, where a different form of cultural compulsion might work with a rapidity similar to Joli Cœur's suggestions to the Xulu man and woman first that they were and then that they were not any longer in love.[10] The biological reality underlying the sexual impulse in the first place, both for the Xulu and the civilized whites (according to Joli Cœur's pamphlet, "The Basis of the Love Emotion") is that, though sexually differentiated, every individual is both male and female, and the "love compulsion" is the "all-too-human cry for [the] restoration of one-ness" or "totality" (228). The spasm of sexual passion allows one to "escape . . . from the lostness of living, the futility of life" and the awareness of death (244). Thus the love compulsion (among the primitives, presumably, this would be simply the "sex" compulsion) occurs when one human being has the power to "*suggest* the possibility" of achieving this escape through sexual intercourse with another, whether that person "be man or woman, homosexual or heterosexual" (244). Moreover, as Joli Cœur articulates Calverton's larger theory of social reform,

> the endurance of a love depends upon the suggestive power people can exercise over each other, just as the endurance of a government depends upon the

socially suggestive power the rulers can exercise over the populace. When that suggestive power disappears, terrorism ensues in physical or psychological form. The husband beats the wife, or the wife, by psychological instead of physical strategy, intimidates the husband, just as a government in a similar state throttles its opponents and intimidates the public into silence. (245)

Readers who have attended to the foregoing account of Calverton's theory of evolution and the possibilities for social reform might be inclined to agree with F. Scott Fitzgerald's response to the novel. Writing to Calverton that the book *"filled me with strange emotions"* that recalled "a conversation we had late one night in which you told me something about your relations with your wife," Fitzgerald offered his criticism, as a friend, that "the more nebulous your thought has been, the more inclined you are to throw a cloud around it . . . and . . . to try to resolve that cloud into a simple declarative fact expressed as an opinion or an apposition, with the naivete of a child pricking a balloon."[11] This is a fair assessment of the novel whose aesthetic qualities are less impressive even than its intellectual clarity. Despite Calverton's passionate beliefs about human nature and primitive communism, none of his characters comes to life. One can ascribe much of this failure to Calverton's limited powers as a novelist, but the novel's failure seems due even more to certain elements in its theory of nature, human nature, and the sexual impulse that defy the reader's (and certainly a novelist's like F. Scott Fitzgerald's) own experience of the natural world—beginning with the idea that nature is not necessarily red in tooth and claw.

More closely related to the exploration of the sex problem in both psychology and fiction during the 1920s and 1930s, it is notable that Calverton attempted here to erase the libido in favor of his somewhat Freudian interest in the struggle between love and death, and more important, in his commitment to behaviorist psychology rather than Freudian psychology as an effective way of dealing with social ills like those represented in the careers of Hitler, Mussolini, and Stalin. As he proclaimed in "Sex and Social Struggle," "Psychoanalysis as an individual therapeutic is significant, but as a social philosophy it is without profound perspective" (*Sex in Civilization* 282). And as he wrote several years earlier, in *The Newer Spirit*, the kind of psychology that most impressed him as being "founded on a basis as objective as that of physical science, is commonly known as behaviorism" (254). Finally, he could not breathe life into narrative accounts that deny the elements of sexual selection from which novelists since *The Descent of Man* had constructed the most compelling stories of courtship and marriage. Joli Cœur claims that his experiments show that human beings are not very selective in their choice of mates: "any man or any woman can fall in love with practically any one, or ones, of a vast multitude of possible persons" (231). Thus, like the character Miriam ("Thy Will Be Done"), who "had no sense of selection" (183), the character Margaret in *The Man Inside* states repeatedly as a refrain that in a number of her relationships she "had no choice in the matter" (152–53). Ultimately in his highly idealized jungle world, "the sexual factor in the physical sense plays little part in [the Xulus'] activities" because they regard it without "mystery," as "most people do food" (234).

In his attempt to verify this theory of red love, then, Calverton simply erases the key elements of the sexual struggle in Darwinian courtship—the lure of attraction in sexual beauty, and combative jealousy among competing males. Still, to give him his due, his purpose in these narratives of the sex problem was to further what he well knew was "still a hazy vision" of "the ideal conditions of a coming society." Attempting to get beyond the Jazz Age's Freudian fascination with the uninhibited libido, he wrote that, "while in the past we have known the costs of repression, it is the future which will introduce to us the costs of freedom." When he gave us these strange stories of sex in civilization, he acted on his belief that "in order to progress we must hazard new seas" (*Bankruptcy of Marriage* 330–31).

Notes

1. Unfortunately this excellent volume is the only substantial study of Calverton. Born George Goetz in 1900, Calverton assumed the name V. F. Calverton when he founded the *Modern Quarterly*, partly, as Wilcox explains, in accord with other radicals during the 1920s, who took on pseudonyms in order "to protect themselves from the wholesale arrests and deportations conducted by the red-baiting Attorney General [A. Mitchell] Palmer" (30–31).

2. Calverton is quoting the feminist Alexandra Kollontai. The substance of this piece in the *Modern Quarterly*, as well as that of his earlier "debate" with Upton Sinclair over the question, "Is Monogamy Desirable" (*Modern Quarterly* 4 [Jan.–Apr. 1927]), is incorporated in Calverton's *The Bankruptcy of Marriage* (1928).

3. For another more well-known discussion of science and Marxism from these years by one of Calverton's associates, see Max Eastman, *Marxism, Is It Science*, in which discussions of Darwin, Freud, Bergson, and the Marxist theory of sex equality, for example, are indexed.

4. Calverton included selections by Briffault in each of his three collections, *The Making of Man* ("Group-Marriage and Sexual Communism," "The Origin of Love," and "Evolution of Human Species"), *Sex in Civilization* ("Sex in Religion"), and *Woman's Coming of Age* ("The Evolution of Woman"), but as Wilcox explains, by 1933 the two fell out as a result of Calverton's stance as an independent Marxist (154).

5. Readers who want to sample Briffault's work in a tidier form might want to consult his later edition in one volume, *The Mothers: The Matriarchal Theory of Social Origins* (1931), but as he notes in the preface to this later work, "for a critical survey of the evidence and for bibliographical references," one must "refer to the larger work."

6. Compare this passage with a similar one in Calverton's and Schmalhausen's preface to *Sex in Civilization*: "The writings of Freud, Adler, Jung, Stekel, Jones, Maeder, Ferenczi and

many others have certainly purported to be more than studies in the specificities of knowledge and reaction. Freud in particular has endeavored to include the universe in his concept of sex; Jung has striven to embrace the most bewildering and enigmatic contradictions of the entire scope of the human mind in his theory of the *endopsychic*, and the tendency to types; Adler has advanced an idea, in his theory of the inferiority complex and the neurotic constitution, that surely strives to leave little unexplained in the mental world," and so forth (8).

7. For discussions of Howells and Frederic in this regard, see my *The Descent of Love* (68, 238–51). Calverton's frequent references to Angelo's grotesque repression clearly reflect the admiration for Anderson that he expressed at length in his chapter, "Sherwood Anderson: A Study in Sociological Criticism," in *The Newer Spirit*.

8. As Calverton wrote in *The Bankruptcy of Marriage*, "Tertullian maintained that the disappearance of man was better than his propagation by sexual intercourse" (324); this point was made frequently in discussions of the sex problem, as by Havelock Ellis, for example, in "Woman's Sexual Nature" (Calverton and Schmalhausen, *Woman's Coming of Age*, 236).

9. The outline for this book is in box 24 of the V. F. Calverton Collection in the Manuscripts and Archives Division of the New York Public Library.

10. For fuller expositions of Calverton's "theory of cultural compulsives" see his introduction ("Modern Anthropology and the Theory of Cultural Compulsives") in *The Making of Man* and his later introduction to *The Passing of the Gods*. In the latter, for example, he explains how "the mind has been trapped by the cultural compulsives" at various moments in history when certain "class interests" have been represented "in psychological form" (22, 14).

11. Letter of November 4, 1936, in Bruccoli, *Correspondence of F. Scott Fitzgerald*, 460–61. Earlier, in 1934, Fitzgerald had thanked Calverton for having arranged for a review of Fitzgerald's own psychological novel, *Tender Is the Night* in the *Modern Monthly* (the later name of *Modern Quarterly*). Fitzgerald also remarked on Calverton's *The Passing of the Gods*, writing that he objected to "the high overtone of economics" but calling him "a modern Lecky" for "*the synthesis of anthropology, sociology and philosophy*" (*Correspondence* 387).

11 "To Be Alive"

John Steinbeck's The Log from the Sea of Cortez
and The Wayward Bus

Largely because of John Steinbeck's long friendship and collaboration with the marine biologist Edward Ricketts, his interest in biology has received more critical attention than that of any other writer discussed in this book. But it was not until 1995 that one of Steinbeck's interpreters began to bring out the essentially Darwinian foundations of his work.[1] This first study served to remind readers of the extent to which Steinbeck was attacked by critics like Edmund Wilson and Leslie Fiedler for having dealt too exclusively with "the processes of life itself . . . the predatory appetite and the competitive instinct that are necessary for the very survival of eating and breeding creatures," as Wilson put it (qtd. in Railsback 6). Many present-day readers of Steinbeck will undoubtedly share Wilson's distaste for the way Steinbeck handles these biological issues, but it is worth emphasizing not only that he was quite aware that his approach would offend many readers, but that the question he and Rickett's posed in *The Log from the Sea of Cortez* is no less troubling now than it was in 1941: "Why do we so dread to think of our species as a species?" (266). "If the reader of this book is 'genteel,'" they wrote, "then this is a very vulgar book, because the animals in a tide pool have two major preoccupations: first, survival, and second, reproduction"; moreover, they insisted, "we are no better than the animals" (70–71). It is also worth emphasizing that their theme—there is "only one commandment for living things: Survive!" (*The Log from the Sea of Cortez* 244)—reiterates Darwin's point in *The Origin of Species*: there is "one general law leading to the advancement of all organic beings,—namely, multiply, vary, let the strongest live and the weakest die" (*The Origin of Species* 208).

While one might think that Steinbeck would have been on safe ground reiterating Darwin's thesis some eighty years after the *Origin of Species*, it is well to remember that when he began to do so more explicitly in *The Sea of Cortez*, the "eclipse of Darwinism" was barely beginning to give way to the revival of Darwinism in what Julian Huxley referred to as "The Modern Synthesis" of Mendelian genetics and natural selection in 1942. Long before that, however, Steinbeck (like most of the writers discussed in this book) had felt the pull of evolutionary biology as a necessary foundation for his work as a writer, and he began his study of zoology at the Hopkins Marine Station in Pacific Grove, California, in the summer of 1923, seven years before he met Ricketts. In the early work for which he is most famous, including *The Grapes of Wrath* (1939), the evolutionary context of his narratives is clearly related to the evolutionary theorists to whom he was drawn and who had also influenced other writers of the 1930s, like V. F. Calverton. Indeed, Steinbeck's interest in Robert Briffault, for example, is well known, and his portrait of Ma Joad in *The Grapes of Wrath* has been described as "pure Briffault."[2] Despite their shared interest in Briffault's *The Making of Humanity* and *The Mothers*, however, Calverton's and Steinbeck's fiction bear little resemblance. Steinbeck had none of Calverton's enthusiasm for the socialist ideology of matriarchy and primitive communism, and as John McCormick concluded in his essay on Ma Joad as a figure from Briffault, "Steinbeck doubts that his America will adopt Ma Joad's matriarchal sense of community as a governing principle" (410).

Nevertheless, both before and after his association with Ricketts, Steinbeck definitely was fascinated with group behavior and mass movements in evolution, and this is reflected in his interest in William Emerson Ritter's studies of the superorganism or organismic wholeness; J. C. Smuts's *Holism and Evolution* (1926); John Elof Boodin's *Cosmic Evolution* (1925); and especially W. C. Allee's *Animal Aggregations: A Study in General Sociology* (1931).[3] Writing to his friend Carlton A. Sheffield in 1933, Steinbeck spoke of his reading such works in an effort to construct "the symbolism of [his] fiction" and remarked that "the fascinating thing to me is the way the group has a soul, a drive, an intent, an end, a method, a reaction and a set of tropisms which in no way resembles the same things possessed by the men who make up the group" (*Steinbeck: A Life in Letters* 76). From this work he produced his unpublished essay, "Argument of Phalanx," where he wrote that "Man is a unit of the greater beast, the phalanx" (Astro 65). In fact, he imagined that his own thinking on this subject had taken the same "direction" of thought that he had found in a number of other writers in fields ranging from physics to anthropology and that this sameness of direction "in itself would indicate the beginning of a new phalanx or group unit" (DeMott xxvii).[4] But even though he would always be interested in group behavior, whether among organisms in a tide pool or migrations of people such as the one in *The Grapes of Wrath*, he never subscribed to the leftist ideology that underlay either Briffault's anthropology or what Allee called his "sociology" (*Animal Aggregations* 3). That is, for all his (and Ricket's) enthusiasm for Allee's descriptions of animal aggregations, he did not share Allee's high regard for Kropotkin's demonstrations "of mutual aid among insects and the larger animals" (360) or for the idea, as Allee wrote in his later book, *Cooperation Among Animals* (1938 and 1951), that it would be "biologically sound" if, in the future, international organizations worked, for example, for the improvement of "living and working conditions . . . among the low income groups," as this "would be based on the great drive toward natural altruism that extends throughout the whole animal kingdom" (205–6).

Even in the powerful conclusion of *The Grapes of Wrath* (1939), when Rose of Sharon feeds the starving stranger from her breast, Steinbeck insisted that he was not reaching for the kind of altruistic symbolism that Allee might have imagined. When his editor, Pascal Covici, asked Steinbeck to do more with the ending, to build up to it as "an integral part of the saga," Steinbeck refused. Covici had felt that "your idea is to end the book on a great symbolic note, that life must go on and will go on with a greater love and sympathy and understanding for our fellowmen." But Steinbeck would not abide the idea that his saga should take any such transcendent direction: "there is no fruity climax," he insisted. He wanted a casual rather than a causal or teleological ending. "If there is a symbol, it is a survival symbol not a love symbol," he wrote, and "it must be an accident, it must be a stranger, and it must be quick" (*A Life in Letters* 177–78). And while some of his best critics still insist that he had written "a gospel of social action" (Astro 135), he maintained (in an interview after the novel appeared) that he had written an age-old story of "battles" for the means of survival. The migrant workers were simply struggling with obstacles placed in their way by other groups, the "financiers who by the principle of ownership withhold security from the mass of the people." While his sympathies are unquestionably with the migrant workers, he suggested that both groups are inevitably bound together in biological conflict. For "the human like any other life form will tolerate an unhealthful condition for some time, and then will either die or will overcome the condition either by mutation or by destroying the unhealthful condition. Since there seems little tendency for the human race to become extinct, and since one cannot through biological mutation overcome the necessity for eating, I judge that the final method will be the one chosen"—that is, to destroy "the unhealthful condition" or obstacle to the individual or group's survival rather than to cohere in communal mutual aid (Benson 386–87).

Still, whether he intended it or not, the biblical echoes in *The Grapes of Wrath* provided many contemporary and present-day readers grounds for believing that, at that high point in his career, his literary symbolism conveyed a kind of teleological vision of evolution, something that resembled J. C. Smuts's *Holism and Evolution*. It seems clear, however, that Steinbeck was more attuned to the developments in evolutionary theory during the late 1930s and 1940s than to the dying strains of anti-Darwinian theories, such as Smuts's, as the eclipse of Darwinism was drawing to a close. Whereas Steinbeck would go on, with Ricketts, to celebrate Darwin in *The Log from the Sea of Cortez*, the statesman and philosopher Smuts (1870–1950) was clinging to the idea that early twentieth-century interpretations of evolution such as his own would "release . . . the human spirit" from "the destructive effects of nineteenth-century science." Writing in 1932, Smuts imagined a "new synthesis" not of Mendelian genetics and natural selection, but of "science, art and philosophy," and on this basis he predicted that "a new religion will arise in which the human spirit can once more rest with firm assurance" ("Some Recent Scientific Advances in Their Bearing on Philosophy" 12). In any case, Steinbeck's critics have noted the change in his work after *The Grapes of Wrath*; DeMott, for example, writes that "during the next few years, Steinbeck moved increasingly away from a communal vision of life" (xxxi), and Astro, clearly disappointed that Steinbeck had abandoned what he took to be the "teleology" of *The Grapes of Wrath*, writes, "Steinbeck was becoming a novelist without a vision" (177).[5] There is certainly a change in Steinbeck's writing after *The Grapes of Wrath*, but it should be seen as partly reflecting the revival of Darwinism that began during those years. This chapter offers a brief examination of two of his most impressive works from the 1940s, *The Log from the Sea of Cortez* and *The Wayward Bus*. These works can be viewed in the context of the literary exploration of evolution and the sex problem. If Steinbeck lacked a vision in these works, it is only in the sense that he refused to offer any teleological or transcendent relief from our responsibility to think of our species as a species.

The Log from the Sea of Cortez: Ecology and Man's Place in Nature

The concept of "Man's Place in Nature" and the term "ecology" both came into being in the wake of the *Origin of Species*, the first in the title of T. H. Huxley's famous book of 1863 and the second in Ernst Haeckel's definition of ecology (in 1866) as "the study of all those complex interrelations referred to by Darwin as the conditions of the struggle for existence," particularly the organism's "friendly and inimical relations with those animals and plants with which it comes directly or indirectly into contact" (qtd. in Brewer 1). Especially after *The Descent of Man* in 1871, when Darwin placed the human being much more squarely within the community of common descent, there were excellent reasons to include the human being as one species of "the animals and plants" whose "friendly and inimical relations" are of ecological interest. But, partly because of the long eclipse of Darwinism, the human's place in nature as one of the ecological players was obscured, and in many ways continues to be obscured. In *The Sea of Cortez*, however, Ricketts and Steinbeck built on W. C. Allee's interest in ecology (in *Animal Aggregations*), as is clear, for example, in their definition of ecology as "the study of the mutual relations between an organism and its physical *and sociological* environment" (273, emphasis mine). But they went quite beyond Allee by, first, emphasizing "our species" in their observations and speculations, underscoring the idea of man's place in nature; second, resting their case for "non-teleological" evolutionary thought (or "'is' thinking") on the theory of "natural selection as Darwin seems to have understood it" (138); and third, giving far more weight to the role of sex in ecology than did Allee, who wrote that "all too frequently one gains the impression that sex forms the main, if not the only, physiological connecting link between the infrasocial and the social animals" (*Animal Aggregations* 4). Giving this kind of scope to "the questing mind" in their exploratory and often frankly speculative *Log*, they produced one of American literature's masterpieces on human nature and ecology (37).

Of the other writers discussed in this book only Jack London, in novels like *The Valley of the Moon* and in his own experimental farming, resembles Ricketts and Steinbeck in retaining a focus on the idea that they were themselves "truly and permanently a factor in the ecology of the region"—though London did not use the term "ecology" (*The Log from the Sea of Cortez* 3). And as London was concerned with the problem of feeding the world's exploding population during the years just before World War I, Ricketts and Steinbeck were concerned with what seemed the pressing issues of their own time, the "general collectivization of human society" and the war that was being waged in Europe but that had not yet spread to the Pacific as they conducted their expedition to the Sea of Cortez in March and April of 1940 (216). Thus they did not hesitate to consider our species as a species or, "when watching the little beasts . . . to trace human parallels." Though acknowledging that "the greatest danger to a speculative biologist is analogy," they insisted that "parallels . . . are downright valuable as regards humans." The greater pitfall, they suggest, is in projecting human conceptions in one's studies of "the industry of the bee, the economics of the ant [with an apparent glance toward Kropotkin's interest in these animals], the villainy of the snake" (96). Indeed, the main thrust of the *Log* is their reiterated faith in the idea that a deeper understanding of ourselves as a species might serve to alleviate our insecurity and enrich our humanity, for if the human species "is still in the state of becoming" it is limited mainly by its "uneasiness of thought and consciousness" (98).

Thus, in their determination to "go wide open" (3) and emulate Darwin in his desire "to see everything" (61), they frequently juxtapose observations of what Darwin called the general war in nature with observations of the human activities related to World War II. In one important example early in the voyage as they sail further into Southern California, they note that "the nature of the animal might parallel certain traits in ourselves" and then they observe a pod of porpoises apparently at play (39):

> The mist lifted from the water . . . the oily slickness remained, and it was like new snow for keeping the impressions of what had happened there. Near to us was the greasy mess where a school of sardines had been milling, and on it the feathers of gulls which had come to join the sardines and, having fed

hugely, had sat on the water and combed themselves in comfort. A Japanese liner passed us, slipping quickly through the smooth water, and for a long time we rocked in her wake. It was a long lazy day, and when the night came we passed the lights of Los Angeles with its many little dangling towns. The searchlights of the fleet at San Pedro combed the sea constantly, and one powerful glaring beam crept several miles and lay on us so brightly that it threw our shadows on the exhaust stack (40).

Describing their entry into the harbor at San Diego, they write, "All about us war bustled, although we had no war; steel and thunder, powder and men—the men preparing thoughtlessly, like dead men, to destroy things. The planes roared over in formation and the submarines were quiet and ominous." The conclusion to this meditation on the parallels between man and the animals is that "the military mind must limit its thinking to be able to perform its function at all." When they ask a gunnery officer, "Have you thought what happens in a little street when one of your shells explodes, of the families torn to pieces, a thousand generations influenced when you signaled *Fire?*" he replied, "Of course not. . . . Those shells travel so far that you couldn't possibly see where they land." Unlike the writers who are determined to be "wide open" so that their "world picture [might] be enlarged" (102), the "good gunnery officer" who proceeds by "not seeing" refuses to "take the responsibility for thinking" (40). Although Steinbeck later played his own role in the thoughtlessness of war by producing the war propaganda that was an embarrassment even to himself, in the *Log* he and Ricketts suggest again and again that there is a certain promise in our efforts to understand how "man is related to the whole thing," how it "is advisable to look from the tide pool to the stars and then back to the tide pool again" (218).

But even before this meditation on war (one of several in the book) they introduce the main theme about the other species and "our own species as a species": that, in view of the history of human warfare and in the absence of "some psychic mutation" to help us change, "so far the murder trait of our species is as regular and observable as our various sexual habits" (18). Not that they are as gloomy on this subject as this might sound. For as they hope to contribute to our better understanding of ourselves, their prevailing mood in the *Log* is a mixture of comic celebration and awe. At the outset they confess their determination to emulate "the true biologist [who] deals with life, with teeming boisterous life, and learns something from it, learns that the first rule of life is living" (28). They question "this myth of permanent objective reality" in scientific observation, acknowledge that their work will be "a factor in the ecology" of the regions they study, and announce their determination "to go doubly open so that at the end we could, if we wished, describe the sierra thus: 'D. XVII-15-IX; A. II-15-IX,' but also we could see the fish alive and swimming, feel it plunge against the lines, drag it threshing over the rail, and even finally eat it" (3). They delight in seeing a school of jumping tuna with the sun glittering on them, for in such places "the sea . . . swarms with life, and probably the ocean bed is equally rich. Microscopically, the water is crowded with plankton. This is the tuna water—life water. . . . Everything ate everything else with a furious exuberance" (48). And alongshore they see areas that "were ferocious with life. There was an exuberant fierceness in the littoral here, a vital competition for existence. Everything seemed speeded-up; starfish and urchins were more strongly attached than in other places" because "of the great surf which beats on this shore" and they sense that in such environments the animals "simply increase their toughness and fight back at the sea with a kind of joyful survival. This ferocious survival quotient excites us and makes us feel good" (60).

In keeping with the period's interest in the sex problem, they frequently observe and join in life's ferocious feeding on life, and they affirm the "bawdiness" of their observations of animals enacting the second of life's "two major preoccupations . . . reproduction. They reproduce all over the place" (70). They comment on how the people they see along the way "are preoccupied with getting enough food and enough children" (102); they joke about their own sexual insecurities and their interest in aphrodisiacs, concluding that "*bêche–de-mer* and the gonads of sea-urchins" are as "over-rated" as the oyster and that "sexual intercourse . . . is the only good one" (69); and they are certainly aware of the great "evil the white man had brought to [the] ancestors" of the Mexicans they encounter: "his breath was poisonous with the lung disease; to sleep with him was to poison the generations" (77). Moreover, they theorize that the human's desire has made him the most destructive of all the species, that "he is the only animal who lives outside of himself," projecting himself into "property, houses, money" to the extent that "when a man loses his possessions a very common result is sexual impotence" (90).

Still, these darker observations about the reproductive drive do not deter them from celebrating this human preoccupation as well. They steadfastly disavow any suggestion, such as John Elof Boodin's (one of their acknowledged authorities on evolution), that "sex love in a normal human being is not just an animal instinct of reproduction" but something that "involves idealization and socialization" and that can "be integrated into the higher pattern activity for abstract truth and beauty" or even, "in rare natures, become love of an impersonal presence in nature" (*Cosmic Evolution* 194). Rather, they record the remark of one of the crewmen that what he "had been considering love had turned out to be simple flatulence" (230). And they reiterate their bawdy point that, as "the first rule of life is living," the true biologist "sits at the feet of living things" and learns that, like the starfish, he must "proliferate in all directions" (28). He "will sing you a song as loud and off-key as will a blacksmith, for he knows that morals are too often diagnostic of prostatitis and stomach ulcers," and so he will "not confuse a low hormone productivity with moral ethics" (29). While this may well be an apology for their own appetites for life, they assert that biologists with physical or psychological ills often produce distorted descriptions of the animals they observe. Therefore, "the man best fitted to observe animals, to understand them emotionally as well as intellectually, would be a hungry and libidinous man" (231).

These biologists develop similar insights when, as anthropological ecologists, they describe the Mexican community of Loreto. There in the nearly fallen mission church they are drawn to the figure Our Lady of Loreto and sense that "this Lady, of plaster and wood and paint, is one of the strong ecological factors of the town of Loreto, and not to know her and her strength is to fail to know Loreto." Just as "a granite monolith" along a beach "would have an effect on animal distribution radiating in circles," she too influences the life patterns here. But they trace her peculiar power to her appeal to the psychological depths of our prehumanity, "the deep black water of the human spirit" (178). Developing one of the major themes in their study of our species as a species and drawing as much on their observations as marine biologists as on modern depth psychology, they recognize that while this "gaudy" Virgin is not in "*good taste,*" she is, like "Isis . . . Artemis, or Venus, or a girl behind a Woolworth counter . . . as eternal as our species" and will be for "as long as we survive." And her most compelling feature is the "look of terror in her face" (178). That is, they suggest that her appeal to "the deep black water of the human spirit" is an aspect of the "mass of sea-memory" that survives in the modern human, rather like the vestigial gill-slits in the human fetus—the unconscious depths of our prehumanity: "what monsters" lurk there, "what enemies, what fear of dark and pressure, and of prey!" (31). Reflected also in the "tidal influences active during the formative times of the early race history of organisms," an "imprint" of which is evident in the "menstrual cycle of women," these depths of the unconscious are alive with the essential evolutionary preoccupations that shape our present lives as they shaped our prehumanity (33). Similarly, speculating on the nature of the human unconscious, they note how certain sounds or smells are "symbols in the unconscious" that "trigger off a response, a little spasm of fear, or a quick lustfulness," and in accord with modern psychology's emphasis on sex, they surmise that there are not only "visual symbols, strong and virile in the unconscious," but those planted by the other senses, as in "the sensitive places . . . just below the ribs, thigh, and lip," the effective musk scent of perfume, or "the smell of a ready woman" (188–89).

"Hungry and libidinous" Steinbeck and Ricketts certainly are in *The Log from the Sea of Cortez*, and in ways calculated to offend the genteel reader who still might "dread to think of our species as a species" (266) or who cannot accept the idea that "life has one final end, to be alive" (244). But to embrace life on these hard terms also required a degree of courage, especially in the early 1940s, and yet they celebrated it with a gentle reverence, as when they entered the church in Loreto or wrote at the end, "our fingers turned over the stones and we saw life that was like our life" (272).

Sweetheart's "Rear End" and the Marriage Problem in *The Wayward Bus*

The Wayward Bus (1947) is a study of the sexual force in the lives of its several characters, each of whom is a kind of case history of various aspects of the sex problem as Steinbeck wanted to present it during those years. Indeed, its major flaw is reflected in the remark by one of its character's (a young college-educated woman named Mildred) that she "knows thousands of case histories" (268). Steinbeck's point about this is that, despite her studies, Mildred still cannot get over the sexual inhibitions that leave her unable to "make the advances" (268), but some readers will justly feel that one's sense of these case histories as case histories disrupts the narrative spell. Steinbeck's narrative technique is to throw his several characters together on a bus named Sweetheart and then to follow them as the central character, Juan Chicoy, drives them through the rural California landscape. Juan is "a fine, steady man," Steinbeck tells us at once, adding repeatedly that "there aren't very many of them in the world" (6). Regarding Juan, Steinbeck's most recent biographer reviews the unfortunate way critics have identified him as Jesus Christ in a long series of mistaken interpretations of the novel as a journey toward redemption. His initials are "J. C.," after all, and the bus is headed toward the town of San Juan de la Cruz. Because of the history of such readings (rather like those that view *The Grapes of Wrath* as a "gospel of social action"), Jay Parini concludes, "*The Wayward Bus* is a woefully misunderstood and neglected novel" (374). This suggestion that there might be a well-deserved revival of interest in the novel was followed a year later when Brian Railsback argued that *The Wayward Bus* contains Steinbeck's fullest "expression of the sexual human" and that it is based on Darwin's theory of sexual selection (88).

The Wayward Bus certainly does rest on Darwin's theory that natural selection and sexual selection are the essential evolutionary mechanisms or "preoccupations," as Steinbeck and Ricketts had driven that point home in *The Log from the Sea of Cortez*. But in *The Wayward Bus* Steinbeck was determined to play off traditional literary forms that the collaborative *Log* had abandoned in favor of the exploratory voyage in natural history. His signals to the literary community are clear in his epigraph from *Everyman* and in the title he originally had in mind, "Whan That Aprille," the first words in Chaucer's General Prologue to *The Canterbury Tales*. With that title he could introduce his cast of characters as a collection of modern pilgrims. More important, his literary allusion would recall both the medieval masterpiece and the reflection on it in T. S. Eliot's famous opening lines to *The Waste Land*, "April is the cruellest month, breeding / Lilacs out of the dead land, mixing / Memory and desire, stirring / Dull roots with spring rain."[6] Whereas, in Chaucer's unified worldview, the April rains produced both organic and spiritual regeneration, the renewed flow of juices in the awakening plants as well as the profane and sacred love in his pilgrims' hearts; in Eliot's *The Waste Land* April is cruel because love and the spiritual promise lie disconnected and dead in the war-torn modern world. Acknowledging these literary landmarks, Steinbeck sets his novel in "the deep spring when the grass was green on fields and foothills, when the lupines and poppies made a splendid blue and gold earth, [and] when the great trees awakened in yellow-green young leaves" with such beauty that it "caught you in the throat . . . and made a pain of pleasure in the pit of your stomach . . . set you breathing nervously, set you panting almost sexually." In short, the "quickening earth [was] frantic with reproduction" (12–13).

Steinbeck's world is resoundingly not a wasteland dominated by impotent characters like Eliot's Prufrock. Although one of his case studies here does seem a clear reference to Prufrock and *The Waste Land*, he dwells on the virile Juan. In contrast with Juan, the businessman Mr. Elliot Pritchard (Steinbeck tended to misspell Eliot's name)[7] displays his biological weakness when "a little shudder of uncertainty came over him" in this (for him) new environment (39); a perfect conformist, he felt that "a man who varied was not a sound man" (41), and we learn that after his only visit to a "parlor house" at the age of twenty "he had had a withering sense of desecration and sorrow" (42). However, if Steinbeck repudiates Eliot's vision of a wasteland, he certainly does tease us with a kind of Chaucerian pilgrimage. Juan Chicoy ends in taking these pilgrims to within sight of San Juan de la Cruz, whose lights they see "winking with distance, lost and lonely in the night, remote and cold and winking, strung on chains" (312). But in this narrative that is redolent with references to sex (as when the landscape "set you panting almost sexually" [13] or when Mildred looks at Juan and "itched with a pure sexual longing" [86]), Steinbeck's underscored "winking" is clear enough, as is his description of Sweetheart. Her front bumper bears "the inscription, still barely readable, 'El Gran Poder de Jesus,' 'the great power of Jesus,'" but both the front and read bumpers bear the "boldly lettered" word Sweetheart (21). Clearly this will be a story of the sexual drive rather than sacred or even sexual love, and the first obstruction to be overcome is that Sweetheart is broken down. She sits in Juan's garage ignominiously "immobilized, her rear wheels off, her end sticking up in the air" (21). Juan, however, is "a magnificent mechanic," and he soon has Sweetheart's rear end in good repair so that the pilgrimage can begin (7).

Each of the characters exhibits his or her own particular difficulty with the sex problem, but by the end of the novel things are distinctly better for several of them. And, although forced to detour when the spring rains wash out a bridge and temporarily delayed when she gets stuck in the mud, Sweetheart drives on. As these pilgrims are part of the "earth, frantic with production" (32), Steinbeck moves them into the evolutionary future, but only as survivors and not as representatives of any kind of progress or phalanx. Instead, reiterating his underlying point that in the frantic spring, "Everybody's nervous" (278), he focuses his interest in all this nervousness on the marriage problem. In effect he poses a post-Darwinian version of the questions that had amused Chaucer in his well-known marriage group of tales (the most famous of which is the Wife of Bath's): how can these representatives of our troubled species endure in a civilized state? In reference to his main character, Juan, Steinbeck's interest in the marriage problem is evident in his repeated image of Juan's wedding ring, which he wears on a ring finger that has been amputated at the first joint. Near the end of the novel, after he and the young woman Mildred Pritchard have engaged in sexual intercourse in an abandoned barn, she "took his hand and rubbed her finger over the smooth skin of the amputation," and he responded, "Don't do that. . . . It makes me nervous" (290). There is much more to say about Steinbeck's view of Juan and marriage, but first it will help to take brief note of the main varieties of troubled sexuality that Steinbeck gives us in these case studies.

Among the women in *The Wayward Bus*, two are unhappily married and three are single and regard their possible future marriages in a variety of ways. Alice Chicoy is "insanely in love with [Juan] and a little afraid of him too, because he was a man" (6), and, largely because of "the black fear that was always on the edge of her mind" that he might leave her, she is often at "a point where she had either to go on into a crazy, hysterical rage that tore the living daylights out of herself" or find temporary relief in an alcoholic binge (31). Steinbeck sympathizes with her anxiety as a "wide-hipped and sag-chested" (5) woman who knows she is "an old bag" whom "nobody wants" (177), with her unfortunate first sexual encounter with a man who hurt and abandoned her, and with her vital capacity, despite these circumstances, to fantasize an encounter with a sexy driver "for the Red Arrow Line" (175). On the other hand, Steinbeck expresses only very limited sympathy for Bernice Pritchard because she "was handicapped by what is known as a nun's hood, which prevented her experiencing any sexual elation from her marriage," a physical disorder with which he associates her headaches, frigidity, repression, and failure as a mother to her daughter Mildred (63). She takes refuge in the pretense of her perfect marriage and her saintliness, but Steinbeck depicts the sickness of this marriage in her hygienic habit of washing "her combs and brushes in ammonia water," a process that also served to clean her engagement and wedding rings and made the "little diamonds shine brightly" (62). She has kept the marriage intact by having strangled her husband's libido, but when the bus breaks down and they take shelter in a little cave, he rapes her and leaves her in a temporary state of neurotic "horror," biting and scratching herself until "the blood flowed down" her waist and into the dirt "on the cave floor" (288).

Of the three single women, one, Norma, who works in the Chicoys' café, is the victim of American popular culture emanating from Hollywood. She "remained faithful" to a "colored picture of Mr. [Clark] Gable in a flying suit with two belts of fifty-caliber ammunition on his shoulders," and at night she took out her secret treasures of "a gold-filled wedding ring and a gigantic Brazilian-type diamond ring," putting herself to sleep by "twisting them on the third finger of her left hand" (10–11). Steinbeck shows her doing beauty exercises "recommended by a picture star," a "grotesque dance" that reveals the depths of her psychic disorder: "Norma was even more submerged that an iceberg" (49–50). While Steinbeck is sympathetic with her plight, as well, he leaves her clinging to a new friend, the single woman Camille Oaks, hoping to share an apartment with her in Hollywood and wistfully murmuring to herself, "Star light, star bright," may I "get the wish I wish tonight" (312). Camille Oaks is a far stronger and more promising character, embodying much of the natural vitality suggested in her name. But if Steinbeck suggests a comparison between Camille and the defining feature in the landscape for miles around the Chicoys' café and garage—"the great white oaks . . . tall and graceful"—he also suggests that even a magnificent oak can be uprooted by the torrential rains, as is the case with "a great old live oak tree [that] came rolling heavily down the stream" to smash into the bridge (7, 184). Thus Camille is vulnerable to three particular aspects in her sexual makeup. First, she bears the scars of a traumatic birth, the "deep forceps marks along her jaws" (114). More important, like some of Steinbeck's women in *Cannery Row*, both her work as a stripper and a sad worldly wisdom about her sexual attractiveness have made her susceptible to another fantasy from popular culture. Her dream derives from the "advertising in the women's magazines" that "never included a man. Just a lovely woman in nice clothes coming down the stairs and guests in the dining room and candles and a dark wood dining table and clean children to kiss good night. That's what she really wanted," Steinbeck writes, "and she knew as well as anything that that was not what she would ever get" (110). Steinbeck is clear in suggesting that a key element in her experience that made her susceptible to this dream is that, because of her powerful sexual attraction, "men couldn't keep their hands off her." The resulting trouble was that "she had to argue or cajole or insult or fight her way out." But "what she hated most about her gift [of sexual attraction], or failing, was the fighting. . . . Men fought each other viciously when she was about" (109). In this novel she spends her time fending off a couple of randy males and in providing half-reluctant support for Norma.

The third and most promising single woman on the bus is the Pritchards' daughter, Mildred, though she is not without her own problems. In introducing her, Steinbeck repeats his point that she was a "fine girl," despite the first of her problems, which was to have been born to her parents. She has inherited her mother's weak eyes but can correct that with glasses, and she is fortunate "not [to have] inherited her mother's physiological accident." But she is an accomplished athlete, considerably taller than both her father and mother, and knows enough about life and herself to realize that she needed to wait "for the time when death, marriage, or accident would free her from her parents." Her sexual experience includes the shock of having been nearly seduced by a "muscular young woman" at her university, but this "was washed away . . . when a male engineering student" bedded her (65–67). Well educated, she had read lots of case histories, knows about the interplay of "irritation and functioning glands," and recognizes that she is "a girl of strong sexual potential" (260). Moreover, she is uninhibited enough to make a pass at Juan, who "fascinated" her with his "dark" complexion and "strange warm eyes": "She felt drawn to him. She wanted to attract his attention, his special attention, to herself. She had thrown back her shoulders so that her breasts were lifted" (82). Most promising, from Steinbeck's point of view, she is self-confident enough to follow Juan to the barn, where their sexual intercourse is not only mutually agreeable but also beneficial. As they leave the barn to return to the bus, Steinbeck stops the rain and causes Mildred to say, "Look at the sun on the mountains. It's going to be beautiful." She feels wonderful (289), and Juan has resolved his anger and frustration from driving the busload of nervous and disagreeable people, as well as the racial "imp of hatred [that had] stirred" in him because of her light eyes and complexion (83). And, of course, he has relieved his sexual frustration. The best of it from Steinbeck's point of view is that now in their more relaxed state, each can push the other to tell the truth about the sexual attraction they feel for each other, admit that it can go no further, and exchange an affectionate goodbye.

As for the men, in addition to Juan and Mr. Pritchard, one is simply a grouchy and disagreeable old man who has "powerful desires" that draw him "pantingly . . . toward young women, even little girls"; finally, "rigid with tension," he has a severe stroke (295). Another, the traveling salesman Ernest Horton, is unmanned or at least "overwhelmed with hopelessness" when the enraged Alice Chicoy tells him, "I won't have you drummers diddling my hired girls," although he had only tried to sell Norma some of his items (58–59). Later we learn that although he often told himself that it would be "pretty nice to have a wife and a couple of kids," he could believe it only "when he was drunk." In his one marriage, he had walked out on the second day, leaving a "frightened and angry wife" (150). And Pimples, the third single male in the story, is a comic figure of festering sexual frustration. "Pimples was [so] loaded with the concupiscent juices of adolescence" that "his body burned with excitements" (223). Repeatedly frustrated in his attempts to attract either Camille or Norma, he finds relief in gorging on sweets and takes his place as a submissive underling to the dominant male, Juan. Juan understands Pimples's inner turmoil and treats him with respect. Once, for example, Juan sympathizes with Pimples's nervous outbreak when a young woman walks by, asking him, "Want to take time out and go over and lift your leg on a tree?" Moreover, he wins Pimples's greater allegiance by understanding his need to go by the more respectable name Kit, and Pimples exclaims to himself, "God damn! . . . There is a man. Why'd I ever work for anybody else?" (120).

Juan Chicoy himself is an interesting figure whose many attributes include the kind of gentle, if ominous, strength he exerts over his wife as well as Pimples. Once, when Alice is in an awful rage at Norma, Juan comes to the door and speaks her name sharply. She cringes in fear, and he moves "toward her as lightly as a creeping cat," "the gold ring on his amputated finger" glimmering in the light. Her whispers, "Don't hit me . . . Oh, please don't hit me," suggest that her terror is not without cause, but Steinbeck repeatedly notes how gently he treated her, as when stroking her cheek gently with the hand "with the stump finger and the wedding ring" and reassuring her, "You'll be all right now" (60). As Steinbeck remarks, Alice "was insanely in love with him and a little afraid of him, too, because he was a man" (6). And Steinbeck certainly regards Juan as the only man aboard Sweetheart who is fit, in the evolutionary sense, to control this collection of nervous pilgrims and get them safely to at least the outskirts of Juan de la Cruz. Moreover, Steinbeck clearly indicates that an essential part of Juan's makeup is his relative freedom, as part Mexican, from the debilitating neuroses of American civilization, an attribute that he associates with Juan's upbringing in primitive religion. His Irish mother had thrown out "the ten thousand pale virgins of the North, and into her had entered [the dark Virgin of Guadalupe] who had blood in her veins and a close connection with people," and his Mexican father assumed that "skyrockets were by nature the way to celebrate Saints' Days. . . . The rising, hissing tube was obviously the spirit rising to Heaven, and the big, flashing bang at the top was the dramatic entrance to the throne room of Heaven" (20–21).

Despite these fertility rites in his ancestry and his own obvious virility, Juan has not won the evolutionary reward of reproductive success. He and Alice have no children. Nor is there any specific indication that Alice is barren, as Steinbeck indicates would be the case with Bernice Pritchard, without medical intervention. In addition to her nun's hood, Bernice "suffered from an acid condition which kept her from conceiving children without first artificially neutralizing her body acids" (63). Still, Juan has the attributes of a successful male in sexual selection: beauty and strength. Women are obviously attracted to him because of his "clear black eyes . . . good head of hair, and . . . dark and handsome face"; his hands are "wide and strong"; his "mouth was full and good, a relaxed mouth" with "the underlip slightly protruding . . . in humor and self-confidence"; and, although we do not know their origin, there are two intriguing scars on his face, an "old scar on his cheek" and "a deep scar [that] was almost white against the pink tissue" of his upper lip, evidence, perhaps, that he is a seasoned warrior in the law of battle. Moreover, there is an odd touch of the peacock in the ornamental feature that Steinbeck repeatedly brings into view, the gold wedding ring that he wears on the amputated finger "as though this finger was no good for work any more and might as well be used for ornament" (14–15).

Steinbeck makes so much of this finger and the wedding ring that one cannot avoid giving it further thought. The finger's sexual appeal is evident in Mildred's desire to rub "her finger over the smooth skin of the amputation" (290), including, perhaps, her attraction not only to his "complete manness" but to the idea that the slight sexual mutilation (a kind of circumcision) has to a degree restrained the wild male (222). Also, it seems, she finds pleasure in possessing the man whose wedding band indicates that he belongs to another. Juan's nervousness when she touches his finger suggests his discomfort with the reminder of his adulterous behavior, his most significant discontent as a civilized neurotic. Indeed, Steinbeck develops this suggestion throughout the novel, most importantly in the way he associates Juan's wedding ring and amputated finger with the mechanical problem that temporarily disables Sweetheart. A product of our mechanized civilization, she too is vulnerable in her "rear end" where the "ring gear" had lost a tooth. Signaling the importance of this detail, Juan tells his helper Pimples to "hold the light close" so that he can inspect "the new ring and pinion gears [that he] was rolling . . . carefully together." "I remember once I put a new ring on an old pinion and she went out right away," he says. He "held the ring gear up sideways and in front of the light turned the pinion slowly, inspecting the fit of tooth against tooth," musing the while on the mystery of why some metal objects hold up better than others. Some metal objects just break down "little by little" and others hold together "almost like a guy with a lot of guts" and "won't bust down no matter what you do." Building to his point, then, Steinbeck describes how "Juan laid his [new] ring gear and pinion on the step of the bus and picked up the old ring from the ground. With his finger he traced the raw place where the tooth had broken out." "Metal's funny stuff," he said. "Sometimes it seems to get tired. You know, down in Mexico where I came from they used to have two or three butcher knives. They'd use one and stick the others in the ground. 'It rests the blade,' they said" (21–22).

As these examples suggest, Steinbeck is interested in the metal of his hero, suggesting that he too, like the rest of these pilgrims, needs to be rested "in the ground." This is the pathway not to any kind of evolutionary progress or transcendent love but merely to the civilized individual's renewal or survival. Juan's hands have been "hammered and hurt" in his civilized labor as a mechanic, but Steinbeck hints at the possibility of some kind of regeneration, for the "shiny" flesh that had "mushroomed where the finger had been amputated" suggests that it is "trying to become a fingertip" (14). Because of the stress and restriction in his marriage, and in his civilized livelihood, Juan almost breaks. As he drove away from their café and garage "he wondered why he stayed" with Alice, thinking that it would cause a lot of "emotional turmoil"; "He'd need another woman right away," and it would not be enough "just to lay a girl"; "Besides, Alice was the only woman he had ever found outside of Mexico who could cook beans . . . properly . . . [with] just enough juice." Juan is amused at this thought, and Steinbeck seems to relish the opportunity to link the gastronomical with the reproductive juices. But Juan goes on here to realize that there was another reason why he stayed with Alice:

> She loved him. She really did. And he knew it. And you can't leave a thing like that. It's a structure and it has an architecture, and you can't leave it without tearing off a piece of yourself. So if you want to remain whole you stay no matter how much you may dislike staying. Juan was not a man who fooled himself very much. (136–37)

Juan not only resists fooling himself, but manages here to articulate the kind of ecological wisdom—involving the "friendly and inimical relations" of human beings in their own social structures, as Haeckel might have put it—that Steinbeck concludes is our best hope if civilized humanity is to withstand the dual stress of the "ring gear" and the "quickening earth, frantic with production." Juan's marriage, he suggests, is like "one of the strong ecological factors of the town of Loreto" in *The Log from the Sea of Cortez*, the figure of the terrified Virgin, made "of plaster and wood and paint" that has such "a powerful effect on the deep black water of the human spirit" (178). Juan's brief sexual encounter with Mildred certainly helps to relieve his nervous stress, after which, as though having rested his metal, he is resolved to return to his wife. Similarly, Steinbeck clearly suggests that the Pritchard marriage had found rest in the sexual violence in the cave. Closing his narrative of the pilgrims aboard "Sweetheart," Steinbeck writes that in the darkness "inside of the bus," Juan addressed the "small metal Virgin of Guadalupe" that sits atop his dashboard, his "connection with eternity" (20): "I ask only one thing. . . . I gave up the other, but it would be nice if you could make it so she was sober when I get back" (310). Whether Juan's return to his ecological niche will lead to a more productive marriage, Steinbeck will not say, but as Juan drives through "the night [that] was very black," "a new breeze had come up, bearing the semenous smell of grass and the spice of lupine" (310).

Notes

1. See Brian Railsback, *Parallel Expeditions*. Perhaps because Railsback was the first to explain and justify Steinbeck's work in this regard, he overstates the case for Steinbeck by suggesting that there is some kind of parallel achievement in Darwin's and Steinbeck's careers. Aside from this volume, the most important works on Steinbeck and biology are by Richard Astro and, in a briefer treatment, by Frederick Bracher.

2. Steinbeck's wife Carol described Ma as "pure Briffault" (qtd. in Astro 133). For a discussion of Steinbeck's interest in Briffault, see Astro, *John Steinbeck and Edward Ricketts*, 48–52, 133. The standard interpretation of *The Grapes of Wrath* in light of Briffault is Warren Motley's "From Patriarchy to Matriarchy: Ma Joad's Role in *The Grapes of Wrath*."

3. For discussions of his reading of these works and others, see Astro's chapter, "The Argument of Plalanx" in *John Steinbeck and Edward Ricketts* and DeMott's *Steinbeck's Reading*.

4. The writers and works he mentions in this well-known remark (in another letter to his friend Carlton Sheffield in 1933) are W. C. Allee (*Animal Aggregations*), Ellsworth Huntington (*Civilization and Climate*), Oswald Spengler (*The Decline of the West*), Vladimir Ouspenski (*Tertium Organum*), Carl Jung (*Two Essays on Analytical Psychology*), Robert Briffault (*The Mothers*), Erwin Schrödinger, Max Planck, Niels Bohr, Albert Einstein, and Werner Heisenberg (DeMott xxvii). DeMott lists no works by the physicists in *Steinbeck's Reading*.

5. Astro believes that "the major portion of Steinbeck's world-view in *The Grapes of Wrath* emerges through the increasing consciousness of [the character] Jim Casy," whom he sees as a "teleological activist" whose "role as a Christ-figure" is so well known that it "needs no further explanation" (129), except that his "Christ-like demeanor is perfectly consistent with his developing teleological character" (131).

6. For a discussion of Steinbeck's tentative title, see Benson, *The True Adventures of John Steinbeck, Writer*, 582. In addition to Steinbeck's references to T. S. Eliot, it seems that he also brought in the other great modernist with whom he had a less literary bone to pick, Ernest Hemingway. One of the pilgrims is a Mr. Ernest Horton, the Horton seemingly a signal pertaining to Hemingway's Horton Bay, Michigan. Steinbeck notes "the kind of shy confidence in his manner" and comments that he seemed to try to protect "himself from insult with studied techniques" (37). When another of the pilgrims, Mr. Elliot Pritchard, first sees Ernest in Alice Chicoy's café, where they are waiting for Juan to fix Sweetheart, Pritchard thinks "there was something queer about him" (40). Soon Ernest Horton pulls a prank on Pritchard and the other guests, pretending that he has an injured foot and taking off his shoe and stocking to display a foot with a horrible wound. The wound, suggesting the famous wounds of Hemingway, is a plastic trick, and Horton is a traveling salesman representing the "Little Wonder Company"; he explains that "it's the psychology that sells it . . . the psychology of taking off your shoe and sock" (45–46). Horton, not a particularly virile male in this collection of males, later declares his intention to go to Mexico because he likes "these fiestas they have," suggesting the famous fiesta in *The Sun Also Rises* (86). About two years before this Hemingway had insulted Steinbeck in a famous incident at a bar in New York City. John O'Hara was there with Steinbeck and proudly showed off a blackthorn cane that Steinbeck had given him. Hemingway doubted that it was real blackthorn and bet O'Hara he could break it, which he proceeded to do, cracking it over his skull. As Carlos Baker remarks, "Steinbeck was disgusted" (*A Life Story* 387, 636).

7. In 1958 Steinbeck remarked, "The Wasteland was certainly in the brilliantly dry and despairing mind of Elliot" (qtd. in DeMott 38).

12 "Night Song"

Africa and Eden in Hemingway's Late Work

"Live all you can; it's a mistake not to. . . . Live, live!" This famous remark by Lambert Strether in Henry James's *The Ambassadors* (1903) brings out what James referred to as the essence of his novel and expands to give the novel what Leon Edel calls "its 'deterministic' post-Darwinian philosophy. We are all moulds, 'either fluted and embossed, with ornamental excrescences, or else smooth and dreadfully plain, into which a helpless jelly, one's consciousness, is poured'" (535–36). The novel builds to the moment when Strether sees Chad Newsome together with his (Chad's) mistress, and, as Edel notes, James wrote of this "momentous and interesting period" in Strether's life shortly after a similar period in his own life, "when he had met Hendrik Anderson . . . and suddenly found himself—after removing his beard—wanting to write things of 'the altogether human order'" (534).

A little more than twenty years after *The Ambassadors* appeared the young Ernest Hemingway was hearing a lot about both Henry and William James from friends like Gertrude Stein. Hemingway's critics have remarked on the deep impression Strether's remark made on him as he wrote his first novel, *The Sun Also Rises* (Lynn 328). There Robert Cohn asks Jake Barnes, "Don't you ever get the feeling that all your life is going by and you're not taking advantage of it?" (*The Sun Also Rises* 11). Whether or not Hemingway would have thought of *The Ambassadors* as a "post-Darwinian" novel, as Edel does, it is clear that his own novel presented a much harsher view of love in light of the theory of sexual selection, the force that accounts for his male characters' combative jealousy. Taking that opportunity to comment on the absurdity of William Jennings Bryan's attack on Darwinism at the Scopes trial (he had just heard the news of Bryan's death), Hemingway joined in celebrating the ancient fertility rites surrounding the bulls and emphasized how that life force undercut the meaning of both sexual and Christian love. He later explained that during those years when the Freudian craze was at its peak he had intended to present "a treatise on basic loneliness and the inadequacy of promiscuity" (*Selected Letters* 767–68).[1]

When he wrote of his first African safari nearly a decade after *The Sun Also Rises*, Hemingway was even more intent on pursuing life, and he declared his intention to return to Africa, "where it pleased [him] to live; to really live. Not just let [his] life pass" (*Green Hills of Africa* 285). Of course he did return to Africa, this time for a longer safari (September 1953–January 1954). There, at about the age Henry James was when he met Henrik Anderson, Hemingway met his African "fiancée" Debba. From this he produced the African manuscript that his son Patrick recently cut into shape as *True at First Light* (1999). Before the safari and after he put the unfinished African manuscript into storage (February 1956), he also worked on the other unfinished manuscript that reflected his interest in Africa and that was edited and published posthumously as *The Garden of Eden* (1986). This chapter will discuss these and a few related works as Hemingway's late explorations of what it means "to live" or, more accurately, to *be* alive, as he put it in "The Last Good Country" (another of his unfinished manuscripts from the early 1950s). In that story a Mr. John Packard tells the young Nick Adams, "You're alive and you're going to do things." Of course this means that Nick "will have things to repent . . . but the thing is to have them " (*Complete Short Stories* 523).[2]

Hemingway's several references to Henry James in *True at First Light* serve to distinguish his own sense of what it means to live from James's. If *The Ambassadors* suggests that James associated what it meant to live with his own intimate relationship with Henrik Anderson or Chad Newsome's with Madame de Vionnet, *True at First Light* drives home Hemingway's assertion that from his own point of view at least half of what it meant to live was to realize his opportunity for sexual intimacy not only with his wife Mary, but with Debba. When his opportunity to sleep with Debba approaches, after Mary had left the safari for a brief trip to Nairobi, Hemingway lies awake in his tent one night and wonders "how Henry James would have handled this situation. I remembered him standing on the balcony of his hotel in Venice smoking a good cigar and wondering what must go on in that town" below him. He "always had great comfort thinking of Henry James standing on the balcony of his hotel looking down at the town and the people passing, all of them with their needs and their duties and their problems." Hemingway thinks of "the sound well-organized life of the canal" and of "James, who knew not one of the places to go, and stayed on his balcony with his cigar. . . . I liked to think of both Debba and James and I wondered how it would be if I plucked the consolatory cigar from James's lips and handed it to Debba who might put it behind her ear." Soon he finds that he "no longer cared to think of the thick, squat figure with the bald head and the ambulatory dignity and line of departure problems and I thought of Debba and the big skin-covered, smoky, clean-smelling, hand-rubbed wood bed of the big house" (232–33).

Bringing out his well-known swagger as a sexual athlete and a deadly shot, such scenes seem calculated to offend. However, it is also important to note that such projections of his legendary manliness are not only those of a braggart but of a self-conscious modern writer who (like Sherwood Anderson or James Joyce) was intent on exploring and confessing his dark sexual fantasies and dreams. In *True at First Light*, this includes the embarrassing comedy of the middle-aged man shaving his head in order to be more attractive to his would-be mate (as James has shaved his beard). As Mr. John ("The Last Good Country") advises the young Nick to have the things of life that he might or might not want later to repent, the writer David Bourne tells himself (in a deleted bit of the "Garden" manuscript) that he must "never leave out anything because you are ashamed of it or because no one would ever understand" (qtd. in Burwell 123). We have seen such troubled efforts at self-analysis earlier in the century by Jack London, Theodore Dreiser, and Sherwood Anderson as they contemplated the male's sexual nature, and all these introspective efforts should be seen as developments in the broader exploration of the evolutionary psyche by theorists such as William James, Havelock Ellis, and Sigmund Freud. In this context, Hemingway's fictional self-analysis is remarkable but not exactly unparalleled, as one of his most insightful recent interpreters has remarked (Burwell 6).

Above all, Hemingway's work is always grounded in the elemental fact that no human can live without dealing with both the sexual need, no matter what complex form that might take, and the need to kill and eat. In this way he fully—and courageously—embraced the idea on which so much of modern psychology was founded, that human life is driven by two kinds of hunger. Although William James had surprisingly little to say on this subject, Freud remarked in *Civilization and Its Discontents*, "I took as my starting-point a saying of the poet-philosopher, Schiller, that 'hunger and love are what moves the world'" (64).[3] And, as Havelock Ellis explained in defining the sources of our dreams, "the great fundamental function of eating is almost as conspicuous as that of loving" (*Studies* 2:2:339). In his great and often appalling emphasis on the first kind of hunger, every human being's inescapable need to kill and eat, along with the force of sexual hunger, Hemingway does seem unparalleled, with the possible exception of Steinbeck in *The Log from the Sea of Cortez*. Of course every human being need not celebrate hunting and killing for its own sake (or for trophies) to the extent that the younger Hemingway too often does in *Green Hills of Africa*. But no one can deny his or her own role in nature's redness of tooth and claw, if only the innocuous thrill a strict vegetarian might feel in sinking one's teeth into a perfect peach. In a meditation on killing and eating in *True at First Light* involving Mary's lion hunt (the second of the book's two main plot lines, the other being the courtship of Hemingway and Debba), Hemingway knows "how abhorrent this would be to real vegetarians." But, he adds, "those who never catch fish, not even a tin of sardines, and who will stop their cars if there are locusts on the road, and have never eaten even meat broth should not condemn those who kill to eat. . . . Who knows what the carrot feels, or the small young radish?" (111). As Santiago remarks in *The Old Man and the Sea*, "the punishment of hunger . . . is everything" (84).[4] And it is encouraging to know that, like Santiago, the aging Hemingway had become more interested in observing than killing animals and that much of his late introspective work is imbued with comic darkness.[5]

Still, that the aging and more gently comic Hemingway retained his focus on the two kinds of hunger is further evident in the two fables he published as companion pieces in 1951, "The Good Lion" and "The Faithful Bull." In the first, which begins, "Once upon a time there was a lion that lived in Africa," Hemingway tells of a lion who (like Santiago who had become "bored" with "eating" [30]) was repulsed by his bad fellow lions who delighted in eating all sorts of animals and "sometimes . . . people too . . . especially . . . Hindu traders." The good lion "had wings on his back" and endured his fellows' laughter "because he only ate pasta and scampi." When he is challenged by "one of the lionesses, who was the wickedest of them all" and who demands to know, "What are you doing here anyway?" he claims that he is from a city (Venice) over which his noble father presides. The wickedest of all the lionesses scoffs at his claim and calls him "a worthless liar and the son of a griffon," and when she threatens to "kill [him] and eat [him], wings and all," he flies into the air and returns to Venice. "What savages these lions are," he thinks, but, "being a lion of culture," he bids them "Adios" and "Au revoir" in his "beautiful Spanish" and "exemplary French." Arriving in Venice, however, he discovers that being in Africa had changed him. After telling his father that he had found Africa to be very savage, he makes his way to Harry's Bar and asks if they have "Hindu trader sandwiches." But first he will have "a very dry martini." As he looks "about him at the faces of all the nice people," the good lion knows "that he was at home but that he had also traveled. He was very happy" (*Complete Short Stories* 482–84).

The companion fable, "The Faithful Bull," features a bull who "loved to fight . . . with all the other bulls," a true champion who was never angry, except "inside himself." His "sharply pointed" horns "hurt him, at the base, when he fought," but he did not care and injured so many of his owner's other bulls that the owner "selected him for breeding" and "turned him into the pasture with the breeding cows." However, being a strange bull and since "he could not fight," he fell in love with "one cow who was young and beautiful and slimmer and better muscled and shinier and more lovely than all the others." As he paid no attention to the other cows, who "meant nothing to him at all," he became worthless to his owner and was therefore sent "to be killed in the ring." There "he fought wonderfully and everyone admired him," and when the matador who finally killed him was told of the bull's strange faithfulness, he remarked, in the fable's last words, "Perhaps we should all be faithful" (485–86).[6] With these obviously playful moral tales about our strange longing for transcendent flight and constant love, Hemingway reiterates the theme of the two hungers that he would sustain in more darkly comic tones throughout *True at First Light*.

Courtship and Anthropology in Africa

In *True at First Light*, as in nearly everything else he wrote, Hemingway presents the theme of the two hungers entwined within a single narrative, a suggestion that, like other evolutionary biologists then and now, he considered sexual selection to be a form of natural selection. Here, the two plot lines at first seem to develop separately, one as the narrative of Mary's quest to kill the lion, conveying Hemingway's point that Mary (like the lioness in the fable) can hold her own as a hunter. This theme is similar to that of Brett Ashley's sexual aggressiveness in *The Sun Also Rises*, for example. But here the female's sexual aggression is linked with her power to kill, as in his first great safari story of Margot Macomber's sexual exploits and her deadly marksmanship. In *True at First Light*, the themes of Mary's hunting and of the Hemingway-Debba courtship are most clearly entwined in his brief description of his copulation with Debba: "We hunted diligently," he writes, "and lay until almost dark on an old blanket on the high side of a hill waiting for a beast to feed out onto the open hillside" (278). Then, "when it was time to go home," and needing to return with meat (in part to justify their absence from the village), the two kill a "Tommy ram" together: Hemingway "lined up on him and with us both sitting down [Debba] had her put her finger on the trigger ahead of mine." He continues, "I felt the pressure of her finger and her head against mine and could feel her trying not to breathe. Then I said, 'Piga,' and her finger tightened as mine tightened on the trigger only a tiny cheating shade faster and the ram, whose tail had been switching as he fed, was dead" (278). At the same time, the narrative of Mary's hunt also touches on her sexual nature, as in many references to Hemingway's and Mary's lovemaking, to the game scout Arap Meina's sexual attraction to Mary (for her androgynous "pure Hamitic face of a boy with a body that was as womanly as a good Masai young wife"), and to her question, "It isn't bad for everybody to be in love with everybody else the way it is in Africa, is it?" (223–24). More explicitly, in reference to Mary's vitality as one well adapted to satisfy the two hungers, Hemingway writes that "we were all hunters and it was the start of that wonderful thing, the hunt"; "Mary was a hunter and a brave and lovely one." He adds only that because "she had come to it late" she experienced the kind of disorientation that a "kitten" feels "when she becomes a cat" and is "in heat for the first time" (156).

To single out the details of Hemingway's theme so baldly obscures his comic accompaniment and will undoubtedly offend many of his readers who would prefer to think of him as a much less hard-bitten Darwinian, or, more unaccountably, as a writer who refuted the Darwinian view of life.[7] But what he calls his gallows humor would have no basis apart from his dark view of life and love: the essential loneliness that "is best taken away by jokes, derision and contempt for the worst possible outcome of anything," he writes (232). Moreover, one can appreciate his dark comedy much more fully, as well as his long-standing interest in Africa, by seeing them in the context, first, of the early twentieth-century fascination with primitivism, as in Sherwood Anderson's *Dark Laughter* and certain novelists from the Harlem Renaissance, especially Claude McKay (who, by the way, admired and once met Hemingway), and, second, in the context of early and mid-twentieth-century anthropology.[8] His early stories of American Indians in Michigan, his satire of Anderson's primitivism in *The Torrents of Spring*, and his own depictions of African people in *Green Hills of Africa* and *True at First Light*—all these reflect his impatience with the idea that there are primitive people who are essentially different from him or that the subconscious in popular Freudianism can be meaningfully associated with the primitive. And while asserting that we must all deal with our needs to kill and eat and to reproduce, that "we were all hunters," Hemingway reserves some of his most derisive humor for the kind of modern anthropology that sought to emphasize the role of culture (or nurture) and to downplay the role of evolutionary biology.[9]

That Hemingway came down resoundingly on the side of nature is unmistakable in the fable of the good lion who was "a lion of culture." Similarly, in "The Last Good Country," Hemingway remarks that Mr. John's wife "loved culture like a lumberjack loved Peerless" (a brand of chewing tobacco), much as Mr. John "loved good bonded whiskey"—because it makes one "feel wonderful." Mr. John allows that "culture maybe was better than religion . . . but it was a cold proposition," and he goes on to counsel young Nick on what it means to be alive (523). In *True at First Light* Hemingway insinuates many ironic remarks about anthropology, tribal laws (including British and American), and religion. Indeed, both this African book as well as *Green Hills of Africa* are in large part essays in a kind of subjective anthropology in which he explores his own inner darkness as part of what he called "the shape of a country" (Foreword to *Green Hills*). In *Green Hills* he did not refer to anthropology as openly as he does in the later book, but one of the major self-exploratory and confessional themes in the book—what he hoped would help to make it "an absolutely true book"—is a direct shot at the widely accepted anthropological principle in the 1930s that there is little or no competition among primitive people. Although on that safari Hemingway's group "tried, in all the shoot, never to be competitive" (86), the book's final words on that subject are the guide Pop's remark, "We have very primitive emotions. . . . It's impossible not to be competitive. Spoils everything, though" (293). And this view is accompanied in the book by references to the gun bearer M'Cola's "old man's healthy laugh" at death and religion: "The Mohammedans and all religions were a joke" (36); religion "was something that gave caste, something to believe in, something fashionable and god-giving . . . something that made you superior to other people" (38–39). Well attuned to this view of life, Hemingway joins in the dark laughter, notably in his "solemn ceremony" each morning while standing in the latrine and looking up at "that fuzzy blur of stars that the romanticists of astronomers called the Southern Cross" (202), and in his closing remark when, standing at Haifa "by the Sea of Galilee" after the safari, he watches the grebes that are never "mentioned in the Bible" and concludes "that those people were not naturalists" (294).

The several volumes of anthropological books that Hemingway owned suggest that he was not close-minded on the subject as much as skeptical. In innumerable ways his writing contradicts even A. L. Kroeber's balanced effort in 1923 (in a book from Hemingway's library), to separate biology from anthropology—his assertion that it "is most misleading" to think "of anthropology as 'the child of Darwin.'" As "the whole history of man . . . [is] much more than an organic matter," Kroeber advises, "a pure Darwinian anthropology would be largely misapplied biology" (8). Hemingway did not know that by the 1950s Kroeber, too, had given ground to the revival of Darwinism.[10] More important, Hemingway seems to smile at the anthropologists whose supposedly objective studies tended to differentiate themselves from their subjects. This is the thrust of Hemingway's comic remarks on anthropology in *True at First Light*, which, for example, he once introduces with this thought about his gun bearer, Ngui: "Walking in the early morning watching Ngui striding lightly through the grass thinking how we were brothers it seemed to me stupid to be white in Africa." Leading to his recollections of having heard a "Moslem missionary" give a "Sermon against the White Man," including "the White Man's heaven" and his way of cursing "the Baby Jesus" in private, this meditation moves to a discussion of snakes. Here Ngui's belief that "snakes are the ancestors of all the Masai" is juxtaposed with stories of "snakes [that] performed biblical feats." Then, writing that snakes "were antipathetic to me and I knew that they were to Ngui too," Hemingway tells how they had agreed to "feel the blood" of an actual snake if they killed one in order to test Ngui's theory that the Masai women's cold hands, and even those of "Italian women," proved their snake ancestry. Hemingway remarks that "this was all in the interests of our anthropological studies which we pursued each day and we kept on walking and thinking of these problems and of our own small problems which we tried to integrate with the greater interests of anthropology" (201–3).

But his playful anthropology in this work mostly concerns his courtship with Debba. This takes him into the field that Bronislaw Malinowski had famously studied in *The Sexual Life of Savages* (1929) or Margaret Mead in *Coming of Age in Samoa* (1928), but Hemingway places himself at the center of his own studies (as he refers to them), self-consciously exposing his own embarrassing obsession with and pride in his sexual exploits. And as he indulges in a kind of locker-room braggadocio, he seems also to challenge his male readers to deny that they have indulged similar sexual fantasies. As he wrote his friend Harvey Breit near the end of the safari, he had his weight down to 186 and had shaved his head "because that is how my fiancée likes it." "My girl is completely impudent," he brags, "her face is impudent in repose, but absolutely loving and delicate rough. I better quit writing about it because I want to write it really and I mustn't spoil it. Anyway it gives me too bad a hardon" (*Letters* 827). But he knows that his pose of youthful virility (at age fifty-five) is outlandish, following it with remarks about how Ngui (at the age of about thirty) has five wives and is looking to "get maybe 2 more," and of how he amuses his African friends with other tall tales. "At night I tell them how we killed George Armstrong Custer and the 7th Cavalry and they think we are wasting our time here and should get the hell to America. It's a lovely country, Harvey." When he did "write it really" in the African manuscript, he confessed that he did actually shave his head, the day after Mary had left for Nairobi, and he knew how perfectly ridiculous he looked: "My head, unfortunately, has much the appearance of some plastic history of a very lost tribe. It is no way as spectacular as the Great Rift Valley but there are historical features of terrain which could interest both archaeologist and anthropologist" (246).

Of course this adolescent masculinity is embarrassing, but like Dick Forest's embarrassing stallion dance in London's *The Little Lady of the Big House* (while chanting, "I am Eros"), it is also a self-conscious confession of a grim comedy in the human male's sexual behavior. He is often inclined not only to polygamous desire (as London, Dreiser, and Anderson boldly confessed) but also to the kind of vain display that the naturalist or anthropologist can more comfortably describe among peacocks or primitive males. As Hemingway wrote of the men in *Green Hills of Africa*, their "tribal marks [of scarification] and the tattooed places seemed natural and handsome adornments and I regretted not having any of my own" (53). In *True at First Light* he asks Ngui "when he had gotten [his] big formal tribal cuts," and Ngui laughs, saying, "You know. To please a girl" (18). Moreover, by emphasizing the scars and associating them with the hunter's weapons as ornamental emblems of his superior appeal, Hemingway always reminds us of the underlying violence of sexual selection in the natural world. Repeatedly in their courtship, Debba fingers the holster of his pistol in admiration: "She liked to feel the embossing on the old leather holster" (35); "she truly loved [the holster], it having been carved better in Denver than anyone had ever been carved or tattooed . . . in a beautiful flowered design" (261). Once, as she was fingering the pistol holster, he "trace[d] the outline of her nose and her lips with [his] fingers," touching her lightly in "a great delicacy of courtship" leading to the kind of love bite that writers and psychologists had long theorized as part of the original sexual hunger. Accepting her invitation to feel where she would have her ears pierced for him, he "kissed them and then bit them a little very gently." "Really bite them with the dog teeth," she says (142–43). Then, ending the scene in which he compares the embossed holster to carvings or tattoos, he has Debba say, "I have all of you in the pistol," and he comments to the reader: "Love is a terrible thing that you would not wish on your neighbor and, as in all countries, it is a moveable feast. Fidelity does not exist nor ever is implied except at the first marriage" (262).[11]

Pursuing his interest in this African courtship, Hemingway includes other materials that he seems to have considered as part of his "anthropological studies" (203), including a remark on Debba's modesty and his interest in the way, at the Ngoma festivities, "the young girls were dancing . . . in a very intense copulative figure" (197).[12] But his broader anthropological study addresses the questions of polygamy, fidelity, and love that surface, for example, in the remark about love as a moveable feast. In an earlier scene, while lying awake one night and listening "to the hyenas talking and disputing over" scraps from butchered game animals, he feels "full of remorse" for having become involved with Debba but then concludes that there is no remedy for it and that he had not started it.[13] Then a leopard coughed "again, hunting, and all the night began to speak about him and I put the shotgun under my leg again and started to go to sleep feeling proud of Miss Mary and loving her and being proud of Debba and caring about her very much" (64). Clearly associating his sexual desire for both women with the nocturnal life of hunting animals, he also imagines that not only Debba but also Mary will accept his polygamous nature. Debba sends word to him that she loves him (to which he responds, "Tell her there is no such word as love") and that "she wishes only one thing, to be a wife if Memsahib, my lady, will accept her. She understands that Memsahib is the principal wife" and is afraid of her (35–36). When Hemingway and Mary are alone they have a playful way of dealing with this conflict, in a set speech that Mary gives "about when I kill the woman who steals your affection." She reminds him that she likes to make the speech, that "it's good for me to make it and it's good for you to hear it." It runs, in part, "so you think that you and he would lead a perfect existence together and at least he would have the love of a woman who understands communism, psychoanalysis and the true meaning of the word love? What do you know about love you bedraggled hag? What do you know about my husband and the things we have shared and have in common?" (107–8).

Later, in another exchange between them, he tries to explain to Mary his excuse for having his affair with Debba and for planning to write about it: "I make the truth as I invent it truer that it would be" if it were not fictionalized. Pursuing this point he explains that "[D. H.] Lawrence tried to tell about it" but failed because he enshrouded it in "so much cerebral mysticism" and because he had too many theories and prejudices. Again, Mary's response, as in her set speech, shows her strength (as a hunter in her own right) and at the same time provides the kind of clear-sighted criticism of his romance that Hemingway wants in order to develop the dark comedy of his self-revelation: she remarks, "I like your fiancée very much because she is a lot like me and I think she'd be a valuable extra wife if you need one. But you don't have to justify her by some writer" (94–95). Still, intent on bringing out the unpleasant truth of what he calls his shameful "nocturnal imagination" (104), Hemingway captures not only Mary's tough-mindedness but her painful insecurity. Preparing to leave for the trip to Nairobi that she knows will free him to be with Debba, Mary tells him, "I don't mind about your fiancée as long as you love me more. You do love me more don't you?" He assures her, "I love you more and I'll love you more still when you come back from town." But as soon as she is gone he remarks both that he "knew how happy [he] would be alone and with the people and the problems and with the country that [he] loved" and, at the same time, that he "was lonely for Mary" (225–27). Soon he shaves his head in order to please his girl and goes courting.

Hemingway refers to this as his "fine, if complicated, life" (304). As though following the advice of Mr. John in "The Last Good Country" (to *have* the things you can have if "you're alive," even though you might later decide to repent them), he *will* have these things of life in the African world, if only as a truthful fiction. In "The Last Good Country," as Nick leads his sister Littless into the secret places he knows within the "virgin timber" (*Complete Short Stories* 515) he thinks to himself, "You should have been an Indian. . . . It would have saved you a lot of trouble" (530).[14] Similarly, "showing signs of wanting to go native," as Carlos Baker describes it (517), or, as it is fairer to say, of exploring himself in the African world, Hemingway tells Mary, "It's just tribal. . . . I'm truly not trying to make things any more complicated then they are" (*True at First Light* 306). Indeed, both Hemingway and Mary had wanted to submit themselves to the African reality. "After all," Mary had remarked in an earlier scene, "we didn't come out here to bring order into Africa. . . . . But we certainly got mixed up in it" (115). However, at this point near the end of the safari, Mary adds the comically critical perspective that Hemingway wants: responding to his remarks about the complications of being "tribal," she observes, "You get too tribal for your own good" (306).

The African safari certainly took them both into a frightening inner terrain where they confronted the two hungers that move the world (to echo Freud once again). And a large part of Hemingway's effort here is to acknowledge (as Steinbeck did in *The Log from the Sea of Cortez* and *The Wayward Bus*) that culture is an undeniable feature of this landscape. But his approach to the cultural phenomena he observes is to expose them to a dark laughter that resembles his critique of D. H. Lawrence's cerebral mysticism. His favorite target for this kind of humor is evident in his repeated references to the "Birthday of the Baby Jesus," in the subplot that involves

Mary's successful quest to kill her lion before Christmas. In the passage introducing the end of this hunt, Hemingway wrote, "There is much mystical nonsense written about hunting but it is something that is probably much older than religion" (156), and earlier, in explaining to the elders that *Mary* (not himself) would kill the lion that had been destroying their cattle and do so forthrightly, he explained, "It was necessary for the religion of the Memsahib that she kill this particular lion before the Birthday of the Baby Jesus. We came from a far country and were of a tribe of that country and this was necessary" (45). He is "appalled by [his] oratory after it was over," but it provided an effective fiction, and it is the subject of many other ironic remarks, including the subplot of Mary's actually wanting to celebrate Christmas. This will involve her trip to Nairobi, where she will purchase gifts (while Hemingway and Debba consummate their affair), and includes Hemingway's point that she had selected a Christmas tree that she didn't know "was really an extra-potent type of marijuana-effect tree" (234).

But he includes these remarks in a pattern of others about African superstitions and cultural practices. And although he cannot ignore these practices, he considers them no less amusing than his own pretense over the "Birthday of the Baby Jesus."[15] An important one of these is Charo's (Mary's gun bearer) practice of what Hemingway refers to as doing "his business" with the animals shot for meat: to *halal* them, that is, to cut their throats before they die of the gunshots in order to make the meat acceptable "for the Mohammedans" (278). Recognizing this ritual need and wanting to protect Charo's conscience, Hemingway once walks as slowly as possible toward an impala he had shot, allowing Charo to "cut the impala's throat and [look up] smiling" (186). Hemingway understands that culture, like fiction, requires a certain amount of lying. But while he pays his respects to such cultural practices, he always deals with them as realities that one must outmaneuver in order to get the meat or, more importantly, in order for him to *have* the main thing in his African life that he knows he might later want to repent—the consummation of his courtship with Debba. There certainly are cultural obstacles, such as when the Widow accompanies Debba in their visits to see that her good reputation is preserved. Once, "the Widow was very tense" and intervened in their intimacy, causing Debba to lose "her lovely Kamba impudence" (63). In a similar incident in the presence of the Widow and Mthuka (another "self-appointed conscience," Hemingway remarks), Debba cannot join in a communal taking of snuff: "I cannot take snuff," she said. "I am unmarried to you and I cannot take snuff." Hemingway writes, "There was nothing to say about this so we did not say anything," but the cultural restrictions do not prevent her at this moment from putting "her hand back on the holster which she truly loved" (260–61).

Despite his dark comic perspective on such customs, however, Hemingway asserts that one should follow them "insofar as he can." In Africa, especially, where it would be absurd for anyone to provide psychological counseling to "be mature. Be well-balanced, be well-adjusted," he asserts that a man should affirm his childlike nature and be as "well-balanced and well-adjusted" as a young gazelle (25). One "should follow his tribal laws and customs insofar as he can and accept the tribal discipline when he cannot. But it is never a reproach that he has kept a child's heart, a child's honesty and a child's freshness and nobility" (26–27). Thus, after Hemingway and Debba do manage to outmaneuver the enforcers of the tribal laws, Hemingway tells the character Keiti that he will act responsibly in bringing up any possible son or daughter born from the relationship. "I will do everything according to Kamba law and custom," he says, "But I cannot marry the girl and take her home because of stupid laws" (279). Earlier he was asked by a Mr. Singh, "Can you justify a European taking an African as his mistress?" He replied, using a more specialized anthropological term, "If a girl loves the man and there is no coercion, to me it is not a sin if adequate provision is made for the issue per stirpes and not per capita" (254–55).

But, far more important than its respectful critique of our amusing cultural practices, *True at First Light* is a formidable and courageous, although often appalling and embarrassing, exploration of the darkness of *life*. Recording his sense of man's true place in nature, Hemingway fixes his attention on how it tastes, how it sounds, what it looks like, and how it feels to be alive. Whereas Dreiser, for example, had contemplated the tyrannous "It" that drives us on, Hemingway wants always to recognize and satisfy the two kinds of hunger. Distinguishing his own efforts to know what it means to be alive from Henry James's detached point of view as an observer on the balcony of civilization or from Lawrence's cerebral mysticism, Hemingway never entertains the idea of evolutionary progress. Rather, considering himself a kind of aboriginal human being with the same elemental needs of his African friends, including their inevitable struggles with the restraints and yet ironic consolations of tribal laws and religion, he penetrates even further into the darkness of common descent. "We were going into the African world of unreality," he writes at the outset, a world

> that is defended and fortified by reality past any reality there is. It was not an escape world or a daydreaming world. It was a ruthless real world made of the unreality of the real. If there were still rhino, and we saw them every day while it was obviously impossible for there to be such an animal, then anything was possible. If Ngui and I could talk to a rhinoceros, who was incredible to start with, in his own tongue well enough for him to answer back and I could curse and insult him in Spanish so that he would be humiliated and go off, that unreality was sensible and logical beside reality. (127–28)

Once, in an effort to justify his night hunting, doing what Mary terms "those terrible night things," Hemingway responds, "We have to study the animals at night"

(224). And when an old Masai man applies to him for work as an interpreter, Hemingway replies, "Would you interpret between me and the animals?" (182). For Hemingway, always determined to explore the reality of our common descent, this is always an essentially religious question.

At the conclusion of one of his plot lines, the hunt for Mary's lion, he "lay down by the lion and talked to him very softly in Spanish and begged his pardon for [their] having killed him, and while [he] lay beside him [he] felt for the wounds. There were four" (169). As Robert Lewis notes, in this rite Hemingway seeks communion with the other world "of the God-man Christ who dies with four wounds" (119). When Hemingway sees that "the flat hard camel flies" buzzing at the dead lion were shifting from the lion to him, he writes, "I drew a fish in the front of him with my forefinger in the dirt and then rubbed it out with the palm of my hand" (*Light* 169). The hardest fact of life in Hemingway's African world is that there is no transcendent communion. He had confronted this frightening truth in the glaring sunlight outside a Spanish church in *The Sun Also Rises*. Having found inside the church that he could not pray, but still believing that it was "a grand religion," Jake entered the square. There "the forefingers and the thumb of [his] right hand were still damp" from the holy water, but he "felt them dry in the sun" (97).

His rite with the dead lion having led to the celebration—"the wild, stooped dancing rush of Wakamba pour[ing] in from behind all the tents singing the lion song" and then to "a fine happy meal"—Hemingway finds himself awake at three o'clock in the morning (170). At this point he remembers a quotation from F. Scott Fitzgerald's writings about his (Fitzgerald's) breakdown: "In a real dark night of the soul it is always three o'clock in the morning." But, "sitting up awake in the African night," Hemingway realizes, "I knew nothing about the soul at all." In fact, before he awoke, he had been dreaming that "I had a horse's body but a man's head and shoulders and I had wondered why no one had known this before. . . . [I]t dealt with the precise moment at which the change came about in the body so that they were human bodies." Having awakened, he recalls, "I could still feel the muscles I had in the dream when my body had been a horse's body. This was not helping me with the soul" (172).[16] Inevitably, Hemingway's meditation on the lion, the soul, and the night is interwoven with his narrative of the courtship, and it leads to this moment following his consummation of the affair and after he has assured Keiti that he will take responsibility for the possible child and that he will abide by "Kamba law and custom." That having been settled, the two talk of a possible hunt together at night. When Hemingway confesses, "I am only learning," Keiti remarks, "Nobody knows the night. Not me. Not you. Nobody. . . . You will [learn it]. But be careful. . . . The night belongs to the animals" (280).

Moments later, realizing that "what Keiti had said was very true," he reiterates his determination to learn it. And then, again in bed, awake at night, thinking of his "great and lovely pleasure to be in camp when Miss Mary should return" and also of his "wonderful pleasure to be with Debba," his thoughts return to the line from Fitzgerald (281). Listening to the night he realizes, "No man is every really alone and the supposed dark hours of the soul when it is always three o'clock in the morning are a man's best hours if he is not an alcoholic nor afraid of the night and what the day will bring" (282). Before Mary had left for Nairobi, the two had lain together in bed listening to "two lions coughing as they hunted," and Mary said, "Us kittens in Africa with our faithful fire and the beasts having their night life. You really love me don't you?" (216). At the end of the African book, as we have it in *True at First Light*, Mary has returned and has suggested, "We'll go to bed early and make love and listen to the night." "Wonderful," he replies (309). In the concluding scene they are together in bed, wondering why they would ever leave this African camp, and Mary offers:

> "Maybe there will be more wonderful places. Don't you want to see the most wonderful places before you die?"
> "No."
> "Well, we're here now. Let's not think of going away."
> "Good."
> The hyena slipped into night song again and took it far up past where it was possible. Then broke it sharply off three times.
> Mary imitated him and we laughed and the cot seemed a fine big bed and we were comfortable and at home in it.

True at First Light is a misleading title for what we might know better as Hemingway's own "night song." In it, wanting to enter "the night [that] belongs to the animals," he goes "far up past where it was possible," sounding even the hyena's note of laughter in order to celebrate everything he knew of *life*.

Dark Eden

One of the most disturbing aspects of the sex problem was Darwin's conclusion, based on the well-known fact "that at a very early embryonic period both sexes possess true male and female glands," that "some extremely remote progenitor of the whole vertebrate kingdom appears to have been hermaphrodite or androgynous" (*Descent of Man* 1:207). No writer explored this question more intensely than Hemingway, especially in *The Garden of Eden*, and ever since its publication in 1986 the subject of androgyny has steadily come to dominate the critical discussion of his work. However, his critics have scarcely considered how his interest in androgyny is related to the extensive exploration of evolution and the sex problem in modern psychology and fiction. Rather, the critical discussion emphasizes psychological and biographical possibilities, centering on his upbringing by a mother who created "a family environment where gender roles were quite fluid." She (Grace Hemingway) fulfilled her "fantasy of being the mother of same-sex twins" by dressing the young Ernest and his slightly older sister Marcelline sometimes as little boys and sometimes as girls (Burwell 17, 20). Much is made of famous photographs of the two-year-old Ernest dressed as a little girl. And other critics address the question of Hemingway's interest in androgyny in order to prove his homoerotic desire or to "construct [his] sexual identity on the border between the heterosexual and the homosexual" (Moddelmog 51).[17]

From another point of view it is worth noting, first, that Hemingway set most of his late self-exploratory work either in Africa or on (or near) the sea, as in the African manuscript, *Islands in the Stream*, and *The Old Man and the Sea* (the exception to this, of course, being his Paris memoir, *A Moveable Feast*).[18] The sea and African settings in all this work serve mainly to focus his narratives on the two engines of life that he had isolated in "The Good Lion" and "The Faithful Bull." And both settings figure importantly in *The Garden of Eden*. There David Bourne works on his African story while living near the sea, where he sometimes fishes and frequently swims in the Gulf of Lions on the Côte d'Azur. Suggesting again and again that his three characters are part of the sea life, to the extent that they tasted of the sea and have hair like seaweed, Hemingway explores the biological darkness—the essential conflict and violence of the natural order—as relentlessly as others had explored only, or mainly, the repressed libido. As always, his meditation on the nature of sexuality undercuts the idea of love, but here more than elsewhere he suggests that the biological fact of our bisexual nature is an undeniable part—but only a part— of the complex violence of natural selection and sexual selection.

In Hemingway's ironic version of the Eden myth, the violence and complexity of sex begins to emerge at once in "the tragic violence" (8) of the sea life that David Bourne engages on the Gulf of Lions when he catches a sea bass. It is also reflected in Catherine's remark to David, "I know I'm a violent girl and you're violent too," (25), as well as in Hemingway's image of the two in bed lying "close together and listen[ing] to the sea" (36). Like the similar scenes of Hemingway and Mary in bed listening to the African night in *True at First Light*, this scene encloses the lovers in the darkness of the natural world. But in this darkness they talk of her androgynous change, and she tells him, "It's the Atlantic ocean. . . . Listen to it." Then considering whether they should stay at this seaside town, he remarks that he would like to stay and, if they do, that he would "like to start to write." The scene closes with her urging him to admit that she hasn't done anything bad to their relationship as a result of her sexual change, but he "did not say anything and listened to the weight of the surf falling on the hard wet sand in the night" (36–37).

As their story develops, then,[19] Hemingway's view of the tragic violence of life expands to include not only David's catching the fish, but also the violence of his father's elephant hunting (in the African story that David is writing all the while), the violence of the main characters' sexual hunger, the violence of sexual betrayal in the triangular affair that develops between the Bournes and the second woman, Marita, and the violence of the conflict within David's and Catherine's relationship over his writing—her resentment of his withdrawing into himself to write and her eventual burning of his manuscripts.

Although we cannot know how Hemingway would have ended the story of this triangular affair, much less the unfinished manuscript as a whole, it is fair to assume, as Robert E. Fleming does, that it would have ended more darkly than it does in the edited novel—more darkly perhaps than even the ending of *True at First Light*, with Hemingway and Mary in bed together as hunting hyenas and lions surround them in the African night.[20] Similarly, it is impossible to tell how Hemingway would have begun his story of the Bournes and Marita had he and not Tom Jenks edited the manuscript. Still it seems perfectly to Hemingway's point that the published novel opens with the information that the recently married Bournes' "hotel was on a canal that ran . . . straight down to the sea." The short first paragraph ends with an image, familiar in Hemingway's sea fiction from *To Have and Have Not* through *The Old Man and the Sea*, of life feeding on life, the primal scene of animal life as it originated not in the garden but the sea: "In the evenings and the mornings when there was a rising tide sea bass would come into [the canal] and [the Bournes] would see the mullet jumping wildly to escape from the bass and watch the swelling bulge of the water as the bass attacked." And Hemingway begins to develop his darkly ironic version of the Eden story in the following paragraph, with a sentence that describes how "a jetty ran out into the blue and pleasant sea" and how the Bournes watched the picturesque "mackerel fishing boats" that were working the spring run "out in the Gulf of Lions. . . . It was a cheerful and friendly town" (3).

Against this backdrop of the pleasantly voracious sea, Hemingway begins (in the novel's third paragraph) to focus on his newlyweds' sexual nature: "They were always hungry but they ate very well" (4). His profuse comments on their hunger and descriptions of their eating include Catherine's question, "Do you always get so hungry when you make love?" and lead in this chapter to David's fishing adventure. Seeking out the place "where he thought fish might be feeding," he immediately hooks one and then endures the long "tragic violence" of overpowering and landing the fish, a feat for which he is celebrated by a "procession of people" (4–9). In short, Hemingway's intention to identify the two essential motives in the lives of his lovers is clear in his remark that "there was only happiness and loving each other and then hunger and replenishing and starting over" (14). Moreover, readers attuned to the modernist analysis of eating and sexuality, of love and pain, or of the primitive cannibalism in sexual hunger cannot miss his suggestions in this chapter and through-out the novel that sexual hunger devours the idea of love.[21] In this first scene empha-sizing their hunger Hemingway dwells on their delight in the eggs they have for break-fast, noting, for example, that their choice of the way "the eggs were to be cooked was an excitement" (4). Elsewhere in the novel he describes how Marita "kissed [David] so hard that she drew blood from his lip" (203), how the boy David and his father each ate "a breast with the heart in it" from two birds that David had killed (172), and how David and Marita dine on "cut up artichoke heart" (243).

From David's initial point of view, in their seaside existence the newlyweds live in a kind of biological Eden: "when they had made love they would eat and drink and make love again. It was a very simple world" (14). But of course the biological reality is highly complicated and fraught with change, as *The Origin of Species* had demonstrated in shattering the vision of a providential design in the natural world. Indeed, this is a familiar refrain throughout Hemingway's career (about how com-plicated things are) and is an essential part of his response to the Darwinian view of life as Darwin expresses it, for example, in the first paragraph of his "Summary and Concluding Remarks" on the "Principles of Sexual Selection": "not only are the laws of inheritance extremely complex, but so are the causes which induce and gov-ern variability"; moreover, "sexual selection" (the means by which "variations . . . are preserved and accumulated") "is in itself an extremely complex affair"; and "hence the manner in which the individuals of either sex or of both sexes are af-fected through sexual selection cannot fail to be complex in the highest degree" (*The Descent of Man* 1:1:296).[22] And as we have seen, one of the most disorienting complications in the nature of human sexuality was the androgynous embryo's threat to the idea of absolute sexual difference. Thus, after Catherine had intro-duced her "simple but . . . very complicated" surprise, that she was "going to be changed," David's response is "No . . . No. Not changed" (*Garden of Eden* 11–12). And before she reappears with "her hair . . . cropped as short as a boy's," David worries over "this thing about the change" (14).

Also at the moment when David is contemplating the change, he thinks how good it will be to get to work again on his writing, but he finds it regrettable that this will require a certain selfish "enforced loneliness" and he was "not proud of it" (14). As their complicated relationship develops, then, and he does begin to write again, David tells himself: "It is all very well for you to write simply and the simpler the better. But do not start to think so damned simply. Know how complicated it is and then state it simply" (37). Now the main threads of the novel (as we have it) are gathered and drawn together as a multithreaded story of David's development as a writer. As it proceeds he will learn a good deal about the nature of bisexuality, in-cluding his awareness that he too quite enjoyed changing and exploring that part of himself: looking at himself in a mirror he said, "You like it. Remember that. Keep that straight. You know exactly how you look now and how you are" (85). He will also discover that he wanted two women at once, "he wanted them both" (132), a central part of the sex problem regarding the male in novels by Howells, Dreiser, and Anderson, for example; finally even "his changing of allegiance" from Catherine to Marita had been an act of violence that he could live with (238). He will, in writing the African story of his father's killing an elephant, discover "his change of feeling toward . . . his father" (182) and later realize that he "was fortunate . . . that his father was not a simple man" (247). And ultimately he will realize that in order to write and to endure he must affirm "the knowledge of loneliness" (201) that had begun when he was a boy and saw the elephant his father had killed, and that comes to him in his present conflict within the triangular affair when he dives "deep down [in] the clear cold water where he missed no one" (132). That is, recognizing the complexity of the natural world as "the unreality that reality had become" for him (echoing his theme in *True at First Light*), he realizes that he "must go back into his own country" of his writing (193). In a world of endless conflict underscored by the essential selfishness of the two hungers, and as this develops into the conflict leading to Catherine's burning his manuscripts, he finally affirms the selfishness of his work that he had originally regretted: "The work is what you have left," he told himself (127); "You better get to work. You have to make sense there. You don't make any in this other. Nothing will help you" (146). "He cared about the writing more than about anything else" (211).

Although the idea that winners take nothing is a familiar landmark in the Hemingway landscape, it is too little appreciated that one underlying reason for this bleak view of life is that, like many other writers of his time, Hemingway (or David) could not console himself with the raw evolutionary reward as Darwin had defined it: survival through reproductive success. This feeling is most memorably expressed at the end of *A Farewell to Arms*, when what he called the "biological trap" closed with the deaths of Catherine and their stillborn child, choked by the umbilical cord. And it is clearly felt in *The Garden of Eden* in the way David eats his and Catherine's eggs ("When Catherine had not come and her egg was getting in danger of getting cold he ate it too" [43]); in frequent references to their eating caviar, as when David remarks, "Everyone's full of charm . . . and sturgeon eggs" (131); and in the way Hemingway describes David and Marita after they make love on the beach. After lifting "very slowly up and gently out and away from her," he "dove under where the water was cold and [he] swam deep," returned to "hold her tight [while] the waves washed against them," and then heard her say, "Everything of ours washed into the ocean."[23] Similarly, Hemingway never expressed any faith in the idea of evolutionary progress that others of his time had sought in love, eugenics, the *élan vital*, civilization, or culture. As David Bourne tells himself, "The writing is the only progress you make" (166). Largely for these reasons Hemingway always insists that the only thing one can claim in a life in which winners take nothing is a sense that one has not only seen it for what it *is*, but has partaken of it—fully, and without cracking up. "The supposed dark hours of the soul . . . are a man's best hours . . . if he is not afraid." And through David he suggests that, for the writer, this form of achieving grace under pressure can come only through the lonely act of composition, where "you have to make sense."

Moreover, Hemingway was also quite aware of the idea that if there is a kind of survival in the creative act, it is essentially only a narcissistic way or preserving one's sense of integrity, one's sense of one's self; that is, a way of staying alive. David's ultimate problem with Catherine's experiments with androgyny is that it poses a natural threat to his own complicated self, in a way that is comparable to the beginning of animal life, as Havelock Ellis and others surmised, when sexual conjugation amounted to "the complete devouring of one organism by another" (*Studies* 1:2:127). We can see Catherine's threat to David's identity in this sequence of her remarks: "I get so hungry," "I'm the destructive type. . . . And I'm going to destroy you" (5); "Now [as she remarks in their changed sex roles] you can't tell who is who can you?" (17); and again, "I'm a violent girl and you're violent too" (25). It is not that he does not like this change of sexual roles, that it is not normal or that he thinks it a sin—only that it leads him to ask himself, "What are you anymore anyway?" (127).[24] When Catherine finally burns his manuscripts (and the identity he had created for himself there), David "felt completely hollow" (216).

In the scene in which Catherine reveals that she had burned the manuscripts, she tells Marita in David's presence that he reads his reviews and clippings "by himself and is unfaithful to me with them. In a wastebasket probably. . . . [W]hat are you to do if you discover the man is illiterate and practices solitary vice in a wastebasket full of clippings?" (215–16). Rose Marie Burwell refers to this as the "masturbatory ritual of [David's] writing" (122), noting that "it is clear even to David himself that he is engaged in a kind of creative onanism" (119), but she does so in order to side with Catherine and further her argument that this is an aspect of David's regression in Hemingway's unsuccessful "attempt to render aesthetic growth through sexual metamorphosis" (108).[25] Rather, Hemingway's portrait of David as writer is part of a pattern of extraordinarily profuse mirror images throughout the novel and constitutes one of the most interesting dimensions of his self-exploration in light of the modernist analysis of evolution and the sex problem. And once again, as is so often the case in Hemingway's presentation of sex, it helps a great deal to compare Hemingway's representation of sexuality with what Havelock Ellis had to say on this subject, in this case on autoerotism and "The Conception of Narcissism."

It is well known that Hemingway began to devour Ellis's *Erotic Symbolism* early in 1920,[26] but it probably was not until 1936 that he was able to read the last volume of *Studies in the Psychology of Sex, Eonism and Other Supplementary Studies* (published separately in 1928), when it was published as part of the famous two-volume edition of the *Studies in the Psychology of Sex* in 1936. Hemingway purchased it that year. In his preface to *Eonism and Other Supplementary Studies* Ellis remarks that with it he "is now finally drawing together the last threads of Studies which have occupied so large a part of my life," the first part having appeared in the year of Hemingway's birth (1899), and in these last studies he cites research that had appeared as late as December of 1925. Ellis's further prefatory remark is worth quoting for the way it reveals how he and the other writers discussed in this book (from Jack London to Gertrude Stein, Sherwood Anderson, and Hemingway) all saw their work with the sex problem. Indeed, they should be regarded as fellow explorers in the new, exciting, and rapidly developing field[27] whose originating impetus can be traced directly to *The Descent of Man, and Selection in Relation to Sex*:

> It may seem that some of the lines of investigation here followed lead away from the familiarly recognizable paths generally accepted as profitable. But as one of our greatest masters in the exploration of the living organism, William Harvey, wrote a few weeks before his death: "Nature is nowhere accustomed more openly to display her secret mysteries than when she shows traces of her workings apart from the beaten path." That which is true of Nature in general is true of the impulse of sex in particular, and none of the explorations, however unfamiliar, recorded in this volume will be devoid of instruction. (*Studies* 2:2:v)

Chapter 6 of *Eonism and Other Supplementary Studies*, "The Conception of Narcissism," begins with a brief history of Narcissus that arrives at "an important stage . . . when Milton . . . represented Narcissus in that feminine shape to which in modern times his attitude has always seemed best fitted, and showed the first Mother of Mankind in the typical Narcissistic attitude of adolescence before she had met Adam." Then he quotes the lines from *Paradise Lost* (bk. 4, 456–69) in which Eve sees her "Shape within the watry gleam," its "looks / Of sympathie and love." She tells Adam that "there I had fixt / Mine eyes till now, and pin'd with vain desire" (*Studies* 2:2:349). Ellis follows this with a brief survey of how, throughout the centuries, poets have "been true to the facts of primitive life" in "dwelling on water as a mirror" and of how writers such as Rousseau, Juan Valera, Wilde, and Tolstoy had described "in themselves or in the creatures of their imagination the mental state of Narcissus" (350–53). Then he describes the development of thought on Narcissism in modern psychology, noting that he had presented "the first generalized description of this psychological attitude" in a paper ("Auto-Erotism: a Psychological Study") in 1898, where he had discussed "that tendency which is sometimes found, more especially perhaps in women, for the sexual emotions to be absorbed, and often entirely lost, in self-admiration" (355–56). By Ellis's account, then, Freud eventually began a series of developing theories of Narcissism, not in the first but the second edition of *Three Contributions to the Theory of Sex* (1910), in which he regarded it as "simply a stage in the development of masculine sexual inversion, the subject being supposed to identify himself with a woman (usually his mother) and so acquiring self-love" (357).

Along the way in his review of the development of thought on the subject of narcissism, including extensive remarks on "the problems of mirror folklore" (371), Ellis twice emphasizes that he had always differed from Freud and others in considering it (and autoerotism, in general) as a normal tendency and not a perversion (358, 362–63). But he draws attention to "the first and most important study by Freud himself in the development of the conception of Narcissism" (in his paper of 1914, "Ueber Narzissismus"), where he concluded that narcissism becomes "the libidinal complement to the egoism of the instinct of self-preservation, a measure of which may justifiably be attributed to every living creature" (357–58).[28]

Showing how the developing theories of narcissism followed this line of thinking about the instinct for self-preservation, then, Ellis notes that "the tendency is increasing to magnify the place of Narcissism in normal life" (366); that "the implication of comparison and selection and preference, even superiority, lies consciously or unconsciously, at the basis of Narcissism" (372); that this brings the "inevitable . . . conception that all creation is essentially an exercise of Narcissism" (374); and finally that it is credible to suggest even that narcissism "is the guiding motive of Nature herself" (375). Indeed, he concludes, "we have moved a long way since the days, only a few years ago" when narcissism "seemed a rather rare and not specially profitable aspect of human invention" (375).

Hemingway's *Garden of Eden* did not simply use or steal Ellis's (and the other psychologists') ideas on creativity and narcissism; rather, he took in these exploratory ideas (as Ellis, Freud, Moll, Jung, and others did) in order to strengthen his own somewhat different exploration of the living organism, as Ellis put it. From Hemingway's perspective such exploration always requires a dive "deep down into the clear cold water" where life began, and it ends in his sense of the essential loneliness in the violent order wherein everything depends upon the instinct of self-preservation (132).[29] This view of life underlies Hemingway's profuse mirror imagery in *The Garden of Eden*, and it includes two important images of animal eyes that serve to impress on David his essential nature in the community of common descent. The first such image appears early in the novel at the end of "the tragic violence" when David lands the sea bass: "He was a handsome and beautifully built fish with great live eyes, and he breathed slowly and brokenly" (8–9). Serving to strengthen Hemingway's constant theme in this novel, his characters' nature as sea creatures, it looks forward to the much more powerful and memorable scene in the

African story within the novel, of "the beginning of [David's] knowledge of loneliness." In this scene the magnificent elephant David's father has shot is itself a sea creature of sorts, "anchored, in such suffering and despair that he could no longer move. . . . as though he was a ship": "He did not move but his eye was alive and looked at David. He had very long eyelashes and his eye was the most alive thing David had ever seen" (199–201).

Regarding the more explicit mirror imagery in the novel, it is important to note that Hemingway uses it to reflect on the nature of all the players in the triangular affair, not only David, as some interpreters suggest,[30] and that the overriding problem is of their self-knowledge as participants in the tragic violence of life. Of course, "nobody knows about himself when he is really involved," as David remarks to Marita (184). But, looking at his mirror image, David does recognize something of his androgynous nature: "You know exactly how you look and how you are" (85). Similarly, he glimpses the idea that in writing about his father he is writing about himself: feeling and welcoming "his father's presence" after a session of writing about him, "He glanced in the mirror and saw he was alone" (147). And in reference to Catherine and Marita, the mirror imagery traces a process of Catherine's disintegrating instinct for self-preservation and Marita's superiority as a sexual competitor for David. When Catherine first looks at herself in a mirror, "her face had no expression and she looked at herself from her head down to her feet with no expression on her face at all" (115). Just before this moment David tells her that she is "talking crazy," and in a later scene she explains that she wants Marita to inherit him from herself "if I'm crazy" (145). Later still she thinks the mirror is "awfully critical" and turns away (133), using it in subsequent scenes only to observe the others (219–20). By contrast, at the end of the novel, after Marita has prevailed over Catherine in the struggle for David, she leaves the bed where "they [had] slept well and naturally" and "looked at herself in the full length mirror. Then she smiled at the mirror" (244). Well equipped with "the instinct for self-preservation" that Ellis and Freud had associated with narcissism, Marita explains to David in the following scene that if any other "young and new and fresh" friends come along, "I'll kill them. . . . I'm not going to give you away to anyone the way [Catherine] did" (245).

No matter how much this might distort the biographical reality of Hemingway's own life and his relationships with women, it does reflect the view of reality that he constructed in *The Garden of Eden*. If Catherine's seductive invitation to David to change suggests her relationship to Eve, she does lead David more deeply into his own complex life as evolutionary biology and modern psychology had described it, and he fully embraces it. Similarly, after his devastating loss of the manuscripts, Marita is Eve-like in her repeated encouragement to eat: "Eat, David, please. . . . Just eat a little. . . . Eat. . . . Just eat now to please me" (234–35). She, too, draws him back into that life in which each of the three players is related to the sea bass that feed on the mullet in the opening scene—near "the hotel . . . on a canal that ran . . . straight down to the sea." Catherine "still tasted of the sea" (162) and "looked as though she had just come out of the sea" (176); David puts "his salty mouth against" Marita's, and, kissing her breasts, says, "They taste like the sea" (241). If they play "under water like porpoises," they sometimes wear "sharkskin" and ultimately participate in the war of nature that Darwin described in the *Origin of Species* and that the other sea animals enact far out at sea as a prelude and backdrop to the three lovers' climactic scene. Just before Catherine reveals that she had burned David's manuscripts, David finds the two women in bed together and, leaving them, looks far out to "three French destroyers and a cruiser, neat and dark, and sharply etched on the blue sea"; the ships "moved in formation working out some problems," maybe "anti-sub maneuvers" (213).[31] Moments later in this scene we see David and Marita swimming far out as the warships are joined by planes.

Clearly, Catherine is a casualty of this war, and many critics have commented on Hemingway's sympathy with her.[32] Others have noted the pattern of imagery that links her ivory color with the prized ivory for which the elephants are killed, as well as the way David's father's hunting is associated with his sexual appetite. But all this is part of the general tragic violence of life that Hemingway confronts again and again in his late work, always in an attempt to accept and ultimately celebrate it. He does so near the end of *The Garden of Eden*, when David and Marita decide to go swimming again, "so [they] won't waste the day." When they enter the "dark and blue sea," their true Eden, there is a note of affirmation in his words, "*Elle est bonne, la mer. . . . Toi aussi.*" Then, he like a porpoise and she a seal, "they swam far out, further than they had ever swum before . . . slowly and strongly" (240–42). Once again one hears the notes of Hemingway's "night song," going "far up past where it was possible" (*True at First Light* 311). When they come ashore tired, Marita remarks that "Catherine wouldn't have gotten tired," but David replies, "The hell she wouldn't. She never swam that far." In her unease, Marita asks, "Do you still love me?" and David assures her, "Yes. Very much." Now the two dine together on "radishes [that] were young and crisp and sharp in flavor" ("who knows what . . . the small young radish" feels? Hemingway asks in *True at First Light*). And then like Santiago and the Good Lion "Marita took a handful of radishes and ate them slowly," and David "cut one of the artichoke hearts" for them to share (242–43).

Notes

1. For an interpretation of *The Sun Also Rises* as a critique of love in light of the theory of sexual selection, see the chapter on Hemingway in my *The Descent of Love*.

2. Subsequent references to this story are cited parenthetically by page number from this volume.

3. As Frank Sulloway notes, Darwin certainly did not invent the idea that "'love and hunger' rule the world," but he, "perhaps more than anyone else in the nineteenth century, singled out the biological importance of the instincts for survival and for reproduction" (252). It is still too little appreciated in literary history that American realism began with William Dean Howells's meditation of this view of life in *Their Wedding Journey* (1871), where he touches on his newlyweds' need to eat and explores more fully their sexual nature. For a discussion of these aspects of the novel, see my *The Descent of Love*. For William James's remarks on killing and eating, see his four paragraphs on "the hunting instinct" in *Principles*, 1030–33.

4. For a brief discussion of *The Old Man and the Sea* from this point of view, see my *Sea-Brothers*, 192–98.

5. Noting Burwell's remark that the African manuscript reveals "Hemingway at his most human, writing of himself with sustained comic irony we have never been allowed to see," Robert W. Lewis suggests that the comic quality is more "sardonic . . . than ironic" and adds that Hemingway's earlier work, as well, reveals that he is "one of our best comic writers" (121). Lewis makes a valid point in his concluding remark in his essay on the African manuscript: "This Hemingway, this mellowed, thoughtful, sardonic naturalist, is a man worth knowing. His extraordinary capacity for both childlike joy and elegiac sorrow is nowhere more well presented than in his 'African Book'" (122).

6. Writing more seriously on this subject during the same years in *Islands in the Stream*, Hemingway has Thomas Hudson's former wife comment on his greatest role, when he played "the Faithful Husband and you were doing it so wonderfully and there was a big spot of natural juices showed on your trousers and every time you looked at me it was bigger" (313).

7. Although Hemingway's critics rarely mention Darwin, even in passing, no reader who is familiar with *The Origin of Species* or, especially, *The Descent of Man*, can fail to see countless moments in Hemingway's work which focus on the workings of natural and sexual selection, as in the scenes of the law of battle among the males in *The Sun Also Rises*, for example, or moments such as his description of the grasshoppers in the first part of "Big Two-Hearted River": "they had all turned black from living in the burned-over land," or the trout in part 2 whose "back was mottled" like "the clear, water-over-gravel color" (*Short Stories* 212, 225). Yet a recent collection of essays, *Hemingway and the Natural World* (1999), contains no references to Darwin. Hemingway's library contained several volumes by and about Darwin, including the *Origin of Species* and *The Voyage of the Beagle* in the Harvard Classics, another edition of *The Beagle*, *The Darwin Reader* (ed. Bates and Humphrey), and *Makers of Modern Science* (edited by Paul B. Sears, author of *Charles Darwin: the Naturalist as a Cultural Force*). It is also widely known that Hemingway read William James's *The Principles of Psychology*, Ellis's *Studies in the Psychology of Sex*, and works on and by Freud. No perceptive reading of James or Ellis could miss the Darwinian foundations of those works. It is not surprising that Hemingway's library contained nothing by Louis Agassiz, but because Hemingway's father was a member

of the Agassiz Club and introduced his son to the pleasures of natural history, one of the most prominent Hemingway scholars concludes that "Hemingway remained throughout his life first and foremost an Agassiz-trained naturalist" (Beegel 75). It is especially puzzling to consider why this essay, on "Hemingway as a Naturalist," makes its case for Agassiz's continuing authority well into the twentieth century in part by noting that "Agassiz's students included such illustrious scientists as William James" (70). As one could not help but conclude from reading *The Principles of Psychology*, James revered Darwin; indeed, as soon as he read Darwin he rejected Agassiz in the strongest possible terms. William wrote to Henry in 1868: "The more I think of Darwin's ideas the more weighty do they appear to me.... Agassiz is unworthy either intellectually or morally for him to wipe his feet on" (qtd. in Ralph Barton Perry, *The Thought and Character of William James*, 102).

8. Hemingway's exploration of primitiveness is more in keeping with what these Americans were doing in the 1920s and 1930s than with Joseph Conrad's *Heart of Darkness*. Noting Hemingway's admiration for Conrad and comparing *The Garden of Eden* with "Heart of Darkness," Comley and Scholes remark on *The Garden of Eden*'s "equivocal but genuine endorsement of transgressive eroticism and its fascination with a truth that can be found only by penetrating to the heart of a dark erotic continent called Africa" (103). But Hemingway's interest in the darkness of killing and eating is quite different from what Conrad was exploring. Still, Comley and Scholes make an excellent point in writing that Hemingway's editors went too far in concealing the darkness of *The Garden of Eden*.

9. For another perspective on the question of Hemingway's primitivism but one that ignores the context of the way this question was debated by a great range of writers during Hemingway's early career (as in Sherwood Anderson and the contributors to the Harlem Renaissance), see Debra Moddelmog's argument that "Hemingway simply moves—into the colonial fantasy regarding black primitiveness and desire" (116).

10. For a discussion of Kroeber and the revival of Darwinism, see Degler's chapter "Biology Redivivus" in *In Search of Human Nature*, especially 218.

11. Most likely there is an editorial error in printing no comma after "and" and one after "as" ("your neighbor and as, in all countries, it is a moveable feast").

12. For example, immediately following a crude train of thought on supposed customs concerning homosexuals, cannibalism, and bestiality ("part of anthropology that I had not yet penetrated"), he thinks that Debba "was a straight Kamba girl replete with modesty and true basic insolence" (249). And here, perhaps, we can see how Hemingway's field work (to put it generously) might reflect something of what he had found in one of his well-worn texts, Havelock Ellis's section on "The Evolution of Modesty," in the volume that also contains "Auto-Erotism." There, after tracing the "fundamental animal factor of modesty, rooted in the natural facts of the sexual life of the higher mammals, and especially man," and after citing lengthy descriptions of modesty among native peoples from all over the world, including the Masai, Ellis concludes with a remark that describes what Hemingway found so charming in Debba and the other African women—their "basic insolence" and "impudence": "Modesty is not ... the last word of love, but it is the necessary foundation for all love's most exquisite audacities, the foundation which alone gives worth and sweetness to what Senancour call its 'delicious impudence'" (1:1:46, 82). Similarly, in what Hemingway calls other "simple studies in our tribal moeurs," undertaken while he was riding to town in a

truck with another African woman, he tells of how a "classically beautiful" Masai woman sat between him and his male friend Mthuka, caressing both men in a "quite shameless" way and laughing when there were visible "reactions to her courtship" (185).

13. Attempting to justify his affair with Debba, Hemingway frequently uses the phrase, "No hay remedio." "It was the saddest thing I knew in Spanish," he tells us, and that is why it was one of the first things he taught Debba to say: "it was probably best for her to learn it early" (63–64). But he is also careful to give us Mary's perspective on the affair, when she tells him that she doesn't "care what you do as long as it's good for you" and as long as he doesn't "hurt other people or spoil their lives. And don't say no hay remedio. That's too easy" (73).

14. Similarly in *The Garden of Eden*, as Catherine and David Bourne get darker and darker in the Mediterranean sun, Catherine wants David to get "darker than an Indian." They will explore "lots of wild places," she says, and that she will get "as Dark as I can. . . . I wish I had some Indian blood" (30–31).

15. In the entry for Charo (Mary's gun bearer) in his "Cast of Characters" in *True at First Light*, Patrick Hemingway comments on the oddities of "ethical behavior in different cultures" in reference to polygamy and polyandry and the Hemingways. Drawing on his own considerable experience in Africa, he notes that his father was then with his fourth wife (Mary) and that she was in her third marriage: "Mary . . . is protected from her husband taking a second wife by the ethics of the West, but not from sequential polygamy, which troubles her a great deal. It is what lies behind her desire to kill a lion . . . in a new and superior way" (315).

16. For Hemingway's dreams of animals, see also a passage quoted by Comley and Scholes from a manuscript in the Kennedy Library in which Hemingway recorded "a dream [he] once had of copulating with a lioness":

> In my dreams I am always between the age of 25 of 30 years old, I am irresistible to women, dogs and on one recent occasion a very beautiful lioness.
> In the dream this lioness, who became my fiancée, was one of the most delightful creatures I have ever dreamt about. She had some of the characteristics of Miss Mary and she could become irascible. On one occasion I recall she did an extremely perilous act. Perilous to me that is. (95–96)

Comley and Scholes do not identify the context of these remarks nor do they comment on the possible fiction here, in what appears to be related to the African manuscript. It could be that Hemingway was playing with the kind of thing he found in Havelock Ellis's voluminous case histories or some of the odd statistics provided by Alfred Kinsey. He enjoyed this kind of play in a letter to Harvey Breit in July of 1950, for example: "Black Dog has gone so sleep now happy that I am writing. He doesn't know what but he loves to hear those keys go. He is a big Springer and a good retriever. I love him and he loves me and Dr. Kinsey can have that for free" (*Letters* 701).

17. In addition to Burwell and Moddelmog, Spilka, Eby, and Comley and Scholes have produced the most important studies of Hemingway and androgyny or gender. Although I take a completely different approach to Hemingway's interest in androgyny or gender from these authors, I do share Moddelmog's sense that "one gets the feeling not only that Hemingway was attempting to comprehend human sexuality, including his own, but that he was

growing tired of the public mask that simplified the complexity of his own desire" (88). Of all these studies, only Comley and Scholes indicate—very briefly and without developing the point—their awareness of or interest in the context of scientific thought on sexuality during Hemingway's career. They write toward the end of their study: "The complexity of human sexuality—especially the potential bisexuality of all humans—were issues that had been given a prominent place in the cultural texts of Fleiss, Freud, and Weininger around the turn of the century. These issues were in the air that Hemingway and other artists of his time were breathing" (144).

18. Earlier in *Green Hills of Africa* he had found himself "thinking of the sea and of the country," there developing a memorable meditation on hunting and killing that leads into the equally memorable lyric tribute to the "one single, lasting thing—the [Gulf] stream" (148–50). And in *The Old Man and the Sea* Santiago's dreams return to the time when had fished along the coast of Africa and had seen "the lions on the beach" (27).

19. Once again it is important to remember that the published novel deals only with the Bournes and their triangle with Marita and that it excises Hemingway's development of the other relationship (of Barbara and Nick Sheldon) and the other triangle (of the Sheldons and Andrew Murray).

20. Discussing the possible endings that Hemingway left with the unfinished manuscript, Fleming concludes that "the Jenks edition of *The Garden of Eden*" distorts the fact that "Hemingway had very deliberately been constructing a tragic novel with his multiple of tales of betrayal, jealousy, and guilt" ("The Endings of Hemingway's *Garden of Eden*" 269–70).

21. See, for example, Freud's remark on "the fact that sexual gratification originates during the intake of nourishment" (*Basic Writings* 603) and, more important, Havelock Ellis's extensive discussion of the love-bite, blood, and the idea that in "the beginning of animal life in the protozoa sexual conjugation itself is sometimes found to present the similitude, if not the actuality, of the complete devouring of one organism by another." ("Love and Pain," a section totaling seven chapters, in *Studies* 1:2:127.)

22. Although there is no reason to conclude that Hemingway did not recognize this Darwinian complexity very early in his career, we do know certainly that this passage is in the volume he acquired shortly after its publication (by Scribner's) in 1956, *The Darwin Reader*, 312. For one early example of Hemingway's interest in this kind of complexity, see his story, "Soldier's Home," in which the young Krebs returned from the war to find that everyone in his town "lived in such a complicated world"; though he "liked" the girls, "they were too complicated. . . . He did not want to have to do any courting"; "He had tried to keep his life from being complicated" (*Short Stories* 147, 152).

23. On this point consider also the discussion between Catherine and David in which Catherine says that with her money "we can have the fun before I have a baby" (27), the scene in which a Colonel Boyle remarks to David, in reference to himself and Catherine, "The get's no good . . . It's kinder to shoot the get" (65), and the scene in which Catherine complains to David of the material he is working within his African story, of "your drunken father staggering around [among "a lot of natives"] smelling of sour beer and knowing which ones of the little horrors he had fathered" (189).

24. Hemingway's questioning of normality in sexual behavior was undoubtedly strengthened by his longtime interest in Ellis and, at about the time he was working on this manuscript, by what he read in Alfred Kinsey's *Sexual Behavior in the Human Male*, and it is expressed

more clearly in the manuscript than in the edited novel. For example, in passages from the manuscript quoted by Moddelmog, Catherine once challenges David, "Who's normal? What's normal?" and in a scene with Marita and David, Marita assures David that their changed roles in lovemaking is "not perversion. It's variety" (78, 82). Regarding sin, David tells himself in the novel, "You're lucky to have a wife like her and a sin is what you feel bad after and you don't feel bad" (21).

25. Burwell writes that Mark Spilka's earlier study, *Hemingway's Quarrel with Androgyny*, had provided her with the key to her thesis of Hemingway's "gender ambivalence" and "attempt to render aesthetic growth" (108). Spilka had concluded that Hemingway's "lifelong quarrel with androgyny . . . was crucial to his creative strength throughout his life" but that he tragically betrayed it near the end of his life, particularly in his decision in *The Garden of Eden* to cast off "Catherine in favor of the supportive adjunct mate, Marita," which amounted to "a casting out of his own creative strength" (336).

26. Lynn writes of how Hemingway "devoured" *Erotic Symbolism* and Conrad's *Victory* early in 1920 (114), but of Hemingway's many biographers and critics only Michael Reynolds, certainly his most distinguished biographer, has given his interest in Havelock Ellis the emphasis it deserves. "How like the writer he became that he should have read Ellis so studiously" in the early 1920s, Reynolds remarks. And Reynolds's sense of the context of Hemingway's interest in Ellis is essential: "Just when Hemingway's sexual life was blossoming, he discovered from [Sherwood] Anderson that one could write about it in ways long forbidden. Deviant behavior, Freudian complexes and basic sexual congress—only hinted at darkly by the preceding generation—were becoming the focus of Hemingway's age. This discovery was crucial to Hemingway's development as a writer" (*The Young Hemingway* 122, 184). Hemingway understood, as did Ellis and Freud, that Darwinian evolution was the bedrock of modern psychology.

27. Earlier chapters here on Norris, London, and Stein, for example, have traced such developments, and in this regard it is worth noting Ellis's comment on Freud and his changing conceptions of narcissism: "Freud himself . . . avoids definitions because his conceptions are always growing and expanding" (2:2:361).

28. It is not clear when Hemingway wrote the parts of the *Garden of Eden* manuscript that play on the profuse imagery of mirrors that reflects Ellis's and Freud's sense of the connection between narcissism and the instinct of self-preservation (Burwell's "Chronology" indicates that he began work on the manuscript in late 1945 and continued sporadic work on it through early 1959); but it is possible that Hemingway found corroboration for the idea of Darwinian theory providing a new mirror for human self-knowledge from the book he acquired in 1953, *Makers of Modern Science*, which included three parts, one by Paul B. Sears on Charles Darwin, one by Gregory Zilboorg on Sigmund Freud, and one by Leopold Infeld on Albert Einstein. In the chapter "A New Mirror" Sears expounds on Darwin's contribution to our self-knowledge, more or less developing the idea that Freud suggested in his famous remark about the three historic blows to human narcissism, those by Copernicus, Darwin (telling us that we are only animals), and himself (in his theory of the powerful subconscious).

29. This scene is one of David's many dives. As noted elsewhere, Hemingway imagined such dives in *The Sun Also Rises* (see my *The Descent of Love* 358–59) and, figuratively, in *To Have and Have Not*, *Islands in the Stream*, and especially in Santiago's contemplation of "the

prisms in the deep dark water" in *The Old Man and the Sea*. For a discussion of such materials in Hemingway's sea fiction, see my *Sea-Brothers*).

30. For important examples see Eby, *Hemingway's Fetishism: Psychoanalysis and the Mirror of Manhood* (especially the chapter "Transvestism, Homeovestism, and the Mirror of Manhood") and Fleming, *The Face in the Mirror: Hemingway's Writers*.

31. Those who know Hemingway will recall the motif of going far out not only in the hyena's night song in *True at First Light* but also in "The Snows of Kilimanjaro," *The Old Man and the Sea*, and his Nobel Prize address, where he spoke of the writer's loneliness and his being "driven far out past where he can go, out to where no one can help him" (Baker, *Life Story*, 529).

32. The deepest reason for his sympathy for Catherine—reflecting something of his complicated relationship with his own father—is that Catherine's father "killed himself in a car. His wife too" (61). Through the character Colonel Boyle, Hemingway suggests that this trouble in Catherine's family background is inherited (as in her own self-destructive nature): "The get's no good," Boyle says, referring to the children that Catherine might bear (65).

Afterword

In their narratives of evolution and the sex problem, the writers surveyed here disagreed on many points, often revealing their personal biases and conflicting political purposes. In general, however, they were embarked together on a quest like Gertrude Stein's to discover "the bottom nature" of "every kind . . . of men and women" (*Everybody's Autobiography* 266). If they gave us varieties of human experience, as William James sought to do in his own work from those years (*The Varieties of Religious Experience* [1902]), they implied their agreement with the idea in his subtitle, that they were also engaged in *A Study of Human Nature*. They shared an interest in the great questions of their time: the sex problem as it had emerged from Darwin's theories of sexual selection, the evolution of mind, and the evolution of race, as well as the general question T. H. Huxley had emphasized in *Man's Place in Nature*.

It is notable that several of the evolutionary questions that most compelled these writers' attention have now receded from view, and they often began to do so within the period itself. For example, the great questions surrounding the evolution of race and Anglo-Saxon supremacy were burning issues for Norris, London, Stein, and the Harlem novelists; but they began to dissolve in London's critique of the Great White Way. Similarly, the related questions of heredity and primitivism that oppressed Fitzgerald, Stein, and the Harlem novelists have receded from view. Largely due to developments in evolutionary biology that led to the modern synthesis, no doubt, these issues (including the question of eugenics) seem irrelevant in the later explorations of Steinbeck and Hemingway. Further, it seems that these oppressive aspects of evolutionary thought arose in the first place out of the human insecurity and self-fear in contemplating the idea of common descent, an anxiety that gave rise to the comforting beliefs in evolutionary hierarchies and deliverance through evolutionary progress. Without suggesting that Steinbeck and Hemingway can represent a period of complete evolutionary enlightenment in American literature, one can say at least that both were on friendly terms with themselves as part of the animal world. There is a kind of liberation in this awareness.

Indeed, in several important ways, all of the writers surveyed here felt liberated by evolutionary science. In this way, their work contradicts the common assumption that Darwinian thought poses a threat to individual liberty and human dignity, that it yields only a demeaning essentialism or a justification for enforcing specious social hierarchies. They were liberated first by the self-knowledge that Darwin offered to any human being who could withstand the initial "*biological* blow" to human consciousness that Freud built on. They were liberated by being able to explore, often in a confessional mode, promiscuous, polygamous, polyandrous, or bisexual desire—and all the other aspects of human sexuality that Darwin, Ellis, and Freud helped define as being within the range of sexual normality, including the underlying power and violence inherent in "the sexual struggle" that Darwin had described. Moreover, many of these writers (London, Anderson, and Jessie Fauset, for example) felt that their new insights could help them find ways to overcome "the old sex antagonism" between men and women (*Valley of the Moon* 78). Among the Harlem novelists, there was a shared sense that Darwin's theory on sex and race had done for biology "what Christ did for theology"—it "democratized" biology (Stribling 219). As Rudolph Fisher put it, evolution was the "savior" of science (*City of Refuge* xiv). It is certainly true that all of these fifteen writers felt empowered by what they could find in evolutionary thought.

Accompanying these writers' high regard, if not reverence, for science is a surprisingly robust affirmation of the human spirit. Its many manifestations include Norris's faith in the sprouting seed and "the enigma of growth," Stephen Crane's faith in the evolution of the human conscience that produced both the tattered soldier's altruism and Henry Fleming's irrepressible shame, Jack London's interest in the early Freudians' idea of the unconscious as soul, Sherwood Anderson's Whitmanesque vision of the body or of the "thing" beyond sexual intimacy that enables one to endure modern life, the soaring spirit of human creativity in Cather's *Song of the Lark,* DuBois's faith in the souls of black folk, or Claude McKay's in the much earthier "marriage of spirits" between his brown lovers in Harlem. To be sure, few of these writers could strike the spiritual note as a dominant theme. In Steinbeck the spiritual need endures as part of human ecology, and Hemingway dramatizes only a poignant longing, as when Jake Barnes watches the holy water evaporate from his fingertips in *The Sun Also Rises* or when Hemingway draws—then erases—the sign of the fish in tribute to the dead lion.

The writers of this period explored the sex problem. But of course none of them individually or as a movement *solved* the sex problem. That sex remains a very important problem for our culture is evident in evolutionary biology's renewed interest in the theory of sexual selection in recent decades and in developments in the highly controversial fields of sociobiology and evolutionary psychology (not to mention such phenomena as the AIDS epidemic or the controversies over cloning and genetic engineering). Still, as they imagined the ways in which Darwin's theory of sexual selection influenced the lives of their characters, many novelists from the 1880s to the 1950s assumed what Michael Ghiselin has called Darwin's "basic point" in *The Descent of Man,* a point that "even good evolutionary biologists usually miss":

"that we live in a competitive world" ("The Individual in the Darwinian Revolution" 126). Indeed, many of these writers sensed that the sexual reality is as fraught with conflict and competition as recent biologists such as Robert Trivers, Geoff Parker, and Tim Birkhead have explained. Noting that there often exists a conflict of interest between males and females over copulation, Birkhead, for example, writes, "It is no longer meaningful to consider reproduction, whether it involves copulation, or simply the release of gametes into the sea, as a collaboration between the sexes. More accurately, it is a potent mix of competition between males and choice by females, which together generate sexual conflict" (*Promiscuity* x).[1] To put it another way, a related study, the highly controversial *A Natural History of Rape: Biological Bases of Sexual Coercion*, by Randy Thornhill and Craig T. Palmer, has recently touched a social nerve that seems even more highly sensitized today than it was when many of the writers discussed here were probing it early in the twentieth century.

Even this limited comparison of our writers with present-day sociobiologists will offend a certain number of literary and cultural historians. For, although the eclipse of Darwinism gave way to a "revival of Darwinism in American social thought" during the last decades of the twentieth century, it also led to the ongoing and very heated "battle for science in the sociobiology debate."[2] The underlying problem in much of this debate remains as it was in 1982, when Ernst Mayr noted that "the part of sociobiology that is being attacked is that which deals with man: Can man's social behavior be compared with that of animals?" (598). In the humanities, of course, the resistance to Darwinian theory is more pronounced. It is especially evident in the stronghold of American cultural studies where—fortunately, and unfortunately—the "traditional American egalitarianism" that resisted the theory of natural selection early in the twentieth-century endures (Mayr 536). It is evident, for example, in the *American Quarterly* review of Carl N. Degler's *In Search of Human Nature: The Decline and Revival of Darwinism in American Social Thought*, "Biology Is Destiny, Once Again" (by the historian Margaret Marsh). This review expresses a good deal of sympathy with the idea that biology is socially constructed and much skepticism over the idea (falsely attributed to Degler) "that turning to natural science *guarantees* a *certain* understanding of what still seem to me to be the varieties of human nature" (334, emphasis mine). Such views and the paucity of thoughtful discussions of Darwin in American literary studies, suggest that—quite apart from the lingering creationism—there is still a partial eclipse of Darwinism in American culture.

This is not to suggest that a greater willingness to consider Darwinian evolution in American literary or cultural studies would end the debate over human nature, only that in literary histories such as this one it would shed a good deal of light on our cultural heritage. It will remind us that many of the writers of this period were sociobiologists in the sense that they accepted Darwin's analysis of the human as a social animal or, in their own time, Havelock Ellis's studies of the human being as a "naturally social animal" (*Studies* 1:xxx). Even in the present-day "battle for science over the sociology debate," wherein Darwin is invoked on all sides, "the central issue" is still "the nature of human nature" (Segerstråle 391). There is much to be learned from our writers' explorations and debates over human nature. For one thing, Segerstråle's conclusion about the role of "moral/political concerns" in the sociobiology debate applies to literary history as well. "Far from being an obstacle to be eliminated," she claims, the "moral/political concerns . . . were in fact a *driving force* both in generating and criticizing scientific claims in this field, and that the field was better off because of this" (408).

Surely American literature is enriched for having been subjected to the varied tests of the fictive imagination that gave us visions of transcendent altruistic love; Bergsonian flights of the creative spirit; tales of "red love"; stories of hereditary determinism; stories of sexual, racial, and psychological conflict between black and white Americans and within the African American community; self-analytical stories of the instincts and emotions; stories that urge an acceptance of our place in the community of common descent; and others that follow the Darwinian pathway toward visions of our place in the ecological web. In these varied ways, American writers have been engaged in composing the human narrative for modern time. They could not agree over what "the true evolutionary epic" *is* (to use Edward O. Wilson's term); but they agreed implicitly with his sense that, "retold as poetry," it can be "as intrinsically ennobling as any religious epic" (*Consilience* 265).

Notes

1. Even writers such as London, Dreiser, Stein, or Hemingway, however, could not have anticipated the variety of astonishing adaptive strategies that Birkhead examines as sperm competition or cryptic female choice. Birkhead explains how the study of such phenomena led to "the most significant discovery of the past two decades—that male and female reproductive attributes co-evolve. . . . Where males coerce females into copulating, females have a range of subtle behavioural and physiological counter-strategies. Where females evolve long and convoluted reproductive tracts [that is, in "the evolutionary battleground on which sexual conflict occurs"] to better regulate sperm uptake, males respond by evolving longer sperm. . . . At any moment in time one sex may have slightly more control than the other, but the battle between the sexes is an evolutionary see-saw—subtle, sophisticated and inevitable" (232–33).

2. These phrases are from the subtitles of Carl N. Degler's *In Search of Human Nature: The Decline and Revival of Darwinism in American Social Thought* (1991) and Ullica Segerstråle's *Defenders of the Truth: The Battle for Science in the Sociobiology Debate and Beyond* (2000).

Works Cited

Parenthetical references to the various volumes of Havelock Ellis's *Studies in the Psychology of Sex*, in two volumes, indicate the volume, followed by the volume within that volume, and then the page number. This departs from the practice used in the "Cumulative Index" in volume 2 of the set.

The texts by Freud are cited from *The Basic Writings of Sigmund Freud*, translated and edited by A. A. Brill, in the Modern Library edition, because many of the authors discussed here would have probably known Freud's work through Brill's translations.

Most of the references to William James's *The Principles of Psychology* are from the standard three-volume set; however, in the chapter on Stephen Crane, James's *Psychology: The Briefer Course* is cited because Crane might have been more likely to study that popular volume than the larger work.

Åhnebrink, Lars. *The Beginnings of Naturalism in American Fiction*. 1950. New York: Russell and Russell, 1961.

Alcock, John. *Animal Behavior: An Evolutionary Approach*. 6th ed. Sunderland, Mass.: Sinauer, 1998.

————. *The Triumph of Sociobiology*. Oxford, U.K.: Oxford Univ. Press, 2001.

Allee, W. C. *Animal Aggregations: A Study in General Sociology*. Chicago: Univ. of Chicago Press, 1931.

————. *Cooperation Among Animals, with Human Implications*. Rev. ed. New York: Henry Schuman, 1951.

Anderson, David D., ed. *Critical Essays on Sherwood Anderson*. Boston, Mass.: G. K. Hall, 1981.

Anderson, Sherwood. *Beyond Desire*. 1932. New York: Liveright, 1970.

————. *Dark Laughter*. 1925. Mattituck, N.Y.: Aeonian, n.d.

————. *Early Writings*. Ed. Ray Lewis White. Kent, Ohio: Kent State Univ. Press, 1989.

————. *Horses and Men*. New York: B. W. Huebsch, 1923.

————. *Kit Brandon*. New York: Scribner's, 1936.

————. *Letters of Sherwood Anderson*. Ed. Howard Mumford Jones and Walter B. Rideout. Boston, Mass.: Little, Brown, 1953.

————. *Many Marriages*. 1923. Ed. Douglas G. Rogers. Metuchen, N.J.: Scarecrow, 1978.

————. *Marching Men*. New York: John Lane, 1917,

————. "Out of Nowhere into Nothing." In *The Triumph of the Egg*, 1921. New York: Four Walls Eight Windows, 1988. 171–267.

————. *Poor White*. 1922. New York: Viking, 1966.

————. "The Rabbit Pen." In *Early Writings*. Ed. Ray Lewis White, 127–35.

———. "Seeds." *The Little Review* 5 (July 1918): 24–31.

———. *Sherwood Anderson's Memoirs*. Ed. Ray Lewis White. Chapel Hill: Univ. of North Carolina Press, 1969.

———. *Sherwood Anderson's Notebook*. New York: Liveright, 1926.

———. *A Story Teller's Story*. 1924. Ed. Ray Lewis White. Cleveland, Ohio: Press of Case Western Reserve Univ., 1968.

———. *The Triumph of the Egg*. 1921. New York: Four Walls Eight Windows, 1988.

———. "Vibrant Life." In *Early Writings*. Ed. Ray Lewis White, 155–57.

———. *Windy McPherson's Son*. 1916. Chicago: Univ. of Chicago Press, 1965.

———. *Winesburg, Ohio*. 1919. New York: Viking, 1966.

Astro, Richard. *John Steinbeck and Edward Ricketts: The Shaping of a Novelist*. Minneapolis: Univ. of Minnesota Press, 1973.

Auerbach, Jonathan. *Male Call: Becoming Jack London*. Durham, N.C.: Duke Univ. Press, 1996.

Baker, Carlos. *Ernest Hemingway: A Life Story*. New York: Macmillan, 1979.

———, ed. *Ernest Hemingway: Selected Letters, 1917–1961*. New York: Scribner's, 1981.

Barkow, Jerome H., Leda Cosmides, and John Tooby, eds. *The Adapted Mind: Evolutionary Psychology and the Generation of Culture*. New York: Oxford Univ. Press, 1992.

Beegel, Susan F. "Eye and Heart: Hemingway's Education as a Naturalist." In *A Historical Guide to Ernest Hemingway*, ed. Wagner-Martin, 53–92. New York: Oxford Univ. Press, 2000.

Bender, Bert. *The Descent of Love: Darwin and the Theory of Sexual Selection in American Fiction, 1871–1926*. Philadelphia: Univ. of Pennsylvania Press, 1996.

———. *Sea-Brothers: The Tradition of American Sea Fiction from Moby-Dick to the Present*. Philadelphia: Univ. of Pennsylvania Press, 1988.

Benson, Jackson J. *The True Adventures of John Steinbeck, Writer*. New York: Viking, 1984.

Bergson, Henri. *Creative Evolution*. Trans. Arthur Mitchell. New York: Henry Holt, 1911.

Birkhead, Tim. *Promiscuity: An Evolutionary History of Sperm Competition and Sexual Conflict*. London: Faber and Faber, 2000.

Bohlke, L. Brent, ed. *Willa Cather in Person*. Lincoln: Univ. of Nebraska Press, 1986.

Boodin, John Elof. *Cosmic Evolution: Outlines of Cosmic Idealism*. New York: Macmillan, 1925.

Bowler, Peter J. *The Eclipse of Darwinism: Anti-Darwinian Evolution Theories in the Decades around 1900*. Baltimore, Md.: Johns Hopkins Univ. Press, 1983.

———. *The Non-Darwinian Revolution: Reinterpreting a Historical Myth*. Baltimore, Md.: Johns Hopkins Univ. Press, 1988.

Boyd, Brian. "Jane, Meet Charles: Literature, Evolution, and Human Nature." *Literature and Philosophy* 22 (Apr. 1998): 1–30.

Bracher, Frederick. "Steinbeck and the Biological View of Man." In *Steinbeck and His Critics: A Record of Twenty-Five Years*, ed. E. W. Tedlock Jr. and C. V. Wicker, 183–96. Albuquerque: Univ. of New Mexico Press, 1957.

Brewer, Richard. *The Science of Ecology*. Philadelphia, Pa.: Saunders, 1988.

Briffault, Robert. *The Mothers: A Study of the Origins of Sentiments and Institutions*. 3 vols. New York: Macmillan, 1927.

———. *The Mothers: The Matriarchal Theory of Social Origins*. New York: Macmillan, 1931.

———. "The Origin of Love." In *The Making of Man: An Outline of Anthropology*, ed. V. F. Calverton, 485–528. New York: Modern Library, 1931.

Bruccoli, Matthew J., ed. *The Great Gatsby: The Revised and Rewritten Galleys*. New York: Garland, 1990.

———, and Margaret M Duggan, eds. *Correspondence of F. Scott Fitzgerald*. New York: Random House, 1980.

———, and Jackson R. Bryer, eds. *F. Scott Fitzgerald in His Own Time*. Kent, Ohio: Kent State Univ. Press, 1971.

Budd, Malcolm. *Music and the Emotions: the Philosophical Theories*. London: Routledge and Kegan Paul, 1985.

Bujic, Bojan, ed. *Music in European Thought 1851–1912*. New York: Cambridge Univ. Press, 1988.

Burrow, Trigant. *A Search for Man's Sanity: The Selected Letters of Trigant Burrow*. New York: Oxford Univ. Press, 1958.

———. "Psychoanalytic Improvisations and the Personal Equation." *The Psychoanalytic Review* 13 (1926): 173–86.

Burwell, Rose Marie. *Hemingway: The Postwar Years and the Posthumous Novels*. New York: Cambridge Univ. Press, 1996.

Buss, David. *The Evolution of Desire: Strategies of Human Mating*. New York: Basic, 1994.

Cady, Edwin H. *The Light of Common Day: Realism in American Fiction*. Bloomington: Indiana Univ. Press, 1971.

Calverton, V. F. "Are Women Monogamous?" In *Woman's Coming of Age: A Symposium*, ed. V. F. Calverton and S. D. Schmalhausen, 475–88. New York: Liveright, 1931.

———. *The Bankruptcy of Marriage*. New York: Macaulay, 1928.

———. *The Man Inside: Being the Record of the Strange Adventures of Allen Steele Among the Xulus*. New York: Scribner's, 1936.

———. *The Newer Spirit: A Sociological Criticism of Literature*. 1925. New York: Octagon, 1974.

———. *The Passing of the Gods*. New York: Scribner's, 1934.

———. "Red Love in Soviet Russia." *Modern Quarterly* 4 (1927–28): 180–91.

———. "Sex and Social Struggle." In *Sex in Civilization*, ed. V. F. Calverton and S. D. Schmalhausen, 242–84. New York: Macaulay, 1929.

———. *Three Strange Lovers*. New York: Macaulay, 1930.

———. *Where Angels Dared to Tread: Socialist and Communist Utopian Colonies in the United States*. 1941. Freeport, N.Y.: Books for Libraries, 1969.

———, ed. *The Making of Man: An Outline of Anthropology*. New York: Modern Library, 1931.

———, and S. D. Schmalhausen, eds. *Sex in Civilization*. New York: Macaulay, 1929.

———. *Woman's Coming of Age: A Symposium*. New York: Liveright, 1931.

Campbell, Bernard, ed. *Sexual Selection and the Descent of Man, 1871–1971*. Chicago: Aldine, 1972.

Carpenter, Edward. *The Intermediate Sex: A Study of Some Transitional Types of Men and Women*. New York: Kennerly, 1921.

———. *Love's Coming of Age: A Series of Papers on the Relation of the Sexes*. 1896. London: George Allen and Unwin, 1948.

Carroll, Joseph. *Evolution and Literary Theory*. Columbia: Univ. of Missouri Press, 1995.

Cather, Willa. *O Pioneers!* 1913. Boston, Mass.: Houghton Mifflin, 1933.

———. *The Song of the Lark*. Boston, Mass.: Houghton Mifflin, 1915.

————. *Willa Cather's Collected Short Fiction, 1892–1912*. Ed. Mildred R. Bennett. Lincoln: Univ. of Nebraska Press, 1965.

————. *Willa Cather on Writing*. New York: Knopf, 1949.

————. *The World and the Parish: Willa Cather's Articles and Reviews, 1893–1902*. 2 vols. Ed. William M. Curtin. Lincoln: Univ. of Nebraska Press, 1970.

Chopin, Kate. *The Complete Works of Kate Chopin*. 2 vols. Ed. Per Seyersted. Baton Rouge: Louisiana State Univ. Press, 1969.

Comley, Nancy R., and Robert Scholes. *Hemingway's Genders: Rereading the Hemingway Text*. New Haven, Conn.: Yale Univ. Press, 1994.

Conklin, Edward Grant. *Heredity and Environment in the Development of Men*. 6th ed. Princeton, N.J.: Princeton Univ. Press, 1929

————. *Laboratory Directions in General Biology*. 2nd ed. N.p., n.d. Seeley G. Mudd Manuscript Library, Princeton University.

Cooke, Brett, and Frederick Turner, eds. *Biopoetics: Evolutionary Explorations in the Arts*. Lexington, Ky.: ICUS, 1999.

Cooper, Wayne F. *Claude McKay: Rebel Sojourner in the Harlem Renaissance*. Baton Rouge: Louisiana State Univ. Press, 1987.

————, ed. *The Passion of Claude McKay: Selected Poetry and Prose, 1912–1948*. New York: Schocken, 1973.

Crane, Stephen. *The Correspondence of Stephen Crane*. Ed. Stanley Wertheim and Paul Sorrentino. New York: Columbia Univ. Press, 1988.

————. *The Portable Stephen Crane*. Ed. Joseph Katz. New York: Viking, 1969.

————. *The Poems of Stephen Crane*. Ed. Joseph Katz. New York: Cooper Square, 1971.

————. *The Red Badge of Courage, An Episode of the American Civil War*. Ed. Fredson Bowers. Charlottesville: Univ. Press of Virginia, 1975.

————. *The Red Badge of Courage: An Episode of the American Civil War*. Ed. Henry Binder. New York: Norton, 1982.

Cronin, Helena. *The Ant and the Peacock: Altruism and Sexual Selection from Darwin to Today*. Cambridge, U.K.: Cambridge Univ. Press, 1991.

Crosland, Andrew T. *A Concordance to F. Scott Fitzgerald's* The Great Gatsby. Detroit, Mich.: Gale, 1975.

Crow, Charles L. "Ishi and Jack London's Primitives." In *Rereading Jack London*. Ed. Leonard Cassuto and Jeanne Campbell Reesman. Stanford, Calif.: Stanford Univ. Press, 1996.

Darwin, Charles. *The Descent of Man, and Selection in Relation to Sex*. 1871. Princeton, N.J.: Princeton Univ. Press, 1981. 2 vols. in 1.

————. *The Expression of the Emotions in Man and Animals*. 1872. Chicago: Univ. of Chicago Press, 1965.

————. *On the Origin of Species by Means of Natural Selection, Or the Preservation of Favoured Races in the Struggle for Life*. 1859. Facsimile of 1st ed. Cambridge, Mass.: Harvard Univ. Press, 1966.

————. *On the Origin of Species by Means of Natural Selection or the Preservation of Favored Races in the Struggle for Life* and *The Descent of Man and Selection in Relation to Sex*. New York: Modern Library, [n.d.].

Davis, Thadious M. Introduction to *The Chinaberry Tree* by Nella Larsen. New York: G. K. Hall, 1995.

———. *Nella Larsen: Novelist of the Harlem Renaissance, a Woman's Life Unveiled*. Baton Rouge: Louisiana State Univ. Press, 1994.

Degler, Carl N. *In Search of Human Nature: The Decline and Revival of Darwinism in American Social Thought*. New York: Oxford Univ. Press, 1991.

DeMott, Robert J. *Steinbeck's Reading: A Catalogue of Books Owned and Borrowed*. New York: Garland, 1984.

Dillingham, William B. *Frank Norris: Instinct and Art*. Boston, Mass.: Houghton Mifflin, 1969.

Diserens, Charles M. *The Influence of Music on Behavior*. Princeton: Princeton Univ. Press, 1927.

———, and Harry Fine. *Psychology of Music: The Influence of Music on Behavior*. Cincinnati, Ohio: by the authors for the College of Music, 1939.

Donaldson, Scott. *Fool for Love: F. Scott Fitzgerald*. New York: Congdon and Weed, 1983.

Dooley, Patrick K. *The Pluralistic Philosophy of Stephen Crane*. Urbana: Univ. of Illinois Press, 1993.

Dreiser, Theodore. *The Financier*. New York: Harper, 1912.

———. *The "Genius."* 1915. New York: Boni and Liveright, 1923.

———. *Hey Rub-A-Dub: A Book of the Mystery and Wonder and Terror of Life*. New York: Boni and Liveright, 1920.

———. *Moods Philosophic and Emotional*. New York: Simon and Schuster, 1935.

———. *Notes on Life*. Ed. Marguerite Tjader and John J. McAleer. N.p.: Univ. of Alabama Press, 1974.

———. *Sister Carrie*. 1900. Ed. Donald Pizer. New York: Norton, 1970.

———. *The Titan*. 1914. New York: Liveright, 1925.

DuBois, W. E. B. *Dark Princess: A Romance*. 1928. Millwood, N.Y.: Kraus-Thomson, 1974.

———. *Dusk of Dawn*. 1940. In *Writings: The Suppression of the African Slave-Trade, The Souls of Black Folk, Dusk of Dawn, Essays and Articles*, 549–802. New York: Library of America, 1996.

———. "The Negro in Art: How Shall He Be Portrayed." Symposium. *Crisis* 31, no. 5 (Mar. 1926): 212–20; 31, no. 6 (Apr. 1926): 278–80; 32, no. 1 (May 1926): 35–36; 32, no. 2 (June 1926): 71–73; 32, no. 4 (Aug. 1926): 193–94; 32, no. 5 (Sept. 1926): 238–39; 33, no. 1 (Nov. 1926): 28–29.

———. Review of *Nigger Heaven* by Carl Van Vechten. *Crisis* (Dec. 1926): 81–82.

———. *The Souls of Black Folk*. 1903. In *Writings*, 357–547.

———. "The Talented Tenth." In *Writings*, 842–61.

———. *Writings: The Suppression of the African Slave-Trade, The Souls of Black Folk, Dusk of Dawn, Essays and Articles*. New York: Library of America, 1996.

Eastman, Max. *Marxism: Is It Science*. New York: Norton, 1940.

Eby, Carl P. *Hemingway's Fetishism: Psychoanalysis and the Mirror of Manhood*. Albany: State Univ. of New York Press, 1999.

Edel, Leon. *Henry James: A Life*. New York: Harper and Row, 1985.

Ehrenforth, Friedemann, "Music, Religion, and Darwinian Science in *The Damnation of Theron Ware*." *Amerikastudien/American Studies* 44, no. 4 (1999): 497–517.

Ellis, Havelock. *The Dance of Life*. Boston, Mass.: Houghton Mifflin, 1923.

———. "Masculinism and Feminism." *Cosmopolitan* (Aug. 1915): 316–20.

————. *Studies in the Psychology of Sex*. 1897–1910. New York: Random House, 1936. 2 vols.

Engels, Frederick. *The Origin of the Family, Private Property, and the State*. 1884. Trans. Ernest Untermann. Chicago: Charles H. Kerr, 1902.

Faggen, Robert. *Robert Frost and the Challenge of Darwin*. Ann Arbor: Univ. of Michigan Press, 1997.

Fauset, Jessie Redmon. *The Chinaberry Tree: A Novel of American Life*. 1931. New York: G. K. Hall, 1995.

————. *Plum Bun: A Novel without a Moral*. 1928. Boston, Mass.: Beacon, 1990.

Fetterley, Judith. "Who Killed Dick Diver? The Sexual Politics of *Tender Is the Night*." *Mosaic* 17, no. 1 (1984): 111–28.

Fisher, Helen. *Anatomy of Love: The Natural History of Monogamy, Adultery, and Divorce*. New York: Simon and Schuster, 1992.

Fisher, Rudolph. *The Conjure-Man Dies*. 1932. New York: Arno, 1971.

————. "Miss Cynthie." In *The City of Refuge: The Collected Stories of Rudolph Fisher*, ed. John McCluskey, 68–78. Columbia: Univ. of Missouri Press, 1987.

————. "John Archer's Nose." In *The City of Refuge*, ed. John McCluskey, 158–94.

————. *The Walls of Jericho*. 1928. New York: Arno, 1969.

Fitelson, David. "Stephen Crane's *Maggie* and Darwinism." *American Quarterly* 6 (Summer 1964): 182–94.

Fitzgerald, F. Scott. "Absolution." In *The Stories of F. Scott Fitzgerald*, 159–72. New York: Scribner's, 1969.

————. *The Beautiful and Damned*. New York: Scribner's, 1955.

————. *Correspondence of F. Scott Fitzgerald*. Ed. Matthew J. Bruccoli and Margaret M. Duggan. New York: Random House, 1980.

————. *F. Scott Fitzgerald: A Life in Letters*. Ed. Matthew J. Bruccoli. New York: Scribner's, 1994.

————. *The Great Gatsby*. Preface by Matthew J. Bruccoli. New York: Collier, 1991.

————. *The Price Was High: The Last Uncollected Stories of F. Scott Fitzgerald*. Ed. Matthew J. Bruccoli. New York: Harcourt Brace Jovanovich, 1979.

————. "Sherwood Anderson on the Marriage Question." In *Critical Essays on Sherwood Anderson*, ed. David N. Anderson, 42–44. Boston: G. K. Hall, 1981.

————. *This Side of Paradise*. New York: Scribner's, 1970.

————. *Trimalchio: An Early Version of The Great Gatsby*. Ed. James L. W. West III. Cambridge, U.K.: Cambridge Univ. Press, 2000.

————. *The Stories of F. Scott Fitzgerald*. New York: Scribner's, 1969.

————. *Tender Is the Night*. 1934. New York: Scribner's, 1969.

————. *The Vegetable or from President to Postman*. 1923. New York: Scribner's, 1976.

Fitzgerald, F. Scott, and Zelda Fitzgerald. *Bits of Paradise*. London: Bodley Head, 1973.

Fleming, Robert E. "The Endings of Hemingway's *Garden of Eden*." *American Literature* 61 (May 1989): 261–70.

————, ed. *Hemingway and the Natural World*. Moscow: Univ. of Idaho Press, 1999.

Flower, Benjamin O. "Life of Charles Darwin." *The Arena* 7 (Feb. 1893): 352–63.

Forel, August. *The Sexual Question: A Scientific, Psychological, Hygienic, and Sociological Study for the Cultured Classes*. Adapt. C. F. Marshall. New York: Rebman, 1908.

Frank, Waldo. *In the American Jungle [1925–1936]*. 1937. Freeport, N.Y.: Books for Libraries, 1968.

———. *The Memoirs of Waldo Frank*. Ed. Alan Trachtenberg. N.p.: Univ. of Massachusetts Press, 1973.

———. *Our America*. 1919. New York: AMS, 1972.

———. "*Winesburg, Ohio* after Twenty Years." In *The Achievement of Sherwood Anderson: Essays in Criticism*, ed. Ray Lewis White, 116–21. Chapel Hill: Univ. of North Carolina Press, 1966.

Fraser, Keath. "Another Reading of *The Great Gatsby*." *English Studies in Canada* 5, no. 3 (1979): 330–43.

Frederic, Harold. *The Damnation of Theron Ware*. 1896. Cambridge, Mass.: Belknap, 1960.

———. *The Market-Place*, 1899. Fort Worth: Texas Christian Univ. Press, 1981.

Freud, Sigmund. *The Basic Writings of Sigmund Freud*. Trans. and ed. A. A. Brill. New York: Modern Library, 1938.

———. *Civilization and Its Discontents*. Trans. James Strachey. New York: Norton, 1961.

———. *The Freud Reader*. Ed. Peter Gay. New York: Norton, 1989.

———. *A General Introduction to Psychoanalysis*. Trans. Joan Riviere. 1922. New York: Washington Square, 1960.

———. *Selected Papers on Hysteria and Other Psychoneuroses*. New York: Journal of Nervous and Mental Disease Publishing, 1912.

———. *The Standard Edition of the Complete Psychological Works of Sigmund Freud*. 24 vols. Ed. James Strachey. London: Hogarth Press and the Institute of Psycho-Analysis, 1953–74.

———. "Thoughts for the Times on War and Death." In *Freud: On War and Neurosis*, 245–76. New York: Arts and Sciences, 1947.

Gallup, Donald, ed. *The Flowers of Friendship: Letters Written to Gertrude Stein*. New York: Knopf, 1953.

Geddes, Patrick, and J. Arthur Thomson. *The Evolution of Sex*. New York: Scribner's, 1914.

Geismar, Maxwell. *Rebels and Ancestors: The American Novel. 1890–1915*. Boston, Mass.: Houghton Mifflin, 1953.

Gelfant, Blanche H. "The Forgotten Reaping-Hook: Sex in *My Ántonia*." In *Critical Essays on Willa Cather*, ed. John J. Murphy, 147–64. Boston: G. K. Hall, 1984.

Ghiselin, Michael T. *The Economy of Nature and the Evolution of Sex*. Berkeley: Univ. of California Press, 1974.

———. "The Individual in the Darwinian Revolution." *New Literary History* 3 (Autumn 1971): 113–34.

Giannone, Richard. *Music in Willa Cather's Fiction*. Lincoln: Univ. of Nebraska Press, 1968.

Gibson, Donald B. *The Fiction of Stephen Crane*. Carbondale: Southern Illinois Univ. Press, 1968.

Giles, James R. *Claude McKay*. Boston, Mass.: Twayne, 1976.

Gould, Stephen Jay, *The Mismeasure of Man*. New York: Norton, 1981.

Groos, Karl. *The Play of Man*. 1899. Trans. Elizabeth L. Baldwin. New York: Appleton, 1908.

Guemple, Michael. "A Case for the Appleton *Red Badge of Courage*." *Resources for American Literary Study* 21 (1995): 43–57.

Gurney, Edmund. *The Power of Sound*. 1880. New York: Appleton, 1924.

Haeckel, Ernst. *The Riddle of the Universe at the Close of the Nineteenth Century*. New York: Harper, 1900.

————, Arthur Thomson, August Weismann, et al., eds. *Evolution in Modern Thought*. New York: Boni and Liveright (Modern Library), 1917.

Hale, Nathan G., Jr. *Freud and the Americans: The Beginnings of Psychoanalysis in the United States, 1876–1917*. New York: Oxford Univ. Press, 1971.

Hall, Gertrude. *The Wagnerian Romances*. New York: Knopf, 1942.

Haller, John S., Jr. *Outcasts from Evolution: Scientific Attitudes of Racial Inferiority, 1859–1900*. Urbana: Univ. of Illinois Press, 1971.

Halliburton, David. *The Color of the Sky: A Study of Stephen Crane*. New York: Cambridge Univ. Press, 1989.

Hamilton, David Mike. *"The Tools of My Trade": The Annotated Books in Jack London's Library*. Seattle: Univ. of Washington Press, 1986.

Hemingway, Ernest. *The Old Man and the Sea*. New York: Scribner's, 1952.

————. *The Complete Short Stories of Ernest Hemingway*. Finca Vigía Edition. New York: Scribner's, 1987.

————. *A Farewell to Arms*. 1929. New York: Scribner's, 1932.

————. *The Garden of Eden*. New York: Macmillan, 1987.

————. *Green Hills of Africa*. 1935. New York: Macmillan, 1987.

————. *Islands in the Stream*. New York: Scribner's, 1970.

————. *The Short Stories of Ernest Hemingway*. New York: Scribner's, 1953.

————. *The Sun Also Rises*. 1926. New York: Scribner's, 1970.

————. *True at First Light*. New York: Scribner's, 1999.

Hoffman, Frederick J. *Freudianiam and the Literary Mind*. Baton Rouge: Louisiana State Univ. Press, 1957.

————. *The Twenties: American Writing in the Postwar Decade*. New York: Collier, 1962.

Hoffman, Michael J. *Critical Essays on Gertrude Stein*. Boston, Mass.: G. K. Hall, 1986.

Howe, Irving. *Sherwood Anderson*. N.p.: William Sloane Associates, 1951.

Howells, William Dean. *The Lady of the Aroostook*. Boston, Mass.: Houghton, Osgood, 1879.

————. *A Modern Instance*. 1882. New York: Penguin, 1988.

Huggins, Nathan Irvin. *Harlem Renaissance*. New York: Oxford Univ. Press, 1971.

James, Henry. *The Bostonians*. 1886. New York: Penguin, 1987.

James, William. "Great Men, Great Thoughts, and the Environment." *Atlantic Monthly* 46 (Oct. 1880): 441–59.

————. *The Principles of Psychology*. 1890. Cambridge, Mass.: Harvard Univ. Press, 1981. 3 vols.

————. *Psychology: The Briefer Course*. 1892. Notre Dame, Ind.: Univ. of Notre Dame Press, 1985.

————. *The Varieties of Religious Experience*. 1902. Cambridge, Mass.: Harvard Univ. Press, 1985.

Jensen, Niels Lyhne. *Jens Peter Jacobsen*. Boston, Mass.: Twayne, 1980.

Kerr, Frances. "Feeling 'Half Feminine': Modernism and the Politics of Emotion in *The Great Gatsby*." *American Literature* 68 (June 1996): 405–31.

Kroeber, A. L. *Anthropology*. New York: Harcourt, Brace, 1923.

Kropotkin, P. *Mutual Aid: A Factor of Evolution*. 1902. London: William Heinemann, 1910.

Kurlansky, Mark. *Cod: A Biography of the Fish that Changed the World*. New York: Walker and Company, 1997.

Labor, Earle. "From 'All Gold Canyon' to *The Acorn-Planter*: Jack London's Agrarian Vision." *Western American Literature* 11 (Summer 1976): 83–101.

———, and Jeanne Campbell Reesman. *Jack London, Revised Edition*. New York: Twayne, 1994.

———, and Robert C. Leitz, III, eds. *The Letters of Jack London*. 3 vols. Stanford, Calif.: Stanford Univ. Press, 1988.

Lachtman, Howard. "Man and Superwoman in Jack London's 'The Kanaka Surf.'" *Western American Literature* 7 (Summer 1972): 101–10.

Larsen, Nella. *Quicksand and Passing*. New Brunswick, N.J.: Rutgers Univ. Press, 1986.

Lawrence, D. H. "A New Theory of Neuroses." *Bookman* 66 (Nov. 1927): 314–17.

Le Conte, Joseph. "The Effect of Mixture of Races on Human Progress." *Berkeley Quarterly* 1 (Apr. 1880): 81–104.

———. *Evolution: Its Nature, Its Evidences, and Its Relation to Religious Thought*. 2nd ed. New York: Appleton, 1897.

———. "The Genesis of Sex." *Popular Science Monthly* 16 (1879): 167–79.

Leopold, Aldo. *A Sand County Almanac with Essays on Conservation from Round River*. New York: Ballantine, 1970.

Lettis, Richard, Robert F. McDonnell, and William E. Morris, eds. *Stephen Crane's* The Red Badge of Courage: *Text and Criticism*. New York: Harcourt, Brace, 1960.

Levenson, J. C. Introduction to *The Red Badge of Courage, an Episode of the American Civil War*. Ed. Fredson Bowers, xii–xcii. Charlottesville: Univ. Press of Virginia, 1975.

Lewis, David Levering. *The Portable Harlem Renaissance Reader*. New York: Penguin, 1995.

———. *W. E. B. DuBois: Biography of a Race, 1868–1919*. New York: Henry Holt, 1993.

———. *When Harlem Was in Vogue*. New York: Penguin, 1997.

Lewis, Robert W. "'The African Book': Hemingway Major and Late in the Natural World." In *Hemingway and the Natural World*, ed. Robert E. Fleming, 111–24. Moscow: Univ. of Idaho Press, 1999.

Lippman, Edward A. *A History of Western Musical Aesthetics*. Lincoln: Univ. of Nebraska Press, 1988.

Locke, Alain, ed. *The New Negro*. 1925. New York: Atheneum, 1968.

London, Charmian Kittredge. *The Book of Jack London*. 2 vols. New York: Century, 1921.

London, Jack. *The Complete Short Stories*. Ed. Earle Labor, Robert C. Leitz III, and I. Milo Shepard. 3 vols. Stanford: Stanford Univ. Press, 1993.

———. *A Daughter of the Snows*. New York: Grosset and Dunlap, 1902.

———, [and Anna Strunksy]. *The Kempton-Wace Letters*. 1903. New York: Haskell House, n.d.

———. *The Little Lady of the Big House*. New York: Macmillan, 1916.

———. *Martin Eden*. 1909. New York: Penguin, 1984.

———. *The Valley of the Moon*. 1913. Berkeley: Univ. of California Press, 1999.

———. *The Sea-Wolf*. 1904. New York: Penguin, 1989.

———. *The Star Rover*. 1915. New York: Macmillan, 1969.

Love, Glen A. "Ecocriticism and Science: Toward Consilience?" *New Literary History* 30 (1999): 561–76.

———. *Practical Ecocriticism: Literature, Biology, and the Environment*. Charlottesville: Univ. Press of Virginia, 2003.

Loy, Mina. *The Last Lunar Baedeker*. Highlands, S.C.: Jargon Society, 1982.

Lynn, Kenneth S. *Hemingway*. New York: Simon and Schuster, 1987.

Marsh, Margaret. "Biology Is Destiny, Once Again." Review of *In Search of Human Nature: The Decline and Revival of Darwinism in American Social Thought* by Carl N. Degler. *American Quarterly* 45 (June 1993): 328–35.

Mayr, Ernst. *The Growth of Biological Thought: Diversity, Evolution and Inheritance*. Cambridge, Mass.: Harvard Univ. Press, 1982.

McCluskey, John, Jr., ed. *The City of Refuge: The Collected Stories of Rudolph Fisher*. Columbia: Univ. of Missouri Press, 1987.

McDermott, John J. "Symbolism and Psychological Realism in *The Red Badge of Courage*." *Nineteenth-Century Fiction* 23 (Dec. 1968): 324–31.

McDowell, Deborah E. Introduction to *Quicksand and Passing* by Nella Larsen, ix–xxxv. New Brunswick: Rutgers Univ. Press, 1986.

McElrath, Joseph R., Jr. *Frank Norris Revisited*. New York: Twayne, 1992.

———, and Douglas K. Burgess, eds. *The Apprenticeship Writings of Frank Norris, 1896–1898*. 2 vols. Philadelphia: American Philosophical Society, 1996.

McKay, Claude. *Banjo: A Story without a Plot*. 1929. New York: Harcourt Brace, 1957.

———. *Home to Harlem*. New York: Harper and Brothers, 1928.

———. *A Long Way from Home*. New York: Arno, 1969.

———. *The Passion of Claude McKay: Selected Poetry and Prose, 1912–1948*. Ed. Wayne F. Cooper. New York: Schocken, 1973.

Mead, Margaret. "Formal Sex Relations in Samoa." In *The Making of Man: An Outline of Anthropology*, ed. V. F. Calverton, 586–602. New York: Modern Library, 1931.

Mellow, James R. *Charmed Circle: Gertrude Stein and Company*. New York: Praeger, 1974.

Meyers, Jeffrey. *Scott Fitzgerald: A Biography*. New York: Harper Collins, 1994.

Miller, Geoffrey. *The Mating Mind: How Sexual Choice Shaped the Evolution of Human Nature*. New York: Doubleday, 2000.

Moddelmog, Debra A. *Reading Desire: In Pursuit of Ernest Hemingway*. Ithaca, N.Y.: Cornell Univ. Press, 1999.

Moers, Ellen. *Two Dreisers*. New York: Viking, 1969.

Morgan, C. Lloyd. "Mental Factors in Evolution." In *Evolution in Modern Thought*, ed. Ernst Haeckel, et al, 166–96. New York: Boni and Liveright (Modern Library), 1917.

Motley, Warren. "From Patriarchy to Matriarchy: Ma Joad's Role in *The Grapes of Wrath*." *American Literature* 54 (Oct. 1982): 397–412.

Myers, Robert M. "A Review of Popular Editions of *The Red Badge of Courage*." *Stephen Crane Studies* 6 (Spring 1997): 2–15.

Nesse, Randolph M. "Evolutionary Explanations of Emotions." *Human Nature* 1 (1990): 261–89.

Norris, Frank. *Blix*. New York: Doubleday and McClure, 1899.

———. "A Case for Lombroso." In *The Apprenticeship Writings of Frank Norris, 1896–1898*, 2 vols., ed. Joseph R. McElrath Jr. and Douglas K. Burgess, 2:127–32. Philadelphia, Pa.: American Philosophical Society, 1996.

———. *Frank Norris: Novels and Essays*. Ed. Donald Pizer. New York: Library of America, 1986.

———. *A Man's Woman*. New York: Doubleday and McClure, 1900.

———. *McTeague*. 1899. In *Frank Norris: Novels and Essays*, ed. Donald Pizer, 261–572. New York: Library of America, 1986.

———. *Moran of the Lady Letty: A Story of Adventure off the California Coast*. New York: Doubleday and McClure, 1899.

———. *The Octopus.* 1901. In *Frank Norris: Novels and Essays*, ed. Donald Pizer, 573–1098.

———. *The Pit: A Story of Chicago.* New York: Doubleday and Page, 1903.

———. "Theory and Reality." In *Frank Norris: Novels and Essays*, ed. Donald Pizer, 1103–5.

———. *Vandover and the Brute.* 1914. In *Frank Norris: Novels and Essays*, ed. Donald Pizer, 1–260.

O'Brien, Sharon. Introduction to *The Song of the Lark* by Willa Cather. New York: Signet, 1991.

———. *Willa Cather: The Emerging Voice.* New York: Oxford Univ. Press, 1987.

Parini, Jay. *John Steinbeck: A Biography.* London: Heinemann, 1994.

Parrington, Vernon L. *Main Currents in American Thought: An Interpretation of American Literature from the Beginnings to 1920.* New York: Harcourt Brace, 1930.

Phelps, Elizabeth Stuart. *Dr. Zay.* 1982. New York: Feminist, 1987.

Pinker, Steven. *How the Mind Works.* New York: Norton, 1997.

Pizer, Donald. "The Biological Determinism of *McTeague* in Our Time." *American Literary Realism, 1870–1910* 29 (1997): 27–32.

———. *The Novels of Frank Norris.* Bloomington: Indiana Univ. Press, 1966.

———. *The Novels of Theodore Dreiser: A Critical Study.* Minneapolis: Univ. of Minnesota Press, 1976.

———, ed. *Theodore Dreiser: A Selection of Uncollected Prose.* Detroit, Mich.: Wayne State Univ. Press, 1977.

Plotkin, Henry. *Evolution in Mind: An Introduction to Evolutionary Psychology.* Cambridge, Mass.: Harvard Univ. Press, 1998.

Powers, Stephen. *Tribes of California.* Washington: Government Printing Office, 1977.

Review of *The Principles of Psychology* by William James. *Atlantic Monthly* 67 (Apr. 1891): 552–56.

Quirk, Tom. *Bergson and American Culture: The Worlds of Willa Cather and Wallace Stevens.* Baltimore, Md.: Johns Hopkins Univ. Press, 1990.

Railsback, Brian E. *Parallel Expeditions: Charles Darwin and the Art of John Steinbeck.* Moscow: Univ. of Idaho Press, 1995.

Rampersad, Arnold. *The Art and Imagination of W. E. B. DuBois.* Cambridge, Mass.: Harvard Univ. Press, 1976.

Raphael, Robert. Introduction to *Marie Grubbe: A Lady of the Seventeenth Century* by J. P. Jacobsen. N.p.: Twayne, 1975.

Reesman, Jeanne Campbell. "Irony and Feminism in *The Little Lady in the Big House. Thalia: Studies in Literary Humor* 12 (1992): 33–46.

———. "London's New Woman in a New World: Saxon Brown Roberts' Journey into *The Valley of the Moon.*" *American Literary Realism* 24 (Winter 1992): 40–54

Reynolds, Guy. *Willa Cather in Context.* London: Macmillan, 1996.

Reynolds, Michael. "Ernest Hemingway 1899–1961: A Brief Biography." In *A Historical Guide to Ernest Hemingway*, ed. Linda Wagner-Martin, 15–50. New York: Oxford Univ. Press, 2000.

———. *The Young Hemingway.* New York: Blackwell, 1989.

Ridley, Matt. *The Red Queen: Sex and the Evolution of Human Nature.* New York: Penguin, 1993.

Ritvo, Lucille B. *Darwin's Influence on Freud: A Tale of Two Sciences.* New Haven, Conn.: Yale Univ. Press, 1990.

Roethke, Theodore. *The Collected Poems of Theodore Roethke.* New York: Doubleday, 1966.

Rosenfeld, Paul. "Sherwood Anderson." In *Critical Essays on Sherwood Anderson*, ed. David. D. Anderson, 74–85.

Rue, Loyal. *Everybody's Story: Wising up to the Epic of Evolution*. Albany: State Univ. of New York Press, 2000.

Russell, Bertrand. *Marriage and Morals*. 1929. New York: Liveright, 1957.

Russett, Cynthia Eagle. *Sexual Science: The Victorian Construction of Womanhood*. Cambridge, Mass.: Harvard Univ. Press, 1989.

Sargent, Frederick LeRoy. "Lincoln and Darwin." *Outlook* 58 (Feb. 5, 1898): 327.

Sears, Paul B. *Charles Darwin. Makers of Modern Science, A Twentieth Century Library Trilogy*. New York: Scribner's, 1953.

Segerstråle, Ullica. *Defenders of the Truth: The Battle for Science in the Sociobiology Debate and Beyond*. Oxford, U.K.: Oxford Univ. Press, 2000.

Shaw, George Bernard. *Back to Methuselah. A Metabiological Pentateuch*. New York: Brentano's, 1921.

Sinclair, Upton. *The Book of Life*. Chicago: Paine, 1922.

Smuts, J. C. *Some Recent Scientific Advances in Their Bearing on Philosophy*. Lecture 1. *Our Changing World-View*. Johannesburg, S. Africa: Univ. of the Witwatersland Press, 1932.

Spengler, Oswald. *The Decline of the West*. Abridged ed. Ed. Helmut Werner and Arthur Helps. Trans. Charles Francis Atkinson. New York: Knopf, 1962.

Spilka, Mark. *Hemingway's Quarrel with Androgyny*. Lincoln: Univ. of Nebraska Press, 1990.

Stein, Gertrude. "Cultivated Motor Automatism; A Study of Character in Its Relation to Attention." *Psychological Review* 5 (May 1898): 295–306.

———. *Everybody's Autobiography*. New York: Random House, 1937.

———. Gertrude Stein: *Writings 1903–1932: Q.E.D., Three Lives, Portraits and Other Short Works, The Autobiography of Alice B. Toklas*. New York: Library of America, 1998.

———. *Fernhurst, Q.E.D., and Other Early Writings*. New York: Liveright, 1971.

———. *The Making of Americans*. In Fernhurst, Q.E.D., *and Other Writings*.

———. *Three Lives*. 1909. New York: Vintage, n.d.

———. *Wars I Have Seen*. New York: Random House, 1945.

———, and Leon M. Solomons. "Normal Motor Automatism." *Psychological Review* 3 (Sept. 1896): 492–512.

Stein, Leo. *Journey Into the Self: Being the Letters, Papers and Journals of Leo Stein*. Ed. Edmund Fuller. New York: Crown, 1950.

Steinbeck, Elaine, and Robert Wallsten, eds. *Steinbeck: A Life in Letters*. New York: Penguin, 1981.

Steinbeck, John. *The Log from the Sea of Cortez: The Narrative Portion of the Book, Sea of Cortez, by John Steinbeck and E. F. Ricketts, 1941, Here Reissued with a Profile "About Ed Ricketts."* New York: Penguin, 1982.

———. *The Wayward Bus*. New York: Viking, 1947.

Stephens, Lester D. *Joseph Le Conte: Gentle Prophet of Evolution*. Baton Rouge: Louisiana State Univ. Press, 1982.

Stewart, Allegra. *Gertrude Stein and the Present*. Cambridge, Mass.: Harvard Univ. Press, 1967.

Stoddard, Lothrop. *The Rising Tide of Color Against White World-Supremacy*. New York: Scribner's, 1922.

Storey, Robert. *Mimesis and the Human Animal: On the Biogenetic Foundations of Literary Representation*. Evanston, Ill.: Northwestern Univ. Press, 1996.

Stribling, T. S. *Birthright: A Novel*. New York: Century, 1922.

Sulloway. Frank J. *Freud, Biologist of the Mind: Beyond the Psychoanalytic Legend*. New York: Basic, 1979.

Sutherland, Donald. *Gertrude Stein: A Biography of Her Work*. New Haven, Conn.: Yale Univ. Press, 1951.

Sutton, William A. *Letters to Bab: Sherwood Anderson to Marietta D. Finley 1916–33*. Urbana: Univ. of Illinois Press, 1985.

Talmey, Bernard S. *Love: A Treatise on the Science of Sex-Attraction for the Use of Physicians and Students of Medical Jurisprudence*. New York: Practitioners, 1916.

Tedlock, E. W., Jr., and C. V. Wicker, eds. *Steinbeck and His Critics: A Record of Twenty-Five Years*. Albuquerque: Univ. of New Mexico Press, 1957.

Thornton, Patricia Pacey. "Sexual Roles in *The Great Gatsby*." *English Studies in Canada* 5, no. 4 (1979): 457–68.

Thornhill, Randy, and Craig T. Palmer. *A Natural History of Rape: Biological Bases of Sexual Coercion*. Cambridge: MIT Press, 2000.

Thurman, Wallace. "Fire Burns." Review of *Nigger Heaven* by Carl Van Vechten. *Fire!!* (Nov. 1926): 47–48.

Townsend, Kim. *Sherwood Anderson*. Boston, Mass.: Houghton Mifflin, 1987.

Tuttleton, James W. "Seeing Slightly Red: Fitzgerald's 'May Day.'" In *The Short Stories of F. Scott Fitzgerald: New Approaches in Criticism*, ed. Jackson R. Bryer, 181–97. Madison: Univ. of Wisconsin Press, 1982.

Van Vechten, Carl. *Nigger Heaven*. New York: Knopf, 1926.

Wagner-Martin, Linda. *"Favored Strangers": Gertrude Stein and Her Family*. New Brunswick, N.J.: Rutgers Univ. Press, 1995.

———, ed. *A Historical Guide to Ernest Hemingway*. New York: Oxford Univ. Press, 2000.

Walcutt, Charles Child. *American Literary Naturalism: A Divided Stream*. 1956. Westport, Conn.: Greenwood, 1973.

Wasiolek, Edward. "The Sexual Drama of Nick and Gatsby." *The International Fiction Review* 19, no. 1 (1992): 14–22.

Wasserman, Loretta. "The Music of Time: Henri Bergson and Willa Cather." *American Literature* 57 (Jan. 1985): 226–39.

Watson, Barbara Bellow. *A Shavian Guide to Intelligent Women*. London: Chatto and Windus, 1964.

Watson, Steven. *The Harlem Renaissance: Hub of African-American Culture, 1920–1930*. New York: Pantheon, 1995.

Watson, Charles N., Jr. *The Novels of Jack London: A Reappraisal*. Madison: Univ. of Wisconsin Press, 1983.

Weininger, Otto. *Sex and Character*. New York: Putnam, 1906.

Weiss, Daniel. "*The Red Badge of Courage*." *Psychoanalytic Review* 52 (Summer 1965): 32–52.

Wertheim, Stanley, and Paul Sorrentino. *The Crane Log: A Documentary Life of Stephen Crane, 1871–1900*. New York: G. K. Hall, 1994.

Wharton, Edith. *A Backward Glance*. In *Edith Wharton, Novellas and Other Writings*, ed. Cynthia Griffin Wolff, 767–1068. New York: Library of America, 1990.